Nazis after Hitler

Nazis after Hitler

How Perpetrators of the Holocaust Cheated Justice and Truth

Donald M. McKale

ROWMAN & LITTLEFIELD PUBLISHERS, INC.
Lanham • Boulder • New York • Toronto • Plymouth, UK

Published by Rowman & Littlefield Publishers, Inc.
A wholly owned subsidiary of The Rowman & Littlefield Publishing Group, Inc.
4501 Forbes Boulevard, Suite 200, Lanham, Maryland 20706
http://www.rowmanlittlefield.com

Estover Road, Plymouth PL6 7PY, United Kingdom

British Library Cataloguing in Publication Information Available

Library of Congress Cataloging-in-Publication Data
McKale, Donald M., 1943–
Nazis after Hitler : how perpetrators of the Holocaust cheated justice and truth / Donald M. McKale.
p. cm.
Includes bibliographical references and index.
ISBN 978-1-4422-1316-6 (cloth : alk. paper) —
ISBN 978-1-4422-1318-0 (electronic)
1. Holocaust, Jewish (1939–1945)—Influence. 2. War crime trials—Germany—History—20th century. 3. Nazis—History—20th century. 4. Nuremberg Trial of Major German War Criminals, Nuremberg, Germany, 1945–1946. 5. World War, 1939–1945—Atrocities. I. Title.
D804.3.M396 2012
341.6'90268—dc23 2011030240

™ The paper used in this publication meets the minimum requirements of American National Standard for Information Sciences—Permanence of Paper for Printed Library Materials, ANSI/NISO Z39.48-1992.

Printed in the United States of America

Contents

Preface

On May 1, 1945, the late-night bulletin from German radio told the world what it had waited far too long to hear: Adolf Hitler had died in Berlin, "fighting to the last breath against Bolshevism." Eventually, the world would learn the truth. Fearful of being caught by the Soviets, paraded "in a cage" to Moscow, and there forced to answer for the global bloody chaos he'd wrought, the Nazi dictator had killed himself. He did so while cowering in a bunker deep below the center of the physically razed Nazi capital. Six days after the radio announcement, Germany surrendered in France to the British and Americans, and on May 9 in Berlin to the Russians.

But now, what would the world do when confronted by the unimaginable? Other questions abounded in May 1945 as World War II ended in Europe. Hitler had started the war in September 1939 when his German armies invaded Poland. Now, with the war over, what did the world realize about what had happened amid the largest armed struggle in history, and what did it already know?

During the conflict, one of the warring nations had done something unprecedented. Nazi Germany, mainly for the reason of racial hatred, singled out an entire people for total physical extermination and, under the cover of a massive war, murdered in systematic fashion nearly six million of that people. The dead were victims of the longest and—in this instance—most fanatical hatred yet known toward a single people: anti-Semitism.

How would the postwar world respond to the Holocaust? What would happen to its several hundred thousand Jewish survivors left in Europe? Tragically, they found little sympathy for what they had suffered—and continued to suffer—from a world exhausted by the largest, deadliest war in history. Some survivors even encountered a persistent—often violent and fatal—postwar anti-Jewish hatred, a hatred that still thrives today in much of the world.

And what about the perpetrators of the Holocaust—the killers and their accomplices? What would happen to them after the defeat and death of Hitler, their Führer, whom they had worshiped and followed so loyally in carrying out the genocide? Would the principal Allied victors of the world war—the United States, Britain, and Soviet Union—bring Nazi and other war criminals to justice, as they had promised during the fighting?

Sadly, in contrast to popular belief widely held yet today, only in a relatively few cases. For a variety of reasons, many chronicled in this book, the postwar world felt little obligation to ferret out and bring the perpetrators to justice. Consequently, the vast majority of them escaped punishment. "For the great bulk of the perpetrators," the acclaimed historian Raul Hilberg wrote in his monumental history of the Holocaust, "there is no report. Most were simply by-passed [by Allied and later German authorities]. By the law they had not lived. By the law they did not die."[1]

When one thinks of the Holocaust and survival, one imagines Jews who somehow lived through the horrific ordeal. The present book, however, examines an entirely different and wholly unfortunate dimension of survival related to the Holocaust—perpetrators of the event who numbered several hundred thousand and who lived after the world war ended but were only rarely, if ever, called to account for their crimes. One scholar has estimated that, since the war, of "approximately 100,000 people investigated in Germany" suspected of committing mass murder and participating in the Holocaust, "only about 6,500 were actually brought to trial, and the large majority of these before 1949."[2]

First, the overwhelming majority of perpetrators acted after the war with impunity and, without Hitler, whom they had followed blindly and so relied on for their positions of power, enjoyed postwar lives of relative comfort, free of consequences or guilt. Others perished of natural causes: heart attacks, old age, dying quietly in their sleep.

Second, most of the relatively few who were judged were brought to justice only long after the war and given minimal prison sentences nowhere near commensurate with their crimes. And even these verdicts and vexingly light prison terms the courts later reduced or rejected outright. This resulted from pressures brought to bear by the Allies, German politicians, their resentful or exhausted constituencies, and even the perpetrators seeking exoneration (not to mention their pensions), as the Cold War grew less temperate.

Third, the overwhelming majority of the perpetrators denied any guilt in and expressed no remorse for what they'd done. Even those few who were brought to trial quickly and executed—like the perpetrators discussed in chapters 3 and 4 at the 1945 Belsen trial and in chapters 8, 9, and 13 at trials in Nuremberg and elsewhere after 1945—went to their deaths unrepentant.

Why should all this matter? Because in the ideological war waged on the post-Holocaust world by the surviving perpetrators, both justice and truth were the first casualties.[3]

Nearly every post–World War II claim of Holocaust perpetrators, insisting on their innocence in what happened, found its way into the mythology of postwar Holocaust denial. Such denial is the most hateful and dangerous new element, along with the violent hatred directed toward Israel by anti-Semites and anti-Zionists, in the post-Holocaust world's racial and anti-Jewish views.

Beginning in 1945, whether placed on trial or living in freedom, the perpetrators carried on what amounted to a massive, never-ending postwar ideological, even propaganda, campaign against Jews. The perpetrators, no longer able to pursue the racial war of systematic mass murder of the Jews they had waged during World War II, continued the attack on those whom they hated the most by cheating both justice for and the truth about what the perpetrators had done. Nearly all the perpetrators declared they had done nothing wrong, that they had not known about the Jewish persecution until the war's end, and that they had little or no responsibility or guilt for what happened. But in making these and other claims denying their involvement in the Holocaust, they in fact justified the Nazi atrocities and anti-Semitism.

They did so by asserting that the victims of the Holocaust—the nearly six million European Jews—were to blame for and even deserved their fate; other perpetrators declared that the number of Jews killed had been exaggerated. Still others maintained that no systematic Nazi policy had existed to destroy the Jews. Moreover, often Nazis on trial for crimes involving the Holocaust alleged that the courts falsified or mistranslated records used against them. Some insisted that Jews conspired from vindictiveness to persecute the perpetrators unjustly. They proclaimed publicly, as the Nazi regime had done so often, that Jews formed part of a vast conspiracy to rule the world. Also, many perpetrators alleged that Germany's and their individual wartime actions were no different from those of the Allies. In fact, they viewed themselves, their families, their friends, and Germany as victims—during the war and after—of the Allies and, of course, international and inimical Jewry.

The perpetrators, therefore, didn't challenge the fact that the Holocaust happened. According to historian Deborah Lipstadt, the perpetrators "admitted that the Holocaust happened but tried to vindicate themselves by claiming they were not *personally* guilty."[4] But the lies of the perpetrators were not merely an effort by the guilty to avoid self-incrimination. Their fabrications represented a virulent anti-Jewish and anti-Allied crusade, taken up and carried on by Holocaust deniers and quasi deniers, once the latter appeared initially between 1945 and 1950, amid the Nuremberg and other war crimes trials.

In a hugely gaping paradox, deniers—who include neo-Nazis, so-called revisionist writers, and other anti-Semites—ignore that the perpetrators admitted the Holocaust happened. Instead, since the late 1940s deniers—and others who hover on the periphery of denial—have used, in one form or another and for varying purposes, the numerous other falsehoods uttered by perpetrators at their trials and elsewhere. In so doing, almost exactly like the perpetrators, the first generation of deniers "defended" Nazi anti-Semitism and the horrors committed in its name.[5] They blamed the Jews for the Holocaust, argued that Jews and others overstated the death toll of the victims, denied the mass of evidence showing the perpetrators' guilt in the Holocaust, disavowed the existence of a methodical Nazi policy to exterminate all Jews the Germans could seize, and insisted that German actions in the world war were no worse than those of the Allies both during and after the conflict.

Also deniers have employed such lies, when convenient, to buttress their biggest lie—that the Holocaust did not happen or that, if something like it did, it had far fewer victims and was nothing criminal or even immoral. The perpetrators, therefore, in the sense discussed above, were the first deniers; they helped advance Holocaust denial without having denied the Holocaust happened. Deniers, on the other hand, almost never admit that many of their claims were also made initially, to one degree or another, by Nazi perpetrators who had survived the war.

In the post-Holocaust world, anti-Semitism has taken on two new elements, both of them dangerous and connected intimately to the surviving perpetrators. First, Holocaust denial—what Lipstadt termed "the growing assault on truth and memory"—originated in Europe and the United States—the former where the Holocaust happened, the latter the country that held at Nuremberg and elsewhere the most widely publicized war crimes trials. Today, the myth of denial is a mainstream belief, a thriving rationale and identity, for many people and some governments in the Arab and Muslim world. Also the myth is still propagated by anti-Semites in Europe and the United States.

Second, many deniers have urged widespread violence against and destruction of Jews and Israel. Those consumed with such hatred and who appear most openly in the Middle East justify denying the Jewish state's right to exist by denying the Holocaust happened. Deniers contend, Lipstadt notes, that "Jews created the myth of the Holocaust in order to bilk the Germans out of billions of dollars and ensure the establishment of Israel."[6] But here, too, much of the inspiration for such claims and behavior originated with Nazism and the surviving perpetrators. The latter, with both their participation in the Holocaust and their postwar disavowals that they had done so, and their blaming the Jews for the Holocaust, left the post-Holocaust world with an example of violence wrought against Jews unprecedented in the long history of anti-Semitism.

Also for many years after World War II, a form of state-sponsored Holocaust denial existed in both the Soviet Union and its Eastern bloc of nations (an issue touched on in chapters 5 and 10). In July 1991, shortly after the fall of the Soviet Empire, Romania's chief rabbi, Moses Rosen, commented that the masses of Romanian Jews killed during the world war "were murdered twice," because for a half century afterward a fact widely known elsewhere was denied or never acknowledged in Romania—more than 211,000 Romanian Jews died during the war, most murdered by their own government.[7] Moreover, Romanian armies invading the Soviet Union with German forces after 1941 assisted the Germans in murdering tens of thousands of Jews in Bessarabia and Bukovina, lands recovered by Romania from the Russians. In the fall of 1941, Romanian troops carried out in the Soviet Black Sea port of Odessa the largest single massacre of Soviet Jews.

Had Nazi Germany and its major Axis allies in the war—Italy and Japan—won the conflict, Hitler intended to expand Nazi racial hatred and the resulting extermination of Jews outside Europe. This included, in his most grandiose imaginings, into the Middle East, plans he'd begun to formalize during the war. "The final crushing of Axis forces in North Africa" in 1943, historian Gerhard Weinberg wrote fifty years later, "ended all prospects for a German occupation of the British mandate of Palestine and the slaughter of its Jewish community."[8] But as Weinberg has also shown, Hitler's second book, a sequel to *Mein Kampf* dictated by the tyrant in 1928 but never published by him, revealed the Nazi leader's belief even before he seized power in Germany in "the necessity of a future major conflict with the United States"—and surely, as the Holocaust would show later and if the opportunity arose, with America's Jews.[9]

Similarly, the Germans had initiated amid the war, and planned to continue implementing it after, the murder of other peoples whom the Nazis despised for racial or other reasons—these victims included the handicapped, Gypsies, homosexuals, Jehovah's Witnesses, Soviet prisoners of war, and other Slavs. The Allied victory in 1945, therefore, spared the earth from domination by an even more horrendous evil of which, most likely, mankind had caught only a frightful glimpse during the war.

In attempting to present and explain the issues in this book most effectively, I followed Thomas Carlyle's axiom. "History," he wrote, "is the essence of innumerable biographies."[10] I've used a biographical approach to relate both the wartime and postwar experiences of thirty, mostly typical, Holocaust perpetrators. I make no pretense, therefore, at providing a comprehensive history of the perpetrators' fate. Instead, each account tells a revealing story about one of the darkest and most tragic episodes in the history of mankind. Two other figures in the book, Bernhard Bechler and Ernst Buchner, weren't perpetrators in the sense of nearly all the others; but the first, a former Nazi soldier, did little in postwar East Germany to punish perpetrators for their crimes, while the second helped steal during the war a mass of art treasures from Jews. Another figure, Hermann Josef Abs, a banker in the Nazi regime, remains an ambiguous one. It seems apparent that Abs was a perpetrator or, at the least, a culpable bystander.

For reasons obvious to most, I've focused my attention on perpetrators less known to the general public. Because of the sharply different yet basic and typical roles they played in the Holocaust, two perpetrators appear most frequently in the book: Franz Stangl, the commandant of the Nazi death camps Sobibor and Treblinka, where altogether over one and a half million Jews perished, who lived after World War II for more than two decades in freedom, and Werner Best, a classic Nazi "desk murderer" mistakenly viewed by history as a savior of Danish Jews, who escaped nearly all punishment and died a "natural" death in 1986. Their stories are main subjects of several chapters, something that I hope provides the reader with a greater context and sense of chronology amid the accounts of other perpetrators. So although the far more notorious Dr. Josef Mengele and Adolf Eichmann—the former avoiding capture and punishment altogether and the latter apprehended finally in 1960—make noticeable appearances within the pages of this book, so much focus and writing has been directed their way that I've limited their presence mainly to their experiences either in the war's final days or in the immediate postwar world.

Likewise, as in the cases of Hermann Göring and Nuremberg and Heinrich Himmler—commander of the Nazi *SS* and police—and the "Final Solution of the Jewish question," where the understanding of one invariably requires the discussion of the other, I've concentrated on their direct relationship to and impact on the Holocaust. The phrase *Final Solution* was a euphemism employed during World War II by German leaders, beginning in 1941 and early 1942, to describe their campaign to murder all Jews under Nazi rule and what, after 1945, Jews and others called the Holocaust.

In selecting Göring, Ernst Kaltenbrunner, Hans Frank, and Alfred Rosenberg out of twenty-two major Nazi war criminals and defendants at the International Military Tribunal (IMT) at Nuremberg during 1945 and 1946 from whom to choose to discuss, I based my selection on similar criteria. Their careers and complicity have received somewhat less attention. In the case of Frank and Rosenberg, the choice was obvious; their policies had a costly and personal impact on masses of Polish and Soviet Jews and on other Poles and Soviet citizens. Looking at their careers and what happened to them at Nuremberg within two chapters (8 and 9) permits contrasts and comparisons between their personalities, actions as overlords (of the so-called Government General in Poland and Nazi Occupied Eastern Territories, respectively), culpability, and defenses that would not have been as effective otherwise.

The pages that follow also show how the perpetrators were aided in their frequent escape of postwar punishment and in their massive assault on truth by many of the courts trying Nazi war criminals. Both the IMT's lengthy final judgment and its sentencing of each defendant barely mentioned the Holocaust, considering it one of many Nazi "crimes against humanity," and focused instead on "crimes against peace." The tribunal's Allied prosecution called few Jewish survivors as witnesses, relying instead for evidence on captured Nazi records that did little to identify the murder of the Jews as the definitive crime—among the many—of Nazism and did nothing to sympathize with the victims' suffering. The Soviet Union refused both during and after the war to acknowledge the suffering of its own Jewish citizens (as noted above, it promoted a kind of state-supported Holocaust denial) and recognized only that of its "Soviet" or "anti-Fascist" peoples. Postwar trials in Poland of several hundred former Auschwitz *SS* personnel resulted in mixed outcomes at best, with nearly 90 percent hardly punished for their criminality.

West German courts after 1950, for various reasons discussed in chapter 11 and elsewhere, tried a tiny percentage of Holocaust perpetrators; nearly all those convicted—in contrast to their monstrous crimes—received light prison sentences. At the trial in France in 1987 of Klaus Barbie, the former *Gestapo* chief in Lyons, none of Barbie's victims who had survived were able to confront him directly; he was all but forgotten when he died in jail four years later.

The failure of nearly every postwar tribunal, no matter where in Europe, to do anything more than barely mention or deal with the Holocaust in punishing its perpetrators represented in itself a form of anti-Semitism. Even when plenty of evidence existed demonstrating that the Nazis had targeted Jews all over Europe for destruction, courts and prosecutors rarely admitted it or focused on it. Their indifference or even outright hostility, for whatever reasons, toward the victims whom the Nazis singled out the most for racial and other hatred, was palpable.

Often the postwar European and other Western press covering war crimes trials repeated the misperceptions produced by the courts of the Holocaust and its perpetrators. Press coverage of the trials, from the first of them, the Belsen trial held by the British, to the later Auschwitz proceedings in West

Germany from 1963 to 1965 and Treblinka trials during 1964–1965 and 1970, was extensive. Reporters from more than twenty nations covered the IMT hearings, over eighty of them representing American publications. Historian Brian Feltman has concluded about the IMT that, although it

> revealed a great deal of information related to the Nazis' attempt to systematically murder the Jews of Europe, and while IMT correspondents regarded such information as fact, [press] reports related to the Holocaust were rarely front-page material. News connected to aggressive war and war crimes commanded significantly more attention than crimes against humanity, but this was simply a reflection of the prosecution's approach to the proceedings.[11]

Like most others working in the historical jungle of Nazi Germany and the Holocaust, I'm keenly aware of how much of my writing both relies and builds on a basis laid by others. This is readily apparent in the present volume, which depends heavily on the research of other historians and writers as well as on original sources. There are numerous scholars whose studies I have used or from whom I have learned much at professional meetings and discussions over the years about the Holocaust. Some of their work appears in the notes and bibliography at the end of this book.

Since the 1980s, the Holocaust Education Foundation of Skokie, Illinois, has supported Holocaust studies in academia. In 2011 the foundation merged with Northwestern University. I'm long overdue in expressing my appreciation publicly to the foundation and its former president and Auschwitz survivor, Theodore Zev Weiss. Since first meeting Zev in 1992, I've gained a great deal from his friendship and the foundation's sponsorship of numerous activities fostering Holocaust education, including helping establish college courses on the Holocaust and producing the "Lessons and Legacies" scholarly conferences and publications. Long into the future, his work in helping create and in leading the foundation will enhance the knowledge of many students, faculty, and others interested in studying the Holocaust; his example inspired much of my teaching of and writing on the subject. The story of Zev and the foundation is told in Anita Wiener's *Expanding Historical Consciousness: The Development of the Holocaust Educational Foundation* (2002).

Before my retirement in 2008 from Clemson University, where I had taught for nearly thirty years, I received much financial and other support for this book from the Class of 1941 Memorial Endowment. The latter was made possible by a generous gift to the university from its class of 1941, in memory of fifty-seven of its members who died in World War II.

Much of the idea for this book originated with Michael Dorr, a superb editor, writer, publisher, agent, and friend. I wish to express my deep appreciation to him, not only for his suggestions for the book, but also for his willingness to read and edit the manuscript. I admire, as well, both his interest in and superior knowledge of the Holocaust.

The *Bundesarchiv* (Federal Archives) in Koblenz, Germany, the Photo Archives of the United States Holocaust Memorial Museum in Washington, D.C., and the archives of Yad Vashem in Jerusalem granted permission for me to use many of the photographs that appear in this book. I received help from Caroline Waddell and Benton M. Arnovitz of the museum, Naama Shilo of Yad Vashem, and Dr. Oliver Sander of the *Bundesarchiv*. Katharina von Kellenbach of St. Mary's College of Maryland kindly provided me with a photograph of her uncle, Alfred Ebner.

Kelly Durham, a good friend and fellow writer, provided me with several valuable ideas for this project. Also I received superb help in the publication process from Susan McEachern, editorial director, and Janice Braunstein, assistant managing editor, at Rowman & Littlefield Publishers. An author could not ask for better editors and publisher.

By far my greatest debt is to my wife, Janna. As she has always done with my work, she encouraged and supported this project fully. Her patience and understanding, especially in putting up with my frequent absences and late-night hours, are remarkable. She and our family are the light of my life, helping make it possible to contend with the darkness of this book's subject—the Holocaust and its perpetrators.

Finally, I should remind the reader that despite the numerous sources cited in the notes and bibliography, all mistakes in this book are, of course, my responsibility.

Abbreviations and Special Terms

Aktion	Literally "action"; a euphemism in World War II used by the Nazis to describe terror operations of the Germans and their foreign collaborators that included the roundup, mass shootings, and/or deportations of Jews.
Aryanization	Nazi term for the German takeover of Jewish property
BSGS	*Bayerische Staatsgemäldesammlungen*; Bavarian State Painting Collections, Munich
BUB	Bohemian Union Bank in Prague
CDU	Christian Democratic Union, Federal Republic of West Germany
CIA	U.S. Central Intelligence Agency
CIC	U.S. Army Counterintelligence Corps
deportation	Mass roundup and transport by *SS* and German police of primarily Jews—but also occasionally of other peoples such as Gypsies—from Germany and much of the rest of Europe to death camps, ghettos, or other facilities in the East where they were murdered.
denazification	An Allied policy adopted in postwar Germany, designed to purge the Germans of Nazism, but implemented by the Allies differently. In the zones of Germany occupied by the Anglo-Americans, especially in the U.S. zone, the authorities attempted an ideological and political screening of millions of Germans, which ended by 1947–1948 amid massive bureaucratic complexities generated by the process. A similar policy was implemented in postwar

	Austria. The Soviet Union carried out in its East German zone a much more limited ideological screening, ended in March 1948, as authorities concentrated on ousting the economic and social elites that had sustained the Nazi regime. A similar policy was implemented in postwar Austria.
DP	Displaced Persons; a description of the millions of refugees or deportees at the end of World War II (including several hundred thousand Jews) who found themselves displaced as a result of the war, often unable to return to their homes, and housed in camps in Germany, Austria, France, and Italy.
Einsatzgruppen	Special employment units; mobile and armed formations of primarily *SS* and German police; used to hunt down and kill Jews and other perceived enemies in the territories in the East conquered and occupied by Nazi armies.
ERR	*Einsatzstab Reichsleiter Rosenberg*, Special Staff of Reich Leader [Alfred] Rosenberg; a German agency that specialized in plundering art treasures of Jews and others in the German-occupied countries of Europe.
euthanasia	Term used by the Nazis as a euphemism to disguise their murder of the handicapped during World War II.
FDP	Free Democratic Party, Federal Republic of West Germany
Final Solution	*Endlösung*, from the Nazi phrase "Final Solution of the Jewish question"; a euphemism for the program developed during late 1941 and early 1942 to exterminate the Jews of Europe and elsewhere.
Gauleiter	Nazi Party district leader.
GDR	German Democratic Republic, the Soviet-controlled government of East Germany from 1949 to 1989.
genocide	A term used during World War II to refer directly to Nazi racial policies then being carried out. The word appeared in the indictments of German officers in postwar trials of war criminals. In 1948 the United Nations adopted the "Genocide Convention," which made genocide a crime in international law. It explicitly bans killing, causing grievous bodily or spiritual harm, preventing births, or transferring children from a targeted group to some other group with genocidal intent.
Gestapo	*Geheime Staatspolizei*, "Secret State Police"; the political police in Nazi Germany.

Higher *SS* and Police Leader(s)	*Höhere SS- und Polizeiführer*; supreme territorial/regional commander(s) for all *SS* officers as well as for police officers within the territory or region. Such commanders were directly responsible to *RFSS* Himmler for implementing policies related to state security and the investigation and treatment of dangerous elements within the realm(s).
Holocaust	Term, widely used since the 1960s, to denote the systematic mass murder of European Jewry by the Nazis during World War II. The word has generally served to separate this particular massacre from other historical instances of genocide. Sometimes the term includes other victims of the Nazis as well, especially Gypsies.
ICRC	International Committee of the Red Cross
IMT	International Military Tribunal at Nuremberg, Germany, 1945–1946
JAFC	Jewish Anti-Fascist Committee, founded in Moscow, likely in 1941
JCRA	Jewish Committee for Relief Abroad, London
Kristallnacht	Literally "night of broken or shattered glass"; the name for the pogrom throughout Germany organized by the Nazis that occurred on November 9–10, 1938.
LRTWC	*Law Reports of Trials of War Criminals*; a fifteen-volume series summarizing the course of the more important trials of individuals accused of war crimes during World War II, excluding the major war criminals tried by the Nuremberg and Tokyo military tribunals. The series was selected and prepared by the United Nations War Crimes Commission.
Mischlinge	Nazi term for part-Jews or Jews of "mixed ancestry"
NATO	North Atlantic Treaty Organization
NCA	*Nazi Conspiracy and Aggression*; an eight-volume, twelve-book series, providing a collection of documentary evidence prepared by the United States and British prosecution for use at the IMT.
NKVD	The abbreviated name for the Soviet Commissariat for Internal Affairs, an agency in charge of state security and forced labor camps.
NYT	*New York Times*
ODESSA	*Organisation der SS Angehörigen*, "Organization of *SS* Members"; an alleged post–World War II clandestine group of former *SS* officials that aided the escape of war criminals from Germany and Europe.

OSS	U.S. Office of Strategic Services
RFSS	*Reichsführer SS*, "Reich Leader of the *SS*"—Heinrich Himmler, who from 1936 held the added title "Chief of the German Police."
RSHA	*Reichssicherheitshauptamt*, "Reich Security Main Office"; a government-*SS* agency established in September 1939 that included the *Gestapo*, criminal police, and Security Service; although officially responsible to Heinrich Himmler, it was run by Reinhard Heydrich until mid-1942, and from January 1943 by Ernst Kaltenbrunner.
SA	*Sturmabteilung*, "storm troopers"; the first Nazi paramilitary organization.
SD	*Sicherheitsdienst*, "Security Service"; the intelligence branch of the *SS*, heavily involved in researching and later implementing the campaigns against Jews and Nazi Germany's other alleged ideological and racial enemies.
Security Police	*Sicherheitspolizei*; a fusion of the various German state political police and criminal police, responsible for dealing with both actual and potential enemies of the Nazi regime; while part of the government, such forces were closely linked to the *SD*.
SMAD	Soviet Military Administration for Germany
SS	*Schutzstaffel*, "protection squad"; an elite Nazi organization headed by Himmler.
TJK	*Trial of Josef Kramer and Forty-Four Others (The Belsen Trial)*; vol. 2 of the *LRTWC* series.
TMWC	*Trials of the Major War Criminals before the International Military Tribunal (Nuremberg, 14 November 1945–1 October 1946)*; a forty-two-volume series of testimony and documents from the IMT.
TWC	*Trials of War Criminals before the Nuernberg Military Tribunals under Control Council Law No. 10*; a fifteen-volume series containing testimony and documents from twelve U.S. trials of almost two hundred German defendants, held between 1947 and 1949. The defendants included diplomats, politicians, jurists, military leaders, *SS* officers, industrialists, and physicians.
Uniformed Police	*Ordnungspolizei*, "Order Police"; city and rural policemen, not in the *Gestapo* and Criminal Police, who handled matters like traffic, patrols, and routine police business. Battalions of Order Police functioned like the *Einsatzgruppen*—they

	carried out mass killings—in the Soviet Union and in Poland. Headed by Kurt Daluege.
UNWCC	United Nations War Crimes Commission; an agency established in October 1943 by Great Britain, the United States, and fifteen other Allied nations to identify and deal with Nazi war criminals.
völkisch	racial nationalist (the Nazi meaning of the word)
Waffen-SS	Armed *SS*
Wehrmacht	German armed forces
WJC	World Jewish Congress
WVHA	*Wirtschaftsverwaltungshauptamt*, "Economic-Administrative Main Office"; an *SS* agency formally established in 1942; it oversaw most *SS* construction and economic activities at the concentration and extermination camps.
ZS	*Zentrale Stelle der Landesjustizverwaltungen zur Aufklärung nationalsozialistischer Verbrechen*, "Central Office of the State Judicial Authorities for the Investigation of National Socialist Crimes," West Germany, created in 1958.

AUTHOR'S NOTE

A useful guide to Nazi terms and their meanings can be found in Richard Breitman, *The Architect of Genocide: Himmler and the Final Solution* (New York: Knopf, 1991), 311–14.

Major German Concentration Camps, 1938–1945

Major Ghettos in Occupied Eastern Europe, 1939–1944
Baltic Sea
Riga
Liepaja
Mikaliskes
Siauliai
Dvinsk
Salos
Svencionys
Vitebsk
Smolensk
Kovno
Vilna
Volozhin
Lida
Minsk
Magil
Grodno
Novogrudok
Diatlovo
Nesvizh
Baranovichi
Slonim
Białystok
Gamel
GREATER GERMANY
UNDER GERMAN OCCUPATION
Minsk Mazowiecki
Warsaw
Brest-Litovsk
Lachva
Pinsk
Łodź
Tomaszow Mazowiecki
Belchatow
Piotrkow Trybunalski
Lublin
Radom
Kovel
Kharkov
Opole Lubelskie
Kielce
Czestochowa
Lutsk
Tuchin
Rovno
Zamosc
Zhitomir
Bedzin
General Government
Berdichev
Theresienstadt
Sosnowiec
Kraków
Rzeszow
Brody
L'vov
Tarnow
Przemysl
Zalochev
Tarnopol
Dnepropetrovsk
Protectorate of Bohemia and Moravia
Nowy Sacz
Drogobych
Rogatin
Berezhany
Vinnitsa
Stry
Chortkov
Stanislawow
Gorodenka
SLOVAKIA (German Ally)
Kolomyia
Mogilev-Podolski
Chernovtsy
ROMANIA (German Ally)
HUNGARY (German Ally)
Kishinev
Kherson
Odessa
0 MILES 100

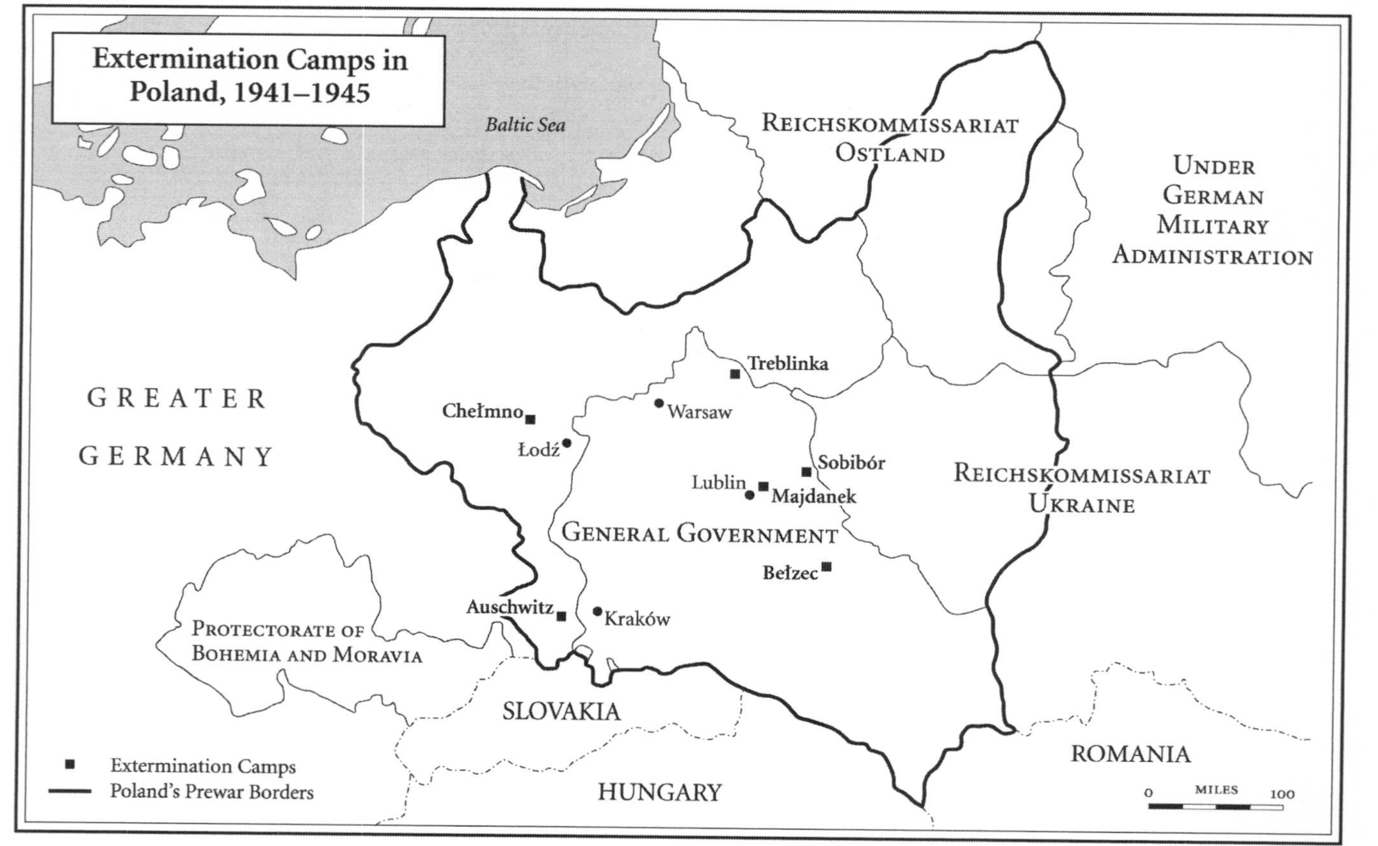
Extermination Camps in Poland, 1941–1945
Baltic Sea
Reichskommissariat Ostland
Under German Military Administration
Greater Germany
Chełmno
Łodź
Treblinka
Warsaw
Sobibór
Lublin
Majdanek
Reichskommissariat Ukraine
General Government
Bełzec
Auschwitz
Kraków
Protectorate of Bohemia and Moravia
Slovakia
Hungary
Romania
Extermination Camps
Poland's Prewar Borders
0 Miles 100

1

World War II and Allied Promises

Before delving into the repulsive figures that make up this book, a brief word is in order about the historical background of World War II that so shaped what happened—or did not happen—to them after the war. At least initially, in the wake of the war's end in Europe in May 1945, the Allied victors captured some leading Nazi officials. The British, Americans, and Russians did so despite the fact that during the war they had made relatively few preparations to identify, among the huge number of German prisoners they held in 1945, either Holocaust perpetrators or other war criminals.

Previously, as the war had dragged on since 1939 with its profligate expenditure of treasure and lives, little support had existed anywhere on the Allied side for assisting Europe's Jews or others, the objects of widespread Nazi racial hatred and persecution. This Allied reluctance to help held especially true before 1943 and 1944, when Allied armies found themselves on the defensive nearly everywhere—in both Europe and the Far East—against the Axis forces.

Early on the morning of September 1, 1939, Germany had invaded Poland, beginning the war. Two days later, Great Britain and France tried to save Poland by declaring war on Germany, but soon Poland lay conquered and divided by Germany and the Soviet Union. A previous Nazi-Soviet pact had helped to seal Poland's fate. In 1940 Hitler's war machine had then turned toward northern and western Europe, conquering Norway, Denmark, the Netherlands, Belgium, Luxembourg, and France. The Nazi armies appeared unstoppable. In late July, Germany launched a massive air assault on Great Britain.

During 1941 the war expanded into a global conflict. Germany overran Yugoslavia and Greece and fought alongside Italy against the British in North Africa. On June 22, Hitler's *Wehrmacht* and Germany's European allies invaded the Soviet Union, breaking the Nazi-Soviet agreement. From that date until the war's end, the majority of fighting in the entire war happened on the massive Eastern front. More people would fight and die there than on every other front in World War II combined. Hitler, despite his having signed an agreement with the Soviet Union, had for a long time hated the Russians or Slavs, claiming they were an alleged inferior and decadent race, ruled by supposedly corrupt and even more wretched "Jewish-Bolsheviks." He intended to conquer the vast Soviet lands for more living space for the racially "pure" Germans. In December 1941, the Japanese attacked the American naval base at Pearl Harbor in Hawaii, beginning the war in the Pacific; shortly thereafter, Germany declared war on the United States.[1]

As early as December 1942, amid increasing reports of mass killings by German armed forces of prisoners of war and civilians in Eastern Europe and the Soviet Union, the Western powers and Soviet government had promised—publicly—swift and sweeping retribution for war crimes committed by the Axis powers. The Allies specified the Nazi attempt to "exterminate the Jewish people in Europe."[2] The announcement clearly warned the Germans: the Allies wouldn't repeat the failed trials that had plagued the aftermath of World War I, when the German Supreme Court had acquitted all but nine of the 896 persons that the Allied powers had charged with war crimes.

On October 30, 1943, Allied foreign ministers meeting in the Soviet capital signed the Moscow Declaration, which confirmed the Allies' intention to hold the Germans responsible for their war crimes and to bring them to justice. In Moscow the Allies agreed on the need to force Germany to surrender and then to implement massive programs of disarmament and denazification there. Simultaneously, Britain, the United States, and fifteen other Allied nations had established the United Nations War Crimes Commission (UNWCC). But by then, historian Gerhard Weinberg reminded the world in 1993, the Germans had exterminated "[a]bout 95 percent of those Jews killed in the 'Final Solution,'" victims of the Holocaust who "came within reach of the Germans only because of the war."[3]

During the winter of 1941–1942, the Soviet government had taken its own steps to deal with perpetrators of such crimes on Soviet territory. By December 1941, German armies had pushed deep into the Ukraine, through the Baltic states to Leningrad, and to within thirty miles of Moscow. But a first major Red Army offensive west of the Soviet capital had stopped the German advance on the city in early 1942. Eventually Soviet military tribunals tried thousands of local Soviet residents, especially Ukrainians and Lithuanians, for collaborating with the invading Germans. A decree of April 19, 1943, directed that corpses of executed Germans and their collaborators should "be left on the gallows for several days so that everyone will be aware that [harsh] punishment will befall anyone who inflicts torture and carnage on the civilian [Soviet] population and betrays his Motherland."[4]

From July to September 1943, military tribunals in Krasnodar, Krasnodon, and Mariupol held a series of open trials of local collaborators. The court in the Caucasus city of Krasnodar tried and convicted eleven collaborators with *Einsatzgruppe* D (a mobile German killing unit of *SS* and police forces operating in the southern Ukraine, Crimea, and Caucasus) charged with participating in German crimes in the region. The indictment rested on evidence provided by a special Soviet state commission for investigating German atrocities, witnesses' testimonies, and defendants' confessions. Defense lawyers were limited to pleading for leniency. Charged with high treason, eight of the defendants received death sentences (carried out publicly in a city square), and three were sentenced to hard labor.

The Krasnodar trial also revealed the German use of specially equipped trucks or vans to murder victims with the engines' carbon monoxide. A *New York Times* article reporting on the trial described "the motor-cars used in the suffocations."[5] The paper provided one of the earliest accounts to reach the American public about atrocities committed by not only *Einsatzgruppe* D but also the three other *Einsatzgruppen*—A, B, and C—operating in Russia. While the Krasnodar court tried only Soviet citizens, both the prosecution and media charged local German commanders, as well as the German military and government, with direct responsibility for the atrocities perpetrated in the region.

On December 18 and 19, 1943, a military tribunal in Kharkov convicted three Germans—officials of the field police, military counterintelligence, and *SS*—as well as a Soviet collaborator of war crimes. All were executed. Some forty thousand spectators watched the public hanging of the four men. The tribunal declared the three Germans guilty of the "executions of tens of thousands of Soviet people" and stressed the culpability of the entire German army in war crimes.[6]

Tellingly, Soviet press reports of both the Kharkov and Krasnodar trials mentioned nothing of the Nazi murder of Jews. Although by 1943 the Soviet government had full knowledge of the Holocaust and possessed massive evidence of the scope of the genocide, the tribunals referred to the executions of Jews as "massacres of Soviet citizens." The indictment in Kharkov termed the vast German ghettoization of Jews the "forceful resettlement of Soviet citizens" to the outskirts of the city.[7]

Such trials contributed to the view that spread among Germans late in the war that if their country failed to win the struggle, they could expect severe treatment from the Soviet Union and, to a lesser degree, from the Western Allies. In the war's final months, vast numbers of Germans, including most war criminals, fled westward to escape the Red Army advance through much of Eastern Europe and into Germany and to evade the Soviets' relentless, merciless reckoning.

Why else had the Allies failed during the war to focus on, identify, and bring to justice Nazi and other war criminals who had carried out the Holocaust? In part, the answer rested with the Allies and the world's general, deeply rooted lack of concern for Jews and for the whole subject of war crimes. Among the Allies, Russia had the most intense, violent history of anti-Semitism, while Western powers (i.e., government officials, the media, and the public) doubted the numerous reports arriving in Switzerland, London, and the United States, all of which confirmed the ever-increasing Nazi atrocities. Similarly, neutral countries such as the Vatican, Sweden, and Switzerland did almost nothing to assist the Jews.

Widespread anti-Semitism, ranging from indifference toward Jews to outright hatred, existed among many officials in the Anglo-American governments, armed forces, and public. Anti-Jewish attitudes permeated both the U.S. Department of State and the British Foreign Office. In the latter, the influential Alexander Cadogan, the permanent under-secretary of state, called the Russians in January 1944 "the most stinking creepy set of Jews I've ever come across. . . . They are swine!"[8]

The State Department's official responsible for refugees, Breckenridge Long Jr., was a paranoid anti-Semite. He believed Hitler's *Mein Kampf* "eloquent in opposition to Jewry and to Jews as exponents of Communism and Chaos."[9] The U.S. secretary of war, Henry Stimson, talked about an alleged Jewish problem in the United States and at no time during the war expressed any strong feelings about the sufferings of Europe's Jews. Before and during the war, few Americans saw Jews from other parts of the world as people for whom to fight and die. Hardly surprising, these laissez-faire views and widespread anti-Jewish sentiments, so embedded in the country's denizens, carried over to the U.S. army. Many officers associated Jews with both Nazism and Communism; the attitude of one of the most well-known generals, George C. Patton, whom a historian in 2000 termed "the crudest sort of racist anti-Semite," was not unusual.[10]

It's unclear how much anti-Semitism—in whatever degree—may have guided the Western Allied decision in 1944 not to bomb Auschwitz. During and after the war a storm of controversy erupted over whether the Allies could have obstructed or mitigated the mass killings of the Jews by aerial bombings of Auschwitz and the railroad lines leading to the death camp. Despite numerous Jewish appeals during the spring of 1944 that the Allies attack the camp in such a fashion, none did so. Disingenuously, many Allied leaders maintained (then and later) that such relief or rescue efforts would divert airpower from military purposes.

But by 1943 and early 1944, the tide in World War II had turned against Germany. This resulted from a combination of factors—the vastly larger industrial, military, and manpower resources of the United States and Soviet Union; the breaking by the British of secret radio codes of the German navy, air force, and police and, after mid-1941, of the Italians; the anti-German guerrilla war fought by partisans in the Soviet Union and Yugoslavia; and the winning by the Anglo-Americans of the wars at sea in the Atlantic and in the air over Western and Central Europe.

During 1943 Soviet armies won massive battles at Stalingrad and Kursk that drove the Germans back on the central portion of the Eastern front. In the West, the Anglo-Americans removed the German and Italian armies from North Africa, forcing the Italians out of the war in September 1943. The Americans and British attacked German-held France beginning on D-Day in June 1944, while the Red Army launched huge offensives along the Eastern front. During the summer and fall, Soviet troops smashed through much of Poland. In Italy, the Western Allies continued their difficult fight against the Germans occupying the country.

Amid the Anglo-American advance toward Germany through France and the Low Countries, Hitler's last-ditch efforts to halt it, using the Nazis so-called miracle weapons—the V-1, a small pilotless plane that carried nearly a ton of explosive, and V-2, a liquid-fuel rocket with a one-ton warhead—and launching the Battle of the Bulge in Belgium, failed. During the spring of 1945, the Allies invaded Germany, the Anglo-Americans in the west and the Red Army in the east. On April 30, just as Soviet forces were about to conquer Berlin, Hitler committed suicide in his bunker below the city. A week later, Germany—amid widespread ruin, devastation, hunger, and disease at home, the legacy of its people fighting and following Hitler to the bitter end—surrendered, finally halting the war in Europe. The war in the Pacific continued until the United States, seeking to end the fighting, dropped enormously destructive atomic bombs on Japan; the Japanese surrendered on September 2.

At the Yalta Conference in February 1945, the Allies had decided that the Allied Control Council—the agency that would coordinate the postwar division of Germany, including Berlin, into Allied zones of occupation—would set the policy for the denazification of the defeated Reich. But only during April and early May, with the British and Americans confronted by ghastly stories emanating from the Nazi concentration, labor, and death camps liberated by the Allies, did the public insist that the Allies punish those responsible for the crimes committed at the camps.

In the United States, mass-circulation magazines such as *Newsweek* and *Life* as well as newsreel films shocked the public with images showing British and American troops uncovering the mass death and persecution at camps in western and central Germany. Many Americans demanded the summary execution of Nazi leaders. In Britain, the government (Whitehall) reflected a similarly popular opinion. As late as April 12, 1945, the British War Cabinet, supporting Prime Minister Winston Churchill's longtime view, continued to argue "that it would be preferable that the Nazi leaders should be declared world outlaws and summarily put to death as soon as they fell into Allied hands."[11]

But President Franklin Roosevelt, who died that very day, had long opposed summary execution of captured German leaders. He and the U.S. government countered that such a policy would lead to charges equating the Allies with the Nazis. Instead, they pressed for postwar trials of Germans involved in wartime atrocities and criminality. By May 1945, the Allies—including the Soviet Union and its leader, Josef Stalin—had agreed to the American proposal and begun extremely belated preparations for trying war criminals.

During the lengthy Allied conference in London, which began on June 26, 1945, the war's victors, now including France, reached an agreement on holding the International Military Tribunal (IMT). The court would try "major" war criminals on charges that the tribunal would prosecute and based on procedures that it would follow.

The resulting charter of the IMT—annexed to the so-called London Agreement of August 8—imbued the tribunal with complete jurisdiction to try individuals charged with

1. crimes against peace, that is, initiating "invasions of other countries and wars of aggression in violation of international laws and treaties";
2. war crimes (atrocities "constituting violations of the laws or customs of war" against civilian populations of occupied territory and prisoners of war);
3. crimes against humanity (atrocities "including but not limited to, murder, extermination, enslavement, deportation, imprisonment, torture, rape, or other inhumane acts committed against any civilian population, or persecutions on political, racial or religious grounds"); and
4. participation in "a common plan or conspiracy to commit any of the foregoing crimes."[12]

In addition, the charter indicted six former organizations of the Germans: the leadership corps of the Nazi Party; the *SS*, along with the Security Service (*SD*) as an integral part; the *Gestapo*; the *SA*; the general staff and high command of the armed forces; and the Reich Cabinet. The Allies agreed as well that they would independently try suspected criminals captured in their respective zones of occupation in Germany and Austria and that criminals involved in atrocities committed in a single region or country would be returned there for trial.

But by the time the London Conference concluded its work, many former perpetrators of the Holocaust had already fled Germany and Austria or disappeared amid the widespread wartime chaos and destruction rampant in those countries. During the war, Weinberg writes in his superb history of the conflict, the German population, "combining fear and apathy with devotion and hope, continued to support the regime until the last days of the war. Only as Allied troops appeared in Germany itself did substantial numbers turn their backs on the system they had served."[13] Anti-Semitism existed in varying degrees, as did admiration for Hitler. Consequently, when the war ended, many of the worst war criminals managed to hide at home—usually with the knowledge and aid of family and friends. When those bases of support couldn't be located, reached, and sustained, crowded Allied internment camps sufficed as transient refuge.

For the Allies, the problematic role of the UNWCC in compiling lists of war criminals didn't help matters. The commission did most of its work in this regard after the war's end. Ultimately it produced eighty lists containing 36,529 names of suspected war criminals, an overwhelming majority of them Germans. In part, both the British Foreign Office and U.S. State Department intervened with the commission to keep the issue of the lists in low profile during the war. The British and American governments feared with the lists, according to Israeli scholar Arieh Kochavi, "possible German reprisals against Anglo-American POWs" and "committing the two governments to take part in the enormous number of war criminals trials to be expected after the end of the war."[14]

Nor later did the Allies agree on the war crimes trials or even on whether to hold them. The British, except for their support of the IMT, conducted only reluctantly a few zonal trials, substantially fewer than did the Americans. The British poorly managed the first major set-piece trial that began on September 17, 1945: the trial of *SS* and others accused of "violations of the laws and usages of war" at the Nazi concentration camp at Bergen-Belsen.[15] Of those in the dock, the tribunal convicted thirty and acquitted fifteen—hardly a model for the other trials that would follow.

On December 20, 1945, the Allied Control Council for Germany issued Law No. 10, entitled "Punishment of Persons Guilty of War Crimes, Crimes against Peace and against Humanity."[16] The law empowered Allied military commanders of the four occupied zones of Germany to conduct, in their respective zones, criminal trials on the charges listed in the law's title. In the case of crimes committed by Germans against Germans or stateless persons, the law authorized the occupation authorities to permit German courts to try the suspects.

But even before Law No. 10, the British had issued a special ordinance regarding "crimes against humanity." It authorized German courts in the British zone of Germany to try all cases of such crimes committed by Germans against other German nationals or stateless persons. Finally, in 1950, following the creation of the Federal Republic of West Germany, the Allies granted German courts permission to try crimes committed against Allied nationals.

In the IMT (and later Nuremberg and other war crimes trials, as well as in the attempted denazification of postwar Germany), the Allies defined the Nazi regime's criminality and extent of participation in both crimes of war and genocide in an unfortunate manner. The definition made possible the rapid reemergence of the German state and society as somehow purged, though only in the most superficial manner, of the criminals and their misdeeds of the past.

First, the Allies had never declared the *Wehrmacht*—the regular German armed forces, through which some twenty million Germans had passed during the war—a criminal organization. Second, they failed to recognize crimes against the Jews of Axis and other countries as "war crimes." Both decisions contributed significantly to the postwar view—widely held and hypocritically false—of the innocence of the German army in the massacre of the Jews. Such failures, Kochavi writes, resulted from "the lack of generosity and outright insensitivity that generally characterized the Anglo-American response to the Holocaust."[17]

Neither the London Charter, nor Control Council Law No. 10, nor the later Allied war crimes tribunals reflected the fact that the Jews formed the major object of Nazi "crimes against humanity." Instead, the Allies included in the category other populations: nationals of neutral countries, stateless persons, and non-Jewish nationals of the Axis powers and their partners. The indictment of the major war criminals before the IMT never mentioned the word *Jews*. Indeed, in the millions of words in the trial transcript, a very small percentage is devoted to the Nazis' monstrous attack on the Jews. The same held true for the tribunal's judgments against the defendants most involved in the Holocaust—both the convicted Nazi organizations and individuals.

Consequently, none of the postwar trials classified the genocide of the Jews—the only people the Nazis targeted for wholesale systematic annihilation—as a separate criminal offense, but rather only one of several atrocities summarized as "crimes against humanity." The Allies placed the Final Solution amid the list of conventional crimes—murder, maltreatment, abduction, enslavement, and robbery—that had been committed for racial reasons. In most trials, the judges convicted the defendants for "crimes against humanity" only when the defendants had perpetrated the acts in connection with "crimes against peace" or "war crimes." The British historian Donald Bloxham concludes that with

> the murder of the European Jews—the definitive crime of Nazism—and the "war of annihilation" between Germany and the USSR that precipitated the genocide . . . the [Allied] war crimes trials did little to clarify conceptualizations of Nazi criminality in the public sphere anywhere. Sometimes they actually muddied the waters by drawing attention away from the victims of Nazi genocide and onto much more ambiguous symbols of suffering. Indeed, the trials had the peculiar effect of helping to elide the fate of the victims.[18]

If originally the Allies had an admirable initial purpose to punish and purge the war criminals, the ultimate result, already by 1948 and 1949, was to cover up the crimes—especially those involved in or associated with the Holocaust—and acquit their perpetrators. By then, the United States and Britain believed themselves faced with a serious Soviet threat to Europe and the West. Rapidly deteriorating international relations led to the Cold War, from which the perpetrators benefited. Both Washington and Whitehall concerned themselves more with integrating West Germany and its new Federal Republic into a Western anti-Communist alliance than with trying and punishing the war criminals. In doing so, the Western Allies sought to recruit to their side the West Germans, who demanded a halt to the war crimes trials and freeing of the convicted. Only the trial in 1961 in Jerusalem of one of the principal Holocaust perpetrators, Adolf Eichmann, provided—in the words of then Israeli president David Ben-Gurion—the "Nuremberg of the Jewish people."[19]

On the other hand, especially for the criminals' Jewish victims who'd survived, much suffering and hardship continued long after the world war. During the summer of 1945 tens of thousands of Jews, mostly in Central and Eastern Europe, barely alive at their liberation, continued to perish in great numbers. Despite efforts by some Allies to rescue them, the survivors couldn't recover from the starvation, disease, and brutality they'd experienced in the German concentration camps.

In addition, during late 1945 and 1946, when they left the camps or their places of hiding from the Germans and attempted to return to homelands (primarily in Poland and elsewhere in Eastern Europe and the Soviet Union), some two hundred thousand to three hundred thousand dispossessed, destitute, and emaciated survivors suffered further discrimination, hatred, and dehumanization. Most had lost their family and friends in the unprecedented genocide and now found themselves bereft and alone. Nearly everywhere the returnees (as shown especially in chapter 10 of this book) discovered that the Nazis had wholly destroyed their once-flourishing Jewish communities.

Although the Allies granted some survivors of Allied or non-Axis countries (especially victims of Nazi political and racial persecution) special status and some postwar assistance, the substantial majority found themselves "stateless," wanted by almost no one, including their native countries and most Allied nations. Many languished for several years after the war in often poorly run and provisioned Displaced Persons (DP) camps in Allied-occupied Germany, Austria, and Italy as well as in France.

Thus, to the critical issue of how the world could stand by during the war and allow the Holocaust to happen, one could add a new, closely related, and similarly crucial issue about the postwar era: how the world stood by with such callous disregard for the Holocaust and its survivors that nations permitted most perpetrators to receive lenient or no punishment at all while its survivors continued to endure discrimination and, in some instances, even death.

2

Four Faces of Genocide

What Happened in the War

Heavily armed guards brought the woman to the main camp office. As she stood there, frightened, dirty, and in tattered clothes, she pleaded in desperation with the tall, sturdily built, haughty German officer, bedecked smartly in his *SS* uniform. "Will you allow me to visit my husband?" she asked.

When the woman, a Polish Jew, turned her back on him, the commandant of the Nazi death camp at Sobibor ordered an *SS* subordinate into the room. The officer signaled to the guard the pulling of a trigger. He made it clear to the guard that the woman standing before them should be shot immediately.

The woman, a Polish Jew from the nearby city of Chelm in southeastern Poland, had arrived at the camp on her own, unannounced, to search for her husband. A few days earlier the *Gestapo* had taken him to Sobibor with a train transport of Polish Jews. The innocent woman didn't know what was happening in Sobibor or that the *SS* had already murdered her husband in one of the camp's gas chambers.

The guard, having received his superior's signal, escorted her brusquely into the large dusty and dirty camp, rife with the rancid odor of dead and burned humans. There he handed her over to a Ukrainian, a German auxiliary guard, who shot her.

Returning from the camp, the *SS* man met the commandant. The latter had waited for the subordinate and asked him whether he himself had executed the woman. When the man replied that a Ukrainian had done the deed, the commandant berated him.

"You coward!" sneered the officer.[1] He wanted all *SS* men in the camp involved individually in the killing of Jews. That made them each a partner in the mass murder—genocide—that was the camp's primary purpose in World War II.

FRANZ STANGL: CAMP COMMANDANT

"I only did my duty," the officer had told himself repeatedly during the war. He'd served Hitler, his Führer, in various *SS* posts, including commandant at the Sobibor death camp. Like Hitler and other fanatical National Socialists, he viewed Jews as allegedly weaklings, racially "inferior," and unfit to live. His absolute obedience to authority, to Hitler and the National Socialist regime, and to the "racial" mission assigned him by *SS* superiors, enabled him to justify his involvement, first in the government's mass murder of handicapped Germans, and then in the extermination of the Jews. Not forced to participate in such horrific operations, he did so, in part, because he craved advancement and material rewards. Also his hardened, masculine nature, a valued attribute among Nazis, added to his willingness to kill.

Franz Paul Stangl, an Austrian, and before the war a police officer and member of the "illegal" Austrian Nazi Party, had served in 1938 and 1939 in the "Jewish department" of the Linz *Gestapo* (the Nazi political police). Part of his job involved traveling through Upper Austria and the Sudetenland (the former Czech territory taken over by Germany) to survey and register Jewish communities. The work assisted the *SS*'s Reich Central Agency for Jewish Emigration in Vienna and after July 1939 in Prague, as well as the agency's head, Adolf Eichmann, a specialist on "Jewish affairs" in the intelligence branch of the *SS*, the Security Service (*Sicherheitsdienst*, or *SD*). The agency, which had its largest branch in Berlin, confiscated Jewish property and either forced the Czech, Austrian, and German Jews to leave the Greater German Reich or suffer or die from impoverishment.

In November 1940, a year into the war, with German armed forces occupying much of Poland, France, and other parts of Western and Northern Europe, Stangl joined the German government's killing program, which Hitler had initiated at the war's beginning and the Nazis had termed, euphemistically, "euthanasia." The program secretly exterminated German and other handicapped and disabled persons. The Nazis judged the victims as unproductive racially and economically and therefore "life unworthy of life."

Stangl held the post of deputy security chief at one of the main euthanasia killing installations or asylums, Schloß Hartheim in Austria. By August 1941, the center, along with five others in Germany, had received and murdered some seventy thousand handicapped Germans, many of them gassed. The Nazis then plundered and cremated their remains.

When appointed to the post at Hartheim, Stangl had listened eagerly to an *SS* superior who described the euthanasia program as a "humanitarian" effort that was "essential, legal, and secret."[2] Stangl's job at Hartheim included helping disguise the truth of how the "patients" had died. He arranged for the dead victims' families to receive the state's false death certificates as well as personal effects such as clothes. He knew that the certificates informed the families "the patient had died of a heart attack or something like that. And they received a little urn with the ashes."[3] In large part from the diligent work of its deputy security chief, only Hartheim among the euthanasia centers retained its secrecy from the German population.

Hartheim and other similar euthanasia asylums served as a form of basic training for Nazi mass killing on a much larger scale—the eventual extermination of the Jews. In killing their own people and learning to live with the stench of cremated corpses, Stangl and others on the staffs of the euthanasia centers felt no guilt later while murdering non-Germans, especially those whom the Nazis viewed as "subhumans" and, like the handicapped, as unworthy of living.

During the spring of 1942, amid the huge German invasion of the Soviet Union, the *SS* sent Stangl, along with numerous other euthanasia personnel, east to German-occupied Poland. There, led by Stangl's fellow Austrian, *SS* Lieutenant-General Odilo Globocnik, they helped implement the euthanasia program's technology and model of mass murder in three newly constructed German death camps: Belzec and Sobibor, both near Lublin, Globocnik's headquarters, and Treblinka, northeast of Warsaw.

The *SS* built these (and three similar camps nearby at Chelmno, Maidanek, and Auschwitz) primarily for one purpose: the systematic killing of all Jews in Europe and anywhere else German forces could seize them during the war. The Nazi leadership around Hitler termed this vast killing campaign, again using a cynical euphemism, the "Final Solution of the Jewish Question." The "question," the Nazis alleged, involved what to do with the world's Jews, although by then the killers already had their answer.

The Germans intended to use Belzec, Sobibor, and Treblinka mainly for the wartime murder of Poland's nearly three million Jews. Later, the Nazis termed this action "Operation Reinhard," named for a principal architect of the Final Solution and deputy chief of the *SS* and German police, Reinhard Heydrich, whom Czech partisans assassinated in May 1942.

In the three camps the *SS* installed what historian Henry Friedlander terms both the "[h]ardware and software" of "the killing technique," much of it borrowed from the euthanasia program. This included not only gas chambers and crematoria (the "hardware") but also the methods of deception (the "software") to lure victims into the death chambers by disguising them as showers, to kill prisoners in assembly-line fashion, to plunder their corpses, such as extracting teeth and bridgework containing gold, and to burn what remained.[4]

Stangl commanded Sobibor from the time it began operating in May 1942 until the following September. During those brief few months, some hundred thousand Jews, arriving by overcrowded transport trains from nearby ghettos in Poland, perished in the gas chambers. The trains stopped temporarily during August and September, in part for repairs on the railroad leading into the camp but mainly for construction of three more gas chambers. The killing facility couldn't keep pace with the numbers of arriving Jews.

At Sobibor, Stangl stood amid the tumult of prisoners at the rail line's unloading platform while the *SS* and prisoners already there stripped the new arrivals of their clothes and remaining little baggage and belongings. He wore a white riding jacket and cracked his whip like a horseman. Sometimes, during the chaos on the platform, he shot his pistol in the air and even into the throng of prisoners around him.

Until the victims' agonizing death in the gas chambers, Stangl attempted personally to disguise what awaited them. On one occasion, a young Jew who worked in a shop making jewelry for the *SS* guards asked the commandant about the fate of his father, with whom the boy had arrived at the camp. The father and other members of the boy's family had died in one of the gas chambers. Stangl, who visited the shop often, replied in a friendly tone: "You are much better off here. This is a much better place to work. Don't worry about him. He is all right."

Only later did the boy discover the truth about what had happened to his family and to the thousands of other Jews sent to the so-called showers. "No one lives," a cousin informed him. "Say *Kaddish* [the Jewish prayer for the dead]." Weeks later, the boy, just to see what Stangl would say, asked again about his father. "He is fine," came the response, "don't worry about him: just do your work."[5]

From Sobibor the *SS* sent Stangl in September 1942 to command Treblinka, the largest of the Nazi death camps in Poland. When he arrived there for the first time, he thought Treblinka "the most awful thing I saw during all of the Third Reich—it was Dante's inferno. It was Dante come to life."[6] Even miles from the camp, as he approached chauffeured by an *SS* driver, he smelled his destination. Corpses rotted along the railroad tracks leading into the camp as well as inside the huge facility itself.

These conditions, along with the failure of the camp's *SS* administration to collect valuable items stolen from the Jews and pass them along to Operation Reinhard headquarters, had led to an inspection of the camp and its temporary closure. Following the camp's reconstruction, Stangl replaced the previous camp commander, and the facility resumed its mass murder.

Between July 1942—when the first transports arrived at Treblinka from the nearby Warsaw Ghetto and elsewhere in Poland—and the fall of 1943—when the *SS* closed the camp and Stangl left it—some nine hundred thousand Jews died in its huge gas chambers. The *SS* organized prisoner detachments that buried the remains in large earthen pits.

Trainloads of victims from Poland and neighboring Slovakia arrived so fast at Treblinka that the camp's three original gas chambers proved insufficient. In the fall of 1942, under Stangl's close supervision, the *SS* constructed ten more chambers, enabling the camp to murder several thousand people in only three hours. When the new gassing installations had been completed, Stangl visited and inspected them with pride. "Finally," he remarked, with cynicism and no emotion, to *SS* officers with him, "the Jewish city is ready."[7]

At Treblinka he took pride and pleasure in his work. He wanted to succeed at his task, as directed by superiors, of eliminating the people sent to the camp and disposing of their valuables as quickly and efficiently as possible. "This is my profession," his twisted mind told him. He "enjoyed it" and it "fulfilled" him. "And yes," he would admit long after the war, "I was ambitious about that; I won't deny that."[8]

He accepted the wholesale murder of the Jews as a necessary fact, thinking of the victims only as cargo, as something inhuman that must be destroyed. "To tell the truth," he told Gitta Sereny, a postwar interviewer, "one did become used to it [the killings]. . . . I rarely saw them as individuals. It was always a huge mass. I sometimes stood on the wall and saw them in the 'tube' [leading to the gas chambers]—they were naked, packed together, running, being driven with whips."[9]

Soft spoken and polite to those he wasn't murdering, Stangl dressed impeccably. He even attended, as he'd done at Sobibor, the unloading of transports dressed in white riding clothes. Following the war, one of the Jews deported from Warsaw, Boris (Kazik) Weinberg, recalled his arrival at Treblinka's train station and what had happened as he crawled off the transport. Jewish laborers opened the freight car doors, showing large numbers of armed Germans and Ukrainians milling around the station platform.

"They started screaming and hitting, and we had to run," said Weinberg. Somehow, along with four hundred other fellow Jews who had arrived with him, Weinberg survived a "selection" of most of the Jews on the train for the gas chambers. His group stood in the camp courtyard and waited for work. Then through a gate the *SS* and Ukrainians brought in workers already living in the camp for a brief time. Immediately, the guards started hitting the workers and dogs bit them. Those in the first rows fell, and then the others collapsed on top of them. Eventually, guards forced them into a nearby wooden hut and, in groups of twenty, removed and shot them. "The scene," Weinberg remembered, "was indescribable."

Stangl arrived soon and addressed the new group of Jewish prisoners, including Weinberg. The prisoners whom the *SS* had just shot, the commandant claimed, had intended to kill the Germans and wipe out the camp. "I have orders to do the same to you," he added, "but I don't want to. There is work here for years." "Whoever works well," he emphasized, "will be treated humanely."

Daily, Weinberg and the other workers sorted, for the *SS*, clothes seized from the masses of murdered Jews, searching in pockets and elsewhere for gold and valuables. The group couldn't work quickly enough. The *SS* and Ukrainian guards, Weinberg recalled,

> would beat us endlessly, until our faces swelled up. Usually every two days they eliminated the weak and the beaten. During roll call the German in charge would remove those who had been beaten, line them up in a row, and transfer them to the ditch we later called "Lazarett." Initially this was just a hole with no fence and no name.[10]

The guards shot anyone placed in the hole.

The money, gold, valuables, and other belongings left by the victims and pillaged by the *SS* provided a source of enormous enrichment for the camp guards as well as for the *SS* and other German institutions. Said one prisoner who survived the camp: "I think that they all became millionaires in Treblinka."[11]

In March 1943, during a visit to Treblinka, Heinrich Himmler, the Reich leader (*Reichsführer*) of the *SS* and chief of the German police, discovered much to his surprise that the corpses of more than seven hundred thousand Jews killed there hadn't yet been cremated or burned, but remained buried in massive earthen pits. He ordered to the camp a special *SS* commando, Unit 1005. It used large excavating machines and groups of Jewish prisoners to exhume and burn the remains of the dead Jews at Treblinka and at many other Nazi killing sites in the German-occupied East.

Such efforts to destroy evidence of the Holocaust accompanied the concern of Hitler and Himmler, heightened by the large ghetto revolt at Warsaw during April and May 1943, that Germany must complete quickly the forcible destruction of the remaining ghettos and labor and death camps in the East. In May, Globocnik, through Himmler, promoted Stangl and the other commanders of Operation Reinhard camps to the rank of *SS* captain. In his recommendation to promote Stangl, Globocnik wrote that the latter was "the best camp commander and had the most prominent part in the whole action."[12] By then the Germans had exterminated nearly all of the Jews who had lived in prewar Poland, with more than a million killed under Stangl's supervision at Treblinka and Sobibor.

Shortly after the *SS* moved to close Treblinka, a prisoner revolt exploded at the camp on August 2. Of the approximately 850 prisoners there, nearly half escaped, but the *SS* caught and shot most of the escapees; only seventy survived. The *SS* executed on the spot some of the prisoners that remained in the camp and forced the others to help close the facility by tearing down the buildings and fences and by removing all traces of the camp. The Germans then planted over some of the land with trees, turned a portion of it into a farm, and murdered the prisoners still there.

Stangl and his boss Globocnik played down the uprising and escape of the Jewish prisoners and tried to keep it a secret. The ambitious Stangl worried that the revolt might end his career and feared being blamed for negligence if *SS* superiors in Berlin learned that prisoners had organized clandestine activity in the camp.

DR. WERNER BEST: THE ADMINISTRATOR

During the first months of 1942, the Final Solution began in France. Since 1940 German troops had occupied northeast France—including Paris—and ports along the English Channel and Atlantic coasts, while a larger and unoccupied area in the south remained under the French-ruled Vichy regime, which collaborated with the Germans. Working from his desk at German military headquarters in Paris, in the deluxe downtown Hotel Majestic, Dr. Werner Best organized the initial deportations of Jews to Auschwitz from the German-occupied portion of France. An *SS* major general, he had received in France in July 1940 an appointment as director of the military command's administrative section.

Immediately on his arrival in July 1940 in Paris, with the full support of his staff of German military officers, the studious Dr. Best seized the initiative. Along with the German embassy in Paris, he implemented numerous measures against French Jews and began by issuing two decrees: one prohibited Jews from entering the German-occupied areas; the other required the registration of Jewish property in preparation for German and French authorities to expropriate it. By December, a massive confiscation of such property—known as *Aryanization*—had begun, including in Vichy.

Despite the presence in Paris of officers of the Nazi Security Police (*Sicherheitspolizei*), *Gestapo*, and Security Service (*SD*), who specialized in "Jewish affairs," the ambitious Best outshone nearly all of them in helping launch the Jewish persecution in France. Moreover, he led the German military command there in preparing for and then implementing the Final Solution. Already on April 4, 1941, in a memorandum, he informed his superior, the German military commander in France, General Otto von Stülpnagel, on the details of Nazi Jewish policy. The clarity and authority with which Best wrote reflected his vast knowledge on the subject. This knowledge resulted, in part, from Best's earlier extensive activity as an administrator in the highest echelons of the *SS* and Nazi Security Police in Berlin.

"Germany's interest," Best told Stülpnagel, "lies in progressively relieving all European countries of Jewry with the goal of achieving a completely Jew-free Europe." To that end, Best continued, one should seek first to expel Jews of non-French nationality and then, as a second step, to intern 35,000 Jews of any nationality (including French Jews) viewed as "dangerous and undesirable." He envisioned eventually the "emigration" of all Jews of French nationality.[13]

A few weeks later, Stülpnagel and Best's administrative staff moved quickly to halt an effort by German Security Police in France to take over from the military the control and imprisonment of Jews. Eager to protect the army's turf in the "Jewish Question" in France, Stülpnagel ordered Best to quicken his implementation of Jewish policy, thereby leaving scant opportunity for the police to pursue its own ascendant ambitions. On May 14, at the urging of Best and his staff, and with the Vichy regime's collaboration, French police arrested 3,733 foreign Jews and placed them in internment camps. Most of the imprisoned had immigrated to France from Eastern Europe after World War I.

The Vichy government, however, refused to intern French Jews—as the Nazis demanded—merely because they were Jews. Consequently, to imprison or proceed otherwise against Jews holding French citizenship, the Germans needed to justify such actions on different grounds. The desired rationale arose during the fall of 1941, when the Nazis linked Jewish policy to another issue.

Previously, Best and the military command's administrative section had rejected massive German shootings of French hostages in reprisal for assassinations of German officers and other attacks on occupation forces by primarily French Communists, who were responding to Germany's invasion of Russia. Hitler and military leaders in Berlin had demanded draconian reprisal measures—namely large-scale shootings of French hostages. But Best and Stülpnagel resisted hostage shooting, fearing that such violence risked the loss of the French population's widespread cooperation with the German occupation. Best and the administrative section maintained in a decree issued on March 26, 1941, to German field commanders and French police: "Hostages should, therefore, be seized only if serious acts of violence are expected *and* other appropriate means [of retaliation] are not available."[14]

Conflict among the Germans over the wisdom of shooting French hostages continued to escalate. Under massive pressure from Hitler's headquarters, Stülpnagel had to announce that one hundred hostages would be shot for each assassination. Amid bitter disagreement involving the Vichy government, Hitler ordered that fifty hostages be shot at once and the other hundred two days later if assassins had not been captured. In late October, ninety-eight hostages were executed, which provoked disgust and outrage both in France and abroad. Following more assassinations of Germans, in mid-January 1942 and pressed to do so by Best and his staff, Stülpnagel suggested to Hitler a substitute for the proposed killings that they knew the Führer would support wholeheartedly. The military commander urged that Germany begin mass deportations of French Jews and Communists "to Germany or the East."[15]

Both Stülpnagel and Best reasoned that, apart from the Communists, the Jews—thanks to the popularity of anti-Semitism in France especially directed at foreign Jews—would receive little sympathy from the French populace as long as there were no public executions. Because the assassins of German officers included Jewish resistance fighters whom the Germans and French had arrested, the Germans could tie together through these repressive measures both their political and ideological mandates.

Simultaneously, Best explained in a German journal his view of what should happen in a Nazi-dominated Europe—a racially based "Greater Region Order," as he termed it—to Jews as well as to other "ethnic" groups who resisted their rulers. In writing that was both blunt and unique even for Nazi officialdom, he argued: "Extermination and expulsion of alien nationalities, when they happen wholesale, do not, based on historical experience, contradict the laws of nature."[16]

Stülpnagel resigned his command over the issue. (Later, in February 1948, facing postwar French prosecution for war crimes, he hanged himself.) But his proposal soon became common practice. An April 10, 1942, a decree from Hitler directed "that for each future assassination, apart from the execution by firing squad of a number of appropriate persons, 500 Communists and Jews are to be turned over to the *RFSS* [*Reichsführer SS*] and the German Chief of Police [Himmler] for deportation to the East."[17]

Even before Hitler's order, Best had begun readying the logistics for deportations. A document—signed by him on January 6, 1942, and produced at the major postwar Allied war crimes trial, the International Military Tribunal (IMT) in Nuremberg—discussed plans for the "deportation" of a thousand French Jews "to the East," either "in February or March."[18]

The German army and *SS* implemented the plans as scheduled. On March 27 the first deportation train, carrying 1,112 Jews, departed from a camp outside Paris for Auschwitz. Between then and the war's end three years later, some 76,000 Jews in France—25 percent of all Jews there—perished in the Holocaust, the majority in the gas chambers at Auschwitz-Birkenau.

Did Best know what awaited the Jews he sent "to the East?" By early 1942, he and the rest of the military command in Paris had few illusions about the Jews' fate.

In Best's administrative section Edmund Bälz, head of the justice division, had received detailed information about the massacre of some 34,000 Jews in Russia at Babi Yar, carried out in September 1941 by German police and *SS* units during barely a two-day period. The news had come from an officer transferred to Paris from the Eastern front. Bälz saw to it that the information became general knowledge within the military administration in the former French capital. "From now on," Walter Bargatzky, another of Best's subordinates in Paris, observed, "there is no more not-knowing in the 'Majestic' [the plush hotel headquarters of Best and the German military administration]."[19]

In fact, Best's earlier police career made it impossible for him not to know the fullest details of the horror unfolding for the Jews. He had long cultivated a German nationalist and Nazi background. His father had died in World War I fighting in France. The son opposed bitterly Germany's postwar democratic government, the Weimar Republic; during 1923 and 1924 he fought actively against the French occupation of the Rhineland. The young Best had joined the *völkisch* (racial nationalist) student movement that called for Germanic or "Aryan" supremacy in the world and for the removal of Jews from Germany's sphere of influence. Jews, *völkisch* writers alleged, formed a powerful racial foe of the Germans both inside the country and elsewhere and could thus never become a part of the German national community.

Best held a doctorate in law. Before Hitler assumed power in Germany in January 1933, he had joined the Nazi Party and *SS* and served as a judge in Hesse. He'd lost his judgeship in 1931, when Weimar authorities found in his possession documents from Nazi gatherings at an estate called Boxheim near Worms. The meetings discussed a plan for overthrowing Germany's government following a supposed Communist revolution.

But once Hitler and his followers took over the government and destroyed the Weimar democracy, Best became a leading Nazi legal theoretician, jurist, and police administrator. As early as March 1933, acting as the new police commissioner in Hesse, he had established the first concentration camp, which housed political prisoners and Jews, in the state at Osthofen.

A year later, he played a key role in the *SS*'s crushing of its much larger militarized party rival, the Storm Troopers (*Sturmabteilung*, *SA*). The killing in Munich and elsewhere of most of the top-level *SA* leaders (including the commander Ernst Röhm), which Hitler had ordered and in which Best participated, opened the way for the emergence of the *SS*—headed by Himmler—as the single most powerful institution in Nazi Germany. Soon it became an independent organization—accountable only to Hitler—that controlled an enormous bureaucratic and economic empire, which included the German police and concentration camps.

Best contributed in a major way to building this hugely powerful domain. Already by 1935, he had risen in the *SS* to the rank of colonel and entered the *Gestapo*. He believed fanatically in the *SS*'s view of itself as Nazi Germany's ideological, political, and racial elite. Soon he served as the closest collaborator of Himmler's deputy, Reinhard Heydrich, in integrating the German police into the *SS* and, therefore, in transforming the police into an instrument of Hitler's personal power. With as much or more loyalty to *SS* ideas and ideals than even Heydrich, Best served in this process as a link to the Nazi Party as well as to the professional and academic world within and beyond the *SS*.

Between 1936 and 1939, government and party decrees removed the police from all state and judicial control, fused *SS* and police agencies, and resulted in the mass appointment of *SS* to police posts. Simultaneously, Best and Heydrich built and united what the latter called the nation's "security corps": the *Gestapo*; the Security Police; the *SD*; and the Criminal Police (*Kriminalpolizei*).

Both Best's administrative work and his publications in legal journals contributed significantly to selling the combined *SS*-police system to German lawyers and other jurists and eventually to making the system independent of regular, restricted state authority. With express reference to Himmler's intentions, Best claimed in a 1939 journal article that the SS-police merger represented "an entirely new type of a unified state security corps."[20] He discussed "militarily trained units" within the new "unified corps borne by the SS." Considering that by then the function of such militarized units resembled that of combat troops, he appeared to support what Himmler had already lobbied Hitler successfully for—expanding, equipping, and militarizing some *SS* formations. Such units would be precursors of the real *SS* soldiers, soon to be given the name *Waffen-SS* (Armed *SS*) that fought in World War II alongside the German army. Also during the war, full *SS* control of a centralized German police—subject to no legal or other restraints—would enable Hitler and Himmler to later carry out the Holocaust and other crimes.

But Best's efforts during 1938 and 1939 to recruit trained jurists like himself for the Security Police alienated Heydrich, whose center of power in the *SS* existed chiefly in the rival *SD* and its intelligence-gathering activities. The *SD* had few officials with academic backgrounds and instead relied for personnel on party members with proven loyalty to Hitler and the regime.

Both Heydrich and Himmler remained suspicious of lawyers. The feud with Best, a vain and sensitive man busy building the Security Police, spilled even into the German press and threatened to undermine Heydrich's efforts to unite the numerous police agencies administratively and to create a leadership structure of the police that served solely the demands of Hitler, Himmler, and the party—not to mention Reinhard's pernicious pursuit of power.

Despite the bitter disagreement, Best assisted the intensified attack by Heydrich and the *SS* on the German Jews. On October 5, 1938, in his role as administrative chief of the Security Police, Best signed a decree ordering all passports held by German Jews to be stamped with a large red *J*. The measure represented a major step in the Nazis' increasing attempts to identify, isolate, and humiliate Jews, to confiscate their remaining property and wealth, and to force them to leave Germany.

During the same month Best participated in deporting thousands of Polish Jews from Germany; Nazi police dumped them across the border in Poland. Amid the crisis that ensued with Poland, which opposed its citizens returning home, Best suggested that the Reich withdraw the Polish Jews to concentration camps. On November 9–10, the Nazis unleashed a tidal wave of violence against Jews and their property all across Germany. Contemporaries termed the massive pogrom *Kristallnacht* ("night of broken glass").

On July 5, 1939, while Hitler made final preparations to initiate the racial war in Europe that he'd always desired and long planned, Best met with police and *SS* officials at Security Police headquarters in Berlin. Best headed up the recruitment and organization of so-called *Einsatzgruppen*, "special employment units," comprising *SS* and police forces that would participate in the forthcoming German invasion and occupation of Poland. Earlier, he had helped establish similar units used in the German takeovers of Austria, the Sudetenland, and the remainder of Czechoslovakia.

On August 29, he and Heydrich met with German army officers to explain the role of the *Einsatzgruppen* and their relationship to the attacking army. The *SS* and police leaders talked in vague terms and appeared little concerned for the army's authority. "Both were somewhat impenetrable," the army's chief quartermaster, Eduard Wagner, commented after the meeting. "Heydrich [was] especially unsympathetic."[21]

Still, the negotiators produced a quick agreement. During September, amid the German conquest of Poland, five *Einsatzgruppen*, each numbering over five hundred troops, invaded that country alongside the German armies. At least initially, the units' "special employment" in Poland involved rounding up and imprisoning or executing Polish political and other leaders as well as Poles and Polish Jews who resisted the invasion.

By then, Dr. Best headed the department for administration and law in the newly created Reich Security Main Office (*Reichssicherheitshauptamt, RSHA*) in Berlin, a large combined government-*SS* police and security agency. In his position Best, serving as Heydrich's deputy, and his department administered and controlled the *Einsatzgruppen*, whose persecution of Poles and Polish Jews grew steadily during the autumn of 1939 and early 1940.

The *Einsatzgruppen* reported daily on their activities to Best in Berlin. Soon the units aimed at launching the Nazi goal of acquiring in the East vastly more "living space" (*Lebensraum*) for the German "master race." The policy involved the forced mass evacuation of Poles and Polish Jews from provinces in western Poland to a neighboring region in the central portion of the former country, termed by the Germans the "Government General." Replacing those expelled from their homes, the *SS* settled German peasants as well as "racial" or ethnic Germans from the Baltic lands and other areas in Eastern Europe.

The persecution of Poles and Polish Jews included their random killing by *Einsatzgruppen* and other German forces. Only a few days into the German invasion, Best established and sent to Poland a sixth *Einsatzgruppe* as well as an independent commando group. Both operated solely as firing squads; their main task was carrying out Heydrich's demand to increase the numbers of daily executions.

Tens of thousands of Jews died. The *Einsatzgruppen* and other armed German units herded them into isolated, terribly overcrowded, hunger-filled, disease-ridden urban ghettos. These wretched areas served as holding centers until eventually, during 1942 and 1943, the Germans deported their inhabitants, nearly three million Polish Jews, to the death camps.

Best, however, didn't remain in the *RSHA* much longer. During the summer of 1940, Heydrich forced him out of the Berlin agency, which had become Nazi Germany's most rapidly expanding center of power. Deeply humiliated but hoping desperately to salvage his career, Werner accepted a transfer to a second-level military post in Paris.

Once there, and no longer dressed in an *SS* uniform but rather in that of an "office" general in the German army, he found himself an outsider. The conservative and nationalist military professionals, suspicious of their new colleague and his party and police background, only gradually learned to respect his administrative abilities and ruthless intent, which included, even in France, his ongoing work as a "desk murderer" of Jews.

ERICH VON DEM BACH-ZELEWSKI: COMMANDER OF KILLING UNITS

The tall, stout, and bespectacled man—with otherwise regular features—had been a longtime follower of Hitler. He'd joined the Nazi Party in 1930 and the *SS* a year later. A former professional soldier from an impoverished aristocratic family, he had achieved by 1939 the rank of general in the *SS* and, amid the world war, two years later took over as Higher *SS* and Police Leader—the commander of mobile killing units—for central Russia. By then, German armies had invaded and overrun vast areas of the western Soviet Union. Otherwise, he seemed poorly equipped for the tasks that his superior, Himmler, gave him. Two of his sisters had married Jews, and for that reason both he and his wife no longer received invitations from fellow military officers to social events. But the Nazi movement had offered Erich von dem Bach-Zelewski a new career.

During July and August 1941, Bach-Zelewski's units and other murder squads (including four large *Einsatzgruppen*) began, on orders of the *SS* and Hitler, to kill masses of Soviet Jews, a campaign that would expand by the fall to killing all Jews in Russia within the Nazis' reach. Historian Gerhard Weinberg has indicated that the Germans' eventual decision to kill all Jews everywhere "could well be influenced by the reaction inside and outside the Third Reich to the first stupendous massacres" carried out by the killing units in Russia.[22]

Himmler had visited the earliest killing sites in Byelorussia, some under the command of Bach-Zelewski. The latter (appointed by and beholden to the *Reichsführer*), with his headquarters at Baranowicze, commanded a mobile-armed *SS* cavalry brigade (part of the *Waffen-SS*) and several battalions of Uniformed Police (*Ordnungspolizei*) operating alongside *Einsatzgruppe* B. Bach-Zelewski's brigade emptied ghettos and hunted down and shot Jews (and other groups whom the Nazis associated with them, such as "Bolsheviks" and armed anti-German partisan or guerrilla fighters). Then the killers buried the bodies in large earthen pits or trenches. Within a year and a half after they'd entered the Soviet Union, the four *Einsatzgruppen* alone had murdered approximately 750,000 Jews and had cooperated increasingly with German army forces in antipartisan operations in the East.

On July 1, 1941, Himmler and Kurt Daluege, head of the German Uniformed Police, had visited Byelorussia, during which Himmler directed Bach-Zelewski to execute two thousand local Jews as punishment for alleged looting. On July 8, Himmler and Daluege turned up in Bialystok, where they spoke again to Bach-Zelewski and other police officers. Himmler urged the police to intervene more against the Jews. The same evening some one thousand local Jews were shot. Four weeks later, Himmler again visited *SS* and police leaders in German-occupied Lithuania and western Russia, where he conferred with Bach-Zelewski on July 31. During that meeting both urged the local armed *SS* and police units to associate Jews automatically with "Bolsheviks," Soviet "partisans," and "looting"—consequently condemning the Jews to mass executions.

Between July 29 and August 12, under Bach-Zelewski's command, the *SS* Cavalry Brigade carried out an initial "cleansing operation" in the Pripet River region and marshes. On orders from Himmler, the brigade shot masses of Jews, including all people suspected of supporting partisans, shipped off women and children, seized food and livestock, and burned villages to the ground. While meeting personally with Bach-Zelewski at the end of July, the *Reichsführer* expressed himself more pointedly: "All Jews must be shot. Drive Jewish females into the swamps."[23]

By August 7, 1941, Bach-Zelewski boasted that the total number of executions of Jews in his sector had exceeded thirty thousand. During the following two days the Germans killed another ten thousand in the Byelorussian city of Pinsk. A week later, Himmler and the chief of his personal staff, the suave *SS* general Karl Wolff, visited Minsk, where they met Bach-Zelewski and Arthur Nebe, another *SS* general, chief of the Criminal Police and commander of *Einsatzgruppe* B. By then, the Germans had begun executing local ghetto inhabitants, but on a limited scale. The ghetto would soon receive shipments of German Jews and serve as a killing center for them.

While in Minsk, Himmler, Wolff, and Bach-Zelewski watched a firing squad kill a hundred prisoners—many of them Jews and women—accused of partisan activity. The executioners did their work poorly, at first only wounding the women. The bloody scene left Himmler visibly distressed. When Bach-Zelewski complained about the psychological repercussions of the shootings on the killers and about the procedure's lack of efficiency, the unit received a short speech from Himmler, in which he demanded that they treat Jews and Slavs in only the most ruthless manner and obey orders unconditionally. He described combat as a law of nature, and against such vermin human beings had to defend themselves. He said that orders for the killings had come personally from Hitler and that he and the Führer alone bore responsibility for them.[24]

Apparently also with Himmler's approval, during late August and September 1941, Bach-Zelewski investigated the possibility of using poison gas to murder Jews in Minsk. First, he invited Herbert Lange—an expert in using carbon monoxide in gas vans or trucks to kill the mentally handicapped—to Minsk. (Lange would serve later as the commandant of the Nazi death camp at Chelmno, where at least 152,000 people would perish during his tenure.) The visit didn't happen, but later Dr. Albert Widmann, the chief chemist of the Criminal Technical Institute in Berlin (a part of the Criminal Police in the *RSHA*), arrived in Minsk.

Previously, Widmann had advised the Nazis' euthanasia program, initiated by Hitler at World War II's onset. The program, using bottled carbon monoxide, liquidated tens of thousands of handicapped Germans. Now the doctor, at Nebe's directive, tested not only the efficacy of killing by gassing, but also—even more horrific and unimaginable—by dynamiting the victims, as tried with handicapped Jews near Minsk. The British historian Peter Longerich notes that Nebe's order to use dynamite "may not have come directly from Himmler," as Bach-Zelewski claimed after the war, "but from himself [Bach-Zelewski]."[25] Eventually, in a mental institution in Mogilev as well as in Novinki and Minsk, patients were killed in airtight rooms with car exhaust fumes introduced from outside.

Following the war Widmann escaped any meaningful punishment for his war crimes. As would happen with Himmler's aide Wolff, a postwar denazification court classified the doctor as merely a "follower" of Nazism and ordered him to pay a small fine. After 1960, during West German trials of several dozen euthanasia and death camp personnel, Widmann denied repeatedly to investigators his involvement in the machinery of mass killings and received a light prison sentence.

As for Bach-Zelewski, his knowledge in the fall of 1941 of the use of gas in the extermination of Jews expanded when he met with Himmler on October 23. The *Reichsführer* was in Mogilev inspecting a factory labor camp under Bach-Zelewski's jurisdiction. According to one witness, Himmler declared that solutions other than shooting would soon be available to kill Jews. Later, Bach-Zelewski would recall that Himmler explicitly discussed the construction of gas chambers. By mid-November, the *SS* had commissioned the Topf company in Erfurt to construct a huge crematorium in Mogilev, and in December the first four-chamber crematorium oven was delivered. The gas chambers were never constructed, and later crematory units were diverted to Auschwitz. Instead, a killing center was created the following spring at Maly Trostinez, closer to Minsk.

Always, with fanatical loyalty, Bach-Zelewski implemented Himmler's directives to kill Jews and others. On August 1, 1941, one of Bach-Zelewski's cavalry regiment commanders informed his men: "No male Jews are to be left alive, no families left over in the towns and villages." During the weeks that followed, the *SS* Cavalry Brigade shot thousands of Jews in villages and towns in Byelorussia—men, women, and children. The total number of Jews murdered in August by the brigade likely exceeded 25,000.

During three days in early September, police units under Bach-Zelewski's command invaded the Minsk ghetto and executed 2,278 persons. On October 2 and 3, *SS* and police murdered 2,200 Jews in Mogilev; two weeks later, in one day Bach-Zelewski's forces murdered 3,726 people. He pushed for the "de-Jewification" of entire areas. According to Longerich, "[t]he mass murder of Jewish civilians that the Cavalry Brigade began so terribly in the first half of August . . . had a radicalizing effect on all the units" under Bach-Zelewski's command.[26] Christopher Browning concludes that the killings in Mogilev "marked the turning point toward genocide" in Byelorussia.[27] Also for *Einsatzgruppe* B, shooting Jewish women and children was now the norm; under Arthur Nebe's direction, it murdered some 45,000 Jews through mid-November. By year's end, Jews were virtually extinct in much of prewar western Soviet territory. As 1941 ended, the total death toll of Jews in Byelorussia amounted to 190,000.

Apparently Bach-Zelewski's work forced him to enter a hospital with stomach and intestinal ailments. Following surgery, his slow recovery prompted Himmler to dispatch the top *SS* physician, Ernst Grawitz, to the bedside of the *Reichsführer*'s favorite general. Grawitz reported in March 1942 that Bach-Zelewski suffered especially from "reliving the shooting of Jews that he himself had conducted and other difficult experiences in the East."[28]

But soon Bach-Zelewski recovered, and in October Himmler appointed him to coordinate all German antipartisan operations in the Soviet Union. Only two months earlier, Hitler had authorized the "extermination" of the partisans by the *Wehrmacht*, *SS*, and police, thereby providing a further blanket approval for atrocities against primarily "Jewish-Bolsheviks." The Führer described Bach-Zelewski as a clever person, one unafraid to take steps not in accord with regulations.

From August to October 1944, Bach-Zelewski commanded troops in Warsaw that helped destroy the revolt of the Polish underground against the German occupation. During the revolt, Soviet army forces waited outside Warsaw as the Germans suppressed the uprising with the utmost brutality. Bach-Zelewski's units killed masses of Polish civilians and helped destroy a large part of the city; for these operations he received the Knight's Cross, the second-highest military decoration in the Third Reich. Before the war's end seven months later, he commanded several other army units.

WALTHER RAUFF: MASS MURDERER BY BULLETS AND GAS VANS

With a June 1944 rank of *SS* colonel, Walther Rauff had progressed impressively since his early days as a former naval officer. His sordid divorce had crippled his professional prospects and forced him to resign from the navy on December 31, 1937. Born in 1906, the son of a banker who had reared Walther with rigid discipline, the youth had been too young to serve in World War I. He had joined the navy in 1924 and, after a period of training as a midshipman during which he saw service in South America and Spain, he rose in 1936 to the rank of lieutenant and received command of a minesweeper. While in the navy, he had met and befriended Heydrich, who had also served in the navy in the 1920s and been forced to resign his commission under similar circumstances.

After Rauff left the navy, Heydrich helped salvage his friend's career. Walther entered the *SS* on April 20, 1938 (Hitler's birthday), and rose quickly in his new organization, in part because of Heydrich's favor and in part because Rauff had the ruthless qualities that made him the type of man who flourished in the *SS*. By 1939 the *SD* had hired Rauff to assist the leaders of the Reich Security Main Office (*RSHA*) in Berlin, Heydrich and Best, in recruiting *SS* and police personnel to serve in *Einsatzgruppen* that followed German army forces invading Poland to murder Polish leaders, intelligentsia, and Polish Jews.

From the start of 1940, following the German conquest of Poland, until early 1941, Rauff served another tour in the navy. But once Hitler decided to shift German war priority from attacking England to invading the Soviet Union, Heydrich arranged for Rauff to return to the *RSHA*. By then an *SS* lieutenant colonel, Rauff headed the *RSHA*'s Section IID, which handled technical matters.

By June 1941, his main duty and that of his section involved providing equipment and supplies for the four *Einsatzgruppen* that entered the Soviet Union behind the massive German armies invading the huge country. Heydrich and other *SS* officials held a series of lectures for *Einsatzgruppen* commanders about the units' "tasks" in Russia, the principal one being, in the words of one of those present, "exterminating the Jews. It was stated that eastern Jewry was the intellectual reservoir of bolshevism and, therefore, in the Führer's opinion, must be exterminated."[29]

In support of such deadly work, Rauff and Section IID negotiated with the German army high command to acquire weapons and munitions—bullets—for the killing units. During the next two years, the units' firing squads murdered some one million Soviet Jews. Simultaneously, when Hitler appointed Heydrich civilian chief of the Nazi-held Protectorate of Bohemia and Moravia, Rauff received a second job, one in Prague to go along with the one in Berlin. In the protectorate's capital he served as Heydrich's deputy in charge of organizing an intelligence office.

Beginning in the fall of 1941, Section IID and Rauff, a friend of Franz Stangl's, played the major role in developing and testing an important invention in the technology of the Final Solution—the mobile gassing van or truck, which the *Einsatzgruppen* employed extensively in Soviet territories to murder Jewish and Gypsy women and children. This involved piping carbon monoxide gas into specially constructed airtight compartments inside motorized trucks or other vehicles. The victims would be killed in transit to the mass graves in which their corpses, pinkish from carbon monoxide asphyxiation, would be dumped; the *SS* timed how long the killing would require (fifteen to twenty minutes) and chose the routes to match the necessary killing time. The interiors of the vans and trucks were lit; often, in desperate efforts to escape, the victims would break the lighting fixtures, but because of the designs implemented by Section IID, they were unable to stop the deadly flow of gas.

For construction of the vans or trucks, Heydrich turned to Rauff, whose jurisdiction in Section IID included all motor vehicles—some four thousand—of the Security Police. In September 1941, Rauff told a subordinate, Friedrich Pradel, chief of the motor pool, about the idea then circulating among Heydrich and others to use carbon monoxide fumes from the truck engines to kill vast numbers of people in the Soviet Union. For the *Einsatzgruppen* operating there, said Rauff, a more "humane method of execution" was needed than shooting their victims.[30] Much later, long after the war, Rauff would claim: "Whether at that time I had doubts against the use of gas vans I cannot say. The main issue for me at the time was that the shootings were a considerable burden for the men who were in charge thereof and that this burden was taken off them through the use of the gas vans."[31]

Rauff asked Pradel to inquire of the motor pool's chief mechanic whether exhaust gas could be directed into a closed truck to kill the passengers. Also Rauff instructed Pradel to discuss with the Criminal Technical Institute how the proposed gas van should function. Initially, Section IID had difficulty in acquiring the necessary large-truck chassis. When Pradel asked the German army's motor pool division to supply several large trucks, it refused to do so. Rauff himself then approached the Saurer truck manufacturer that provided five chassis.

Pradel and his mechanic visited the body-making company of Gaubschat and contracted it to build airtight compartments for the chassis. Christopher Browning has described the subsequent mechanical work that made the trucks into killing machines:

> When work on the first chassis was finished, [the mechanic, Harry] Wentritt brought the converted Saurer, which now looked like a furniture van, to his garage. He inserted a T-joint in the exhaust pipe and bored a two-inch hole in the floor of the rear compartment. A perforated U-shaped pipe was welded on

> the inside and a nozzle on the outside of the hole. When the T-joint and the nozzle were joined by a pipe and the regular exhaust pipe was capped, exhaust gas was diverted into the rear compartment.[32]

The mechanic then drove a completed truck to the nearby Criminal Technical Institute, where Albert Widmann showed other chemists there how, by adjusting the timing of the ignition, one could maximize the amount of poisonous gas in the exhaust. One of the chemists, wearing a gas mask, measured the amount of carbon monoxide produced in the sealed compartment. Some days later, probably at the end of October, the gas van appeared at the Sachsenhausen concentration camp, where the *SS* and chemists tested it again. Forty naked Russian prisoners died in the van from poisoning.

Immediately, Rauff and Section IID placed orders with Gaubschat for thirty more airtight compartments. According to Browning, while the "initial intention" in constructing the gas van "may have been to facilitate the Einsatzgruppen killing operations on Soviet territory," it had also become available by the end of 1941 "as one potential solution to SS planners pondering the means for killing the European Jews."[33]

During 1942 and 1943, the *RSHA* sent at least five or six vans to assist the killing operations of *Einsatzgruppe* A in the Baltic states and *Einsatzgruppe* B in Byelorussia. *Einsatzgruppe* C, operating in north and central Ukraine, used six more gas vans. In the southern Ukraine, which included the Crimea and the area reaching east to the Caucasus, *Einsatzgruppe* D employed the vans to murder Soviet prisoners of war and civilians, most of them Jews.

In May 1942, Rauff received a field report from the *SS* chemist Dr. August Becker, who had worked in the euthanasia program and advertised himself as a "gassing expert." (At the war's end, the Allies captured the report and used it in war crimes trials at Nuremberg; Becker served three years in prison for his membership in the *SS* and in 1959 was sentenced to ten years imprisonment for his role in gassing Jews, but he was released from detention in 1960 for poor health.) Becker wrote from the Ukraine and discussed the "overhauling of vans" for *Einsatzgruppen* C and D, describing technical problems that plagued the vehicles. Some stopped "completely in rainy weather," he complained, causing difficulties in the killing procedure:

> It is only a question now whether the van can only be used standing at the place of execution. First the van had to be brought to that place, which is possible only in good weather. The place of execution is usually 10–15 km away from the highways and is difficult of access because of its location; in damp or wet weather it is not accessible at all. If the persons to be executed are driven or led to that place, then they realize immediately what is going on and get restless, which is to be avoided as far as possible. There is only one way left; to lead them at the collection point and to drive them to the spot.[34]

Becker also reported to Rauff on another issue. It involved hiding the vans from their Jewish and other victims:

> I ordered the vans of group D to be camouflaged as house-trailers by putting one set of window shutters on each side of the small van and two on each side of the larger vans, such as one often sees on farm-houses in the country. The vans became so well-known that not only the authorities, but also the civilian population called the van "death van," as soon as one of these vehicles appeared. It is my opinion, the van cannot be kept secret for any length of time, not even camouflaged.[35]

The *SS* employed the vans or trucks as well to kill Jews in Serbia and continuously at the Chelmno extermination camp in German-annexed Polish territory. At least 215,000 Jews died at Chelmno until the Nazis closed the camp in April 1943, and after it reopened briefly in late 1944 and early 1945. It's estimated that altogether in the Soviet Union and Serbia, the vans murdered at least 150,000 persons, mostly Jews.

During the summer of 1942, the *RSHA* sent Rauff to North Africa to command a special German police detachment (an *Einsatzgruppe Afrika*), which planned to exterminate the Jews of Cairo once the regular German army unit, the *Afrika Korps* of Field Marshal Erwin Rommel, arrived in the city. Also Rauff's death commando stood ready to accompany Rommel's forces if they advanced into Palestine, where it would have murdered the roughly half-million Jews then living there.

During the battles in 1942 in North Africa between the *Afrika Korps* and the British Eighth Army, and with the death camps in Poland in full operation, Nazi propaganda broadcasts in Arabic to the Muslim world by Arab exiles in Berlin, including the radical Palestinian cleric and mufti of Jerusalem, Haj Amin Al-Husayni, incited listeners to mass violence against Jews. A broadcast on July 7 urged, "You must kill the Jews, before they open fire on you. . . . Your sole hope of salvation [from "British imperialism"] lies in annihilating the Jews before they annihilate you."[36] Deportation of Jews from Western Europe to Sobibor and Auschwitz-Birkenau had just begun.

But when Rauff discussed with Rommel at Tobruk the liquidation of the Jews of Cairo, the field marshal, disgusted with the idea, refused to talk about it and sent Rauff on his way. Nevertheless, later that same year in Tunis, Rauff led a police unit that rounded up 4,500 Jews for slave labor and stole jewels, silver, gold, and religious artifacts from Jews. Himmler ordered Rauff to ship the Jews to Italy and to apportion them from there to various extermination camps in Poland. Clearly, this all pointed to Nazi intentions to extend the Holocaust from Europe to the Middle East and North Africa. Only the defeat of Rommel's forces by Anglo-American troops in the major battles of

El Alamein (November 1942) and in Tunisia (May 1943), which removed the German and Italian armies from North Africa, ended such a threat.

Nevertheless, during the final year and a half of the war, as the fighting turned against Germany and its Axis allies, Nazi propaganda broadcasts to the Arab world claimed that the Jews had "kindled this war in the interest of Zionism." Also the Nazis told the Arabs repeatedly, "The Americans, the British, and the Jews are all conspiring against Arab interests."[37]

When Italy defected in September 1943 from the Axis alliance with Germany and Japan, Rauff took over as chief of the *SD* and Security Police in German-occupied northwestern Italy. His subordinates, with his implicit approval, doled out particularly brutal reprisals for acts of resistance to occupation forces. As the war drew to a close in Europe in April 1945, an Italian mob nearly lynched Rauff in Milan. Another of the many Austrians involved in the Final Solution, he surrendered to the Allies and attempted to gain credit with them for the surrender of German forces in Italy. But the Americans arrested and interned him in a prisoner of war camp in Rimini. A U.S. Army intelligence report described him as "most uncooperative during interrogation" and "a menace if ever set free, and failing actual elimination, [he] is recommended for life-long internment."[38]

3

Leaving Auschwitz

The mood in the huge camp near Krakow in Upper Silesia grew ever more tense. If they kept quiet on the long snowy nights in early January 1945, they could hear Red Army artillery to the East. A Jewish teenager, Hans Frankenthal, and many of the tens of thousands of other prisoner–forced laborers still breathing at the huge Auschwitz-Monowitz labor camp used their fingers to calculate the days when Soviet troops might arrive at the camp to liberate them, ending their suffering and the long world war.

Monowitz was part of a huge complex of concentration and death camps known collectively as Auschwitz. The latter comprised mainly an original camp, Auschwitz I; a larger facility nearby, also for killing and forced labor, Birkenau (Auschwitz II); Monowitz (Auschwitz III); and numerous smaller satellite camps in the surrounding area. The region, formerly under Polish rule, had been incorporated in the fall of 1939 into Germany after its occupation of western Poland.

Earlier, Frankenthal had heard that Himmler had ordered the *SS* to blow up the several gas chambers and crematoria at Birkenau. Nearly euphoric, Hans and his fellow prisoners hoped that the "selections" for gassing prisoners unable to work would stop. The furnaces still intact at Birkenau could not keep up with incinerating the masses of prisoners who continued to die. Bodies piled up all over Monowitz. The killing was nothing new to Hans and his brother, Ernst. In March 1943, the boys had lost their parents, both of whom the *SS* had gassed at Birkenau, shortly after the family arrived at the camp.

But now, nearly two years later, with the Red Army nearby, rumors abounded. The Germans, the prisoners whispered, might still try to kill them.

Three of Hans's friends, he recalled later, members of a small anti-Nazi camp resistance, were so "firmly convinced that the Germans were not going to leave anybody alive" for the Russians to find, that they "organized an escape."[1] Within a few days, the *SS* had captured and hanged the escapees.

As the Red Army approached the camp, the Final Solution continued and even quickened its pace. Then, late in the evening of January 18, 1945, the camp bell sounded. Amid the bitter cold and snow, Hans and thousands of other shivering prisoners, dressed only in filthy, raggedly thin, striped camp uniforms, assembled in the courtyard. There the *SS* directed that all prisoners who could walk ready themselves to leave the camp immediately. The prisoners had no blankets or anything else to help shield them from the frigid weather.

Neither Hans nor anyone else expected an evacuation—apparently not even the *SS*. By then, the Soviet armies had fought the Germans to within a few miles of the camp. The *SS* men, fearing for their lives at the enemy's hand, sought to remove prisoners and other evidence of the mass death at Auschwitz. The *SS* had orders to evacuate the prisoners to the west, away from the advancing Soviet troops.

Hans had never seen the guards "so edgy" and worried. "They were actually more nervous than we were." For the first time, at least in his experience, "nobody took a head count" or "roll call" in Auschwitz. Instead, people ran around in "a state of confusion," including the *SS*, who fired guns "frantically" into the air.

When the main camp gate opened, Hans recounted long after the war, many prisoners bolted through it "like a herd of wild animals." For a brief moment, he considered staying behind at the camp; he suffered from an inflamed knee and could walk "only with great difficulty." His block chief and friend at the camp, Ede Besch, however, persuaded him to leave. "It can't last that long," Besch told him. "Wherever they make us go, I'm sure the Red Army won't be far behind." The prisoners dragged themselves out the gate and northward, stumbling through heavy snowdrifts. Yelling and cursing, guards pointed guns at them. Numerous prisoners, too weak, exhausted, and cold to continue, fell behind.

Hans and his brother Ernst heard the first gunshots. It didn't take long to realize that the *SS* shot the stragglers or left them to freeze and die along the road. The boys tried to remain at the front of the weary, slow-moving columns to avoid the much more dangerous rear. Some nine thousand prisoners had left Monowitz. Soon, the number swelled to tens of thousands more as other prisoners, many numbed by the freezing temperatures and threatened with frostbite, joined the already deadly march from Auschwitz's nearby satellite camps.

The long lines moved throughout the night and following day. Hans nearly collapsed. "I have no idea how many people have been murdered," he remembered thinking years later. But at the moment, there was no relief; the "death march" continued. He and other prisoners would end up first in central Germany, doing forced labor producing V-2 weapons at the Dora-Mittelbau concentration camp, and then at Theresienstadt, a large ghetto established by the Germans north of Prague in the Nazi protectorate of Bohemia-Moravia. In early May 1945 Soviet troops liberated the ghetto.[2]

FIRST POSTWAR REPORTS

Although neither Hans nor his prisoner friends did so, thousands of other prisoners sent in early 1945 on similar long "death marches" from Auschwitz and other Nazi concentration-and-labor camps in the East—together with many of the camps' *SS* guards—ended up in northwest Germany at Bergen-Belsen, one of the Nazis' large concentration camps. Almost immediately upon liberating Bergen-Belsen in mid-April 1945, the British army began learning firsthand about the savagery of the *SS* personnel and the massive killing facilities at Auschwitz.

On May 6, two weeks after she arrived at Bergen-Belsen, the first civilian relief worker at the camp, Jane Leversen, a British Jew, reported to the Jewish Committee for Relief Abroad (JCRA) in London on what she called the "horrors" that had befallen Belsen's tens of thousands of prisoners, at least a third of whom were Jews. "A very considerable number of the internees," she wrote the JCRA, "have spent anything from six months to two or three years in other concentration camps." Survivors had told her about Ravensbrück, the camp for women north of Berlin; Theresienstadt, the Jewish ghetto near Prague; and the Warsaw Ghetto.

Then Leversen discussed in startlingly vivid and generally accurate terms the camp "which is spoken of most frequently" by survivors "and with the most dread." It is likely that her description of Auschwitz for the JCRA represented the first postwar report of the camp, much of it accurate and gleaned from eyewitnesses, to reach the Anglo-American world:

> [I]t was here that many of the internees were branded with their numbers. Auschwitz had a crematorium where people were burnt alive, and also gas-chambers where, I am told, it took two minutes to kill people. I have also been told that a number of people were crucified here, with their feet uppermost. The horrors of Belsen camp are, I am quite sure, beyond imagination of those who have not seen them, but they are as nothing compared to Auschwitz. Internees were forced to stand and watch their dearest relatives and friends being forced into the crematorium, and to listen to their shrieks as they were roasted; similarly with the gas-vans, and similarly with the crucifixions. I know a girl

> of 27, Polish, a bacteriologist by profession, whose job it was to sit for twelve hours per day, at the entrance to the crematorium, noting down the numbers, in nationalities, of those who were killed there, with them appealing to her as they passed, to help them; she did this for seven months. There seems to have been no discrimination about the people who were burnt; it seems that the internees were paraded in "exercise grounds" every morning, and Guards [*sic*] walked through them, dividing them into two groups in each enclosure, and then said which side was to go to the death chambers on that particular day. I know mothers who saw their own children killed, husbands their wives, brothers their sisters, etc. There is no need further to labour these horrors, but it must always be remembered that those whom we meet later, in the outside world, have lived through these nightmare experiences. It seems that a large number of Auschwitz internees were transferred to Belsen; some came by rail, in open trucks, but one very large group was forced to march for three days through the snow last winter, two six-hour forced-marches per day, without even a pause "to relieve themselves." The agony of this journey was indescribable—exhaustion, pain, frost-bite. Many died by the way. It was quite fantastic.[3]

Would her readers in London believe all that she had told them? Leversen wondered. "I trust," she concluded in her report, "that it will be recognized that I have tried to write objectively."

Especially the British heard at Bergen-Belsen about one of the doctors at Auschwitz. If, in the postwar world, Auschwitz became eventually the arch-symbol of the Holocaust, Josef Mengele became the supreme personification of the sheer and unexampled evil that had characterized the camp.

In the days and weeks following the liberation of Bergen-Belsen, the British arrested forty-five *SS* and other German camp officials. Most had served at and evacuated Auschwitz in January 1945. Preparing to bring the accused to trial, the British located and questioned numerous former Auschwitz prisoners, the majority Jews. Repeatedly, the survivors mentioned Mengele and gave the postwar world its first glimpse of one of the most wanted and abominable of Nazi war criminals.

Edith Trieger, a twenty-year-old Slovakian Jew, recounted how she had observed "a selection to choose people for the gas chamber" carried out during October 1944 "inside the block in which I lived." She continued, "Dr. Mengele was in charge of the selection" along with a female *SS* guard and supervisor of women prisoners, Irma Grese—one of Mengele's principal accomplices in the mass murder. Those selected included primarily the elderly and sick:

> All the women in the block had to undress. I was excused as I was a Block Leader. Those selected were taken to my room to await removal to the gas chamber and I was ordered to keep those selected in my room. . . . I was made

> to stand in front of the doorway of my room with my hands outstretched. The selected persons endeavoured to escape by passing under my arms and between my legs. When an opportunity occurred, I let them do so and they ran out into the street. Grese saw this. One or two got away, but Grese caught the majority and beat them with her hands and kicked them until they were forced back into the room. All the girls were naked.[4]

Another prisoner, Klara Lebowitz, a Czech Jew, had "often seen Grese with Dr. Mengele selecting people for the chamber and for forced work in Germany." When Grese observed a mother and daughter or sisters trying to stay together in selections for forced work in Germany to avoid being sent to the gas chamber, she "would beat them until they were unconscious and leave them lying on the ground."[5]

In rare instances, Mengele chose a victim for the gas chamber and then, during the gassing, intervened to save him or her. A Polish Jew, Regina Bialek, herself one of the persons rescued, recounted the unimaginable horrifying experience:

> On 25th December, 1943, I was sick with typhus and was picked out at a selection made by Doctors Mengele and [Karl] Tauber along with about 350 other women. I was made to undress and taken by lorry to a gas chamber. There were seven gas chambers [*sic*] at Auschwitz. This particular one was underground and the lorry was able to run down the slope and straight into the chamber. Here we were tipped unceremoniously on the floor. The room was about 12 yards square and small lights on the wall dimly illuminated it. When the room was full a hissing sound was heard coming from the centre point on the floor and gas came into the room. After what seemed about ten minutes, some of the victims began to bite their hands and foam at the mouth, and blood issued from their ears, eyes, and mouth, and their faces went blue. I suffered from all these symptoms, together with a tight feeling at the throat. I was half conscious when my number was called out by Dr. Mengele and I was led from the chamber. I attribute my escape to the fact that the daughter of a friend of mine who was an Aryan and a doctor at Auschwitz had seen me being transported to the chamber and had told her mother, who immediately appealed to Dr. Mengele. . . . I think that the time to kill a person in this particular gas chamber would be from 15 to 20 minutes.[6]

JOSEF MENGELE: HEALER TURNED KILLER

The handsome, dark-haired, highly educated *SS* doctor had murdered—by his own hand or indirectly—at the huge Auschwitz-Birkenau camp at least several hundred thousand Jews, as well as many Gypsies and Slavs. His *SS* camp colleagues had also participated widely in the killing. Rarely did he reflect on his gruesome work. Still, several events stuck involuntarily in his mind. Particularly one.

During a selection of Jews arriving at Birkenau by train from a Polish ghetto, a mother had refused to permit the *SS* to separate her from her thirteen-year-old daughter. When the *SS* doctor intervened, the woman bit and scratched him—*him*, an officer and doctor!

Instantly, he shot both the mother and daughter. Unfazed by what he'd done, Josef Mengele ordered the entire transport, comprising hundreds of Jews, including those previously selected for work, to be gassed. As he did so, he commented with no emotion, "Away with this shit!"[7]

Unlike Nazi death camps at Treblinka, Sobibor, and Belzec, which oversaw as their primary task the murder of all Jews, Auschwitz had a dual purpose: as both a death and concentration camp. While the Germans murdered some one million Jews at the camp, the *SS* there sought also to exploit as many camp prisoners as possible as forced laborers, including at Monowitz, in Germany's war and related industries. To accomplish this mandate, the Germans instituted at Auschwitz the now-infamous selections, whereby they separated men and women still able to work from those intended for killing in the gas chambers. The conduct of many of these selections fell to *SS* physicians at the camp.

Mengele, while working at Auschwitz from May 1943 to October 1944, functioned as the head doctor at the Gypsy family camp at Birkenau. In that role, he worked in hospitals and clinics in other sectors of the huge facility. "Thus," according to Helena Kubica, senior curator at today's Auschwitz-Birkenau State Museum, "for all practical purposes his authority as SS doctor extended over the entire Birkenau camp."[8] In the fall of 1944, following the killing of the camp's remaining Gypsies, Mengele served as chief physician of Birkenau's hospital for male prisoners. While at the camp, he—along with numerous other *SS* camp physicians—transformed himself from someone educated to be a healer, who'd taken an oath to uphold such a duty, into a torturer and murderer. Prisoners called him the "Angel of Death."

He dealt with Auschwitz's food shortages and typhus outbreaks by sending up to four thousand women a day to their deaths. Personally, he selected hundreds of thousands of Jews—either on the camp's railroad ramps, as the victims crawled off arriving trains, or in the camp's hospital and other blocks—for killing in Birkenau's four huge gas chambers and crematoria.

As the death trains from all over Europe pulled into the camp, Mengele often stood on the platform with *SS* guards and Jewish prisoners. The latter, dressed in dirty and ragged striped uniforms, were ready to unload the masses of Jews (including many who had died en route to the camp) and their few paltry belongings.

Watching the grim scene, Mengele stood—sober, seemingly detached, sometimes whistling to himself—dressed impeccably in his *SS* uniform. Seeking to deceive the new arrivals about their *real* fate as the *Gestapo* had done when packing them into the trains, he announced loudly that whoever felt strong enough to work should go to one side of the ramp; those who didn't feel well he ordered to the other side. The latter group, he said, would receive "easier work." Thus, the initial selection for gassing of the prisoners who had just arrived began. Within a few hours, the group that had chosen or been sent by Mengele for less work—usually the elderly, women, and children—had perished in the gas chambers, their remains destroyed in the crematoria or in large earthen pits, where the *SS* burned the bodies.

The *SS* sent Jews who survived the initial selection—both men and women—into the adjacent concentration camp portions of the huge facility. Most prisoners who worked and died—eventually, nearly inevitably, and often quickly—from slave labor, physical deprivation, and torture saw the crematoria's smoke and smelled the murder of their loved ones as well as of many others.

In May 1943, when typhoid struck the camp, Mengele ordered in a two-day period the extermination of sixteen hundred Gypsies. In November 1944, only weeks before he fled Auschwitz, Mengele arranged the gassing of some forty thousand women who had been subsisting on a daily ration of six hundred calories. Earlier the same year, he approved the killing of one thousand young boys who couldn't touch the top of a soccer goal.

His criminal medical interests centered mainly on Gypsies and identical twins, as well as on dwarfs, hunchbacks, and persons with other deformities—some as young as five and six years of age, often pulled from the arriving trains and separated from their parents. He'd use them in his so-called research, where he sought to increase the number of births of twins in order to double the rate of "Aryan" (a term the Nazis used erroneously for Germanic peoples) children for Hitler. In other experiments he injected the eyes of children with dyes to see whether he could turn them Aryan blue. Instead, he blinded many "patients." Following the tests, he sent the children routinely to the gas chambers and then had the corpses dissected. In further inhuman fashion, he displayed samples of their eyes, from pale yellow to bright blue, on his office wall.

Frequently, the mass murderer took gifts of candy and clothes to the children, joked with them, even hugged and kissed them. But then, a few hours or a day later, he'd torture them with barbaric experiments or kill them with phenol or other injections and fatal operations. In numerous instances, he murdered children purely for postmortem examinations. Some of the unsuspecting victims grew even to like Mengele, substituting him for their absent fathers the Germans had killed, and called him, innocently, "good uncle."[9]

A few Jewish survivors worked with or near him at Birkenau. Olga Lengyel, a Jew from Transylvania deported in May 1944 to Auschwitz along with her husband, two sons, and parents, had an assignment in the camp hospital during which she saw the "Angel of Death" and his behavior often. Whether or not he played a role later in the murder of Lengyel's family is uncertain.

Before seeing Mengele for the first time, Lengyel had heard from older inmates that the doctor was "good looking"—this despite the gap between his two front teeth. Later, she too admitted to finding him physically "handsome" and "attractive." Yet, she realized once she saw him, "there was a certain wildness in Mengerle's [*sic*] eyes that made one uneasy."

During his selections of prisoners in the barracks or camp yards, Lengyel observed that he never uttered a word: "He merely sat whistling to himself while he pointed his thumb either to the right or to the left, thus indicating to which group the selectees were to go. Though he was making decisions that meant extermination, he was as pleasantly smug as any man could be."[10]

On other occasions, Mengele forced prisoner-mothers to kill their own babies. In August 1944, Mengele ordered Ruth Huppert, a twenty-two-year-old Czech Jew who had lost her entire family (father, stepmother, and older sister, as well as most of her aunts, uncles, and cousins) in the Holocaust, to stop feeding her infant daughter. Another prisoner suggested to Huppert, "It's another of Mengele's experiments; he wants to see how long a newborn infant can live without being fed." The child's slow death broke her mother's heart—the most unspeakable of horrors she recounted many decades later in her memoirs.

Finally, Huppert could no longer think rationally. After a while, she had no will left. She did it. She killed her own child. "Mengele," she wrote, "had turned me into a child murderer."[11] Killing seemed so easy to the handsome, well-educated doctor.

In October 1944, Huppert joined some five hundred other women prisoners, mostly Hungarian Jews who were young, strong, and could work, whom the *SS* shipped out of Auschwitz to a labor camp at Taucha near Leipzig, a satellite of the Buchenwald concentration camp. The women worked at a factory that produced antitank rocket launchers. On April 14, 1945, when the *SS* evacuated the camp, forcing most prisoners to leave on a "death march," Huppert and several other fellow prisoners, including a young Czech Jew and her future husband, Kurt Elias, managed to remain behind—suddenly freed.

IRMA GRESE: BEAUTIFUL SADIST

The twenty-one-year-old woman, described by those who survived her torture of them as both "beautiful" and "mad," had left Auschwitz-Birkenau on January 18, 1945. She returned to the Ravensbrück women's camp, north of Berlin, where she'd trained as an *SS* guard and supervisor of women prisoners at Nazi concentration camps and perfected the art of beating and murdering alleged political and racial enemies. In March, she arrived at Bergen-Belsen. There, too, she beat and killed prisoners continually; inmates called her the "Bitch of Belsen." At least five thousand female guards like her manned the Nazi concentration and death camps, comprising about 10 percent of the camps' personnel.

Irma Grese, when arrested in late April 1945 by the British, denied to interrogators all responsibility in selecting prisoners for death at Auschwitz. She blamed it on Mengele: "I know from the prisoners that there were gas chambers at Auschwitz and that prisoners were gassed there. Dr. Mengele came in the camp at Birkenau and sorted out the people unfit for work for these transports."[12] Similar to other *SS* officials and guards held captive by the British, she disavowed nearly all involvement in the mistreatment of camp inmates. Nevertheless, she admitted knowing the reason for the selections, during which she, other *SS* guards, and prisoner foremen assembled and kept order among the prisoners paraded before Mengele and other camp doctors.

Following each such horrific event, Grese had kept a written account of the number of prisoners chosen. She noted for British interrogators how *SS* administrators had informed her, while employing euphemisms to conceal the fate of persons selected, that the latter "had gone to another camp in Germany for working purposes or for special treatment [*Sonderbehandlung*], which I thought to be the gas chamber. I then put in my strength book [for estimates of numbers of prisoners] either so many for transfer to Germany to another camp, or so many for S.B. (Sonder Behandlung)."

"It was well known to the whole camp that S.B. meant the gas chamber," she repeated.[13] She denied, however, that she'd selected prisoners to die and even claimed to have hidden mothers and children being chosen. But belying her professed concern and revealing her wrathful attitude and anti-Semitism, she accused the Jewish prisoners of controlling the camp and of causing her problems: "I was once denounced by the Jews for having done this [allegedly saving some prisoners from death] and was put under arrest for two days in my room. Jews were used as spies in this camp and had certain privileges."[14]

Since her childhood, Grese had shown a keen enthusiasm for Nazism. Her father, an agricultural worker, had prohibited her and a sister from joining the Nazi youth group for girls. When, at nineteen, she told him that she'd joined the *SS* as a guard at Ravensbrück and discussed her duties there, they argued and he expelled her from the house.

Her embrace of Nazi ideology had turned Grese from a coward into a bully. During her school days, often shy and frightened, she had run away from quarrels and fights with other girls. However, as an *SS* woman she found her courage guarding and supervising female prisoners at Ravensbrück, Birkenau, and Bergen-Belsen, places of horror where brutality was the norm and where she could act violently with impunity; the prisoners dared not hit back or retaliate in some other way.

Because of Grese's physical appearance, many prisoners had difficulty believing that she was so extraordinarily brutal. Fela N., a Polish Jew who'd lost her parents and several brothers and sisters in the Holocaust, had seen Grese often at Bergen-Belsen during the treacherous so-called *Appelle* (roll calls), in which prisoners stood for hours, silently and at attention, while the *SS* counted them. Later, she told a postwar interviewer:

> I remember her [Grese] very well. She did such terrible things, especially with our block. Her face, you know, was so beautiful. Large blue eyes and beautiful golden hair. Beautifully dressed in such a trim SS costume and a stick in her hand and a large dog. She would come to us every day, and before she would arrive we had to wait three, four hours for her. From 8:00 in the morning to 11:00 in the morning we were called to the camp square without washing, without food, without anything. We had to stand there in the rain and snow and frost, that was all the same. Stand lined up, four or five abreast. The block senior was inside the block and waiting until she came. We had to stand, we couldn't sit down. We wanted to sit down even on that wet, muddy ground. But we had to stand at attention till Irma Grese came. Then she would come. She had once prohibited us to have anything on our head.[15]

When Grese discovered a woman with something atop her head, she called her large guard dog. The latter "would jump at the girl and gnash his teeth as if he was going to bite":

> Irma Grese did not permit him to bite. She did not want that. She just wanted to horrify us. She wanted to cause anguish and terror, and that was much worse. So she would throw down this blanket [a small rag, cut by prisoners from gray blankets and thrown over their heads to protect them from the rain and snow, and prohibited by the *SS*] together with the person and kick her and beat her with her whip. . . . And then, afterward, when Irma Grese would talk to the block senior, she would ask how many people there were, how many had died and so on, and so on, and show such a beautiful countenace, such a kind face. Indeed, nobody could tell that just a moment ago she had made such scenes and was so bad, that she could be so merciless to other people.[16]

Grese had arrived at Birkenau in March 1943. On one occasion the *SS* commandant at Auschwitz, Rudolf Höß, wanted to make the young Grese "hard" toward prisoners. When another female guard had shown compassion to inmates, *Reichsführer SS* Himmler, then visiting Auschwitz, personally gave the guard twenty-five blows on her buttocks. Höß forced Grese and other female camp personnel to watch the punishment and ordered Grese to deal the last two blows.

She learned brutality well. Notorious for her sadism, Grese beat prisoners with a whip and walking stick as well as with her fists; she kicked and trampled them with her heavy jackboots; she set her violent dog on them; she assisted Mengele in the selections of victims for the gas chambers; and she wore a pistol, using it to beat and shoot prisoners.

Among her most gruesome actions, she sought out buxom Jewish women and cut their breasts open with her whip. She then took the victims to a woman prisoner doctor, who performed a painful operation on them while Grese watched—according to one inmate doctor who survived Auschwitz—with cheeks flushed, swaying rhythmically and foaming at the mouth. At another time, a prisoner physician, Gisella Perl, had to perform an abortion on Grese, who threatened to kill Perl if she talked about it but promised to pay her with a coat. The doctor never received the payment.

During 1944, Irma had supervised a punishment company (*Strafkommando*) for women prisoners, mostly Hungarian Jews. The women, numbering nearly a thousand, did backbreaking work in a quarry outside the camp. At a forced rapid pace they loaded stone and sand onto iron trucks and pushed them along a narrow-gauge railway. A strand of wire three to four feet high surrounded the quarry, which prisoners were not allowed to leave. Around the wire guards stood at intervals.

After the war a former prisoner, Helena Kopper, told the British that each day Grese, working with interpreters, chose "certain of the Jewish women prisoners and ordered them to get something from the other side of the wire." When the prisoners approached the wire, the guard nearby challenged them. But because nearly always Grese picked non-Germans, they didn't understand the guard, walked on, and were shot. Kopper testified that Grese "was responsible for at least 30 deaths a day, resulting from her orders to cross the wire, but many more on occasions." It was always Kopper's job, the latter continued, "ordered by Grese, to count the dead, and I, together with some other women, used to load the bodies into one of the railway wagons after working hours. The bodies were subsequently removed by ambulance."[17] Other former prisoners supported Kopper's account.

Grese and other female guards participated often in the nonstop persecution and killing of prisoners at Auschwitz. For this reason, she advanced rapidly, becoming *SS* roll call leader and eventually one of the head officials of the women's camp at Birkenau.

In September 1945, a British military tribunal at Lüneberg placed on trial Grese and forty-four other former camp officials (including several more female guards) for "violations of the laws and usages of war" and "ill-treatment" of prisoners at both Bergen-Belsen and Auschwitz. Journalists observing the sensational proceedings seemed fascinated with young Grese's beauty. In one of its first reports on the trial, the *New York Times* remarked how the "21-year-old blonde . . . managed to maintain the defiant contemptuous look that marred her undeniable good looks." The paper's later accounts of the trial referred to her as "blonde" and "smartly dressed."[18]

During the proceedings, a host of witnesses—mostly Jewish women formerly imprisoned at Birkenau and/or Belsen—testified, usually in depositions, to Grese's utter cruelty. They recounted how she'd beaten them and other prisoners repeatedly—shooting many others—and of her prominent role in selections of victims for the gas chambers.

In her own testimony, she admitted to carrying a whip, a walking stick, and a pistol at Birkenau and other camps and using them solely for occasional beatings of prisoners. Yet, despite her appalling actions, it was *Irma* who felt victimized by her work in the camps. Brimming with self-pity, this "beauty" testified on one occasion during the trial:

> The conditions in the concentration camps were bad for everyone, including the SS. The only time that I was allowed to go home for five days was after I had finished my training in Ravensbrück. I told my father about the concentration camp and he hit me and told me never to enter the house again.[19]

Even when captured at Belsen (amid the piles of dead prisoners) in April 1945, she had insisted on her own unjust victimization and affronted innocence. In a statement given eventually to the British—and read on October 5 into the Belsen trial record—she blamed "the brutal treatment of internees at the [concentration] camps" on *SS* chief Himmler (by then long dead from suicide). Continuing to excuse her behavior, she made a calculated admission, recorded by the British, in which she attempted to defuse her particular crimes by obscuring them in the morass of *SS* amorality:

> But I suppose I have as much guilt as all the others above me. I mean by this that simply by being in the SS and seeing crimes committed on orders from those in authority and doing nothing to protest and stop them . . . makes anybody in the SS as guilty as anybody else. The crimes I refer to are gassing people at Oswiecim [Auschwitz] and the killing of thousands at Belsen by starvation and untended diseases. I consider the crime to be murder.[20]

On October 16, 1945, her normally calm behavior in the courtroom dissolved into tears and shouts. After hearing her sister, Helena, testify on her behalf, Irma broke into violent sobbing, mopping her red eyes with a handkerchief that hid her face. But two hours later, when Grese stepped to the stand to deny the charges against her, she had recovered her composure. Yet during questioning, once again her voice betrayed her, becoming increasingly strident. Nearing the end, she was screaming, "I never shot a prisoner. I never shot anyone."[21]

In defending her to the court, the British officer acting as her legal counsel, Major L. S. W. Cranfield, presented his client not as a beast but rather as the scapegoat of Belsen. He viewed corporal punishment as perfectly acceptable in a prison, even, amazingly, when inflicted on women. Such behavior, he told the judges, seemed "reasonable conduct in the circumstances." His persistent use—and that of other defense counselors—in the courtroom of the word *prison* instead of *camp* (be it concentration, slave labor, or death) implied that justifiable legal grounds existed for the Nazis to confine inmates. Attempting to buttress his absurd claim, he cited instances of prisoner beatings in Allied countries, mentioned chain gangs in the American South, and noted that British police in India used bamboo whips—all deplorable acts, but even when linked together, they still did not render acceptable Grese's moist sadism.

Her attorney went so far as to insist that Grese was guiltless, especially in selections of prisoners for the gas chambers. "Before the parade [selection] took place," Cranfield argued, she "did not know what it was for" and "had no part whatever in deciding who was to be selected or in selecting anybody" herself. He termed the evidence against her "exaggerated and unreliable," and even accused the witnesses who had testified to her murderous activities of venting a vendetta: "The Nazis have aroused racial passion all over the earth, and I do not think it is unnatural or surprising that those young Jewesses should be vindictive towards their former warders, or to seek to avenge themselves upon them."[22]

The criticisms by Grese and her counsel of evidence used against her, as well as their attack on the "vindictive" Jews testifying against her and allegedly controlling the camp, would emerge among some of the earliest Holocaust deniers. The latter watched the trials of war criminals closely. One, a French fascist, Maurice Bardèche, contended in 1947 that at least a portion of the evidence regarding the concentration camps, such as Auschwitz and Belsen, had been falsified. Bardèche argued not only that "the Nazis were not guilty of atrocities," but that "the true culprits were the Jews themselves."[23]

But Grese's behavior at the trial often contradicted her claims of innocence. She shook with laughter when the wife of Josef Kramer, the chief defendant in the trial and former commandant at both Birkenau and Belsen, testified that her husband was a kind-hearted family man who had worried about the camps' prisoners having "to sleep on bare floors" and lacking "medical dressings."[24] Irma giggled as well when on other occasions the defense sought to portray those on trial as well-meaning victims of circumstances and inescapable superior authority. It seemed to matter little to her that she sought to portray herself as such a person.

On November 17 the tribunal convicted Grese and ten other defendants of mass murder and sentenced them to death; nineteen defendants received prison sentences, most of them ten years or less in length; and fourteen were acquitted. (Later the terms of sentences of those imprisoned would be truncated.) At the sentencing, among the defendants only Grese remained openly defiant.

In his closing speech, the chief prosecutor, Colonel T. M. Backhouse, focused on the selections. In a rare moment during the trial (but all too absent in later Allied trials of Nazi war criminals), Backhouse discussed their primary target:

> We have been accustomed in the last eight weeks to talk quite airily about selections and we have got quite used to the words "gas chamber." . . . I again submit that every person who took part in these parades, knowing what they were for, took part in a deliberately, carefully organized murder, not of one person but of a whole race—an attempt to destroy the whole Jewish race, an attempt to destroy the strength of Poland, one of our Allies, and an attempt to destroy by fear many other people. The martyrdom of the Jews, in so far as it concerns Allied nationals and was employed on those persons who came into the power of the Germans and into the power of the personnel of Auschwitz, was a war crime which has not been equalled.[25]

His words—and the evidence presented by the prosecution—mocked the court's penchant for light prison sentences and acquittals, which would soon become obvious. At the start, neither the British government nor its military had favored such trials until the United States and Soviet Union urged them into compliance and enforcement (however halfhearted). In sharp contrast, simultaneously a U.S. military court in Bavaria sentenced to death thirty-six of forty former Dachau concentration camp officials and guards it tried.

On a cold, snow-swept morning in mid-December 1945, in the northwest German town of Hamelin, the scene of the legend of the Pied Piper, the British hanged the breathtaking Grese. Royal engineers had erected gallows in the yard of a local ancient prison situated along the banks of the Weser River. But unlike the piper, whose entrancing, beautiful playing persuaded the town's children to follow him, never to return, neither Grese's beauty nor her lies and denials persuaded her postwar judges to ignore the horrific crimes she'd perpetrated.

Apparently, on the eve of her execution, she sang in her cell—much as Mengele, on whom she had tried to hoist much of the blame, had whistled on the rail platforms of Auschwitz during those heady days when German victory had seemed inevitable. Irma had learned nothing from her capture or her trial and expressed no remorse for her sadistic crimes. She went to her death convinced of her own reasonable rectitude.

MENGELE: IMPRISONED AND RELEASED BY THE AMERICANS

His demonic shadow, along with several thousand "lesser" such figures, towered over the camp. He'd never cared about the prisoners—especially not during early January 1945. By then, he too could hear the Red Army's approach to Auschwitz-Birkenau. The Soviets—or Bolsheviks, as the Nazis favored terming them—had advanced almost completely across Poland and were nearing the huge Auschwitz complex of camps that lay on the eastern border of Germany. Well aware that the war was lost and that capture by Allied troops meant a death sentence, he decided to run and hide. Unlike most other *SS* men, he had no tattoo of his blood type under his armpit, so he stood a good chance of eluding identification and capture.

On January 18, 1945, Mengele fled Auschwitz-Birkenau, along with most other Nazi officials there. Amid the hurried evacuation and attempted destruction of the camp's crematoria and gas chambers by the *SS*, they left. Although he took with him documents containing the results of his hideous research, only a few months earlier he had sent—for safekeeping—a collection of skeletons of dwarfs and handicapped persons (mostly Jews and Gypsies murdered either by him or by other *SS* men) to an "anthropological" institute in Berlin.

Upon leaving the death camp, Mengele remained for a time at the nearby Gross Rosen concentration camp in Lower Silesia. From there, he moved westward through Czechoslovakia and into eastern Germany, where the war's end found him disguised as a regular German army doctor in a retreating military unit. Caught in a no-man's land in Saxony between Soviet and American troops and fearing capture, he gave a nurse friend his research records for safekeeping.

Despite his notoriety among Auschwitz-Birkenau survivors, startlingly he didn't become an infamous public figure immediately following the war. After the Soviets liberated the Auschwitz camps on January 27, 1945, Mengele's name recurred in survivors' testimony given to the Soviet and, eventually, British armies. His name appeared on lists of major war criminals compiled by both the United States and the UNWCC (the latter established in October 1943 by Great Britain and the United States).

In the weeks after the war, the Allies hunted Mengele. On June 11, 1945, in the small Austrian town of Autenreid, three U.S. military policemen appeared at the door of Mengele's wife, Irene, and demanded to know his whereabouts. She insisted that she knew nothing and thought her husband probably dead.

Meanwhile, amid massive postwar chaos, destruction, and multitudes of displaced persons clogging the roads in Germany, Mengele made his way undetected through several Allied checkpoints and arrived in Weiden, a town in northern Bavaria. There, the U.S. Army apprehended and interned him for several weeks; in July 1945 he was transferred to a prison camp at Ingolstadt.

Even though he gave the captors his real name, they either had insufficient information about him or never checked the name carefully enough against the lists of wanted Nazi criminals. Numerous such lists existed, and the Allies faced an enormous task investigating some several million prisoners of war held in camps throughout Germany and Austria. Inefficiency and lack of coordination characterized relations among the various groups of U.S. occupying forces. Nor, apparently, did special units of U.S. military intelligence hunting war criminals visit the Weiden and Ingolstadt camps. While in custody, Mengele received false identity papers from a fellow German doctor to whom the Americans had given a good-conduct certificate.

Mengele's new identity gave him the alias "Fritz Hollman."[26] Believing him "clean," the Americans released Mengele in September 1945. By then, the U.S. Army had begun rotating into Europe new troops to man the American zones in Germany and Austria. Most arrived directly from the United States and saw neither combat nor the horrors of the Nazi camps. Often they felt differently toward the German captives, even expressing sympathy toward them, and seemed less concerned with their Nazi backgrounds and what such histories implied.

In the fall of 1945, Mengele arrived at a friend's house, the veterinarian Albert Miller, in the Bavarian town of Donauwörth on the Danube River. Desperate to avoid Allied recapture, the physician-turned-mass-killer denied everything that his family, friends, and others whispered about his wartime activities. Hiding at Miller's house, he insisted on his complete innocence, a claim that both he and nearly every other Holocaust perpetrator would make in the years to come. Miller's wife recalled later about the day Mengele knocked at the door: "He said, 'Good day, my name is Mengele.' Later my husband came home and we had dinner. I remember him [Mengele] saying, 'Don't believe everything you hear about me. It's not true.'"[27]

The same night of his arrival, U.S. Army intelligence officers arrested Miller for questioning about the latter's wartime Nazi activities. Mengele, undiscovered, hid in a back room. Miller's arrest scared Mengele. He left Donauwörth in the middle of the night and, during the next few weeks, moved east into Saxony. In a risky journey into the Soviet zone of occupation, he managed to locate his nurse friend to retrieve his notes from Auschwitz.

Meanwhile, Mrs. Miller contacted Mengele's family in the nearby Bavarian town of Günzburg. Not only did the Millers inform his family of his safety, but they also kept his visit a secret from the American authorities. Mengele's biographers, Gerald Posner and John Ware, noted that the Millers' readiness to help reflected an attitude prevalent in the Günzburg area. There was a widespread readiness to believe that the allegations against Mengele were false. The town had driven out its 309 resident Jews after the Nazis came to power. And broadcasts across Germany by the overseas service of the BBC, claiming that the SS had engaged in monstrous acts of carnage, were viewed as Allied victory propaganda.[28]

Beginning in late October 1945, concealed by friends and now using the name Fritz Hollman, he found shelter at a small mountain farm near the Austrian border, where he worked as a farmhand. He contacted his wife, parents, and other relatives in Günzburg, all of whom claimed to American authorities that Mengele had died. The parents owned a local firm that produced agricultural machinery and were well loved by the townspeople and local German authorities. The family was more hostile toward the Allies than most residents; an American bombing raid had damaged the Mengele factory in January 1945. Mengele attempted unsuccessfully to convince his wife to join him with their son and eventually leave Germany. But she was living with another man, he learned, and sought a divorce through Germany's legal system.

For the remainder of the year, American authorities applied no pressure on Mengele's family. The Americans accepted his wife's doorstep denial as a satisfactory answer in their hunt for the war criminal. Meanwhile, in January 1946, at the IMT in Nuremberg during the testimony of a French woman who had survived Auschwitz, Mengele's name "appeared in the trial record for the first time," as one of the American prosecutors, Telford Taylor, recalled later.[29] After some months passed, however, the Americans believed Mengele dead. In 1947 they notified his wife.

WILHELM BOGER: THE INTERROGATOR

Wilhelm Boger, too, made his way from the horrific camp and for nearly two decades avoided any punishment for his crimes there. Even the Nazis had investigated him, one of their own sadistic murderers. Prisoners had known him by the names "Beast of Auschwitz," "Black Death," "Terror of Auschwitz," "Advancing Death," and "Devil of Auschwitz." To an *SS* court probing into Wilhelm Boger's activities and those of his superior *SS* officer, Rudolf Höß, at Auschwitz, Boger had testified in October 1944: "We don't kill nearly enough of them [prisoners at the camp]. Everything was done for the Führer and for the Reich."[30] He despised both Jews and Slavs.

While at the original Auschwitz camp (Auschwitz I) from 1942 to 1945 as an *SS* staff sergeant and investigator in the camp's Political Department, Boger had earned an infamous reputation for arresting, interrogating, and murdering prisoners. His authority extended as well to nearby Birkenau (Auschwitz II). A native of Württemberg, he had a longtime Nazi past: he'd joined the Hitler Youth in the early 1920s and, when Hitler became chancellor of Germany in 1933, the Nazis appointed him a member of the auxiliary police that helped to hasten the Weimar Republic's collapse and the Nazis' ruthless seizure of power.

At Auschwitz the Political Department interrogated prisoners accused of political opposition either inside or outside the camp, including organizing escape attempts and resistance groups. Department members used raw violence—beating, kicking with their large boots, or in other ways physically abusing them—to force the prisoners to admit to accusations against them.

Shortly after arriving at the camp, Boger judged the methods of interrogating prisoners as much too humane. He ordered Lilly Majerczik, a multilingual secretary in the department, to attend his questioning of prisoners so that she could translate and write down their statements. She realized that "all the SS people in the camp abused the prisoners," but Boger, she thought, "was by far the cruelest. He noticeably wanted to be 'number one.'"[31] Often, his beatings of prisoners left them covered with blood and physically unrecognizable.

He soon introduced an invention for torture that satisfied even his sadistic imagination. He built a "swing," a primitive contraption consisting of a long wooden pole that rested horizontally on two supports. A former prisoner, Hermann Langbein, described after the war an interrogation on the so-called Boger swing:

> The swing is the Political Department's favorite form of torture. An inmate has to sit on the floor and draw up his knees. His hands are bound in front and pulled over his knees. A pole is placed under the hollows of his knees and over his lower arms, and the inmate is hung from this pole with his head down. Then he is rocked back and forth, and with each swing he gets a slap on his buttocks. All this would be bearable, but, worst of all, the tormentors hit his genitals. Boger . . . takes direct aim at these. The inmates who are sent to the bunker have to strip and get only thin dungarees but no underwear. I never imagined that testicles could swell so horrendously and turn blue and green. Those coming from the swing cannot sit or lie for days. If someone has not talked despite this torture, he is picked up again after two days. By that time even the slightest touch is hellishly painful. If an inmate is put on the swing again, he has to be made of steel to keep his mouth shut.[32]

Frequently, such "intensified interrogations"—in the words of the *Gestapo*—culminated in Boger or other *SS* men beating the prisoner to death. Prisoners who managed to survive the torture were likely shot by the *SS* at the "Black Wall," an execution site in the Auschwitz main camp.

The killings often resulted from the *SS* seeking to "evacuate" or "clean out" the arrest cells at nearby Block 11. Boger and the Political Department administered that block. Its basement contained twenty-eight cells, including the "standing bunker[s]," the name for four cells, each smaller than a square meter. A prisoner ordered to a standing bunker had to enter by crawling through a small opening near the floor. Each dark cell had only one air hole. The *SS* locked the condemned into the bunker, where lying down was an impossible feat, for a number of nights, and then compelled them to march to work during the day. On numerous occasions the Germans imprisoned several inmates simultaneously in a single standing bunker.

Of 2,137 inmates, more than half of them Jews, brought to the Political Department between 1941 and early 1944, 821 died while incarcerated there. Hardly a Jew left the bunker breathing. Other victims included Poles, Russians, Germans, and Austrians.

Inside Block 11, Boger exerted immense influence—even over his *SS* superiors, whom he pressed to murder as many prisoners as possible. Willingly and fanatically, he immersed himself in the killing process. During Block 11's evacuations he and other *SS* men removed prisoners from their cells, gave them quick mock trials to determine their already decided fates, and then the *SS* carried out the "verdict[s]" immediately—nearly always at the Black Wall.

During the fall of 1943, with the consent of the Nazi hierarchy (obsessively meticulous, even when being euphemistic, in its recordkeeping), the *SS* investigated such actions and dubious attributions. It did so, however, only because enemy radio, most notably the BBC, had broadcast reports—which had reached the West through the Polish government-in-exile in London—of widespread torture and murder at Auschwitz and because many of the victims killed at the Black Wall were Poles. If Boger had been discerning enough to execute only Jews, in all likelihood, no investigation would have occurred. When Arthur Liebehenschel, the new Auschwitz commandant, prohibited using Boger's "swing," Wilhelm responded angrily: "How can these pigs be made to talk if they can't be hit?"[33] But little more resulted from the *SS* investigation.

A few low-ranking *SS* officers received mild punishments for filling their pockets with prisoners' property rather than delivering it directly into the *SS* coffers. The latter's perverted code of ethics regarded such "corruption" as dishonorable but extolled torture and killing for the Fatherland. Most appalling but also easily anticipated, the investigators ignored the mass killing of the Jews at Auschwitz. Why would they do otherwise? It was the camp's raison d'être.

On its railway platform during selections of arriving Jews for the gas chambers, Boger behaved as cruelly as ever, ensuring that most of those disembarking from the trains in terror, deprivation, desperation, and confusion never spoke to the prisoner commandos working on the platform. On one occasion a truck carrying Jewish children entered the camp and stopped at the barracks housing the Political Department. A boy, four or five years old, jumped out. He played with an apple in his hand.

Boger saw the child. Grabbing the boy by his feet, he smashed his head against the wall. Boger's *SS* assistant ordered Dounia Wasserstrom, a female prisoner serving as an interpreter in the department, to wash the wall. Shortly thereafter, Boger summoned Wasserstrom to translate something for him. When she entered, she saw in horror: "He was sitting in his office eating the boy's apple." Fifteen years later, long after the end of World War II, Wasserstrom, who couldn't look at a child without weeping, remarked, "Since that moment I have no longer wanted to have children."[34]

At the war's end in May 1945, amid the mass confusion and movement of so many peoples throughout his defeated country, Boger managed to escape Allied capture and reach Ludwigsburg, his hometown. There he hid for several weeks. "But then," he recounted later, "I was betrayed by a former inmate of Auschwitz and arrested by the Americans."[35] How revealing that he used "betrayed" for a former prisoner's justice-driven action.

On July 5 he testified while in U.S. Army captivity about Auschwitz, during which he sought to exonerate himself of any wrongdoing at the camp and to make himself and other *SS* officials into unwitting victims of the criminals populating the highest levels of the *SS*. Boger told his captors:

> Auschwitz! Unimaginable capital crime unique in the history of mankind! A big scientific investigation of this course of events by scholars from all over the world will find those who are truly guilty and absolve the German people in its totality as well as the mass of SS men, those pitiful slaves of the greatest sadist of all time, RFSS Himmler.[36]

In 1946 in Bavaria, Boger fled from a U.S. Army transport carrying him to Poland for trial and made his way to Württemberg, where he hid among relatives and friends. "At that time," he observed later, "it was still apparent that Germans stuck together because they all knew me and no one reported me."[37]

For two years he lived as a fugitive in Unterrath near Schwäbisch Hall and after 1950 worked in Stuttgart-Zuffenhausen at a local Heinkel engine factory. Like the vast majority of eight thousand former *SS* personnel who'd served at Auschwitz, he returned to a comfortable freedom and a normal law-abiding life. Most escaped all punishment for their war crimes.

Boger, whose unremarkable facial features and stature belied his violent meanness, remained among those fortunate unrepentant degenerates for nearly thirteen years after the war. But finally, in October 1958, West German authorities arrested him. While in prison awaiting trial, he lacked the slightest shred of guilt. His distorted remorselessness, along with the publicity he received in the West German news media, apparently made him feel like a movie star. Major newspapers such as the *Frankfurter Rundschau* and *Frankfurter Allgemeine Zeitung* focused primarily on him because he had invented the torture machine—the infamous "swing" named for him.

His only regret, he wrote his wife, was not having written his memoirs. In December 1963 a court in Frankfurt am Main tried Boger, along with nineteen other former Auschwitz perpetrators, all of whom represented a cross-section of criminals who had participated in the camp's atrocities. During the so-called Auschwitz trial, which lasted from December 1963 to August 1965, neither Boger, who became the most famous of the defendants, nor any of the other accused showed even a minuscule amount of repentance. Historian Rebecca Wittmann terms the trial "by far the largest, most public, and most important ever to take place in West Germany using West German judges and West German law."[38]

Boger's defense attorneys denounced the prosecution for trying the "small men" involved in the Holocaust, including (of course) their client, and—with some justification, which nonetheless failed to extricate their client from responsibility—argued that most so-called bureaucratic or desk murderers or even those officials with greater murderous authority at Auschwitz remained untouched and unpunished. Boger, one attorney maintained, without convincing anyone except the defendant, had acted at Auschwitz from humble ambition and had merely followed the orders of superiors, but never from baser motives such as National Socialism, anti-Semitism, or racial hatred.

In August 1965 the court found former *SS* staff sergeant Wilhelm Boger guilty of mass murder—both as an accomplice and as a principal perpetrator of joint, as well as individual, murder—of Jews, Poles, and other Auschwitz inmates. Since West German law prohibited capital punishment, he received the harshest sentence the court could give: life in prison plus—because the tribunal viewed him as an "excess" perpetrator—five more years. Only five other defendants received life sentences; the remaining eleven got sentences of three to fourteen years.

Over a decade later, when summoned from his prison cell to serve as a witness at another trial of Auschwitz killers, Boger revealed that his incarceration had done nothing to make him reflect on or regret his savage, merciless crimes. "I feel neither guilty nor punished," he began his testimony. Then, full of self-pity, he added: "I have to bear my fate."[39]

A bit later, he tried to justify to his questioner his "service" in the war. "We were soldiers," he declared.[40] He actually believed his own rhetoric and viewed himself a war hero. And of course, by "we" he meant the guards and officers at Auschwitz. Unlike his many victims at the camp, whom he had beaten and shot to death some thirty-five years earlier, he died quietly in prison in April 1977 of natural causes. And for nearly half of those years, he had lived in freedom and comfort.

4

A Liberation of Contrasts

Frightened and cold, six of them huddled amid thick bushes and rough sand along the beach. One early October night in 1943, a young Leo Goldberger and others in his family waited anxiously and eagerly for the promised signal—a blinking light from a Danish boat offshore. Only waves lapping at the shore broke the dark silence.

As the tiny group readied to enter the frigid water, Leo wondered to himself: "Why is this all happening? What had we ever done to be in hiding, escaping like criminals? Where would it all end? And why in God's name did the signal not appear?" For days he and his family had heard rumors that the Nazi forces occupying Denmark planned an *Aktion*—literally "action," a German terror operation that included the roundup and mass executions of Jews and/or their deportation to other killing sites.

Finally, the lights flashed. Into the sea Leo and the family waded, walking out some one hundred feet. The waves reached up to the young boy's chest. "We are off!" he thought, shivering profusely but full of excitement.

His father carried Leo's two smaller brothers on his arms. His mother held onto a bag of socks she'd taken with her to mend. Leo clutched a flashlight. An older brother tried valiantly to carry the family's suitcases but finally had to let them drop in the water. The Goldbergers lost to the sea the last of their meager belongings—a few clothes, some treasured papers and family photos, and, in Leo's case, a newly acquired police flashlight. But they saved their lives. Leo recalled later how the small desperate group of Copenhagen Jews was

> hauled aboard the boat, directed in whispers to lie concealed in the cargo area, there to stretch out covered by smelly canvases; in the event German patrols were to inspect the boat, we would be passed over as fish. There seemed to

> have been some twenty other Jews aboard. As we proceeded out toward the open sea my father chanted a muted prayer from the Psalms. A few hours later—bright lights appeared along the coastal outline of Sweden. Wonderful, peaceful Sweden.[1]

Once safely in the new country, Leo had a brief moment to reflect on his liberators. "What a magnificent feat!" he told himself. "And to think that for the Danes the rescue seemed only natural. For them it was the only way." Yet, in his mind, what the Danes had done would remain "a moral object lesson of how we all ought to behave in the face of injustice and suffering."

BEST AND THE DANISH JEWS

Not everyone in Copenhagen thought so. Dr. Werner Best, now Hitler's Reich plenipotentiary in German-occupied Denmark, sat worriedly at his office desk. What could possibly make Hitler and his other superiors in Berlin, he asked himself repeatedly, understand how and why, during the previous night, the first of Europe's Jews had been liberated? How could he persuasively exonerate himself of responsibility for this unprecedented failure in the Nazis' racial policy? Nearly all of Denmark's seven thousand Jews had escaped a roundup by Nazi police—yet another *Aktion*—for deportation to the East.

Best, Denmark's highest-ranking Nazi political official and diplomat, chose his phrasing carefully while crafting his report to the German foreign ministry. With a stroke of arrogant boldness and a penchant for distortion that nearly all of the Nazi Party's upper echelons possessed, he decided to portray the failed *Aktion* as a major success.

"From today forward," he emphasized to the ministry on October 2, "Denmark can be considered free of Jews."[2] The Danish Jews had left the country, he declared. The facts that most had fled by sea to neutral Sweden (which he downplayed) and to freedom (which he didn't mention at all) weren't highlighted. The German police had seized the remaining several hundred Danish Jews for deportation, which he did emphasize.

Three days later, when the ministry inquired why German Security Police had captured so few of Denmark's Jews, Best responded in a tone both sharp and defensive. The Danish Jews, he claimed, had learned of the planned *Aktion* nearly a month earlier and had prepared their escape. Germany had insufficient police and naval forces in Denmark to monitor the country's eastern coast and to prevent the mass exodus of Jews across the strait to Sweden. This had happened despite his repeated pleas for extensive police and military assistance.

Still, Best strove mightily to put a positive, even triumphant, face on the incident. He told the foreign ministry, "Since the objective goal of the Jewish action in Denmark was the de-Judaization of the country and not the most successful head-hunt, it must be recognized that the Jewish action achieved its goal. Denmark is free of Jews, as no Jew who falls under the relevant regulations can legally live and work here any longer."[3]

Despite the German military occupation of Denmark since 1940 and the involuntary collaboration of the Danish government (a parliamentary monarchy), thousands of Jews had escaped because of widespread Danish assistance—ranging from the king, Christian X, to ordinary Danish citizens and police. Shortly before and especially during the night of October 1–2, 1943, the Jews fled to Sweden in rowboats, fishing vessels, and numerous other seacraft. Of the 481 Jews who remained and German police seized, the latter sent 454 to Theresienstadt, the ghetto near Prague, and twenty to the German concentration camps Ravensbrück and Sachsenhausen. Three managed to escape en route.

The vast majority of deported Danish Jews survived the war in part at least because their fate attracted immediate and continued world attention. Already on October 3, a *New York Times* article reported from Stockholm on Sweden's offer of aid to Denmark's Jews and concluded: "[I]t is believed here that the Danish Jews are facing the same fate as those in other countries under the German heel. In other words, they will be shipped to Poland, German-occupied Russia and never will be heard from again."[4]

In June 1944 the Nazis, for propaganda purposes, permitted the International Red Cross to visit Theresienstadt. There they showed the inspectors the allegedly good treatment of Danish Jews. To impress their visitors and defuse any percolating international outcry, the Germans reduced crowding in the camp—but they did so by deporting some 7,500 non-Danish prisoners to their deaths at Auschwitz. This was an integral though appalling principle of the Holocaust: where some survived, others more often than not perished as a primary or secondary result.

What had the Danish Jews escaped or, in fact, been liberated from? Best had long believed removing Jews from the German sphere of rule anywhere an absolute necessity. Since the mid-1930s, his career was based on facilitating the Nazi persecution and even killing of Jews, first from his desk in the *Gestapo* and *RSHA* in Berlin, and then from military headquarters in German-occupied France. In Denmark, for at least a month before it happened in early October 1943, Best planned and organized the *Aktion* to ensnare the Danish Jews and send them—he knew fully their fate—to certain death in the East.

He had arrived as Reich plenipotentiary in Denmark on November 5, 1942, after barely surviving a disastrous near end to his career. A few months earlier, while still in France, he had tried in a blundering and unsuccessful fashion to repair relations with his old rival and nemesis, the powerful Heydrich, who was not known for ever exhibiting a forgive-and-forget policy toward his factional foes.

Amid this crisis, which depressed him deeply, Best had appealed to Himmler through a letter to the *Reichsführer*'s adjutant, Karl Wolff. Not only did Best request a meeting with Himmler, but also he assured Wolff "that I have remained the old National Socialist and SS man, in whose loyalty and good will he [Himmler] will never have to doubt."[5] The thought of losing Himmler's trust and favor terrified Best, as well it might, since Himmler was often the sole protective barrier between Heydrich's vengeful intrigues and his intended victims. Further, such a loss would mean the ambitious Best's exclusion from the inner circle of leadership of the *SS*. His entire professional, political, philosophical, and, most crucially, personal identity rested on belonging to this elite Nazi group.

During early June 1942, he'd breathed a sigh of relief (as did many others, including perhaps Himmler himself, always wary of his brilliant, ruthless, upstart underling) when he learned of Heydrich's assassination by the Czech resistance. Events beyond Best's control had saved him and his career. Shortly thereafter, both Himmler and the German foreign minister, Joachim von Ribbentrop, supported Best's entry into the foreign ministry and his eventual appointment in Denmark as Reich plenipotentiary. A ministry spokesman explained publicly that Best's designation as "plenipotentiary" instead of "envoy" had little political significance, since Best, as a division chief in the ministry, held the rank of ambassador and therefore could not have been appointed to the higher grade of envoy.

For the *SS*, sending Best to Denmark as Germany's top civilian official offered an opportunity to take into *SS* hands the administration—based on *völkisch* principles—of a country of non-Germans of "Nordic blood." This would enable the *SS* to recruit in Denmark "Germanic legions" (voluntary military units) and to prepare the country for its postwar integration into the so-called Greater Germanic Reich.

During his first months in Denmark, Best continued the German practice of indirectly exploiting a country both economically and strategically, in this case by supervising the Danish political administration rather than exerting control directly and publicly. He concerned himself with ensuring valuable Danish food deliveries to the Reich and with protecting German military security in Denmark. German troops occupied the country and its bases on the Baltic and North Sea coasts, thereby helping to defend Nazi-controlled northern Europe from an Allied invasion. The latter, at this point, was a lingering, if not looming, menace for many Nazi leaders equipped with even a modicum of foresight.

Frequently, Best found himself in conflict in Denmark with the local German military commander, General Hermann von Hanneken. An economic policy specialist in the army and former official in the Reich economics ministry, Hanneken initiated violent measures against the Danes to increase their food deliveries to Germany and to suppress Danish resistance to the German occupation. Best, however, opposed Hanneken's brutal policy, implementing instead a more reasonable treatment of the Danes. The Reich plenipotentiary regarded himself primarily as Ribbentrop's man and Germany's diplomatic representative in Denmark whose orders were to keep Denmark docile, quiet, and cooperative with the Germans. But Best's policy had little success; Danish resistance to and sabotage of the German occupation steadily increased.

Although by early 1942 the Nazi leadership had decided to seize Danish Jews in order to deport and murder them, the plan held no intrinsic certainty or even probability of success. In reality few such Nazi-initiated *Aktionen* did—only with the indolent indifference or outright involvement of local collaborators did the odds for success increase exponentially. In the case of Denmark, the Copenhagen government defended the rights of its Jewish citizens, who had enjoyed civil and political equality for over a century. As long as Danes retained principal authority in most internal political affairs, the Germans would confront difficulty and resistance in pursuing their goal of capturing the country's Jews without having to expend substantial effort and in overcoming Danish opposition.

Consequently, Best pursued a relatively restrained policy toward the Danish Jews. In January 1943, he emphasized to his superiors in Berlin that imposing a harsh policy against the Jews would inevitably undermine German occupation policy, namely collaboration with the Danish monarchy. No Danish government, he said, would implement anti-Semitic legislation, and Germans would be forced to establish their own occupying administration. He confirmed this general view again in April.

Nevertheless, he had discussed with officials in the "Jewish section" of the German foreign ministry implementing measures for, as he termed it, "a later total solution of the Jewish question in Denmark."[6] In April, Ribbentrop asked Best for a comprehensive report on the "Jewish Question" in Denmark. Best replied that a registration of Danish Jews had begun for an eventual "comprehensive ruling" on the matter.

At the end of August 1943, however, German policy in Denmark changed completely. Steadily increasing anti-German, Dane-incited disturbances, including mass strikes and frequent sabotage, intensified the Germans' concerns for the adverse effects of such defiance on the local armaments industry. The Danish resistance, encouraged by recent German military defeats and by British agents arriving in Denmark, had begun to initiate local anti-Nazi revolts. German occupation forces had responded with increasing violence, including killing and wounding a number of Danes. Best's policy of reasonableness had failed to make the Danes cooperative.

For some time previously, Hitler had pressed for a "tough" policy against the Danes. On August 29, at the Führer's order, Germany proclaimed martial law in Denmark. It replaced the Danish government with a German military and police dictatorship headed by Best. The latter himself had urged such a radical change. Best's desire to implement his own personal rule in Denmark led him to intensify the existing internal crisis, primarily "by activating the 'Jewish question' in Denmark."[7] Mass arrests that same day included three leaders of the Jewish community in Copenhagen. The combination of arrests, the declaration of martial law, and rumors of an impending *Aktion* against Danish Jews led to widespread nervousness among the latter. On August 31, the Germans forcibly entered a Copenhagen law office and seized documents of the Jewish community.

Amid the Danish uprising in August, a temporary mood of despondency gripped Best. Despite his ambitions for greater personal power in Denmark, he had observed a near total collapse of his efforts to supervise a peaceful administration of Denmark in accordance with his *völkisch* ideal for ruling a non-German people of "Nordic blood."

But not all was lost to Best or to his racial idealism. In his view, the proclaimed martial law and direct German control of Denmark now offered an unparalleled opportunity to enact the long-discussed "solution of the Jewish Question." On September 1, to help restore order in the country and round up its Jews for deportation, he requested from Berlin further German police battalions and officers. Peter Longerich concludes: "Thus the deportation of the Jews would also open up the way for a transition to a police regime, and it would immediately provide Best with the troops he needed."[8]

On September 8, Best dispatched a telegram to the German foreign ministry proposing officially what the Nazi leadership wanted to hear—the impending seizure of Danish Jews. The telegram left the impression as well that Best was pursuing the more ruthless and uncompromising policy in Denmark urged by Hitler himself.

"With the successful implementation of the new course in Denmark," Best explained in the telegram, referring to martial law, "in my view a solution of the Jewish Question and Free Mason Question should now be in sight." He discussed what he knew such a "solution" would mean for the Danish Jews:

> To seize some 6,000 Jews (including women and children) suddenly and take them away, the police forces . . . I have requested must be used almost

> exclusively in Greater Copenhagen, where far and away most of the local Jews reside. Additional forces must be ordered for use from the commander of German troops in Denmark. For transportation [of the Jews], ships come into consideration in the first line, and these should be requested immediately.[9]

He ended the telegram by urging that Berlin approve his proposal and by requesting "a decision on which measures I should take." Both the foreign ministry and Eichmann's *Gestapo* department IVB4, for "Jewish affairs and evacuation," in the *RSHA* agreed quickly, giving on September 16 their formal consent for the *Aktion*; Hitler approved it the following day.

Simultaneously in Copenhagen, at Best's orders, Nazi police confiscated the membership rolls of the Jewish community. The Germans justified the seizure on the false pretext that the records were needed to investigate "criminals." During the ensuing days Best perfected final arrangements for the planned *Aktion* and requested from Germany even more police units and large ships in which to deport the Jews.

On September 20, Rudolf Mildner, a new commander of the Nazi Security Police in Denmark, arrived in Copenhagen. Previously, he had worked as *Gestapo* chief in the Polish city of Kattowitz, a post in which he'd deported thousands of Jews to their death at Auschwitz. By then, however, most Danish Jews expected an imminent Nazi attack on them. Beyond the other ever-more conspicuous indications that the Germans planned such an assault, the Jews noticed the newly arrived German police units, which marched through Copenhagen in daylight and spoke openly about why they were there. Already some Jews had left their homes and fled to Sweden, while many others, such as the Goldberger family, began arranging to escape across the strait.

On the German side, such developments didn't remain unnoticed. Both Best and Mildner expressed increasing skepticism about the success of the planned, practically publicized, and now problematic *Aktion*. The newly arrived German police units had no knowledge of local areas in Denmark. The units also had insufficient manpower to search for thousands of Jews hidden in the Danish capital and countryside. Nor could the Germans count on the cooperation of Danish police or Jew-hating citizens in the hunt for Jews, as Mildner had in Poland.

Indeed, already a day after Mildner's arrival, he cautioned against deporting the Jews prematurely. On September 22, Hitler reconsidered the issue but ordered continued planning for it despite concerns that the *Aktion* might fail and what such a failure might suggest about the already besieged sense of Nazi invincibility. Three days later, Mildner flew to Berlin for final instructions on the roundup and deportation.

The difficulties facing Best and the Germans mounted. Hanneken, the German military commander in Denmark, refused to provide troops to assist in the *Aktion*. Such forces had to remain on alert against any suspected Allied invasion of Denmark through Jutland or elsewhere. Worse still, the German navy had taken few precautions to prevent the flight of Danish Jews across the sea to Sweden. Unreliable Danish ships were left to perform most of the coastal surveillance. The German commandant of the harbor in Copenhagen allowed German ships to dock there for repairs, thus leaving less room for deportation ships.

Best informed the German leadership of his concerns about such issues. Now, suddenly, he worried that the planned roundup of the Danish Jews would complicate Germany's—and his—already difficult situation in governing Denmark. Thus, in large measure to avoid such a prospect, and in doing so protect himself and his own political aspirations, he decided "to let the date for the wave of arrests leak out" and allow "the escape of the Jews" from Denmark.[10]

When one of Best's staff, a shipping adviser, Ferdinand Georg Duckwitz, already skeptical of the German plans, learned from Best the date for the *Aktion*—October 1 and 2—he passed the information, apparently on his own initiative, to several Danish politicians. They, in turn, alerted Danish Jews, who set in motion with the help of vast numbers of Danes the subsequent rescue effort.

On the morning of October 1, Best telegrammed Ribbentrop and noted the "rumors over the impending Jewish Aktionen" that had arisen in Denmark "directly after the declaration of martial law." These, he continued, had now "increased to a near panic level."[11] Germany must reckon, therefore, he warned, with the *Aktion* being at least a partial failure.

Amid the aftermath of the abortive *Aktion*, an anxious Best defended and defined what had happened as ultimately a success, but Hitler and other Nazi leaders, possibly to avoid further scrutiny and publicity over the genocidal debacle, appeared surprisingly unconcerned. In addition, Himmler's support of Best most likely saved the latter from losing his post in Denmark and spared him the resulting certain destruction of his career. Best had coveted, and curried tirelessly, the *Reichsführer*'s support and now, at last, that pursuit had borne fruit.

So had Best's initiation on September 8 of the attempted deportation of the Danish Jews, however dismal its outcome. Himmler confirmed this understanding to Best on October 12. "In any case," Himmler said, "the Jewish Aktion is correct. It will make waves for a brief time, but in general it will help deal with the chief saboteurs and malicious agitators."[12] The fanatical anti-Semitism of the *Reichsführer*, Hitler, and other Nazi officials led them to view "saboteurs" and "agitators" everywhere as Jews. This persistent misperception would cause great grief to the latter but would also doom the occupiers, who on some level never fully fathomed that the threats to their overarching authority would never vanish with the "disappearance" (slaughter) of the last Jew; the threats and resistance were national and, therefore, enduring.

Once again, as he'd done in the *RSHA* in 1939 and 1940 and in France in 1942, Best had succeeded in both protecting and furthering himself by helping to attack Jews. But unlike his intended victims in Denmark, most other Jews still alive in Europe in late 1943 continued to suffer. Longerich observes that despite the turning point of the war against the Germans in the winter of 1942–1943, making more difficult their implementation of deportations in cooperation with other Axis or collaborationist countries,

> the Germans did not abandon their policy, since precisely in view of the worsening military situation they saw the intensification of the persecution of the Jews and the associated compromising of their "partners" as an important safeguard for the cohesion of the block [of states] under their rule. Attitudes towards the "Jewish question" became an important gauge for the German side, on which they could read the loyalty of their partners.[13]

The Germans compelled most Jewish survivors to wait another year and a half for liberation, until the war's end in the spring of 1945 and the Allies' defeat of the Reich. And even after that, the horror for many simply continued. For some it seemed as if it had gone on and would go on forever.

JOSEF KRAMER: "BEAST OF BELSEN"

"I shall never forget," he thought about the camp, "the mass of human beings and corpses in the barracks I entered."[14] The sheer number of former prisoners, many Jews, still dying at Bergen-Belsen overwhelmed Zwi Azaria. A Yugoslav officer and rabbi liberated from a German prison in Celle, he'd entered the huge Nazi concentration camp in late April 1945, barely two weeks after British troops freed it from German rule.

Immediately he had assumed the role of army chaplain (and eventually also a new name, anglicized as Hermann Helfgott), assisting in easing the suffering and promoting the rehabilitation of the camp's survivors. Well educated in rabbinical studies and philosophy, Azaria gained rapid popularity among the British, who would soon appoint him chief rabbi for the British zone of occupation in Germany.

At the liberation of Bergen-Belsen, some thirteen thousand dead lay unburied, their decaying corpses strewn or piled everywhere. Before the British arrived, the camp's *SS* guards had sought to hide as many of the dead as possible. At gunpoint, prisoners had dug mass graves in a remote corner of the camp, into which they dumped bodies. The dead, both buried and unburied, had perished from starvation, disease, and overcrowding or were killed by the *SS*, many on orders of the camp's last commandant, Josef Kramer.

Numerous instances of cannibalism had characterized the camp's final weeks. For prisoners who had lived in various German concentration camps and then, toward war's end, arrived at Bergen-Belsen, the latter seemed the worst, most inhuman of all the German camps. Kramer's brutality—especially toward the Jewish prisoners—persisted even after Himmler ordered explicitly that the killing cease.

Shortly after arriving at the camp, Azaria, walking among the living dead, suddenly heard a weak voice: "Help me, Zwi, please." It was an old friend. Azaria ran about looking for a doctor and shouting hysterically. As he returned, however: "I found my friend completely still. His eyes seemed to say 'thank you.' He was at peace."

Feeling "helpless in this sea of misery," and one of only two rabbis among other chaplains, he "took over the macabre task of giving the numerous dead in the camp a decent burial. . . . People were still dying after liberation. They had gone too far to be saved."[15]

Nothing could have prepared Azaria or anyone else—including Allied troops and their commanders—for the horrors they found at Bergen-Belsen and many other Nazi camps. Located in northwest Germany near Hannover, the camp held at its liberation on April 15, 1945, nearly sixty thousand prisoners, roughly half of them Jews. Since late 1944, camp conditions had worsened significantly. On December 1 of that year, it had confined 15,257 prisoners, but during the ensuing months tens of thousands of Jewish and other "death march" survivors had poured in from camps elsewhere in Germany or in the East, including Auschwitz. During the camp's last months, complete chaos reigned. Prisoners lacked water and food; many perished from starvation and a typhus epidemic. Sanitation was nonexistent; inmates defecated and urinated where they sat or lay.

From January to April 1945, at least thirty-five thousand prisoners perished. One, Anne Frank—the Dutch teenager who had kept an extraordinary and extraordinarily moving diary while hiding with her family and some friends in a house in Amsterdam before their betrayal, arrest, and deportation to Auschwitz—had died at age fifteen at Bergen-Belsen with her sister, Margot, in March 1945.

In just the first weeks following the liberation of Bergen-Belsen in late April, some thirteen thousand more former prisoners died there, as Zwi Azaria, British troops, and foreign newsmen visiting the camp witnessed helplessly. Huge dirt-moving machines buried the dead in mass graves.

The horrific scenes at Bergen-Belsen repeated themselves with fearful frequency throughout the vast number of other Nazi camps liberated in Central Europe. On April 12, 1945, the U.S. Third Army occupied Buchenwald, near

Weimar in central Germany; on April 29 American troops reached Dachau in Bavaria; and on May 4 they discovered Mauthausen in Austria. For its part, the Soviet army liberated Sachsenhausen on April 22 and the women's camp at Ravensbrück on April 30, both north of Berlin, and Theresienstadt near Prague on May 8. In the ensuing days and weeks following liberation, thousands more Jews and other former prisoners perished in the camps in which they had been imprisoned. Even in death, they were unable to die in true freedom—beyond the camps' perimeters.

He knew why it had all happened. Set a world apart from the camp's prisoners over whom he exercised a murderous rule, he expressed no emotion about either the mass death at the camp or the latter's takeover by the British. The powerfully built, round-cheeked, and dark-whiskered *SS* officer hated Jews and other "races" whom the Nazis had pronounced as inferior, but whom they believed (paradoxically, in view of their supposed inferiority) to menace their goal of one day dominating under Hitler—the leader they worshiped as Führer—first Europe and then the world.

When British troops arrived at Bergen-Belsen on April 15, 1945, Josef Kramer, commandant of the camp since December 1944, stood proudly at its entrance with a group of other neatly dressed, well-fed *SS*, *Wehrmacht*, and Hungarian officers. Immediately the British disarmed and arrested them.

"What type of prisoners have you got in here?" one British officer asked Kramer.[16] The officer was Derek Sington, the first Briton to arrive in Bergen-Belsen following the German surrender of the camp hours earlier under the terms of a limited German-British truce. Sington, a German-speaking captain and head of his army unit's psychological warfare section, led a British amplifying group to tour the camp in jeeps and a van. Using loudspeakers, the group informed those inmates still cognizant of anything beyond their own impending death that the Germans had capitulated and that the Allies had taken over. (Three weeks later, Jane Leversen, the postwar relief worker at Belsen, reported to the JCRA on the bitterness of camp survivors at "the fact that the British military commander drove round Camp No. 1 on the first day of liberation, in the same car as the German military commander, 'for all the world as though we [the survivors] were an exhibition.'"[17])

"Homosexuals and professional criminals," Kramer replied to Sington's query, "as well as some Bibel Forscher [Jehovah's Witnesses]." He watched the Briton carefully. "And political prisoners?" "Oh yes, there are the Häftlinge [prisoners]," he said in a friendly, confiding way.[18]

Kramer volunteered nothing about the thousands of Jews—dead, dying, and barely living—scattered throughout the camp. He acted unashamed of and showed no feeling toward the hell on earth that surrounded him. It was an inferno he had helped to create and fuel, with its mountains of corpses, its vast suffering populace, and its nauseating stench.

Prisoners had called him the "Beast of Belsen." Riding on a jeep running board, he led Sington and other British troops through the massive compound, with its filthy, disease-ridden, and rickety wooden huts, and among crowds of starving, raggedly clothed prisoners. Kramer's sole concern at the moment, he told Sington, consisted of doing nothing "without authority from the [local] Wehrmacht commandant." He added that he dared not "enter the camp unarmed." When the British asked Kramer for personal documents of the tens of thousands of prisoners in the camp, he responded, wholly indifferent, "They have all been destroyed."

As Sington's jeep arrived at the camp's potato field, which Kramer claimed disingenuously prisoners had plundered following the liberation, the British officer saw three *SS* guards. They'd just beaten a prisoner, then "lying on the ground with blood on his face and rolling his eyes."[19] When Kramer chose to ignore *SS* guards shooting starving prisoners who had raided the camp kitchen and potato patch seeking food, the British quickly made clear that they were now in control at Bergen-Belsen.

Sington ordered the camp's last commandant "to pick up one of the bodies and carry it away himself." Kramer insisted that only "in the last few days" had conditions at the camp worsened, and he further denied any role in making them so.[20] Hate continued to consume him for Germany's "racial" enemies at the camp—the Jews and Slavs.

Since taking over as commandant five months earlier, he knew that he had helped to transform Bergen-Belsen from a much less severe facility for prisoners—when it had functioned as a transit (or holding) camp principally for Jews Germany might use as hostages when bargaining with the Allies—into a deadly concentration camp. Once in command, he replaced a major portion of the prisoners' self-administration with so-called *Kapos* (brutal prisoner-foremen who pushed slave laborers to exhaustion and often death) and with equally ruthless prisoner elders (*Blockälteste*) in charge of prisoner blocks or barracks.

Kramer's complete disinterest in the lives of his prisoners had led, in significant measure, to the camp's massive disorganization and resulting enormous number of casualties. Nevertheless, hoping to ingratiate himself with the British, he requested desperately needed medicines and food and maintained that the *SS* had abandoned him in the war's closing stages and left Bergen-Belsen bereft of supplies. The appeal appeared to influence some British officers favorably toward Kramer. However, the officers chose to ignore the fact that a *Wehrmacht* supply store only two miles from the camp had some eight hundred tons of food. Until the British liberated Bergen-Belsen, its commandant had not asked for the obviously available provisions.

In his first statement to British interrogators, Kramer denied that gas chambers, mass executions, whipping, and other cruelty had existed at Auschwitz-Birkenau. He'd served from May to December 1944 as commandant of the infamous camp. While there, he had presided over the murder of some 437,000 Hungarian Jews shipped to the camp in 147 trains as well as of several thousand Gypsies.

But at his war crimes trial in September 1945 (that also tried other SS personnel who had worked at Auschwitz and Bergen-Belsen), after he finally admitted that Birkenau had gas chambers, he was questioned about what he'd said earlier. His British defense counselor, who described Kramer as "the scapegoat of Belsen," asked why he had initially denied the presence of the chambers. He replied that first, one of his superiors, Oswald Pohl, chief of the *SS* Economic and Administrative Office (*Wirtschaftsverwaltungshauptamt, WVHA*), had told him, "I should be silent and should not tell anybody at all about the existence of the gas chambers." He'd still felt bound, he continued, by his word of honor to Pohl and the highest levels of the Nazi leadership to treat the extermination machinery as a secret. He had changed and made his admission only because "these persons to whom I felt bound in honour—Adolf Hitler and Reichsführer Himmler—were no longer alive and I thought then that I was no longer bound."[21]

Yet in the next breath, Kramer testified that he'd hardly known about the gas chambers. He alleged that Rudolf Höß, commandant of all the Auschwitz camps between 1940 and 1943, had told him that he (Kramer) "had nothing to do with either the gas chambers or the incoming transports [trains carrying Jews]." Kramer even proclaimed on the stand, "I did not know what the purpose of the gas chamber was."

During cross-examination, the British prosecutor, Colonel T. M. Backhouse, zeroed in on Kramer's previous contradictory testimony and statements. He got the defendant to admit that while he had commanded the Natzweiler-Struthof concentration camp in eastern France—before he arrived at Auschwitz-Birkenau—he had built a gas chamber there and even forced into it eighty prisoners to die.

Then Backhouse asked the defendant: "When Kommandant Pohl demanded your word of honour not to talk about the gas chambers [at Birkenau], why was it that you could not tell anybody if it was all legally proper and above board?" Trying to evade answering, Kramer responded, "I do not know. Nothing could be said about concentration camps in the outside world."

Immediately Backhouse followed up: "Was not that because all of you knew that they were an outrage against decency?"

Still Kramer claimed total innocence. "No," he said. "We never spoke about them with the outside world, and I, as Hauptsturmführer [captain], had no right to ask a General about such a case."

The prosecutor pressed him further. "Was the purpose of the gas chambers not a part of the determination of your Party to try and exterminate the Jewish race and all the intelligent people of Poland?" Kramer, beginning perhaps to realize the futility of his denials, equivocated: "I do not know."

Nevertheless, a few moments later, Josef denied having been present at and taking an active part in selections of prisoners for the gas chambers—this, despite witness after witness having told the court that he had done so. He persisted in trying to perpetuate the secrecy of the Nazi annihilation of Jews and protect himself. When asked by the judge advocate, C. L. Stirling, why, in his (Kramer's) opinion, both Auschwitz-Birkenau and Bergen-Belsen had admitted old and weak Jews no longer able to perform forced labor useful to the Reich, Kramer insisted: "I do not know, I had nothing to do with the reasons why these people were sent into my camp. I was there to receive them. Whether it was a political enemy or a Jew or a professional criminal had nothing to do with me at all. I received the bodies, that was all."

But along with many other German officials involved in the Final Solution, he and they had made a crucial distinction among the prisoners—they had attempted purposely to murder all Jews. Eventually, and most reluctantly, during a re-examination by his defense counsel, did Kramer admit as much. When asked "if it was part of the doctrines of your Party to exterminate the Jewish race," the former camp commandant replied curtly, "It was part of it."

In his initial denial that gas chambers had existed at Auschwitz-Birkenau, and in his effort to keep the Final Solution a secret, Kramer not only sought to protect himself from incrimination. He also broke with most surviving Holocaust perpetrators who, when placed on trial and/or forced to testify in court, admitted that the mass murder of the Jews had happened. Nevertheless, Kramer's failed attempt to deny the existence of gas chambers anticipated the claim invented already in the late 1940s by Holocaust deniers that there were no such killing facilities in the Nazi camps, but that "gas chambers were used for disinfection."[22] Also he confessed eventually that a plan had existed to destroy the Jews.

The trial of Kramer and forty-four other former camp officials (including the gorgeous and ghastly Irma Grese) and *Kapos* had begun on September 17 at Lüneburg in the British zone. The so-called Belsen trial—in which Kramer found himself the lead defendant—was the first major war crimes trial following the war.

Unfortunately, the British military, as well as some in Whitehall, remained divided over whether the Allies should prosecute former German leaders. Such uncertainty and lack of resolve on the part of some officials contributed to the poor preparation for and mismanagement of much of the trial. The ill-conceived prosecution also likely influenced the British decision not to charge Kramer or any of the other defendants in the Belsen trial with murder.

Instead, the charges alleged primarily that "members of the staff at Bergen-Belsen/Auschwitz concentration camp responsible for the well-being of the persons interned there, in violation of the laws and usages of war were together concerned as parties to the ill-treatment of certain persons causing the[ir] deaths."[23] The Germans, however, hadn't designed the Auschwitz complex of camps for the "well-being" of inmates but for their murder; it served primarily as an extermination camp. Prisoners at Bergen-Belsen had perished from premeditated savagery and neglect—not merely from "ill-treatment."

The indictment, which made no mention of Jews, reflected clearly this misperception. The part of it devoted to "war crimes" at Auschwitz did not refer to either gas chambers or mass murder. The prosecution's opening speech included only one reference to Jews—the near precise estimate of forty-five thousand Greek Jews taken to Auschwitz, of whom it was noted only sixty survived. One wonders, in this regard, what encouragement such legal proceedings would eventually give Holocaust deniers and other anti-Semites.

Consistent with British prejudices, the prosecution called as its initial witnesses members of the British army involved in liberating and subsequently administrating Bergen-Belsen as a DP camp. Astoundingly, the first survivor examined was the only Briton, a non-Jew, known to have lived through the Nazi camp. The prosecution relegated Jewish witnesses, who had seen far worse horrors than the soldiers and almost anyone else, to giving affidavits or depositions or to testifying late in the trial. In cross-examining the Jews, British officers serving as defense counselors, including Kramer's, disputed the witnesses' accounts of both Bergen-Belsen and Auschwitz.

Similar to his pretrial claims, Kramer insisted that at Bergen-Belsen he'd tried desperately to prevent the tens of thousands of deaths. His defense counsel, an English military officer, produced a letter that the former commandant had written to Berlin on March 1, 1945, addressed to the *SS* inspector of concentration camps, in which he urged that the *SS* send no more Jews to the camp because the typhus outbreak was causing nearly three hundred deaths per day.

The letter, as well as Kramer's behavior when he surrendered Bergen-Belsen, impressed many British officers. The lawyer argued to the court that concentration camps had been legal in Germany and that therefore those who worked in them couldn't be punished for obeying orders. He even suggested that murder in the camps didn't qualify as a war crime.

The tribunal convicted Kramer, and the British hanged him on December 12, 1945. Two days later, they executed ten other former *SS* officials (including Grese) convicted along with Kramer of persecuting and murdering prisoners at Bergen-Belsen and Auschwitz. But the court sentenced numerous others who had served at both camps to ten years or less in prison, and the tribunal found a good number of defendants not guilty.

Moreover, while the trial introduced the name of Auschwitz, it focused—with unfortunate consequences—much more substantially on Belsen and very little on the differences between the two camps. According to Donald Bloxham:

> The majority of defendants were drawn from Belsen, and even those who had played significant roles at Auschwitz remained connected primarily with Belsen. It remained "the Belsen trial," and the majority of newspaper reports on issues pertaining to Auschwitz had either come after, or in the context of discussion of Belsen. . . . [T]here was certainly no consistent differentiation between the extermination camp and the concentration camps to counteract the barrage of photographs and reports of the latter at the close of the war in Europe. This lack of clarity was perpetuated at [the IMT in] Nuremberg in the greatest single forum for the investigation of Nazi criminality.[24]

Such misperceptions about the former Nazi camp system and about its principal victims—the Jews—did not remain confined to the courtroom. In reporting on the Belsen trial, the Allied-controlled Western press transmitted the false views to the public. Both the *New York Times* and *The Times* (London) covered the prosecutor's opening speech and—like it—emphasized Belsen and then described Auschwitz, erroneously, as a camp with "very much the same routine as Belsen." When the papers reported the prosecutor's mention of four million murdered at Auschwitz (a number far in excess of current expert estimates of the total dead at the camp), they referred solely to "people" cremated, not Jews.

The only licensed German paper in the Western Allied zones, the *Frankfurter Rundschau*, reproduced the British description of Kramer as "the beast of Belsen," thereby accepting and reflecting the trial's bias toward that camp. Yet when the paper detailed the scale of the Birkenau gas chambers, it mentioned nothing of Jews. When Kramer admitted that "as a rule" Jews were the only people at Birkenau required to attend selections, the *Times* (London) report of his statement made no mention of Jews and concentrated more on the former commandant's denials than on his admissions. Following Kramer's testimony—during the fourth week of the eight-week proceedings—both British and American press coverage of the trial declined noticeably (the only exception was the *New York Times* reporting on the "blonde" Grese).[25] Both the *Times* (London) and *New York Times* received the trial's end with virtual silence, reproducing the verdicts only mechanically and with little comment on their significance.

A flood of public criticism, especially from the French, who wished to retry the fourteen *SS* officials acquitted at Belsen, greeted both the flawed trial and its verdicts. But the trials to follow (including the IMT) would be, in many instances, equally if not more flawed, biased, arbitrary, and often downright unjust—though not in the ways the defendants and their apologists would later claim. Many of the future trials would aid the Holocaust perpetrators in cheating, in some instances, justice, and in almost every instance, truth.

BEST IMPRISONED IN COPENHAGEN

With the war's end only days away, liberation for Werner Best in Denmark meant, first, staying alive, and then, above all, avoiding postwar punishment for what he'd done in Nazi Germany and elsewhere to help build and provide victims for Hitler's machinery of mass killing.

During April 1945, Best never considered committing suicide or trying to escape Copenhagen and the advancing Allies. "If I try to flee and am captured anywhere," he thought, "I'd be too ashamed." And what about taking his own life? "No, that would be laughable."[26] He feared his own death more than anything else. Of the terrible irony in this he seemed wholly oblivious. Had he not spent several years knowingly helping or attempting to send to their deaths numerous other people?

When news of Hitler's death reached him in Copenhagen on May 2, he made his way quickly to northern Germany. At Plön, a small lakeside town not far from the Kiel Bay, he joined Himmler and traveled with the *Reichsführer* farther north to the German-Danish border. On May 3 at Flensburg, the headquarters of the new Nazi government under Karl Doenitz, commander of the German navy since 1943, Best participated in a meeting of German military and political leaders. The discussion centered on whether or not to end the war and capitulate to the Allies, whose armies occupied nearly all of the war-torn Reich.

Doenitz began the meeting by noting that only German troops in Norway and Denmark were still fit for action. He posed the question of whether such forces should delay surrendering and thereby give as many East Germans as possible (who were fleeing the Russians) a chance to get to the West. Most of the military leaders present urged continuing the fight in the north. But Best opposed it. If fighting broke out in Denmark, he argued, it would likely unleash a revolt of tens of thousands of Danish resistance fighters. This could leave some three hundred thousand Germans already in or near Denmark—refugees and wounded—without protection. The meeting produced no decision on what to do.

Shortly afterward, Best returned to Copenhagen, to his wife and their five children. On May 4, German forces in Denmark, the Netherlands, and northwest Germany surrendered. The next morning, Best went to the Danish foreign ministry and, acting as a former German official with diplomatic status in Denmark, asked for protection for himself and his family.

Following the war's end two days later, he remained at his home in the Danish capital but under house arrest. He'd convinced himself that eventually the Danes would free him. Denmark and its leaders, he believed, knew the extraordinary debt they owed their country's former Reich plenipotentiary. In his view he'd worked continually during the war's last year and a half to moderate and preserve legality in Nazi occupation policy in Denmark and to enable the country to survive the war unscathed by the destructive fighting. In contrast to most of the rest of Nazi-occupied Europe, Denmark had suffered minimally.

And for that, Best expected payback. Repeatedly, he'd defied even Hitler's orders to implement vigilante measures against the anti-Nazi Danish resistance. Since the fall of 1943, the latter's acts of sabotage against German occupation forces and assassination of German and Danish Nazis had increased steadily. Best opposed the secret "counter-terror" unit of the Nazi Security Police sent by Hitler and Himmler to Denmark. The unit responded to each case of sabotage or assassination with a corresponding German action—usually murder or bomb attacks—against Danish officials or their property.

Nevertheless, in no way had Best pursued a mild course against the resistance. He had used occupation tribunals to pronounce numerous death sentences that German Security Police and the *Gestapo* carried out almost instantly. For the "idealistic" lawyer in Best, and due to his *völkisch* thinking, racially the Danes were "Nordic" kin of the Germans, and, therefore, they deserved an occupation regime based on the rule of law, even if the Germans had to employ legal measures to murder them.

Nevertheless, at a meeting of his military leaders on November 19, 1943, Hitler had criticized his chief diplomatic and political representative in Denmark to those present. "Undiplomatic," he called Best, for not agreeing fully to the vigilante-style counterterrorism policy. The possibility of an Allied invasion of Denmark, said the Führer, made the "security situation" there a sensitive one that required the "sharpest of policies" against the Danish resistance. He ordered the German military commander in Denmark, Hanneken, to carry out far-reaching "measures of atonement" for attacks on German troops, which led immediately to the shooting of twenty-four Danish saboteurs (Hitler considered insufficient the execution of fifteen a few days earlier).[27]

Eventually, the ongoing Danish opposition and Best's "soft" response infuriated Hitler. On July 5, 1944, the dictator met with Best at Hitler's mountain retreat at Obersalzburg. During a tense confrontation, Hitler accused his underling of disobeying his orders and demanded that the Reich plenipotentiary halt his "legal" policy toward the Danish resistance and support the counterterror unit in Denmark. On July 30, only a few days after the assassination attempt on Hitler at his East Prussian headquarters, the Führer issued a "terror and sabotage" decree, ordering the use of counterterror methods in all areas occupied by German forces.[28]

Both Hitler and Himmler had lost confidence in Best's ability to control Denmark. They undermined his authority while increasing that of his German subordinates in Copenhagen, the local Security Police chief and Hanneken, the *Wehrmacht* commander. On September 21, meeting again with Hitler, Best intended to protest the usurpation of his power and to offer to resign. Hitler neither let him speak nor protest, and he refused to accept his subordinate's resignation. Despite Best's conflict with Hitler and Himmler, the *SS* promoted him to the rank of lieutenant general, the grade next to the highest in the organization. Obviously, no superior questioned his ultimate loyalty to them or to the National Socialist ideology and cause.

Surely, Best kept thinking while under house arrest in the Danish capital, soon the Danes would release him and his family. So he was stunned when, on May 21, 1945, Danish police transferred him to the prison in the Copenhagen fortress. Immediately, feelings of intense pessimism and depression, so characteristic of Best in crisis situations, fell over him. He remained despondent for weeks.

Meanwhile, during the summer of 1945, the Danish government established laws and judicial bodies to try Danes, perhaps as many as forty thousand, suspected of wartime collaboration with the Germans. In the absence of any clear international law on the issue, the government moved much more slowly in prosecuting and punishing former German occupation officials. In September 1945, Denmark adhered to the London charter establishing the IMT and other subsequent war crimes tribunals at Nuremberg. This consent obligated Denmark to try war criminals involved in occupying the country and in perpetrating atrocities within its borders.

But problems remained. For example, could the Danes prosecute Best, a former Nazi official with diplomatic immunity during the occupation? If so, could the Danes produce sufficient evidence to convict him? By what measure or law could that be accomplished? While the Allies had captured tons of Nazi records, understaffed teams of Allied intelligence officers and translators had only begun to sift through a small portion of the mountain of material and to make it available to war crimes prosecutors.

Not surprising, therefore, during the fall of 1945, Copenhagen sought to avoid placing Best on trial in Denmark by offering him to another country for prosecution. The search had little success. First, fearing that insufficient evidence existed to convict Best, Britain declined the Danes' offer. Then the Americans at Nuremberg refused to try him for his role in the *Gestapo*. (At the time, U.S. prosecutors had sketchy knowledge of the organization and operation of the Nazi political police.)

During the spring of 1946 the Danes asked the French government to try Best, but Paris replied that it knew nothing about him. The Danes even transferred Best briefly to the French capital, but the French assertion was wholly improbable. Could France not remember the former Nazi administrator who, only four years earlier, had supervised much of the French administration, including its police and judicial bodies?

The truth existed elsewhere—in French politics rather than in simple human justice: a trial of Best in Paris would provide greater problems for the French than a trial in Copenhagen would for the Danes. Such a Parisian tribunal would implicate much of the wartime French administration—especially its police and informants—as collaborators. In that role, the French had cooperated in such policies as murdering hostages, fighting the anti-Nazi resistance, and deporting Jews and Communists to places such as Auschwitz.

Still a prisoner in the Copenhagen fortress, only gradually did Best realize that he had little to fear from a spontaneous act of revenge by the former Danish resistance or from a wholehearted effort by the Danes to place him on trial. By August 1945, his depression had given way to a delusional mood in which he viewed his imprisonment as a temporary honor and his Nazi career as one of heroism and political innocence.

He produced this wholly mythical image of himself, first, in Danish interrogations of him, and second, in extensive notes and memoranda he wrote about his career and about different leaders and aspects of the Nazi regime. In each instance he sought to develop a consistent story, free above all of incriminating information.

With little documentary or eyewitness evidence available to prove otherwise, Best concealed successfully his responsibility in helping Himmler and Heydrich build the murderous *SS*-police system. Simultaneously, he ignored as much as possible the German occupation in France and Denmark. He avoided completely his involvement in the *Einsatzgruppen* killings of Polish Jews and Poles, the deportation of French Jews, and the Jewish policy and counterterrorism measures in Denmark.

During his interrogations and in his writings, he portrayed the war and resulting Nazi occupation of much of Europe as merely expressions of a "natural" effort to fight for the interests of one's own people. He maintained that the writings of the nineteenth-century German nationalist philosopher, Johann Gottlieb Fichte, had influenced him and many other Germans. Such a view, he believed, exonerated individual German participants, including him, of any responsibility for the Nazis' war goals and the unprecedented murderous means expended to achieve them.

He styled himself as an apolitical German in Hitler's service, wholly without ambition and without opportunities to influence state policy. About Lutz

Count Schwerin von Krosigk, Hitler's former minister of finance whom Best admired, he wrote in October 1945: "His high ethos of duty and service to the state always strengthened me. His view of the old Prussian nobility and officialdom that service to the state was more important than politics corresponded to my basic instincts."[29]

While in the *Gestapo*, he insisted, he had served only as an "administrative specialist" in personnel and financial questions and had nothing to do with police measures. In France he'd worked exclusively on "administrative" questions and had always, when necessary, opposed attempts of Nazi officials in Berlin to implement harsher political and occupation policies.

Of Hitler, Best praised the former Führer as a political "prophet" whose alleged greatness existed in his combining "National Socialism, anti-Semitism, and the Greater German plan" into a "teaching" and proclaiming it to the masses. Hitler's sole mistake or downfall, claimed Best, was the Führer's attempt to control everything and his inclination "to burn all bridges behind him politically and militarily. . . . [T]o push forward the 'prophet's' war of ideology to an uncompromising end."[30]

Not surprisingly, when writing about Himmler, Best said much less, and most of that was far from laudatory. Discussing the onetime *SS* and police chief too much or too favorably could very well implicate Best in the Nazi regime's widespread criminality. To protect the picture of innocence and idealism he'd fashioned so carefully for himself, he had to ignore what had made the regime exceptional and the role of the *SS* in that exceptional "laurel": the Nazis' nearly triumphant attempt to establish an imperialist *völkisch* new order in Europe through a policy of war and genocide, much of it aimed principally at Europe's Jews.

In March 1946, French authorities transferred Best from their custody in Paris to the U.S. interrogation camp at Oberursel near Frankfurt am Main. The Allies requested his presence at Nuremberg.

5

Soviet "Liberators"

Their joy at being among the first freed in the East from Nazi persecution wouldn't last long. "When the Russians came" in the summer of 1944, Maria Epstein thought, "we really believed we were liberated. Unfortunately, our elation was short-lived, and we were left with a grim reality."

The Red Army had liberated Epstein, her husband, and their two-year-old daughter from a German forced labor camp outside the western Soviet city of Minsk. The Germans had occupied the city since the end of June 1941, during the first days of their invasion of the Soviet Union. But now the Epsteins, at their liberation, had nowhere to go and no other family left; the Germans had murdered her parents and his and most other family members.

The couple, Polish Jews, remained in Minsk, capital of the Soviet republic of Byelorussia (White Russia) until the Allies defeated Germany in May 1945. But the Epsteins found their Soviet "liberators" full of distrust toward people (especially Jews) who had survived the Nazi occupation of the Soviet Union and neighboring Poland. The Soviet secret police started to recruit people to spy on the two, "and ironically, anti-Semitism became rampant again":

> In the cafeteria, Jews had to sit at separate tables. Once more we were second-class citizens. Since the Russians suspected us of collaboration [with the Nazis], they started a forced evacuation of the survivors, and the Jews were the prime targets. Just like before the war, the knock on the door at night meant an imminent arrest and a sentence to Siberia. My husband always had a piece of bread in his pocket just in case.[1]

Maria and her husband, living in perpetual fear of the worst descending upon them, watched as Soviet police arrested several friends and sent them to labor camps. Constantly under surveillance, without money, food, and clothing, and perpetually exhausted, their "spirits had once again been broken. This so-called liberation was in fact a very bitter one."[2]

Yet for one brief magical moment during a summer evening in 1944, around 7 p.m., the Epsteins had known an indescribable joy. They had heard people screaming, "The Russian tanks are here!" They ran outside. In the first tank they saw a young Soviet soldier. His face, covered with dirt and soot, looked tired. "We all ran to him, crying, kissing and hugging him." Tears streaming down her face, Maria carried her daughter whom she'd managed, miraculously, to give birth to during the war and to save.

The Red Army had rescued the young family of Polish Jews from the Holocaust. When the Germans invaded Russia in June 1941, nearly five million Jews lived in the country. By mid-1944, the Germans had killed over one million of them. Deported from Poland by the Nazis in 1941 to the Soviet Union, the Epsteins managed to survive the Nazi massacres of Soviet and Polish Jewry. Among the first Jews liberated in the war, Maria believed that she had "never experienced a feeling of such intensity."

During the war she and her husband had survived four years near the Minsk Ghetto in German labor camps and factories. They had witnessed or learned about some of the worst Nazi atrocities. The Germans and their collaborators, a unit of armed Latvians, worked the Jews like slaves and "slowly dehumanized us and stripped us of our dignity." Always hungry and poorly dressed, the Epsteins, Maria thought, "forgot that a different life existed. The past was something unreal, like a dream that had disappeared forever."

More and more, the two heard terrible news about the nearby Minsk Ghetto, where from July 1941 to October 1943, *SS* and German police battalions murdered some hundred thousand Jewish inhabitants in repeated *Aktionen*. She remembered long after the war:

> Every day somebody else was missing, every day the Germans made room for more Jews by burning the old ones alive. The Minsk ghetto became a central point where Jews were being brought from surrounding villages and towns to be sent to extermination camps. . . . During the raids, inhumane SS men had an opportunity to unleash their blood-thirsty instincts on innocent people. They stripped infants and children from mothers' arms and killed them by smashing their heads on the stone walls.[3]

At the factory Maria and her husband saw several co-workers shot to death by the *SS* solely because they had fastened the patches with yellow Jewish stars on their shirts using safety pins, different from German orders. Despite the impossibility of the situation in Nazi captivity, a glimmer still existed in Maria, a hope that she and her family would somehow survive. "We all believed," she thought, "that one day all the evil would disappear and our lives could be restored. It was worth it to go on living just to wait for this moment, so we fluctuated between feelings of hope and despair."[4]

Only in March 1945, after the Russians had liberated the Epsteins and after they had suffered continued discrimination at the hands of their liberators, would the Soviet government permit them to return to Poland. For years thereafter, they struggled to survive in a hostile, sometimes deadly, though not (as under Nazi rule) genocidal, world.

THE WAR AND POSTWAR TRAGEDY OF SOVIET JEWRY

The Soviets seemed little interested in the Holocaust in their country. As the war ended, many Soviet Jews refused to believe that anti-Semitism existed within the postwar Soviet system. One, Vasily Grossman, was an assimilated Ukrainian Jew and a patriot who'd seen firsthand the horrors of the war and the Holocaust that had ravaged his country.

When the Germans invaded Russia in 1941, the Soviet army had declared Grossman unfit for military combat and instead appointed him, at the rank of lieutenant colonel, a special correspondent for the army's newspaper, the *Red Star*. A relatively well-known novelist in his mid-thirties, he spent most of the rest of the war as a frontline reporter.

During early 1943 he had learned for the first time of the German atrocities against Soviet Jews. He'd arrived in Elista, a town in the northern Caucasus some two hundred miles south of Stalingrad. An *SS* commando there had massacred the local Jewish population. Grossman wrote in his notebook: "Death of ninety-three Jewish families. They'd smeared the children's lips with poison."[5]

A few months later, while at Kursk reporting on the huge German-Soviet tank battle there, Grossman noticed a renascent anti-Semitism expressed by his own government and culture. Like many other fellow Soviet idealists, he believed that the heroism of the Red Army at Stalingrad, a battle ending in January 1943 with the army's first major defeat of the Germans, would not only win the war but would also change Soviet society forever. Victory would create a new, more free and open Russia—not only for Jews but also for other Soviet minorities.

Accompanying the Red Army as it advanced through the Ukraine, Grossman heard about just one of many atrocities committed by the Nazis. He recorded details of it in his notebook:

> People who had come from Kiev told me that the Germans had surrounded with a ring of troops a huge mass grave in which the bodies of 50,000 Jews killed

> in Kiev in the autumn of 1941 were buried. They were hastily digging up the corpses, putting them on trucks and taking them to the West. They tried to burn some of the corpses on the spot.[6]

His words referred to the *SS*'s earlier slaughter of Jews at Babi Yar, a large ravine outside Kiev. The German Sixth Army and Ukrainian militia assisted. During September 29–30, 1941, firing squads murdered 33,771 Jews, over half of the Ukrainian capital's Jewish population. Later at the site, tens of thousands more people died: more Jews, plus Gypsies, partisans, and Communist Party members. In October 1943, Soviet civilians slipped through the front lines and reported that Nazis had ringed off the ravine and were attempting to eliminate traces of the killings by exhuming the corpses and burning them.

Although hardened to massive battlefield death, such information so shocked Grossman that he wrote an article entitled "Ukraine without Jews," in which he observed poignantly: "There are no Jews in the Ukraine. . . . All is silence. Everything is still. A whole people has been brutally murdered."[7] But *Red Star* refused to publish the essay.

Increasingly, Grossman realized, Soviet authorities didn't welcome his reports on what the world would later term the Holocaust. Stalin and, as a result, the Kremlin refused to accept any special categories of suffering. Without qualification they defined all victims of Nazism on Soviet land as "citizens of the Soviet Union." Official reports on atrocities, even those describing corpses wearing yellow stars, avoided any mention of the word *Jew*. The Stalinists refused Grossman's articles addressing this conspicuous omission as well as other Soviet suffering; this suppression was partly because, based on his interviews with witnesses, the *Red Star* correspondent described how numerous local Ukrainians had participated in the Nazi killings and subsequent looting of the victims' possessions.

When Soviet forces liberated Berdichev in January 1944, Grossman learned that his mother and other family members had died in the ghetto there in one of the first German massacres of Jews in the Ukraine, which began on September 5, 1941. Terribly burdened with a sense of guilt at failing to move his mother to Moscow before the German invasion, he wrote an article, "The Killing of Jews in Berdichev." Once again, Soviet authorities censored his work.

When Red Army troops arrived in late July 1944 at the Nazi death camp Maidanek, near Lublin in southeastern Poland, Grossman's superiors replaced him with another journalist to write about the Nazi crimes there. The substitute correspondent avoided any emphasis on the Jewish identity of victims in his article. But when Soviet troops farther north reached the site of Treblinka, which Himmler had ordered destroyed to conceal the crimes there, Grossman was allowed to go there and write about what the Russians found. He interviewed some forty Jewish survivors of the camp, who had hidden in surrounding forests. His article, entitled "The Hell Called Treblinka," appeared in a Soviet journal and is generally considered one of his most powerful pieces of writing. Later, prosecutors at the IMT in Nuremberg quoted from it:

> Thrift, thoroughness and pedantic cleanliness—all these are good qualities typical of many Germans. They prove effective when applied in agriculture and industry. But Hitler has put these qualities of the German character to work committing crimes against humanity. In the labour camps in Poland, the SS acted as if it was all about growing cauliflowers or potatoes.[8]

Nevertheless, when the war ended in Europe in May 1945, because of the immense hardships of wartime Soviet Jews, Grossman and other Jews believed that Stalin and the Moscow government would lead a comprehensive postwar campaign against anti-Semitism. The Jews pinned their desires on their country recognizing the wartime loyalty and sacrifice that Soviet Jews had displayed so amply: more than one million served in the Red Army; many died in the fighting and/or received decorations for their heroism. Now, Grossman thought, no one could possibly hate Jews after what had happened to them.

He was very wrong. Contrary to the expectations of Grossman and many other Soviet Jews, they discovered soon how deeply anti-Semitism infected the Stalinist regime. Stalin himself held rabid anti-Jewish views. In that respect, he and the anti-Bolshevik Hitler were in complete accord; the 1939 Nazi-Soviet pact allowed the Germans to invade Poland and consequently butcher the Jews there and until June 1941 helped sustain the Nazis' war effort in the West. One of Stalin's subordinates and later successor as Soviet leader, Nikita Khrushchev, who himself disparaged Jews and refused to admit that they had suffered more than non-Jews on Soviet territory, noted Stalin's "hostile attitude toward the Jewish people":

> I remember when I was working in Moscow, some kind of trouble at the Thirtieth Aviation Factory was reported to Stalin through Party channels and by State Security. During a meeting with Stalin, while we were sitting around exchanging opinions, Stalin turned to me and said, "The good workers at the factory should be given clubs so they can beat the hell out of those Jews at the end of the working day."[9]

As early as 1913, even before the Bolshevik Revolution, Stalin prepared the trap that eventually, after World War II, caught and mercilessly destroyed members of the pro-Soviet Jewish organization, the Jewish Anti-Fascist Committee (JAFC). The JAFC, formed in Moscow most likely at the end of 1941, had supported the Russian war effort both financially and with propaganda favorable to the Soviet Union.

But Stalin, possessing already in 1913 the Bolshevik Party's final word on the rights of national minorities in Russia, had defined the "nation" to exclude Russian Jews from any form of nationhood. The Jews, he had written, had no closed settlement region, no peasant class, no national market, no common language. After World War II his regime accused the JAFC and Soviet Jews of seeking their own nation and of cultivating "divisive" national leanings.

At the war's end, the JAFC's determination to publish what it called the *Black Book*, which contained damning information on the Holocaust in the Soviet Union, put the committee on a collision course with the Soviet dictator. During the final months of 1945, the book's editorial staff, which included Grossman, received considerable criticism from Ilya Ehrenburg, Grossman's Jewish friend and noted *Red Star* correspondent. Ehrenburg disapproved of Grossman's wish to include in the *Black Book* liberal documentation on the activity of traitors in the German-occupied territory, especially Ukrainians and Lithuanians, who had eagerly collaborated with the German extermination of Jews.

By year's end, Grossman put together a new staff and assumed the post of chief editor. Meanwhile, the JAFC distributed early drafts of the book to numerous foreign Soviet-friendly organizations. During late 1946 the Kremlin unleashed a hysterical campaign—led by Andrei Zhdanov, the Communist Party's chief ideologist and cultural policeman—against all efforts in art or literature that supposedly undermined Soviet patriotism and "nationality." On October 12, 1946, the Soviet minister of state security sent a note to the party's Central Committee about "the nationalist tendencies of the Jewish Anti-Fascist Committee."

In February 1947, the government accused the JAFC of sending manuscripts to foreign countries without permission. A Soviet official complained, "The idea that the Germans robbed and murdered only the Jews goes through the entire book. The reader gets the impression that the Germans went to war against the USSR with the sole purpose of annihilating the Jews."[10]

In the fall of 1947, Stalin himself forbade publication of the *Black Book* in Russia, even while he supported the creation of the new state of Israel. A censored edition of the book, eliminating extensive material on the local Soviet peoples' cooperation in murdering Jews, was published in the United States and in other foreign countries.

It took nearly fifty years, until after the fall of the Soviet regime in 1991, for researchers to uncover the original uncensored manuscript in the Moscow archives of the *KGB* (the Soviets' former secret police). In 1993 the book—in its original form—appeared in Russia. It remained largely unnoticed, and the German edition in 1994 was also widely ignored. In the original version, Albert Einstein, the Nobel Prize–winning physicist—forced to emigrate from Germany when Hitler came to power in 1933—living in the United States, wrote in the foreword:

> The Jewish people have lost more than all other afflicted peoples through the catastrophe of the last few years. Therefore, if we truly want to strive for a righteous redress, the Jewish people have to be given special consideration in the reorganization of peace. The fact that the Jews cannot be considered a nation in formal political terms, because they do not have a country or a government, should not be a hindrance. They should be dealt with as a unified group, as if they were a country. Their status as a unified political group has been proven to be a fact by the actions of their enemies. . . .
>
> The existence of the Jews in parts of Europe would be impossible for years to come. The Jews have made it possible to settle in Palestinian soil through decades of hard work and voluntary financial aid by other peoples. All of these sacrifices were taken with the understanding that the official promises made by the governments involved after the last war would be kept. This was the promise that a safe haven be created for the Jewish people in the old homeland of Palestine. . . . Therefore, after the Jews—especially the Palestinian Jews—honorably earned a name for themselves, one must emphatically call attention to that promise. Palestine has to be opened to Jewish immigration within its economic capabilities.[11]

By the end of 1947, the Cold War between the Soviet Union and the West had begun in earnest. Not surprisingly, the JAFC's contacts with the United States and other foreign countries made it even more suspect to the xenophobic Stalin and his sycophantic underlings (including an ambitious and ruthless Khrushchev).

Increasingly the government had implemented the doctrine of Russo-Slavic nationalism, thereby intensifying the Russification of Soviet minorities that had begun somewhat haphazardly before the war. The campaign affected Jews most acutely because the government's official anti-Semitism could sustain its streamlined unimpeded course only by not recognizing the shredded currents inherent therein. But when JAFC leaders asked the government to counter anti-Jewish attacks—at the very least with moral indignation and vocal denunciation—Soviet officials accused the Jews and committee of engaging in anti-Soviet "nationalism." In November 1947 the government shut down the JAFC and denounced its members for allegedly engaging in espionage for foreign countries. (Two months later, the Soviet police in Minsk would murder the committee's former chairman.)

Until Stalin died in his bed on March 5, 1953, his regime waged an open war against the Jews, during which it charged them with promoting "rootless cosmopolitanism." It conducted massive purges of Jews from cultural areas, the military, and industry. *Pravda*, the Communist Party's paper, denounced Jewish theater critics for their alleged inability to understand the Russian national character. The government went further and arrested most of the JAFC's former leaders (except for Grossman and Ehrenburg). The Soviet powers that be interrogated and tortured them. In May 1952 they were placed on trial. Before the closed proceedings began, the court had decided on its guilty verdicts. By August, all but two had been executed.

The immediate postwar destruction of the JAFC paralleled what amounted to a broader frontal attack on Soviet Jews and the Holocaust in Soviet culture. Although the Kremlin did not deny that six million Jews died in the war, among them many Soviet Jews, and that the Nazis had singled out Jews for annihilation, it viewed the Holocaust as part of a larger issue—the murder of "Soviet civilians" or "citizens." Soviet literature ignored the term *Holocaust* completely; only in the early 1990s, after the fall of the Soviet regime, did "holocaust," transliterated from English, appear publicly. In the decades after World War II, history textbooks in elementary and secondary schools made no references to Jews except for a single mention of "terrible Jewish pogroms."

The six-volume official Soviet history of the war ignored Jews. The *Great Soviet Encyclopedia*, while it mentioned that the Nazis had carried out a policy of mass extermination of Jews, said nothing about the Holocaust. Nevertheless, during the 1950s a well-known controversy arose over the construction of a monument to the Jewish victims at Babi Yar. In 1959 the writer Viktor Nekrasov protested plans to turn the site into a park and soccer stadium. Another writer, Yevgeny Yevtushenko, published a poem, "Babi Yar," condemning anti-Semitism. Dmitri Shostakovich, the composer, included the poem in his Thirteenth Symphony. Thus, Soviet officialdom did almost nothing to expose the public to even the most basic details of the Holocaust. Only during the 1960s did a few books appear—including some translations from other languages—that provided more information.[12]

In explaining why this and other tragedy and humiliation continued for Soviet Jewry long after the world war, British historian Richard Overy has linked it both to Russia's long history of anti-Semitism and especially to the Soviet leadership's failure to understand what had happened in the war. "The most crushing blow," Overy concludes, "came with the persistent refusal of the [Soviet] regime to recognize that the German race war had been directed at the Jewish people as such."[13]

As noted earlier in this chapter, Stalin and his subordinates feared that knowledge of the Holocaust might raise Jewish consciousness—and, therefore, nationalism—and lessen the Russification of Soviet Jews. In addition, Stalinist authorities, always seeking to legitimize their power, wished to do nothing that might undermine the virtual—and official—postwar cult in Soviet society worshiping Stalin and the country's victory in World War II.

In this regard, during 1945 and 1946 a fiercely paranoid Stalin refused to believe that Hitler had committed suicide in his Berlin bunker and ordered the Soviet secret police to assemble for him an extensive dossier on the Nazi dictator. The police produced a file 413 typewritten pages thick, edited and published recently as *The Hitler Book.* It was remarkable for two particular qualities: first, it contained a detailed, intimate portrait of the Führer; and second, it mentioned nothing of the Final Solution—or even Hitler's anti-Semitic ideology.

Apparently, only Stalin's death saved Grossman and Ehrenburg from a fate similar to the JAFC defendants as well as many other Soviet Jews arrested and executed. The Kremlin compelled Grossman to issue a letter of repentance for writing a novel about the war without mentioning Stalin. The novel was further condemned for reducing the achievements and role of the Communist Party in the world war's victory.

Both men likely would have faced trial in connection with the so-called Doctors' Plot, which *Pravda* announced two months before Stalin died. The Kremlin accused a group of Soviet doctors, most of them Jewish, of conspiring to kill Soviet leaders—Stalin foremost. Until then, Grossman and Ehrenburg had escaped persecution, primarily because of their notoriety and heroism as war correspondents. Did Stalinists plan another major campaign, a new Great Terror resembling that of the 1930s, whose principal victims would be Soviet Jews? A likely accurate speculation, since Stalin stood with Hitler as one of the greatest mass murderers in history.

Despite his disdain of Stalinism, with its overripe lies about the war and its betrayal of the Jews, Grossman never lost his faith in the Russian soldier or in the huge sacrifices that made up what the Soviet government called the "Great Patriotic War." During the 1950s he worked on what would be his masterpiece novel, *Life and Fate*, a story about Stalingrad, one of the most devastating and decimating of German-Russian battles, and the Stalinist dictatorship.

The Soviet government refused to allow the book's publication; the police even seized nearly every copy of the manuscript. When he died in 1964, Grossman assumed that his greatest work had been suppressed forever. But he'd given a copy to a friend and eventually, Soviet dissidents—including the physicist Andrei Sakharov—smuggled it out of Russia to Switzerland, where it was ultimately published. Like so many other Jews victimized by the Holocaust, Grossman never got over his guilt and horror at the fate of his loved ones—especially what his mother, killed by the Germans, had suffered.

REPORTS AND TRIALS

On May 29, 1945, the Soviet Union demanded in its official report on Auschwitz, which outlined what the Red Army had found when it liberated the camp four months before, that "[a]ll . . . who personally participated in the murder and torture of the prisoners at Oswiecim [Auschwitz], must be brought before the court of nations and pay the severe penalty they merit."

The lengthy report, appearing in the weekly English-language newsletter issued by the Soviet Embassy in the United States, discussed the conclusions of an "Extraordinary State Committee" that investigated the camp after its liberation in late January 1945 by the Red Army. The committee based its findings on the

> interrogation and medical examination of 2,819 prisoners of Oswiecim camp who were saved by the Red Army, a study of German documents discovered in the camp, the remains of the crematorium and gas chambers blown up by the Germans as they retreated, bodies found on the territory of the camp, and belongings and documents found in camp warehouses and barracks of the people from various countries of Europe who were killed by the Germans.[14]

In the report the world had one of its first accounts of the technology and machinery of annihilation, including details of the construction and operation of the gas chambers, at Auschwitz. Also the report revealed the gruesome specifics of how "German-fascist professors and doctors," including Josef Mengele, "widely practiced medical experiments on living persons, displaying monstrous inventiveness." It outlined as well the "organized monstrous death-conveyor system" of slave labor at Auschwitz.

But if the Soviet report provided an important survey of what had happened at Auschwitz, it mentioned nothing about what, in fact, the Nazis had used the enormous camp primarily for—to murder at least one million Jews deported there from throughout Europe. Indeed, the report identified only one Jew at the camp—"a Jewess from Greece named Bela," killed by x-ray sterilization experiments conducted on female prisoners by a camp doctor, Horst Schumann (who, like the vast majority of perpetrators, was never brought to trial for his involvement in the Nazis' euthanasia program and for his pointless and painful medical experiments at Auschwitz). Instead, those annihilated at Auschwitz were "citizens of the Soviet Union, Poland, France, Belgium, Holland, Czechoslovakia, Yugoslavia, Rumania, Hungary, and other countries. . . . The German executioners were especially savage in their treatment of Soviet prisoners." But not of Jews, at least according to the report.

The postwar Soviet trials of Holocaust perpetrators—who had murdered some one million Soviet Jews—also reflected the ambivalence of Russian officialdom toward the murder of Jews in their country. Beginning in December 1945 and lasting into the first months of 1946, the Soviets held public trials in numerous cities, including Minsk, Riga, and Kiev.

The timing of the trials corresponded purposely with the IMT in Nuremberg. Soviet officials emphasized repeatedly that the trials represented part of the international effort to punish war criminals; the extensive publicity surrounding the trials was intended to demonstrate that the Soviet Union had suffered the utmost devastation and human loss, something the Moscow government would use in bargaining with the other Allies over assets in Germany.

In contrast to similar Soviet trials during the war (discussed in chapter 1), the postwar trials introduced crimes related to the Holocaust as one of the principal charges against the defendants. The massive extent of the Holocaust in the country and the involvement in it of the *SS*, regular German armed forces, and civilian administration provided the Soviet tribunals with a significant opportunity to convict the majority of the defendants.

While the indictment included a wide net of war crimes perpetrated in the former German-occupied Soviet territories, the courts paid particular attention to the Holocaust, especially in areas with large prewar Jewish populations. In Kiev, Riga, and Minsk alone, some twenty-six of forty-one defendants stood accused of organizing or participating in the murder of Jews. Evidence against them included captured Nazi records as well as eyewitness testimony. In addition, interrogations sometimes accompanied by brutal treatment of the defendants nearly always produced confessions from them.

The government-controlled Soviet press covered the trials extensively but downplayed the Holocaust, camouflaging it as the "sufferings of the Soviet people." Newspapers referred ambiguously to the murdered Jews as "Soviet citizens" or "civilians." The word *Jew* rarely, if ever, appeared in print. In this regard, the press—like most every other area of Soviet culture—reflected the Stalinist regime's anti-Semitism and its wish, officially and publicly, to suppress the memory of the Holocaust and any sympathy for its victims among other Soviet peoples.

Yet despite the language and policy of the press toward the trials, the trials exposed the overwhelming tragedy of the Soviet Jews. They revealed to the country the scope of what had happened to the Jews and made it part of the history of the "Great Patriotic War."[15] The trial of former *SS* Lieutenant General Friedrich Jeckeln provided a telling example. He was Erich von dem Bach-Zelewski's fellow Higher *SS* and Police Leader South—for the Ukraine—and later northern Russia, the highest-ranking defendant among the onetime *SS* and police officials.

Jeckeln, a stalwart Nazi since the 1920s, was distinguished looking in his uniform, but there was nothing distinguished about his deeds. During the first months of the German invasion of the Soviet Union in 1941, he had managed to involve the *Wehrmacht* in the Ukraine in massacring local Jews. The police battalions he commanded had execution totals far higher than other similar mobile killing units elsewhere in the Soviet Union, and Jeckeln's initiative earned Himmler's enthusiastic approval.

Between July 27 and August 27, 1941, Jeckeln's *SS* and police units in the Ukraine, independent of the deadly march east of *Einsatzgruppen*, reported to Himmler's command staff of having murdered 7,261 persons, of which "*an astounding 94 percent* of the victims were Jews." His units carried out some of the worst massacres in the Ukraine: they shot 23,600 Jews at Kamenets-Podolsky; another *Aktion* followed in Berdichev, where Jeckeln's units killed 1,303 Jews, "among them 875 Jewesses over twelve years of age." Altogether during August the Higher *SS* and Police Leader South's firing squads alone killed 44,125 persons, "mostly Jews." Jeckeln also assisted *Einsatzgruppe* C. When its *Kommando* 4a moved into Kiev, two detachments of his Uniformed Police helped to kill nearly 34,000 Jews at Babi Yar, the ravine outside the city.

In October, Himmler transferred Jeckeln to the Baltic region and Byelorussia, where, in response to Hitler's demand, the *Reichsführer* wanted more rapid progress in killing Jews. At the ghetto in Riga, between November 29 and December 9, at least twenty-four thousand Jews, including eight thousand children, some deported from Berlin, were shot by Jeckeln's murder units. The killing of Jews from the Reich, however, had neither been expressly ordered by Himmler nor forbidden. Not only did Jeckeln meet his superior's deadly expectations, he just as mercilessly plundered Jewish property and belongings. In Riga, he controlled a huge warehouse and, according to Raul Hilberg, "spent hours sorting jewelry on his desk."[16]

A month later, following Himmler's directive, Jeckeln liquidated the Salaspils concentration camp, located near Riga, which held Jews from all over Europe. In a deposition he gave on December 14, 1945, preceding his trial, he admitted that his killing units completed the task by June 1942, when nearly eighty-seven thousand Jews at Salaspils had been murdered. To facilitate the killing, the Germans had used gas vans. At the war's end, the Red Army captured Jeckeln and other German officials who served in the Riga military district.

Jeckeln's trial in Riga lasted from January 26 to February 3, 1946. He acknowledged his direct involvement in the murder of Jews, but like many perpetrators on trial at Nuremberg, he insisted that he had merely carried out his superiors' orders. He had received the command directly from Himmler in November 1941 to liquidate the Riga Ghetto, including Jews just deported there from Berlin. According to Jeckeln, the *Reichsführer* had also ordered the Higher *SS* and Police Leader to kill "all Jews in the Ostland [the area encompassing the Baltic states and Byelorussia] down to the last man."[17] He told interrogators as well that in February 1942 he had received a letter from

Reinhard Heydrich, informing him that Göring had "gotten himself involved in the Jewish question, and that Jews were now being shipped to the East for annihilation only with Goering's approval."[18]

On February 3, 1946, the court convicted Jeckeln of organizing the "complete extermination" of three hundred thousand "Soviet citizens of Jewish nationality" in the Baltic area and two hundred thousand in Byelorussia.[19] The same afternoon, the Soviets executed him and five other German generals found guilty with him.

BERNHARD BECHLER: DENAZIFICATION DIRECTOR

In one of the many ironies—as well as insults—of the postwar era for Jewish survivors, Bernhard Bechler was a former professional officer in the German army and enthusiastic National Socialist. But in postwar Soviet-occupied East Germany, he directed in his province of Brandenburg the denazification (or purge) of former Nazi Party members from the government, economy, and society.

Denazification in the Soviet zone did almost nothing to punish individual Germans for their participation in the Holocaust. Nor did it attempt to lessen the widespread anti-Semitism that had produced and fueled the Nazi persecution of Jews. Instead, the purge reflected the views of the Russians and their German Communist allies that German fascism—Nazism—had resulted from monopoly capitalism. Eliminating Nazism required an antifascist drive to destroy the whole socioeconomic and political system.

To help legitimize itself with its nearly seventeen million people, the new Soviet-controlled East German zone made worship of the former anti-Nazi Communist resistance a key part of the antifascist campaign. This meant expropriating private property, nationalizing key industries, and creating, politically, a broadly based—but carefully controlled—antifascist order. The Soviet Military Administration for Germany, known by its German acronym SMAD, removed several hundred thousand former Nazis from the civil service, police, education, and economy, and replaced them with reliable Communists. But the Soviet zone—and eventually the Moscow-dominated East German regime established in 1949—needed experienced administrators, and hence SMAD ended denazification already in early 1948.

Brandenburg, the largest of five provinces in the Soviet zone, included the area—less Berlin—west of the Oder-Neiße border. Bechler served as minister of interior in the new provincial government, created by the Soviets on July 4, 1945. German Communists appointed by Moscow held the other major offices.

Why place a former Nazi officer in charge of purging the province of former Nazis? The Red Army had captured Bechler during the Battle of

Stalingrad. While a prisoner of war in the Soviet Union, he'd become an active member of the National Committee for a Free Germany. The committee represented a Soviet effort during the war to develop an alternative government for Germany comprising German prisoners of war and political refugees. Had Bechler, therefore, gone over to the Soviet side, as seemed obvious to the Russians? Or should one believe his ex-wife, who called him after the war an outspoken supporter of Hitler and the only National Socialist in the family?

Accompanying the Red Army, Bechler had entered Germany in the spring of 1945 as an operative of the National Committee for a Free Germany. Even before the Red Army advanced on Berlin in April, he had established a so-called front school, which had some sixty members trained to take control of administrative activities in Brandenburg.

Immediately on his appointment to Brandenburg's government, the former Nazi made denazification a top priority of his ministry. None of his eventual policies, however, indicated even a remote interest in uncovering and purging former Nazi perpetrators of Jewish persecution. Neither he nor anyone else in the provincial government or SMAD showed the slightest concern for what Nazi Germany had done to Jews.

In July 1945, during Bechler's first meeting with the province's district magistrates and mayors, the former Nazi soldier ordered that "all the remaining [Nazi] party members will have to be released" from government service throughout the province. In his guidelines regarding the purge in Brandenburg, he emphasized that every German shared in the "responsibility for this war," but he made no differentiation among the levels of guilt.[20] Nor did he define what "this war" had meant or whom it had affected so horribly.

During August an order from SMAD—refusing to allow German officials such as Bechler to implement the purge, instead preferring to issue commands that it expected the Germans to carry out—reaffirmed his previous directive. While the military order made no distinction between dismissing active and nominal members of the Nazi Party from all positions in the provincial administration, it also mentioned nothing about removing party members involved in persecuting and exterminating Jews.

Even the purge of former party members proceeded slowly. Numerous factors, in large part other pressing tasks, undermined the denazification campaign in 1945: clearing wartime rubble, erecting housing, securing the fall harvest, processing thousands of Displaced Persons, and combating lawlessness. Many Brandenburg officials argued that, like Bechler, former Nazis employed in the government had an "irreplaceable" expertise in addressing such issues. For practical reasons, allegedly, one couldn't afford to remove the ex-Nazis.

Eventually, throughout East Germany the Soviet leadership viewed unworkable a blanket dismissal of former Nazis from the administration. By the end of 1946, onetime party members made up 21 percent of the Brandenburg government's employees. Many more former party members owned businesses or other properties. In October 1946 SMAD moved to denazify such persons by implementing several measures, including registering them and former German army officers, using both groups in forced labor battalions, expropriating their land and personal belongings, and denying them voting rights in subsequent elections.

Concerned about the effects the seizures of former Nazi-owned businesses or other properties had on the province's economic reconstruction and activity, Bechler attempted to limit the extent of the confiscations by restricting the definition of persons liable for expropriation. He defined the categories of the most likely candidates for such expropriation as "officeholders of the NSDAP [Nazi Party]," "leading members" of the party, and the party's "influential supporters." He intended in such guidelines to ensure that "small greengrocers or similar businessmen will not be thrown out of their shops and have their property expropriated."[21] Of course, unspoken was the irrefutable fact that even numerous "small greengrocers" had benefited immeasurably from the Nazis' expulsion of Jews from the economy.

What purposes did confiscating such property or dismissing employers of former party members serve? For one thing, Bechler claimed in January 1947, such measures honored those who had allegedly suffered the most under Nazism. Following rigid Soviet ideology, Bechler celebrated the heroic antifascists, by which he meant the anti-Nazi, primarily Communist, working-class resistance. "Every true antifascist," he proclaimed, "is responsible to the innumerable dead and to the other victims, who established a lasting legacy in the fight against fascism and in the struggle for the creation of democracy."[22]

And what about financial compensation for the now-largest group of "innumerable dead" among Germans, whom Bechler refused to acknowledge—German Jews and especially their surviving descendants? Before killing their victims, the Nazis had seized their property and businesses.

Neither Bechler nor the rest of the Brandenburg government (not to mention the Soviet military) said or did anything to return such properties to their rightful owners or redress their loss with even the most paltry gesture. Nor did East German and Soviet authorities consider providing survivors some portion of the property and other wealth expropriated from party members. The new rulers in Soviet-occupied Germany ignored totally the vast losses of German Jews in property and belongings.

In Brandenburg, during 1947 and early 1948, denazification boards, staffed by Germans and established by the Soviets, exonerated a tiny number—less than 1 percent—of former Nazis who showed that they'd continued in Nazi Germany their relationships with Jews or aided them in avoiding deportation. (The systematic deportation of Jews from Brandenburg had begun in April

1942.) The boards, including the province-level body headed by Bechler, issued such judgments not because they recognized the Jews as a unique group persecuted by Hitler's regime, but because they viewed the assistance of Jews by party members as antifascist activity.

According to the average defendant testifying before the boards, no one had supported mistreating the Jews or any other group; few had joined the party out of conviction; and those who'd done so quickly saw their error. Admissions of remorse were rare, confessions of actual guilt almost nonexistent. The boards in Brandenburg and Bechler's ministry nearly always accepted the claim of former party members—despite their having joined the party before or shortly after the Nazis seized power in Germany in 1933—that they had opposed or had no knowledge of the Jewish persecution.

Most of the general population of Brandenburg, numbering nearly 2,500,000, believed similarly. The people, concerned more with shortages of food and housing—and with a generally grim day-to-day existence under the Soviet thumb—than with politics, disliked denazification; few agreed to serve as prosecution witnesses for the boards. Both Soviet and German Communist officials retained a keen memory of Nazism's popularity among Germans. After 1945, such officials worried about how best to prevent its revival. The Soviets responded to the perceived threat with a two-pronged approach: imposing a dictatorship over what they viewed to be a dangerous people, and avoiding large-scale, direct confrontations with the Germans' Nazi past.

In March 1948 the Soviets discontinued denazification throughout their zone. By then, the Brandenburg boards and Bechler's ministry had convicted and punished only a tiny proportion of the twenty-nine thousand former Nazis—a small quantity of the population—who had appeared before the boards.

Hardly surprising, the same political views dominated the postwar court trials of Nazi criminals in the Soviet zone of East Germany and, after 1949, in the Russian-controlled German Democratic Republic (GDR) and East Berlin. Near the end of World War II, as the Red Army advanced into eastern Germany, the Soviet Commissariat for Internal Affairs, the *NKVD*, established numerous prison camps at the battlefronts (*Frontlagern*). Before May 1945, the Soviets had arrested nearly three hundred eighty thousand persons, mostly Germans, and interned eighty-eight thousand in the camps. Once Soviet armies forced Germany's surrender, the *NKVD* created in the Soviet-occupied eastern Germany so-called special camps (*Speziallagern*). These were in fact concentration and forced labor camps interning primarily Germans. It's estimated that from mid-1945 to 1950 the camps held at least one hundred fifty-seven thousand prisoners, which included thirty-five thousand non-Germans.

Soviet government directives, issued initially in December 1944, made clear that the Soviet Union had a much greater concern for "the labor supply question" than for "the punishment of Nazis and denazification."[23] Statistics from the former GDR appear to bear this out. Between 1945 and 1964, Soviet-dominated German courts convicted 12,807 persons of "Nazi and war crimes"; of the convicted, 118 received death sentences, 231 life in prison, and 12,458 varying terms of imprisonment.[24] The figures gave no indication of how many—if any—of the convicted had participated in the persecution and killing of Jews or members of other groups.

In comparison, during approximately the same period, between 1950 and 1962, the West Germans investigated thirty thousand former Nazis, indicted 12, 846, tried 5,426, and acquitted 4,027; of those sentenced, only 155 were convicted of murder. One scholar's assessment of the West German figures—that they "show a relatively high figure for acquittals and a low number of heavy sentences"—could apply as well to the East German numbers.[25]

KARL CLAUBERG: AUSCHWITZ DOCTOR

How much did Moscow's attitudes and policy toward Jews influence its wholly negligent punishment of one of the few former Nazi murderers at Auschwitz captured after the war by the Soviet Union? From 1942 to 1944 Karl Clauberg, a fellow physician of Mengele at Auschwitz, had experimented in involuntarily sterilizing Jewish, Gypsy, and other female prisoners at the camp. These bestial experiments, conducted under the tissue-thin premise of "legitimate" scientific study, resulted in untold suffering and death for his victims.

During May 1941, Clauberg, a noted prewar German gynecologist and obstetrician, university professor, and enthusiastic National Socialist (who'd risen eventually in the *SS* to the rank of lieutenant general), had approached Himmler initially about what the doctor termed, in a memorandum, "nonsurgical sterilization of inferior women." A year later, Clauberg—a short, bald, and chubby creature—asked permission from the *SS* leader to conduct his experiments at Auschwitz. These involved injecting irritant chemicals into the uterus by means of a syringe. He planned, he informed the *Reichsführer* confidently, to perfect a mass sterilization method for "unworthy women" as well as to produce fertility in "worthy women."[26]

The ambitious Clauberg envisioned making himself a Nazi hero. He would do so, he thought, by contributing in a revolutionary way to the plans of Himmler and Hitler to complete in the course of the war the racial or demographic reordering of much of the landmass of Eurasia, during which tens of millions of Jews and Slavs would be slaughtered, sterilized, or deliberately starved to death.

His letter produced results. In July 1942, Himmler ordered Clauberg to begin the latter's proposed experiments at the Ravensbrück concentration camp. Shortly thereafter, the diabolical physician received permission to use facilities at Auschwitz to continue his work. There Clauberg had numerous prisoner doctors for assistants, including a Polish Jew, Wladyslas Dering (the subject of a famous libel case in England in 1964 involving medical experiments at Auschwitz). A principal aim included discovering—by performing the procedures in (what Himmler and other *SS* officials termed) "major dimensions" on Jewish women in the camp—a method by which the victims could be sterilized without awareness of what was being done to them. Himmler pledged all those involved to secrecy.

During the next year Clauberg worked busily in Block 10 of Auschwitz I, the so-called experimental block. To fool his victims, he informed the women before injecting them with the irritant fluid—without an anesthesia—that they were undergoing artificial insemination. The injections, however, caused inflammation of the ovaries, excruciating pain, and often death. Estimates of the number of women sterilized in this vicious fashion range from seven hundred to several thousand.

In June 1943, Clauberg sent his first report to Himmler, in which he claimed to have "almost perfected" his method. The time was not far distant, the self-aggrandizing doctor assured the *Reichsführer* proudly, when he would be able to say that one doctor, with ten assistants, could sterilize a thousand women in one day.[27] Eager to please Himmler, Clauberg exaggerated his progress and his method's effectiveness. He never discussed how one could expect to maintain secrecy in such a mass procedure. Meanwhile, Himmler approved other *SS* doctors' proposals (like those of Horst Schumann) to experiment at Auschwitz with using x-rays to achieve mass sterilization.

Alina Brewda-Bialostocki, a Polish Jew and physician imprisoned at Auschwitz in September 1943 who worked in Block 10, recalled after the war that Clauberg never used antiseptics in injecting the oft-deadly chemicals and that everything pointed to the supposition that he was not what he pretended to be. She noted that at least "1 or 2 times" a prisoner nurse, Sylvia Friedman, had called Brewda-Bialostocki to help,

> because women who had been injected by Clauberg had gone into shock. I remember that one woman lay on the X-ray table, with the instrument still in the vagina, i.e., uterus.
>
> From discussions with fellow prisoners, I heard repeatedly that Prof. Dr. Clauberg administered his injections very brutally, so much that with women who defended themselves instinctively or screamed loudly, Sylvia had to intervene by hitting them. . . . Dr. Clauberg's treatment of the women convinced me that he could be no professor.[28]

Another Polish Jew, Jiri Beranovsky, an electro engineer, imprisoned in Auschwitz in March 1941, worked eventually on the equipment in Clauberg's operating room in Block 10 and on the X-ray machine. Beranovsky testified after the war that he knew Clauberg "personally" and that

> I had occasion to observe the preparations he made for these experiments. In Block no. 10 the windows were boarded up with wood, so that one could neither see out of the block nor into it. In this way the block was isolated from the rest of the camp, also from the yard that separated Blocks no. 10 and no. 11 from one another. In this block [no. 11] were prisoners whom the camp Gestapo had condemned to death. They were also executed in the yard. Block no. 10 was always locked up and opened only with the ring of a bell. Only Dr. Clauberg and Dr. Döring [Dering] could enter this block. In addition, as skilled workers, we had occasion to go inside to make necessary repairs, but always, to be sure, accompanied by the SS. Neither the nurses nor the women subjected to the experiments could leave the block. . . .
>
> Dr. Clauberg carried out his first operations with the assistance of Dr. Döring [Dering] in Block no. 20, opposite Block no. 10, before the latter's operating room was completed. . . . The experiments had a terrible effect on the women, which I had occasion to observe—it was quite enough when Dr. Clauberg or an assistant entered the block: immediately the women scheduled for the experiments broke into a frightful whining and crying. The fear they had of the experiments was obvious. After the experiments, performed by Dr. Clauberg, a few of the women languished, others to my knowledge died from them. I cannot estimate their number [the dead], because the bodies were removed at night and taken to the crematorium. The average number [of women in Block 10] was between 400 and 600. . . . That the administration of the concentration camp was concerned greatly about keeping these experiments secret is confirmed by the fact that during the evacuation of the entire camp the women of Block no. 10 were isolated from all the other prisoners. I know that at the time of the camp's liquidation, there were only about 150 women in Block no. 10, which meant that the others had been taken out dead. As I mentioned already, the transporting [of the dead] was always done at night, so that I was not a firsthand witness to the removal.[29]

After leaving Auschwitz in 1944, Clauberg returned to his private clinic nearby at Königshütte. When the Red Army approached the area in January 1945, he fled west. During his flight he took the time to continue his sterilization experiments at Ravensbrück, the Nazi women's camp. The war's end found him in northern Germany, in Schleswig-Holstein, seeking to join there a last group of loyal *SS* leaders surrounding Himmler.

On June 8, 1945, the Russians captured Clauberg. The Soviets placed him on trial in 1948 for the part he had played in the "mass extermination of Soviet citizens," not of his principal victims, Jews. His crimes against "Soviet citizens" alone should have led to his execution or, at least, to life imprisonment. It did not.

Nor would the Western Allies and Germans insist on his being properly punished. The Soviets sentenced him to twenty-five years imprisonment. But in October 1955, following the death of Josef Stalin and after West Germany and the USSR had completed various diplomatic agreements, Moscow amnestied and returned Clauberg, who had served barely seven years of his sentence, to West Germany as part of a repatriation of German prisoners. In Germany, at least initially, neither judicial authorities nor medical groups (many of whose members included numerous former Nazis) made moves to punish Clauberg despite substantial evidence and knowledge of his murderous experiments at Auschwitz.

Wholly unrepentant, Clauberg, after returning from Russia to West Germany, even boasted of his "scientific achievements." "I was able," he told the press proudly—but falsely—in an interview about his work at Auschwitz and Königshütte, "to perfect an absolutely new method of sterilization . . . [which] would be of great use today in certain cases."[30]

Only in late November 1955, after pressure from groups of Jewish survivors and others, did West German authorities arrest Clauberg. For a considerable time the German Chamber of Medicine, the official body of the profession, resisted taking any action that would remove his title of doctor of medicine.

Nor did the former wartime Western Allies press for his punishment. A group of onetime prisoner physicians of Auschwitz issued an impressive declaration condemning Clauberg's actions there as being "in total disaccord with the sworn duty of every doctor," and bitterly decrying the fact that "such medical practitioners who . . . put themselves at the service of National-Socialism to destroy human lives . . . are today in a position to practice once more the profession which they have profaned in such a scandalous manner."[31]

Only reluctantly did the Chamber of Medicine revoke Clauberg's license. But like so many of his former Nazi colleagues, he cheated justice to the end. The fifty-nine-year-old died on August 9, 1957, shortly before facing trial in a Kiel court that charged him with repeatedly inflicting grave bodily injury on Jewish women inmates at Auschwitz. One could have added—and causing widespread death.

6

In the Custody of Leniency

He hadn't given much thought to fleeing the enemy. Only vaguely had the prospect of a German loss in the war crossed his mind. Instead, something far more immediate concerned him: the possibility of losing, in the next few moments, his job and livelihood. Before opening the door to the office, he paused, expecting the worst. Since the Jewish prisoners had revolted three weeks earlier in Treblinka, he'd fretted that Himmler or someone else high up in the *SS* hierarchy would hold him responsible for what had happened at the camp.

"It's my hardest time," Franz Stangl thought to himself. "I'm sure I'll get all the blame."[1] He feared the ruin of his career, one in which he had supervised the extermination of masses of people at Treblinka, Sobibor, and Schloß Hartheim. He'd performed the work dutifully, seeking to fulfill his superiors' orders with ambition and zeal.

Now he had a directive to appear at the office of Odilo Globocnik, his commander in Nazi-occupied Poland, who had just received from Himmler an appointment as Higher *SS* and Police Leader in the Trieste area of northeast Italy, a region infested with heavily armed anti-German Yugoslav partisans. One had to question whether or not the new assignment rewarded this *SS* officer for his leadership since the end of 1941 in carrying out the mission given him by Hitler and Himmler—the extermination of nearly all of Poland's three million Jews, some third of whom had perished under Stangl's command in Treblinka's gas chambers.

In late August 1943, when Stangl, full of apprehension but as always dressed immaculately in his *SS* uniform, entered Globocnik's headquarters in Lublin, Stangl's superior rose from his desk. The two exchanged the Hitler salute, clicking their boot heels loudly. Stangl feared both Globocnik and what the latter seemed likely to announce; perhaps his boss would send him to the Eastern Front.

But Stangl received instead a most welcome surprise. "You are transferred as of immediately to Trieste," Globocnik informed him, "for antipartisan combat." The German army in Italy, Globocnik explained, needed reinforcements. The recent fall from power in Italy of Hitler's major European war ally, the Fascist dictator Benito Mussolini, and the landing of Allied forces in southern Italy had increased anti-German partisan activity in the country's northern portion. To fight the partisans, Globocnik would take with him *SS* men (including Stangl) and Ukrainians, whom he'd commanded in Poland.

Stunned by the news, Stangl thought "my bones would melt" with relief. Instead of the worst he could imagine for his professional life, he'd survived. "I was going to get out [of Germany]. And to Trieste, too—near home" in Austria. Breathing more easily, he returned to Treblinka but stayed there only "three or four days," just long enough to prepare for the last transports of Jews to arrive at the camp for killing before the *SS* dismantled it.[2]

STANGL: DOUBT IN TRIESTE

Stangl traveled to Trieste in mid-September 1943 as part of a convoy that included Globocnik and 120 others from Globocnik's staff in Poland as well as ten from Treblinka and from the earlier euthanasia program in Germany. One in the group, *SS* Major Christian Wirth, known as the "savage Christian," had supervised extermination camps at Belzec, Sobibor, and Treblinka along with Globocnik and had served previously as a roving inspector of euthanasia installations in Germany and Austria. Stangl had worked closely with and as a subordinate of Wirth since Stangl's job at Hartheim.

But now for the first time Stangl seemed concerned, even doubtful, about his and Germany's future. He believed that the Nazi leadership viewed as "an embarrassment" him and the others it had shipped off to a faraway and perilous wartime region. He remembered later, after the war: "They wanted to find ways and means to 'incinerate' us. So we were assigned to the most dangerous jobs."[3] In Nazi jargon "incineration" meant eliminating their own men by sending them to a dangerous war front from which no one expected them to return. For a regime tainted with likely the worst single crime in history—the Holocaust—as well as other criminal actions, and desperate to hide as much of its murderous activities as possible, Stangl and the others sent to Trieste knew too much for their own or their superiors' good. If some died in action, as Wirth, the target of partisans, did in 1944, then so much the better.

Stangl found troublesome the recent German defeats in Russia and North Africa and the failure of the Reich's submarine campaign in the war in the Atlantic. The overarching military victory he and other Nazi leaders had always expected so confidently now appeared much less certain. What, he worried to himself, would happen in the end to Germany? And to himself and his family?

A year earlier, the Allies had announced that if they won the war, they intended to capture and punish Nazis and their collaborators whom they grouped together as war criminals. He knew that category surely included him—a commander of death camps who had murdered some million innocent civilians. Not surprisingly, Stangl now appreciated being out of Germany.

He remained in northern Italy until the spring of 1945. As part of Globocnik's security force, he participated in widespread manhunts searching for Jews as well as for Communist and partisan members of the anti-Nazi resistance. In Trieste, Globocnik's staff transformed an old rice factory, the Risiera di San Sabba, just inside the city, into a transit camp for Jews destined for Auschwitz and into a site for interrogation of suspected partisans.

At San Sabba the *SS* interned more than twenty thousand prisoners and killed many of them, mostly by striking them in the head with a heavy club. Some evidence also exists that the *SS* gassed prisoners and burned their bodies in a crematorium. The Germans deported some 650 Jews from San Sabba to Auschwitz or, at the end of 1944, to concentration camps within Germany.

Stangl led antipartisan operations, especially against Yugoslav Communists, and roundups of Jews in Fiume, Abazia, and their environs. On one occasion he narrowly escaped death; during a Christmas leave in 1943, partisans ambushed and assassinated his *SS* replacement while the officer carried out a rural security patrol that Stangl, if not away, would have made.

In early March 1944 he returned home for a week's leave to visit his wife, Theresa, and family in Wels, a city in Upper Austria. Theresa had just given birth to their third child. He confided that in Italy "they had ordered him to be on the lookout for Jews." But, he maintained, he wouldn't do so. "What do they think I am?" he asked. "A headhunter? They can leave me out of this now."

She believed his claims, as she recalled after the war: "I don't think he had anything more to do with this Jewish business."[4] She, too, knew what awaited captured Jews but had chosen to ignore both it and her husband's involvement. During the fall of 1942, while Stangl still commanded Sobibor, she and their two daughters had visited him in Poland and had lived a few miles from the camp. From a drunken *SS* man she had first learned about what occurred at Sobibor: "The Jews are being done away with," the man had told her.

"Done away with?" she asked. "How? What do you mean?"

"With gas," he said. "Fantastic numbers of them."

When she questioned her husband about what she heard and about his role at the camp, he lied to her: "You must believe me. I have nothing to do with any of this. My work is purely administrative and I am there to build—to supervise construction, that's all." Then she asked, "You mean you don't see it happen?" He answered, "Oh yes. I see it. But I don't *do* anything to anybody." Later, she admitted, "I finally allowed myself to be convinced that his role in this camp was purely administrative—of course I *wanted* to be convinced, didn't I?"[5]

In mid-March 1944, after a pleasant leave, Stangl returned to Italy, where he worked in a much safer job, as a supply officer for a construction project in the Po valley. The endeavor employed nearly five hundred thousand Italian workers building last-ditch German military fortifications against the advance of Anglo-American troops north. While there, Stangl likely met numerous persons who would later assist his postwar escape through Italy.

Once he realized that Germany's defeat was imminent and the war at an end, Stangl suffered from symptoms of intense emotional stress and, eventually, a heart attack. In May 1944 he had viewed the dead body of Wirth, one of his previous bosses and a fellow mass murderer, whom Yugoslav partisans had apparently killed. Throughout the spring of 1945 he recovered in a field hospital in Trieste. As soon as doctors discharged him, the *RSHA* ordered him to report to its headquarters in Berlin, where he found "things" in an "unholy mess." Only a few days before Germany's surrender, he managed to secure a ride to the German-Czech border and from there went on foot to his family in Upper Austria.

He feared not only the widespread enemy air raids, the destruction of whole cities, and the pervasive confusion everywhere but also summary punishment from even Nazi civilian authorities for not fighting to the war's bitter end. He traveled with much difficulty to police headquarters in Linz, Vienna, and then back to Berlin. In each location he found massive physical wreckage from Allied bombing, *SS* and other Nazi officials fleeing, and everything in disarray.

In order for him to escape arrest by the Allied armies advancing ever closer, his wife pleaded with him to remain home and remove his uniform. "Get into a pair of the headmaster's trousers," Theresa urged him. "Put on civvies and stay here. Here we can hide you: it would be best." But he refused, less on principle than the practical threat such an action entailed. "If I take off the uniform," he told her, "the Gauleiter [Nazi Party district leader] will find out and I'll be hanged as a deserter, even at this late date. Yes, the Gauleiter is still sitting in Linz."[6] Instead, Stangl left home again.

HERMANN GÖRING: PRIZE PRISONER

During his first hours in U.S. Army custody in Bavaria on May 9, 1945, nothing happened to dissuade Hermann Göring from the delusion that he was no mere prisoner of war, but rather an emissary acting on behalf of the German Reich in armistice discussions with the Western Allies. Apparently unknown to, or ignored by, Göring, the world war had ended in Europe. That same day other German officials surrendered their massively destroyed and defeated nation to the Russians in Berlin; they were repeating a similar ceremony enacted two days earlier in France, where the Germans ended the war with the Anglo-Americans.

Among the leading former German officials still alive and known to the world, Göring was considered by the Allies to be the most important—the prize—of those the Allies had captured in the first postwar days and weeks. These prisoners included the onetime champagne salesman and Nazi foreign minister Joachim von Ribbentrop, the governor general of Poland Hans Frank, known as the "Butcher of Poland," the chief Nazi civilian administrator of the German-occupied Soviet Union, Alfred Rosenberg, Himmler's deputy in the *SS* since 1943, Ernst Kaltenbrunner, and the *Wehrmacht*'s highest-ranking officers.

Altogether between 1945 and 1949, the Americans would intern one hundred thousand former Nazi officials. In all three Western Allied zones of occupation in Germany, the United States, Britain, and France imprisoned almost two hundred thousand former Nazi leaders, but the Allies, and later West Germany, would try and punish only a minuscule fraction for war crimes.

The rotund, churlish Göring was a longtime drug addict with a voracious appetite for accruing power and for plundering private and public art collections for his own self-aggrandizing sense of culture. He had lived in opulence that none of his peers approached. Since 1939 and almost to the end of Hitler's regime he had served as *Reichsmarschall* (the Führer's designated successor) and since 1935–1936 as commander of the *Luftwaffe* (air force) and head of the Four-Year Plan (a huge government office that prepared and enabled the German economy to wage war). Few—if any—among his captors knew yet that during the war his influence with Hitler had dwindled steadily and that his last-minute request that he be allowed to succeed the Führer had led to Hitler's expulsion of him from the Nazi Party.

Troops of the Seventh U.S. Army, Thirty-Sixth Division, headquartered at Kitzbuehl, Austria, captured Göring while he and his wife traveled in a convoy—of more than twenty vehicles and seventy persons, including advisers, servants, and guards—from a castle in Bavaria, at Fischhorn, toward the nearby mountains. Along the roads—packed with retreating troops and refugees—the group got stuck often in traffic jams and amid advancing American army units. During one such instance U.S. Army First Lieutenant Jeremy Shapiro, assigned to capture Göring, recognized and arrested him. Shapiro had visited Fischhorn first only to discover that his quarry had left; since then, he had scoured the country for the former *Reichsmarschall*.

When the two met, they saluted. To Shapiro's surprise, both Göring and his wife appeared delighted to see the lieutenant. Not only had the Görings escaped the *Gestapo*, whom they feared had orders to seize or kill them, but Göring also remained so full of illusions about his political authority that he continued to believe he could negotiate with the Allies an honorable peace for Germany. Before leaving Fischhorn, he had sent emissaries to the nearest U.S. Army headquarters with a letter proposing "discussions" with the Allied commander in Europe, General Dwight D. Eisenhower. He surrendered to Brigadier General Robert J. Stack, assistant commander of the Thirty-Sixth Division.

Göring had appeared on all the Allied lists of war criminals. During his first day in captivity the Americans treated him as a prisoner of war of high rank. They permitted him to retain his solid gold marshal's baton and, together with his family, to dine with the American general in Bavaria. But the next day, apparently on Eisenhower's orders, his captors made clear that they regarded him not as a prisoner of war but rather as a war criminal. Stripping him of his *Reichsmarschall*'s insignia, the two medals and the huge diamond ring he wore, and the baton, they shipped him to Kitzbuehel, next to a collection camp, a beer cellar in Augsburg, and after a stay at Mondorf—codenamed by the Allies "Ashcan"—in Luxembourg, to Nuremberg.

Initially, American officers viewed Göring with avid curiosity; some even requested his autograph, while others drank and talked—he spoke reasonably good English—freely with him. Afterward, the officers completed a report on him to U.S. Army headquarters that concluded:

> Although he tried to soft-pedal many of the most outrageous crimes committed by Germany, he said enough to show that he is as much responsible for the policies within Germany and for the war itself as anyone in Germany. . . . On the other hand, he denied having had anything to do with the racial laws and with the concentration camps, with the SS and the atrocities committed both in Germany and outside.[7]

Göring's role in planning and assisting Germany in its intent to wage war interested American authorities the most. Only later, once his trial began before the IMT, did his participation in the Nazi persecution of Jews become more evident. When an American psychologist interviewed him in his prison cell at Nuremberg about the attack on Jews, Göring disclaimed any involvement: "I was never anti-Semitic. Anti-Semitism played no part in my life." In fact, he claimed that he'd saved and helped many Jews.

He blamed the wartime "atrocities" against the Jews primarily on Nazi propaganda minister Joseph Goebbels, "that clubfooted fanatic" who "had influenced Hitler to become more anti-Semitic," and on the Jews themselves, with their alleged "anti-Nazi movement in the Jewish press." Göring chose well when naming Goebbels as sole scapegoat for Germany's anti-Semitic policies. Following his adored Führer's example, Goebbels committed suicide with his wife in Hitler's bunker on April 30, 1945—but not until the wife had killed their six small children—and therefore couldn't respond to being burdened by Göring with responsibility for the persecution of Jews.

Seeking to exculpate himself further with his captors, Hermann continued lying:

> I never had any feeling of hatred toward the Jews. I realize that it looks stupid that it is hard to understand how a person like myself who made anti-Semitic speeches and who participated as number two man in a regime that exterminated 5 million Jews can say that he was not anti-Semitic. But it is true. I would never have made this policy.[8]

About Auschwitz and the other death camps, he pleaded complete ignorance: "I didn't know anything about it."[9]

Initially, the Allies knew little or nothing of how, two years into the war and shortly after German armies invaded the Soviet Union with initial stunning success, Göring had played a key role in assisting Hitler and Himmler in their efforts to facilitate the Final Solution. Perhaps more than any other single Nazi document, a deceptively simple directive—a mere three sentences dated July 31, 1941, and signed by Göring—had sealed the fate of European Jewry.

In the order that he issued as head of the German war economy and as a result of Hitler having placed him in 1938 in charge of the "Jewish question," Göring authorized Reinhard Heydrich, Himmler's deputy in the *SS* and fellow architect of the Holocaust, along with Hitler, to prepare the "organizational, technical, and material matters for bringing about a complete solution of the Jewish question within the German sphere of influence in Europe." Göring ended by directing Heydrich "to send me, in the near future, an overall plan . . . for the accomplishment of the final solution of the Jewish question which we desire."[10]

Six months later, Heydrich called the Wannsee Conference in Berlin, where he hoped to work out the relevant details with chief German government ministry officials for the mass slaughter of the Jews. At the start of the meeting he noted his authority from Göring to coordinate a Final Solution to the Jewish question. As later events showed, the words *Final Solution* had but one meaning in the Nazi vocabulary—extermination.

When considered alongside other actions taken by Hitler and his closest Nazi associates regarding Jews in Europe under German rule, the Göring directive illustrated that such leaders had begun irrefutably the decision-making process that would eventually, by late 1941 and early 1942, lead to the Holocaust. They prepared to extend Germany's unfolding mass murder of Soviet Jews—begun several weeks earlier with the German military invasion of the Soviet Union—to all Soviet and, eventually, European Jews.

Göring's authorization was crucial for Heydrich, Himmler, and the *SS* to realize the unprecedented genocidal campaign by gaining assistance from official German government and other agencies as well as offices not under *SS* jurisdiction. With the directive in hand, Heydrich and other *SS* leaders could—and did—demonstrate to any such hesitant or indifferent offices that the highest levels of the regime had ordered and supported the campaign.

Beginning in the fall of 1941 and early 1942, Göring's authorization, either because he'd received an order from Hitler to do so or because he knew of the Führer's wishes on the subject, opened the way for the *SS* to construct in Nazi-occupied Poland the first extermination camps, which would use poison gas to murder several million Jews. Shortly after the Allies arrested Göring, a major setback to his postwar posturing occurred. They captured the critical document.

KURT DALUEGE: UNIFORMED POLICEMAN

At almost the same moment they seized Göring, the Allies captured *SS* General Kurt Daluege on the north German seacoast. Throughout the war Daluege had commanded the Nazi Uniformed Police (Order Police, or *Ordnungspolizei*), local police units responsible primarily for everyday law enforcement. But apart from these mundane duties, numerous Uniformed Police battalions had also served as mobile units participating in the mass killing of Jews and Slavs in Poland, in the Nazi protectorate of Bohemia and Moravia, and in the Soviet Union.

Immediate Allied postwar information, however, tied Daluege only to German measures of retribution for the Czechs' mid-1942 assassination of Heydrich, whom Hitler had appointed Reich Protector of Bohemia and Moravia. Retaliating for Heydrich's death, the Nazis had murdered all the men in the Czech town of Lidice, sent the local women to concentration camps, and leveled the town physically. Not yet sated, the Germans carried out further mass arrests and executions. In the aftermath an approving Hitler had appointed Daluege as Heydrich's successor.

But soon his dual role as Reich Protector and as Uniformed Police chief overwhelmed Daluege. He quarreled endlessly with other Nazi officials and caused a scandal when he appointed an old friend, Walter Jurk, as the administrator in Bohemia and Moravia of property and valuables seized from murdered Czech Jews. Jurk disappeared with a substantial portion of the stolen wealth (from which Daluege had also profited).

Long before his contentious, bitter relations with other Nazi officials, Daluege had contributed significantly to establishing the machinery of mass murder that would make the Holocaust possible. Between 1935 and 1939 he assisted Himmler in uniting the German police with the *SS*, thereby removing a check to that organization's unchecked ambitions. Historian Edward Westermann shows how Himmler and Daluege indoctrinated the police in Nazi ideology and created within it a militarized organizational culture built on a fanatical anti-Semitic and anti-Bolshevik ideology.

By 1940, the first year of the war, the number of Uniformed Police stood at more than one hundred twenty-five thousand, divided among some one hundred battalions. Throughout the conflict the Uniformed Police under Daluege's command participated, along with other German police and *SS* formations, in persecuting Europe's Jews and other alleged racial enemies of Germany. Following the German conquest of Poland in 1939, Uniformed Police battalions operated in both the German-occupied western Polish territories and the so-called Government General (a badly overcrowded Nazi "reservation" or territory for unwanted Polish Jews and Poles). There, they conscripted such "racial enemies" for forced labor and also guarded Jewish ghettos.

For one battalion in the huge Warsaw Ghetto, shooting Jews was a routine part of its daily duties. On November 11, 1939, following another battalion's massacre of several hundred Jews (including women and children) in the Polish village of Ostrów Mazowieck, Daluege ordered that no policemen should discuss this or other similar *Aktionen* in public. Employing a euphemism to conceal such killings, he further directed commanders of police formations returning home, "These men are to be sworn to secrecy concerning the conduct of *special tasks* that they were delegated during their duty [in Poland]."[11]

On July 8 and 9, 1941, barely two weeks after German armed forces initiated their massive invasion of the Soviet Union, Daluege accompanied Himmler on a visit to Byelorussia (White Russia) and met with battalions operating there. They conferred initially with *SS* and police officers in Bialystok. Himmler urged the police to intervene more against the Jews, considering the latter "partisans" and, by implication, "looters." Daluege, who embraced with enthusiasm Himmler's orders regarding the killing of "Jewish-Bolsheviks," spoke to a police regiment, telling it "Bolshevism must now be eradicated once and for all."[12] The police, he continued, should take pride in the destruction of the world enemy. He urged a more radical role for police in cooperating with the *SS*, *Einsatzgruppen*, and *Wehrmacht* in massacring local Jews.

Thereafter the police battalions entered local villages and towns, searched the Jewish quarters for "looters," and shot masses of Jewish men, women, and children. In Brest-Litovsk, around July 12, a battalion shot several thousand Jewish civilians; immediately prior to the killings, Daluege, Bach-Zelewski, and other *SS* commanders had visited Brest. Well into 1943, the battalions continued their bloody rampages in the Soviet territories.

Daluege participated also in the origin of the Final Solution. On July 29, he flew to Lithuania to see Himmler, who was visiting his Higher *SS* and Police Leader for the area, Hans-Adolf Prützmann. Daluege returned the next day to Berlin for, as he told Himmler, an important meeting. Historian Richard Breitman speculates that the Berlin meeting "likely involved Heydrich and his subordinates," who had decided on removing the large numbers of Jews by sending them east for forced labor and/or killing. Both Daluege's Uniformed Police and other German police units would play a role in the deportations of Jews to the East. On July 31, Heydrich "took a big step" toward such a policy, acquiring from Göring, Hitler's head of the war economy, authorization to prepare a plan for the future "final solution of the Jewish question."[13]

In the attack on the Soviet Union, more than four hundred Uniformed Police officers and 11,640 policemen joined the *Einsatzgruppen* and some three million *Wehrmacht* troops. In addition, during the last half of 1941 and the beginning of 1942, Daluege, at Himmler's directive, established auxiliary police formations in the German-occupied areas of the Soviet Union, comprising Ukrainians, Balts, and Byelorussians whom the Soviet army had not conscripted, and commanded by German police. During 1942, these forces numbered more than three hundred thousand and assisted the German mobile killing units in the repression and massacre of Jews.

Rumors spread during the war that Daluege suffered from mental illness. Likely the stories related to his syphilis, a form of which, he claimed, he had inherited from his father. Following a heart attack in June 1943, he asked Hitler for a temporary leave from his official duties, which the Führer granted, but not before awarding his minion the gift of a landed estate in western Poland. At the end of 1944, Daluege and his family moved to the new domain, but with the Red Army approaching rapidly, they had to flee west, first to Berlin and then to northern Germany.

Following his capture on May 8, 1945, in Lübeck, Daluege, a large man with hooked nose, beady eyes, and somber facial expression, claimed to the

Allies that—despite his command of the Uniformed Police—he "knew nothing" of the German attacks on or killing of Jews in Germany or elsewhere. Only once, he said, had he witnessed the burning of a synagogue in Munich, but it had happened so quickly. "What could I do?" he protested.[14]

He strove to distance himself from the former Nazi officialdom above him by insisting that he "didn't get along well" with Himmler and that the Uniformed Police had no military functions. In fact, he and Himmler were close friends. Nor did the police, he maintained, belong to the *SS*. Did he feel guilty of anything? "No."

An American army psychiatrist, Leon Goldensohn, who interviewed Daluege, concluded that the latter was lying, that he was "the kind of executive who would neatly and obsessively be well informed about everything his forces did." The interviewer described the former police chief as "insensitive, hard-boiled, capable of great ruthlessness, amoral, conscienceless. . . . Getting a sincere or emotionally meaningful answer from him is like trying to bail water from a long-dry well."[15]

In the first weeks of Germany's invasion of the Soviet Union in 1941, British intelligence had learned about the Uniformed Police's mass executions of Soviet Jews and knew much more—what a liar and criminal Daluege was. But the British didn't share their information with the Americans. The former had broken the Uniformed Police's secret radio code and intercepted and read the battalions' reports to the *RSHA* in Berlin.

The United States considered including Daluege in the small group of major Nazi defendants being brought to trial before the IMT. Instead, in January 1946 at the urging of the Czechs, the U.S. extradited him to Czechoslovakia, which possessed sufficient evidence for a court to try him for persecuting and slaughtering Czechs following Heydrich's assassination. Ironically, given the lack of evidence regarding him and the Uniformed Police available then to Allied prosecutors, had the Allies placed Daluege on trial at Nuremberg he would likely have received a lesser punishment. At his trial in Prague in October 1946 the court convicted him of a long list of war crimes, including the expropriation, enslavement, and murder of Czechs and the use of his position as Reich Protector to enrich himself financially. The Czech court sentenced him to death.

But the trial proceedings rarely mentioned his extensive persecution of Czech Jews. Under heavy pressure from Soviet forces having overrun and occupied Czechoslovakia, the Czech government recognized only "Czech" citizens and refused to acknowledge the Holocaust and resulting Jewish suffering. During the trial Daluege—wholly unrepentant to the end—claimed that he had a clear conscience and, ignoring his crimes, said, "I am beloved by three million policemen."

His belief in Hitler remained unshaken. He appeared perplexed when the court refused to accept a claim of innocence based on his insistence that he'd only followed Hitler's orders. He asserted that he could no longer recall the German policies he'd implemented. He sought to place responsibility for them on other Nazi officials—despite the presentation in court of documents captured by the Western Allies, Czechs, and Soviets, documents signed by Daluege that proved his guilt.

On October 15, hoping it would work in his favor and persuade the court to spare his life, he even attempted to feign mental illness. Eventually, however, in the words of Jaroslav Drabek, a witness against him, Daluege "saw that no one believed him." While awaiting execution a week later, he tried unsuccessfully in his prison cell to commit suicide. Full of self-pity, he uttered last words typical of Hitler's fanatical followers. He complained: "I do not die as Christ did, but as a political criminal. My work as chief of the Orpo [Uniformed Police] has not been appreciated."[16]

STANGL: ESCAPING AN AUSTRIAN PRISON

Desperation and fear accompanied him. Germany had surrendered and the U.S. Army now occupied much of the surrounding Austrian countryside. When he left home fleeing the Americans, Stangl told his wife nothing. Not even that he'd gone to his mother's place in Ebernsee, near Salzburg. The enemy, he reasoned, mustn't be able to force her to reveal where to find him. Then he moved to a village on the Attersee, where he hid at the home of a friend, a police officer with whom he and his family had stayed occasionally on holidays.

While on the move every few days, Stangl considered others he could trust to hide him, but it mattered little. At the friend's Attersee home, someone "denounced" him "to the Americans."[17] Whether the policeman did so, Stangl never knew. His friend claimed that a police subordinate had told American soldiers an *SS* officer lived at the house. Immediately, a local U.S. Army unit took Stangl into custody.

The Americans imprisoned him in a camp at Bad Ischl, not far from Salzburg. Meanwhile, knowing nothing of his whereabouts, his wife decided to look for Stangl. She left their three young children with local schoolteachers and began walking to nearby American POW camps. When she arrived at Bad Ischl, she went to the office of the U.S. Army Counter-Intelligence Corps (CIC). There, she found only Austrians working for the Americans and told them for whom she searched.

"Oh yes, he's here. We'll get him for you," came the reply. Within minutes they brought Stangl to her and, with a guard nearby, the two talked briefly.

"The prison," he complained bitterly to her, neglecting to recall the Nazi death camps he'd commanded during the war, "was awful. It was a real cage." At the moment she didn't seem to mind what she heard: "[A]t least I knew where he was."[18]

Not long thereafter, in July 1945, his captors transferred Stangl to a much larger POW camp at Glasenbach, also near Salzburg, but a complex of several holding facilities with numerous categories of prisoners. Altogether Glasenbach had nearly twenty thousand inmates. There, too, Stangl resented his less-than-luxurious accommodations. He lived in Barrack 16 with two thousand other men. For nearly a year he and other prisoners slept on the floor. "There were neither bunks nor blankets," he fumed.

But to Simon Wiesenthal, a former Jewish victim of the Nazi camps, Glasenbach seemed a virtual spa. The alumnus of Mauthausen and postwar Nazi hunter visited Glasenbach several times to assist the American search for war criminals. He observed:

> The internees were well-fed and sunburned, and they led a pleasant life. They had amusing company from another part of the camp, where wives of high-ranking Nazis and some women who used to be concentration-camp guards were interned. . . . The internees of the Americans, at least, lived like guests. They got medical care and cigarettes. In many cases, these "prisoners" were living better than the civilian population outside the gate.[19]

In May 1946 the prisoners received permission to build wooden frames with planks to sleep on. A few months later, they constructed wooden chests in which to lie. During the spring of 1947, Stangl admitted that things improved. He received a bunk and blanket as well as parcels of provisions from his family. Every week Stangl's wife made a six-hour round trip to bring him packages. But the authorities at Glasenbach refused to let her see him.

Apparently the Americans imprisoned Stangl primarily because he had been a member of the *SS*. A routine U.S. interrogation revealed only "his anti-partisan activities in Italy and Yugoslavia"; the interviewer never questioned him "about any other war or prewar assignments."[20] Nor did Stangl volunteer such information. In this, like many other similar Allied interrogations of German POWs, apparently the questioner lacked the evidence necessary to identify and prosecute war criminals. Allied investigators had only begun sifting through and organizing the tons of Nazi records that Allied armies had captured. American and British military officers investigating Nazi criminals and crimes—despite the officers' moral indignation at what many had witnessed in the liberated Nazi camps—faced an incredible number and variety of German POWs, who often disguised themselves as civilians, and of displaced persons of all nationalities. To make sense of the stories investigators heard, they needed not only more evidence but also many hundreds more staff trained and fluent in foreign languages and knowledgeable about European cultures.

By the time the CIC interrogated Stangl, U.S. and British occupation personnel had begun replacing the soldiers who had fought in the war with new troops, who, for the most part, felt considerably more sympathy for the Germans—more even, in some instances, than for their victims. In Austria, clearly an "enemy" of the Allies during the war, the confusion for occupying forces increased even more than in Germany because the Allies had declared Austria a "liberated country." Under the circumstances, what did that mean precisely?

One consequence was that nearly anyone, including Stangl, who wished to hide his Nazi activities could do so with little difficulty. Possibly, had Stangl not worked in Austria during 1940–1941 at Schloß Hartheim, the Nazi euthanasia facility, he'd never have attracted attention in 1947. To be sure, by then, at war crimes trials held by the United States at Nuremberg, what had happened at Treblinka had surfaced repeatedly. But prosecutors possessed relatively little information about the camp. So few persons survived Treblinka, and those who did rarely surfaced to identify Stangl or other former camp officials by name.

Meanwhile, authorities of the new Austrian republic began to investigate the euthanasia program at Schloß Hartheim. By requesting information from Allied POW camps in Germany, Austria, and Italy, the Austrians discovered that the United States held Stangl at Glasenbach. In the late summer of 1947 the Austrians asked the United States to hand him over for trial; soon the authorities transferred him to a civilian prison in Linz.

In his new confinement his wife visited him often, in a private room and for as long as they wished to talk. She noticed the "openness" of the prison and its surprisingly lax security. It is unclear how much Stangl had told her during and after the war about his work in the euthanasia program and later as a mass murderer at Sobibor and Treblinka. After the war she alleged that she'd known nothing. Once the Hartheim trial opened in Linz, she read a newspaper account of the proceedings, which described the killings of the handicapped at Hartheim. During the trial, prosecutors identified Stangl as Hartheim's police superintendent.

Immediately, she confronted Stangl with the paper. "Is this true? Why didn't you tell me? Didn't you know I'd stand by you?" "I didn't want to burden you with it," was his reply.

She seemed little affected by what had happened at Hartheim. Her husband's fate at the Linz trial and his potential punishment—probably several more years in prison—concerned her far more. She told the postwar interviewer, Gitta Sereny, she "never thought for a moment he was in danger of being sentenced to die. Why should they?" she told herself. "He had never killed anybody." And at Treblinka? "As far as I knew—or at least rationalized and accepted—in Treblinka too he was never responsible for anything but the valuables." She'd persuaded herself "that what had happened," what her husband "had been involved in was part of the war, that awful war. And it was over."

She begged him to escape: "Finally I told him I couldn't take any more; I said if he didn't get out, get himself a job abroad and send us money to live, the children and I would end up dead. I said I was at the end of my strength."[21] He agreed.

A few days later, on May 30, 1948, he and another inmate, Hans Steiner, a former *SS* officer, walked out of the prison and, undetected, left Linz. Stangl carried with him a rucksack containing some of his wife's meager savings and jewelry, to help finance his escape, and tin cans of food. He possessed as well an identity card of a former *SS* comrade at the prison, on which Stangl had replaced the photograph with his own. Possibly, the comrade acted as part of an alleged postwar underground organization popularly called—by Nazi hunters and others—*ODESSA* (*Organisation der SS Angehörigen*, Organization of *SS* Members), or as part of a much more general so-called rat line, which assisted former *SS* members in fleeing Germany and Austria. Recently writers Gerald Steinacher and Guy Walters have cast doubt on the existence of *ODESSA*. The comrade urged Stangl to escape to Rome where, he said, a Catholic churchman would help the fugitive.

A day after the escape, an Austrian police officer visited Stangl's wife at their home in Wels. "Is your husband in the house?" he asked. When she said "no" and then invited him to search the dwelling, he declined. "Aside from this," she would recall many years later, "no one ever came to ask me anything."[22] Eventually, the provincial court in Linz issued an arrest warrant for the escapee.

KARL WOLFF: THE ALLIES' FAVORITE

The Allies would not place on trial the elegant, smooth *SS* general they took into custody in northern Italy on May 13, 1945. Long after the war, the officer's German biographer, Jochen von Lang, wrote: "He was one of the unknown giants of Hitler's Reich, who worked in the shadows. Only the top five hundred in the party and state knew his name and his functions."[23]

Karl Wolff, silver haired, aristocratic looking, and amiable, had served from 1933 to 1936 as Himmler's personal adjutant. From then to September 1943 he'd held the post of chief of the *Reichsführer*'s personal staff and as its liaison officer with the Führer. Although in this role Wolff hadn't acted as one of the driving forces behind the Final Solution, nevertheless he possessed extensive knowledge of its machinery and participated in it.

During August 15–16, 1941, he accompanied Himmler to German-occupied Byelorussia, to Minsk to inspect the work of *Einsatzgruppe* B. As part of that visit both men watched a unit of the *Einsatzgruppe* push 120 Soviet Jews into a ditch and shoot them. Himmler's later speech to the unit, for which Wolff was present, sought to convince its members that their murderous actions were not only lawful, because Hitler had personally ordered them, but also a type of combat in defense of oneself against what the *Reichsführer* characterized as vermin. During the remainder of the summer and fall, Wolff traveled with Himmler to inspect *Einsatzgruppe* A in the Baltic countries and *Einsatzgruppe* D in the southern Ukraine.

Almost simultaneously, Wolff participated in the Holocaust in Yugoslavia, which the Germans had occupied since early April 1941. He intervened with Himmler to protect *SS* Major General Harald Turner, chief of military administration in the Yugoslav territory of Serbia, from being removed by local German military officials. The latter disapproved of Turner's ordering four thousand Jews and two hundred Gypsies shot in retaliation for Serbian partisan attacks on German troops.

A few months later, in April 1942, secure in his post again and continuing to order the killing of Jews and Gypsies, Turner thanked Wolff in a letter because, as Turner wrote, "I am sure that this is all due to your influence." Then he added, describing the killings and his own bloodthirstiness:

> Already some months ago, I shot dead all the Jews I could get my hands on in this area, concentrated all the Jewish women and children in a camp and with the help of the SD [Security Service] got my hands on a "delousing van" [a euphemism for gas van], that in about 14 days to 4 weeks will have brought about the definitive clearing out of the camp, which in any event since the arrival of Meyssner [August Meyszner, a Higher *SS* and Police Leader, who arrived in Serbia in January 1942] and the turning over of this camp to him, was continued by him.[24]

On July 16, 1942, at the onset of the German offensive toward Stalingrad in the Soviet south and the Caucasus mountains, the *Wehrmacht* refused to release any trains to transport Polish Jews to the nearby death camps at Treblinka, Belzec, and Sobibor. Wolff telephoned a close contact in the Reich transportation ministry, State Secretary Albert Ganzenmüller, who assured him that the ministry would make cars and locomotives available for the transports.

Twelve days later, Ganzenmüller informed Wolff in a letter: "Each day since July 22, a train leaves with 5,000 Jews from Warsaw via Malkinia to Treblinka. A train also leaves twice a week with 5,000 Jews from Przemysl to Belzec." On August 13, Wolff replied:

> With particular pleasure I took note of your report that for fourteen days now a train has been leaving daily for Treblinka with 5,000 members of the chosen

> people, and that in this manner, we have been able to carry out this population movement at increasing speed. . . . I thank you again for your efforts in this matter and ask you at the same time to continue giving your attention to these things.[25]

In September 1943, with nearly three million Polish Jews exterminated already, mostly in death camps, Hitler sent Wolff as German military governor to northern Italy and Germany's official envoy to its figurehead ruler, Benito Mussolini. Convinced by the end of February 1945 that Germany had lost the war, Wolff established contact through Italian and Swiss intermediaries with Allen Dulles, the representative of the U.S. intelligence agency, the Office of Strategic Services (OSS). In Switzerland, behind Hitler's back, Wolff negotiated to surrender all German forces in Italy on May 2, six days prior to the general cease-fire in Europe.

Wolff insisted to his Allied captors that he'd saved the northernmost portion of the country, the South Tyrol, from much greater war and destruction. Also he maintained that he'd rescued both Allied and German soldiers from nearly a week of fighting and, therefore, countless casualties. But above all, he hoped that he'd saved himself from postwar punishment by the enemy.

Indeed, in thinking about his own future, he guessed correctly. For his "service" at the war's end, Wolff remained, among the captured Nazis, an Allied favorite. Dulles, the OSS, and other sympathetic U.S. officials used their influence to prevent the Allies from placing the *SS* general on trial at Nuremberg. Instead, the Americans and British interrogated him numerous times about other captured Nazis, most of them on trial. When he testified in court, the Allies permitted him to do so in full military uniform. (They'd yet to sift through the mass of captured German documents that contained records incriminating him.)

Wolff maintained repeatedly that he had nothing to do with crimes against Jews. Although the Allies knew of Wolff's former position as Himmler's right-hand man and Hitler's close confidant, they accepted his dubious assertions wholeheartedly. Even Wolff's anti-Semitism, which he expressed occasionally but openly to Allied officials, didn't trigger their suspicions. During a February 1947 interrogation, the former *SS* general complained furiously:

> A Jew is killed in the gas chamber in a few seconds, without having an idea or even knowing it. My comrades and I have been allowed to die once every night for twenty-one months. This is much more inhumane than the extermination used on the Jews. Too much has been grossly exaggerated.[26]

Outbursts from perpetrators like Wolff, claiming that the murder "used on the Jews" had been overstated, had echoes in the same allegation made by the earliest Holocaust deniers. According to Deborah Lipstadt, "[w]ithin a few years after the liberation of Europe" such deniers moved toward claiming "that the death of six million Jews was not only greatly exaggerated but a fabrication."[27] Also evident in his comments, Wolff defended both Nazi atrocities and anti-Semitism. Clearly, he and deniers were of the same mind.

Two months later, Wolff claimed to an American interrogator that before the war's end, he'd never heard about the *Einsatzgruppen*. Apparently he couldn't recall that along with Himmler, he had visited in Minsk and watched over one hundred people murdered there by *Einsatzkommando* 8—a unit of *Einsatzgruppe* B—and a police battalion. But in June 1947 at the trial of former *SS* Lieutenant General Oswald Pohl, chief of the *SS* Economic-Administrative Main Office (*Wirtschafts-Verwaltungshauptamt*), the U.S. prosecution produced for the first time Wolff's exchange of letters in 1942 with Ganzenmüller arranging for the transportation of Jews from the Warsaw Ghetto to the Treblinka extermination camp. (The U.S. military tribunal sentenced Pohl—whose *SS* business empire had provided concentration camp inmates as forced laborers to private German industries and sold Jewish possessions that included jewelry, gold fillings, hair, and clothing to provide funds for the Reich government—to death; he was executed in June 1951, despite intense West German efforts to gain amnesty for him.)

Still, the Allies made no move to indict Wolff. The OSS, in fact, recruited several of his former *SS* aides in Italy to work for U.S. intelligence, planning to use them to spy on the Russians and Eastern Europe in the emerging Cold War. Commenting on the Allied treatment of Wolff, Donald Bloxham observes:

> It could be said that, just as during the Holocaust the aiding of the Jews by the Allies was subordinated to the effort to win the war, afterwards the will to punish those responsible for the genocide was often undermined by the determination to gain a decisive superiority over the USSR.[28]

Meanwhile, in November 1948 a German denazification court—whose judges were Germans and part of a general postwar program to which the Allies subjected many Germans—sentenced Wolff to four years' hard labor for his *SS* membership. During the proceedings, the defendant claimed that he had never taken anti-Semitism seriously as an element of the Nazi Party program. About the Ganzenmüller incident, Wolff testified, "I was not aware of anything criminal happening."

Whereas his exchange of letters with Ganzenmüller would lead sixteen years later to Wolff's sentencing as an accomplice to mass murder, the denazification authorities used the exchange only to prove that Wolff knew that Jews were being persecuted. But von Lang wrote in 2005: "Anyone able to observe the happenings in Hitler's Reich from the lofty standpoint of a minister or as an SS Obergruppenführer [lieutenant general], had to at least have an idea of [*sic*] something dreadful was taking place. Wolff, however, would never admit that."[29]

The denazification court, however, bungled the appointment of its judges, apparently from laziness, and this made an appeal by Wolff inevitable. Consequently, another court reversed the verdict, and during 1949 a new hearing was held. In the interim, Wolff requested and received a number of so-called Persil (the name of a best-selling German brand of laundry detergent) certificates or letters and submitted these character references to the court.

The letters, which "whitewashed" his past and supported his freedom, came from noted friends. Signatures included those of Dulles and numerous prominent former Nazis. As a result, the court classified him first as a former "lesser offender" (category III of denazification charges) and later as a "follower" (category IV) in the Nazi regime. (See chapter 12 for a discussion of the categories.) According to his *SS* rank, however, the court should have declared Wolff a "major offender" (category I).

Subsequently released from prison, he became a highly successful advertising agent in Cologne and later built from his earnings an elegant lakeside villa on the Starnberger See. But finally his vanity and exhibitionism proved his undoing. In 1961, during the Israeli trial of Adolf Eichmann—chief of the *Gestapo*'s wartime "Jewish office" and a crucial implementer of the Final Solution by his vigorous deporting of Jews to the East—Wolff published his memoirs, ghostwritten and serialized in the Cologne newspaper *Neue Illustrierte*.

Under a banner headline "Eichmann's Boss: Heinrich Himmler," Wolff provided "a portrait" of the former *Reichsführer SS*. The paper's introductory paragraph to the reminiscences proclaimed: "For the first time since the collapse of the thousand year Reich, a man who belonged to the innermost vicious circle around Himmler for ten years speaks. . . . Wolff reports the facts, and gives his personal opinion, which is not that of the editors. . . ."[30]

Wolff saw himself as the leading witness, and readers should judge and issue a verdict. To be sure, the publication drew the public's attention and, more importantly, that of the Bavarian Ministry of Justice, to his wartime activities as a key figure in Himmler's immediate entourage and in the creation of the *SS* empire. Bavarian authorities arrested Wolff in 1962 and placed him on trial. Two years later—and seventeen years after the Allies had uncovered his damning correspondence during 1942 with Ganzenmüller—a Munich court charged him at last with complicity in the murder of at least three hundred thousand Jews, primarily those deported in 1942 and 1943 to Treblinka from the Warsaw Ghetto. The court refused to accept Wolff's continued denials of knowledge of the death camps and on September 30, 1964, sentenced him to fifteen years in prison. The prosecution, disappointed at the sentence, had sought life imprisonment. A year later, the West German Federal Supreme Court denied Wolff's request for an appeal.

Even then, however, eventually West German authorities softened the punishment—significantly. In view of his "otherwise blameless life" and his self-serving contribution to shortening the war, the Bonn government released Wolff from prison in 1971. In July 1984, he died in peace and of natural causes—and, like so many other Holocaust perpetrators, barely punished for his crimes.

HEINRICH HIMMLER: SUICIDE

At mid-afternoon of May 23, 1945, three German prisoners, each dressed in civilian clothes, appeared before Captain Tom Selvester, the British officer in charge of Interrogation Camp No. 031, near Lüneberg in northern Germany. The British had no idea who the captives were but suspected they had deserted from the *Wehrmacht*.

One of the Germans—short, pudgy, balding, wearing a patch over one eye—asked to see Selvester privately. The unremarkable man hoped to communicate personally with the captain and possibly even to conduct discussions with him about the release of himself and the others captured with him.

The prisoner (described later by Selvester as "ill-looking and shabbily dressed") had long lost all sense of reality. In April 1945, to save himself and his coveted power, he attempted unsuccessfully to approach the Allies—through a Swedish official—for peace negotiations. When Hitler, also disconnected from reality and utterly deluded, learned of his most loyal follower's betrayal, he stripped his underling of all the latter's powers. The man—now in British custody—continued to deceive himself that the Allies would consider him an acceptable leader of a newly reconstituted Germany and would negotiate with him on equal terms.

Once Selvester and the German were alone, the latter removed the patch covering his eye and donned thick glasses. Since his capture nearly three days earlier, he'd passed unnoticed, but now his identity was immediately obvious. In a soft voice he announced: "Heinrich Himmler."[31]

To confirm the former *Reichsführer*'s identity and interrogate him, Selvester sent for intelligence officers. While he waited, he ordered guards to search Himmler. He also offered the prisoner a British army uniform in exchange for the civilian clothes his captors had removed from him. But when the *SS* chief saw what he'd be required to put on, he refused; apparently, he feared that someone would photograph him dressed in the uniform of the enemy and publish the picture.

Later, the captain described Himmler's behavior, noting that he "gave me the impression that he realized things had caught up with him. He was quite prepared to talk, and indeed at times appeared almost jovial. . . . I found it impossible to believe that he could be the arrogant man portrayed by the press before and during the war."[32]

Himmler was transferred a few miles to the British Second Army's interrogation center to be interviewed by senior military intelligence agents. Once there, an army doctor and other officers still suspected that he carried poison. That evening, while they strip-searched the notorious prisoner, he crunched on a vial of cyanide carefully hidden in a gap between his teeth. Despite frantic efforts to prevent him from swallowing and to pump out the poison, the former chicken farmer and major Holocaust perpetrator died after fifteen minutes.

One British officer exclaimed in frustration: "The bastard's beat us!"[33] But had the doctor and other officers who searched and examined Himmler done so too carelessly? They all knew who their prisoner was. A few weeks earlier, one of the officers, Sergeant-Major Edwin Austen, had failed to prevent Hans-Adolf Prützmann (one of Himmler's *SS* generals and a principal figure in carrying out the Holocaust in the Soviet Union) from committing suicide when he also bit into a cyanide capsule concealed in his mouth.

Such suspicions of bungling aside, on the evening of May 23, 1945, suddenly and shockingly, Himmler—the man so crucial in conceiving, creating, and controlling the Holocaust as well as inflicting widespread suffering and decimation on millions of other innocent victims—had breathed his last.

Nearly a week earlier, seeking to evade capture and culpability, Himmler and a small party of *SS* associates had disguised themselves as rank-and-file German soldiers and were trying to escape the British zone of occupation in northern Germany. Himmler wanted to join his family in Bavaria. The group left, via automobile, the Schleswig-Holstein town of Flensburg, the site of the last headquarters of the Nazi regime, which had resoundingly rejected Himmler's offer of service.

Heading south, the group eventually reached the Elbe River, where, leaving its cars behind, it crossed the water on a fishing boat. From there, the group walked farther south. The former leader, who once enjoyed his own private railroad car, was now no better off than hundreds of thousands of ordinary Germans wandering homeless on the roads. On May 20, Himmler and two adjutants left the main group to continue on their own. By then, Himmler was wearing civilian clothes and the eye patch and carrying the identity papers of a Heinrich Hitzinger, one of the many Germans sentenced to death by a Nazi court and now incapable of protesting the usurping of his name.

Soon the trio ran into a squad of Russian troops who failed to recognize them but handed them over to British soldiers stationed nearby. Despite his capture, the former *Reichsführer* must have felt somewhat fortunate. Breitman comments: "Himmler undoubtedly preferred to be in British hands; he considered the Anglo-Saxons part of the Nordic family of races. It is also hard to imagine what fate the Russians would have devised for him."[34] The three prisoners were shipped around for a couple of days until, on May 23, they ended up at Interrogation Camp No. 31.

By pointing the way with their suicides, Himmler, Hitler, Goebbels, and several other prominent Nazis deserted the many subordinates to whom they had delegated carrying out the Final Solution and other mass killings and to whom they'd promised to assume ultimate accountability. Only a few days before his capture and death, Himmler had summoned *SS* leaders from Nazi concentration camps around Germany to Flensburg and had issued his last "noble" order: escape—as he intended to do. "Disappear into the Wehrmacht!" he instructed them.

Unlike the *SS* as an institution, the *Wehrmacht*'s role in the Holocaust remained—and would for far too many years—largely ignored or simply unknown to the world, which thereby helped the German army and most of its perpetrators to escape punishment for their crimes. The German-Jewish refugee and philosopher Hannah Arendt, in her 1963 book *Eichmann in Jerusalem*, was one of the first postwar observers to identify the German armed forces as participants in the Holocaust:

> These mobile killing units [the *Einsatzgruppen*], of which there existed just four, each of battalion size, with a total of no more than three thousand men, needed and got the close cooperation of the Armed Forces; indeed, relations between them were usually "excellent" and in some instances "affectionate" (*herzlich*). The generals showed a "surprisingly good attitude toward the Jews"; not only did they hand their Jews over to the *Einsatzgruppen*, they often lent their own men, ordinary soldiers, to assist in the massacres.[35]

In part because most such crimes of the *Wehrmacht* happened in the Soviet Union and the British and Americans remained largely uninterested in such actions, the Western Allies—over the protest of the Russians who were outvoted—left the German army off the list of organizations declared criminal at the IMT in Nuremberg. While the United States placed on trial during 1947 and 1948 and sentenced to varying terms in prison nineteen former German army and air force generals for ordering the shooting of hostages and for committing other similar war crimes, the British only reluctantly (and because of pressure to do so from the United States) placed two former high-ranking German officers on trial—Albert Kesselring in Venice in 1947 and Erich von Manstein in Hamburg in 1949. Both received prison sentences, but the British commuted Kesselring's in 1952 and released Manstein (whose case is discussed in chapter 13) in 1953.

During the summer of 1945, Western Allied intelligence and interrogation units knew, as yet, few details about methods and personnel involved in exterminating Jews. Only gradually would the British learn that the group captured with Himmler, along with the seizure of others in his original party of *SS* refugees, had included several leading *SS* officers and participants in killing Jews and other victims of Nazi hatred. These included:

- Otto Ohlendorf, an *SS* lieutenant general since 1944, who had commanded *Einsatzgruppe* D, which—as he boasted at war crimes trials later (see chapters 7 and 13)—massacred nearly one hundred thousand Jews in the Soviet Ukraine and Crimea between June 1941 and April 1942;
- Rudolf Brandt, Himmler's personal secretary, who had involved himself in assigning *SS* personnel to concentration and death camps; in confiscating Jewish valuables at the camps; in facilitating deadly medical (especially sterilization) experiments on Jews at Auschwitz; and in utilizing Jews and other prisoners as slave labor in the camps; and
- Karl Gebhardt, the *SS*'s chief clinician and Himmler's attending physician, who had participated in the often-deadly sterilization of—and medical experiments on—Auschwitz inmates.

Clearly, the Allied efforts, however well intentioned, were faltering seriously. Even the most powerful Nazi bigwig and "architect of genocide" next to Hitler had benefited from the Allies' lenient custody.[36]

STANGL: LINZ, ROME, AND DAMASCUS

After he walked unnoticed out of prison in Linz, and with insufficient money to ride a train, Franz Stangl left the city on foot. He'd decided that to avoid recapture by the Austrians or Allies he must leave Europe. During the next week, possibly with the assistance of *ODESSA*, or more likely the general "rat line," he and fellow (former *SS*) fugitive Steiner traveled some one hundred miles southeast, toward the Italian border. On arriving in the Styrian capital of Graz, Stangl sold his wife's jewelry for a few Austrian schillings.

He knew the city well, but what allegedly happened there both surprised and scared him. As he passed by a local "construction site," a man hollered at him. When a worker ran suddenly in his direction, he thought the worst: someone had identified him and intended to take him into custody.

The man, tall and blond with a handsome face, drew nearer, shouting: "Herr Captain, Herr Captain!" Just as Stangl readied himself to run, he gasped with relief.[37] He recognized the man as Gustav Wagner, a fellow Austrian and Stangl's former deputy commander at both Sobibor and Treblinka.

Stangl had met Wagner initially while the two worked in the euthanasia program at Schloß Hartheim. At Sobibor, Wagner's proficiency as a mass murderer and torturer of Jews, whose victims called him the "Human Beast," had led Himmler to promote him to the *SS* rank of master sergeant. One survivor recalled about him, "He didn't eat his lunch if he didn't kill daily. With an axe, shovel, or even his hands. He had to have blood." Said another, "He was an Angel of Death. For him, torturing and killing was a pleasure. When he killed, he smiled."[38] He had huge shoulders and hands that killed emaciated Jewish prisoners merely by punching them in the stomach or slamming them to the ground. After the war, a U.S. military tribunal at Nuremberg had tried Wagner *in absentia* and sentenced him to death.

The two men, talking quietly, stood near the street. Stangl told his former deputy commander that he and Steiner were heading to Italy and, hopefully, into hiding somewhere outside Europe. Wagner begged Stangl to let him come along. "Please, please," he urged repeatedly. When Stangl agreed, the enthusiastic Wagner, walking with his distinctive looping lurch, joined him immediately without even bothering to return to the construction site or to his apartment for a few belongings.

Numerous skeptics doubt Stangl's account—given long after the war to Sereny—of meeting Wagner accidentally in Graz and of their subsequent escape together to Italy. They suspect that he lied to conceal or protect those who likely helped the two escape. Not only did former Nazis assist *SS* officers in leaving Germany and Austria, but Roman Catholic priests and monks also aided Nazi refugees in moving south into Italy along a "monastery route," or part of what observers have termed the "rat line." Some Catholic officials during the war had sheltered Jews fleeing for their lives, but after 1945 a few such persons worked with refugees so much—or they had pro-Nazi sympathies—that they rarely differentiated among their guests and merely helped any traveler on his way.

Allegedly, Stangl's small group traveled across the rugged Tyrolean mountains, crossed the border into Italy, and continued moving south into the Trentino-Alto Adige, stopping in Merano and, eventually, Florence. From there, the trio rode a train most of the way to Rome. Whether or not Stangl and his companions crossed into Italy with church assistance or with other contacts that he and Wagner had made during their work late in the war in Italy, Stangl sought aid from the church when he arrived in the Italian capital. Allegedly someone had told him that a Catholic churchman there, a "Bishop Hulda," an Austrian at the Vatican, "was helping Catholic SS officers."[39]

Bishop Aloïs Hudal served in Rome as rector of a school of theology and as father confessor to the local Catholic-German community. A notorious anti-Semite and admirer of Hitler, Hudal had aided Nazi war criminals in leaving Europe. Apparently, his close friend, Pope Pius XII, supported the bishop's activities. If the pope and his undersecretaries at the Vatican didn't know that Hudal assisted central figures who'd carried out the Holocaust and other war crimes, they nevertheless, according to church historian Michael Phayer, "had every reason to suspect it with Hudal as [the central figures'] agent."[40]

Phayer concludes that "the evidence unquestionably points to the Holy See's assistance to fleeing Nazis," which involved "pressuring South American states to accept them." For the Vatican "the positive qualifications of these refugees as anti-Communists outweighed any possible negatives connected with membership in the Nazi Party."[41] But Stangl, for his part, had no experience in or knowledge of fighting Communists—except with Jews, whom he and other Nazis equated with "Bolsheviks."

Before his ascension to the papacy, Pius XII had served as a Vatican envoy to Weimar Germany. During World War II, despite extensive knowledge of the German massacre of Jews, the Holy Father had remained silent about the Holocaust. On October 16, 1943, he'd done nothing decisive while the Germans rounded up over a thousand of Rome's Jews under the Vatican's very windows and deported them to Auschwitz. Nor had the war changed the Catholic church's centuries-long prejudice against Jews as disbelievers in, and so-called killers of, Christ. At the war's end Pius opposed the Allied and other trials of Nazi war criminals and their collaborators.

Besides assisting Stangl and Wagner, Hudal also helped Eichmann and Mengele leave Europe. The bishop protected the Austrian Otto Wächter, a former high-ranking *SS* officer and Nazi governor of Galicia sought widely by the Allies and Jewish intelligence in Israel because of his role in killing hundreds of thousands of Polish and other Jews. Wächter died in Rome while receiving the church's last rites from the bishop.

On arriving in Rome, Stangl allegedly "had no idea how one went about finding a bishop at the Vatican." Supposedly, while walking across a bridge over the Tiber River, he found himself suddenly "face to face with a former comrade: there, in the middle of Rome where there were millions of people." He knew the man from their days in prison at Glasenbach. During the war the acquaintance had served in France as an *SS* and police officer. While being extradited to France to be tried for war crimes, he had escaped and fled to Rome.

He asked Stangl, "Are you on your way to see 'Hulda?'" Stangl replied, "Yes. But I don't know where to find him." His comrade gave him directions to Hudal's office. It took him a mere half hour to walk there. The bishop entered the room, where his visitor, a major Nazi war criminal, waited. Hudal held out both his hands: "You must be Franz Stangl. I was expecting you." During the meeting he provided Stangl with money and a place to live in Rome and promised to have travel papers made for him.

Two weeks later, the bishop called Stangl to his office and handed him "a Red Cross passport." Shortly thereafter, Hudal gave him an entrance visa to Syria and a ticket for travel there on a ship. Hudal even arranged a job in a textile mill for Stangl in Damascus. During all this, as Stangl wrote his wife later, "no one questioned him about himself—still less that he had to fill out any sort of questionnaire."[42]

By mid-July 1948, six weeks after his escape, the onetime mass murderer had arrived in Damascus. He wrote his wife that "he had a room in an Arab house and had found [Nazi] friends who had got there ahead of him, and soldiers too—and there were some generals who had come there from Egypt. His letters sounded relaxed, calm, liberated."[43] Syria—one of numerous Arab League nations that despised and had attacked the newly proclaimed state of Israel—welcomed the military and other expertise of several former Nazi officials who surfaced in Damascus.

Meanwhile, Stangl's fellow escapee, Steiner, returned to Austria, but Wagner followed his former superior to Damascus. Back in Europe, few details had emerged about the Treblinka death camp and its *SS* leaders. Still, the information *was* there, if only someone were interested enough to investigate. But no one was, and no one did.

7

Nuremberg, Number Two, and the Substitute

He could barely conceal his pride at being locked up together with, in his view, so much fame. It all seemed to lift his spirits. Beginning in March 1946, the Allies imprisoned Werner Best in Nuremberg for use as a witness at the International Military Tribunal (IMT). Between October 1945 and November 1946 in the city's so-called Palace of Justice, the court placed on trial twenty-two former "major" National Socialist leaders—one, Martin Bormann, Hitler's private secretary and head of the Nazi Party chancellery, *in absentia*. They were charged with crimes against peace, war crimes, crimes against humanity, and conspiracy to commit the foregoing crimes. Both at the same time and later, at Nuremberg, Dachau, and elsewhere in Germany, Allied military courts tried several thousand other "lesser" Nazi war criminals.

The Palace of Justice, a large and stoutly built structure located on a main boulevard in Nuremberg, included a prison, an office building, and a courthouse. The Allies had worked to repair the main courtroom—damaged some in the war by bombs—and enlarge it to accommodate an audience of several hundred persons.

After Best had spent nearly a year in isolation in a Copenhagen jail, his new addresses in prisons at Oberursel and Nuremberg left him excited and in awe: "The prosecution as well as defense call as witnesses the best known people of the last 10 years. There are more field marshals than I have ever seen in one group. Many Reich ministers, a group of state secretaries, almost all the *Gauleiters* still alive, and other interesting people."[1] And now, he thought immodestly, this number included himself—a former top-level *SS* and *Gestapo* official and Reich plenipotentiary in wartime Denmark.

Best seemed little concerned about his new internment. He'd found in news accounts of the IMT much less in its proceedings about the defendants' persecution of Jews than about the former Nazi leaders' planning and implementing aggressive war and about their violating the laws of war, such as mistreating POWs and hostages. To fellow prisoners he denounced as "senseless" the IMT and the later trials of lesser Nazis planned by the Allies. The world, he complained, had "wholly new, and no less disastrous, problems"—namely empowered Soviet Communism—confronting it than vanquished Nazism.

Partly to justify to himself—or to excuse—his own role in Nazi criminality, he praised those on trial at Nuremberg. To Best, they seemed "to be no worse intellectually and morally than the people who govern many other states, if only a madman had not stood at the head."[2] Like so many other former Nazi leaders, as well as most Germans generally, he blamed Hitler and conveniently took no responsibility himself for what had happened under his authority and in his name under Nazism.

BEST AS DEFENSE WITNESS

Initially Best remained unclear on whether the Allies would prosecute him in one of the later Nuremberg trials or would permit his use at the IMT as a defense witness. His interrogators concentrated on his role in and knowledge of the *Gestapo*, which the tribunal would declare a criminal organization, along with the leadership corps of the Nazi Party and *SS*. Early in the Nazi regime, the government had detached the *Gestapo* (the secret state or political police) from the general German police.

Eventually, the *Gestapo* acquired jurisdiction in the Nazi concentration camps and received such extensive powers of arrest and imprisonment that German courts of law could almost never conduct formal reviews of or limit its activities. Before the war it had worked closely with the *SD* to eliminate alleged Jewish influence in Germany, including in the economy, and to force Jews to emigrate. In November 1938, during the weeks following *Kristallnacht*, the *Gestapo* participated in the mass arrests of Jews and in the pillaging of Jewish-owned art in Munich and elsewhere.

By the war's onset, the political police could search, arrest, and detain Jews and other so-called enemies of the state at will. During the war, after March 1941, the *Gestapo* arranged for and carried out—through Eichmann and his department IVB4, staffed by numerous other "Jewish experts"—most of the massive deportations of Jews from all over Europe to death camps in the East. Some *Gestapo* members served in the *Einsatzgruppen* that, in 1941 in the Soviet Union, began massacring Jews and Slavs.

On July 31, 1946, Best took the stand at the IMT as a witness for the *Gestapo*. His testimony provided a classic example of careful evasion and purposeful falsification about both the *Gestapo* and his own activities in the Nazi regime. During lengthy questioning by Dr. Rudolf Merkel, the lawyer for the *Gestapo*, Best portrayed the political police as a blameless tool in the hands of others, especially Hitler and Himmler. It had no philosophical or political bases, he claimed, and operated solely as a professional police force to prevent "political crimes."

In one exchange Merkel asked, "Did not the Gestapo also carry out actions which were not demanded of it through the general police directives?" Yes, Best replied, but "to carry out [such] actions" the police

> were an instrument for the carrying out of matters which were alien to the police sphere. I might say they were misused and abused along these lines. As the first case of this type, I remember the arrest of about 20,000 Jews in November 1938. This was a measure that was not necessary from the police point of view, and would never have been done by the Secret State Police on their own initiative, but they had received this order from the Government for political reasons.[3]

What had Best known about the *Einsatzgruppen* and their role in the war? He mentioned nothing of his key role in 1939 in the formation and use of such units in German-occupied Poland. Instead, he answered falsely that in Denmark and Norway such forces "very frequently objected to the measures they were ordered to carry out by the central agencies, measures which would have led to a severe treatment of the local population." No such units had existed there.

He added, lying completely to the court, "The Security Police and I severely protested against the deportation of Danish Jews." A bit later, he told Merkel: "I actually sabotaged this action" against Hitler's orders, which "would have cost me my life."[4] In fact, as shown in chapter 4, while serving as Germany's chief political official in Denmark, and despite his fervent attempts in 1943 to deport Danish Jews, most of them—an extreme rarity in the Final Solution—managed to escape to freedom, an outcome Best would've thwarted if he could have.

When questioned about wartime France and the Nazi shooting of hostages (mostly French Communists) ordered by Hitler, Best emphasized how the German military command, which included him during 1941 and 1942, had opposed the killings. The military feared the shootings would damage or destroy the widespread French cooperation with the German occupation. But he failed to mention how he and the military in Paris had proposed to Hitler a substitute for the killings, which the Führer had adopted readily—the mass deportations of Jews and Communists in France to Germany or to "the East."

And, asked Merkel, had Best a judgment "concerning the orders to the Gestapo or parts of it, to carry out actions, deportations, and executions?" In reply, the witness lied again, in the process concealing the enormous power and jurisdiction given the political police by the Nazi state. "I have already said," he insisted, "that these were measures quite alien to the Police, as they had nothing to do with the ordinary activities of the Police and were not necessary from the Police point of view." The Nazi policeman, Best continued, if ordered by Hitler or another political superior, had to obey—"each individual official had to take it upon himself as an obligation to carry out the decree."[5]

Unfortunately, despite holding a mass of captured *Gestapo* and other Nazi records as evidence, the Allied prosecution couldn't contradict Best. Frequently, prosecutors appeared confused about the structure and function of the vast network of Nazi police and *SS* organizations. In cross-examining Best on August 1, Whitney Harris, the assistant U.S. prosecutor, showed little interest in the former Nazi or in the particulars of his role in fulfilling the Nazi regime's mandate and his own vaunting ambition. Instead, Harris focused his questioning almost exclusively on the role of the *Gestapo* in the German killing of prominent Danes and of Soviet prisoners of war.

Questioners, including Harris, asked Best nothing remotely related to the witness's numerous criminal actions against Jews. Only at the end of his interrogation of Best did Harris ask him if he had signed a document submitted to the tribunal regarding "the deporting of Jews and Communists from France" that had to be delayed "for a while because of lack of transportation." To that Best answered, "Yes."[6] But the prosecutor didn't pursue the issue.

In this, as in every other interrogation, Best protected himself by avoiding assiduously discussing any subject that could incriminate him. To prepare for such questionings, including his appearance before the IMT, he rehearsed and polished ahead of time what he would say. As part of such efforts, on arriving in Germany in the spring of 1946, he'd written a lengthy biography, whose wording—even entire sentences—he used often in interrogations or cross-examinations. In this way he hoped to avoid contradicting or impugning himself and others. But he no longer portrayed himself to interrogators as a loyal Prussian and apolitical administrative specialist, a view that present Allied information—although still relatively limited—rendered unbelievable. Instead, he fashioned a picture of himself as a political idealist influenced by early nineteenth-century German nationalists, and one who had opposed in the *Gestapo* and later in wartime France and Denmark the disreputable actions of radical National Socialists.

One IMT prosecutor did express frustration at Best's testimony. The Englishman, Sir David Maxwell-Fyfe, told the court on August 29, 1946: "Best, the enslaver of Denmark, gave evidence before you for the Gestapo. Having seen the documents that were presented to him in cross-examination, can you believe one word of what he said?"[7] Unfortunately, Best's smooth, sidestepping, and distorting defense of the political police and himself helped persuade the Americans in October not to hold a later trial of the *Gestapo*, with Best as one of the chief defendants.

Still, following his appearance at the IMT, the Allies continued to intern and question him. When, on September 19, 1946, U.S. Army intelligence officers, both German emigrants who'd left their country in the 1930s, interviewed him, he denied completely any knowledge of—or involvement in—the Final Solution.

"The Jews," his questioners began, "were your enemies. Did the thought of their extermination not give you much worry?" Without hesitation, Best responded: "I never thought about the annihilation of the Jews. In numerous discussions I have expressed the sole view that they represented for me a nationality like any other, that they were people no better or worse than anyone else, that no one knows the value of others."

One of the interrogators pressed Best further: "Whoever subscribed to the foundations of the [Nazi] party acknowledged its attitude toward the Jewish question, and there is no instance known to me that the party protested against the murder of the Jews. How did you oppose this? What did you do to prevent the murder of 5–6 million Jews?" He replied, evading the question, "There is nothing about the extermination of the Jews in the party's program."

"What do you think about the killing of 5–6 million Jews?" Best claimed ignorance. "I heard of it here first."[8]

The words stunned his listeners. Both had lived in the Weimar Republic and, for a time, in Nazi Germany. How could a former chief functionary of the *Gestapo* and *SS* assert that he'd not viewed the Jews as inferior and had only just learned of their extermination? They found equally incomprehensible—even absurd—Best's other claims. After joining the Nazi Party, he declared, he'd never changed his attitude toward Jews. Nor, he added, was the original racial nationalist (*völkisch*) philosophy of National Socialism the source of Nazi criminality, but rather Hitler's departure from such ideals.

On February 27, 1947, Danish police officials arrived at Best's prison cell in Nuremberg to return him to Denmark. Thus far, almost two years after the war's end, neither the Allies nor anyone else had uncovered his criminality in the Holocaust. He left Nuremberg brimming with satisfaction and confidence.

OTTO OHLENDORF'S ADMISSION OF "INNOCENCE"

He testified before the IMT on January 3, 1946, as a prosecution witness. The relatively small, youthful-looking, thirty-eight-year-old—whose physical appearance belied the opposite of the usual brutish thug image embodied so well by the likes of defendants Hermann Göring and Ernst Kaltenbrunner—made a straightforward admission that stunned even the twenty-two major Nazi defendants in the dock.

He provided the tribunal with its most vivid—and only—account of the German mass murder of Soviet Jews by a Nazi official who had participated in it. Otto Ohlendorf, a former *SS* lieutenant general and wartime chief of the *SD*, had commanded *Einsatzgruppe* D, a mobile killing unit attached to the German Eleventh Army that operated in the southern Ukraine, Crimea, and Caucasus. As head of the *SD*, in the words of Israeli scholar Robert Wistrich, Ohlendorf had provided "for the benefit of the [Nazi] leadership" intelligence information "of a unique kind in the Third Reich, prying into the lives and thoughts of ordinary citizens in Nazi Germany and acting as a secret and relatively candid recorder of 'public opinion.'"[9]

But the IMT's interest in Ohlendorf centered on his role as commander of *Einsatzgruppe* D. Shortly after he took the stand, the American trial counselor Colonel John Amen asked him what orders he had received in 1941 as commander of the mobile killing unit. "The instructions were," Ohlendorf replied, "that in the Russian operational areas of the Einsatzgruppen the Jews, as well as the Soviet political commissars, were to be liquidated."

Amen followed up: "And when you say 'liquidated' do you mean 'killed'?"

"Yes, I mean 'killed.'"

Where had such instructions come from? "Himmler," Ohlendorf said, "told me that before the beginning of the Russian campaign Hitler had spoken of this mission. . . ." He added that Himmler had emphasized to him and other *Einsatzgruppen* commanders "that the leaders and men who were taking part in the liquidation bore no personal responsibility for the execution of this order. The responsibility was his, alone, and the Führer's."[10] His statement, which Ohlendorf repeated a year and a half later at his own trial at Nuremberg, was accepted by jurists and historians as fact until the early 1970s. By then, however, other evidence would emerge that placed Ohlendorf's claim about the timing of the killing directive in question. This issue is dealt with in more detail in chapter 13.

Then Amen inquired about the involvement of the German military leadership in the mass killings. The IMT had indicted not only two former members of the High Command of the German Armed Forces, Alfred Jodl and Wilhelm Keitel, but also the entire General Staff and High Command as a criminal organization. Nevertheless, many Allied military and other officials widely and erroneously assumed the innocence of the German army in the mass killings of Jews and other peoples.

But in a rare moment at the tribunal, the prosecutor raised the subject. Earlier in the questioning, Ohlendorf had noted that at the start of the invasion of

Russia, "a written agreement" existed between the *RSHA* and *Wehrmacht* regarding the use of the *Einsatzgruppen* "in the operational areas." Amen asked him: "Do you know whether this mission of the Einsatz group was known to the army group commanders?"

Ohlendorf acknowledged that "[t]his order and the execution of these orders were known to the commanding general of the army." With regard to *Einsatzgruppe* D, he said, the commander of the Eleventh Army—after September 1941, General Erich von Manstein—had directed or supervised the killing unit's activities in two ways: first, that the Eleventh Army had ordered "liquidations were to take place only at a distance of not less than 200 kilometers from the headquarters of the commanding general"; and second, that "the army commander requested the Einsatzkommandos in the area to hasten the liquidations, because famine was threatening and there was a great housing shortage."[11] Ohlendorf even mentioned that army troops had participated in shooting Jews.

Then Amen asked, "Do you know how many persons were liquidated by Einsatz Group D under your direction?"

With no emotion and unrepentantly, even boastfully, Ohlendorf replied: "In the year between June 1941 and June 1942 the Einsatzkommandos reported 90,000 people liquidated."

"Did you personally," Amen asked, pursuing the shocking revelation, "supervise mass executions of these individuals?" The answer: "I was present at two mass executions for purposes of inspection." Ohlendorf explained how his units had carried out the massacres. They had rounded up Jews "on the pretext that they were to be resettled. After the registration the Jews were collected at one place; and from there they were later transported to the place of execution, which was, as a rule an antitank ditch or a natural excavation. The executions were carried out in a military manner, by firing squads under command."[12]

"And," Amen pressed him further, "after they were shot what was done with the bodies?" "The bodies," Ohlendorf said, "were buried in the antitank ditch or excavation." He described how the *SS* confiscated the dead victims' property, including clothing and valuables such as gold and silver, and sent it to Berlin, to the *RSHA* or Reich Ministry of Finance. During the spring of 1942 the mobile killing units had changed their method of execution for some victims: "An order came from Himmler that in the future women and children were to be killed only in gas vans." About the vans and their use, in which one truck killed fifteen to twenty-five persons simultaneously, Ohlendorf testified:

> The actual purpose of these vans could not be seen from the outside. They looked like closed trucks, and were so constructed that at the start of the motor, gas was conducted into the van causing death in 10 to 15 minutes. . . .

> The vans were loaded with the victims and driven to the place of burial, which was usually the same as that used for the mass executions. The time needed for transportation was sufficient to ensure the death of the victims.[13]

Eventually, a Soviet judge, Major General I. T. Nikitchenko, asked Ohlendorf if, while *Einsatzgruppe* D had operated in the Soviet Union, it "had the objective of annihilating the Jews and the [Soviet political] commissars?" After Ohlendorf had answered "Yes," Nikitchenko queried him, "For what reason were the [Jewish] children massacred?" The former mass murderer stated matter-of-factly: "The order was that the Jewish population should be totally exterminated."[14]

Bizarrely, Ohlendorf didn't view his testimony and admissions as constituting a confession but as an avowal of his innocence. When, during cross-examination, the defense counsel for the *SS* asked whether he had "no scruples in regard to the execution" of the orders given the mobile killing units, Ohlendorf replied, "Yes, of course." But "how is it," the lawyer continued, that the orders "were carried out regardless of these scruples?" In his reply the witness revealed irrefutably his underlying remorseless state of mind: "Because to me it is inconceivable that a subordinate leader should not carry out orders given by the leaders of the state."

The questioner persisted: "Was the legality of these orders explained to these people under false pretenses?" Ohlendorf responded, "I do not understand your question." He went on to explain his apparently straightforward but actually convoluted rationale: "Since the order was issued by the superior authorities, the question of illegality could not arise in the minds of these individuals, for they had sworn obedience to the people who had issued the orders."[15]

The Soviet deputy prosecutor, Colonel Y. V. Pokrovsky, also examined Ohlendorf. The Russian appeared concerned to emphasize that the *Einsatzgruppen* hadn't murdered solely Jews. "Were Jews only," he asked, "handed over for the execution by the Einsatzgruppe or were Communists—'Communist officials' you call them in your instructions—handed over for execution along with the Jews?" "Yes," Ohlendorf responded, noting apparently what Pokrovsky wanted to hear. "Activists and political commissars."[16]

GÖRING: A TROUBLESOME NUMBER TWO

Finally, during the defendant's seventh day on the stand, the prosecutor raised the subject that the accused feared most. When it happened, suddenly the vastly slimmed-down but still jowlish and loud man being questioned felt himself perspire even more than usual. And with good reason. Hermann

Göring had much to hide as Hitler's former second-in-command and now, with the Führer dead, the lead Nazi defendant at the IMT. His trial, consequently, drew the most global public attention of any such war crimes proceeding.

Along with Hitler, Himmler, and Goebbels—all suicides—Göring had a complete view of the machinery of destruction used by the Germans against the Jews. He knew the details of the *Einsatzgruppen* operations in Russia and saw the whole scheme of the deportations in the rest of Europe. On one occasion, Goebbels, in March 1943, in his diary (found and published after the war), quoted Göring as speaking about what had already happened to the Jews: "On the Jewish question, especially, we have taken a position from which there is no escape. That is a good thing. Experience teaches that a movement and a people who have burned their bridges fight with much greater determination than those who are still able to retreat."[17]

Two years later, Göring found himself a prisoner of the Allies at Nuremberg, on trial as a war criminal. When asked by Gustave Gilbert, an American prison psychologist, to autograph his indictment and to add his opinion of it, Göring had written, in his usual cynical vein: "The victor will always be the judge, and the vanquished the accused."[18] This view of Göring, popular among many Germans and others at the time—who decried alleged "victors' justice" at Nuremberg—and adopted eventually by Holocaust deniers, cast Germany as the victim and, by implication, denounced the Allied war crimes trials and denazification programs. A newspaper critical of the Nuremberg trials, the *New York Daily News*, declared that the defendants' "real crime was that they did not win."[19]

A few months before his appearance on the stand at Nuremberg, Göring had tried to dismiss with contempt the testimony before the tribunal of the prosecution witness, Ohlendorf. Ohlendorf had related in gruesome detail how the *Einsatzgruppe* he'd commanded during late 1941 and the beginning of 1942 exterminated tens of thousands of Jews in Russia. Shortly after the questioning of Ohlendorf, Göring had sneered, "Ach, there goes another one selling his soul to the enemy! What does the swine expect to gain by it? He'll hang anyway."[20]

But now, with the wholly unrepentant Göring himself on the stand, to his surprise and relief his questioner spent only a few minutes asking him about his responsibility for the Final Solution. Previously, his defense lawyer, who'd questioned him extensively before the court, hadn't even mentioned the Nazis' so-called Jewish question. But once the Allied prosecution cross-examined the defendant, it too did little to acknowledge or inquire into his pivotal role in the genocide of the Jews.

Instead, throughout the nearly nine days Göring spent on the stand—March 13–16 and 18–22, 1946—his questioners focused primarily on his role in the

Nazi conspiracy to wage World War II. They grilled him about his participation in Hitler's seizure of power in Germany; about the country's rearmament and its takeover of Austria and Czechoslovakia; about the Nazi conquest of Poland and France and invasion of Russia; about the use of masses of foreigners as slave labor; and about the persecution and killing of prisoners of war.

On trial at Nuremberg, the once-powerful *Reichsmarschall* saw as his sole task—now that his beloved Führer had killed himself and the Allies had defeated and destroyed Germany so completely—the imperative to set an example of loyalty to Hitler. Above all, Göring wanted to demonstrate to the twenty other former major Nazi leaders in the dock with him that he—still, in his mind, acting as the *Reichsmarschall*, the once–number two man to Hitler—was in full charge of what remained of the wreckage of Nazism. It mattered little that, in the war's final days, Hitler had accused Göring of betraying the Führer, stripped him of his offices, and expelled him from the Nazi Party.

He proved the most formidable and troublesome of the defendants on the stand. Almost no one in the courtroom—among the judges, prosecutors, or other officials—anticipated his intelligence and resourcefulness. Gilbert, the prison psychologist, had given each of the twenty-one defendants an IQ test, on which Göring scored third highest. Göring's behavior, both before and during his testimony, worried Allied officials. One, an alternate judge and famous English jurist, Sir Norman (later Lord) Birkett, kept notes during the trial and summarized his thoughts after the first day of Göring's testimony:

> Goering is the man who has really dominated the proceedings, and that, remarkable enough, without ever uttering a word in public up to the moment he went into the witness box. . . . He has followed the evidence with great intentness when the evidence required attention, and has slept like a child when it did not; and it has been obvious that a personality of outstanding, though possibly evil qualities, was seated there in the dock.
>
> Nobody seems to have been quite prepared for his immense ability and knowledge, and his thorough mastery and understanding of the detail of the captured documents. He has obviously studied them with the greatest care and appreciated the matters which might assume the deadliest form.[21]

On the stand Göring made no secret that he'd done all he could to rearm Germany for Hitler; to expand the economy for such a purpose, including implementing forced *Aryanizations* of Jewish property; to make the Reich immune to blockade; and to build an air force as rapidly as the economy and training programs permitted. With barely concealed arrogance he accepted responsibility for Germany's *Anschluss* with Austria in 1938. His decisions, he insisted, had nothing to do with armed aggression, but with his effort—as head of Germany's war economy—to accumulate or allocate scarce resources for his country.

Often contentious and bellicose toward his accusers, at every opportunity he boasted about his importance in Hitler's Germany. "All in all," he told Robert H. Jackson, the chief U.S. prosecutor and an associate justice on the U.S. Supreme Court, on March 18, 1946, "I do not believe anyone had anything like the influence on the Führer that I had."[22] When asked three days later by General R. Rudenko, the Soviet prosecutor, who were Hitler's closest associates, Göring declared without hesitation: "The close collaborators of the Führer as I said before were first I, myself."[23]

Much was expected from Justice Jackson's cross-examination of the defendant. The Allies worried about the effectiveness of Göring's performance. "No one on the Allied side," Göring's biographer wrote later, "wanted to see Goering emerge as the hero of the trial. It was the hope of everyone that Mr. Justice Jackson would cut him down to size."[24]

But that did not happen. Jackson's cross-examination of the defendant lasted nearly three full days, during March 18–20. The prosecutor appeared shaky on his facts, giving Göring repeated opportunities to correct him. This Göring did, not in his usual arrogant fashion, but "with an air of great courtesy and mock-humble helpfulness."[25] In addition, Jackson framed his questions so that the defendant time and again could launch into long, and often irrelevant, answers.

By early afternoon on March 19, Jackson, irritated and frustrated, fumed to the court, "I respectfully submit to the Tribunal that this witness is not being responsive, and has not been in his examination. . . . It is perfectly futile to spend our time if we cannot have responsive answers to our questions." In a rage, he threw down his earphones, whereupon the judge adjourned the court for the day.

The following morning, Jackson urged the tribunal to permit Göring to answer questions with only a "yes" or "no." He complained that he could not "discharge" his duties "if the defendant is to volunteer these statements without questions which bring them up."[26] A few moments later, he began asking Göring about "public acts taken by you in reference to the Jewish question."[27] When he questioned Göring about the latter's directive of July 31, 1941, to Heydrich, the deputy chief of the *SS*, Göring admitted little about its contents or meaning—only that he'd signed the decree and addressed it to Heydrich. The short directive, a copy of which Jackson had in hand and read into the court record, had ordered Heydrich, in the first paragraph, to make preparations for "a complete solution of the Jewish question in the German sphere of influence in Europe" and, in the last paragraph, to plan for "the Final Solution of the Jewish question which we desire."

By July 1941, the Nazi use of the terms *complete solution* and *Final Solution* would soon mean the extermination of the Jews. Not surprisingly, Göring complained to the court about the translation of the document and objected to reading in it the German word *Endlösung* as "Final Solution," insisting that it read instead as "total solution." Obviously, Göring wanted to disassociate himself from the term *Final Solution*.

Unfortunately, neither Jackson nor any other Allied prosecutor made an effort to ask Göring about the distinction, in this regard, between the words *total* and *final*. Nor did the prosecution inquire further about the document or its meaning. Jackson alluded to only its second paragraph when he noted that in the directive, Göring had "ordered all other governmental agencies to co-operate with the Security Police and the SS in the Final Solution of the Jewish question." But the former *Reichsmarschall* avoided the issue. "There is nothing," he replied, correcting his questioner, "about the SS here [in the document], only about the Security Police, a governmental agency."[28]

Jackson didn't follow up. It's unclear whether he realized that Göring's directive in 1941 had helped so significantly in setting in motion the Nazi mass slaughter of the Jews. In the next few weeks, the *Einsatzgruppen* and German police battalions began killing every Jew they could seize in Russia. Also, six months after Heydrich received the order, the *SS* leader held the Wannsee Conference, attended by numerous high-ranking Nazi government and police officials, including Eichmann. At the meeting, Heydrich noted that both Göring and Hitler had entrusted him with preparations for the Final Solution. Those present worked out the main blueprint for the destruction of Europe's Jews—transporting them to death camps in the East.

Jackson appeared much less interested in the defendant's participation in the extermination of Jews than in his prewar role in removing Jews from the German economy. He asked Göring extensively about his responsibility for the Reich's anti-Semitic decrees issued during 1938 and 1939, both before and after the *Kristallnacht*. Göring admitted that during a meeting of Nazi officials in his office in Berlin following the pogrom that devastated the Jews remaining in Germany, he had declared to Heydrich: "I wish you had killed 200 Jews and not destroyed such valuable property."[29]

Then Jackson asked Göring about his wartime looting of art treasures by the trainload from Nazi-occupied countries. The accused maintained—again lying—that he'd only built an art collection for the future cultural interest of the German state. By the end of his cross-examination of Göring, Jackson had done little to add to the case against the defendant. Birkett commented later: "Certainly there has been no dramatic destruction of Goering as had been anticipated or prophesied."[30]

The Western press followed Göring's testimony with enthusiasm, revealing his sometimes-humiliating command of the court, including his verbal clashes with Jackson. According to historian Brian Feltman, "Göring was without question at his best on the stand and seemed to hold a strange power over the [press] correspondents, many of whom gave his performance glowing reviews, often describing him as brilliant and ingenious."[31]

At the end of the day's questioning, the scant time Jackson had spent on Göring's participation in the extermination of Jews apparently left the latter pleased with his performance. That evening he told his co-defendants smugly, "If you all handle yourselves half as well as I did, you will do all right. You have to be careful—every other word can be twisted around."[32]

The following day, March 21, when Sir David Maxwell-Fyfe cross-examined Göring, the British prosecutor returned briefly to the subject of what exactly the defendant had known of the Final Solution when it had happened. Maxwell-Fyfe read to the court from the minutes of a conference in April 1943 among Hitler, his foreign minister Joachim von Ribbentrop (one of Göring's co-defendants), and the regent of Hungary, Miklos Horthy. The minutes showed that the German leaders had demanded that Hungary, a German ally in the war, surrender its nearly seven hundred thousand Jews for killing. Ribbentrop told Horthy "that the Jews should be exterminated or taken to concentration camps. There was no other possibility." Immediately, Hitler confirmed Ribbentrop's explicitly murderous statement, noting about the three million Jews in Poland, most of whom the Germans had killed already: "If the Jews there did not want to work, they were shot. If they could not work, they had to perish. They had to be treated like tuberculosis bacilli, with which a healthy body may become infected."

The prosecutor then read from another document that recorded the minutes of a wartime meeting between Göring and Hinrich Lohse, Nazi civilian commissioner for the so-called *Ostland*, the conquered Baltic states and Byelorussia. The minutes quoted Lohse as informing the *Reichsmarschall*: "There are only a few Jews left alive. Tens of thousands have been disposed of."

When Maxwell-Fyfe asked Göring whether, "in the face of these two documents," he could still say "that neither Hitler nor yourself knew that the Jews were being exterminated," the defendant claimed that the document incriminating him had been mistranslated. His assertion had no basis in fact—only in his effort to avoid answering the question. Maxwell-Fyfe continued to press the issue: "Will you please answer my question? Do you still say neither Hitler nor you knew of the policy to exterminate the Jews?"

Göring persisted in his denial: "As far as Hitler is concerned, I have said I do not think so. As far as I am concerned, I have said that I did not know, even approximately, to what extent these things were taking place."

"You did not know to what degree, but you knew there was a policy that aimed at the extermination of the Jews?"

"No, a policy of emigration, not liquidation of the Jews. I knew only that there had been isolated cases of such perpetrations."[33]

Göring questioned repeatedly the documentary evidence used against him, much like that done by fellow perpetrators Irma Grese and, as shown in chapters 9 and 14, respectively, Alfred Rosenberg and Adolf Eichmann. This would provide critics of the war crimes trials, including German apologists and the earliest Holocaust deniers, fuel for their claim that the trials used falsified records. In 1947, a few months after Göring's testimony, the assertion appeared in a book published by Maurice Bardèche, a French fascist and denier. He and other deniers watched the IMT proceedings closely. In addition, Göring's refusal to acknowledge the existence of the Final Solution as a German policy played into the hands of deniers, who would also claim that Germany had no such wartime policy.

Maxwell-Fyfe, in his brief exchange with Göring regarding the latter's knowledge of the Holocaust, ended his questioning regarding it. Most of his interrogation of Göring focused on other—wholly unrelated—issues, including the wartime Nazi murder of captured British Royal Air Force officers, the delivering of Russian prisoners of war to the *Gestapo*, and the defendant's dubious testimony about his alleged attempt to prevent war by negotiating behind Hitler's back.

Much of the rest of the afternoon the Soviet prosecutor, General Rudenko, asked Göring about the German invasion and occupation of the Soviet Union. Only at the end of his cross-examination—almost as an afterthought—did the Soviet official ask the former number two Nazi about the *Einsatzgruppen*:

> You must have known about the mass extermination of the Soviet citizens from the occupied territories of the Soviet Union. . . . Is it not true that the Einsatz Kommandos and their activities were the result of the plan prepared in advance for the extermination of Jews and other groups of Soviet citizens?[34]

"No," came the adamant reply from the stand. "Einsatz Kommandos were an internal organ which was kept very secret."[35] The *Reichsmarschall* lied—again. In reality, nearly every major German government agency, including Göring's air ministry, had received copies of the *Einsatzgruppen* reports from Russia.

The next day, March 22, his last on the stand, the questioning of Göring ended during the morning session. In his cell that evening—as he'd done earlier—he couldn't help but admire his performance during the previous two days. "Well," he queried Gilbert, the psychologist, in his typically arrogant manner, "I didn't cut a *pretty* figure did I?"

Still again, the brief time spent by prosecutors on the Final Solution and his role in it appeared to lift his spirits. Continuing to support the fiction of his innocence in the genocide, he bellowed to Gilbert: "For heaven's sake, do you think I would ever have supported it if I had the slightest idea that it would lead to mass murder?" A few seconds later, he added: "I only thought we would eliminate Jews from positions in big business and government, and that was that. But don't forget they carried on a terrific campaign against us too, all over the world."[36] He still believed the age-old myth propagated by anti-Semites like himself and by the former Nazi regime that an international conspiracy existed among Jews to establish their global domination. Perhaps not surprising, nearly every Holocaust denier would make the same claim—Germany before and under Hitler had been the victim of an alleged powerful "world Jewry" that conspired against the country.

In yet another insult to the millions murdered by the Nazis, much earlier in the trial Göring had scoffed at the horribly graphic film of German concentration camps—mountains of emaciated bodies piled high at Dachau, Buchenwald, and Bergen-Belsen, and many of them pushed by bulldozers into immense ditches for graves—taken at the war's end, shown to the court by the American prosecution. The general counsel for the U.S. Office of Strategic Services, Commander James Donovan, explained that the film "has been compiled from motion pictures taken by Allied military photographers as the Allied armies in the West liberated the areas in which these camps were located."[37]

The film shocked most of those in the courtroom, including many of the defendants. Except one. Later, when Göring discussed the day's evidence presented against him, he did so with his typical sneering insolence: "It was such a good afternoon too. . . . And then they showed that awful film, and it just spoiled everything."[38]

In reality, during the heady days in the war of Nazi triumphs and Allied timidity, he'd been only too pleased to sanction and facilitate the Final Solution as long as it expanded his power, prestige, personal connections, and private wealth. Besides, the Third Reich was supposed to have lasted a thousand years, to have conquered and crushed all opposition. The seemingly inevitable victors had never considered with any serious reflection that possibly their fortunes might turn and they might find themselves forced to account for prior orders issued at their instigation and actions done at their direction. Now, less than a year after the Nazi defeat, no matter how self-congratulatory he may have felt about his performances on the stand, Göring was not so self-deluded as to discount that a reckoning was on its way.

ERNST KALTENBRUNNER: THE STAND-IN?

He complained to his accusers in Nuremberg that they had singled him out for trial only to serve as a substitute for the dead Himmler. The IMT had indicted as criminal six former Nazi organizations, including the *SS*, its intelligence arm, the *SD*, and the *Gestapo*. Allied prosecutors chose *SS* Lieutenant General Ernst Kaltenbrunner to stand trial because in the fall of 1945 he was the highest-ranking *SS* officer still alive and in custody whose responsibilities linked him to the *Gestapo*, the *Einsatzgruppen* in Russia, and the horrors of the concentration and death camps.

Since early 1943, Kaltenbrunner, a large, even hulking, scar-faced Austrian and fanatical Nazi, had headed the powerful Reich Security Main Office (*RSHA*), which directed the operations of the *Gestapo* and Security Police organizations. In this position he had succeeded Heydrich, whom the Czech underground had assassinated in 1942. While the *RSHA* didn't administer directly the concentration, slave-labor, or death camps, nevertheless it authorized arrests of individuals or large groups for imprisonment in them; it determined the length of detention; it issued orders for executions; and it had responsibility for transporting to the camps persons marked for internment there or, in the case of the death camps, for extermination.

On May 16, 1945, in the Austrian Alps, U.S. Army forces captured Kaltenbrunner. Long on Allied lists of major war criminals, he'd left his family in Austria and hidden with several companions in a hunting lodge high in the mountains southeast of Salzburg. But in a rare instance, a local hunter had betrayed him to the U.S. Army. When agents of the U.S. Army's CIC brought Kaltenbrunner face to face with his mistress, who'd borne him infant twins six weeks earlier, she "confirmed Kaltenbrunner's identity by impulsively embracing him."[39]

In contrast to most other leading German officials arrested by the Allies, the latter knew little about Kaltenbrunner. Unlike longtime major Nazi officials such as Göring, Ribbentrop, Hans Frank (governor general of Poland), Alfred Rosenberg (Reich minister for the occupied eastern territories), or Julius Streicher (the Nazi district leader of Nuremberg and, next to Hitler, the vilest of anti-Semites), Kaltenbrunner had risen to prominence in the Nazi regime only during the last two years of the war, which contributed to the Allies' sparse knowledge of him. Often described by his captors as a brutish thug and one who ranked low on the IQ test given to the defendants at the IMT by Gilbert, he was nevertheless a well-educated lawyer.

After ten weeks of imprisonment and extensive questioning in London, the Allies transported Kaltenbrunner in September 1945 to Nuremberg. On October 19 the IMT served him an indictment charging him with perpetration of war crimes, crimes against humanity, and participation in a conspiracy to commit such crimes. Gilbert, as he did with the others, asked the prisoner to sign the indictment and write his view of it. Kaltenbrunner complied, scribbling: "I do not feel guilty of any war crimes, I have only done my duty as an intelligence organ, and I refuse to serve as an ersatz [substitute or stand-in] for Himmler."[40]

Initially, American officials who interrogated him in prison hardly inquired about his role in the extermination of Jews. He told one, "I am not the disagreeable, uncouth fellow the public probably thinks because of all the atrocities committed under Himmler's rule, and of which I am totally innocent."[41]

He believed the Allies would surely reward him with leniency for his efforts near the war's end to step into Himmler's place as a mediator of peace. In this regard, he had sought contact with both the International Committee of the Red Cross (ICRC) and Allen Dulles, the European head of the U.S. Office of Strategic Services. Between March 12 and 14, 1945, he met Carl Burckhardt, president of the ICRC, and officials of the German foreign ministry. But in the words of Israeli historian Leni Yahil,

> Their talks ended with the Germans consenting to have food sent to the prisoners on the death marches and allowing the Red Cross to supervise the distribution of the parcels within the camps. But the concrete results of this agreement were meager. It was not until the final days of the war, for example, that a Red Cross representative managed to get into Mauthausen. And when asked actually to release the prisoners from the camps, the Germans responded with evasions.[42]

Before the IMT Kaltenbrunner hoped to persuade his accusers that he'd served Hitler primarily as a blameless intelligence official; in February 1944 the *RSHA* had taken control of the foreign and counterintelligence department of the *Abwehr* (military intelligence). On the morning of April 11, 1946, a few minutes before Kaltenbrunner began his courtroom testimony, Gilbert visited him in his jail cell. The huge prisoner—described by Telford Taylor, the chief U.S. prosecutor, as "the most ominous-looking man in the dock" who "had no friends there"[43]—appeared calm, unlike earlier when, at the start of the trial, he'd suffered a near stroke from tension and agitation. He hinted to the visitor what his defense would be—evading responsibility for everything regarding the concentration camps. He bragged to the American: "That organizational chart of the RSHA—I will be able to demolish that myself in a few minutes."

"But what about the mass murders?" he was asked.

"That is just it," he retorted, without a trace of a sense of guilt. "I can prove that I had nothing to do with it. I neither gave orders nor executed them. You have no idea how secret these things were kept even from me."[44]

A few moments later, on the stand at the IMT, Kaltenbrunner responded to a question from his defense counsel: "[T]he special assignments which had been given to Heydrich, such as, for instance, the assignment with regard to the Final Solution of the Jewish problem, were not only not known to me at the time but were not taken over by me." He claimed ignorance of firsthand knowledge of the concentration camps and denied repeatedly that he'd visited Mauthausen, the main camp in his native Austria: "I heard gradually more and more about conditions in concentration camps."[45]

When had he learned first of Auschwitz and that it was an extermination camp? "Himmler," he replied, "told me that in 1944, in February or March. That is, he did not tell me, he admitted it." What had Kaltenbrunner done when he heard about Auschwitz and the Final Solution? He claimed, "Immediately, after receiving knowledge of this fact, I fought, just as I had done previously, not only against the final solution, but also against this type of treatment of the Jewish problem."

When pressed for details about what he'd done, he said: "First I protested to Hitler and the next day to Himmler." He insisted also that the Jewish persecution had ended in October 1944 and sought to take responsibility for its alleged halt: "I am firmly convinced that this is chiefly due to my intervention, although a number of others also worked toward the same end."[46] According to Kaltenbrunner's biographer, Peter Black, "The evidence that has survived renders such disclaimers ludicrous."[47]

The next day, April 12, 1946, Colonel John Amen, the U.S. trial counselor, cross-examined Kaltenbrunner. He presented the former *RSHA* chief with wartime documents from his own hand or that of other Nazi officials implicating him, with affidavits of prosecution witnesses, and with inconsistent statements he'd made.

Still the defendant, unfazed, denied everything. Did he "assume no responsibility for anything done in connection with the program for the extermination of the Jews?"

"Yes," came the quick reply. Did he "likewise deny" that Heinrich Müller, the brutish head of the *Gestapo* (Department IV in the *RSHA*), "always conferred with you with respect to any important documents?"

"Yes."

Amen read into the court record affidavits of several former Nazi prisoners at the Mauthausen concentration camp. Two had worked at the camp's crematorium during the war, burning bodies of Jews and others; they testified to having seen Kaltenbrunner visit the camp at least "three or four times." One, Johann Kanduth, recounted: "Kaltenbrunner went laughing into the gas chamber. Then the people were brought from the bunker to be executed, and then all three kinds of executions: hanging, shooting in the back of the neck and gassing, were demonstrated. After the dust had disappeared we had to take away the bodies." In response to the affidavits, Kaltenbrunner insisted "that not a single word of these statements is true."[48]

Amen introduced still another affidavit, one from Hans Marsalek, a former Mauthausen prisoner who, on the night of May 22–23, 1945, had taken in writing for the Americans the deathbed confession of the camp commandant,

SS Colonel Franz Ziereis. The latter, whose "baby face," according to Holocaust writer and filmmaker Joshua Greene, belied his deadly sadism, had "ordered prisoners thrown into the crematory fires" and the "kitchen staff to overturn pots of soup so he could watch starving prisoners lick the spillage before it was absorbed in the dirt."[49] Ziereis died after American troops wounded him as he attempted to escape from a hunting lodge in Upper Austria. Marsalek quoted the dying Nazi as admitting that nearing the war's end, he'd received the following directive regarding the camp inmates:

> According to an order by Reichsführer Himmler, I was to liquidate all prisoners on the instructions of SS Obergruppenführer Dr. Kaltenbrunner; the prisoners were to be led into the tunnels of the Bergkristall works of Gusen and only one entrance was to be left open. Then I was to blow up this entrance to the tunnels with some explosive and thus cause the death of the prisoners. I refused to carry out this order. . . .
>
> A gas chamber camouflaged as a bathroom was built in the Mauthausen Concentration Camp by order of the former garrison doctor, Dr. Krebsbach. Prisoners were gassed in this camouflaged bathroom. In addition to that, there ran, between Mauthausen and Gusen, a specially built automobile in which prisoners were gassed during the journey. . . . I myself never put any gas into this automobile; I only drove it. But I knew that prisoners were being gassed. . . .
>
> Everything that we carried out was ordered by the Reich Security Main Office, Himmler or Heydrich, also by SS Obergruppenführer Müller or Dr. Kaltenbrunner, the latter being Chief of the Security Police.[50]

After reading Marsalek's statement, Amen questioned Kaltenbrunner about it: "Do you still say that you had nothing to do with the order referred to or the matters set forth in the affidavit?"

"I maintain that most emphatically," the defendant said curtly.

Yet another postwar affidavit submitted to the court from Kurt Becher, a former *SS* colonel and close associate of Himmler, maintained that on April 27, 1945, only a few days before Germany surrendered, he—Becher—had visited Mauthausen. While there, Ziereis, the camp commandant, told him "in strictest secrecy" that Kaltenbrunner, in opposition to Himmler's directive forbidding any further last-minute extermination of Jews, "gave me the order that at least a thousand persons would still have to die at Mauthausen each day." In commenting on the affidavit, Kaltenbrunner insisted that he had ordered "the entire camp with all its inmates be surrendered to the enemy."[51]

In an affidavit, another prosecution witness, Alois Höllriegl, remembered about Kaltenbrunner, "I was on guard duty at the time and saw him twice." A former *SS* man at Mauthausen, Höllriegl too provided the Allies with a statement read by Amen: "He [Kaltenbrunner] went down into the gas chamber with Ziereis, commandant of the camp, at a time when prisoners were being gassed. The sound accompanying the gassing operation was well known to me: I heard the gassing taking place while Kaltenbrunner was present. I saw Kaltenbrunner come up from the gas cellar after the gassing operation had been completed."[52]

Kaltenbrunner testified also on April 12 that he had known the meaning of the Nazi phrase *special treatment*, a euphemism for killing Jews. But when the prosecutor, Amen, placed before him an affidavit of Josef Spacil, a former *SS* brigadier general, noting that he [Spacil] had witnessed personally meetings of Kaltenbrunner and his subordinate, *Gestapo* chief Heinrich Müller, regarding whether "one or the other case should receive 'special treatment' or if 'special treatment' was to be considered," Kaltenbrunner denied meeting Müller about "official matters." Instead, he claimed, "I met Müller when we were lunching together."[53]

Kaltenbrunner's defense suffered also from the testimony before the IMT of Rudolf Höß, the commandant at Auschwitz from May 1940 to December 1943. Höß testified on April 15, 1946. Kaltenbrunner's counsel subpoenaed Höß, apparently believing the latter would enhance his client's defense by shifting the entire responsibility for the Holocaust away from the *RSHA* to another *SS* agency, the Economic-Administrative Main Office (*Wirtschafts-verwaltungshauptamt*, or *WVHA*). Both Kaltenbrunner and his counsel had sought to distance him from not only *Gestapo* chief Müller but also from Eichmann and Oswald Pohl, the head of the *WVHA*. During the war, within the huge *SS* bureaucracy, the *RSHA* had dealt with arrests and isolating the Jewish population as well as with transports to the death camps. The *WVHA* had charge of killing the victims, plundering their property, and sending it to the *Reichsbank* in Berlin and other Nazi institutions. All this represented a further attempt by Kaltenbrunner to narrow his sphere of responsibility in the Nazi regime to the latter's intelligence service.

But Höß's testimony damaged Kaltenbrunner severely. The former camp commandant described in blunt and grisly detail not only how Auschwitz operated but also his (Höß's) role after 1943 as a department chief in the *WVHA*, "responsible for co-ordinating all matters arising between RSHA and concentration camps under the administration of WVHA. I held this position until the end of the war. Pohl, as Chief of WVHA, and Kaltenbrunner, as Chief of RSHA, often conferred personally and frequently communicated orally and in writing concerning concentration camps." He testified further: "While Kaltenbrunner was Chief of RSHA orders for protective custody, commitments, punishment, and individual executions were signed by Kaltenbrunner or by Müller, Chief of the Gestapo, as Kaltenbrunner's deputy."[54]

Similarly, Kaltenbrunner's case took a hit from the testimony before the IMT of Dieter Wisliceny, one of Eichmann's former subordinates in the *SD* and *Gestapo* involved in the deportations of Jews to Auschwitz. Wisliceny, who is discussed in more detail in chapter 14, had testified in January 1946. He maintained to the court that Kaltenbrunner and Eichmann had a close relationship. Both men had come from the Austrian town of Linz, and Eichmann had once told Wisliceny that "if he [Eichmann] had any serious trouble, he could go to Kaltenbrunner personally."[55]

Long before he headed the *RSHA*, he'd known about what occurred inside the concentration camps. He had participated eagerly and fully in the war of annihilation against European Jewry. When Kaltenbrunner was appointed to head the *RSHA* in early 1943, the death camps' gas chambers had been operating for some eight months. (Deportations had started more than a year earlier.)

He inherited from Heydrich a smoothly functioning apparatus operated by an experienced *Kommando*—the infamous *Gestapo* Department IVB4—led by Eichmann. The *Kommando* arranged for the roundup and deportation of Jews from all over Europe. "Kaltenbrunner," Peter Black notes, "needed only to make certain that the apparatus continued to function smoothly. . . . [His] personal knowledge of and involvement in the annihilation of the European Jews remained constant and consistent."[56]

But Ernst was no deskbound killer skulking and hiding within the myriad mundane halls of bureaucracy. As early as February 22, 1943, he had received from Himmler's office foreign press clippings on the "accelerated annihilation of the Jews in occupied Europe." Two months later, he discussed "Jewish affairs" and other related issues on the telephone with Richard Glucks—the *SS* inspector of concentration camps with responsibility for the camps' medical "care," i.e., human experiments, and yet another likely suicide in May 1945—and Himmler. In late May 1943, Himmler sent Kaltenbrunner to a meeting in Poland to press the *SS* policy goal that "the evacuation [deportation] of the last 250,000 Jews in [the Government General], which for some weeks will undoubtedly excite unrest, must be completed as quickly as possible despite all difficulties."[57]

Kaltenbrunner believed that Russian Jews formed the backbone of the partisan movement; consequently, he supported the killing of large numbers of Jews by the *Einsatzgruppen* and other *SS* and police formations. Kaltenbrunner admitted such during a postwar Allied interrogation of him at Nuremberg prison: "[T]hough usually careful to say nothing about the Jews except that he did not know what was happening to them, Kaltenbrunner slipped and declared that the death of many Jews was not incomprehensible, since the 'partisans' in Poland, White Russia, and the Ukraine were largely organized by Jews." He told interrogators: "All partisan activity, every resistance movement, every form of espionage, had the Jew as its organizers, as the principal mainstay of the Bolshevik idea; he was the decisive element in every hostile action."[58] According to Black, "It is clear that, in the East, Kaltenbrunner saw the Jew as the major enemy."[59]

Within days of his appointment as *RSHA* chief, Kaltenbrunner sought eagerly to demonstrate his willingness and ability to assist in evacuating Jews to the East—*ipso facto*, the death camps in Poland. Throughout German-occupied Europe he supported Eichmann's deportation teams in their efforts to round up and ship European Jews to extermination camps. (Thanks, to a prominent degree, to the new *RSHA* chief's "facilitation," deportations occurred during early 1943 from Greece and the Theresienstadt Ghetto in the German Protectorate of Bohemia and Moravia; in May from the Warsaw Ghetto; and in February 1944 from the Netherlands.)

His most spectacular, consistent efforts to accelerate the extermination of the Jews occurred in 1944 in Hungary, since late 1940 an ally of Germany. He and the *RSHA*, reflecting Hitler's personal wishes, aspired to annihilate the entire Jewish population—numbering seven hundred twenty-five thousand—on Hungarian territory. Primarily for that purpose, and to prevent Hungary from leaving the war as Italy had done, on March 19 Germany occupied Hungary and placed in power there a new government headed by the Germanophile prime minister General Döme Sztójay (convicted and shot in Budapest in 1946). Three days later, Kaltenbrunner met with Sztójay in Budapest and persuaded him to cooperate in the "speediest solution" to the Jewish problem and in the deportations of Hungarian Jews for "labor purposes" to Auschwitz. At every opportunity he pressed for sending the largest possible number of Jews.

After completing his mission, Kaltenbrunner returned to Berlin. He left the details of the deportations to Eichmann and his *Kommando* in Budapest, but even then he was not left out of the loop. The *RSHA* chief received regular reports from his subordinates. The *RSHA* also helped to provide railroad cars and timetables for deportations of Hungarian Jews, which began in mid-May 1944. By the fall, the Germans had shipped over four hundred thousand Jews to Auschwitz, most of whom were gassed. Even as Soviet troops approached Budapest to liberate it from Nazi rule, Kaltenbrunner demanded further deportations of Jews.

As early as June 30, 1944, Kaltenbrunner had "demonstrated his powers of intervention in the deportations from Hungary."[60] That day he wrote the mayor of Vienna, *SS* General Hanns Blaschke, informing the latter that he, Kaltenbrunner, agreed to Blaschke's request, sent three weeks earlier, for Jewish labor for the Austrian capital. He had diverted, Kaltenbrunner said, four trainloads of Hungarian Jews—numbering twelve thousand—bound for Auschwitz to the labor camp at Strasshof near Vienna. Most aboard the transports could not work and would have to die. "Women unable to work and children of those Jews who are all kept in readiness for special action," Kaltenbrunner said, using another popular Nazi euphemism to express murder, "and therefore one day will be removed again, have to stay in the guarded camp also during the day."[61]

According to Raul Hilberg, the Hungarian Jews in Austria "were laid 'on ice.'" A new branch of Eichmann's *Kommando* in Vienna had jurisdiction over them: "They wore stars, were allowed to have no money, were not permitted to shop or to smoke, and were forced to work in industry for no wage. A thousand of the Jews died. A few were sent to Bergen-Belsen, a few to Auschwitz."[62]

Amen read into the IMT record the original copy of Kaltenbrunner's letter to Blaschke, signed by the *RSHA* chief with the intimate or familiar German greeting, "Yours [Dein] Kaltenbrunner." But immediately its author insisted: "That is not my signature. It is a signature either in ink or it is a facsimile, but it is not mine." Previously, however, Amen had collected samples of his signature that matched perfectly the one on the June 30, 1944 letter.

Not even Gilbert could persuade Kaltenbrunner of the incredulity of his defense. "Frankly," he told the defendant, "I doubt if many people can believe that you, as nominal Chief of the RSHA, had nothing to do with concentration camps and knew nothing about the whole mass murder program."

In a conversation with the psychologist following the *RSHA* chief's testimony, Kaltenbrunner protested, "You Americans . . . seem to think that our whole RSHA was nothing but an organized gang of criminals." When the psychologist agreed with that assessment, Kaltenbrunner proclaimed, "Then how can I defend myself against such prejudice?"[63]

He'd been a victim, he said, of others—of the dead Himmler, the assassinated Heydrich, and the missing Müller, on whom he blamed the Final Solution. In reality, Kaltenbrunner had opposed even Himmler when, in the fall of 1944, the *Reichsführer* ordered that the deportations of Hungary's remaining Jews be suspended. (This order was less an act of benevolence than a cynical opportunity Himmler acted on; he intended to use the Jews as bargaining chips with the Western Allies to secure his own safety.) But Kaltenbrunner still clung to his claims of "innocence." In Kaltenbrunner's memoirs written in prison for his children, Black finds "[m]ost remarkable . . . the absence of any guilt, remorse, or even reflection on the millions of innocent people who had been murdered by the regime that he served or who had died as a result of its policies."[64]

BEST: FROM SELF-IMPORTANCE TO SELF-PITY

The journey, under police guard, from Nuremberg to Copenhagen lasted eight days. On the way Werner Best spent time in prison cells in several north German cities. Amid it all, however, he remained full of eager—even happy—anticipation. He felt confident that, in Allied eyes, his recently completed testimony at the IMT had exonerated him—and possibly the defendants—of any wartime criminality.

Surely, he thought, on his arriving in the Danish capital, his police escort would place him as a privileged prisoner in the Tre Kroner fortress. Soon, following a nearly two-year separation from them, he'd see his wife and five children. (They'd lived since the war's end in a Danish internment camp.) Above all, considering his wartime "moderation," Best expected the Danes to release him quickly. They must recognize (so he viewed it) his heroism as the former Reich plenipotentiary, the highest-ranking German civilian official in wartime Denmark (though subordinated to the German foreign ministry), in saving the country of Hans Christian Andersen from much suffering and destruction or the effects of total war. Once freed, he imagined, grateful Danish officials would call him as a witness in trials of former Danish Nazi Party leaders, whom he had sidelined only because of his pragmatic tyranny.

But when he reached Copenhagen, his inflated sense of importance and fairy-tale outlook collapsed suddenly and completely. The police delivered him to the city's central prison and placed him in solitary confinement. Predictably, Best had another psychological breakdown. His resulting depression, which lasted for weeks, expressed itself often in hours-long, uncontrollable fits of crying.

The prison physician, Max Schmidt, met Best for the first time on March 12, 1947. A few days later, the doctor prescribed for the prisoner strong doses of psychiatric drugs. Best, when talking to Schmidt, complained bitterly about his incarceration, and especially about what he termed his captors' unjust and undeserved treatment of him. The doctor, describing their meetings, recorded in his diary: "He is full of self pity; one torments and tortures him. . . . He assured me while he cried that I was the only one who understands him, for which he was very thankful; but I have never been able to establish a deep personal contact with him."

Hoping to stabilize his patient's condition, the physician arranged for Best to meet his wife Hilde outside the prison, their first visit in two years. But the encounter produced the opposite of what Schmidt had intended:

> During the trip he [Best] cried, despite the bright sunshine, and complained that his wife was such a [physical] wreck to look at. His wife, on the contrary, had said nothing about her experiences in internment camps; she sat there peacefully, with a detached dignity and non-pushy confidence. Best, in contrast . . . cried during the entire visit, like he had been whipped. He clung to his scrap of paper on which he had written out everything that he wanted to say.[65]

Best's wife treated him coolly. She criticized his whiny attitude, his lack of toughness, and his willingness earlier to testify at Nuremberg. In the days after the meeting, he reacted to her disapproval with panic. His fits of crying intensified. He spent hours trying to justify himself to her. On April 7 he scribbled her a lengthy letter protesting that her "contempt is unjustified," particularly because he'd sat longer in postwar prison cells than nearly all the other former Nazi bigwigs he'd seen at Nuremberg. He even threatened in the letter to commit suicide and included a last testament. But on Schmidt's advice Werner never sent the letter.

Following the Bests' next meeting, which proceeded more smoothly, a determination seized him: he must convince her of his hardiness and hardness. "Tough and flexible like steel," he described himself in a letter to her that he, in fact, sent, henceforth promising to act honorably—"like a soldier serving his time."[66] But his resolve would be tested strenuously when the Danes indicted him.

8

Nuremberg

"King Frank"

He was a waffler. Rarely has a waffler acquired such designations as "decisive" or "courageous." But Hans Frank, a lawyer, did manage to collect like dead moths numerous honorific posts at the highest (Reich) levels of both the Nazi Party and government—in the process, his emaciated ego aspiring to the full swell of a bullfrog's throat.

Yet he was more than a man of mere titles. Much to the sorrow of Jews and Poles, he believed he was (like his Führer, with whom he spent his life hopelessly currying favor) a leader not to be denied—instead of just a waffler. After Hitler designated him in October 1939 governor general of a planned Nazi "reservation" or territory in central Poland for unwanted Polish Jews and Poles, Hans declared proudly his intent to name his new domain after the Vandals, ancient German barbarians. But Hitler bestowed a more utilitarian, institutional name: the Government General. Little did the world realize then that during the next six years of war and killing, the province Frank ruled would be the centerpiece of a new dark age descending on the earth, a land reduced to a vast, reeking cemetery. The Germans, in the words of Gerhard Weinberg, set about "wrecking the existing features of civilization the way the barbarian invasions had once snuffed out whatever advances had been made in the ancient Mediterranean world."[1]

Initially, the Government General served as a special Nazi category of exploited territory. There the Germans experimented with the most extreme policies for ruling occupied territories and for subjugating subject peoples. But by the end of 1941 and during 1942, it became the wretched dwelling place of four of the six Nazi death camps: first Belzec, and then Sobibor, Treblinka, and Maidanek.

HITLER'S LAWYER

Frank, the governer general, had first seen Hitler in Munich in January 1920 at a meeting at which Hitler spoke. Captivated by what Frank termed in his postwar prison memoirs, *In the Face of the Gallows* (*Im Angesicht des Galgens*), the "immense and irresistible power" of Hitler's speeches, the anti-Semitic and anti-Communist twenty-year-old law student (son of a disbarred lawyer and swindler of older, affluent women) joined the tiny German Workers' Party, later renamed the Nazi Party. In 1923 he entered the *SA*. He completed his law degree and participated a year later in Hitler's Beer Hall Putsch. By 1930, he was serving as the party's lawyer, defending in court both Hitler and many oft-violent Nazis.

Also in 1930, apparently in response to a threat of blackmail from a relative of Hitler alleging that he had a Jewish ancestor, the Führer entrusted Frank to research the former's family genealogy in nineteenth-century Styria, in the rural northwesterly part of Lower Austria, bordering on Bohemia. Frank discussed his findings in his postwar memoir. The lawyer's investigation, however, produced no surviving factual evidence of any such Jewish connection—only Frank's conjecture in his memoirs that "the father of Hitler . . . could have been a half Jew." Supposedly this had resulted from an affair involving Hitler's grandmother, Fraulein Maria Anna Schicklgruber, and the son of a well-to-do Jewish family, the Frankenbergers, in the town of Graz.[2] Or, according to Frank, who at times appeared confused in his account, perhaps Maria Anna had an affair with a Graz butcher, Leopold Frankenreiter. Also, letters were allegedly exchanged for years between Maria Anna and the Frankenbergers.

But, Frank said, Hitler claimed that he knew from talking with his father, Alois, and grandmother that his grandfather had not been the Jew from Graz. Only one certainty resulted from Frank's inquiry: the illegitimacy of Hitler's father. Most likely, the latter was the child of a mill worker and non-Jew, Johann Georg Hiedler, a second cousin of Fraulein Schicklgruber. Five years after the birth of the child, Johann married her and legitimized her son. Later, Adolf's father changed his name from Hiedler to Hitler.

Frank's story—hinting at the possibility, despite having no proof, that Hitler had a "half" Jewish father—gained considerable attention after World War II. "But," Hitler's most definitive biographer, British historian Ian Kershaw, concludes, "it simply does not stand up":

> There was no Jewish family called Frankenberger in Graz during the 1830s. In fact, there were no Jews at all in the whole of Styria at the time, since Jews were not permitted in that part of Austria until the 1860s. A family named

> Frankenberger did live there, but was not Jewish. There is no evidence that Maria was ever in Graz. . . . No correspondence between Maria Anna and a family called Frankenberg [*sic*] or Frankenreiter has ever turned up. . . . Equally lacking in credibility is Frank's comment that Hitler had learnt from his grandmother that there was no truth in the Graz story: his grandmother had been dead for over forty years at the time of Hitler's birth.[3]

Following the Nazi seizure of power in Germany in 1933, Hitler named Frank not only a *Reichsleiter* in the party but also the Bavarian minister of justice and in 1934 Reich minister without portfolio. In addition, Frank served as president of the Academy of German Law, a self-created, self-aggrandizing organization in which he sought to reformulate German law on the basis of National Socialist political and racial principles.

But the minister-lawyer, according to his British biographer, Martyn Housden, "showed such commitment to legal formalism that fateful conflicts soon arose with some of the most important centres of power in the Reich."[4] Frank clashed with Himmler over killings by *SS* men in Aschaffenburg and over the murder at Dachau of three prisoners by *SS* guards. In June 1934, during the Night of Long Knives and the brief imprisonment of *SA* leaders, including their commander Ernst Röhm, before their executions, Frank even challenged Hitler—who had ordered the purge—by opposing the killings. In the end Hitler threatened Frank with the fate of the *SA* leaders, whereupon the minister-lawyer retreated from his stalwart stand and the *SS* shot Röhm and his subordinates. It was not the first time, certainly, and it certainly wouldn't be the last time that his resolve crumbled.

While he held Nazi posts with flowery and formidable-sounding titles, Frank had little influence on Hitler, his closest associates, or the development of policy. One of the ironies in this Nazi lawyer's career was that he entrusted his fate to the Führer, who mistrusted and despised both the law and lawyers, preferring that Himmler and the *SS* "make" the law. By 1936, the *Reichsführer SS* headed the German police and controlled the concentration camps; gradually, the police accumulated such extensive powers of arrest and imprisonment that German courts of law could almost never conduct formal reviews of it or limit its activities.

THE "BUTCHER OF POLAND"

Only when Hitler appointed Frank governor general in Poland at the start of World War II did Hans assume political importance (not to mention an official limousine, a Mercedes, and a private railroad car) and begin accruing the crimes for which he'd be tried and executed at Nuremberg. Immediately he established his residence in the southern Polish city of Krakow, in the huge

Wawel castle that had served as the home of Polish kings from the ninth to the eighteenth centuries. The city served also as the Government General's capital.

He wrote with excitement to his wife, "Brigitte, you are going to be the queen of Poland. . . . The Burg [castle] is marvelous, Gold on the windows and in all of the rooms, the art treasures—enormous."[5] It also wasn't far from the Krakow Ghetto and the more distant but still discernible Plaszow concentration camp. In fact, Jewish workers labored at Wawel until they were dragged away and gassed—with or without Frank's consent is unclear, but every interpretation leaves the almighty governor general looking either a little more impotent or a lot less human.

Frank lived like a king himself, plundering—in collusion with his wife, whom he had married in 1925 and, despite their oft-embittered marriage, who bore him five children—artwork and other treasures. This included seizing for himself the Black Madonna of Czestochowa, Leonardo da Vinci's *Lady with an Ermine*, a Rembrandt, and a portrait of a young man by Raphael (lost to this day), as well as other precious items from Polish Jews and Poles, whom the Germans deported into the Government General by the hundreds of thousands from Polish lands to the north and west that Germany had annexed.

Brigitte, accompanied by *SS* men, raided ghettos, stealing furs, jewelry, other valuables, and foodstuffs. For a time, the Franks established a fur warehouse, where they sold the contents at bargain prices. Frank, who dealt also with swindlers and black marketers, sold much of the plundered goods in Germany and elsewhere for immense profits. Moreover, he shipped food and property to his private estate in southern Germany. Not surprisingly, his income increased enormously, as did the frequency of his deposits into his personal bank account in Munich. But the governor general's undisguised avarice and corruption would eventually catch the attention of Himmler, his major political rival, who sought Frank's removal from his post.

Frank had stressed to his underlings in his usual patronizing, pontificating tone that the Germans must reassure the Poles that if they behaved, they would have nothing to fear. But the Polish people had a great deal to fear. Frank was a racist and anti-Semite; for him, the Poles ranked only slightly higher than the Jews in his hierarchy of alleged subhumanity. The Germans had designated the expanse of their country as an enormous area for ruthless experimentation in how best to subjugate and exploit the "inferior" Slavs and to eliminate Jews of all nations. During 1939 and 1940 the Nazis used the Government General as a dumping ground for the alleged racially inferior, forcing the Jews into overcrowded and disease-ridden ghettos, where they were compelled to labor for the German war economy.

While many of his victims starved and died or were killed randomly by the *SS* and German police, "King Frank"—or the "Butcher of Poland" as many would also call him—threw lavish banquets and feasts at the castle for his friends and political subordinates. A skilled pianist, the new "monarch" often entertained his guests by playing Chopin; behind the grand piano the plundered sixteenth-century "masterfully carved wooden statue" known as the Beautiful Madonna presided involuntarily.

Frank, his biographer has written, "did not take a good photograph. The impression he made face-to-face could be appropriately negative."[6] His pale face, swollen cheeks, hooked nose, and black, shiny, receding hair made him look variously childish, senile, and vain. His own son Niklas, a toddler at the time, would later recall his despised father's face as porcine and bat-like. Despite the many public speeches he gave during his political career, his voice remained shaky, and he talked often in sound bites to make a good impression.

While juggling party intrigues, a less-than-happy marriage, and numerous affairs (from a Polish countess to the Polish help), Frank pursued two principal aims in the Government General: produce (and maintain) a position of power for himself and secure Hitler's favor. But in both cases, he fell significantly short of his ambitions. Much like Alfred Rosenberg in German-occupied Russia (the subject of chapter 9), Hans found his civilian authority in his domain subordinated to the powerful Himmler, specifically to the latter's local *SS* and police leader, *SS* Lieutenant General Friedrich Wilhelm Krüger. (He would commit suicide on May 9, 1945, a day after Germany's surrender; having overseen in the Government General the liquidation of the ghettos, the extermination camps where 1,700,000 perished, and the expulsion of 110,000 Poles, it was unlikely that he would've been spared the gallows.)

Frank succeeded in limiting the *Wehrmacht*'s influence, in establishing an understanding with Hermann Göring for close cooperation on the economic exploitation and plundering of Polish Jews and Poles, and in wriggling out of Himmler and Martin Bormann's (Hitler's deputy Führer of the party) efforts to ensnare and depose him on charges of corruption. But his efforts to issue orders to the often-murderous *SS* and police—which had Hitler's backing—failed.

Consequently, directives from Hitler and Frank's rivalry with Himmler led the governor general to veer increasingly in the direction of a brutal and destructive policy toward the nearly three million Polish Jews, many of whom the Nazis deported to and ghettoized in his territory. As shown in the following pages, he assisted the steadily growing Jewish persecution and, by late 1941, the implementation of the Final Solution. He objected not because of what was being done in his dominion, but rather because he wasn't always kept in the genocidal loop and consulted. The Holocaust affronted his ego, not his ethics.

During late 1939 and early 1940, the *SS* planned and began carrying out the first deportations of Poles and Jews to the Government General from the Reich and areas of western Poland newly annexed to Germany. The placing of Jewish deportees in the first ghettos in the Government General, especially near Lublin, happened under miserable and subhuman conditions such that during the first six months "some 30 per cent of those transported had died."[7]

Frank promulgated decrees aimed at exploiting both the property and labor of the Jews while excluding them from normal economic life. He despised the Jews the most, whom he referred to as "lice," "human vermin," and "mincemeat." On November 25, 1939, he exhorted his administrators in the Government General at a meeting in Radom: "Make short work of the Jews. What a pleasure, finally for once to be able to tackle the Jewish race physically. The more that die, the better."[8] On December 1 he marked all Jews ten and older by compelling them to wear yellow stars on the right sleeves of their outer and inner clothing.

But during the spring of 1940, because of massive overcrowding and chaotic conditions in the Government General, of complaints of such by Frank, and of pressures placed by the deportations on the transport systems moving German troops in Western Europe, Göring, Hitler's head of the war economy, suspended deportations of Jews into the territory. The Nazi idea of the Government General becoming a "reservation" for all Jews under German control had proved impractical.

During the summer and fall of 1940, the governor general and Krüger—along with many Nazi bigwigs such as Eichmann in Berlin—supported a plan to deport all of Europe's Jews, including those in the Government General, to the French island of Madagascar. But the so-called Madagascar Plan to solve the "Jewish question" proved wholly unrealistic and, if ever implemented, disastrous and deadly for the Jews in question.

Meanwhile, deportations of Jews and other "undesirables" to the Government General resumed. In early October 1940, Nazi leaders in Vienna and East Prussia asked Frank to take fifty thousand Jews from their local regions into the Government General. Frank refused, but Hitler held the view that "it is irrelevant how large the population in the General Government is."[9] The Führer planned to deport more Jews and Poles into the Government General from the western Polish territories annexed by Germany to make room for the resettlement in the territories of ethnic Germans from Romania and the Soviet Union.

At the end of 1940, Hitler resolved an argument between Nazi Party leaders in East Prussia and Danzig-West Prussia, both of whom demanded the removal of Jews from their areas. Some forty-eight thousand more former Polish citizens, Jews and non-Jews, were deported into the Government General from East Prussia, West Prussia, and Upper Silesia. A short while later, other large-scale deportations began into Frank's domain.

Frank now felt increased pressures of overcrowding, chaos, and hunger at the arrival of more of the despised and unwanted. On March 26, 1941, he claimed that Hitler had agreed recently that the "General Government would be the first area to be made free of Jews." But that was only a long-term goal of the Nazi hierarchy, which Frank apparently recognized. That same day he spoke of Hitler's determination "within the next 15 or 20 years to make the General Government a purely German land."[10] Also Frank stressed the importance of the forced-labor groups of Poles and Jews to the German war economy. Simultaneously, he worked on construction of the large ghetto in Warsaw.

Shortly before the German attack on the Soviet Union, Frank told the Nazi propaganda minister Goebbels, "[I]n the General Government they are already looking forward to being able to get rid of the Jews." On June 19, Hitler gave Frank assurance that in the near future, the Jews would be removed from the Government General, turning it into "transit camps."[11] During the previous months, the highest echelons of the Nazi leadership had concluded that, in some shape or form, large deportations of Jews "to the East," including apparently from Poland, would accompany the planned invasion of Russia.

The massive assault on the Soviet Union began on June 22, as did the Hitler-mandated use behind the frontlines of *Einsatzgruppen* to kill as many of the several million Soviet Jews as possible. The seemingly successful campaign provided the ultimate impetus for Hitler, Himmler, Heydrich, and Göring to move toward adopting the most radical of measures to deal with the vastly increasing number of Jews now falling under German control: the Final Solution.

On August 1, Hitler joined Eastern Galicia, a portion of Poland under Soviet rule since October 1939 and overrun by the *Wehrmacht* on its way into Russia, to Frank's Government General. This added another five hundred thousand Jews to those already under his and Krüger's "benevolent" rule. *Einsatzgruppe* C, sweeping through Galicia, carried out mass executions of local Jews en route to the Ukraine.

According to historian Christopher Browning, "The notion of killing Jews in the General Government struck a responsive chord among Frank's men, who felt beleaguered on a number of fronts at this momentum."[12] Frank joined other Nazi officials in complaining even more sharply to Hitler and Himmler about the overcrowding of their territories with Jews. He reminded Hitler of the Führer's recent permission to deport Jews from the Government General.

To provide a kind of "Jewish reservation" for such deportees, he pressed—unsuccessfully—Hitler's chancellery in Berlin for Germany to annex land farther east in Byelorussia, including the Pripet Marshes and area around Bialystok. In the region Frank proposed for annexation, thousands of its indigenous Jews were being murdered—"cleansed"—by *Einsatzgruppe* B and other mobile killing units. On July 22, Frank mentioned again—this time in his diary—Hitler's recent approval for deportation of Jews from the Government General and announced that the "clearance" of the Warsaw Ghetto would be ordered soon.

But on October 17, 1941, Frank met in the Government General's city of Lublin with *SS* Major General and Lieutenant General of Police Odilo Globocnik, Himmler's highest-ranking official in the territory. During the meeting Frank learned that Hitler had approved clearing all nonworking Jews out of the Lublin district and sending them "over the Bug River," which formed part of the eastern boundary of the Government General with the German-occupied Soviet territories.

Browning concludes about the significance of such developments: "Moreover, Frank obviously realized that the alleged deportation over the Bug was a euphemism for killing, since he had no intention of deporting Jews into the district of Galicia and he knew that deportations to Rosenberg's territories [to the east in the Soviet Union] were foreclosed." Four days before, Rosenberg had told Frank personally that there was no possibility for the "Jewish population of the General Government [to] be [deported] to the occupied Eastern territories."[13] From that moment on, Peter Longerich concludes, Frank and his subordinate officials began to think about a Final Solution of the "Jewish question" in the Government General.

By then—if not before, as some historians have argued—Hitler had decided on the total physical destruction of European Jewry—and on its beginning soon—in the East. In a meeting on October 13 with Globocnik and Krüger, Himmler must have informed them of his and the Führer's decision to kill Jews by gassing them—a proposal proffered to Eichmann by Christian Wirth, a former Stuttgart policeman and key figure in the Nazi murder by gas of euthanasia victims. Globocnik likely received at the meeting the assignment to build the Belzec extermination camp. Simultaneously—as noted in chapters 2, 6, and 7—other Nazi officials in Berlin and the East were experimenting with mobile gas vans as killing chambers.

Four days later, after meeting with Globocnik on October 17, Frank knew the *real* meaning of the phrase "over the Bug." Between October 14 and 21, he held a series of meetings with his district administrators in Warsaw, Lublin (where he conferred with Globocnik), Radom, Krakow, and Lemberg (Lvov). The meetings contributed to the growing radicalization of Jewish policy in the Government General.

In Lublin, the death penalty was introduced for Jews who left the local ghetto, effectively launching a manhunt for Jews living outside it. A decision also directed that initially "1,000 Jews [were to be] moved across the Bug." In Krakow, it was decided "that an ultimately radical solution to the Jewish Question was unavoidable, and that no allowances of any kind . . . could be made." The head of the health office in the Government General summarized the attitude of King Frank and the region's German ruling class: "There are only two ways: we condemn the Jews in the ghetto to death by starvation or we shoot them."[14]

But there was also another way.

Soon, within the Government General, construction began on gas chambers at Belzec, while *SS* officials explored a site at Sobibor for the same purpose. Just outside the Government General, to the west, the Germans made preparations at Chelmno to begin gassing tens of thousands of Jews from the nearby Lodz Ghetto.

On December 12, 1941, Frank attended a meeting in Berlin with Hitler and the party's national and district leaders, including Rosenberg. During the gathering the Führer made clear that the Final Solution would begin in the spring of 1942. Also, apparently Frank learned that no Jews would be deported from the Government General. At almost the same time, he heard from Heydrich that the latter was inviting most government agencies, including the Government General, to send representatives to a meeting on the "Jewish question" he'd called for January 1942 at a villa on the Wannsee in Berlin.

Frank returned to the Government General and on December 16 addressed his subordinate officials. He repeated to them what he'd heard in Berlin from Hitler and Heydrich, namely, that few, if any, Jews would be deported from the Government General. With this in mind, he informed his listeners, "As far as the Jews are concerned, I want to tell you quite frankly, that they must be done away with in one way or another. . . . We must annihilate the Jews, wherever we find them and wherever it is possible."

He mentioned the forthcoming meeting called by Heydrich for January 1942, the result of which, he said, would be "[a] great Jewish migration." What should be done with the Jews? Berlin, he said, had instructed him, "So, liquidate them yourself." Frank then discussed the large numbers of Jews in his territory:

> The Jews represent for us also extraordinarily malignant gluttons. We now have approximately 2,500,000 of them in the Government General, perhaps with the Jewish mixtures and everything that goes with it, 3,500,000 Jews. We cannot shoot or poison [as the *SS* was preparing to do] those 3,500,000 Jews; but we shall nevertheless be able to take measures which will lead, somehow, to their annihilation, and this in connection with the gigantic measures to be determined in discussions with the Reich. The Government General must become

free of Jews, the same as the Reich. Where and how this is to be achieved is a matter for the offices which we must appoint and create here.[15]

Longerich has claimed that Frank's remarks, while they indicated "the method and time-frame for this mass murder were still undecided," illustrated that "the leadership of the General Government" had decided "to achieve" exterminating the victims soon.[16] Browning concluded that "Frank at least knew from his conversations in Berlin" that the conference—of representatives from government agencies—called by Heydrich for the next month would "deal with a problem implicit in Hitler's speech, namely, how the Jews were to be killed."[17]

Frank's state secretary in the Government General, Dr. Josef Bühler, attended the Wannsee Conference on January 20, 1942. (Sending a subordinate to such a meeting only fortified one's deniability of knowledge of mass murder, if such an approach became desirable later.) According to the official minutes of the meeting prepared by Heydrich and Eichmann, and not surprising given the view of Frank and others that soon they should begin exterminating Jews in the Government General, Bühler urged that the Final Solution begin in his territory "as soon as possible." The 2.5 million Jews in the Government General, he said, were overwhelmingly "unfit for work."[18] Clearly, he proposed that the majority of the Jews in the Government General should be murdered within the territory itself.

On March 5, 1942, Himmler met with Frank in the *Reichsführer*'s private train at Hitler's headquarters. Also present were the head of the Führer's chancellery, Hans Lammers, and Bormann, to ensure that the governor general wouldn't impede or block either the death-camp killings scheduled in the Government General or the seizure by the *SS* of the belongings of dead Jews. With the help of Lammers and Bormann, Himmler used an ongoing *SS* investigation into the rampant corruption of King Frank and his administration to persuade him to agree to improve the relationship between the *SS* and Government General, not to mention its efficiency. The *SS* and police assumed authority over all of the territory's security and resettlement issues (including, especially, all Jewish affairs).

King Frank crumbled quickly and consented to even greater *SS* authority in the Government General. His vision of unified power and the annihilation of the Jews under his own hand in Poland vanished, a victim of his weakness, cowardice, and fear. The outcome of his surrender? The authority of the *SS* had grown decisively over that of Frank's civil administration. Only a few days later, massive gassing began in the Government General—killings not under Frank's direction, as he preferred, but controlled by others.

During the subsequent action code-named by the *SS* "Operation Reinhard"—after Heydrich, who had died on June 6, 1942, assassinated by the Czech government-in-exile and members of its resistance—nearly three million Polish Jews perished. The *SS* and police cleared the ghettos and deported the victims for gassing from throughout the Government General: beginning in March 1942 to Belzec, in the easternmost part of the territory; in July to Sobibor, east of Lublin, and to Treblinka, northeast of Warsaw; and in the fall to Maidanek, adjacent to Lublin. Just outside the Government General, in Upper Silesia, Auschwitz began operation, murdering Jews deported there from all over Europe; Chelmno also started mass gassings. Meanwhile, throughout 1942 and 1943, the *Einsatzgruppen* and other mobile *SS* and police units continued in routine fashion to kill every Jew they could in the Soviet Union.

The Final Solution raged furiously—much of it in Frank's Government General. A substantial majority of the Polish Jews died during 1942, many amid the inhuman clearing of the ghettos (what the Germans termed *Aktionen*) that, according to Longerich, represented "the largest single murder campaign within the Holocaust":

> The effectiveness of the [clearing] campaigns themselves was based on the element of surprise and calculated terror, designed to throw the population of the ghetto into a panic and prevent any resistance. The Jewish councils [an internal ghetto administration] were informed a short time before the imminent "resettlement," and the Jewish police were forced to help drag the people from the houses, usually in the early hours of the morning. If the clearing of a ghetto lasted days or even weeks, an attempt was made to conceal the planned extent of the overall operation and cover the ghetto with a series of shock operations. . . .
>
> Throughout the entire process people who hid or failed to follow instructions were shot, but also often murdered on an utter whim. After the execution of the "actions" the streets of the ghettos were often scattered with corpses.[19]

On May 18, 1942, Frank confronted his wife and confessed the most gruesome things to her, but he didn't do so out of remorse. Rather, he used the extermination of Jews as a ploy to seek a divorce from her under the gallant guise of protecting her and the children from the inevitable fallout. Furthermore, he had just begun a passionate affair in Munich with a former sweetheart from his days as a youth. But Brigitte refused his noble offer.

Some three months later, on August 1, 1942, he gave a speech in Lvov, the capital of Galicia, commemorating the annexation of the region to the Government General a year earlier. Then on August 24, he met with his administrators from throughout the Government General, during which he discussed policies designed and adopted by his regime to deprive the territory's remaining Jews of the most basic necessity of life—food. Not only did he note the hunger rations introduced into the Warsaw Ghetto, but he also referred to new food regulations implemented throughout the Government

General, none of which improved the devastating situation for the Jews still there in ghettos or for many Poles.

Callously—and doubtless casually and with pride—he declared that the regulations condemned more than one million Jews to death: "That we sentence 1,200,000 Jews to die of hunger should be noted only marginally. It is a matter of course that should the Jews not starve to death it would, we hope, result in a speeding up of the anti-Jewish measures."[20] Such "measures" could only have meant those carried out in the death camps and by the *Einsatzgruppen*.

And they *were* "speeding up," as were the intrigues of Himmler and Krüger, who with scorn ridiculed Frank's repeated and failed vacillation with them and likened him to a jumping jack. In late November, because of their encroachment and interference, Frank proffered his resignation (as he had done on occasion before) to Hitler, who refused it.

On January 25, 1943, at a conference in Warsaw of his civilian administrators as well as of Globocnik, Krüger, and other cold-blooded officials, Frank listened as Krüger, who also served as Frank's chief of security, reported, "In colonizing this territory with racial Germans, we are forced to chase out the Poles. . . . The Poles say: After the Jews have been destroyed then they [the Germans] will employ the same methods to get the Poles out of this territory and liquidate them just like the Jews."

Frank closed the meeting by commenting on the devastating blow to the Germans in the war—deep inside the Soviet Union, their decimated Sixth Army was about to surrender at Stalingrad. He issued a warning to his listeners:

> The situation of the Reich is presently very serious and decisive. The war is beginning to become hard and show its seriousness. . . . We are now duty bound to hold together. Everyone must show understanding for others, [and] he must be convinced that he is doing his best. . . . We must remember that we who are gathered together here figure on Mr. Roosevelt's list of war criminals. I have the honor of being Number One. We have, so to speak, become accomplices in the world historic sense.[21]

Clearly, Frank knew he was a war criminal or at least a major accessory to mass murder. His remarks likely reflected as well the Western Allies' announcement a few days earlier of "unconditional surrender," issued at the Anglo-American conference at Casablanca, by Prime Minister Winston Churchill and President Franklin Roosevelt. The declaration stated that the Western Allies would conclude no separate peace with such a criminal regime as the one ruling in Berlin. Frank's words on January 25—in the face of a decisive looming German defeat in the Soviet Union—encouraged the recognition and sustenance of Germany's ongoing policy toward the Jews.

Having committed horrific crimes, Frank and his underlings had little choice but to cling to the prolonging of the war and to Hitler's genocidal plan to kill as many Jews as possible within the shortest possible period of time. If the Führer's racial war succeeded, there would be (ideally) no survivors to condemn them.

To this end, the Nazis were intent, as Frank had said, on speeding it up. By early 1943, nearly 80 percent of all Holocaust victims had already died. As for the Government General, Frank observed in July 1943 that while the territory once had nearly 3,500,000 Jews, a mere 203,000 were left. In large part for this reason, unbeknownst to Frank, he was rapidly becoming obsolete.

His conflicts with Himmler continued, and Hitler—who supported the *Reichsführer*—removed Frank from all his party offices and banned him from public speaking. Yet in his typical fashion, the Führer pursued a policy of divide and rule among his lieutenants. He allowed the ongoing, interloping agencies to go on interloping, while reaffirming Frank as governor general. (For multiple reasons, he even rejected another of Frank's half-hearted attempts to resign his post.)

In March 1943, Hitler even talked about Frank with Goebbels. The propaganda minister recorded the exchange in his diary, discovered and published after the war:

> The Fuehrer no longer has any respect for him [Frank]. I argued with the Fuehrer, however, that he must either replace Frank or restore his authority. . . . Added to everything else Frank has an unfortunate divorce matter on his hands in connection with which he is behaving in a way that is not exactly noble. The Fuehrer refused to let him get a divorce. This, too, serves to play havoc with the Fuehrer's relationship to Frank. Nevertheless he wants to receive him within the next few days to determine whether he can still be saved, and if so, to strengthen his authority once more. Frank is not acting properly in this whole situation. He vacillates between brusque outbursts of anger and a sort of spiritual self-mortification. That's no way, of course, to lead a people.[22]

Frank the "waffler," therefore, still remained in his post in Krakow. Despite his conflict with the *SS*, he continued in the massacre of the Jews to consent and contribute to the wishes of both Hitler and Himmler. Housden emphasizes about Frank that in his many speeches to his administrators, in which he repeatedly "denigrated the worth of Jews," he

> led the Government General by example and made it much easier for his staff to accept and adopt similar values. Hans Frank helps us understand how bureaucrats in the East managed to avoid asking questions, evaded feelings of guilt and lived with what was happening around them. He was creating a consensus for annihilation.[23]

His active support, including implementing policies that resulted in the deaths of tens of thousands of Jews by starvation, helped render the immoral—worse, the amoral—possible and the resulting human cost incalculable. Speaking to lawyers in Berlin in April 1942, Frank made "brazenly clear that Jews had to vanish completely from the Reich."[24]

The huge revolt during April and May 1943 in the Warsaw Ghetto and similar uprisings at Treblinka (August 2) and Sobibor (October 14) only served to confirm to the Nazis the supposed Jewish threat to them and Germany. Frank met on October 19, 1943, with *SS* and *SD* leaders and told them that the Jewish camps had become an acute danger for the security of the Germans. Obviously, Hitler and Himmler agreed because the *SS* swiftly shut down Treblinka and Sobibor as well as various forced-labor camps in the Government General. During November 3–4, 1943, some two thousand to three thousand *Waffen-SS* and police troops from the Government General and Reich, as well as a special detachment from Auschwitz, killed forty-two thousand Jews—primarily in three labor camps in the Lublin area.

Also that same month, following a decree issued by Frank himself, the *SS* dismantled a concentration camp filled with Jews in the Krakow district and deported its inhabitants to Auschwitz or, for those inexplicably "blessed," to the Plaszow forced-labor camp on the outskirts of Krakow. At Plaszow the *SS* regularly carried out mass executions three to four times per week.

On January 25, 1944, Frank confided to a secret press conference: "At the present time we still have in the Government General perhaps 100,000 Jews." Nearly 98 percent of Polish Jews had been made "to disappear," words Frank had used three years earlier amid the planning phase for the Final Solution.[25] Although apparently he hadn't visited the death camps in his territory or at Auschwitz (as he claimed later at his war crimes trial), he knew about them. How much firsthand information he had about what was in fact happening in the camps is unclear. But according to Housden, Frank "knew well enough that annihilation was becoming a reality."

Four days later, on the evening of January 29, 1944, while he traveled in his private railroad car for Lvov, the Polish Home Army finally caught up with Frank. It was a bold assassination attempt (several months before German officers and anti-Nazi opponents tried to assassinate Hitler at his military headquarters in East Prussia) that involved detonating explosives on the railroad track and firing weapons at the train itself. The "King of Poland" was deeply unsettled by the attempt on his life at a time when he was trying to bring the Poles to the side of the German cause.

He had urged in Berlin the German adoption of a new Polish policy, aimed at improving the treatment of Poles to encourage their forced labor and "productivity" of food for the Reich. Was his belated "beneficence" toward the Poles because he feared increasingly the possibility of war crimes trials for him and other leading Nazis? He had never offered during the war a "new policy" for the Polish Jews.

Despite Frank's major role in helping implement the Holocaust, likely the principal reason Hitler had unleashed the world war, the governor general last met with the Führer on February 6, 1944, some fifteen months before the war's end in Europe. With the conflict turning against Germany and its allies, with nearly all of Poland's Jews dead, and with the huge death camps in the Government General dismantled (except for Maidanek outside Lublin, which the Russians liberated in July 1944), the Führer had no more time for his loyal underling. King Frank had served his master's principal mission in the war. As such, he could be discarded—and was. The waffler was on his own.

In Housden's words, Frank's story is "about how an individual becomes corrupted." How did it happen? He cites Frank's "obedience to a charismatic Führer" and "an acceptance of anti-Semitism." But not least, Frank dealt in genocide because

> his position dictated it. He was the self-important Governor General who wanted to lead his territory to a place in the history books and who wished to control every aspect of what went on there. The Holocaust was part of the deal. Although a unique policy, it was [in his ambition] just another aspect of Nazi politics. . . . Once Frank understood what was expected, he took up the initiative as his own. He was not dragged to crime kicking and screaming; he was prepared to buy into it with innovation and ingenuity.[26]

CAPTURE IN GERMANY

His German "monarchy" in Poland came to a quick and informal end. On January 17, 1945, with Soviet troops advancing from the east and nearly surrounding Krakow, even penetrating its northern suburbs, Frank prepared to evacuate the city with his staff to Germany. He hated to leave what he believed was his personal "imperium."

As recounted in his bombastic memoirs, written while he stood trial later at Nuremberg, during his final moments in "his" castle he stood alone in the large coronation hall of the Polish kings of centuries earlier. What a splendid view of the wonderful old city, he thought to himself as he walked under the castle's dome and descended into its vault. The latter contained the graves of the former sovereigns. Full of vainglory and nihilism, he counted himself their modern heir.

Meanwhile, outside the castle, his minions were busy incinerating incriminating records and transforming them into great quantities of black smoke and ash. To have ordered such a destruction of records was not merely a matter of protocol but a subtle admission from Frank that certain documents couldn't survive the war without condemning him.

Soon he departed the castle and Krakow in a convoy of automobiles carrying some twenty-five people. He traveled northwest, crossed into the Silesian portion of eastern Germany, and settled for a few days in a small castle near Breslau. With the Red Army in rapid pursuit behind them, he and several subordinates burned most of the remaining official papers they'd brought with them from Krakow—but not the huge official diary he'd kept while governor general, the vast documentation of his criminality and culpability. Ironically, and revealing both his arrogance and obtuseness, he thought his official diary might one day exonerate him.

On January 23, Frank and his small entourage headed south to Bavaria, visiting briefly Bad Aibling, presumably so he could see his mistress. Then they stopped in Neuhaus am Schliersee and established in a local restaurant (a far cry from Wawel castle) a new headquarters for the grand, now-nonexistent Government General. He contacted Hitler's chancellery in Berlin, informing it that he stood ready to serve the Führer once again—but by then the contact had little to do with reality except that the episode illustrated Frank's die-hard dedication to Hitler—to the bitter end.

On May 4, three days before Germany's surrender in the war, Lieutenant Stein, a soldier of the U.S. Seventh Army, which had overrun Bavaria, showed up at the café headquarters of the Government General in Bavaria—the authority of which reached no farther than the surrounding two hundred square meters. He called out, "Which one of you is Frank?" Such were the less-than-distinctive features of a less-than-distinguished career. (Even the burned body of an archvillain like Goebbels was identifiable despite its blackened, shriveled form.)

But not Frank. The former German "king" of Poland had to say, "I am," at which point Stein announced, "You're coming with me," and arrested him unceremoniously.[27] Having realized since 1943 that the Allies viewed him as a war criminal and now trying, possibly, to gain his captors' favor, Hans turned over to them his official and massive diary, comprising some three dozen volumes and totaling eleven thousand typewritten pages. These records—ironically—would help mightily to hang him at Nuremberg seventeen months later, though he foolishly thought their contents would give evidence of his championship of the Poles and his opposition to Himmler and exculpate him from his other more cowardly and cruel statements and acts.

The Americans placed him in a prison in nearby Miesbach, where he was forced to run a seventy-foot gauntlet, during which Allied soldiers beat him. Seeing "the future as black and threatening," he twice attempted to take his own life. But army doctors did not abandon Frank; on each occasion they saved the prisoner. "I tried to commit suicide," he lamented later to U.S.

prison psychiatrist Leon Goldensohn, showing his self-pity, "because I sacrificed everything for Hitler. And that man whom we sacrificed everything for left us all alone."[28]

Soon he found himself transferred to a POW camp near Berchtesgaden and Hitler's former mountain retreat (he had visited the palatial residence often but now could see it only in the distance from behind barbed wire that enclosed the camp). Shortly thereafter, the army moved him again, this time to Mondorf-Les-Bain, a small town in Luxembourg; there he joined other senior Nazis held in a former luxury hotel converted to a prison (called "Ashcan" by the Allies).

On August 12, 1945, the Americans moved Hans and other major war criminals to Nuremberg to stand trial before the IMT. During one of his first interrogations, Frank professed ignorance of the former Nazi death camps in Poland (and elsewhere) and denied any responsibility for them. Although Auschwitz lay barely thirty miles from Krakow and his former castle residence, he claimed that he knew nothing of what had happened there. "One passed it on the train," Frank said, then added, "It was a huge camp. One could always see the barbed wire."

"Didn't you often also pass Maidanek?" asked the interrogator.

"I don't know about that. One passes a lot of things."[29]

He worried: would his captors find out the truth? (He still hadn't realized that the Allies *had* the truth of his complicity—courtesy of Frank himself: his official diary in which his statements, decrees, and views were so assiduously recorded for posterity.) Toward the end of the questioning and seeking to save himself, he blamed Himmler and even Hitler for murdering the Jews. And insisted on his own innocence.

TRIAL BY DIARY

Once imprisoned in his small—nine by thirteen feet—cell in Nuremberg, he made similar claims to other interrogators as well as to the prison psychologists and—most importantly—to the IMT. The tribunal received the general indictment of both the individuals and organizations declared criminal on October 20, 1945, and arraigned Frank on three charges: crimes against peace; crimes against humanity; and conspiracy to commit the "foregoing crimes."

His response to the indictment was a mix of the sanctimonious, subservient, and self-serving—all qualities that he'd exhibit throughout the trial: "I regard this trial as a God-willed world court, destined to examine and put to an end the terrible era of suffering under Adolf Hitler [an era in which Frank had been a prominent, ambitious, and willing accomplice]."[30]

For the next two months in the court, not much happened to Frank. He sat in the dock with crossed arms and wore large sunglasses; sometime during the trial he converted to Catholicism. But on December 13, in the morning session, the prosecution began to zero in on him. First, James Donovan, a member of the U.S. prosecution, showed the court a film, captured by U.S. troops near Augsburg, Germany, and recorded, he noted, "by a member of the SS." The movie, he told the court, offered "undeniable evidence made by Germans themselves, of almost incredible brutality to Jewish people in the custody of the Nazis, including German military units. . . . It is believed by the Prosecution that the scene is the extermination of a ghetto by Gestapo agents, assisted by military units."[31]

Frank twitched nervously. Ghetto? In his former territory? And one that "exterminated" and not merely "liquidated"? Amid a dramatic silence in the courtroom he and the other former Nazi bigwigs on trial watched the film. As he did so, he perspired more with every violent scene: German troops dragging old men and naked women out of houses—dead bodies strewn in the streets—an elderly woman pushed past the camera while a man in *SS* uniform watched.

Immediately following the film, matters worsened for Frank. Rising to address the tribunal, a U.S. assistant trial counsel, Major William Walsh, began presenting evidence of Germany's starvation and killing of Jews in Poland. Soon, he "turned to that fertile source of evidence," as he termed it—Frank's diary that the former governor general, expecting it would explain and exonerate him, had turned over to U.S. troops at his capture.

From the diary entry for December 16, 1941, Walsh read to the court much of the text of Frank's address to his staff that day, in which he used phrases such as the Jews "must be done away with in one way or another," "[t]hey must disappear," "[w]e must annihilate the Jews," and "liquidate them yourselves." The document, Walsh told the tribunal, indicated something significant: "The methods used to accomplish the annihilation of the Jewish people were varied and, although not subtle, were highly successful."[32]

The next morning, Walsh resumed his presentation and returned immediately to the diary. First, he discussed the use by the Germans of deliberate starvation as a major means "for the annihilation of the Jewish people." Introducing the diary's entry for August 24, 1942, he summarized Frank's speech to a conference of Government General administrators and *SS* officers and highlighted the passage in which Frank had noted that reducing food rations in the ghettos virtually condemned "1,200,000 Jews to die of hunger."

A bit later, after Walsh presented to the court the *SS* report on the violent crushing of the Warsaw Ghetto uprising in the spring of 1943, he referred again to Frank's diary. He noted from it Frank's estimate in his speech of

December 16, 1941, that between 2,500,000 and 3,500,000 Jews lived in the Government General. Walsh then turned to the diary's entry for January 25, 1944, and quoted Frank as writing that "perhaps 100,000 Jews" remained in the territory. Walsh commented about the comparison of the two entries: "In this period of 3 years, according to the records of the then Governor General of Occupied Poland, between 2,400,000 and 3,400,000 Jews had been eliminated."[33]

A moment later, providing yet another document regarding the total number of Jews killed by the Germans, the U.S. assistant prosecutor read from an affidavit of Dr. Wilhelm Hoettl, a former official in the *SD*, who quoted Eichmann as saying: "Approximately 4 million Jews had been killed in the various concentration camps, while an additional 2 million met death in other ways, the major part of which were shot by operational squads of the Security Police during the campaign against Russia."[34]

Thus, the death toll of Jews that prosecutors had provided to the IMT reached roughly six million. (The tribunal's indictment of both the accused individuals and six former Nazi organizations had placed the number slaughtered at 5,721,800.) For the dethroned "King Frank," being mentioned—in almost the same breath as Eichmann—had to cause him serious concern.

During an intermission the prison psychologist, Gustave Gilbert, asked Frank about "the cold-blooded statements in which he spoke of letting a million Jews starve." Frank responded that "he had made such statements in his days of blind Nazi fanaticism." But, obviously seeking to curry Gilbert's favor by asserting a disingenuous motivation for his strategic miscalculation, he added that he "had turned all his diaries and writings over to the American Military Government . . . so that the truth of the whole ugly episode could finally be brought to light, let the axe fall where it may."[35]

But in the courtroom—on December 13 and 14, 1945—the prosecution's presentations left Frank heavily incriminated. Back in court following the Christmas break, on January 10, 1946, Lieutenant Colonel William Baldwin, another assistant U.S. trial counsel, presented to the tribunal the prosecution's initial statement on Frank's accountability for the criminal actions of the Nazi regime. Baldwin emphasized the defendant's clashes with the *SS*, his mistreatment of Poles and Ukrainians, and his recruitment of them for slave labor for the German war economy. The prosecutor quoted from Frank's diary of January 14, 1944: "Once the war is won, then, for all I care, mincemeat can be made of the Poles and the Ukrainians and all the others who run around here; it doesn't matter what happens."[36]

In contrast, Baldwin spent only a few minutes on Frank's role in the "Jewish question." Like other prosecutors, he relied heavily—though not exclusively—on Frank's voluminous diary for evidence. He told the tribunal:

> These facts are from the diary of the man himself. . . . The supreme authority within a certain geographic area admits that in a period of 4 years' time up to 3,400,000 persons from that area have been annihilated pursuant to an official policy and for no crime, but only because of having been born a Jew. No words could possibly reveal the inferences of death and suffering which must need be drawn from these stark facts.[37]

In summarizing the prosecution's case against Frank, Baldwin said to the court: "As Governor General the Defendant Frank, we feel, must be held responsible for all concentration camps within the boundaries of the Government General. These include, among others, the notorious camp at Maidanek and the one at Lublin and at Treblinka outside of Warsaw." The U.S. assistant prosecutor concluded his presentation by using for a final time Frank's own words from the diary. He explained that on January 25, 1943, "prophetically enough" Frank had told subordinates they were doubtless "on Mr. Roosevelt's list of war criminals" and admitted that he was almost certainly "war criminal Number One."[38]

Frank took the stand on April 18, 1946. His testimony, his biographer observed, which lasted a half day, "fluctuated between emotional confessions of guilt (a characteristic which singled him out as unique among defendants) and weasel-words designed to deflect blame."[39]

The defendant's counsel, a young Munich attorney, Dr. Alfred Seidl, questioned his client: "Did you ever participate in the annihilation of Jews?" Frank's answer seemed at the moment a stunning confession of guilt, a singular rarity in the court. As he talked, everyone in the chambers listened intently, many shocked at what they heard, so shocked that his equivocations and qualifications about his "guilt" were easily overlooked:

> I say "yes" and the reason why I say "yes" is because, having lived through the 5 months of this trial, and particularly after having heard the testimony of the witness [Rudolf] Hoess [former *SS* commandant of Auschwitz], my conscience does not allow me to throw the responsibility solely on these minor people. I myself have never installed an extermination camp for Jews, or promoted the existence of such camps; but if Adolf Hitler personally has laid that dreadful responsibility on his people, then it is mine too, for we have fought against Jewry for years; and we have indulged in the most horrible utterances—my own diary bears witness against me. Therefore, it is no more than my duty to answer your questions in this connection with "yes." A thousand years will pass and still this guilt of Germany will not have been erased.[40]

That last seemingly noble utterance clicked with history's faulty and feeble memory, so much so that for many who are aware of the IMT and

Frank's role, his "admission" remains his defining moment—and not his later retraction. Telford Taylor, the chief U.S. prosecutor, would conclude in his memoirs: "Hans Frank admitted his guilt in his own way, but that was a long way from pleading guilty to the Indictment."[41]

Was it an admission of guilt or a defensive parry? And what, in fact, had Hans admitted or said "yes" to? How had he confessed to participating in the Holocaust? Only in two ways: by having "fought against Jewry for years" and by having "indulged in the most horrible utterances" against Jews, amply recorded in his diary—"my own diary bears witness against me"—the only totally accurate statement embedded within his four-sentence "confession." Otherwise, denials, distortions, and lies riddled his pronouncement. Guilty were Hitler, the *SS*, and Germany—but not him, not really.

Perhaps most damning of all, Frank's "speech" at the IMT was too busy playing hide the guilt to express either remorse for or a sense of the suffering inflicted on and endured by the persecuted and dead Jews and other Poles; sorrow for Germany was the only sentiment expressed. Once again, when it suited their purpose, the perpetrator and his passive-active supporters were in the foreground, playing the "victims" of Hitler and the *SS* who "laid that dreadful responsibility on" them. Such claims by perpetrators like Frank, seething with self-pity and who believed themselves victims at the hands of vengeful Jews and/or the Allies or even Hitler, doubtless influenced numerous postwar Holocaust deniers, who would make the same allegations.

During continued questioning by his counsel, Seidl, Frank denied that he had looted art treasures and libraries in the Government General. He admitted to having established ghettos and to forcing Jews to wear badges for identification and to do forced labor. When had he heard "for the first time about the concentration camp at Maidanek?" Frank replied, "[I]n 1944 from foreign reports." What did he know "of the conditions in Treblinka, Auschwitz, and other camps?" Again, he professed ignorance: "Auschwitz was not in the area of the Government General. I was never in Maidanek, nor in Treblinka, nor in Auschwitz." Much like he had claimed in interrogations before the trial, he insisted he had known nothing of the camps.

But during cross-examination, L. N. Smirnov, an assistant Soviet prosecutor, caught Hans in his lie. Smirnov showed the defendant a document presented by his own defense counsel—a report, compiled by Frank in June 1943 and addressed to Hitler. The report mentioned how the "Polish intelligentsia" held "against the Germans alleged similar cruelties, especially in Auschwitz." A couple of sentences later in the report, Frank had noted: "It is said that there are concentration camps at Auschwitz and Maidanek where likewise the mass murder of Poles is carried out systematically."

But hadn't Frank earlier, Smirnov queried him, testified that he had "heard of Maidanek only at the end of 1944?" In the communication to Hitler, dated

June 1943, he had "mentioned there both Maidanek and Auschwitz."[42] Frank tried to extricate himself from the snare by asserting that he had heard about the mass killings of the Poles at Maidanek in 1943 and of the Jews in 1944.

Also making Frank's alleged profession of guilt suspect was his response to the testimony before the tribunal three days earlier of Rudolf Höß, the commandant of Auschwitz from 1940–1943, about the gassing of Jews at the camp. Höß had appeared at the request of Ernst Kaltenbrunner's defense counsel.

Frank rationalized Höß's testimony by remarking afterward to fellow defendant Alfred Rosenberg that what had happened at the camp had been no worse than supposed Allied atrocities: "They are trying to pin the murder of 2,000 Jews a day in Auschwitz on Kaltenbrunner—but what about the 30,000 people who were killed in the bombing attacks on Hamburg in a few hours?—They were also mostly women and children.—And how about the 80,000 deaths from the atomic bombing in Japan?—Is that justice too?" Rosenberg laughed. "Yes, of course—because we lost the war."[43]

During the trial Frank wrote his memoirs, published in 1953 by his wife and promoted by her until her death in 1959. In the book's nearly four hundred pages, he spent barely five discussing the Holocaust. Regarding the killings, he insisted that he had known nothing during the war of the Final Solution and that he had had no authority over the Jews. The responsibility for their massacre fell on the dead Hitler and Himmler—especially Hitler, whose "blind rage as it became evident to him that the war could be lost, brought forth the ghastly plan for the extermination of the Jews." Without any factual evidence to support it, Frank even speculated that Hitler had done so because "it is not absolutely impossible that Hitler's father could have been half Jewish."[44]

Thus, with the eloquence of the waffler ("not absolutely impossible," "could have been") and with a grandiosity reminiscent of the Führer himself, he attempted (and, in part, succeeded) to out-Goebbels Goebbels—who merely imitated his Führer's death—by not just dying with Hitler but by explaining him while simultaneously indicting the Jews for their own near-annihilation. Much as he did at the trial, Frank confessed to nothing under the guise of confessing to several things: "I too was an anti-Semite. I joined the voices. I also carry a heavy guilt in the larger intellectual concept. I have assumed this guilt."[45]

Guilt as a "larger intellectual concept"? *Only* an anti-Semite? Really? Was that all? Many decades later, one of his sons, Niklas Frank, obviously ashamed of his father and infuriated by his life of corruption and cowardice, called him "a bloody footnote to the history of our times. . . . [A] nauseating mess." Bitterly but eloquently, the son acknowledged in his *In the Shadow of the Reich* (a mix of biography, memoirs, and scathing indictment) what Hans Frank never could or would: "My father was a criminal."[46]

9

Nuremberg

"Fred" the "Endowed Seer" and Verdicts and Sentences

He always overestimated himself. And now, at war's end, he suffered as well from delusions that he still held power and influence as a former high-level Nazi administrator. Recovering from a badly inflamed left ankle, he lay in a naval hospital in Flensburg, the city near the German-Danish border that served as the headquarters of Hitler's handpicked successor government (that had surrendered only a few days earlier). While there he wrote a letter to the commander of British forces occupying northwestern Germany, Field Marshal Bernard Montgomery. In the message, handed to a British officer, he placed himself at Montgomery's "disposal."

"I waited" for a response, he remembered later, "but nobody called for me."[1] Instead, after a week had passed, on May 18, 1945, British military police arrested him. Within a few days, his captors sent him by automobile to nearby Kiel and from there by plane to Luxembourg and an Allied prison.

"INNOCENT" IDEOLOGUE?

Even within the hierarchy of the Third Reich, Alfred Rosenberg's importance had always been far more official than actual. Hitler had conferred on him—one of the Führer's earliest mentors in the Nazi Party who became the semiofficial "philosopher" or ideologue of National Socialism—a host of formal (and bloated) titles (though the ever-humble Rosenberg preferred "The Father of National Socialist Literature"): Reich leader (*Reichsleiter*) in the Nazi Party; member of the *Reichstag*; chief of the party's "Foreign Policy Office"; "Commissioner of the Führer for Safeguarding the Entire Intellectual and Philosophical Instruction and Education of the National Socialist Party"; and, during the war, head of the "Special Staff of Reich Leader Rosenberg" and "Reich Minister for the Occupied Eastern Territories." Not bad for a failed architect, though the wartime honors, as hollow as all the others, would lead to Rosenberg's name being placed on the hangman's dance card. But, according to one historian: "In actual practice, he [Rosenberg] was elbowed aside" by his rivals in the party and government bureaucracy.[2]

Nevertheless, despite, and most likely because of, his lack of decisive efficacy, Rosenberg—or Fred, as friends called him affectionately and party rivals referred to him derisively—played a key role in the Holocaust. He not only helped to develop and disseminate the National Socialist ideology of racial hatred and anti-Semitism, but during the war he also led the Nazi plundering of art and other treasures of Europe's Jews. He also headed the Nazi civilian administration in German-occupied Russia that helped the *SS* implement its policies of ghettoization and extermination of at least one million local Jews.

Rosenberg was born in the Russian Baltic province of Estonia to parents of mixed Baltic, German, and uncertain ethnic origin and humble beginnings (his grandfather was a struggling cobbler). His father was an impoverished invalid; his mother died soon after his birth. Rosenberg had studied at universities in Riga and Moscow, but in 1918 he fled the Bolshevik Revolution. "So life pulled me," he wrote later in his *Memoirs* while on trial at Nuremberg in 1945 and 1946, "and I followed."[3]

He reached Berlin first and then Munich, which captured his heart. There, he connected with other anti-Bolshevik émigrés from Russia. During 1919 he joined extreme right-wing political groups such as the Thule Society and the German Workers' Party (renamed the Nazi Party in 1921). His very first pamphlet, *The Trace of the Jews in the History of the World* (1920), was rife with racial hatred beneath a pseudoscientific veneer of logic.

But despite his impressive anti-Communist stance and activities, Rosenberg's Eastern and Russian origins always rendered him suspect among all the contending factions within the Nazi Party. Nor did Rosenberg's Jewish-sounding surname help his cause or credibility. Suggesting that his anti-Semitism was a response to this scorn and suspicion is likely too simplistic a solution, though it certainly was a factor. Indeed, his background included Latin, Slavic, and Jewish ancestry, but not a drop of Germanic or German "blood." As for the Russian Revolution, its violence never directly touched Alfred, who fled and then used his sick wife as an excuse to avoid fighting with the White Russians against the Bolsheviks.

An important figure in the party's early days, Rosenberg impressed Hitler with his "learning"—mostly acquired from crank literature saturated with nationalism, anti-Bolshevism, and anti-Semitism—though his readings of Friedrich Nietzsche, he noted in his memoirs, "struck me as alien" and "did not enlighten me any further."[4] Especially noticeable were Rosenberg's books attacking Jews and Freemasons. His anti-Semitic writings were extreme, speculative, uncritical, and morally vile. He believed Bolshevism was an invention of Russian Jews and linked old anti-Semitic stereotypes with the new fear of a Communist global revolution.

Much of his time Rosenberg spent annotating, publishing, and spreading *The Protocols of the Elders of Zion*, a pre-World War I tsarist police forgery alleging a Jewish conspiracy to rule the world. His later book, entitled *The Myth of the Twentieth Century* (1930), which many Nazis deemed second only to Hitler's *Mein Kampf* as a Nazi bible, and which an exceedingly minuscule number of them read cover to cover, preached a hodgepodge of mystical, pseudoscientific racial and anti-Semitic ideas.

On November 10, 1938, during what would become known as the "Night of Broken Glass," Rosenberg witnessed firsthand in Germany the destructive results of his and others' racial drivel. Later, in his *Memoirs*, he touched briefly on the pogrom, but only to distance himself from responsibility for the rampant and organized terror unleashed upon the Jews. He portrayed himself as innocent even of knowledge of what had happened. Although he claimed to have seen "many broken windows and a burnt-out synagogue" in Berlin, he insisted that the "total extent" of the damage "I learned only here at Nuremberg [at his trial]."[5]

In reality the destruction was devastating; across Germany and Austria, 7,500 businesses were destroyed; 171 synagogues were torched; 26,000 Jews were incarcerated in concentration camps, of whom 91 were murdered; and an unknown number of Jewish women were raped. To add economic woe to the traumatic aftermath, the insurance money due to the Jews for their ruined businesses, which amounted to one hundred million *Reichmarks*, was paid directly to the German government, and the Jews were fined one billion *Reichmarks* as punishment for allegedly having caused the night of destruction. Rosenberg's claim to have learned of the extent of the devastation to the Jews only at Nuremberg was ludicrous.

Mainly because of his ineffectiveness in various Nazi political offices in the 1930s, Rosenberg had little influence to exert in party and government circles when it mattered most. Yet during the war, Hitler placed him in charge of several enterprises requiring solely a determination to destroy European Jewry. In this regard, the Führer had complete confidence in his loyal, malleable minion.

Already during the fall of 1940, Rosenberg won a power struggle over a multitude of other high-level Nazi figures for control of the plundering of Jewish-owned and so-called Germanic artworks in German-occupied Western

Europe. But in the long run, this factional victory would only strengthen later the prosecution's case against Rosenberg at Nuremberg.

On September 17, Hitler issued a directive mandating that Rosenberg have sole jurisdiction over the looting of the treasures. For that purpose, Alfred headed the most effective agency the world has seen, a party organization with the title of Special Staff of Reich Leader Rosenberg (*Einsatzstab Reichsleiter Rosenberg*, or *ERR*). Initially, the *ERR*—which had a complex web of officials, work details, and groups throughout Western Europe and portions of Eastern Europe—looted museums, archives, and libraries of the declared enemies of National Socialism, that is, the Jews.

Even before 1941, Rosenberg acquired nearly three-fourths of the *ERR*'s wartime lootings, including in France and much of it from Jews. The agency confiscated almost four thousand pieces of art owned by various branches of the Rothschild family alone. To fend off continued powerful German rivals (including Göring) for the looting of artwork, as well as to acquire more funds for his operation, Rosenberg joined forces with the powerful *Reichsmarschall*.

In the Netherlands, a special office associated with the *ERR* but directed by Artur Seyss-Inquart, the Nazi Reich commissioner in the Netherlands (an Austrian Nazi tried after the war by the IMT and executed in 1946), confiscated at least 1,114 paintings from the art collections of Dutch Jews. In 1941 in German-occupied Greece, Rosenberg's thieves quickly plundered Greek and Jewish treasures, including archives and libraries.

Moreover, the *ERR* looted treasures in Eastern Europe and, after mid-1941, the occupied Soviet Union. It sent most of its plunder to Frankfurt am Main, where Rosenberg had established in 1939 the Institute for Research on the Jewish Question (*Institut für die Erforschung der Judenfrage*). The facility contained a large library, which held a portion of the approximately three million books looted by the Nazis from Jews throughout wartime Europe. In addition to helping rob the Jews, the institute infamously provided the German foreign ministry and police with information on Jews in foreign countries that assisted the ministry and police in locating them for imprisonment or murder. On March 28, 1941, in a speech at the formal opening of the institute, Rosenberg proclaimed that all political and other problems would be solved "for Germany . . . when the last Jew has left the area of Greater Germany" and "for Europe . . . when the last Jew has left the European continent."[6]

"INNOCENT" VISIONARY?

On July 17, 1941, a month after Germany's invasion of the Soviet Union, Hitler named Rosenberg Reich minister for the Occupied Eastern Territories, thereby giving him responsibility for civilian administration in the areas of conquered Russia no longer directly under German military command. Rosenberg's ministry included the *Reichskommissariat Ostland* (the Baltic states and Byelorussia) and *Reichskommissariat* Ukraine. He accepted the post, believing that it would enhance his power and influence significantly in the Nazi regime. ("So life pulled me, and I followed.")

As part of its work there, the *ERR* looted treasures throughout the territories in Rosenberg's jurisdiction. Apparently, the new minister's main qualifications for the post were his limited pseudoknowledge of the East and his proclaiming himself an expert on the region. His appointment to head a new and large government agency, often called the "Eastern ministry," added yet another layer to the invariably complex bureaucracies already involved in the Soviet Union: Göring's economic pursuits, Himmler's expanding *SS* and police empire (in the Ukraine under the real occupation chief, Erich Koch, *Gauleiter* of East Prussia), the organization of Fritz Todt, which procured foreigners as slave labor and controlled infrastructure, and the *Wehrmacht*, which competed often for control of occupation policy.

Most of Rosenberg's Nazi competitors viewed him as a joke and a fool—unfortunately, for Russians and Jews under German occupation, he was a deadly fool at that, committed to "Aryan" colonization through depopulation via sterilization, deportations, and mass murder. Regarding the treatment of Soviet Jews, Rosenberg differed only in detail—not in intent or principle—from the policy of extermination carried out by the *Einsatzgruppen* and other police and *SS* units on orders of Himmler, Heydrich, and the *RSHA*.

Even before his appointment as minister, Rosenberg had approved in the spring of 1941 the first draft of Heydrich's eventual memo of July 31 to Göring, which the latter signed and, in so doing, charged Heydrich with preparing "an overall plan . . . for the accomplishment of the final solution of the Jewish question which we desire." Heydrich had approached Rosenberg with the draft apparently because, at the time, Heydrich considered deporting the Jews of Europe to the yet-to-be conquered territory in Russia.

But by the time of Germany's invasion of the Soviet Union in June 1941 and of Rosenberg's appointment a month later, German policy had begun to shift toward killing vast numbers of Soviet Jews whom German forces could seize. By the fall, the killing campaign would expand to murdering all Soviet Jews. Immediately, clashes occurred between Himmler and Rosenberg over authority in the East, in which Rosenberg viewed the mass murder of Jews and the planned *SS* Germanization of Soviet lands as disruptive for economic and war production. The killings didn't concern Rosenberg, only the timetable and his total lack of control in his territories over Himmler (whom Hitler made responsible for security—that is, killing Jews and other "unwanted" Soviet citizens) and other Nazi rivals as well as over the *SS* and *Wehrmacht* in the field.

Initially, Rosenberg envisioned that under his authority, the occupied Soviet Union would secure the German food supply and provide labor and production for the war economy. In time, the western Soviet territories would form a series of German satellite states (the Ukraine, White Russia, and Baltic region) to provide a future protective barrier against what existed farther East—the allegedly inferior Muscovite "Asiatic horde," the Great Russians, now controlled by "Jewish-Bolsheviks."

About the "Jewish question," he sent memoranda to his administrative subordinates that called for—in addition to ghettoization, forced labor, and other discriminatory measures for Soviet Jews—"partial preliminary measures" in anticipation of a much broader European-wide solution of the question after the war.[7] Despite his proposals suggesting a different postwar time schedule for the same agenda, the systematic murder of Jews continued. In the Ukraine his chief administrative underling there, Erich Koch, a formidable rival in his own right and one whom Rosenberg had recommended for the job, cooperated with the mobile killing units.

Later, at his trial at Nuremberg, Rosenberg—who portrayed himself after the war as an innocent visionary for Hitler's empire in the East—attempted to conceal that he had known the brutal and unstable Koch for many years and that he had urged (albeit reluctantly, fearing Koch would act too independently) Koch's appointment in the Ukraine. Instead, at the trial he blamed Koch, whose whereabouts at the time were unknown, but whom the British captured in May 1949, whom the Poles tried as a major war criminal in 1958, and who spent the rest of his life in prison until his death in 1986, for most of the killings and other horrors that happened in Rosenberg's ministry in the Ukraine.

Rosenberg took this position during his testimony at the IMT on April 17, 1946, but the dramatic and skillful cross-examination by American prosecutor Thomas Dodd exposed the shabbiness of Rosenberg's stance and his blatant deceit. When Dodd confronted him with one of his own signed ministry records, dated April 7, 1941 (Document Number 1019-PS, U.S. Exhibit 823), which noted that "the undersigned would recommend the Gauleiter of East Prussia, Erich Koch, as Reich Commissioner in Moscow" and described Koch as "an absolutely ruthless person both as regards the military representation and also the eventual political direction," a deflated Rosenberg found himself forced to admit he had lied.[8] Revealingly, his *Memoirs*, written during the trial, focused very little on his role as minister of the Occupied Eastern Territories.

Thus, Rosenberg had recommended a known thug and butcher to administer the Ukraine for him and only opposed Koch when contemptuously the latter would usurp his superior's authority. Rosenberg had no redeeming explanation for his obvious lie, no distorting spin to discredit Dodd's proof, no alternate interpretation of his own words then condemning him before the tribunal, no verbose speech to sputter. Not even a single monosyllabic word to fall back on.

RACIST MURDERER

On September 14, 1941, Rosenberg passed on (via his liaison officer at the German army high command, Otto Bräutigam, who would serve after the war in the West German foreign ministry) the idea of deporting Jews from Central Europe to the East (Poland and western Russia) as a "reprisal" for Stalin's sudden displacement of Volga Germans to Siberia. But by then, Hitler, Himmler, Heydrich, and Göring—with millions more Jews having fallen under German rule in Poland and the Soviet Union—had made an exceedingly radical decision: to move from ghettoizing Jews to implementing the systematic, organized Final Solution, that is, deporting them all to the East and, upon their arrival at specially constructed killing centers, exterminating them. Also as part of the annihilation process, the *Einsatzkommandos* operating in Soviet territories expanded the range of their executions of local Jews by murdering women and children while at the same time collaborating with the *Wehrmacht* and Nazi civilian authorities to confine the survivors of these massacres in ghettos.

The ghettos played a complementary role in the unfolding extermination policies. Established in German-occupied Soviet areas from late July 1941 on, they served several purposes of the Nazis: to keep the Jewish population under control, free up living space elsewhere for German settlement, provide sources from which the Germans set up Jewish labor gangs for military and other tasks, and exclude Jews from participation in the economic life of their original communities. Rosenberg, in a directive to his ministry's chief office in the Ukraine previous to Koch's appointment to lead it, described the "establishment of ghettos and labor gangs" as the "key solution" to the "Jewish problem."[9]

On October 13, in a personal conversation, Hans Frank, the Nazi head of the Polish Government General, suggested to Rosenberg that the "Jewish population of the General Government be [deported] to the occupied Eastern territories." Rosenberg replied that at the time there was no possibility "for the implementation of resettlement plans of this kind." However, Rosenberg declared himself willing in the future "to encourage Jewish emigration to the East, particularly since the intention existed to send asocial elements within the Reich to the thinly inhabited Eastern regions."[10]

Beginning in late October 1941, deportations of German and other Central European Jews to the occupied Soviet territories, to ghettos in Minsk, Riga, and Mogilev, began. Once there, many were killed immediately in mass shootings;

others perished from near starvation and disease. Simultaneously, officials from Rosenberg's ministry, from the Nazi euthanasia program (for murdering the handicapped), and from the *RSHA* began discussing in Berlin the possibility of establishing gassing installations in Riga and Mogilev. Soon, in the former Poland, the first death camps, Chelmno and Belzec—using gas vans and other gas chambers—started operating, Belzec in the Polish Government General.

On November 15, 1941, Rosenberg had a long meeting with Himmler about the "Jewish question" and about coordinating the work of the latter's Higher *SS* and Police Leaders in the Soviet Union with the Reich minister's civilian officials. Three days later, Rosenberg briefed German journalists in Berlin, during which he declared that the "Jewish question," which involved "some six million Jews" still living in the east,

> can only be solved in a biological eradication of the entire Jewry of Europe. The Jewish question is solved for Germany only when the last Jew has left German territory, and for Europe when not a single Jew lives on the European continent up to the Urals. That is the task that fate has posed to us.[11]

He instructed the press, however, to divulge no details to the public of what was happening in the East, except for using common phrases about "Bolshevism and its destruction." Later, at Nuremberg, Rosenberg attempted to minimize the damning impact of that statement and others by claiming that, by Jewry, he didn't mean Jews as people, just the cultural and political influence of Jews as a race. Regarding Rosenberg's comments to journalists on November 18, 1941, Christopher Browning asserts: "If Rosenberg was still unsure exactly how and in what area in the east the Jews of Europe were fated to die, he now knew that a 'biological eradication' of all European Jews was the clear goal. And the same can be said for all those to whom he spoke."[12]

Three weeks later, Rosenberg attended a party for top echelons of the Nazi leadership. Hitler hosted the gathering at his private apartment in Berlin. The Führer issued no explicit directive but made unmistakably clear to the guests that his prophecy of January 1939—when he had told the German parliament (*Reichstag*) that "should the international Jewry of finance succeed, both within and beyond Europe, in plunging mankind into yet another world war, then the result will not be a Bolshevization of the earth and the victory of Jewry, but the annihilation of the Jewish race in Europe"—had to be taken word for word.[13] Further, his statement resolved any ambiguity about the timetable for implementing the Final Solution: it would proceed during the following spring and not be delayed—as apparently Rosenberg and others had thought—until after the war.

Two days after the party, Rosenberg met again with Hitler, discussing with him the draft of a major foreign policy speech that the Reich minister planned to deliver in Berlin but never did. Rosenberg had written the speech before Germany's declaration of war on the United States, in which he apparently threatened severe retaliation against the Jews of Eastern Europe in response to "New Yorker Jews" calling for Germany's encirclement. He noted in a memorandum on December 16:

> I remarked on the Jewish question that the comments about the New York Jews must perhaps be changed somewhat after the conclusion (of matters in the East). I took the standpoint not to speak of the extermination (Ausrottung) of Jewry. The Führer affirmed this view and said that they had laid the burden of war on us and that they had brought the destruction; it is no wonder if the results would strike them first.[14]

A week later, his "Eastern ministry" replied to its commissioner for the *Ostland* (the Baltic states and Byelorussia), Hinrich Lohse, who had protested the mass executions by the *SS* of Jews in the region, including some deported there from Central Europe. On November 15 Lohse had asked the ministry to clarify whether "all the Jews in the Ostland are to be liquidated" and whether this was to happen "without concern for age and sex and economic interests," the latter referring to the *Wehrmacht*'s need for "skilled workers in munitions factories." After Rosenberg's meeting with Himmler and his listening to Hitler in Berlin, his ministry on December 22 informed Lohse that, from "oral discussions" that had taken place, "economic concerns . . . should be fundamentally disregarded in dealing with the [Jewish] problem."[15] All doubtful cases were to be resolved directly with the *SS* leadership in the *Ostland*. Like Hitler, Himmler, and the others, Rosenberg was a racist murderer.

On January 20, 1942, two high-ranking officials from Rosenberg's ministry, Dr. Alfred Meyer and Dr. Georg Leibbrandt (both longtime fanatical Nazi Party members, Meyer would kill himself in May 1945, and Leibbrandt would escape postwar criminal proceedings when such action was turned over by the United States to a Nuremberg-Fürth district court and discontinued—inexplicably—in 1952), attended the Wannsee Conference in Berlin, during which Heydrich and Eichmann discussed in the most direct, bluntest terms the forthcoming "Final Solution of the Jewish question." Heydrich listed the numbers of Jews believed to be in each European country, which totaled eleven million and which the *SS* planned to deport for killing. Most of those present at the meeting already knew of the mass killings of Jews in the Soviet Union; the *RSHA* had distributed *Einsatzgruppen* reports—marked "top secret"—to most government ministries.

No one objected to what they heard, and several reacted enthusiastically. Already the extermination camps at Chelmno and Belzec were operating; others, including Auschwitz, would start killing masses of Jews in the spring of 1942. Although sending subordinates may have been an attempt at providing

Rosenberg with deniability—should that ever be necessary—it is inconceivable that Meyer and Leibbrandt didn't report to Rosenberg what had occurred at the Wannsee Conference.

For the remainder of World War II, the huge killing operation (i.e., the racial war) became one of the major activities of numerous Nazi government ministries or agencies—increasingly often, to the detriment of the German military war. Already on January 29, 1942, barely a week after Wannsee, Rosenberg's Eastern ministry convened the first of several meetings during the rest of the year to discuss the definition of a Jew and the concept of *Mischlinge* (persons of mixed ancestry with one or two Jewish grandparents) in the Occupied Eastern Territories.

Previously, apart from some exceptions, the Germans had spared *Mischlinge* from persecution. But Rosenberg's ministry took a radical view of the issue by urging that every person with a Jewish parent or grandparent be defined as a Jew—and thus be targeted for destruction. This suggested that the days of *Mischlinge* were numbered, especially if Germany won the war. Likely, Rosenberg advocated this extreme position in an effort to help him assert his authority and control over the rival Nazi interlopers running rampant throughout his realm and to impress Hitler.

Meanwhile, in the Occupied Eastern Territories, Rosenberg and his ministry did nothing to stop—and even cooperated in—the continued slaughter of Soviet Jews by mobile killing units and some *Wehrmacht* troops. Nor did he and the ministry stop anti-Jewish, pro-Nazi Ukrainian gangs from murdering Jews. Also Rosenberg remained involved in the plunder of Jewish property in Western Europe.

To the war's end, despite the retreat by 1944 of German forces from the Soviet Union, Rosenberg stayed on in his ministry in Berlin ("I still went dutifully to my office," he wrote in his memoirs, "around which the bombs fell almost constantly").[16] There, he continued to concern himself solely with fighting his Nazi rivals for authority in his own—now wholly meaningless—domain. Full of jealousy for those who nearly always bested him (especially the propaganda minister Goebbels, Himmler, and Martin Bormann), he found himself completely excluded from Hitler's presence. He never again saw the Führer privately after November 1943.

In early April 1945, he suffered "an inflammation and hemorrhage" in his ankle, which confined him to the heroic state of being bedridden. During that month of convalescence he even "managed to get hold of a sufficient quantity of cyanide," but, unlike his rivals Goebbels and Himmler, he lacked the mettle for suicide.[17] Eventually, he fled with his wife and fifteen-year-old daughter to Flensburg, the site of the new German government under the leadership of the Hitler-appointed Admiral Karl Doenitz, who would receive at Nuremberg ten years' imprisonment for that "honor."

When no one took Rosenberg seriously, he left. ("So life pulled me, and I followed.") On May 11, 1945, his ankle suffered a relapse, and he was admitted to the naval hospital. The following day, he wrote Field Marshal Montgomery. Soon after, the British apprehended him. As a British pilot flew him and a guard in a twin-engine plane, the self-important Rosenberg still thought his destination was Montgomery's headquarters instead of Mondorf Prison in Luxembourg. There he'd wait with other war criminals until shortly before the start of the IMT at Nuremberg.

"INNOCENCE" ON TRIAL

He learned nothing from his imprisonment and trial at Nuremberg. In May 1945, he told his British captors that the Nazi state went wrong because of the machinations, not of himself, but of the Himmlers and Bormanns. He believed the ideas of Nazism remained as sound as ever but the party had failed such principles, which he had helped provide. Even amid Germany's devastating defeat, he held the delusion that the party had forced the British and Americans at long last to see the necessity for an alliance with Germany against the Bolsheviks and Jews.

Six months later, Rosenberg—medium-sized physically, with graying light brown hair, receding hairline, and a round, calm face that exuded a superficial amiability—sat in his prison cell at Nuremberg and responded to the IMT's indictment against him. The tribunal charged him on all four counts: crimes against peace; war crimes; crimes against humanity; and participation in "a common plan or conspiracy to commit any of the foregoing crimes." He declared his innocence to Gustave Gilbert, the American psychologist assigned to the prison to monitor the mental health of Rosenberg and the other major war criminals on trial. "I must reject an indictment for 'conspiracy,'" Rosenberg complained. "The anti-Semitic movement was only protective."[18]

Once the trial began, his continued virulent anti-Semitism showed through repeatedly in interviews with Gilbert and a U.S. Army psychiatrist, Leon Goldensohn. On December 15, 1945, in his third-floor cell, where he had his own collected works to use in preparing his defense, he asserted to Gilbert his innocence in the Nazi genocide of the Jews and even blamed the Jews for their persecution. Equally baseless was his confidence that he would never be found guilty and executed. After all, what were his crimes?

On February 3, 1946, both Goldensohn and Gilbert interviewed Rosenberg, again in his cell. The prisoner continued to deny that the *Protocols of the Elders of Zion* were fraudulent. He then persisted in blaming the Jews for their persecution by the Nazis. Goldensohn's notes of the conversation recorded Rosenberg's bigoted and senseless claims: "The cause of the Jewish question was, of course, the Jews themselves. The Jews are a nation, and like every nation, have a nationalist spirit. That's all very well, but they should be in their own homeland."

A few moments later, Rosenberg raised the subjects of "different types of blood" and "the differences between races," asking: "Would, for example, a blood transfusion from a Negro cause any character differences to ensue if given to an Aryan?" He didn't know, he said, answering his own question quite seriously and with—what the interviewers called—a "philosophic" smile.

He then added, cynically, "That would be a brutal experiment such as was done in the concentration camps." He smiled again, as if to imply that he'd scored a triumph of reasoning. But the doctors pressed him for his opinion. "[S]uppose," they asked him, "a Nazi soldier were injured and given some Jewish blood, or Negro blood. Would character changes occur?"

"It wasn't proven," came the reply. "Negroes beget Negroes [*sic*], Jews Jews, so it must be that blood will tell."[19] What else could one expect from such a "genius," one who petitioned the court to have his co-defendant Hans Frank, otherwise known as the "Butcher of Poland," act as his defense counsel?

He repeated similar calumnies when he took the stand at the IMT in mid-April 1946. During nearly three days of testimony his questioners—both prosecutors and defense counsel—focused on Rosenberg's early career in the Nazi Party, his status as "party philosopher," his relations to the pro-Nazi Norwegian politician Vidkun Quisling, who helped the Nazis occupy Norway in 1940 (and who would be tried and executed by firing squad at 2 a.m. on October 24, 1945), his willing collaboration in the ruthless conscription of Soviet peoples for forced labor in Germany, and his participation in the aggressive war against the Soviet Union.

Often, Rosenberg failed to answer questions that required a simple "yes" or "no," instead launching into verbose, convoluted discourses that bore little relation to the questions asked him. On at least four occasions, even his defense counsel, Dr. Richard Thoma, suggested, "I think you should be a little briefer." The American prosecutor Thomas Dodd complained to the court, "This defendant continues to make a speech."[20]

Thoma recognized early in conferences with Rosenberg that representing the latter would be no easy matter. The lawyer—as recorded in his memo of November 13, 1945—attempted to develop a defense strategy for his client. The counsel proposed that Rosenberg enter a guilty plea and acknowledge the criminal culpability of the Nazi regime, similar to what Albert Speer, Hitler's former minister for armaments and war production, had done. Thoma reminded Rosenberg of what he had told the lawyer:

> But as you note, what had terrible results for your ideology were its very real demands that only through hate could we redeem the world. Then you should have protested against those consequences. You say that you knew Jews were being killed in gas chambers, only you had not been able to believe it. Yet, you saw the disastrous influence of a Himmler, Kaltenbrunner, Bormann, etc. . . . You declare that you should not be convicted solely because of your ideology, but you admit that you were terrified at its consequences.[21]

According to his biographer Ernst Piper, Rosenberg "never spoke of gas chambers," although "[n]aturally, in reality he knew everything about the 'Final Solution.'"[22] Apparently Rosenberg told Thoma that he would consider the counsel's proposal that he plead guilty. But he did not do so. In fact, he pursued the exact opposite course, persisting to the end in defending National Socialism and the crimes that it—and he—had committed.

When Thoma asked him in court about his role in the "Jewish question," the defendant tried to portray himself as a friend of the Jews. Alfred insisted that early in the Nazi regime, he had proposed to the party that it "make efforts to solve this problem in a chivalrous way." Later, "when things occurred which were regrettable" (meaning the mass killing of Jews), he denied knowledge of what happened and blamed the *SS*.[23]

Again, he claimed innocence when asked about his wartime organization, the *ERR*, that seized artworks and other valuable "ownerless" properties abandoned by or taken from Jews and other people in both Western and Eastern Europe. He denied any plundering of such treasures on his part and told the court that Hitler had established the *ERR* for "the safekeeping and the transporting of these objects of art into the German Reich."[24] But in yet another deft cross-examination, Dodd was able to get Alfred to admit that his ignorance was willful and that his learning of Nazi criminality was acquired in the earliest days following the Nazis' seizure of power.

Although the prosecution spent relatively little time asking him about his knowledge of and role in the Final Solution, Dodd succeeded during cross-examination in trapping Rosenberg in lies and contradictions and in compelling him to admit his involvement in the policy. First, the prosecutor asked, "Did you ever talk about the extermination of the Jews?" Rosenberg attempted to avoid answering: "I have not in general spoken about the extermination of the Jews in the sense of this term." Dodd pressed him: "You will get around to the words. You just tell me now whether you ever said it or not. You said that, did you not?" He acknowledged that, in December 1941, while discussing with Hitler a speech that he (Rosenberg) planned but never delivered, he had done so.

Then the prosecutor asked: "[Had you] written into your speech remarks about the extermination of Jews?" The defendant—by now visibly nervous—responded, "The word does not have the sense which you attribute to it."

Dodd wasn't satisfied. "I will get around to the word and the meaning of it." But had Rosenberg, he inquired again, used the word *extermination*?

Still the accused tried to evade the issue: "That may be, but I do not remember."

"Well then," said Dodd, "perhaps we can help you on that." He then showed Rosenberg the latter's memorandum written about his discussion with Hitler regarding the planned speech. What did Rosenberg mean, Dodd asked him, when he had written in the memo "'I took the standpoint not to speak of the extermination (Ausrottung) of Jewry?'"

The once-arrogant Nazi "philosopher" and plunderer of Jewish and other treasures now began to squirm in his chair, as he continued trying to quibble about the meaning of the German word *Ausrottung*. First he complained that "[t]ranslations from German into English are so often wrong." Then he suggested that the word "means 'to overcome'" something.

Dodd would have none of the defendant's chicanery: "Are you very serious in pressing this apparent inability of yours to agree with me about this word or are you trying to kill time? Don't you know that there are plenty of people in this courtroom who speak German and who agree that that word does mean to 'wipe out,' to 'extirpate'?"

A moment later, the prosecutor observed: "I want to remind you that this speech of yours in which you use the term 'Ausrottung' was made about 6 months after Himmler told [Rudolf] Hoess [*SS* commandant of Auschwitz], whom you heard [earlier] on this witness stand, to start exterminating Jews. That is a fact, is it not?"

Rosenberg tried to divert attention elsewhere: "No, that is not correct, for Adolf Hitler said in his declaration before the Reichstag [in January 1939]: Should a new world war be started by these attacks of the emigrants and their backers, then as a consequence there would be an extermination and an extirpation."

"Well, actually," Dodd retorted, "the Jews were being exterminated in the Eastern Occupied Territories at that time and thereafter, weren't they?" (During that period Rosenberg had been Reich minister of the territories.)

Again, the accused didn't answer. Increasingly desperate not to incriminate himself further, he claimed that "in speaking here of [the] extermination of Jewry," there was "a difference between 'Jewry' and 'the Jews.'"

But Dodd refused to let him off the hook: "I asked you if it was not a fact that at that time and later on Jews were being exterminated in the Occupied Eastern Territories which were under your ministry? Will you answer that 'yes' or 'no'?"

At last, the defendant could no longer dodge the truth. "Yes," he said. "I quoted a document on that yesterday."[25]

Immediately, Dodd followed up by reading to the defendant from a series of documents, all written by Rosenberg's highest-ranking officials in the

Ministry for the Occupied Eastern Territories and all found by the Allies after the war in Rosenberg's ministry office. Each document reported on the mass executions of Jews in the regions administered by the officials, primarily in the Baltic states and Byelorussia. Not only did Rosenberg disbelieve that the documents had been "found in my office in Berlin," but also he refused to admit that the initial *R* on two of them was his own, thereby showing he had seen—and approved—them at the time they were written. He claimed only to know that in the Soviet territories under his jurisdiction, "a large number of Jews were shot by the police."

An incredulous Dodd countered that he believed Rosenberg obviously had known—and sanctioned—what his underlings did: "I think you will agree that in the Ukraine your man [Erich] Koch was doing all kinds of terrible things. . . . So that five people at least under your administration were engaged in this kind of conduct, and not small people at that." When Rosenberg evaded answering again, the court's president, Geoffrey Lawrence (Lord Justice of Great Britain and North Ireland), cut him off and ordered, "Will you answer the question first? Do you agree that these five people were engaged in exterminating Jews?"

Finally, the accused conceded his knowledge of and involvement in the mass killing of the Jews: "Yes. They knew about a certain number of liquidations of Jews. That I admit, and they have told me so, or if they did not, I have heard it from other sources."[26]

Despite all the evidence presented against him and the other defendants at the trial, and despite his admissions of culpability in the Holocaust and other Nazi crimes, Rosenberg never changed his mind regarding what he'd done. Similar to Göring and other perpetrators, Rosenberg's unsuccessful effort at questioning the evidence used against him nevertheless likely inspired public critics of the war crimes trials, as well as later Holocaust deniers, to allege that the trials used falsified records. By 1947, a year after the IMT ended, the assertion appeared in a book by Bardèche.

Throughout Rosenberg's life, and especially during his trial, when his life was most gravely at stake, not only did he feel no regret, but instead, in his *Memoirs*, he attacked angrily both the Allies and Jews. In this respect, too, he agreed with—and added fuel to—the claims of American and other relativists and German apologists who served as precursors to Holocaust deniers. Already during the spring of 1946, William Langer, an American isolationist and senator from North Dakota, citing the Allies' postwar mass transfer of ethnic Germans from Czechoslovakia and Poland, accused the United States of a "savage and fanatical plot" to destroy millions of German women and children.[27]

Rosenberg alleged the same. His trial, it seemed, had no effect on him—except to make him hate even more. The Allies, he claimed, were no better than the Nazis:

> To be sure, the victims of Auschwitz, Maidanek, etc., are held against us and have heavily incriminated the German nation. However, the millions of murders, expulsions, and deportations now taking place in Germany under the very eyes of the victorious Allies, speak just as forcefully against our accusers.[28]

Still a rabid anti-Semite, he sought to justify his hatred—and in doing so, he provided even more material for so-called revisionist writers who sought to relativize or lessen Germany's wartime actions and for the earliest Holocaust deniers. He blamed the Final Solution once again on the Jews: "The war against Jewry came about because an alien people on German soil arrogated the political and spiritual leadership of the country, and, believing itself triumphant, flaunted it brazenly." He remained an ardent racist, a self-professed "endowed seer," who warned the United States against its "fourteen million Negroes and mulattoes [and] four to five million Jews" destroying the country.[29]

The editors of his *Memoirs* observed, "[H]e did not recant under the threat of final punishment, but remained faithful to the twilight world of demigods and demons he had originated—an unregenerate Nazi to the end."[30] The millions of Jews who suffered unimaginably as a result of his rigid fidelity to a fanatical ideology would've been grateful if he had exhibited a bit less "faith."

VERDICTS AND SENTENCES

Between September 30 and October 1, 1946, the IMT, after long and often acrimonious deliberations, decided the fates of the defendants. The court based its findings on a huge mass of evidence, oral and written. The transcript of the IMT's sessions ran to more than fifteen thousand pages. The tribunal had over three hundred thousand affidavits submitted to it, used some three thousand documents (most of them German records captured by the Allies), and heard oral testimony from two hundred witnesses.

The tribunal acquitted only three of the twenty-two men on trial: the *Reichsbank* president and minister of economics, Hjalmar Schacht; Reich chancellor before Hitler and the latter's vice chancellor and ambassador to Austria and Turkey, Franz von Papen; and radio chief in Goebbels's propaganda ministry, Hans Fritzsche. Ironically, the trio cowered in their former prison for three days to avoid being arrested by the German civil administration.

The others were less fortunate. Seven received terms ranging from ten years to life imprisonment, but three of them (two of whom had been sentenced to life in prison) would be released early for health reasons—a consideration millions of the war's victims never enjoyed. Twelve were sentenced to death;

that number included Martin Bormann, who had disappeared in Berlin at the war's end, convicted and sentenced *in absentia*. (In 1972, construction workers near the Lehrter railway station in West Berlin uncovered the remains of what proved eventually—using DNA tests in 1998—to be Bormann's.)

The eleven other defendants had dates with the hangman. Four of them—Göring, Kaltenbrunner, Rosenberg, and Frank—still insisted in their final words to the tribunal, spoken on August 31, 1946, that they had no role in the genocide of the Jews. Göring proclaimed the German people victims of Hitler and the Allies; the people, he alleged, were wrongfully punished, "free of guilt," and "without knowledge of the grave crimes which have become known today."[31] Similar to his earlier testimony, his words would play into the hands of postwar Nazi sympathizers, especially deniers of the Holocaust, who made the same claims. The tribunal convicted Göring—despite his calling on God and the German people to attest to the sincerity of his selfless patriotism—on all four counts of the indictment, including the charge of "crimes against humanity."

It seemed that no one believed Kaltenbrunner's stance of ignorant innocence—except, of course, Kaltenbrunner. Most assuredly, the judges didn't. Nevertheless, in sentencing Kaltenbrunner to death for war crimes and crimes against humanity, the IMT relegated to a secondary place his "leading part in the 'Final Solution' of the Jewish question." The court's judgment against him recognized his role and culpability in the Jewish persecution only after it presented a much lengthier discussion of his involvement in other crimes: the "mistreatment and murder of prisoners of war"; "the murder and ill-treatment of the population" in Nazi-occupied territories; and the "enforcing [of] a rigid labor discipline on the slave laborers." Only then was the genocide of Jews noted.

Rosenberg, besides praising National Socialism in his final statement, professed to be completely bewildered that his impassioned ideology and racial philosophy would lead to such an unexpected and murderous outcome. After all, he only ever sought to dispossess and segregate the Jews—to treat them in a "chivalrous" manner. The judges begged to differ; they found him guilty, like Göring, on all four counts of the indictment.

Frank, who had earlier proclaimed that Germany's guilt would not be erased for a thousand years, had backpedaled by asserting that the crimes committed by the Russians and others against the Germans now negated that guilt. His waffling didn't spare him either, the IMT finding him guilty of war crimes and crimes against humanity.[32]

The four defendants, along with the seventeen others on trial, were summoned individually to hear their respective sentences. Immediately afterward, the American psychologist Gilbert observed them carefully. About the four men focused on here, he noted:

> It was my duty to meet them as they returned to their cells. I asked each one what the sentence was.
>
> Göring came down first and strode into his cell, his face pale and frozen, his eyes popping. "Death!" he said as he dropped on the cot and reached for a book. His hands were trembling in spite of his attempt to be nonchalant. His eyes were moist and he was panting, fighting back an emotional breakdown. He asked me in an unsteady voice to leave him alone for a while. . . .
>
> Kaltenbrunner's clasped hands expressed the fear that did not show in his insensitive face. "Death!" he whispered, and could say no more.
>
> Frank smiled politely, but could not look at me. "Death by hanging," he said softly, nodding his head in acquiescence. "I deserved it and I expected it, as I've always told you. I am glad that I have had the chance to defend myself and to think things over in the last few months."
>
> Rosenberg sneered agitatedly as he changed into his prison overalls. "The rope! The rope! That's what you wanted, wasn't it?"[33]

But both the IMT's lengthy general judgment and its sentencing of each defendant reflected the court's lack of focus on the Holocaust and its centering instead on "crimes against peace." For instance, in the tribunal's three-page decision against Göring, his participation in the attack on Jews received barely a paragraph's attention. Almost as an afterthought, the court mentioned his directive of July 31, 1941, ordering Heydrich to produce "a complete solution of the Jewish question." But the court failed to note that the directive had also commanded its recipient to "plan" for "the final solution" of the "question." Most disappointing, the finding said nothing of the directive's crucial role in the *SS* recruitment of German government agencies to assist in the genocide of the Jews. Similarly, the tribunal's 112-page general judgment contained just five pages on the Nazi "persecution of the Jews" and mentioned the Final Solution only twice—a sterling example of what Ambrose Bierce's devil might have used to illustrate his definition of "historical footnote."[34]

The French prosecutor at the IMT, François de Menthon, was uncomfortable with the very concept of "crimes against humanity"—he preferred "crimes against peace."[35] Throughout the trial, he made no reference to the deportation or murder of Jews. The American prosecutor, Telford Taylor, did not even notice this striking omission until many years later.

Also during the trials, the Allied prosecution called few Jewish survivors as witnesses. How could that have happened? How could the tribunal have produced such "Holocaust-less" proceedings as well as judgments? Given the enormous crimes of the Final Solution and the considerable knowledge of it that had accumulated among the Allies since 1941, why did the IMT and other war crimes tribunals so minimize—in the words of Donald Bloxham—"the Jewish factor" in its proceedings?[36]

Allied prosecutors relied most heavily for their evidence on the vast store of captured Nazi documents available to them. The records—which did little to identify the murder of the Jews as *the* definitive crime of Nazism and did nothing to sympathize with the victims' suffering—provided, in the view of chief U.S. prosecutor Robert H. Jackson, nearly everything he and his colleagues needed to make the Allied case. But Bloxham has suggested other reasons for the "ambiguities characterizing the responses of the liberal democracies to the Holocaust," both before and during the IMT and in later Allied trials:

> At base, the accepted [Allied] view of [Nazi] anti-Semitic activity was a quintessentially liberal one: though violence against a minority group was despised, outbreaks of anti-Semitism were interpreted as reactions to Jewish "difference," or . . ."the irritant of Jewish particularity". . . . [T]his classic, assimilationist theory could not account for the level of Nazi antisemitism. Initially, therefore, [Allied] responses featured ambivalence towards reports of atrocities in the USSR based on experience of atrocity stories in previous wars, but also on a suspicion of the vagaries of "Slav imaginations" and a belief in the inclination of Jews to "magnify their persecutions." Subsequently, there was an unwillingness to commit to any strategy either of rescue for the victims or punishment for the perpetrators, despite the verification of atrocity reports and the issuance of general declarations pertaining to the Axis and its crimes. Allied reticence was characterized by denials—many grounded again in a liberal-universalist refusal to single out the treatment of any group as unique—that the Jewish fate required a specific consideration over and above that of other groups or of the universal aim of winning the war. There was also fear on either side of the Atlantic about the consequences in terms of the post-war world of allowing Jews to air their grievances: it was felt that anti-Semitism would be stirred up in those countries whose nationals were to be subjected to what might be attributed to Jewish vengeance; and, relatedly, that a strong moral claim might result for a separate Jewish state [in Palestine].[37]

The Soviet Union, as shown in chapter 5, had made clear long before the IMT—even during the world war—that it refused to acknowledge the suffering of its own Jewish citizens and recognized that of only its "Soviet" or "anti-Fascist" peoples. With such a view, Stalin, too, sought to avoid any "strong moral claim [that] might result for a separate Jewish state"—albeit one in his own country.

JUSTICE EVADED (GÖRING), JUSTICE ENACTED (KALTENBRUNNER, ROSENBERG, AND FRANK)

Two weeks later, after his request to be shot was denied and shortly before his scheduled execution, he cheated the hangman by committing suicide in his Nuremberg cell. How did Hermann Göring die? How could he have taken his own life in such a heavily guarded prison?

Göring had seen his wife, Emmy, for the last time on October 7, 1946, when she visited him in the prison. The two of them were separated—as with all their visits—by a wire-and-glass partition. "Do you really think they will shoot you?" she asked him. "You may be sure of one thing," she quoted him later as saying, "they won't hang me. . . . No, they won't hang me." Immediately, she knew what that meant.

The Allies had scheduled his execution by hanging—and that of the ten other war criminals given the death sentence (including Frank, Kaltenbrunner, and Rosenberg, and excluding the absent Bormann)—for 2 a.m. on October 16. Although the time of the executions was supposed to be kept a secret from both the prisoners and press, during the previous evening (October 15) rumors spread through Nuremberg that the time had come for the condemned men. The prisoners themselves could hear the sound of hammering from the prison gymnasium, where U.S. Army troops readied three gallows, and the noise of cars arriving outside all alerted the inmates that this was going to be execution night.

Everyone who saw Göring that evening in his cell found him in a bitter and depressed mood. He despised the Allied Control Council's insistence on hanging him and the other prisoners instead of shooting or killing them in some other way. Hanging, apparently, was unbefitting such "royalty."

The prison chaplain visited Göring around 7:45, the prison doctor and a guard at 9:30, and when the latter left, another guard, U.S. PFC Gordon Bingham, locked the cell and kept his eyes on Göring through the small porthole in the door. The prisoner, dressed in a nightshirt, lay in bed, mostly on his back. At 10:30 the guard at the cell door changed. All seemed normal.

A few moments later, the new guard, U.S. PFC Harold Johnson, noticed that Göring "brought his hands across his chest with his fingers laced and turned his head to the wall." He "lay that way for about 2 or 3 minutes," whereupon he "placed his hands back along his sides." Soon Johnson noticed that Göring "seemed to stiffen and made a blowing, choking sound through his lips."

Immediately, Johnson knew something had happened and called for help. Other guards and the chaplain raced to the cell; they unlocked the door and pushed it open. The chaplain felt Göring's pulse on his right arm, which dangled over the side of the bed. "Good lord," he mumbled, "this man is dead."

The *Reichsmarschall* had smashed a capsule between his teeth, releasing and swallowing its contents: cyanide. Doctors found glass fragments in his mouth. But how had it happened? According to Telford Taylor, who analyzed the question and the evidence in his 1992 memoir *The Anatomy of the Nuremberg Trials*: "The truth has not yet been proven."

Göring had left four letters (three dated October 11) under the blanket on his bed. One was a suicide note addressed to the strict and disliked—by the inmates—prison commandant, Colonel Burton Andrus. Göring claimed to Andrus that, since his imprisonment, "I have always kept the poison capsule on my person." Originally he had three capsules, he said, "one left in my clothing, so that it would be found in the search." The other two he'd hidden "so well that, in spite of the frequent and very thorough searches," they couldn't be found. He had taken one of the capsules, he said, which "was almost impossible to find." The other "was still in my little toilet case" hidden in "a round container of skin cream."[38]

Taylor found the suicide letter "vaguely written" and "not convincing." The former prosecutor at Nuremberg concluded: "Goering's main purpose in this letter appears to be to crow over Andrus and his men by boasting of his own ability to hide the capsule in his cell."

So where had the capsule that killed Göring come from? In November 1975, his wife had written another former Nuremberg prosecutor, the German Robert Kempner, telling him, "[A] friend whose name she would not give, had passed the poison to her husband in Nuremberg." Taylor believed that Emmy Göring's "statement about a secret friend" was "probably true."

Who was the "friend," the cyanide dealer? Taylor thought it likely "a tall, burly American first lieutenant," Jack "Tex" Wheelis, one of several junior officers who had keys to the baggage room—where Göring's belongings were stored (including possibly the capsules)—and who seemed to have a "lack of judgment, especially when he showed us a watch given him by Goering." He had "formed a friendship with Goering" and had his photograph taken with the prisoner, who had autographed it: "To the great hunter from Texas."

Wheelis died in 1954, but twenty years later, his widow showed a writer inquiring into the suicide "a solid gold Mont Blanc fountain pen with Goering's name inscribed on the cap, a large and elaborate Swiss wristwatch bearing his name in facsimile signature, a solid gold cigarette case, and a handsome pair of gloves." The widow added, "All these gifts . . . were given to [my] husband for favors done on behalf of Frau Goering and her little daughter."[39]

Was Wheelis the culprit? Likely, if Göring had such assistance. Similar to so many others already in the immediate postwar world, it appears that Wheelis had little or no feelings either for the sheer evil that Göring represented or for the suffering of his many victims—Jews as well as others.

Between 1:29 and 2:57 a.m. on October 16, 1946, the ten remaining imprisoned Nazi leaders condemned to death were taken one by one from their cells. Guards led them with their hands cuffed behind their backs down the corridor, across a yard, and into the gymnasium, where each climbed thirteen steps to the scaffold. There, the handcuffs were removed, his hands were bound again with black silken cords, his ankles were confined, a hood was pulled over his head, and the noose was fitted around his neck. The American executioner John C. Woods then pulled the lever, hanging each in turn.

Although Woods had executed nearly 350 prisoners in his deadly career, his was the rare case of practice not making perfect. The executions were essentially botched. The design for the gallows was flawed. As some of the condemned's bodies dropped, the trapdoor snapped back, smashing the bones in their faces. Rumors spread that the condemned hadn't died from broken necks but from strangulation. As a British Foreign Office official wrote, the truth was "not a pretty one."[40] But neither were their lives.

Ernst Kaltenbrunner was the third of the ten to hang. His voice was steady as he uttered his final words: "I have served my German people [terrorizing tens of thousands in the process and killing millions more] and my Fatherland with a willing heart. I have done my duty in accordance with the laws of the Fatherland. I regret that crimes were committed in which I had no part. Good luck Germany." After the ruined state in which twelve years of Nazi rule had left the country, it needed good luck—not to mention the millions of postwar Allied (i.e., American) dollars in reconstructive aid. Kaltenbrunner's mendacity did not fail him, even in his last moments. In the same breath (his last) that he acknowledged that "crimes" (a rather paltry word to encompass the death and devastation he had wreaked) had been "committed," he also distanced himself from them and from any responsibility for them. He died as he'd lived: a self-serving liar.

Alfred Rosenberg was fourth to die. He was pale, close to collapse, and—finally—at a loss for words. He did not speak. His verbosity failed him. It had never been nearly succinct enough for last words. So gravity pulled him, and he followed.

Fifth to hang was Hans Frank. According to one eyewitness, Father Sixtus O'Connor, who accompanied the condemned, when they came for him he was kneeling, hands folded, in his cell. As he was led to his death, he was smiling, they chatted "about this and that," and then he almost bounded up the steps to the scaffold. He had thanked Andrus for his "great kindness," and his final words echoed that sentiment, the sudden convenient resurgence of his newly found Catholic faith and his craven eager-to-please nature: "I pray to God to take my soul. May the Lord receive me mercifully. I am grateful for the treatment I have received in prison."[41] But there was no mention of a thousand years of inerasable guilt. After having rescinded that prediction, he didn't try to reclaim it on the gallows. In that, he didn't waffle.

Soon, the cremated remains of Göring, Kaltenbrunner, Rosenberg, Frank, and the others would be scattered near Munich into Solln's Konwentz Brook. As the ten Nazis were finally held to account and hanged, many of the Allied officers and other observers present, to steady their nerves, removed packs of Lucky Strikes from pockets and jackets and began to smoke.

10

Poland

Occasional Trials amid a Continuing Holocaust

The leaflet advertised a message of terror: BEAT THE JEWS. FOR THE MURDERED POLISH CHILDREN.[1] This hate-filled writing appeared in August 1945 in Poland, almost a year after the Red Army's liberation of the country. The leaflet reflected the belief of many Poles in the age-old myth of "blood libel"—that Jews allegedly murdered Christian children for use of their blood in religious rituals.

Throughout much of Christian Europe's history, most especially in the Middle Ages, such false accusations or claims against Jews had resulted in the arrest and killing of many of them by mobs. Now, in 1945, these and other similar leaflets represented what amounted to death warrants for Polish Jews who, having survived the Holocaust, had returned to their homeland. The writings threatened the returnees with the worst violence if they remained in the country and informed them that they had only a short time to leave.

Of the more than three million prewar Polish Jews, some 200,000–250,000 survived the Nazi Final Solution. Either before the war or during the initial months of German occupation, roughly 70 percent of survivors had fled the country, principally to the Soviet Union. The Red Army had evacuated some to Russia following the Nazi-Soviet agreement of 1939 (dividing Poland between Germany and the Soviet Union) and the subsequent Soviet occupation of eastern Poland. Other Polish Jews had survived Nazi concentration, forced-labor, and death camps; the war's end found many of them in Germany and Austria. Still other Jews in Poland had lived through the horror by managing to hide among the Poles or as partisan fighters.

Beginning in late 1944 and continuing through 1945 and into 1946, thousands of the survivors, many haggard and destitute, wandered back to their former Polish villages and homes. A substantial number came from the

Soviet Union, following a repatriation agreement signed on July 16, 1945, by Moscow and the new Soviet-controlled Polish Communist government.

RISING TIDE OF HATE

A continuing Holocaust, however, greeted those returning. Along with its seizure of power in Poland, the new Communist government encouraged and sponsored anti-Semitism. Polish and Soviet authorities ignored the suffering of Polish Jews in the Holocaust, refused to acknowledge their identity as Jews, and asserted that Nazism had persecuted only Poles, Russians, and other Slavs.

In fact, the Communists never championed Jewish "interests" of any kind. Instead, with few exceptions, they ignored the suffering of Poland's Jewish citizens at the hands of their neighbors both during and after the war. "The Communist Party," historian Jan Gross concludes in his book on anti-Semitism in postwar Poland, "aimed to distance and insulate itself as much as it could from the 'Jewish question' in order to gain a modicum of legitimacy in the eyes of the Polish population, and adopted what at best can be described as an attitude of benign neglect in matters Jewish."[2]

The Soviet-controlled Polish government made no mention at the postwar Auschwitz museum and memorial that the Germans had used the huge former complex of camps to murder almost exclusively—at least a million—Jews. When Victor Klemperer, a Jewish survivor living in East Germany, visited the former camp in May 1952, he recorded in his diary what he saw and heard on his guided tour. About the gassing and torture that had gone on at the camp, the guide had emphasized, "We have allowed it—but on the whole we don't like it, *human beings* were murdered here, without distinction of nation, of faith . . . only human beings."

People murdered without regard to their faith? Klemperer seemed to ask this question and mourned the tour's omission of the word *Jew*: "The details (figures, precise statements: 'here stood'. . .'135 Russians were shot here'. . .etc. etc.) has [*sic*] been learned, the grief and the horror and the sympathy are genuine. The Polish state has, in other words, turned Auschwitz into an obligatory educational institution."[3]

Such a policy gave the lie to the stereotypical belief and myth of "Judeo-Communism" (*zydokumuna*), espoused by a large portion of the Polish population. Jews, the claim asserted, had a special affinity for Communism and dominated the party and government. The popular Polish identification of Jews with Communism, which several years of Nazi propaganda had only intensified, blended well with the long tradition in Poland of religious—predominantly Roman Catholic—and other prejudices against Jews.

Amid the hostility and hatred Polish Jews encountered on their return home, they searched frantically for missing family and friends. Some returnees expected regret, sympathy, or compassion—in a word, remorse—from the world for what had happened in the Holocaust. Others didn't expect such understanding but only desired to be allowed to return home and live in peace.

But the expectations nearly always proved illusory. The German death camps and firing squads had ensured that few—if any—relatives, friends, or prewar Polish and other East European Jewish communities had survived. Where once thriving and bustling communities existed, now most returnees found only physical ruin, few if any Jews remaining, and personal rejection. Nearly always, local inhabitants—many of whom had assisted in and profited financially from the Nazis' wartime spoliation and even murder of Jews—refused to return property, much of it looted from the families of survivors and dead Jews.

The Communist government also involved itself in the takeover of Jewish property. Beginning in 1945, it issued a series of laws that temporarily placed abandoned (ownerless) and formerly German properties in the trusteeship of the state and that permitted the state to keep the properties or to transfer them to individuals. "Abandoned" property applied primarily to formerly Jewish possessions.

After the war Poles commonly dug up local murder sites and Jewish remains in search of valuables, including gold tooth fillings. At Treblinka and Belzec scavengers made enormous excavations. Even after the Nazis had killed them, the Jews continued to be a source of wealth for those who despised them.

Overwhelmed, disillusioned, and desperate, some Jews survived only to commit suicide after the liberation—in some instances, decades later. For Holocaust survivors the past was always present. Between November 1944 and October 1945, Poles murdered 351 Jews. Random attacks on and murders of Jews occurred daily on Poland's roads and trains and in small towns and large cities.

In October 1945 a report in the *New York Times* by one of the paper's correspondents traveling in Poland described pogroms, "anti-Jewish riots" in the country "with heads broken and synagogues ransacked." Anti-Semitism there, he concluded, "has been revived to a degree likely to impel the ultimate emigration of most of the few remaining Jews. . . . Jews feel that there is not much of a future for them in Poland. Observers estimate that 90 percent would emigrate if they had a chance."[4] The report calculated that only eighty thousand Jews were left in the country. In fact, the figure would become substantially higher, in large part because of the repatriation, during the spring and summer of 1946, of about 136,000 Polish Jews from the Soviet Union.

A PAPAL APPEAL FOR ARTHUR GREISER

Awaiting trial, a former World War I pilot and failed businessman before his Nazi career, the thickset, round-faced German sat in a closely guarded Warsaw prison cell. The Red Army had captured him in the spring of 1945. Not unlike many Poles, he hated Jews and cared nothing for and thought little about their postwar plight. "Why should I?" he mused. Indeed, he despised them even more than he disdained the "subhuman" Poles.

During the war, Arthur Greiser had served as the Nazi governor and *Gauleiter* of the Warthegau (Polish western regions annexed to the German Reich). The area included the city of Lodz and its large Jewish ghetto. From 1939 to 1945, he'd been in charge of deporting some 630,000 Jews and Poles (most destined to be exterminated) in order for the *SS* to settle Reich citizens from Germany, as well as 537,000 ethnic Germans from Eastern and Southeastern Europe, into the denuded area.

In Greiser's district the *SS* had established the first operational extermination camp at Chelmno—in large part because during 1941 Greiser had pressed Hitler and Himmler to remove the Jews from the Lodz Ghetto and make the district "Jew free." For months the Reich governor led a grass-roots movement in the district to eliminate the Jews. In July 1941, an *SS* major in the Warthegau, Rolf-Heinz Höppner, had informed Eichmann about discussions on the subject in Greiser's office. Solutions proposed, said Höppner, "sound in part fantastic," but in his view, "thoroughly feasible." Plans developed to construct a labor camp for some three hundred thousand Jews, although the facility would not be a complete answer to dealing with the district's large Jewish population. According to Höppner, "This winter there is a danger that not all of the Jews can be fed anymore. One should weigh earnestly if the most humane solution might not be to finish off those of the Jews who are not employable by some quick-working device. At any rate, that would be more pleasant than to let them starve to death."[5] While Greiser had not made up his mind about such proposals, near the end of the year the Jews of the Warthegau were being gassed in Chelmno.

By the fall of 1941, Greiser had managed to limit the number of additional German Jews that Berlin intended to send to Lodz. Following Greiser's negotiations with Eichmann, some twenty-five thousand Jews and Gypsies were deported to the ghetto instead of 60,000, the originally planned number. Chelmno functioned as the center for murdering Jews in both the ghetto and the rest of the Warthegau. Estimates of the numbers of Jews killed from there vary widely, with the most realistic figure hovering around 215,000.

But after the war, a Polish tribunal and prosecutors concerned themselves primarily with Greiser's record of cruelty toward Poles. Based on captured German records and on the evidence of witnesses presented to it, the court concluded, "without any possibility of doubt," that

> as a result of direct or indirect orders from the accused, thousands of Poles and Jews lost their lives, their property was destroyed or removed, Catholic and Protestant churches were ruined, schools and teaching centers shut down. The accused, again on his own initiative, issued such orders as those for severe restriction of Polish fertility, for limitation of the food allowed to sick children and pregnant women.[6]

Early in the war, Greiser had declared in a speech: "We are the masters and we must behave like masters. The Pole is a servant and must only serve. We must have iron in our backbones and never admit even the thought that Poland could ever rise again."[7]

Accepting the indictment almost wholesale, the court emphasized Greiser's role in deporting Poles for forced labor or death in concentration camps such as "Fort VII," near Posen; in summarily executing Polish intelligentsia, clergy, and others; in seizing Polish property; in restricting the Polish language in schools; in destroying Polish culture and science; and in removing Poles from the economy.

But while Jews counted for little in the Communist- and Soviet-dominated tribunal, the indictment and trial did not ignore Greiser's persecution and murder of Polish Jews. The indictment described the German wartime effort "systematically to exterminate the Jews" and how "more than 300,000 persons, practically all Jews, perished in Chelmno," the "extermination camp" that had "served the Warthegau" and Lodz Ghetto.[8] But in the final analysis, the tribunal's judgment lumped Poles and Jews together, making no reference to the Final Solution, instead emphasizing the destruction of Polish culture and "the Polish element."[9]

Long after Greiser's trial, a telling Allied-captured Nazi document surfaced. In a letter to Himmler, dated May 1, 1942, Greiser had written (using a euphemism for mass murder) of "the action involving special treatment of some 100,000 Jews in my district," to which Himmler and Heydrich had agreed as compensation for the planned deportation of Jews from the Reich to Lodz. The "special treatment," said Greiser, could be "concluded in the next 2–3 months."

According to Peter Longerich, "If Himmler and Heydrich had to 'authorize' this mass murder, we can assume that the suggestion [for it] must substantially have come from Greiser." Some time during the summer or autumn of 1942, Hitler gave Greiser, "when he [Greiser] again addressed the 'Jewish question' in his Gau a free hand—special authorization was no longer required to murder a certain number of people."[10]

On March 19, 1943, Greiser had written Himmler noting that he (Greiser) had visited the special *SS* and police *Kommando* at Chelmno, where they murdered Jewish deportees in gas vans. Greiser had issued death orders for many victims from Lodz and elsewhere in the Warthegau. Within a few weeks the *SS* closed and destroyed the camp but re-established it (for a few months) in 1944.

In June 1944, on the basis of an agreement between Himmler and Greiser, those inhabitants of the Lodz Ghetto either unfit for work or no longer needed by the ghetto administration were murdered with gas vans at the specially reactivated Chelmno camp. By mid-July more than seven thousand people died in this manner. Then, in August, the great majority of the remaining Lodz Ghetto dwellers, some sixty-eight thousand, were deported to Auschwitz, where nearly all died in the gas chambers.

Greiser, a year and a half earlier in writing to Himmler, had praised the Chelmno gas van *Kommando* to the *Reichsführer*: "The men have not only fulfilled the difficult task that has been set for them loyally, bravely and in all respects appropriately, but also their soldierly conduct is exemplary." After receiving Himmler's permission "to invite some of these men to be my guests" during their upcoming leave from Chelmno and "to give them a generous allowance," Greiser appeared at the camp together with his staff, consisting of fifteen high-ranking *SS* officers.

There, he addressed the *Kommando*: "I want to thank you on behalf of the Führer for the work you have done in Chelmno." Then he entertained the killers at a farewell party in a nearby hotel, where, according to one of them, "After a short while everyone was drunk and fell asleep at the table."[11]

At his postwar trial—despite the overwhelming evidence of his war crimes presented by prosecutors—Greiser showed himself wholly remorseless for what he'd done. He pleaded "not guilty," maintaining adamantly his innocence of the charges against him and blaming his role in the deaths of Jews and Poles on superiors.

"Most of the discriminating decrees and regulations signed by him, or issued under his authority," claimed his defense counsel, "were enacted and put into effect on express orders of Hitler or Himmler, and in his actions he was always strictly supervised by the central German authorities." Greiser alleged that "I had no influence whatsoever" in the killing of Jews, deportation of Poles, and other war crimes. He had no authority, he insisted, over the police or *SS* in his region, which "always took their orders and instructions directly from Berlin, and particularly from Himmler."[12] He suffered now as a scapegoat, he claimed, for the crimes of his bosses, Hitler and Himmler—an assertion that drew derisive laughter from the courtroom's spectators.

On July 21, 1946, escorted to his well-earned execution for war crimes, Greiser stepped into the bright Polish daylight. The fifty-nine-year-old former Nazi official and still fanatical anti-Semite had spent his final hours reading the Bible. That morning, weak-kneed and mumbling prayers, he climbed the scaffold stairs where the hangmen awaited him. He declared that he still wanted to live (and his Jewish and Polish victims didn't?) "to tell the whole truth" about himself and his role in the war.[13] But truth telling or its counterpart, truth denying, no longer was pertinent to Arthur's plight.

At the execution, fifteen thousand Poles watched silently—among them few, if any, Jews. Those present hoped to witness justice for what Greiser had done to many of them and their families. One of the executioners placed a hood over Greiser's face, tightened the noose around his neck, and then opened the door in the floor below him. He was hanged in Poznan in front of the lavish Ludowikovo palace, where he resided while governor of the Warthegau.

The day following his execution, the Vatican city newspaper, *L'Osservatore Romano*, confirmed previous media reports that Pope Pius XII had agreed to Greiser's appeal and had interceded with the Polish government urging that the German war criminal's "life be spared." The paper emphasized the pope's full awareness of Greiser's wartime atrocities, including his ruthless anti-Catholic persecution, but nevertheless, Pius had followed the example, the paper claimed, of the "Divine Master who on the cross prayed for those who had crucified Him."[14]

The pope had sought clemency for Greiser despite the latter's conviction two weeks earlier by the Polish Supreme National Tribunal for numerous war crimes (including waging aggressive war on—and participating in—what amounted to genocide against the "Poles"). Pius issued his appeal for mercy even as in Poland the pervasive postwar killing of Jews continued with apparently nary a whisper of protest from the Vatican.

While some observers expressed puzzlement at the last-minute papal intercession on behalf of Greiser, it hardly surprised many others. During the war Pius XII had said nothing publicly to condemn the mass slaughter of European Jews—despite his receiving countless dispatches describing the genocide and requests that he speak out. He held a long-standing secret antipathy toward Jews, whom he despised more for their alleged potential Bolshevism than perhaps for their Jewishness.

Pius XII believed that Jews had brought misfortune on themselves. He suspected that the church's intervention on their behalf could draw the church into alliances with forces—mainly Communist Russia—that he feared and that he believed to be a greater danger to Christianity than Nazism. With such views, all was possible and permissible. The Holy Father didn't even protest openly during the war the German killing of Catholic priests in Poland.

Yet Pius found his voice enough to criticize the IMT, and during 1945 and after, the Vatican assisted *SS* and other Nazis in escaping to the Middle East or Latin America. The standards for receiving such church-sponsored assistance were less than negligible. More murderers than innocent refugees benefited from this papal *deus ex machina*. Despite the continued widespread killing of Jews in postwar Poland, Pius issued his appeal on behalf of Greiser. Those murders seemed less crucial or urgent than advocating for the life of a war criminal. On the matter of the Jewish blood still being spilled, he continued his ignoble policy of silence.

THE POGROM

Almost simultaneously with Greiser's trial, on July 4, 1946, the single most deadly postwar pogrom in Poland (and elsewhere in Eastern Europe) killed forty-two Jews at Kielce, a town north of Krakow. The frenzied violence left dozens more badly injured.

Tragically, the pogrom happened amid the worst era of bloodshed and death for Jews in postwar Poland, from an August 1945 pogrom in Krakow to the uprising and murders in Kielce nearly a year later. According to Jan Gross: "How many Jews altogether were killed in this period is difficult to estimate. The most careful conservative figures range between 500 and 600; more widely accepted estimates put the total at around 1,500."[15]

Nearly eighteen months earlier, when the Red Army had liberated Kielce from German control, only two of the twenty-four thousand Jews in the city before the war had survived the Holocaust. Just two. The mind reels when forced to reflect on such figures—statistics of an unbridled moral depravity. Later, some 180 Jews—former inhabitants who had survived the Nazi camps or had hidden in nearby forests, as well as Jews from other locales—gathered in the city's Jewish Committee building and tried to piece together and reestablish their lives. An equal number of Jews lived elsewhere in the town.

But anti-Semitism ran at a fever level in Kielce. In early July 1946 local non-Jews accused the small Jewish community of "blood libel" or "ritual murder" in the disappearance of a local eight-year-old Polish youth, Henry Blaszczyk. In actuality the boy had returned home after visiting playmates in a nearby village, where his family had lived a few months earlier. Regardless of the reality, his father (initially while in a drunken stupor) maintained to local police that Jews had kidnapped the child. The boy, said the father, had managed to escape. Similar charges of so-called blood libel had helped to fuel the pogrom in August 1945 in Krakow.

Once news of the story spread in Kielce, on July 4 mobs gathered around the Jewish Committee building. The police intervened, but only to confiscate the few weapons owned by the Jewish inhabitants. Soon, Polish security service and army troops arrived. Witnesses do not agree who fired the first shot—a policeman, a soldier, or, as some suggest, one of the Jews—but, as Gross notes, "Like a starter's signal, it spurred those present on the scene to deadly violence."[16]

Police entered the building forcibly, beat Jews, and threw some out windows. The soldiers acted similarly. In the courtyard outside, mobs gathered and beat and murdered Jews, all the while robbing them of their possessions and clothing. Bitter conflicts—administrative, personnel, and otherwise—between the police and security service paralyzed law enforcement's ability to halt the rapidly escalating violence.

Before he died, apparently shot in his office by policemen, the Jewish Committee's chairman, Dr. Seweryn Kahane, tried to telephone a high-ranking security service officer to ask for help. The officer was on the other end of the line and recalled after the pogrom: "I then heard a loud shot and silence in the receiver."[17]

After midday Polish workers from a local foundry arrived at the Jewish building; their appearance unleashed the pogrom's second surge. Wielding tools, iron bars, and other improvised weapons, they murdered fifteen to twenty Jews in little more than an hour. Elsewhere in the city, rampaging mobs murdered Jews in their homes or dragged them into the streets before killing them.

The whole area turned into a "vast killing field," covered with "bloody mementos" long after the pogrom. A foreign journalist who visited Kielce the following day recalled about the pogrom's main site:

> The immense courtyard was still littered with blood-stained iron pipes, stones and clubs, which had been used to crush the skulls of Jewish men and women. Blackening puddles of blood still remained. . . . Blood-drenched papers were scattered on the ground. . . . I picked up some. . . . These were letters addressed to the victims by their relatives in Palestine, and Canada, and the United States.[18]

Only hours after the pogrom, to investigate what had happened and to assist the remaining Jews in Kielce, Poland's Central Jewish Committee sent to the city Yitzhak Zuckerman. He had survived the Warsaw Ghetto uprising in 1943 and was a cofounder of *Brichah* (meaning "escape" or "flight" in Hebrew). A postwar Zionist relief organization comprising mainly Holocaust survivors, *Brichah* assisted Jews in Poland and elsewhere in Eastern Europe to immigrate illegally (primarily through Central and Southern Europe) to Palestine.

Convinced that the pogrom had resulted from "a well-organized plot" involving the local police, other citizens, and Soviet provocateurs, Zuckerman recalls in his memoirs the horror he'd found:

> Then I went out into the streets of Kielce by myself. And once again, it looked like a ghost town. I returned to our base. The army was in its place—it wasn't clear what the army was guarding. I chatted with people in the building and yard in order to get eyewitness accounts. Everyone knew his own story. But these were the survivors. Some were our members and others were ordinary Jews. I didn't know the leaders of the local community. I asked to be taken to the morgue, where I saw dozens of bodies; and, meanwhile, more bodies of Jews killed on the roads were brought in. I saw pregnant women whose stomachs were ripped open. I can't describe the sight. And that wasn't in 1942, that was in 1946! There's no need to waste words on my feeling at that time in view of the sights of Jewish men and women, young and old, of all classes, laid out there, slaughtered.[19]

It's little wonder that Zuckerman left Poland at the beginning of 1947 and settled in Palestine. Two years later, he helped to found in northern Israel Beit Lohamei Haghetaot, the Ghetto Fighters' kibbutz. To perpetuate the memory of the ghetto fighters and Jewish resistance to Nazi genocide, the kibbutz created a museum and educational institute that teaches about the Warsaw Ghetto rebellion and Holocaust. In 1961, Zuckerman testified for the prosecution at the trial of Adolf Eichmann in Jerusalem.

Not long after the Kielce pogrom, local Poles destroyed a monument erected in the city's Jewish cemetery with the names of the forty-two victims of the massacre. (Only in 1987—over four decades after—would the Polish government permit Jews to rebuild the memorial.) News of the Kielce killings shocked even Polish Jews who had experienced the open postwar discrimination and violence.

In official government statements issued immediately following the pogrom, the word *Jew* hardly appeared. A few days after the pogrom, the Communist government conducted a pseudoinvestigation of what had happened. This culminated in several trials that convicted only seven of the perpetrators—despite the fact that several thousand Kielce residents had participated in the bloodbath. This charade of justice only intensified the fear and horror gripping Polish Jews.

Both the Communist Party and government, deeply engrossed in winning the Polish population's support, knew that most Poles felt no sympathy for Jews. The regime did not wish to alienate the nation's populace by carrying out a thorough unsparing investigation of the pogrom and by meting out appropriate justice to as many of the killers as possible.

Throughout Poland the pogrom met with mass approval, with the exception of a few intellectuals courageous enough to denounce it. Nearly every Polish clergyman, along with Pius XII and the Vatican, refused to condemn the pogrom, anti-Semitism in general, or the spurious accusation of blood libel. When asked to add his name to a petition opposing the mass killings, Polish Catholic Bishop Czeslaw Kaczmarek declined to do so. Instead, he chaired a secret church commission that issued a report denying Poles had cooperated during the war in the Nazis' mass killing of Polish Jews. The report also accused Jews of supporting Communism. Kaczmarek's commission claimed later, "Jews are responsible for the lion's share of the hatred that surrounds them."[20] (Numerous Nazi perpetrators of the Holocaust—and later deniers of it—made the same irrational claim.)

Following the pogrom, most of the remaining Polish Jews—possibly as many as two hundred thousand—left the country in droves. Assisted in large part by *Brichah*, they managed to travel, often with much difficulty, to the West by train as well as by most every other means, including on foot. At the end of 1946, the number of Jewish DPs, living often in poorly provisioned camps in the Western zones of Germany and Austria, had risen to nearly two hundred four thousand. The American areas contained 183,600—or about 90 percent of them. Jewish DPs in Italy numbered over twenty-one thousand. From there, many would seek transport to Israel, the United States, or elsewhere in the West.

AMON GOETH: A COURT'S RARE ADMISSION

The Kielce killings and subsequent mass exodus of Jews from Poland, which the Polish Communist government encouraged and even facilitated, nevertheless may have had another consequence. Possibly such events persuaded the government-controlled Polish national tribunal, concerned momentarily about foreign (especially Western) opinion, to make a rare acknowledgement in its postwar trials of war criminals—that Jews had been victims of a purposeful Nazi genocide.

In its verdict of September 5, 1946, the court sentenced to death Amon Goeth, an Austrian, former *SS* captain, and commandant of the German forced-labor camp at Plaszow, near the city of Krakow in the Government General. Based on Nazi records captured by the Russians and Poles and on the testimony of numerous witnesses to Goeth's crimes, the prosecution showed that he "was responsible for the atrocities committed as part of a general pattern of the German policy aiming at complete extermination of the Jewish population in Europe."[21]

The tribunal convicted Goeth for his role in the barbarous evacuation of Jews from ghettos in Tarnow and Krakow. The court found Goeth guilty of committing atrocities during the closing down—the Germans called it "liquidation"—in March 1943 of the Krakow Ghetto. During the *Aktion* the German police murdered Jews wholesale on the spot. According to the prosecution: "The total number of Jews murdered on this occasion reached about 4,000, among which were many women and children. Amon Goeth himself shot many people."[22] The Germans sent the remaining Jews, possibly as many as ten thousand, to Auschwitz, where they perished in the gas chambers. Only a few hundred Jews from the ghetto deported to nearby Plaszow survived.

Also in June 1942, Goeth had directed the removal of some six thousand Jews from the Tarnow Ghetto to the Belzec death camp, where nearly all were murdered immediately. In September 1943, Goeth headed the liquidation of the ghetto. The prosecution asserted, and the court agreed: "Goeth himself shot between thirty and ninety women and children and sent about 10,000 Jews to Auschwitz by rail, organizing the transport in such a way that only 400 Jews arrived there alive, the remainder having perished on the way."[23] He had viewed his shooting of Jews as a sporting event, as a hunting game.

While commandant at Plaszow during 1943 and 1944, he continued to indulge his twin pleasures of torturing and murdering. From the balcony of his villa, he used his rifle to shoot and kill over five hundred Jewish prisoners himself as they worked or walked in the camp. In addition, the indictment at his postwar trial accused him of causing "the death of about 8,000 inmates by ordering a large number of them to be exterminated."[24]

In September 1944 he was relieved of his position, and in November the *Gestapo* arrested him on charges of stealing property from the inmates at Plaszow, which, according to Nazi law, had become the property of the Reich. But the crisis of impending defeat spared Goeth a trial, though *SS* doctors diagnosed him as mentally ill and committed him to a sanitarium, where the Americans found and arrested him in May 1945. Poland requested his extradition and tried him in Krakow.

Given the conspicuous and callous nature of his crimes, the overpowering case against him, and, at the time of his trial in August and September 1946, the continuing massive physical attacks on Jews in Poland and their flight from the country, the tribunal believed apparently that it couldn't ignore—as it had done in previous trials of perpetrators of the Final Solution—that the Germans had targeted Jews for destruction. In this instance the court couldn't simply refer to the victims as solely Poles or Polish "citizens."

Still, Goeth had no conscience about what he'd done. He pleaded "not guilty" and attempted to deny the evidence against him, to blame other Nazis for what had happened, and to lessen the extent and severity of the crimes he'd committed. The Polish government denied his appeal "for mercy" and hanged Goeth, age thirty-seven, on September 13, 1946.[25] The hangman twice misjudged the length of rope required to hang the former commandant, and it wasn't until the third try that he died. (In 1993, Goeth's career received international notoriety with his depiction in the film *Schindler's List*, which told the story of a German businessman who saved the lives of more than a thousand Polish Jews at Plaszow by employing them in his factories.)

RUDOLF HÖß: TRIAL OF THE DEATH DEALER

The Warsaw regime's recognition of the extraordinary suffering of Polish Jews in the war apparently didn't last long. By the time the Polish tribunal placed on trial in March 1947 Rudolf Höß, the *SS* commandant of Auschwitz from 1940 to 1943 and during several months in mid-1944, nearly all the Jews who had survived had managed to leave Poland for DP camps and other destinations farther west and south in Europe. At the trial both the prosecutors and tribunal claimed that "Poles"—not Jews—"constituted the largest group of murdered from among the registered inmates" at Auschwitz.[26]

In reaching this wholly unfounded conclusion, the court ignored the vast evidence—including Höß's own testimony before and at the trial—showing that, in fact, the Nazis had used Auschwitz almost solely for the mass murder of Jews from all over Europe and elsewhere. With few Jews remaining in Poland and with anti-Semitism still rife there and in Russia (including among the Communist elite in Moscow and Warsaw), the Communist-controlled tribunal sought to portray the camp as representing "fascist" aggression intent on persecuting Poles and one that only the Soviet Union had defeated.

Almost a year earlier, the British had captured Höß, a former *SS* lieutenant colonel, in northern Germany. By the time Germany surrendered in May 1945, he'd made his way to Ravensbrück, the women's concentration camp north of Berlin; there, a rumor claimed that he had died in an automobile accident. In reality, he'd fled, along with numerous other *SS* officers, north into Schleswig-Holstein, where, at Flensburg, he had taken leave of Himmler for the final time and, with false papers provided by the latter, disguised himself as a naval petty officer. Apparently unrecognized, and released in late May by the British from an internment camp, he lived under the alias "Franz Lang" with his family near Flensburg and worked as a farm laborer.[27] In March 1946, British intelligence located and arrested him.

He was subpoenaed at the IMT as a witness for the defense of Ernst Kaltenbrunner, the head after January 1943 of the *RSHA*, the agency that controlled not only the German Security Police and *SD* but also the *Gestapo* and much of the concentration camp system and administrative apparatus for carrying out the Final Solution. But the plans of Kaltenbrunner's defense counsel misfired. Höß admitted that the Germans had singled out the Jews for destruction in the war.

Once he took the stand, an American prosecutor, Colonel John Amen, asked him about information he had provided in an affidavit. "The 'Final Solution' of the Jewish question," said Höß, "meant the complete extermination of all Jews in Europe. I was ordered to establish extermination facilities at Auschwitz in June 1941." Until December 1943, while he had commanded Auschwitz, he added,

> at least 2,500,000 victims were executed and exterminated there by gassing and burning, and at least another half million succumbed to starvation and disease making a total dead of about 3,000,000. This figure represents about 70 or 80 percent of all persons sent to Auschwitz as prisoners, the remainder having been selected and used for slave labor in the concentration camp industries; included among the executed and burned were approximately 20,000 Russian prisoners of war . . . who were delivered at Auschwitz in Wehrmacht transports operated by regular Wehrmacht officers and men.[28]

Höß overestimated the number of persons killed altogether at Auschwitz; nevertheless, possibly as many as one and a half million Jews had died there. The former camp commander shocked nearly everyone in the courtroom when he described the process of choosing the victims newly arrived at the camp for killing:

> The way we selected our victims was as follows: We had two SS doctors on duty at Auschwitz to examine the incoming transports of prisoners. The prisoners would be marched by one of the doctors who would make spot decisions as they walked by. Those who were fit for work were sent into the camp. Others were sent immediately to the extermination plants. Children of tender years were invariably exterminated since by reason of their youth they were unable to work. . . . [Also] at Auschwitz we endeavored to fool the victims into thinking that they were to go through a delousing process. Of course, frequently they realized our true intentions and we sometimes had riots and difficulties due to that fact. Very frequently women would hide their children under the clothes, but of course when we found them we would send the children in to be exterminated. We were required to carry out these exterminations in secrecy but of course the foul and nauseating stench from the continuous burning of bodies permeated the entire area and all of the people living in the surrounding communities knew that exterminations were going on at Auschwitz.[29]

After removal of the bodies from the gas chambers, Höß continued, "special Kommandos [of camp prisoners] took off the rings and extracted the gold from the teeth of the corpses," and "[t]his gold was melted down and brought to the Chief Medical Office of the SS at Berlin."[30] Even the defendants in the dock listened in gloomy silence to Höß's testimony.

Before Höß took the stand at Nuremberg, the U.S. prison psychologist, Gilbert, had interviewed him in his cell. When asked whether he had understood the "enormity" of what his superiors had ordered him "to undertake," Höß replied in a quiet, apathetic voice: "At the moment I could not oversee the whole thing, but later I got some idea of its extent.—But I only thought of the necessity of it, as the order was put to me."

Had he thought about the consequences of his murderous job at the time he'd started it? Hardly, Höß responded: "It didn't occur to me at all that I would be held responsible. You see, in Germany it was understood that if something went wrong, then the man who gave the orders was responsible. So I didn't think that I would ever have to answer for it myself."

"But," his examiner started to ask, "what about the human—?"

"That just didn't enter into it," was Höß's answer, before the psychologist could finish the question.

"When did it first occur to you then that you would probably be brought to trial and hanged?"

"At the time of the collapse—when the Führer died."[31]

A few days later, following Höß's testimony before the IMT, the psychologist, curious about what had made Höß believe exterminating Jews "was right," asked him "how he got his anti-Semitic views." Höß responded that he'd read "every week for many years" the books and other writings of Nazi leaders: Hitler, propagandist Goebbels, party ideologue Rosenberg, and, occasionally, anti-Semitic publisher Streicher, whose lurid anti-Semitic *Der Stürmer* at its height enjoyed a circulation of nearly five hundred thousand. In addition, he listened to their speeches and read the ideological pamphlets and other educational material of the *SS*.

Such sources preached constantly the idea that Jewry was Germany's enemy and that, in Höß's words, "sooner or later there would have to be a showdown between National Socialism and World Jewry—that was even in peacetime." And how had it influenced him? "I took it all as fact—just as a Catholic believes in his Church dogma. It was just truth without question; I had no doubt about that." The war, he continued, further intensified his hatred of Jews:

> Then, after the war started, Hitler explained that World Jewry had started a showdown with National Socialism—that was in a Reichstag speech at the time of the French campaign [*sic*, the speech was in January 1939]—and the Jews must be exterminated. . . . Goebbels expressed himself more and more sharply against the Jews. He did not attack England or Holland or France, so much as the Jews, as our enemy. . . . [I]t was always stressed that if Germany was to survive then World Jewry must be exterminated and we all accepted it as truth.[32]

In other discussions with Gilbert, Höß admitted that he'd developed no strong feelings for other people, even those closest to him. He mentioned growing up as a child in "a very strict Catholic tradition" and with a father who "was really a bigot." Höß had led a loner's life: "I never had friends or a close relationship with anybody—even in my youth." Even his marriage had suffered from "estrangement" and the lack of "a real spiritual union."

Still, in his listless voice the former commandant and mass murderer insisted: "I am entirely normal." But Gilbert concluded about Höß:

> There is too much apathy to leave any suggestion of remorse and even the prospect of hanging does not unduly distress him. One gets the general impression of a man who is intellectually normal but with the schizoid apathy, insensitivity and lack of empathy that could hardly be more extreme in a frank psychotic.[33]

In May 1946, Britain sent him to Poland for trial. During the trial, held in Warsaw, he admitted to nearly all the claims in the indictment, though he questioned its accuracy in placing the total number of victims killed at Auschwitz at "about 4,000,000 people mainly Jews." The figure, he suggested, was much lower.[34] In a memorandum he wrote in Krakow prison in November, he claimed that during "the summer of 1941" Himmler had told him that Hitler "had ordered the Final Solution of the Jewish question," and that "We the SS have to carry out this order."[35] Only recently have historians raised doubts about the statement's accuracy, challenging not only Höß's dating of his meeting with Himmler to the summer of 1941 but also his claim that by then Hitler had ordered the Final Solution.

Though Höß described himself as being "firm and often harsh," he denied at his trial that he'd committed personally "any acts of ill-treatment or cruelty" against camp prisoners. But Primo Levi, a former Italian chemist, Auschwitz survivor, and celebrated writer whose postwar works examined his experiences and the enormity of man's potential for inhumanity—begged to differ. In an essay assessing the nature and veracity of Höß's memoirs, composed while he was in custody, Levi, who as a prisoner was well placed to know, asserted that the commandant "had an affair with an Auschwitz prisoner and extricated himself by sending her to her death."[36]

Höß's entire defense rested on his insistence that he'd only carried out orders received from his superiors. But the tribunal used captured Nazi records, as well as statements from a large number of former Auschwitz prisoners, to convict and sentence him to death. When news of his impending execution circulated, a crowd of thousands, many of them former inmates, converged on the gallows. The size of the throng, which government officials hadn't expected, caused them serious concern.

The threat of such a crowd transforming spontaneously into a mob was palpable. As Auschwitz's former victims waited restlessly, a uniformed official declared that the execution had been postponed indefinitely. Reluctantly and slowly, the crowd dispersed—once more thwarted in their desire to see justice done, this time by an inexplicable bureaucratic decision. The "Death Dealer"—in the words of the editor of Höß's memoirs—had eluded death.

But the following day, April 16, 1947, he wasn't so lucky. After a priest heard his confession, Höß enjoyed his final request—a cup of hot coffee made from a small American stash and brewed by a Polish woman. He drank slowly, but the coffee was soon gone. Before being led to the gallows, he uttered his final words, "I am very sorry for what I have done to the Polish people. I ask that they forgive me."[37] Yet no remorse for Jews, his main—and intended—victims.

Photographers from a second-storey window worked their cumbersome cameras and captured the image of his final walk. He mounted the gallows, received the noose, which the hangman tightened, and stared without expression till the trapped door dropped. He was hanged next to the house inside the former Auschwitz I camp where, only four years earlier, he had lived with his wife and five children and where he had sent—according to the latest and most accurate postwar estimates—over a million innocent men, women, and children to their deaths.

In his memoirs, published posthumously, Höß emphasized with pride his deeply held *petit-bourgeois* sense of duty and absolute obedience to authority. He had concerned himself at Auschwitz with only one thing: executing his orders from Himmler and others, which meant administering with maximum efficiency the camp's equipment of mass murder, from the arrival at the camp of the deportation trains to the gassing and burning of the victims.

Yet in his horribly twisted mind, he felt himself a victim. He described how he suffered under the acts that he forced others to commit: "Believe me, I felt like shrinking into the ground out of pity, but I was not allowed to show the slightest emotion. . . . Today I deeply regret that I didn't spend more time with my family. I always believed that I had to be constantly on duty. Through this exaggerated sense of duty I always made my life more difficult than it actually was."[38]

Thus, his regrets had nothing to do with those whose slaughter he had supervised. His concern focused only on his own self-pity and alleged suffering. His anti-Semitism remained solidly intact. In this regard, Höß, like a multitude of other perpetrators, a number of them major figures in this book, likely encouraged the claims of Nazi apologists and Holocaust deniers. Repeatedly deniers have insisted that vengeful Jews and Allies made the Germans and their former Nazi rulers the real wartime and postwar victims.

Many years later, Primo Levi commented on the memoirs and how they expressed Höß's wholly merciless and deceitful nature: "In regard to the Jews his false notes become more strident. He feels no conflict, his Nazi indoctrination never collides with a new and more humane vision of the world. Quite simply, Höss has understood nothing, he has not transcended his past, he is not cured."[39]

Shortly after writing these words about Höß, on April 11, 1987, Levi committed suicide by jumping from the interior landing of his third-storey apartment in Turin to the ground floor below. Contrary to the view of many observers, Levi had never recovered from the awful pain and humiliation he and other survivors experienced at Auschwitz and other Nazi camps. And perhaps he could no longer endure a world of such profound intolerance and indifference. Fellow Holocaust survivor and author Elie Wiesel noted that Levi had died at Auschwitz forty years earlier.

OTHER TRIALS

Because it revealed the enormous dimensions of the crimes perpetrated at Auschwitz, Höß's trial in 1947 met with considerable response in Poland and worldwide. But simultaneously, trials in Poland of other former Auschwitz *SS* personnel resulted in mixed outcomes. On the one hand, similar to the Höß case, at the end of 1947 the world watched closely the verdicts handed down by a Krakow court to forty other members of the former Auschwitz *SS* force. That tribunal sentenced twenty-three defendants to death (later, two received pardons), six to life sentences in prison, seven to fifteen years in prison, and three to sentences of ten, five, and three years, respectively. The court even acquitted one *SS* man.

Postwar district tribunals in Poland meted out far lesser punishments to 590 other Auschwitz *SS* personnel. The courts passed death sentences against only six *SS* men and two *SS* women supervisors, sentenced three *SS* men to life in prison, and acquitted six. Sentences to the remaining defendants—nearly 97 percent—ranged from fifteen years to six months in prison. Among the latter group, the courts' most common sentence was three years in prison, the verdict based mainly on the ground that the defendant had been a member of the *SS* and not on their damning individual behavior.

Most Polish tribunals and prosecutors lacked a full understanding of Auschwitz's power structure and of the varying importance of the positions held by the defendants. Many of the judicial proceedings—carried out in haste and in an assembly-line style—resulted in obvious errors. Most egregiously, the courts acquitted or gave lenient sentences to numerous defendants who had terrorized prisoners and contributed actively to the death of hundreds of thousands of people brought to Auschwitz for their immediate extermination.

Down to the present day, even when one includes the West German trials of Auschwitz *SS* personnel between 1963 and 1976 and trials in other countries, some 90 percent of such personnel who had worked at the huge complex of death and concentration camps at one time or another avoided postwar arrest and punishment. Aleksander Lasik, a Polish scholar, has estimated, based on "camp documents" and "personnel files of nearly 6,500 members of the Auschwitz SS personnel," that "a total of 7,000 to 7,200 men and women supervisors served in Auschwitz" between 1940 and 1945. Further, he has calculated that "about 6,500 former members of the Auschwitz SS personnel survived the capitulation of the Third Reich."[40] But altogether, at the most, it is likely that no more than six hundred of them were brought to justice.

11

Memory in West Germany

Long and Short

Already on May 4, 1945, several days before Germany's surrender, at least one survivor of the Holocaust in Germany received a hint that in the future search for and punishment of perpetrators, Germans would do their utmost to render it impotent. Why wouldn't they forget easily or ignore what had happened? Why wouldn't they most likely exonerate both Hitler and themselves of the war and German atrocities? Why wouldn't they hide or protect the war criminals among them? What else were friends for?

That day, Victor Klemperer—a German Jew, Dresden professor, and husband of a non-Jew, whose mixed marriage had saved him from deportation to certain death in the extermination camps in the East—had spoken with two German soldiers on their way home, whom he met in Munich. Klemperer and his wife Eva were living with friends in the Bavarian capital following the massive Allied bombing of Dresden on February 13–14, 1945.

Klemperer recorded in his diary that the soldiers had just listened to a radio account of Berlin's surrender to the Soviet army and of Hitler's death. One of them observed, "If anyone had told me that, even four weeks ago, I would have shot him down—but now I don't believe anything anymore." He went on to critique Germany for wanting too much in the war, for overreaching and overdoing things, and for committing atrocities in Poland and Russia. "But the Führer," he concluded, "probably knew nothing about it."

Then both claimed that one couldn't blame Hitler for what had happened, because, they alleged, Himmler had been in charge of the government. Klemperer didn't disagree—despite his deep, determined desire to do so. "Still they believe in Hitler," he said to himself in disbelief, thinking about the massive wartime destruction and suffering all around him and throughout Germany: "He [Hitler] undoubtedly had a religious effect."[1]

A week later, Klemperer asked a German woman whether she'd heard anything about the fate of Hitler or other Nazi leaders. "No," she replied in a curt, surly tone.

Still fearful for his life, Klemperer didn't press her. He realized that the fate of Nazi officials "no longer interested her. The 3rd Reich is already almost as good as forgotten, everyone was opposed to it, 'always' opposed to it; and people have the most absurd ideas about the future."[2]

Two weeks later, he had another encounter with the rapidly appearing amnesia of the defeated Germany. On this occasion a woman had told him, "What is 'Gestapo,' I've never heard the word. I've never been interested in politics, I don't know anything about the persecution of the Jews." He responded to the woman's affront to history and memory in his diary:

> Is this true not-knowing or has it come into being only now? Of the Dachauers [former concentration camp inmates, many of whom were now refugees in Munich, "conspicuous in their white-and-blue-striped linen"] she always says only: "The convicts," she talks to them, yet nevertheless keeps a fearful distance. Her father, she says, was a Social Democrat, her husband—she does not know where he is—an "unpolitical" mechanic. What is the truth of this not-knowing?[3]

For a Jewish survivor, such responses seemed both frightening and unreal. Even Klemperer, isolated during the war, had known about the mass killing of the Jews. As early as March 1942 he'd heard of Auschwitz "or something like it," mentioned "as the most dreadful concentration camp. Work in a mine, death within a few days."[4] For a long time, he retained a quiet hope that there would be news from Jewish friends or acquaintances who had steadily disappeared all around him. Other sources of information confirmed the rumors that permeated the lives of every German, but no more compellingly than those of German Jews yet to be deported.

Klemperer's wife, Eva, had visited with an army corporal, an "Aryan" family friend home on leave from the East and from prosecuting the war against Soviet Russia. The soldier told her about the massacre of Jews at Babi Yar in the Ukraine during September 29–30, 1941. "Ghastly mass murders of Jews in Kiev," he said. "The heads of small children smashed against walls, thousands of men, women, adolescents shot down in a great heap, a hillock blown up, and the mass of bodies buried under the exploding earth."[5]

On October 17, 1942, Klemperer concluded that Auschwitz "appears to be a swift-working slaughterhouse." A week later, he decided that all conversations among Jews about the war and the problems of the Germans militarily in Russia "lead to the same reflection: 'If they [the Germans] have time, they'll kill us first.'"[6]

Yet Victor seemed to believe that such information described only isolated atrocities. He didn't realize that these nuggets of secondhand news reflected in small part the larger, wholesale, systematic genocide suffered by the victims of the Final Solution. By the end of 1942, far-reaching rumors had spread throughout Germany about the gassing of Jews, but similar to Klemperer, most Jews still did not—or could not—grasp what those scraps of information meant.

NAZI HUNTER IN THE MAKING

He had fainted in the arms of his American rescuer. A few days after U.S. troops liberated him from Mauthausen in Austria on May 5, 1945, as he walked in the surrounding countryside, the thirty-seven-year-old Polish Jew and former engineer dropped by a farmhouse. He conversed briefly with an Austrian peasant woman. By one glance at his gaunt face and physique and his loose and striped rags for clothes, she could tell from where the visitor hailed. Nodding in the direction of the concentration camp, she asked him, "Was it bad over there?"

"Be glad you didn't see the camp from the inside," Simon Wiesenthal replied.

"Why should I have seen it?" she asked. "I'm not a Jew."

Wiesenthal winced. Implicit in the woman's reply was a prevailing attitude of "this is what happens to Jews" and "this is what happens to the rest of us."[7] Her comment would help transform Wiesenthal into a tenacious postwar hunter of Nazi war criminals. In the weeks and years to come, he would hear many Austrians and "good Germans" volunteer to him that they "knew nothing about what was happening" under Nazi rule and had even "saved some Jews." To this, he replied with incredulity:

> If all the Jews had been saved that I was told about in those first few months, there would have been more Jews alive at the end of the war than when it began. I also stopped believing after a while when people tried to convince me they knew absolutely nothing. Maybe they knew not the whole truth about what went on inside the death camps. But all of them must have noticed *something*. . . . People knew what was going on, although many were ashamed and chose to look the other way so they wouldn't see too much. Soldiers and officers on leave from the eastern front came home and talked about massacres of the Jews there. People knew much more than they admitted, even to themselves, which is why today so many suffer from an acute sense of guilt.[8]

Wiesenthal, remaining in Austria, worked initially for a local U.S. Army war crimes unit until 1947, when he established his own similar organization, the Jewish Documentation Center, first in Linz, later in Vienna. In offering his services in late May 1945 to the Americans, he told them that he had spent time in thirteen Nazi concentration camps, the last Mauthausen:

> Every house I built is gone. I have lost my mother, my father, my wife, and ninety relatives in Poland. Poland is for me a cemetery. Every tree, every stone would remind me of whole tragedies. How can you ask me to live in a cemetery? . . .
>
> You liberated me, you saved my life, but I don't know what to do with my life. I have nobody and nothing to live for, but I could find a meaning for my life by helping you with your work. I've seen a lot and I have a good memory. Men and women have been murdered before my eyes. I can give you names and dates and sometimes addresses. I can help you find the criminals and, when you interrogate them, the most important thing is to ask the right questions—and I have those.[9]

Once he embarked on his newly chosen profession, few Germans or Austrians ever welcomed seeing Wiesenthal. He made them remember. And why in the world would they want to remember? Voluntary amnesia has always had its appeal. But Wiesenthal dedicated his postwar life to making certain that for them forgetting itself would be too conspicuous—too painful.

A "FAMILY HISTORY"

In January 1979, only a few miles from the former Nazi camp at Dachau, an eighteen-year-old woman in Munich was determined to watch the initial broadcast of what would quickly be recognized as a landmark television miniseries—the all-star, Emmy-winning *Holocaust.* Despite the airing of the American docudrama throughout much of West Germany, Bavaria's regional channel refused to broadcast it. The teenager's mother also attempted to prevent her from seeing it.

The series aired first in the United States in April 1978—where it earned a near 50 percent market share—and was subsequently watched also by hundreds of millions of people around the world. It personalized the Holocaust by focusing on the experience of a single German Jewish family and a German family; in the latter the husband was an ambitious *SS* member who turned eventually into a merciless and cruel war criminal. The miniseries profoundly influenced public opinion in West Germany as well as globally. It especially raised awareness of the Holocaust among younger Germans such as Katharina von Kellenbach. Moreover, the telecast helped to convince the West German government to revoke its statute of limitations concerning the punishment of Nazi crimes.

Many years later, von Kellenbach, in an essay she wrote for the American journal *Holocaust and Genocide Studies*, recalled the near-perfect wall of "silence" in her family about the Holocaust. Her history lessons in school had marginalized the Nazi persecution of Jews. She learned about the Third Reich only in the sixth, ninth, and eleventh grades, but those courses "had examined the period 1933–45 through the NSDAP [Nazi Party] political platform, tracing the constitutional and institutional shifts from democracy to dictatorship and back." The classes didn't include lengthy discussions of such subjects as anti-Semitism or the Holocaust. But von Kellenbach remembered seeing concentration camp films, with their "gruesome photo materials," and taking "a class trip to nearby Dachau."[10]

She realized that what she learned in school, church groups, and the media "could not be discussed safely inside my family. My questions were never considered innocent and conversations around the dinner table quickly turned antagonistic." She lived the dichotomy of second- and third-generation post-Holocaust German children—that is, the presence of the Holocaust in mass media, history classes, and public discussion alongside "its emotionally charged absence inside the family." For her, the consequences had a stunning result:

> I concluded (inexplicably) from my family's inability to communicate about history that the "bad guys" no longer existed. My aspiring, middle-class world seemed to have no connection with the horrors of the war. Obviously the perpetrators were monsters, and nobody I knew fit that description. The normalcy of postwar German life depended upon the virtual disappearance of those who had implemented the National Socialist vision of an Aryan *Herrenrasse* (master race).[11]

But in the early 1970s, von Kellenbach, then barely a teenager, attended a family gathering in Stuttgart. There, a relative handed her a newspaper article. It reported that German authorities had accused her uncle, Alfred Ebner, of killing twenty thousand Jews in 1941 in Nazi-occupied Byelorussia but that his trial had been discontinued due to his health. As she read the article, she recalled later, Ebner sat "peacefully (and apparently in good health) across the table from me. He was a regular guest at family gatherings, and I had often visited his family's house in Stuttgart before my family moved to Munich." The experience influenced the young—and perceptive—von Kellenbach. Suddenly, she had questions:

> What was I to make of the fact that my relatives did not censure him? Wouldn't my family treat him as a murderer if he had killed one person? The fact that he sat among us unperturbed implied that the murder of tens of thousands never happened. I wondered how and where he did it, and who his victims were.[12]

When she tried to find answers and asked relatives about Ebner, they brushed her off. "Of course, he didn't do these things, these are all lies," they told her. "Leave this old man his deserved peace, he has suffered enough." The family met her questions "with stony silence." Occasionally, when she asked a family member, "each attempt was received as an attack and rebuffed with increasing hostility."

She never learned anything about her uncle's past. The family viewed Ebner as a casualty of war and victim of postwar vindictiveness. "Eventually," she admitted, "I forgot (repressed?) this knowledge." On the other hand, she didn't blame her failure to remember or to pursue the matter solely on "family resistance." She had her own "protective shields," namely that "the idea of a mass murderer upon whose knees I had sat as a child brought the horror too close to home." This made "seemingly irresistible" the "desire to deny and minimize evil" in her midst.

But years later, von Kellenbach "remembered." In 1983 she moved to the United States to pursue a graduate degree in religious studies. There, she met Jewish survivors and their children, during which she experienced a stunning revelation:

> My self-image as a "good German" who had nothing to do with Nazism collapsed as the memory of that newspaper article flooded back. In that moment, I became aware of the monumental "vanishing act" that had erased consciousness of the perpetrators. I realized that my forgetfulness was not accidental but the result of the endemic evasions that characterized Germany's postwar culture. While I experienced myself as the blameless victim of my family's "conspiracy of silence," my lack of precise knowledge also colluded with the perpetrators' desire to conceal their crimes. As my Jewish peers shared their families' painful stories, I felt a growing sense of urgency to break through the mantle of deception and to become much more direct and deliberate in my search for truth. For the sake of maintaining honest and authentic relationships with my Jewish friends, I had to take a stance against the erasure of the Holocaust and confront my family's secrets.[13]

In 1989, two years after Ebner's death, she began collecting information on him from archives in Germany, Israel, and the United States. During her exceedingly bold but difficult quest, she "felt the weight of betrayal of my family and of the contradiction between my own childhood experience of Ebner as a personable family man and his actions during the Holocaust."

To the question—"Did this truly happen?"—she found a devastating answer. "The historical record," she wrote in 2003, having become a religion professor in the United States, "shows that Ebner was directly responsible for the implementation of Nazi extermination policies."[14] Also his trial in a West

German court, discussed later in this chapter, produced a similar conclusion. Yet her uncle was never convicted.

For von Kellenbach, however, in uncovering and confronting the crimes of her uncle, she had lived what she believed. "It is the moral task of more recent generations," she concluded, "to resist" the "vanishing acts" of the perpetrators, the "silence" of their families, and the erasure of the Holocaust. "To face one's own closeness to horrific crimes is a painful process that requires great honesty and courage."[15] She had plenty of both, and more—one of the rare exceptions in a post-Holocaust world that more often manifested those who felt or showed little concern or remorse for what happened.

ALFRED EBNER'S REAL PAST

One of relatively few Nazi participants in the Final Solution brought to trial by West German courts, Alfred Ebner had killed both because of personal impulse and because of his official government position. Beginning in 1950, shortly after the creation of the Federal Republic—and quite apart from the unsuccessful effort of Best and other former Nazis to force from Western Allies a wholesale amnesty of Nazi war criminals convicted by Allied tribunals—the Allies authorized German courts to try all Nazi crimes, even those perpetrated against Allied nationals.

An early and fanatical follower of Hitler, Ebner had joined the Nazi Party and *SS* in 1931. He had enrolled in a special Nazi school to educate future political leaders for the party and the government that the Nazis expected to establish in short order. When the world war began, he fought briefly in France in the *Wehrmacht*. Shortly after Germany invaded Russia, the Nazi hierarchy sent him to the East.

In September 1941 he arrived in Pinsk, a city and surrounding area that held some thirty thousand Jews in formerly eastern Poland (but in the fall of 1941 part of Nazi-occupied Byelorussia). Appointed deputy commissioner of the region's Nazi civilian administration, he was responsible for the local Jewish inhabitants. Already during August 7–8, 1941, an *Einsatzgruppe* unit had killed between eight thousand and eleven thousand Jewish men from Pinsk.

In his commissioner's post Ebner controlled the destiny of more than twenty thousand Jews who had survived the first mass killing in the Pinsk area. From the fall of 1941 to December 1942 he supervised the systematic confiscation of Jewish property, the exploitation of Jewish labor, and the methodical starvation of the Jewish population. In May 1942 he organized the ghettoization of the Pinsk-area Jews, mostly women and children. The massive overcrowding and the lack of water, food, and wood for cooking and heating in the ghetto rendered it a death trap for the inhabitants. At least forty died per day.

Between October 29 and November 2, at Himmler's directive, Battalion 306 of the Nazi Uniformed Police marched Pinsk's remaining Jews from the ghetto and shot them in large trenches or ditches. Only a handful survived the massacre; most of those had hidden from the killers or had joined the partisans operating in the surrounding Pripet marshes.

After the war Ebner lived with his family in Stuttgart and operated a business until his arrest in January 1962 and indictment two years later before the city's regional court. On January 3, 1966, the authorities transferred the case to a court in Frankfurt am Main. Finally, in March 1968, over two decades since the actual events on which the charges were based, the prosecution indicted Ebner and members of Police Battalion 306 for "several hundred cases of malicious and cruel murder."[16]

But despite his responsibility for implementing Nazi extermination policies, Ebner was never convicted. What had happened? Where was justice? Where was memory?

WEST GERMAN "JUSTICE"

The Federal Republic of West Germany, founded in May 1949, prosecuted a tiny minority of the estimated several hundred thousand former Holocaust perpetrators. This held true even after the Bonn government created in 1958 the Central Office of the State Judicial Authorities for the Investigation of National Socialist Crimes (*Zentrale Stelle der Landesjustizverwaltungen zur Aufklärung nationalsozialistischer Verbrechen*, or *ZS*).

Established in Ludwigsburg through an agreement with West German states, the *ZS* investigated Nazi crimes—committed primarily in the East—and collected information on perpetrators in the form of documents or eyewitness testimony, evidence it then forwarded to the appropriate state's prosecutor's office for possible criminal prosecution. Eventually the *ZS*, according to one historian, would provide "a staging ground for 30,000 cases, with almost 13,000 indictments filed and 5,426 cases tried."[17]

Altogether, from the war's end in 1945 to 1992, the West Germans investigated 103,823 persons suspected of participating in or committing Nazi crimes. Of this number, courts convicted only 6,487 (of which 5,513, or 85 percent, were condemned for "nonlethal" crimes). Thirteen were sentenced to death (before the Federal Republic abolished the death sentence), 163 to life imprisonment, 6,197 to temporary imprisonment, and 114 to only fines. If one excludes defendants prosecuted for robbery or assault charges, the disturbingly low number shrinks further. Between May 1945 and January 1992,

West German courts tried only 1,793 cases related to Nazi capital crimes committed during the world war. Of those, 974 led to convictions, while 819 ended with either the court acquitting the defendants or terminating the proceedings for other reasons.

In May 1955 an agreement among the United States, Great Britain, France, and West Germany included the provision that German courts could not investigate or prosecute anyone whom the Allied occupation powers had investigated earlier. The overwhelming majority of *SS* personnel who had served at the Auschwitz camps, as noted in chapter 10, avoided postwar arrest and punishment. Of the four thousand former *Einsatzgruppen* members who, between the fall of 1939 and 1944, slaughtered well over one million Jews in Poland and the Soviet Union, nearly all escaped retribution. By 1948, the Western Allies had captured, and a U.S. tribunal had placed on trial for war crimes, barely two dozen of them. Later, West German courts tried only a tiny number of other former *Einsatzgruppen* members.

In the Federal Republic, nearly all of the convicted—in contrast to their crimes of mass murder—received light prison terms. How did such miscarriages of justice in West Germany happen? As punishment for the crime of murder, West German law mandated a maximum sentence of life in prison. But the new Bonn government, under its first chancellor Konrad Adenauer, chose not to prosecute Nazi criminals using the charges or legal procedures of the IMT. Instead, the government wanted to utilize the long-standing German penal code (with its Nazi revisions repealed).

In contrast to the IMT charter, the code provided for lesser penalties (the IMT had executed some of the worst criminals convicted) and distinguished between "perpetrator" (murderer) and "accomplice" or "accessory" (those who aided and abetted murder). In 1951 the Allies submitted to massive German pressure and permitted West Germany to try Nazi criminals—but only on the basis of the penal code. Most Germans resented the Nuremberg trials and denazification process and pressed for the pardon and reintegration into society of ex-Nazis convicted of even serious crimes.

Moreover, West German law—as a condition for convicting defendants as perpetrators—required evidence of individual acts of murder by the accused. For a murder conviction, prosecutors also had to show in the killings the presence of "base motive" (e.g., racial hatred). But while most pertinent available Nazi records provided statistical numbers of the murdered and/or vague accounts of what had happened, rarely did they discuss the perpetrators' name, will, motive, and intentions. Further, the places of daily systematic killing of thousands of nonregistered Jews—the death camps and *Einsatzgruppen* execution sites in Russia—left little or no trace of the victims.

For all these and other reasons West German courts had difficulty finding proof of the perpetration of murder and, therefore, seldom applied the maximum punishment. Instead, the courts judged many defendants as accomplices or accessories who, in fact, had ordered, arranged, or supervised mass killings but who hadn't been shown to have committed themselves an act of murder. More often than not, such persons received much lighter prison sentences than some of their former subordinates, whom the courts convicted of shooting or otherwise killing Jews themselves.

EBNER: A TYPICAL EXAMPLE

In Ebner's case, the prosecution attempted to show that he was a perpetrator or co-perpetrator because he'd wanted to murder Jews. A high-level civilian administrator, he enjoyed authority over the local police and Ukrainian militia and coordinated with the police battalions employed in the mass executions. "More than the shooters," von Kellenbach wrote in 2003, "he carried direct responsibility for the fate of the Jews in his district."

To attain a murder conviction, the prosecution argued in the indictment that Ebner had acted because of "racial hatred." He "so hated Jews himself" that he "wanted the measures against the Jews as his own, and he had a personal interest in the execution of these measures." But the procedures and rules of West German law made it difficult to prove that Ebner had acted out of such "base motives." He denied any personal hatred of Jews and insisted that he'd never been taught anti-Semitism. When questioned about his Nazi ideological training, he declared: "Regarding the Jewish race, there were no special comments or instructions. . . . We were not trained in racial hatred. We were possibly told that the Jews are not the ideal race."[18]

He knew that admitting to anti-Semitism made him liable to a murder conviction, so he lied about his deeply held anti-Jewish beliefs and presented himself as merely a loyal civil servant, just a cog, in Hitler's Germany. He had only followed orders, he claimed, and, when doing so, had been "humane towards the Jews." Nevertheless, documents signed by him made clear that he'd slashed in half food rations for the Pinsk Ghetto. The indictment, though, charged him with personally shooting Jews on two occasions because the victims had smuggled a piece of butter into the ghetto.

According to his niece, Ebner's "administrative responsibility for murder proved especially difficult to prosecute." In pretrial hearings the judges dismissed three charges because witnesses couldn't verify that he'd done the shootings. But testimony confirmed that in the summer of 1942, he ordered the creation of a list of forty "sick and mentally retarded" Jews whom later the police shot. Again in November 1942 he "selected" ten more Jews for execution, though eventually they were spared. In each case Ebner led the persons to the trucks that transported them out of the ghetto for killing.

But the judges dismissed the charges for lack of evidence. They speculated that the victims "might have found their death at the hands of a third party, independently of the defendant." In von Kellenbach's words: "This seems disingenuous, to say the least. Obviously, as the deputy area commissioner, Ebner did not have to perform the shootings himself."

Ebner's case never went to trial. On December 2, 1971, the court suspended the proceedings against him for reasons of alleged poor health. He had complained of "dizziness, lack of concentration, forgetfulness, and difficulty thinking." The court accepted a medical expert's diagnosis that he suffered from "pseudo-dementia," thereby making "it impossible for the defendant to stand trial."

Similar to many other court cases dealing with Nazi crimes, for the reason of an alleged minor ailment the proceeding against Ebner ended without a conviction. The court suspended its proceedings permanently on August 25, 1978. In the meantime, apparently in good health, Ebner appeared regularly at family gatherings in Stuttgart and on at least one occasion sat across a table from his niece.

He died peacefully in 1987, in her words, "his involvement in the genocide unacknowledged, unrepented, and unpunished." To the end, with von Kellenbach an exception, his family claimed him as a victim of the war and of postwar harassment. He'd suffered, it was alleged, undeserved accusations, questions, and mistreatment in a hostile postwar world. After all, according to the family view, "If it weren't for the Jews," neither the Holocaust nor the investigations and trials of persons like Ebner would have occurred.[19] In this twisted scenario the Jew had become the cause, catalyst, and perpetrator. Incredibly, anti-Semitism and the dehumanization of the Holocaust's real victims continued—fostered by both West German society and its legal system.

Franz Stangl in front of the commandant's hut in Treblinka. Stangl holds a horsewhip. He was the second commandant of Treblinka, arriving in August 1942 from Sobibor. *Source*: U.S. Holocaust Memorial Museum, courtesy of Jacob Rader Marcus Center of the American Jewish Archives

Franz Stangl. *Source*: U.S. Holocaust Memorial Museum, courtesy of Jacob Rader Marcus Center of the American Jewish Archives

Reinhard Heydrich, *SS* lieutenant general, chief of the *RSHA*, and deputy Reich protector of Bohemia and Moravia, as he appeared in January 1942, a few months before his assassination by Czech partisans. *Source*: Bundesarchiv, Bild 183-B20373. Photo: Friedrich Franz Bauer

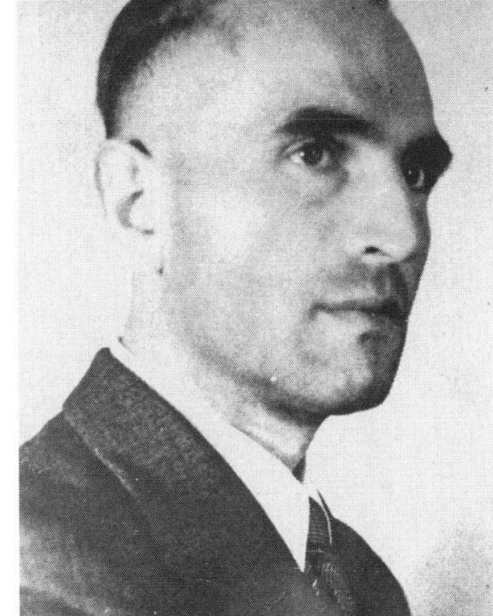

Werner Best in 1942. During the war, he served as deputy head of the *RSHA*, administrative chief of the German military command in France, and Reich plenipotentiary in Denmark. *Source*: Bundesarchiv, Bild 183-B22627

Erich von dem Bach-Zelewski, center, Higher *SS* and Police Leader for central Russia, reviews Uniformed Police in Minsk in 1943. *Source*: Bundesarchiv, Bild 101III-Weiss-046-14-1. Photo: Weiss

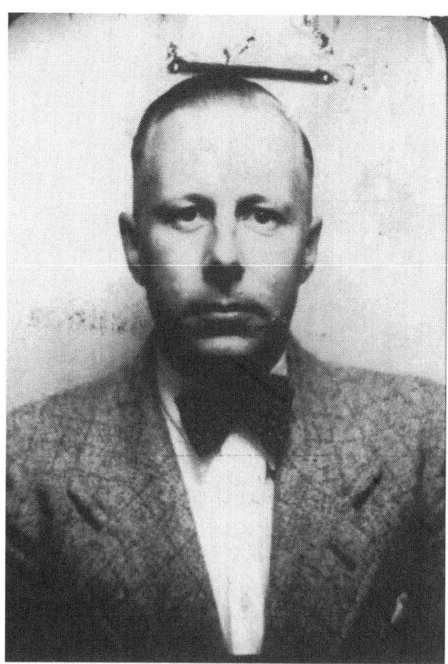

Walther Rauff, senior *SS* official in the *RSHA* Technical Department and developer of the gas vans. *Source*: Yad Vashem Photo Archives

SS officers socialize in July 1944 on the grounds of the *SS* retreat Solahütte outside of Auschwitz. From left to right: Josef Mengele, *SS* physician at Auschwitz; Rudolf Höß, former commandant of Auschwitz; Josef Kramer, commandant of Auschwitz-Birkenau; and Anton Thumann. *Source*: U.S. Holocaust Memorial Museum Photo Archives

Irma Grese, known as the "Bitch of Belsen," a female *SS* guard in Auschwitz-Birkenau, Ravensbrück, and Bergen-Belsen concentration camps. She was convicted by a British military tribunal at Lüneburg of committing crimes against humanity and was executed by hanging. *Source*: U.S. Holocaust Memorial Museum Photo Archives

Irma Grese and Josef Kramer await trial in September 1945 before a British Military Tribunal. *Source*: U.S. Holocaust Memorial Museum Photo Archives

Wilhelm Boger, an *SS* staff sergeant in the Political Department at Auschwitz from 1942 to 1945. *Source*: Yad Vashem Photo Archives

Dr. Karl Clauberg, center, gathers with other *SS* officers in September 1944 for drinks following the dedication of the new *SS* hospital at Auschwitz. *Source*: U.S. Holocaust Memorial Museum Photo Archives

Odilo Globocnik, in uniform as an *SS* colonel in 1938–1939. During the war, he was promoted to *SS* major general and lieutenant general of the Police; he served as *SS* and Police Leader for the Lublin district in Government General Poland and as Higher *SS* and Police Leader in the Adriatic region. *Source*: Bundesarchiv, Bild 146-2007-0188

Hermann Göring, center, second in command to Hitler in Nazi Germany, talks with Brigadier General Robert J. Stack, assistant commander of the U.S. Thirty-sixth Infantry Division (right) and Major General John Dahlquist, commander of the Thirty-sixth Division, after Göring's arrest in the Grand Hotel at Kitzbuehl in Tyrol, Austria. *Source*: U.S. Holocaust Memorial Museum Photo Archives

Kurt Daluege, right, chief of the German Uniformed Police, looks at a photograph with *Reichsführer SS* Heinrich Himmler, during their meeting on October 7, 1942, at *SS* headquarters in Hegewald near Zhitomir, Ukraine. *Source*: U.S. Holocaust Memorial Museum Photo Archives

Karl Wolff, center, *SS* lieutenant general and personal adjutant to *Reichsführer SS* Heinrich Himmler, converses in 1941 with Himmler, right, and Rudolf Schmundt at Rastenburg [East Prussia], Germany. *Source*: U.S. Holocaust Memorial Museum Photo Archives

Otto Ohlendorf in November 1943. During the war, he served as head of the *SD* in the *RSHA* and commander of *Einsatzgruppe* D, attached to the German Eleventh Army, that operated in the Ukraine. *Source*: Bundesarchiv, Bild 183-J08517. Photo: Schwarz

Hermann Göring, flanked by two military policemen, testifies in March 1946 at the IMT. *Source*: U.S. Holocaust Memorial Museum Photo Archives

Ernst Kaltenbrunner (right) watches with other *SS* officials in 1941 as the commandant of Mauthausen concentration camp, Franz Ziereis, points out something to Heinrich Himmler, while the officials view the quarry during an inspection tour of the camp. In January 1943 Kaltenbrunner succeeded Reinhard Heydrich as chief of the *RSHA*. *Source*: U.S. Holocaust Memorial Museum Photo Archives

Portrait of Hans Frank, German governor-general of Poland from 1939 to 1945. *Source*: U.S. Holocaust Memorial Museum Photo Archives

Portrait of Alfred Rosenberg, Nazi racial ideologue and Reich minister for the Occupied Eastern Territories. *Source*: U.S. Holocaust Memorial Museum Photo Archives

Governor-General Hans Frank hosts *Reichsführer SS* Heinrich Himmler at a dinner held at Wawel castle during his visit to Krakow. *Source*: U.S. Holocaust Memorial Museum Photo Archives

Alfred Ebner in 1975. From the fall of 1941 to December 1942, Ebner served as deputy commissioner in the German civilian administration in Pinsk in Nazi-occupied Byelorussia. *Source*: Photo courtesy of Katharina von Kellenbach

Arthur Greiser, deputy *Gauleiter* of Danzig, and from 1939 to 1945 *Gauleiter* and Reich governor of the Warthegau, the Polish western regions annexed to Germany. *Source*: U.S. Holocaust Memorial Museum Photo Archives

Commandant Amon Goeth stands half-dressed with his rifle on the balcony of his villa in the Plaszow concentration camp. *Source*: U.S. Holocaust Memorial Museum Photo Archives

Hermann Josef Abs, left, German banker during the Nazi era and after, at a reception in the Beethovenhalle in Bonn in 1961. At the time, Abs served as chair of the managing board of the Deutsche Bank. At right is Ludwig Erhard, West German Minister of Economics; in the center is Karl Blessing, president of the German Bundesbank. *Source*: Bundespresseamt, B 145 Bild-00082636. Photo: Egon Steiner

Franz Schlegelberger, state secretary in the Reich Ministry of Justice. During 1941–1942 he served as acting Reich Minister of Justice. *Source*: Bundesarchiv, Bild 183-B05039

Hanns Albin Rauter served during the war as Higher *SS* and Police Leader and Commissioner General for Public Safety in the Nazi occupation administration in the Netherlands. *Source*: Bundesarchiv, Bild 183-1982-1021-509. Photo: Porsche

Portrait of Robert Wagner, *Gauleiter* and Reich governor of Alsace-Baden. *Source*: U.S. Holocaust Memorial Museum Photo Archives

Portrait of German Field Marshal Erich von Manstein from June 1946 at the IMT commission hearings investigating the Supreme Command of the German Armed Forces. *Source*: U.S. Holocaust Memorial Museum Photo Archives

Defendant Adolf Eichmann, former chief of the *Gestapo*'s "Jewish department," IVB4, during World War II, takes notes during his trial in Jerusalem in May 1961. The glass booth in which Eichmann sat was erected to protect him from assassination. *Source*: U.S. Holocaust Memorial Museum Photo Archives

Alois Brunner, an *SS* officer who served among others as assistant to Adolf Eichmann in the *Gestapo*'s "Jewish department." *Source*: Yad Vashem Photo Archives

Portrait of Franz Novak, an assistant to Adolf Eichmann in Department IVB4 of the *Gestapo*. *Source*: U.S. Holocaust Memorial Museum Photo Archives

Klaus Barbie, 1942, served in the *Gestapo* in Lyon, France. *Source*: Yad Vashem Photo Archives

12

Pseudo-Purges and Politics

He soon learned firsthand the bitter truth—and how it permeated postwar German politics. Denazification boards in Schmallenberg called Hans Frankenthal and his brother Ernst, both survivors of Auschwitz, to testify as witnesses in hearings against former local Nazis and their sympathizers. Most of the proceedings proved—as so much else in the postwar world—that only the victims of Nazism cared about what had happened to them.

Appearing before the local board in 1946, Frankenthal testified first against Robert Krämer, a livestock dealer who as early as 1937 had been observed breaking windows of the town shop owned by Max Stern, a Jewish cloth merchant in Schmallenberg. To make sure every resident saw what had happened, Stern covered the windows with cardboard.

But at Krämer's denazification hearing, a farmer friend, Kewekordes, testified for the defense: "I didn't see or hear anything with regard to the windows." Frankenthal found Kewekordes's statement such a bald-faced lie that he couldn't restrain himself in the courtroom. He shouted at Kewekordes, "They're showing a movie in town right now called Der Meineidbauer [The Farmer Who Perjured Himself]—why don't you go see it!"

What, Frankenthal thought to himself, would the board do with Krämer, a former Nazi collaborator? He couldn't believe what he witnessed at Krämer's hearing. During the *Kristallnacht* in 1938, Krämer had supplied straw to Nazi storm troopers who used it to set the local synagogue ablaze. Nevertheless, the board decided not to remember this or anything about Krämer's longtime cooperation with the Nazis; instead, it "exonerated" him rather than classifying him at least as a "lesser offender." Frankenthal mused long after, "And when the Cold War began, things got even worse. Denazification was a farce."[1]

DENAZIFICATION

Western Allied authorities had established the denazification boards in Schmallenberg and elsewhere at the local level in West Germany and had staffed them with anti-Nazi Germans. The composition of board members reflected the mistaken belief of the British, American, and French occupiers that Nazism was principally a political phenomenon (not a racial and cultural one), which the Allies could eliminate by removing or purging Nazis from positions of power and replacing them with "acceptable" Germans, thereby establishing democracy. But, more often than not, anti-Nazi was not equal to or interchangeable with a pro-Jewish stance. Quite the contrary—as the Frankenthal brothers discovered.

Denazification began at the war's end in 1945, when the Allies dissolved and outlawed the Nazi Party and its affiliated organizations. During that summer and fall the Allies arrested automatically and interned hundreds of thousands of former middle- and lower-level Nazi political officials as well as economic and cultural leaders. The occupying powers banned such persons from continued employment and from use of their property (business, land, and housing).

In March 1946 the United States, Britain, and France created in their zones denazification boards to investigate former Nazi leaders as well as millions more adult Germans, like Robert Krämer of Schmallenberg, for their affiliation with or relationship to Nazism. The boards collected evidence about defendants, including questionnaires completed by them and statements about them from witnesses. Based on their investigation, the boards classified the accused into one of five categories: I—"major offender" (criminals); II—"offender" (active supporters of the Nazi Party); III—"lesser offender" (persons who had collaborated, but in less serious ways); IV—"follower" (opportunists who had joined Nazi organizations but not participated in their activities); and V—"exonerated."

For persons placed in categories I through III, penalties ranged from imprisonment in a labor camp from two to ten years to confiscation of property (I—all property save necessities; II—property in whole or part; and III—property acquired by political means, like *Aryanization*), prohibition to hold public office, loss of claims for pensions, restrictions on housing and residence, and payment of fines. The so-called followers (IV) paid fines of varying amounts. According to Allied law, former Nazi Party members and officials who wished to continue their careers, especially in political administration, had to receive a classification below II ("offender").

Initially, the occupying powers supervised denazification in their respective zones, but this endeavor, for numerous reasons, proved to be an enormously difficult task. The United States processed some 12,753,000 cases in its zone alone (most of which never reached the trial stage). By 1950, only three hundred persons remained in labor camps under sentences imposed by denazification boards. The Germans, who assumed control of denazification as prescribed by Allied law, proved even more inadequate in their efforts than had the Allies.[2]

KARL LÖFFLER: COLOGNE'S *GESTAPO* CHIEF

He had headed the "Jewish desk" of the Cologne *Gestapo* during the main waves of deportations of that city's Jews from October 1941 to September 1942, and again in October 1944. "Evacuation to the East," his office euphemistically termed the deportations—employing a phrase that concealed the victims' transport in train cars to their deaths in ghettos and other killing sites in Eastern Europe. By 1943, of the 14,816 Jews in Cologne a decade earlier, the *Gestapo* had rounded up and deported nearly four thousand. During 1944 the Germans even deported those Jews in "mixed marriages" and so-called Jews of mixed ancestry (*Mischlinge*); some eleven thousand died at Auschwitz. At the war's end, only forty to fifty Jews in the city survived by hiding.

Karl Löffler, Cologne's "local Eichmann," directed the deportations. Löffler knew fully what awaited deportees at journey's end. Seldom did he administer physical force personally to the assembled Jews placed on the trains headed east. But prior to the deportations he met with many of the Jews daily and, through personal arbitrary decisions, determined which of them should live and which should die.

He did spare a few local Jews, but without a qualm he condemned most to death. Mothers' pleas or young people's tears or those seeking to save loved ones failed to move him. On some occasions he even escorted Jews publicly from their crude, overcrowded ghetto in the city's western suburb of Müngersdorf to the waiting trains. Most Cologne citizens, aware of the disappearance of the city's Jews, remained indifferent to what had happened.

In October 1945 the British arrested Löffler at his family home in Cologne and placed him in a POW camp in the Ruhr valley town of Recklinghausen. At fifty-eight years old, his life appeared over. During his first months of internment the IMT in Nuremberg tried twenty-two leading German war criminals and sentenced twelve to their death and seven to lengthy prison terms; it acquitted only three.

Most observers at the time expected that Löffler and all other former *Gestapo* perpetrators of Nazi terror and genocide would receive similar severe punishment—either from an Allied court or a denazification board.

But shortly after the end of the IMT, denazification authorities in Cologne began receiving letters and affidavits—the so-called Persil certificates—from prominent Cologne citizens in support of Löffler.

During early 1947 two local clergymen—one the second–most powerful Catholic official in the city, the other the head of the local Protestant church—wrote British authorities urging them to take mercy on the former *Gestapo* chief. Other letters from private individuals and former colleagues provided further glowing testimony to Löffler's supposed good character and anti-Nazi sympathies. The letters built a seemingly convincing case that Löffler deserved to be spared from prosecution and to receive every consideration in the denazification process. Nothing made this image more believable, however, than the support he received from a few members of the tiny remnant of Cologne's Jewish community, especially from its head during the late 1940s and early 1950s, Moritz Goldschmidt.

On July 4, 1949, Goldschmidt wrote the Cologne denazification authorities about Löffler's work as a former *Gestapo* chief: "In this capacity he [Löffler] displayed tolerance in every sense of the word to the Jewish religious community." Goldschmidt urged the authorities "to take these things into consideration in your judgment."[3]

Nothing uncommon existed in the large number of letters written for Löffler; nearly every former Nazi under postwar investigation assembled for himself many such references. Almost always, former Nazis could count on family and friends to vouch for their innocence of Nazi activity or to protect and even hide them from Allied and other authorities (as in the cases of Stangl and Mengele).

What made Löffler's letters unusual, however, was who wrote them and—more unanswerable—why. The high-ranking church leaders, for example, supported him because they possibly had something to hide from the Nazi era that Löffler knew about and threatened to expose publicly. Or perhaps, like so many pro-German, anti-Semitic, anti-Bolshevik churchmen, they simply sympathized with the agenda and "achievements" of the Nazi leadership.

But far more rare were letters from Jews. Why Goldschmidt did so apparently resulted from the fact that he and his family had survived the Holocaust while most other Cologne Jews had not, and that possibly he'd paid Löffler to spare him and his loved ones from deportation and, in hindsight, didn't wish this to be revealed. Or perhaps Goldschmidt had deceived himself into thinking that the *Gestapo* chief had spared him and his family when the real reason they'd survived was that his wife was Catholic.

Despite these letters of heart-warming support from most unusual sources, Löffler was not the upstanding, humane opponent of Nazism and Jewish persecution they claimed him to be. A former Cologne *Gestapo* official who hadn't joined the Nazi Party and whose denazification board had exonerated him gave the following testimony about Löffler to prosecutors on October 21, 1952:

> The leading figure in the Jewish department was Löffler. He was commonly known as a great Jew hater. It may be that he had occasionally helped [people out] in individual cases. But such measures were not born out of humanitarian compassion; rather, they were tied to advantages of a material nature. Only in this way can I possibly explain the positive testimony that the head of the Cologne Jewish Community Goldschmidt has provided.[4]

Still others testified to Löffler's numerous crimes perpetrated against thousands of defenseless and innocent people. A Cologne couple, Friedrich and Regina Löwenstein, held Löffler personally responsible for the death of their son, Rudolf, at Auschwitz. They and an aid committee for Nazi victims, the Cologne branch of the Association of Persons Persecuted by the Nazi Regime, charged that Löffler had known fully about the death camps to which he'd helped deport thousands of Cologne Jews, including the Löwensteins' "half Jewish" son. The Löwensteins—Friedrich a Jew, Regina a Catholic—provided documentary evidence showing how, in July 1942, Löffler had arrested and deported Rudolf Löwenstein, a *Mischling* who, because he hadn't violated German law, couldn't be deported legally.

Nevertheless, on May 13, 1952, Löffler claimed to West German authorities that he had known nothing about the fate of deported Jews. He couldn't have known, he insisted, because the *Gestapo* had transferred him from Cologne to its Brussels office "at the beginning of 1942" before the Cologne deportations began. But a copy of the Cologne *Gestapo*'s organizational chart of April 1942—thus during the middle of the city's deportations—listed him as head of the "Jewish desk." In fact, his transfer to Brussels had come much later, in September 1942, and in July 1944 he'd returned to the Cologne office, a full three months before the last deportation transport left the city.

Originally, in 1948 the denazification board classified Löffler as a category III Nazi, a "lesser offender"—not an unusual category for *Gestapo* officers who'd held his position. The classification prevented Löffler from returning to police service and from receiving his pension. But outraged at the judgment and nearing retirement, he appealed the board's decision. Incredibly, the authorities granted him a new classification—category V, the status of fully "exonerated" of Nazi activity—that provided him the pension he sought.

West German authorities favored Löffler (as they did with so many other former Nazis and Holocaust perpetrators), but it didn't end there. In the fall of 1955 the state government of North Rhine-Westphalia decided, in calculating Löffler's pension, to factor in his years in the *Gestapo*. Three years later, the state refigured his pension once more, this time to reflect all of his promotions in the former, now-discredited and criminalized political police. Fully "rehabilitated" and compensated, Löffler lived several more years to a ripe old age. About his case and those of other former *Gestapo* men like him, historian Eric Johnson writes:

> Even though they were never adequately punished for what they had done, Karl Löffler . . . and other Jewish affairs specialists were nonetheless serious war criminals, no less than, and perhaps even more than, some of the more obviously brutal and fanatical Gestapo colleagues with whom they served.
>
> It is important that these men not be viewed as upstanding, correct, and decent career police officers who were forced against their will to join and remain in the Gestapo, as they presented themselves in their disingenuous postwar self-portraits. Nearly all Gestapo officers created self-serving and deeply false characterizations of themselves as they tried to escape prosecution. . . . They were ardent anti-Semites and convinced Nazis who had believed fully in Nazi ideology.[5]

In short, Löffler's postwar story repeated itself *ad nauseum* all across Germany. Between 1946 and 1950, of the roughly 3.66 million denazification trials in the British, American, and French zones of occupation, only around twenty-five thousand—far less than 1 percent—led to classification of those prosecuted in the two highest categories of Nazi "offender." In contrast, some 150,000 persons—including many former *Gestapo* officials like the "tolerant" Löffler and other civil servants—received classification as "lesser offenders," and around a million as "followers" of Nazism. In May 1951 the Federal Republic granted many such persons amnesty, which entitled them to re-employment in public life and pensions.

HERMANN JOSEF ABS: THE "NON-NAZI" BANKER

A devout Catholic who never joined the Nazi Party, Hermann Josef Abs was "merely" responsible for the bank's "foreign policy." In 1938 he became a member of the managing board of the mighty *Deutsche Bank*, the largest in Germany. His presence on the board added significantly to the bank's principal asset—its wide range of foreign contacts. Once Hitler began in 1938 Germany's expansion in Europe, the bank's foreign connections gave it, in the *Aryanization* of Jewish property outside the Reich, the desired competitive edge over its major financial rivals.

Born in 1901, Abs studied economics and law at the University of Bonn before accepting in 1929 a post with Delbrück, Schickler & Co., one of

Germany's large private banks. While advancing rapidly up the bank's corporate ladder, he traveled widely and continued studying his profession not only in Germany, but also in Paris, London, New York, Amsterdam, the Far East, and South America. Eventually, in addition to his native tongue, he spoke fluent English, Dutch, French, and Spanish.

After 1933 a key person in Hitler's government viewed Abs as a rising star in the financial world. This was Hjalmar Schacht, the new president of the *Reichsbank* and Hitler's economics minister in charge of German rearmament. (Though brilliant in many aspects, Schacht was a conflicted, inevitably corrupted figure who sought to play the German government and its anti-Nazi opposition against each other for his own benefit and safety; the IMT tried him and acquitted him in 1946.) Schacht, recognizing Abs's commercial and diplomatic skills, entrusted him with numerous sensitive foreign missions. One involved attending international meetings at which Abs and other German representatives opposed efforts by Germany's creditors to obtain repayment of loans made to the country after World War I.

Abs's connections to Nazi power extended even beyond Schacht: clients of Delbrück, Schickler & Co. included Hitler himself and the Nazi "philosopher" Alfred Rosenberg. By the end of the 1930s, according to journalist-historian Tom Bower: "There were few people of any importance in the whole world of banking whom Abs did not know well, and scarcely any who did not know of and respect him."[6]

Long before Abs joined its managing board in 1938, the *Deutsche Bank* had cooperated with the Nazi regime in carrying out the most important aspects of *Aryanization*: the removal of Jewish members from the bank's leadership. This purge eventually developed into a much larger—racially driven—dismissal of all Jewish employees, and into the brokering of transfers of property from Jewish into "Aryan" hands, which amounted to huge losses for the "sellers." By 1938, when confiscating Jewish-owned property and businesses became official state policy, the bank had already assisted in the forced transfer of 330 companies from Jewish to "Aryan" ownership.[7]

The bank's anti-Semitic actions not only reflected the demands of Hitler's regime but also resulted from the bank's financial vulnerability following the Great Depression and from the ever-present threat that the Nazi government might decide to nationalize the institution. *Deutsche Bank* acted less from the profit motive than from the opportunity to expand its market both by replacing Jewish with "Aryan" customers and, in competition with other large German banks, by gaining business—including foreign. Yet, no doubt disingenuously, Abs emphasized "Profit is good, but it's not everything. As man does not live in order to breathe, he does not go about his business with the exclusive aim of making profit."[8]

After 1938 *Aryanizations* escalated inside both Germany and German-annexed Austria and Czechoslovakia. Skillfully, Abs exploited this trend to the advantage of *Deutsche Bank* and, in at least one major instance, also to that of his family. Inside Germany the bank, with Abs playing a leading role in transactions often involving foreign investors and sellers, bought up shares—or otherwise received commissions in brokering the *Aryanization*—of several large Jewish businesses. These included Mendelsohn's bank in Berlin and Adler & Oppenheimer, a leather producer. The *Aryanization* of Adler & Oppenheimer, because members of the two families lived outside Germany, proved complicated and lasted nearly three years, until 1941. By then, because three members of the families lived in German-occupied France and the Netherlands, the *Deutsche Bank* took part "in what was also a ransom operation, in which lives were to be exchanged for the consent to a financial transaction."[9]

Long after the world war, in 1970 Abs claimed that he had helped the original owners of Adler & Oppenheimer and delayed the *Aryanization*. A member of the Adler family supported his argument, recalling that during the *Aryanization* negotiations, Abs had told a Nazi official: "Adler (Eagle) is a proud old bird and Oppenheimer is what we call a 'good wine,' so what do you want to 'aryanize' about the firm?"[10] Abs tried hard to find suitable purchasers for the large firm, made difficult not only for the reasons noted above, but also because of the number of interests and competing Nazi government and party agencies seeking to shape the outcome of the process.

In addition, Abs figured prominently in the *Aryanization*, concluded in December 1939, of a final property held by the vast German-Czech coal empire, the Petschek concern. He arranged for the expropriation of a Petschek-owned company and small coalfield in western Germany; in the process, and surely not an accidental by-product, he preserved and increased his personal interests—his family's minority shares—in the business.

While making money in such actions on behalf of the *Deutsche Bank*, occasionally Abs assisted the major Jewish victims—most notably Mendelsohn and the Petscheks—in acquiring the best possible settlement, which even then was below market value. In this respect, at the highest levels German banking operated during the Nazi regime much as it had before and much as it has since. It relied on networks of personal contacts, friendships, intermarriages, and collegiality among interlocking boards of directors and trustees. When Jews were integrated into such networks, often bankers like Abs proved reluctant (at least at first) to throw them entirely to the Nazis' mercy. Less anti-Semitism and more economic and political-strategic motives—seeking to secure from the Hitler regime the best possible conditions for competition and profit—appeared to drive the *Deutsche Bank*'s policies.

But once Germany embarked on its aggressive expansion beyond the Reich—first into Austria and then into Czechoslovakia—the *Deutsche Bank*, fiercely competing with other financial institutions such as the *Dresdner Bank*, succeeded in acquiring extensive foreign investments through *Aryanizations*. Far fewer personal relations existed in this context to serve as a brake to the German banks' predatory and greedy interests.

Only days after Germany's *Anschluss* with Austria in March 1938, the *Deutsche Bank* sent Abs and other officials to Vienna to begin negotiations for acquiring Austria's largest bank, the *Creditanstalt*. During the next two years the *Deutsche Bank* helped to fashion—and then headed—a large German banking consortium that seized control of the *Creditanstalt* and used the latter to rapidly *aryanize* Austrian business. Moreover, the now-German-owned Austrian bank served as a major Nazi conduit for *Aryanizations* in neighboring lands, especially in the German-occupied Czech territories of Bohemia and Moravia. During the process, Wilhelm Keppler, Hitler's economic adviser and Reich commissioner for Austria, remarked to an Austrian banker: "Abs was still the best of them all" in brokering *Aryanizations*.

In 1939 to direct *Aryanizations* of Czech banks, Abs urged the *Deutsche Bank* to appoint the young Walter Pohle, whom British historian Harold James describes as "energetically inventive and destructive" in his work.[11] Barely thirty-one years old and, before joining *Deutsche Bank*, a former employee of the Reich Economics Ministry, Pohle had worked earlier with Abs in *Aryanizations* in Germany. In Prague, Pohle pursued aggressively the incorporation into the *Deutsche Bank* of various branches of the Bohemian Union Bank (BUB). Bluntly, he proclaimed the BUB "a Jewish enterprise [that] must therefore . . . be pronounced an aryanized enterprise as quickly as possible."[12] Pohle arranged the transfer of BUB's highest-value accounts to the *Deutsche Bank* and then used the BUB to expropriate masses of other Czech-Jewish property—including banks. He sold much of the acquired assets to the *SS* and to Germany's large iron, steel, and mining conglomerate, the Hermann Göring Works. A state-owned gigantic industrial firm, it employed seven hundred thousand workers and amassed capital of four hundred million marks (roughly equal to $160 million), which aided Göring in amassing (along with the art he plundered from Jews and others) his huge fortune.

During the first years of the war, Abs, as director in charge of *Deutsche Bank*'s foreign department, financed much of Germany's early wartime industrial expansion. This was especially true in countries overrun by the *Wehrmacht* in eastern and southeastern Europe, where his clients integrated factories, mines, and transport systems into, in Bower's words, "a series of industrial empires unmatched in European history."[13] During the twelve years of Nazi rule the *Deutsche Bank*'s wealth quadrupled. By 1945, its directors sat on 197 different company boards in Germany and elsewhere in Europe.

Despite not joining the Nazi Party, Hitler never doubted Abs's loyalty. The banker's alleged tie to the anti-Nazi resistance remains unproved. Regularly, he spoke publicly and wrote about the anticipated new postwar Europe under German rule. Following the war, he justified his role during the Nazi era as a bank director by claiming that he was only preserving a longtime German institution, the *Grossbank* (major or big bank).

But to James, "In retrospect, [this] does not seem a very good justification" for what the *Deutsche Bank* did under Abs's leadership. In the British writer's judgment, the bank's participation in the "despoiliation" of Jewish property "was a crucial link in the cumulative radicalization of a process of discrimination that ultimately led to genocide." Even more damning, "some of the directors of BUB lost their lives as a consequence of their dismissal and Pohle's intrigue. This constitutes responsibility."[14]

Much of Abs's postwar fate rested with the bitter divisions between the British and Americans over denazification and how to rebuild the German banking system and economy necessary to reconstruct the war-shattered country. On the afternoon of May 3, 1945, the forty-three-year-old Abs left his suite in Hamburg's luxury Vierjahreszeiten Hotel. He fled arriving British troops and hid in the nearby home of a friend, remaining secluded there for the next six weeks until the British, who knew his name well, located him.

Immediately, several highly placed London bankers and acquaintances of Abs from the 1930s jumped to his defense. They persuaded the British military government to employ Abs not only to reconstruct the banking system in the British zone but also to re-establish the *Deutsche Bank* throughout Germany. The decision, however, infuriated the Americans, who demanded Abs's arrest and extradition to the American zone for interrogation.

After much conflict among the Allies over the issue, the British agreed grudgingly to permit the Americans to interrogate Abs but only in Hamburg, not in the U.S. zone. For three days in the fall of 1945, a U.S. Army major, described by John Kellam, who was an accountant in the banking section of the British military government present at the interrogation, as "a Jewish official from the US Treasury," questioned Abs. But the interrogator suffered from the same problem as the vast majority of Allied interrogators in the first postwar months—he didn't know the correct answers to his own questions.

Abs's performance impressed the British official present, Kellam, who recalled many years later, "We all felt Abs had stood up very well. The Americans wanted to get their eye-for-an-eye revenge. I knew that the Germans had blotted their copybook, but we had to live with them for the next three hundred years." Another British functionary, Edward Hellmuth, an executive in Britain's Midland Bank and involved in the denazification of German finance and banking in the British zone, claimed that the Americans "didn't appreciate" Abs's "banking experience" and believed him, erroneously, "a Nazi. But he wasn't a member of the party, so we gave him protection."[15]

Nevertheless, confronted with continued and intensified U.S. pressure for Abs's arrest, the British stripped him of his forty-five bank directorships. But in late 1945 the Americans remained dissatisfied with only Abs's dismissal from his banking posts. On January 16, 1946, the British bowed at last to U.S. demands and arrested Hermann as a suspected war criminal. When a British accountant involved in denazification visited Abs in Hamburg's Altona jail to ask the banker for advice on rebuilding the German economy, Abs—the non-Nazi, selfless "patriot" concerned with his country's welfare—refused to talk with him. His cooperation, he said, depended on his release from jail. Three months later, the British freed him; the accountant drove Abs "to his apple farm at Remagen in the French zone." Later, the Englishman remarked, apparently with satisfaction, "I winkled him out of American hands."[16]

Abs remained free despite a U.S. military government study of the *Deutsche Bank*, conducted during 1946 and 1947, which recommended the bank's liquidation and the indictment and trial of its leaders as war criminals. Although Yugoslavia condemned Abs to death *in absentia* as a war criminal, the Allies only interrogated him several times at Nuremberg. Unable—and unwilling—to arrest Abs and make him the centerpiece of a large war crimes trial of former *Deutsche Bank* and other German bank officials, the U.S. nevertheless placed on trial in Nuremberg during 1947 and 1948 twenty-four former German industrialists.

The main defendants included Friedrich Flick, the coal and mining magnate; Alfred Krupp, the iron and steel baron; and Carl Krauch, head of *I. G. Farben*, the giant chemical company. During the so-called *Farben* trial, Abs sat in the public gallery to demonstrate to the defendants, some of them his former clients at *Deutsche Bank*, his "moral support."[17] As a result of the industrialists' trials, thirteen received prison sentences of one to eight years; ten were acquitted; and one was dropped from prosecution because of ill health.

In March 1948, despite misgivings of General Lucius Clay, the U.S. military governor in Germany, the Western Allies hired Abs to help spearhead the rebuilding of the West German economy. The Allies appointed him deputy chief of the German Credit Institute for Reconstruction (*Kreditanstalt für Wiederaufbau*) and president of the new German central bank (*Bank Deutscher Länder*), both of which supervised the distribution of the U.S.'s Marshall Plan funds to West German industry. Between 1951 and 1953 he served as the representative of the West German government and Chancellor Konrad Adenauer in renegotiating prewar foreign debts with the Allies.

Simultaneously, and most ironically, Abs participated in German negotiations with Jewish survivors—including Paula and Rolf Levi and the Petschek brothers—for the restitution of at least a portion of their property seized by the Nazis. But his involvement in the matter was no less tangled than it had been earlier in the *Aryanizations*. In assisting with restitution after 1945 he participated in many different guises and represented diverse interests—"sometimes those of new owners," as James noted, "sometimes those of the victims of Nazism, as well as the interests of the Deutsche Bank at a time when that institution no longer existed."[18]

Abs's importance in the postwar West German economy gave him influence not only among Germans but also with the Americans. By 1949 and 1950, the United States hoped that expanding German industry would help the West in opposing Communism in the Cold War. Abs argued to John J. McCloy, the U.S. commissioner for Germany, that a key to German recovery and cooperation was the release of the German industrialists convicted and imprisoned by the Americans.

That the new East German Communist government placed Abs in 1950 on a "war criminals" list didn't lessen his sway with the United States. He joined Adenauer and many other West Germans in emphasizing to McCloy and the Americans that the United States could secure Germany's friendship and assistance against the Soviet Union much more easily if it freed the industrialists and the several hundred other war criminals. By the end of 1951, the United States had granted clemency to—and released—most of the convicted.

When the *Deutsche Bank* reopened in 1957 in Frankfurt am Main, Abs assumed control of the managing board, a post he held for ten years; thereafter, he chaired the bank's supervisory board and from 1976 until his death in February 1994 held the title of honorary chair. He also served on the boards of some two dozen companies until 1965, when a West German law limited the number of corporate board posts a person could hold simultaneously. He appeared at the height of his influence, moving easily among the West German political elite, including Chancellor Konrad Adenauer and the longtime economic czar, Ludwig Erhard.

In 1970 a book by East German writer Eberhard Czichon accused Abs of war crimes, including claiming that he cooperated willingly with the Nazi regime in *Aryanizations*. Both Abs and the *Deutsche Bank* sued the author and won the case in a Stuttgart court. At the time of Abs's death at age ninety-two, no one had managed to link him directly to the Nazi persecution of Europe's Jews or to the Holocaust. In this regard, the 1948 statement by an American economic adviser in Germany that "we just didn't have a handle with which we could cut him off" held true as late as the 1990s.[19]

But at the end of the decade the net around his slippery activities and that of the *Deutsche Bank* in the Holocaust began to tighten. On two occasions the discovery of previously unknown or unreported bank documents surprised—very unpleasantly so—the institution. First, in 1997 balance sheets turned up showing that during the Nazi regime the bank had engaged in purchasing and selling gold, all of which the Third Reich stole and some of which was so-called victim gold—that is, gold in the possession, or from the teeth, of murdered Jews. Quickly, this revelation triggered the bank to form a historical commission to delve more deeply into the bank's history during the National Socialist era.

Two years later, the bank reported the discovery of other similarly damning records. They showed that during the war the bank's Kattowitz branch in Poland had financed a midsize construction firm involved in building the *I. G. Farben* synthetic rubber (*buna*) factory at the Monowitz (Auschwitz III) concentration camp. The firm had received slave labor from the nearby Auschwitz I and Auschwitz II (Birkenau) camps. Still other documents revealed bank loans to other companies that constructed both *SS* barracks and crematoria at Auschwitz. The bank also funded a company whose subsidiary manufactured the Zyklon B gas used at the camps to murder Jews.

At the time of these disclosures, the bank had pending a proposed multi-billion-dollar acquisition of the U.S. financial institution Bankers Trust; bank directors hoped to blunt public criticism of its merger plans by publicizing the Auschwitz connections before journalists or others did so. By then, the world had finally begun—for the first time since the late 1940s—to address the issue of recovering the enormous assets of Holocaust victims that the Nazis and others had looted in wartime.

Jewish organizations in the United States and the American government led the way in recovering victims' assets paid to Jewish survivors. In 1998, Swiss banks (which, in order to retain the money in the accounts, had insisted that survivors provide proof of death for relevant family members—a distasteful and impossible demand under the circumstances) were forced finally to pay restitution to Jewish and other victims, and a year later similar pressures led large German corporations to agree to compensate former slave laborers. But even then, lawyers consumed in fees and commissions a huge percentage of the sums awarded. In fact, those survivors still living received a paltry average of a few hundred dollars each per month.

Who knew about—and sanctioned—the *Deutsche Bank* loans for construction at the death camp? The head of the bank's historical institute, Manfred Pohl, told a news conference that bank officials at Kattowitz were well aware of the facts: "It is clear that this was known as high up [as possible] at the main office in Katowice. It is not certain whether it was known in Berlin [at bank headquarters]."[20] But, he added, the loans would have had to be approved from Berlin to proceed.

This admission implied that Abs and other bank directors knew of—and consented to—the loans. Abs, Pohl explained, had sat on the board of directors of *I. G. Farben*, the parent company of the *buna* plant in Auschwitz and of a subsidiary, Degesch, which controlled the manufacture and distribution of Zyklon B. In November 1999, Pohl remarked in an article in the German newspaper *Die Zeit* that the world was finally getting to know "the Abs in the Third Reich."[21]

Was Abs, therefore, a Holocaust perpetrator to some degree? One may harbor strong suspicions that he was, but the world still awaits a firm answer to the question. Eventually, the revelations would lead to the bank sponsoring further studies of it and Abs by professional historians such as James and the German scholar Lothar Gall. But the information outraged many Jews and others. Some accused the *Deutsche Bank* of hiding evidence of the institution's financial dealings with the Nazis. Publicly, the director of the Simon Wiesenthal Center in Los Angeles, Rabbi Marvin Hier, cited the U.S. military government's 1946–1947 report linking the bank to financing companies involved with Auschwitz. The center had received a copy of the report in 1983. According to Hier: "The U.S. government certainly has this report. All the Allies certainly have this report. The bank knew about it."[22] But only when a profitable merger appeared to be endangered by scandal did the bank's death grip on the truth slacken.

DR. ERNST BUCHNER: ART THIEF

Few symbolized more than Ernst Buchner did the Nazis' enormous plunder of Jewish property and other wealth. First in Germany and Austria, and later in wartime Europe, the art museum director, along with many other Germans, stole or arranged for the theft of works of art owned by Jews and others valued in May 1945 at $2.5 billion ($20.5 billion today). Altogether, the Nazis looted an estimated 220,000 artworks from both museums and private collections throughout Europe. Only a few thousand such works have been recovered to date.

The many art thieves in Hitler's Germany concluded a "Faustian bargain" with the National Socialist regime and its art policies. After the war, moreover, not unlike nearly every other criminal Nazi art "expert," each avoided even the most minimal punishment. "The Nazi leaders," art historian Jonathan Petropoulos concludes, "could not have dominated the artistic sphere or amassed such [art] collections without the assistance of figures in the art world."[23]

Dr. Ernst Buchner, born in Munich in 1871, his father an academic painter, grew up revering high culture and believing, in this regard, in German national superiority. After World War I he graduated with a degree in art history from the Ludwig Maximilian University in Munich. During the 1920s he held junior staff positions at various Munich art collections, and in 1928 he received the directorship in Cologne of one of Rhineland-Westphalia's finest museums. He published extensively in scholarly journals, in which he exhibited his knowledge of Bavarian art and the broader fields of Northern Renaissance and German Baroque painting.

In July 1932 the forty-one-year-old Buchner realized his longtime ambition: he received the post of director of the Bavarian State Painting Collections (*Bayerische Staatsgemäldesammlungen, BSGS*) in Munich. In the world of German art museums, the appointment ranked second in importance, just behind the head of the Berlin network of such institutions.

Primarily to protect himself in his plum new post from the recently established Hitler government, he joined the Nazi Party in May 1933—one of nearly a million "March opportunists" who applied for and received party membership. Buchner felt vulnerable because of a Nazi press attack on "his relation to Jews," especially his friendship with Professor August Levy Mayer, the curator and sole Jewish employee of the *BSGS*. Not surprisingly, when Hitler's government forced Levy Mayer's dismissal because of his "Jewishness," Buchner did nothing to defend his subordinate and supposed friend.

Apparently also the *BSGS* caught Levy Mayer dealing art for himself on the private market, which violated the museum's policy. The Nazi newspaper, the *Völkischer Beobachter* (*Racial Observer*), called him a "Jewish art parasite" and announced that he had been placed under "protective custody" (*Schutzhaft*), a device that enabled the German police to arrest and imprison suspects deemed a "threat to the state" for any length of time without trial.[24]

By 1938, Buchner had become well acquainted with Hitler and numerous other top Nazi leaders, including Göring and Rosenberg. Spurred onward by his professional ambition, by the tantalizing promise of closer proximity to government power, and by an utter lack of sympathy for Jews, he cooperated in the *Gestapo*'s confiscation of Jewish artwork. Between 1939 and 1944 he bought at least twenty-eight works, including paintings by Eugène Delacroix and the important Bavarian painter Wilhelm Trübner, which had been seized from Jews. The *BSGS* collections grew from some 10,500 to 12,000 paintings while he served as its director. He also played an important role in the seizure of Jewish collections and the *Aryanization* of Jewish art dealerships in Munich.

By late 1942, Buchner had assisted in the German plunder in unoccupied France of several of the greatest artworks of Northern Europe, including the Ghent Altarpiece by Flemish masters the Van Eyck brothers. The altarpiece contained the famous painting *The Adoration of the Mystic Lamb*, completed in 1432. The seizure of the Ghent Altarpiece was followed by the German theft of another Dutch treasure. Buchner led an expedition that confiscated an altar at Leuven called *The Last Supper*.

Buchner stored some of the paintings and other artwork outside Munich at Schloss Neuschwanstein, one of the buildings under his control that housed more than twenty-one thousand artworks seized from French Jews. Hitler and the Germans viewed the confiscation of the Van Eyck altarpiece as revenge for the perceived unfairness inflicted on Germany after World War I by the Treaty of Versailles. During that earlier war, the Germans had removed some of the altarpiece from a cathedral in Ghent to Germany; after 1919 the Allies had returned it to Belgium. In July 1942, Buchner had written a museum curator, justifying the seizure of the altar: "In consideration of the reparations and the screaming injustice of the Versailles Treaty, nothing stands in the way of an immediate return of the [altar] panels."[25]

Along with other German art dealers such as Dr. Hans Posse and Karl Haberstock, Buchner helped Hitler amass a huge collection of art for the planned so-called *Führermuseum* at Linz in Austria. The dictator intended the grand architectural structure and its looted collection to honor him following the global victory the Nazis anticipated. For the Linz project, Buchner appraised 250 works from the Schloss Neuschwanstein collection that the Vichy government had confiscated from Jews in France. Besides supervising the Schloss, he oversaw the Austrian salt mine near Altaussee that housed, by war's end, a vast array of paintings, sculptures, and other art objects looted by the Nazis.

The Americans arrested Buchner on June 18, 1945, and held him initially at police headquarters in Munich. Cooperating with his captors, the museum director described in lengthy interrogations the massive German plunder of art under Hitler and helped to recover a small portion of the stolen works. Charming and charismatic, he impressed the Americans favorably. One intelligence officer remarked about him: "Honest and straightforward in his attitude. Nothing that he told us turned out to be a falsehood—an unusual case in this group."[26]

Despite his cooperation the U.S. removed Buchner from his post. Only by trial before a denazification board could he resume his career. A board in Munich, hearing his case in 1948, received mixed evidence regarding his activities during the Nazi regime, but in the end it ruled him a "follower"—primarily because it possessed incomplete information about his ardent involvement in removing the Van Eyck altar and in confiscating other works of art. The board's decision showed as well its reluctance to view noncapital offenses as serious crimes.

Petropoulos demonstrates how Buchner's classification permitted his rehabilitation. Immediately, Buchner applied for reappointment to his former position, but the U.S. occupation government had filled it with someone else. In September 1948 the Bavarian state government provided him financial support to research and write art history until a suitable post became available.

After the war, first the Allies and then the Germans had difficulty finding experienced art personnel who hadn't compromised themselves under Nazism.

His rehabilitation appeared complete in April 1953, when he received reinstatement as director of the Bavarian State Painting Collections. Shortly thereafter, the University of Munich appointed him an honorary professor. He retired in 1957 after involving himself in the reconstruction of Munich's historic museums, which the Nazis—including himself—had helped to destroy with the war.

On leaving the *BSGS*, he received praise from the president of the West German Federal Republic, Theodor Heuss, and an award from the Bavarian minister president, Wilhelm Hoegner. The politicians thanked him for his service on behalf of the Bavarian government; two years later, the state gave him a prestigious service medal.

Buchner died in June 1962 of natural causes. According to Petropoulos, neither the Americans nor the German authorities who evaluated Buchner's career in Nazi Germany "grasped the real significance of his behavior. . . . This inclination to turn a blind eye to complicity in Nazi criminal endeavors of course extended beyond the art world, but the case of Ernst Buchner follows a typical pattern of collaboration during the Third Reich and rehabilitation after the war for many within his profession."[27]

The Americans, though, came closest to recognizing the vile importance of Buchner's actions in assisting the Nazis. In July 1945 a U.S. intelligence officer and art specialist wrote:

> No amount of passive resistance could counterbalance the moral effect of his official allegiance. Buchner, one of the countless "white" Germans, prominent men in their communities who, in spite of an inner dislike for Nazism and a realization of its evils, nevertheless agreed to act as its representatives, through a mixture of personal ambition and fear of consequences of standing aside. These men bear a heavy responsibility to the mass of their compatriots, for they provided the fanatics and criminals with the necessary cloak of respectability. . . . [I]t is recommended (a) that Buchner be kept under house arrest at the disposition of the Monuments, Fine Arts and Archives authorities, Third U.S. Army for consultation, and (b) that he be placed on the list of those officials who are to be prohibited permanently from holding any position in a newly constituted German fine arts administration.[28]

And yet the opposite happened.

13

Other Trials and Amnesty

He thought nothing of the many Jewish victims—most dead—of his actions during the Third Reich. Amid his postwar outbursts of self-pity and feelings of persecution, he ignored completely how, several years earlier, he had signed a vast number of orders for the imprisonment of Jews and others, had organized the *Einsatzgruppen* that operated so lethally in Poland, and had initiated the brutal deportations of Jews in France.

Like so many other former Nazis in captivity, as well as numerous Germans in the postwar era, the weepy Werner Best engaged in a grotesque inversion of reality. "Every concentration camp," he convinced himself, "was more humane than the gruesome prison machinery that delivers isolated [former Nazi] inmates to a hellish torment of nerves."[1] He wanted to hear nothing of the horrors perpetrated by him and other Nazis. These—including Allied films of mountains of bodies in the camps at the war's end—he described and dismissed as "purely propaganda."[2]

The more he indulged in such delusions, the brighter and purer the picture he portrayed of himself became. During the summer of 1947 he wrote a series of anecdotal stories (at the suggestion of his lawyer, who believed the writing would take Best's attention off his misery and troubles with his wife) about the inner world of high-level Nazi politics. In these essays Best rendered himself as being a most pious, important, and yet nonpolitical protagonist caught among, and to some degree against, leading personalities of the regime—including Heydrich, Ribbentrop, and Göring—enraptured with themselves and their power. Most of the accounts, written in the form of novellas, had less-than-sensational-sounding titles: "The Secretary of the Gestapo Chief"; "Croats in Berlin: A Story of Göring, Gestapo, and Murder of the King"; and "Ribbentrop's Courier."[3] None of the stories contained anything of significance about the Nazi bigwigs. While Best awaited his fate at the hands of the Danes, he could not help but notice that the Allies and other countries continued to place on trial and convict at least some second-tier Nazi war criminals like him.

OHLENDORF ACCUSES THE VICTIMS

A year and a half had passed since he had appeared as a witness before the IMT, and now Otto Ohlendorf found himself on trial. During 1947 and 1948 the U.S. military held in Nuremberg a series of twelve trials of so-called lesser war criminals—physicians, industrial and financial leaders, and members of various branches of the *SS*, German army, judiciary, and foreign service. One of the proceedings began in July 1947 against the chief defendant, Ohlendorf, and twenty-three other officers and members of *Einsatzgruppen.*

One of those on trial in the so-called *Einsatzgruppen* Case was Paul Blobel, an unsuccessful architect who proved to be wildly more successful in the destructive realm than in the creative sphere. A colonel in the *SS* and *SD*, he had led a *Kommando* of *Einsatzgruppe* C on its killing spree from June 1941 to January 1942 in the Soviet Union, through the Volhynia and Ukraine to Kiev. His victims numbered sixty thousand, including those unfortunates at Babi Yar. In this context perhaps his excessive drinking was understandable, but it exacerbated a liver ailment and he was relieved of duty. Upon his recovery, from mid-1942 until October 1944, he headed a series of special groups, comprising in large part Jewish prisoners and known collectively as "Unit 1005." The groups moved throughout the German-occupied East, exhuming masses of bodies of mostly slain Jews, cremating the remains on pyres and scattering the ashes. During nearly two years of such horrific work, Blobel's unit dug up and burned more than two million corpses.

During the *Einsatzgruppen* trial, Ohlendorf recounted much of what he'd told the IMT about his mobile killing unit, *Einsatzgruppe* D, and its massacre of Jews in the southern Ukraine and Crimea. He affirmed the deep involvement in the unit's bloody work of Army Group South, commanded by Erich von Manstein. Ohlendorf had "constant contact with the army." He saw Manstein "in the Crimea on duty, as well as privately" and had "personal discussions with him about the question of military commitments of my unit."[4]

He blamed his own criminality on Hitler and Himmler, whose directives, he insisted, he had been bound to follow. He testified that even before the German invasion of the Soviet Union began in June 1941, his superiors had issued a "special order" to him and other *Einsatzgruppen* leaders "to protect the rear of the [German] troops by killing the Jews, Gypsies, Communist functionaries, active Communists, and all persons who would endanger the security." His "immediate feeling" about the order had been one of "general protest," as he had considered it unjustified.

Had he known, asked the presiding judge Michael Musmanno, "about plans or directives which had as their goal the extermination [of such groups] on racial and religious grounds?"[5] No such plans existed, Ohlendorf claimed, for either the Slavs or Jews. Yet he admitted, as he had at the IMT, that his *Einsatzgruppe* D had murdered some ninety thousand Soviet Jews.

For many years after his testimony, most judges and historians accepted his claim—along with other similar evidence—as proof that prior to the German attack on the Soviet Union, Hitler, through Himmler, had given a clear order to murder all Soviet Jews. But recently, at least one historian has claimed that Ohlendorf in fact constructed his testimony about an alleged early comprehensive order to murder the Jews for the purpose of defending himself and his wartime actions.

By the early 1970s, notes Longerich, other former *Einsatzgruppen* leaders (during trials for and investigations of their criminality) had remembered something different—"a step-by-step mode of receiving orders, a 'framework order,'" once the invasion of Russia had begun, "which was intended to be 'filled in' on the initiative of the commandos and by subsequent orders." Longerich concluded: "Ohlendorf put formidable pressure on his co-defendants in order to be able to claim that he had been acting upon orders received, thereby reducing to a minimum the extent to which he had himself been free to act with respect to the atrocities of several *Einsatzkommandos*."[6]

Apparently by the end of August or beginning of September 1941 at the latest, *Einsatzgruppe* D had received the decisive order to move from random killings of Ukrainian Jews to their mass murder. The directive may have come from Ohlendorf. In 1969, one of the *Einsatzgruppe*'s commando leaders testified that Ohlendorf had visited him in early September 1941 and revealed "that there is now an order from the Führer according to which all Jews are to be killed indiscriminately."[7] Other commando leaders interrogated in the 1960s testified similarly.

Most incredibly, at his trial Ohlendorf blamed the Jews for the wartime genocide that befell them. Perhaps more than any other single Holocaust perpetrator, his testimony included multiple claims the likes of which would appear eventually in the writings and utterances of postwar Holocaust deniers. During the war, he and his defense counsel insisted, the Jewish victims had posed a danger to German armed forces and therefore deserved annihilation. In reality, the overwhelming majority of those slaughtered were drawn from innocent civilian populations and were not members of any political or military resistance.

In an opening statement to the court, Ohlendorf's counsel, Dr. Rudolf Aschenauer, set forth the perverted argument that the *Einsatzgruppen* and their commanders operating in the Soviet Union had acted merely to defend themselves:

> The prerequisite for self-defense is an unlawful attack, i.e., an attack which the attacked person does not have to tolerate. The attack need not yet have started. Self-defense is also admissible in the face of an imminently *threatening attack*. . . . Therefore, *also the state, as such, the existence of a nation, the endangered vital interests of a nation* can be defended in self-defense.[8]

When cross-examined by chief prosecutor Benjamin Heath, Ohlendorf tried to justify the killing of Jewish and Gypsy children by *Einsatzgruppe* D. The prosecutor questioned him: "Will you explain to the Tribunal what conceivable threat to the security of the Wehrmacht a child constituted in your judgment?"

"I did not have to determine the danger," Ohlendorf responded, "but the order [I received] contained that all Jews including the children were considered to constitute a danger for the security of this area."

His accuser rebutted him: "Will you agree that there was absolutely no rational basis for killing children except genocide and the killing of races?" The defendant remained adamant, still attacking his former victims:

> I believe that it is very simple to explain if one starts from the fact that this order did not only try to achieve security, but also permanent security because the children would grow up and surely, being the children of parents who had been killed, they would constitute a danger no smaller than that of the parents.[9]

He added: "I have seen very many children killed in this war through [Allied] air attacks, for the security of other nations, and orders were carried out to bomb, no matter whether many children were killed or not."[10] He defended the Jewish massacres as a necessary task historically to secure *Lebensraum* (living space) for the German Reich in the East.

Also he claimed that Allied actions in the war were equally as destructive as Germany's. He declared that history would regard his firing squads as no worse—in referring to the dropping of the atom bombs on Japan— than those who, "by pushing of a button," had killed "a much larger number of civilians, men, women, and children, even to hurt them for generations."[11] For Germany, therefore, those who had suffered and died in the Final Solution had supposedly produced their own destruction. The *SS*, Nazi police, and other armed forces, he insisted, had only defended themselves.

Nor had Ohlendorf finished with his twisted, hateful claims and untruths. Not the Jews, but rather he and his fellow killers in the dock and the German people had suffered persecution. In a closing statement he denounced the war crimes trials as unjust:

> I have been now in the Palace of Justice in Nuernberg for 2½ years. What I have seen here of life as a spiritual force, in these 2½ years in Nuernberg, has increased my fear. Human beings who under normal conditions were decent citizens of their country were deprived of their basic conception of law, custom, and morals by the power of the victors. . . . Thus, this legal, moral, and ethical suffering of the German people became greater than the material one which threatens its physical existence."[12]

The tribunal remained unimpressed but provided the defendants considerably more justice and fairness than Ohlendorf (or Paul Blobel) had ever offered those screaming, naked people he and his minions had herded to the edges of deeply dug ditches before gunning them down. On April 9, 1948, the court sentenced Ohlendorf and thirteen other defendants in the *Einsatzgruppen* Case, including Blobel, to death by hanging and most of the remainder to terms in prison.

But why did Ohlendorf, Blobel, and the others ordered hanged remain alive three more years? Why didn't the Western Allies carry out the death sentences of such confessed mass killers immediately? The answers revolved around the growing public indifference and the increasing political pressures brought to bear on the British and Americans.

On the one hand, a mixture of public malaise toward the war (desiring the past to be past) and pragmatic optimism about the present (after all, the war had been concluded decisively in the Allies' favor) encouraged the view that it would be more profitable to look ahead than to remain focused on events swiftly sinking into history. (Of course, the *Einsatzgruppen* had robbed their victims of this luxury of choice—or any choice, for that matter.) In addition, the Cold War and the resulting U.S. concern to enlist West German support against Communist Russia led the Americans to bow increasingly to German demands for clemency for its convicted war criminals.

As a result, only four of the fourteen were ever executed; the rest had their sentences commuted to life imprisonment, and most of those were later further reduced, some to time already served. Amid widespread protest among West Germans against it, the United States executed the quartet, including Ohlendorf and Blobel, in Bavaria's Landsberg prison on June 7, 1951—thereby granting the condemned three more years of life than they had permitted the Jews and other victims.

FRANZ SCHLEGELBERGER: DAGGER BENEATH HIS ROBE

An experienced German legal official who had worked in the Reich Ministry of Justice since 1921, Franz Schlegelberger rose a decade later to the office of state secretary in the ministry. When the Nazis took over the German government in 1933, he joined the great majority of German legal officials who, by hiding their lethal discrimination and persecution under their judicial robes, supported the new regime. The national-conservative Schlegelberger didn't join the Nazi Party until 1938 but nevertheless welcomed the government's revival of nationalism, authoritarianism, and militarism—even at the expense of corroding the German judicial system itself.

Before the war both he and the Ministry of Justice cooperated with the rest of the government to innovate and implement anti-Jewish measures that isolated German Jews and left them unprotected by the law. He involved himself extensively in *Aryanizing* Jewish property. During late 1938, in the wake of *Kristallnacht*, he signed a decree preventing Jews whose property had suffered injury or damage arising from the "occurrences" of the massive pogrom from seeking compensation in the courts. By 1939, for the small number of Jewish businesses still remaining in Germany, he issued orders enforcing the boycott of such firms by German civil servants and Nazi Party members.

Once the war began, Schlegelberger participated in the judiciary's intensification of the persecution of Jews. From the spring of 1941 to August 1942, he served as acting Reich Minister of Justice. In his new post he drafted proposals for special penal laws for Poles and Jews in the Occupied Eastern Territories.

Especially in this way he and the ministry contributed—openly and willingly—to the Final Solution by turning German law nearly wholesale into a weapon of racial extermination. In line with the killings planned by Hitler, the *SS*, and the police, the ministry issued the "Criminal Law Decree for Poles and Jews," much of which Schlegelberger drafted and which took effect in January 1942.

Essentially, the law opened the door for the unconditional execution of Poles and Jews, whom it deprived of any legal protection whatsoever. In the decree's words Poles and Polish Jews "are sentenced to death, or in less serious cases to imprisonment, if they demonstrate their anti-German mentality by spiteful or inflammatory actions . . . or if they demean or damage the reputation or the well-being of the German Reich or the German people by *any other behavior*."[13]

Meanwhile, toward the end of 1941, Schlegelberger and the ministry involved themselves increasingly in helping exterminate Jews. On November 21, the acting Reich minister received a letter from Heydrich inviting him to attend, with other government agency and *SS* leaders, an upcoming conference in Berlin to discuss what the *SS* chief termed the "Final Solution" of the Jewish question. In the letter Heydrich mentioned nothing of killings, only that "the Jews have been evacuated in continuous transports from the Reich territory, including the Protektorat of Bohemia and Moravia, to the East, ever since October 15, 1941."[14] What happened to the deportees and the meaning of *Final Solution* Schlegelberger and the other recipients of the invitations either understood or could deduce. Most already knew of the mass killings of Jews. Their respective offices had received copies of the reports from the *Einsatzgruppen* in Russia.

In Schlegelberger's stead his subordinate, the notorious jurist Roland Freisler (who, after August 1942, serving as president of the People's Court, which provided quick justice in cases of treason, delighted in mocking and screaming at the accused who came before him even as he sentenced 90 percent of them to death or life imprisonment) attended as a representative of the Ministry of Justice at the conference held at a villa on Berlin's Wannsee on January 20, 1942. During the meeting, Heydrich discussed how "Europe will be combed through from west to east" for Jews, most of whom would be worked to death and the rest "dealt with accordingly." Consequently, the mass killing of Jews no longer involved solely the *SS* and police; now the elite of the government administration—such as Schlegelberger and the Ministry of Justice—had signed on.

Following the Wannsee conference, Schlegelberger busied himself with another of its major subjects: the Reich's policy toward the nearly two hundred thousand *Mischlinge*. On April 5, in connection with what he termed the "Final Solution of the Jewish problem," he proposed that the government view so-called *Mischlinge* of the second degree—persons with one Jewish grandparent—equal to Germans and exempt them from evacuation. In contrast, for *Mischlinge* of the first degree—individuals with two or more Jewish grandparents—he agreed with a suggestion from the German interior ministry that the regime should sterilize them. In a secret letter to Hans Lammers, the head of Hitler's Reich Chancellery, and six other Nazi party and government agencies, he proposed: "Those half-Jews who are capable of propagation should be given the choice to submit to sterilization or to be evacuated in the same manner as Jews."[15]

The proposal resulted not from an effort by Schlegelberger or other like-minded government functionaries to save *Mischlinge* from the Final Solution. Instead, it represented a step, demonstrated a half century later by Annegret Ehmann, a German historian, on "the path leading to the second phase of the extermination policy—the 'Final Solution of the Mischling and mixed marriage question.'"[16]

During 1943 and 1944 the Nazi government killed Jewish children of mixed ancestry at Hadamar, one of Germany's euthanasia centers. After mid-1944 all *Mischlinge*, including the so-called privileged ones of the second degree, remaining in the government bureaucracy were removed. In February 1945 the *SS* deported Jewish partners in mixed marriages to the Theresienstadt Ghetto. Only the Allied victory over Germany in the war saved the *Mischlinge* from extermination.

During the spring of 1942 the escalating war added to Hitler's growing concern about keeping the German home front loyal to him. The Führer responded to this concern by expanding police and other terror and by attacking Schlegelberger and the Ministry of Justice as too lenient. On April 26 he denounced in a *Reichstag* speech the judiciary and civil service and threatened to "relieve of their office judges" who failed to pass more-brutal and less-formal sentences in all court cases.[17] Despite the already unprecedented legal terror in Nazi Germany, Hitler compared the legal system—its courts and judges—unfavorably with the unrestrained actions of the police. His deep-seated mistrust of the judiciary intensified to a fever pitch.

In response, Schlegelberger made immediately clear to courts what he—the acting Reich minister—expected: judges must mete out the harshest punishments. Despite his preening objection to the German police's frequent revision of sentences issued by courts, the minister ordered—personally—at Hitler's request the incontrovertible murder of at least one German Jew. Schlegelberger assured the Führer that he would, himself, take action if Hitler informed him of other sentences that met with the dictator's disapproval. From spring 1942 onward, on the order of the Ministry of Justice, as part of the genocidal killing of Jews, judicial authorities handed over to police hundreds of Jews in prisons and jails to be removed to concentration camps or deported.

Still, the ever-restive Hitler remained discontented with the legal system and its sixty-six-year-old chief minister. On August 20, 1942, Schlegelberger received his retirement notice, a letter of appreciation from Hitler, and a substantial payoff of one hundred thousand *Reichsmarks*. Hitler replaced him with Otto Georg Thierack, the bloodthirsty president of the feared People's Court, which tried cases that included treason and assassination or attempted assassination of political leaders. Recently, Thierack—the last Nazi minister of justice—had overseen a massive rise in the number of death sentences that the People's Court had handed out. Arrested after the war, he would commit suicide in 1946 in a British prison camp—one more perpetrator eluding public accountability for his public crimes.

Schlegelberger's trial, which included fourteen other defendants from the former Nazi judiciary, opened before U.S. judges on January 4, 1947. He and his fellow defendants—placed on trial at Nuremberg in what the United States called the "Justice Case"—represented a cross-section of the German judiciary that had served Hitler. Schlegelberger, one of the lead defendants, attempted to justify why he'd played such a leading role as a longtime professional jurist in Nazi Germany in destroying the rule of law and implementing Nazi racial policy.

His defense counsel, in an opening statement before the tribunal, insisted that "all" of his client's "activities" during the Third Reich "were aimed at preventing or at least modifying the course set by Hitler's dictatorship."[18] As alleged evidence for the claim, the counsel cited Hitler's *Reichstag* speech of April 1942 and the dictator's removal a few months later of Schlegelberger as acting minister of justice. But his counsel barely mentioned Schlegelberger's deep involvement in transforming German law into an unlawful instrument of racial persecution and extermination.

On the stand or in other testimony, Schlegelberger himself mentioned little or nothing of the extermination of the Jews. Nevertheless, the prosecution produced numerous documents—among the total of 2,093 exhibits and 138 witnesses examined in the Justice Case—in the defendant's own hand or that he'd signed. These incriminated him in the persecution of Jews and demonstrated clearly his knowledge of deportations and their more-than-likely destination.

In his final statement to the court on October 18, 1947, Schlegelberger attacked the tribunal and, like so many of his fellow Nazi criminals, portrayed himself as a victim of the Allies. "The charges and insults of the prosecutor," he complained, "do not apply to me. My life is not compatible with the intention of crime."[19]

The court rejected forcefully Schlegelberger's and the other defendants' proclamations of their innocence. Nearly all the defendants—especially Schlegelberger—had maintained that they'd remained in their judicial posts solely to protect the administration of German justice from falling into the lawless hands of forces such as the *SS*. The tribunal's judgment against Schlegelberger declared the opposite:

> The evidence conclusively shows that in order to maintain the Ministry of Justice in the good graces of Hitler and to prevent its utter defeat by Himmler's police, Schlegelberger and the other defendants who joined in this claim of justification took over the dirty work which the leaders of the State demanded, and employed the Ministry of Justice as a means for exterminating the Jewish and Polish populations, terrorizing the inhabitants of occupied countries, and wiping out political opposition at home.[20]

In another place, the judgment noted, memorably: "The dagger of the assassin was concealed beneath the robe of the jurist."[21] The court sentenced

Schlegelberger to life in prison, as it did three other defendants in the Justice Case; six received prison terms that varied from five to ten years; one committed suicide before trial; and another was dropped from the proceeding for ill health. Nearly immediately, however, both the U.S. and West German authorities began undoing the results of the trial. The U.S. released Schlegelberger "provisionally" for health reasons in 1950; in July 1951 he emerged as fully "exonerated" from a delayed denazification board hearing.

The new West German government approved his pension, which included service during the Nazi years and even his postwar time in prison. Consequently, at a moment when a skilled German worker earned about 400 marks per month, Schlegelberger received a monthly pension of 2,894 marks, plus 160,000 marks in back payments. Only in 1959 did the government terminate his pension following repeated complaints about it in the German parliament (*Bundestag*).

Even then he was not without legal recourse—unlike the Jews and Poles he had dispossessed of their legal standing. Eventually, he reached a settlement on financial compensation with a federal administrative court. The leniency shown Schlegelberger was both routine and widespread toward former Nazi jurists. According to historian Nikolaus Wachsmann: "The [West] German judiciary showed no great desire to tackle the Nazi past."[22] Already in 1949, a U.S. report revealed that in Bavaria alone, 752 of 924 judges and prosecutors were former Nazis—or 81 percent. The United States and Britain, agreeing to the policy, claimed it necessary for rebuilding the German legal system.

THE DANISH VERDICTS ON BEST

He thought it would never happen. But in June 1947 the Danish Ministry of Justice initiated an investigation for a future trial of Best and three other former Nazi leaders of the German occupation of Denmark. The latter included Otto Bovensiepen, commander after January 1944 of the local Nazi Security Police, and Hermann von Hanneken, German military commander in Denmark after September 1942.

Best decided early on not to testify at the trial nor to participate in interrogations of him beforehand. He hoped thereby to avoid having to answer accusations directly during questioning and entangling himself in contradictions. Neither would he run the risk of losing his nerve in interrogations or cross-examinations and of betraying himself with emotional eruptions, such as crying.

Nevertheless, the investigation and trial intensified Best's self-pity and depression, which found ever new, ever more infantile, forms of expression. To every testimony and other piece of evidence favorable to him he responded with euphoria, and to everything incriminating he fell into utter despair. After particularly damaging testimony by a fellow defendant, he wrote to his wife full of discouragement and vowing, "I will never request a plea for clemency."[23]

Best again threatened to kill himself and contrasted angrily and self-righteously the alleged injustices against him with what he'd done during and after the war. "How many have I helped!" he grumbled on November 1, 1947. "No one helps me!"

Eventually, he tried to inspire the impression that he was insane (not unlike Rudolf Hess, Hitler's former deputy Führer, during his capture and imprisonment by the British after he flew in May 1941 to Scotland). On January 21, 1948, he attempted to justify himself further to his wife. "Until 1945," he asserted, doing more than hinting at his anti-Semitism,

> I had proven strength and courage like any other of the "prominent" in our state! In 1946 I stood resolute in Nuremberg and fought courageously in the frontline in the dangerous struggle with the American-Jewish angels of revenge. Since 1947 I have shown in Denmark that I am no weakling and coward, because I am the first and sole "war criminal" to have refused to testify and defend myself, in order to protest and demonstrate before world history against the legally inadmissible, politically insane, and morally unjust proceeding.[24]

During the investigation of Best the prosecution concentrated on three areas: his overall responsibility for the German occupation in Denmark between late 1942 and the war's end—and thus for all the occupation's violations of international law or Danish war crimes laws; the German policy of counterterror against the Danish resistance; and the *Aktion* in 1943 against the Danish Jews.

Best's defense centered on his argument that he'd sought to protect Denmark's sovereignty and territorial integrity from greater injury by the war. Such efforts had been opposed, he and his defense counsel contended, by both England and the Communist-dominated Danish resistance, which engaged in acts of terror and sabotage against the occupation. This, Best claimed, had produced the massive German counterterrorism policy in Denmark, which had killed numerous Danes in the resistance. Hitler had ordered the policy, and German police commandos—whom the Führer had not subordinated to the Reich plenipotentiary—carried it out. Above all, Best's lawyer argued, employing the standard excuse of most German war criminals, the defendant had always done his duty and obeyed orders of his superiors, thereby acting "honorably" in the interests of his nation.

By April 1948, Best's psychological condition had stabilized sufficiently that the Allies asked that he be returned to Nuremberg, this time to testify in one of the twelve American trials of "lesser" Nazi war criminals—in the so-called Wilhelmstraße trial of officials of the former German foreign ministry (its headquarters set on Berlin's Wilhelmstraße). Until his reappearance at Nuremberg, the greatest problem for Best in preparing for his own trial in Denmark involved his role in the 1943 planned *Aktion* against Danish Jews.

Previously on this issue, Best's testimony had been (despite his foremost efforts at uniformity) contradictory and—although unknown to prosecutors—filled with lies. Initially, during an Allied interrogation on August 31, 1945, he'd manufactured the story that *Gestapo* chief Heinrich Müller (who, in the closing days of the war, vanished, never to be held accountable) had informed him in September 1943 that "certain aggressive German circles" intended in Denmark "to launch a pogrom." Best maintained that he'd protested against such plans to his superior and to the foreign ministry. He insisted that when his protests proved ineffective, he had warned, through fellow Nazi officials in Copenhagen, Danish Jews.

The ever-cagey Best based his August 1945 testimony on the belief that the war had destroyed the foreign ministry's files on Denmark. The Allies, he thought, could never prove him wrong. Therefore, he gave interrogators a version that exonerated both him and all others who'd participated in planning the German *Aktion* against the Jews.

Best added yet another fabrication during an interrogation in February 1947. He'd received, he said, a phone call on September 7, 1943, from the foreign ministry's liaison at Hitler's headquarters. The caller informed him of the Führer's decision to proceed with the Danish *Aktion.* In response, he alleged, he telegrammed the ministry on September 8 opposing the attack. No less contradictory postwar testimony regarding Best's role in the *Aktion* came from his former collaborators in occupied Denmark, including shipping adviser Ferdinand Georg Duckwitz.

On April 14, 1948, Best testified at the Wilhelmstraße trial in Nuremberg, during which he emphasized the above claims of his innocence in formulating and fervently striving to implement Nazi policy toward the Danish Jews. His testimony helped, regarding the issue, to exonerate not only him, but also the foreign ministry officials on trial. Other equally self-serving diplomats confirmed his version of events, including Hitler's supposed decision on September 7, 1943. But the court possessed no documentary evidence of the dictator's order that day for the *Aktion*, nor has anyone else found it since.

Back in Denmark, Best was present as his trial opened on June 16, 1948, in the Copenhagen municipal court. In his favor the prosecution possessed few records on his role in conceiving and realizing the *Gestapo* and *RSHA*'s anti-Jewish policy. Apparently his accusers knew nothing of his responsibility for implementing the deportations of French Jews.

Nevertheless, Duckwitz's contradictory testimony—initially claiming before the trial that Best hadn't participated in Duckwitz's warning of Danish

Jews, yet at the trial saying that, in fact, Best had done so—did little to bolster the former Reich plenipotentiary's credibility before the court. More damaging to Best, in the court's view, was the evidence against him given on the stand by one of his co-defendants, Bovensiepen, the former chief of German Security Police in Denmark. He portrayed Best as primarily responsible for the deadly Nazi policy of counterterrorism against the Danish resistance.

On September 20 the court issued its verdict. It sentenced Best and the Security Police chief to death and gave the other two co-defendants, including Hanneken, prison terms. The tribunal held Best—as Germany's highest-ranking official in wartime Denmark—responsible for the counterterrorism measures. Regarding the planned Jewish *Aktion*, the court concluded that Best's September 8, 1943, telegram had, in fact, set in motion the *Aktion* and hadn't countered, as he claimed, the alleged order for the attack already issued by Hitler.

The judgment against Best satisfied the expectations of a majority of the Danish public. Some observers saw the decision as the Danes' political statement to the Western powers, that is, as an effort to demonstrate most starkly to the British and Americans Denmark's anticollaborationist course during the war. But the relatively late time that the verdict was handed down worked to Best's advantage. Had he received the sentence one or two years earlier, closer to the war's end, when most Danes (especially former resistance members) were still focused on ensuring the punishment of former Nazis and their collaborators, the sentence most likely would have been carried out—quickly.

By the fall of 1948, increasingly the attention of Danes, as well as of the Western powers and West Germans, had shifted away from the war crimes trials and toward the rapidly unfolding and unstable Cold War. For one thing, seeking to expel the Western Allies from the divided Berlin and thus from the Soviet zone of occupation in eastern Germany, the Russians had blockaded the former Nazi capital. For another, Britain, the United States, and France had begun efforts with German leaders to found a new democratic West German state to oppose the Soviets' maneuvers and measures to impose a Communist Germany.

Amid the rapidly changing political atmosphere in Western Europe, the chances that Best and his three co-defendants could appeal their sentences improved substantially. A state court began hearing the pleas on May 9, 1949, with Best refusing, as he'd done earlier, to testify. The trial ended a few months later with a verdict that caused a sensation: the court sentenced Best to five years in prison, four of which it gave him credit for having already served. In one year he'd be a free man. Even more stunning, the court accepted his claim that he had neither helped initiate nor prepare the Danish-Jewish *Aktion*. Nor, the court concluded, had the counterterrorism measures of the Nazis violated international law.

The judgment produced widespread indignation and criticism among Danes and the country's press. Soon, the angry protests forced the Danish minister of justice to take Best's case to Denmark's Supreme Court. In March 1950 the court announced its decision in the form of a sentence only: Best received twelve years in prison instead of five. The judgment satisfied the Danish public and press; for them the issue of German war criminals had begun to lose much of its insistent significance.

Best, with no further possibility of appeal, pressed immediately for an amnesty or pardon. In his twisted, deluded mind he deserved a pardon because all war crimes trials had been a farce, and especially because in Hitler's Germany he and other Nazi officials had acted always for "honorable" or "higher" reasons, a rationale eerily resonant of Auschwitz's commandant Rudolf Höß. On May 20, 1950, Best wrote to a friend:

> Correctly interpreted, the "war criminals trials" are a page of fame for our people. Because to my knowledge it has not been established that a single defendant acted from personal, "criminal" motives. All acted solely from conviction or on orders (unlike the plunderers, defilers etc. of 1945!).[25]

Doubtless he had heard of Himmler's similarly perverted and frightening wartime creed. In a long speech delivered on October 4, 1943, to senior *SS* officers in Poland, the *Reichsführer* had urged them onward to complete the Final Solution—or, as he termed it, "the evacuation of the Jews, the extermination of the Jewish people." He had praised the *SS* for implementing the killings and still, with "exceptions caused by human weakness," remaining "decent fellows." In a horrific description Himmler termed the subject "a page of glory in our history which has never been written and is never to be written."[26]

THE DUTCH VERDICT ON HANNS ALBIN RAUTER

It mattered little that during his postwar trial a court in The Hague produced massive evidence—including eyewitnesses and Nazi documents originating from himself—that revealed how Hanns Albin Rauter and wartime police forces subordinate to him had taken, in the court's judgment, an "active part in the persecution of the Jews in the Netherlands."[27] Arrested at the war's end in 1945 and extradited to the Netherlands for trial for war crimes, Rauter insisted on his innocence. He'd merely followed orders from superiors, he told the court in May 1948, and he had "no knowledge" that Dutch Jews deported to the East "would be ill-treated or exterminated."[28]

Following Germany's conquest of the Netherlands in 1940, Rauter—one of numerous Austrians in the Nazi occupation administration—had served as

Himmler's Higher *SS* and Police Leader in the country and simultaneously as its "commissioner general for public safety." As Himmler's deputy in the Netherlands, on the "Jewish question" Rauter both collaborated with and acted independently of his nominal superior in the occupation, the *Reichskommissar* for the Netherlands, Arthur Seyss-Inquart (later tried and convicted by the IMT and executed).

Rauter commanded not only German police and *SS* in the Netherlands, but also Dutch police and a unit of the Dutch *SS*. Because of the Nazis' persecution of Dutch Jews and the eventual onset of the Final Solution, increasingly the German occupation had to rely on police power. This meant that Rauter, his police, and the *SS* bureaucracy became ever more important and powerful.

Already in early 1941, in reprisal for Dutch and Jewish resistance in Amsterdam to the oppression of Jews, he decreed that four hundred Jews would be deported to Germany for forced labor. The deportees ended up at Mauthausen, where the *SS* worked them like slaves in nearby stone quarries. Most died from exhaustion. On March 12, 1941, Seyss-Inquart defended this brutal action in a speech, ominous in its tone for all Jews: "The Jews are not Dutchmen. They are those enemies with whom we can come neither to an armistice nor to a peace."[29]

After the *SS* and police crushed the Amsterdam uprising and in June seized another group of Jews in the Dutch capital to send to their deaths at Mauthausen, no such further demonstrations happened in the Netherlands. During the following months, widespread discriminatory legal measures against Dutch Jews—confiscating their property and forcing them to wear yellow stars—culminated in their systematic roundups and imprisonment in two large concentration camps, Westerbork and Vught.

The Germans used the camps primarily as transit stations for the eventual deportations of Jews to Germany or Poland, where slave labor or extermination awaited them. In the summer and fall of 1942, with the Final Solution well under way at Auschwitz and elsewhere in the East, Eichmann ordered from *Gestapo* headquarters in Berlin the start of massive deportations from the Low Countries.

Rauter had charge of the Dutch Jews. Under his direction the *SS* and police placed tens of thousands of victims on trains and shipped them to the East—the majority of the 102,000 Jews from the Netherlands murdered in the Holocaust. Amid the persecution few Dutch did little to hide or rescue Jews from the Germans and almost certain death.

A Dutchman betrayed Anne Frank, the Jewish teenager who hid with her family and some friends in Amsterdam—in what Anne called, in her diary, the "Secret Annexe"—from July 1942 to August 1944. After the annex's divulgence to the *Gestapo*, most of the Frank family and the other occupants, including the daughter-diarist, died at Auschwitz or Bergen-Belsen. Three months before the betrayal, Anne sensed the growing danger to her and her family from the Dutch. She confided in her diary on May 22, 1944:

> To our great sorrow and dismay, we've heard that many people have changed their attitude toward us Jews. We've been told that anti-Semitism has cropped up in circles where once it would have been unthinkable. This fact has affected us all very, very deeply. The reason for the hatred is understandable, maybe even human, but that doesn't make it right. . . .
>
> I have only one hope: that this anti-Semitism is just a passing thing, that the Dutch will show their true colors, that they'll never waver from what they know in their hearts to be just, for this is unjust!
>
> And if they ever carry out this terrible threat, the meager handful of Jews still left in Holland will have to go. We too will have to shoulder our bundles and move on, away from this beautiful country, which once so kindly took us in and now turns its back on us.[30]

During Rauter's postwar trial the court produced many of his numerous progress reports to Himmler, including one of September 10, 1942, in which he informed the *Reichsführer*: "The rounding up of the Jews is making us rack our brains to the uttermost. I will on no account fail to make use of any influence I may have for what is gone is lost. . . . [S]o that with this the great purge can begin in Holland. . . . I am harnessing up everything that can exercise police or assistant police functions. . . ."[31]

Two weeks later, he declared to Himmler that he'd accounted for some fifty thousand Dutch Jews, including thirty thousand Jews "pushed off" to Auschwitz. He promised: "Every Jew found anywhere in Holland will be put in the large camps. As a result no Jew, unless a privileged one, will be seen any longer in Holland." Simultaneously, he announced that "Aryans who hide Jews or help them over the border, and who have forged identity papers, will have their property seized, and the perpetrators will be taken to a concentration camp."[32]

Seventeen months later, on March 2, 1944, Rauter, brimming with pride, announced to Berlin the results of his work: "The Jewish problem in Holland properly speaking can be considered as solved. Within the next ten days the last full Jews will be taken away from Westerbork camp to the East."

Earlier, Rauter had ordered his *SS* and police subordinates to act ruthlessly and pitilessly in carrying out the ordered deportations. "This is not a nice job," he told them, echoing Himmler's words when the latter addressed *SS* and police leaders in Poland in October 1943. "[I]t is a dirty work, but it is a measure which, seen historically, will have great significance. . . . There is no room for tenderness or weakness. The one who does not understand this, or who is full of pity or silly talk about humanism and ideals, is not fit to lead in these times. . . . And this is what is going to happen. Not one more Jew will remain in Europe."[33]

In the late evening of March 6, 1945, the Dutch anti-Nazi resistance nearly succeeded in killing Rauter. As he traveled by automobile on the road between Arnheim and Apeldoorn, the attackers ambushed the vehicle, shooting Rauter several times and wounding him severely. The would-be assassins fled, and a few hours later he was discovered and taken to a hospital. He survived the attack, and the next day, at his order, as a reprisal 263 prisoners were taken from Dutch jails and concentration camps and shot to death.

During his postwar trial five years later, despite the court's reproducing his words and the above-mentioned documents ordering the elimination of the Dutch Jews, Rauter denied to the court any responsibility for Germany's deliberate destruction of most of Dutch Jewry. He claimed that the court had no jurisdiction or right to try him. Some of the Dutch population, his defense counsel argued, by resisting the wartime German occupation (established with the surrender of Dutch armed forces in 1940), had "violated the laws and customs of war and had thereby relieved the accused of the obligation to abide by such laws and rules."[34]

Nevertheless, the court sentenced Rauter to death. His claim that he didn't know during the war what would happen to the Jews he deported to the East the court found impossible to believe, and it declared him guilty of that charge and also of persecuting numerous other Dutch. An appeals court upheld the verdict in January 1949, which Dutch authorities carried out on March 24 near the town of Scheveningen. He died by firing squad, but not before he allegedly gave the order himself to shoot. The Dutch buried him in a secret place.

ROBERT WAGNER: A FRENCH VERDICT

"France's Nuremberg" is what the *New York Times* called it.[35] But the trial appeared to prove the sad postwar point that the French disregarded generally what had happened to the Jews in wartime France. In May 1946 a French military court in Strasbourg convicted and sentenced to death Robert Wagner and several of his leading Nazi Party subordinates. During the war Wagner, with his high forehead, remaining hair neatly combed over, and defiant stare, had served as the German chief of civil administration of the French province of Alsace, incorporated from 1940 to 1945 into Germany.

Historically, Germany and France had disputed (and at one time or another had claimed) control of two French provinces, Alsace and Lorraine. The court convicted Wagner and the others in the dock of having forced French citizens during the war to bear arms for Germany and of having murdered numerous Frenchmen. But, once again, amid the charges in the trial, the court mentioned little of the defendants' persecution of tens of thousands of Alsatian and other Jews.

Wagner's longtime fanatical service to Hitler and to the Nazi cause in Alsace and the neighboring German state of Baden had continued until April 29, 1945. That day, only hours before Hitler's suicide in Berlin, Wagner dismissed his staff at Bodmann on Lake Constance. After discovering that his wife had committed suicide, he emerged from hiding and surrendered to the Americans on July 29. The U.S. Army interrogator who interviewed him noted the former Nazi leader's "ferocious fidelity to Nazi ideology."[36]

Wagner, long devoted to the *völkisch* (racial nationalist) and anti-Semitic principles of Nazism, had participated in 1923 in Hitler's so-called Beer Hall Putsch. During that violent Nazi uprising in Munich, Hitler had failed to overthrow the Bavarian state government, a prelude to his planned destruction of the German democratic government, the Weimar Republic. Two years later, after an early release from prison for his putsch and treason, Hitler named Wagner leader (*Gauleiter*) of the Nazi Party's organization in Baden. In 1933, when the Nazis assumed power in Germany, Wagner became Baden's Reich governor.

Thereafter, he directed a steadily increasing persecution of Baden's roughly twenty thousand Jews. First, he ordered that all Jews from state and municipal positions, which included teachers and university personnel, be removed. The Nazi-dominated state agencies and courts implemented racial legislation stripping Jews of their legal rights. The state government facilitated an extensive *Aryanization* of Jewish businesses. During the nationwide pogrom on *Kristallnacht* in November 1938, amid the unrestrained violence against Jews, the Nazis in Baden murdered at least one Jewish woman. Many Baden Jews reacted to the pogrom by emigrating.

In 1940, only a few days after the German conquest of France and Wagner's appointment as the civilian leader of Alsace, he had carried out—at Hitler's directive—two of the first wartime Nazi deportations of Jews from their homelands. Similar to the expulsions of Jews from western Poland in late 1939 and 1940, the Germans moved the Jews of Alsace and Lorraine into the unoccupied zone of France. In Alsace, where most Jews in the two provinces lived, they had to meet daily at Mulhouse and clean the town's streets.

On July 16, 1940, assisted by French authorities, Wagner assembled the Jews of Colmar together at the local police station. Each Jew received a suitcase and two thousand francs (forty-five dollars at the time, based on an exchange rate of forty-four francs to the dollar). The police then crowded the victims into trucks, drove them across the demarcation lines into Vichy France, and dumped them at night on a deserted country road. On September 28, Hitler demanded of Wagner and party leader of the Palatinate Josef Bürckel that in ten years they be able to report these French areas as

"German, furthermore as purely German"; he said he would not ask "what methods they had applied" to achieve the Germanization.[37]

By October, anti-Jewish pressure from Wagner and other Nazi administrators in Alsace had intensified so acutely that German and French military officials met to conclude an agreement. The latter provided for the deportation of all Jews of French nationality from Alsace and Lorraine into unoccupied France. According to Wagner at his trial in 1946, the expulsions involved twenty-two thousand Jews from Alsace alone. The number of deported, in fact, amounted to several tens of thousands more.

On October 22 and 23, 1940, Wagner deported the remaining German Jews from nearby Baden. The *SS* moved forcibly some seven thousand Jews from both Baden and the Saar-Palatinate in twelve transports to southern (unoccupied Vichy) France, where the French authorities imprisoned them. According to Longerich, "It seems that the Gauleiters [Wagner and Bürckel] themselves were responsible for the initiative for these deportations, which were explicitly approved by Hitler."[38] Many of those expelled died of malnutrition and disease at the Gurs concentration camp in southwestern France; others perished after 1942 in deportations from France to the East and its extermination camps.

At his trial Wagner admitted that he'd desired a Nazi victory in the world war and declared that Nazism was his faith, Germany his religion. As part of his defense, he said next to nothing about persecuting Jews and claimed ignorance of many facts alleged in the indictment against him.

Before his execution on August 14, 1946, and wholly unregretful for his crimes, he praised a dead trinity by exclaiming, "[L]ong live Greater Germany, long live Hitler, long live National Socialism."[39] These hollow words, while reflecting his fanatical commitment to Hitler and *völkisch* ideology, were absurd in view of Germany's total defeat and devastation, much of which his beloved Führer had ordered and/or approved. Wagner's brutal rule, and that of other Nazis, in Alsace alienated the local citizenry and contributed significantly to the rapid postwar reintegration of the province firmly into France.

ERICH VON MANSTEIN: LONG DELAYED BRITISH "JUSTICE"

The British had arrested him in the summer of 1945 and imprisoned him for two years. But they didn't want to place him on trial. As one of Nazi Germany's former field marshals and arguably its most brilliant military commander, Erich von Manstein came from the classic Prussian mold, the type of soldier that numerous British officers had learned to respect. In Britain, both an official and public disdain existed for trials of Axis soldiers, especially prominent ones like Manstein.

During 1947 widespread protests in the British army and government greeted the trial by a British military court in Italy—and its sentencing to death—of the former commander of German forces in Italy, Field Marshal Albert Kesselring, for authorizing the reprisal murder of Italian citizens. The uproar led eventually to commutation of his sentence and to his premature release.

Among Britons there was discontent with war crimes trials in general. The IMT added to the British attitude when in the fall of 1946 it failed to convict the German general staff and high command among the former Nazi organizations and declare them criminal (although the Soviet judge opposed the decision). Nevertheless, both the tribunal and, later, the Americans in particular pursued and brought to trial individual members of the German Armed Forces.

As for Manstein, he was born in Prussia in 1887, the son of Eberhard and Helene von Lewinski, but was adopted by an uncle. The Lewinskis had Jewish origins, including a distant relative named Levi. Consequently, the king of Prussia (and German emperor) "granted special permission for Erich to take his uncle's name."[40] Manstein became a professional soldier and, once Hitler assumed power in 1933, rose rapidly in rank to lieutenant-general and was assigned to the army general staff. In World War II, he helped plan the German invasions of Poland and France and held commands of armies in Operation Barbarossa against the Soviet Union. Hitler promoted him to field marshal on July 1, 1942.

Late in the war, German conspirators who attempted to kill Hitler on July 20, 1944, had contacted Manstein about joining the plot. But he refused to do so, declaring that as a Prussian field marshal, he owed absolute loyalty to Hitler and the German state. Still, he never betrayed the plotters. In late January 1945, he moved his family from its home in Liegnitz to western Germany. He surrendered to British Field Marshal Bernard Montgomery, and British troops arrested the charming but arrogant German officer on August 23, 1945.

Since then, Whitehall had done little to investigate Manstein for war crimes or other charges. During and after the war he enjoyed acclaim as possibly Germany's most talented staff officer and field commander. Shortly after Germany invaded the Soviet Union, he had assumed command of the Eleventh Army, which operated in the southern Ukraine, Crimea, and Caucasus. Fourteen months later, in November 1942, following a series of victories over the Red Army in the Crimea and his promotion to field marshal, Manstein took control on the Eastern Front of the newly formed German Army Group South.

In his 2006 book, Wolfram Wette observes that Manstein, while commanding the Eleventh Army, "repeatedly received precise reports" about the "systematic murder of Jews" in the area of his responsibility, carried out by *Einsatzgruppe* D.[41] For the operational area covered by the Eleventh Army, it's estimated that as of April 1942, *Einsatzgruppe* D had killed one hundred thousand Jews.

In addition, during October 1941, one month after Manstein took command of the Eleventh Army, the Romanian Fourth Army fighting alongside the Germans murdered sixty thousand Jews in and near Odessa, the city and Black Sea port with the largest Jewish population in the Soviet Union. According to Wette, Manstein's

> reaction to the reports is unclear. On the surface, he either ignored them or declared the information on the scale of the killings to be unreliable. Despite full knowledge of the murders and, in his view, catastrophic strategic errors on Hitler's part, his motto was, "Prussian field marshals do not mutiny." His views on the duties of a soldier, and in particular on the absolute loyalty a Prussian officer owed to a legitimate government, were such that he could not take action against them, even when he was aware of war crimes being committed on a mass scale. He must have dealt with the knowledge that he himself had Jewish forebears by repressing it.[42]

Later, while commander of Army Group South, Manstein informed a small group of officers on his staff of his Jewish background. This apparently led his ordnance officer, Lieutenant Alexander Stahlberg, to tell the commander of Stahlberg's similar ancestry. Nearly five decades after the war, Stahlberg related his conversation with Manstein to Bryan Mark Rigg, an American graduate student living and doing research in Germany.

While Stahlberg and Manstein played chess one evening, Stahlberg told his superior he'd heard that the *Einsatzgruppe* assigned earlier to Manstein and the Eleventh Army had murdered one hundred thousand Jews. When Manstein didn't respond, Stahlberg told him: "Dear Field Marshal, I feel the need to tell you this because I'm of Jewish descent myself." Manstein paused. "That's very interesting," he said. But immediately he turned his attention back to the chessboard.

When Stahlberg asked him about the huge numbers of Jews being slaughtered, the field marshal stared at him. "Do you really believe that?" he asked. Stahlberg responded that he did. "Well," Manstein declared, "if this really happened, they're only Jews."[43]

During Manstein's first months in captivity, American prosecutors preparing for the IMT attempted unsuccessfully to persuade him and several other British-held German generals to testify against Jodl and Keitel, the leaders of the former high command of the *Wehrmacht* then on trial before the tribunal. Manstein and the others signed a statement pointing the finger of blame for Germany's defeat and sorry state in 1945 at Hitler and away from the army.

Toward the end of the IMT, on August 9 and 10, 1946, Manstein appeared as a witness at the tribunal for Jodl and Keitel. Early in his testimony, he sought to distance himself from Himmler, who had "wanted to replace the Army by his SS; and in my opinion the generals of the Army were particularly persecuted by him with hatred and libel."[44] Manstein blamed on Himmler his own dismissal by Hitler in March 1944.

Eventually, Manstein addressed the subject that no former Nazi, whether witness or defendant, wished to mention: the murder of the Jews. The lawyer for the high command officers asked him about the *Einsatzgruppen*, no doubt because during the previous January Ohlendorf, the chief of *Einsatzgruppe* D attached to Manstein's Eleventh Army, had testified to the IMT that he'd received orders from the army commander.

Manstein admitted that, possibly, Ohlendorf "reported to me once," but he denied all knowledge of the extermination of Jews. He knew nothing, he said, of the ninety thousand Jews slaughtered by *Einsatzgruppe* D and noted by Ohlendorf, because such "Jews who were mentioned were not murdered in my zone of command." He insisted that he "did not receive a report on the shooting of Jews," although he'd "once heard of a rumor."

Regarding his troops' involvement in the killings, Manstein contended: "That units of my army could have participated in the shooting of Jews, I consider quite out of the question. . . . If a unit or officer of my army had participated in anything like that, it would have meant his end." He knew only that the *Einsatzgruppen* "were organized to prepare for the political administration; that is to say, to carry out the political screening of the population in the occupied territories of the East." He didn't elaborate on what such "screening" involved.[45]

Under cross-examination by Telford Taylor, the U.S. prosecutor, he repeated that "I knew nothing of the plan of extermination" of Jews.[46] Had he, Taylor questioned, ever issued during the war an order to his troops similar to one decreed by a fellow army commander in October 1941, to "support [the] program to liquidate the Jews and commissars?"

"No," Manstein declared. Taylor—who wrote later in his memoirs that "I did not for a moment believe Manstein's claim that he knew nothing of the massacres" by the *Einsatzgruppen*[47]—placed in evidence a new document, signed by Manstein on November 20, 1941. In part it read:

> Since 22 June the German people have been engaged in a life-and-death struggle against the Bolshevist system.
>
> This struggle is not being carried out against the Soviet Armed Forces alone in the established form laid down by European rules of warfare. . . .
>
> The Jewish-Bolshevist system must be exterminated once and for all. Never again must it encroach on our European living space.

> The German soldier has not only the task of crushing the military potential of this system. He comes also as the bearer of a racial concept and as the avenger of all the cruelties which have been perpetrated on him and on the German people. . . .
>
> The soldier must appreciate the necessity for the harsh punishment of Jewry, the spiritual bearer of the Bolshevist-terror. This is also necessary in order to nip in the bud all uprisings which are mostly plotted by Jews.[48]

Manstein argued—feebly—that he couldn't remember the document but admitted that he'd signed it. Still, he maintained that neither he nor his troops knew anything about the killings of Jews. Nevertheless, Taylor termed the former field marshal's appearance on the stand a "debacle," believing his "credibility was shattered."[49]

Obviously, the British disagreed. For three years, while he remained in prison, they did nothing to prosecute Manstein. Even pressure during the fall of 1947 from the United States on Whitehall to try him and two other former Nazi commanders—Field Marshals Walter von Brauchitsch and Gerd von Rundstedt—for issuing and distributing criminal orders on the Eastern Front, failed to persuade the British to place them on trial. By then, the United States had assembled further captured Nazi records incriminating Manstein on all charges in the London Charter and forwarded these documents to the military governor of the British zone. The new evidence discredited decisively the testimonies before the IMT of Manstein and the other commanders.

One new document relating to Manstein, a report, dated April 16, 1942, by Ohlendorf to Eleventh Army headquarters, concerned the "freeing of Crimea of Jews." Another report observed, "The Jewish question in this vicinity has been solved."[50] Other directives showed that Manstein had ordered the *Einsatzgruppen* to work closely with—and sometimes under—*Wehrmacht* officers.

Still, the British remained unmoved. Finally, in the fall of 1949 they found themselves forced by public pressure to try the then sixty-seven-year-old Manstein alone, in order to avoid having to permit the extradition of the field marshal and the three other officers (Brauchitsch, Rundstedt, and Colonel-General Adolf Strauss) to Poland or the Soviet Union, since the British distrusted both countries' legal procedures. Among the four officers, British physicians declared only Manstein medically fit to stand trial.

While waiting in prison, Manstein and the others complained bitterly about the conditions in which they lived. A letter of Manstein somehow found its way into the *Manchester Guardian*. The missive condemned his alleged suffering, what he described as "torment and torture," and presented a litany of grievances. He disliked living—since the scheduling of the trial—under a twenty-four-hour guard. His wife, he complained, could visit him only for an hour each day and his children not at all. He criticized his captors for, in his view, keeping him in ignorance about his future. He and his fellow former officers had endured endless humiliations. "We are being confined like criminals," he protested.[51]

Likewise, he criticized his involuntary return by the Allies to Nuremberg in 1948 so that he could serve as a witness in a U.S. trial of thirteen former officers of the high commands of the German Armed Forces. Later, he denounced publicly the fact that he hadn't been allowed to testify. In truth, he'd refused to take the stand.

Hardly surprising—given the widespread antipathy in Britain to trying soldiers—he received sympathy from numerous politicians. These included the former prime minister, Winston Churchill, who bizarrely and deplorably contributed to Manstein's defense fund. In June 1945, Churchill had confessed that he "did not see the German admirals and generals, with whom [the British] had made arrangements, being made to stand with their hands above their heads." In October 1948, amid the heated debates on the possible trial of Manstein and others, he described as foolish the desire "to make a feature of such squalid long-drawn vengeance [as trials] when the mind and soul of Germany may once again be hanging in the balance."[52] Many Britons, amid the Cold War crisis, which included the Soviets' 1948–1949 blockade of Berlin, didn't believe it necessary for Britain to prosecute Germans who had murdered Russians, Poles, and Jews. After all, Germans like Manstein hadn't killed Englishmen.

The following summer, as Manstein's trial approached, the field marshal's defense fund received contributions from supporters like poet T. S. Eliot, who had his own anti-Semitic views that sometimes cropped up in his poetry. Many Germans, while delighted at such support, remained puzzled by the great affection that most of the British public held for Manstein. Increasing numbers of Germans thought it overwhelming proof that the British sought help of Germany and its officer class against Soviet Communists. Moscow interpreted British sympathy for Manstein similarly, calling Churchill "Warmonger No.1"[53]

The trial opened on August 24, 1949, in Hamburg. The principal charges against Manstein included the slaughter of Soviet POWs, the use of such prisoners for slave labor, and the mass killings of Jews. Regarding the last accusation, he admitted knowing of the Jewish persecution but asserted that it had originated only for "religious" reasons. He'd never heard, he said, of concentration camps or atrocities. Of Hitler's many orders against the Jews that he received, he had either changed them or not issued them to his forces. Some Führer directives he had to pass on, solely because he had no alternative but to obey his superior.

Manstein's defense counsel, Reginald Thomas Paget, a British Labour Party MP and admirer of the field marshal, argued that Ohlendorf had exaggerated wildly the reports he'd submitted to Manstein's headquarters. The *Einsatzgruppe* leader had inflated the numbers of Jews his unit had murdered to impress Himmler. Instead of the alleged ninety thousand killed, the counsel put the number at near three thousand. He spent considerable time portraying Ohlendorf as a wildly boastful and unreliable *SS* officer. Manstein's staff hadn't passed on *Einsatzgruppe* D's reports to the field marshal because the staff didn't wish to upset him.

The defense lawyer bought wholeheartedly the popular but erroneous argument of many Germans that Nazi atrocities against Jews and the *Wehrmacht*'s alleged complicity in them were solely the figment of Communist and anti-German propaganda, similar to the supposed exaggerated Allied propaganda of World War I. He maintained that "the German Army in Poland behaved well [though] some synagogues [were] burned, [and] occasional indignities were imposed on the Jewish population."[54]

In this regard, Manstein and his counsel not only made claims similar to other Nazi war criminals, but also their assertions—aimed, in effect, at justifying Nazi atrocities and anti-Semitism—played into the hands of the earliest Holocaust deniers. The latter had begun appearing by the time of Manstein's trial. This first generation of deniers not only argued that Nazi atrocities against the Jews "were exaggerated or even falsified," but also they asserted that whatever happened to the Jews had been deserved "because the Jews were Germany's enemy."[55]

On another occasion Manstein's counsel contended that no difference existed between Manstein's "Jewish-Bolshevist" order of November 1941 and the postwar Allied rule of "nonfraternization" with Germans. Such a gross claim seemed delusional at best; whereas the former directive urged the elimination of Jews and Bolsheviks, the latter sought to prohibit Allied troops from engaging in friendly relations with Germans. Manstein and his counsel "consistently ignored the fact that Germany was the aggressor against Russia."[56]

Repeatedly, Manstein defended himself as bound by duty to obey Hitler's orders. This line of his defense had thus far succeeded only in securing convictions and executions for many prior defendants. In this regard, it seemed not to matter an iota that he'd alleged—erroneously—to his postwar captors that he alone, among the former German army commanders, had challenged and argued frequently with the Führer on military strategy. Such conspicuous contradictions were not explored but simply ignored.

On December 19, 1949, the court sentenced Manstein to eighteen years' imprisonment for "war crimes," primarily for neglecting to protect civilians. It acquitted him, however, of the charge of responsibility for atrocities against Jews. For whatever reasons, the judges appeared to ignore how—by a very wide margin—Jews formed the most notable civilian victims of the *Einsatzgruppe* attached to the Eleventh Army. The court discounted the substantial evidence of the field marshal's involvement and that of a portion of his troops in killing Jews.

Of the 632 Nazi war criminals executed after conviction by British and U.S. postwar military courts (not counting the IMT), the number included no generals in the regular armed forces. The Western Allies executed only subordinate officers, most of whom pleaded that they'd followed superior orders, much as Manstein had claimed. Not only did he and fellow superior officers benefit from his own courtroom defense, but so had most other former Nazis (though not the leading lights of the benighted regime).

He and his counsel had contended, in Tom Bower's words, "that the handful of deaths in Russia were justified, and were, in any case, only carried out in the best military tradition of 'an honourable soldier just obeying orders.'"[57] Now, following the trial, only a small step remained for ex-Nazis and numerous other Germans to excuse many more atrocities perpetrated by the Germans and even to denounce the Allied trials as tainted with the very crimes of which the Allies were accusing the Nazis.

The British interned Manstein in a fortress, where his family and a secretary assisted him in writing his memoirs. Soon, his sentence was commuted to twelve years; in August 1952 the British gave him a medical parole after he had served roughly three years of a fifteen-year sentence. Eight months later, he received a full release from prison. He worked briefly as a military adviser to the Federal Republic, during which he assisted in rebuilding the German army.

His memoirs appeared in print in 1955. The book, entitled *Verlorene Siege* (*Lost Victories*) might more accurately have been titled *Lost Memories* or *Lost Truths*. The book, received as a classic of military history, actually represented a classic example of numerous memoirs of former Nazis (such as those by Karl Doenitz, Heinz Guderian, Keitel, Kesselring, Erich Raeder, Walter Schellenberg, and Curt Prüfer) invariably filled with inaccuracies, distortions, omissions, and even pure inventions, which the authors used to conceal their roles in the Nazi regime and its criminality. Manstein omitted completely any mention of the Holocaust and of his involvement—and that of the *Wehrmacht*—in it. He even intimated that he'd opposed Hitler's "political measures in the east" that "ran entirely counter to the requirements of his strategy."[58]

In the book's foreword, Basil Liddell Hart, a British military officer and celebrated historian, praised Manstein as a "military genius" and the book as "one of the most important and illuminating contributions to the history of World War II." Unfortunately, Liddell Hart was too dazzled by his access to former Nazi generals and their flattering welcome of him to exercise a more scrutinizing view of them and their actions. In 1970, the Englishman's 766-page *History of the Second World War* appeared; it made no mention of the Holocaust and other German atrocities. According to Gerhard Weinberg, "The single most difficult task all those [scholars] working on World War II in Europe and North Africa face is the need to penetrate the fog of distortion and confusion generated by the vast German memoir literature, especially that of . . . Erich von Manstein."[59]

On June 9, 1973, the former field marshal, living in Irschenhausen near Munich, suffered a stroke and died (at age eighty-five). The Federal Republic buried him with full military honors.

BEST: FREEDOM AMID ALLIED AND OTHER PARDONS

Early on the morning of August 29, 1951, Werner Best walked away from the Copenhagen prison a free man. He'd spent barely six years in Danish custody (and none in Allied detention). Within hours the Danes whisked him to the German border as one might drive an ant off of a picnic blanket. He crossed into Germany and soon joined his wife and five children living in Rumel near Moers on the Lower Rhine River.

Efforts by the Germans—and by Best himself—to obtain his release had begun much earlier. During the spring of 1949 he'd received a visit in prison from West German industrialist and transport magnate Hugo Stinnes Jr. Best had known Stinnes since the 1930s and during the war had channeled Danish contracts to his shipping firm. The industrialist, a power in the conservative North Rhine-Westphalia branch of West Germany's Free Democratic Party (FDP), notorious for its neo-Nazi leanings, worked actively for the release of German war criminals from Allied and other prisons.

Following his Copenhagen trip, Stinnes commissioned a close friend and fellow FDP member, the Essen lawyer Ernst Achenbach, to provide Best and his Danish defense counsel with legal advice and to work for Best's release. (Werner knew Achenbach from when they had worked together as Nazi occupation officials in France during the war.)

Like Best, Achenbach had a past. While working in the political section of the German embassy in Paris, he helped to set in motion the deportations of Jews in France. In 1944 he left the German foreign ministry, when foreign minister Ribbentrop removed the head of its department for "Jewish affairs" for conspiring—vanity of vanities, but expressive of the departmental rivalries rife in the Reich—to overthrow the minister, that is, Achenbach himself. Achenbach exited the ministry before the German defeat; his departure helped him after 1945 in developing the baseless legend that he'd been an "opponent" of the Nazi regime.

Best's renewed contact with Achenbach provided Best with a major, almost invaluable advantage. The West German lawyer had served as a defense attorney at Nuremberg in 1947 and 1948 for former Nazis tried by the United States, particularly in cases involving the German chemical firm *I. G. Farben* and the German foreign ministry. Ernst had ties to numerous groups of former officials and soldiers from the Nazi era as well as to West German industry. Achenbach counted among his close friends in the FDP Thomas Dehler, the West German government's first minister of justice.

Best, too, had friends and personal acquaintances serving as officials in the new Federal Republic, particularly in the ministries of foreign affairs, justice, and the interior. He'd worked with many of them in the Nazi civil service. The republic's first chancellor, Christian Democratic Party leader Konrad Adenauer, had hired numerous former Nazi officials to help construct and operate the burgeoning bureaucracy.

Adenauer believed—apparently the United States and Britain agreed—that establishing a functioning democracy required less memory and justice for Nazi crimes and more "integration" of those who had "gone astray." To many observers—especially those Jews whom the Nazis had persecuted—it must've been very dispiriting to see the return *en masse* of former Nazi officials to government.

Especially following Best's second trial in Denmark in mid-1949, in which the court accepted his false claim that he'd neither helped initiate nor prepare the *Aktion* to deport Danish Jews, his friends and others in the Bonn regime viewed him as a "rescuer of Jews."[60] In their minds, he embodied the role of a martyr, one emblematic of all former Nazis still "wrongfully" imprisoned.

Not surprisingly, given the public misperception of the facts, during late 1949 and 1950 the Federal Republic established contact with German prisoners in Denmark and attempted to influence Danish authorities to lessen the prisoners' sentences or, ideally, to end them entirely. When visited in prison in mid-June 1950 by a lawyer from the Federal Republic's Central Office for Legal Protection, Best demanded that the West German government place pressure on Denmark for his immediate release: "For its key thrust in negotiations, the federal government must make its economic cooperation with Denmark—in passing or explicitly—dependent on the release of the German prisoners."[61]

The Danish government, seeking to improve its trade and other contacts with West Germany, viewed Best and other German prisoners in Denmark as a burden on and obstacle to such goals. But the Danish public wouldn't approve an immediate release or pardon of the prisoners. At one point, Copenhagen considered handing the prisoners over to Britain for placing in Allied custody in Germany. The German prisoners, Best included, protested bitterly.

The prospect of incarceration in a British prison, probably under worse conditions than in Denmark, pushed Best into another tiresome psychological breakdown—including threatening suicide anew. On December 16, 1950, the ever-reliable Achenbach informed Best's Danish counsel that delivering Best to the British would constitute "clearly an insult to our [German] national dignity." Germany, as well as Denmark, he stressed, had

> every reason to worry about other things, such as, e.g., the defense of Western Europe against Bolshevism. . . . Therefore, a radical final stroke must be drawn in Europe through the past, if one day Danish resistance fighters and German National Socialists will not face the same fate, namely to perform slave labor together in the Urals.[62]

Despite the obvious distortions and exaggerations that infused such statements, in Bonn there was full agreement; Adenauer's chancellery intervened with the British to help stop the planned prisoner transfer. Simultaneously, the policies of the Federal Republic and Western Allies regarding war criminals improved Best's prospects with Danish authorities.

Under growing demand from its own willfully amnesiac population, the West German government illustrated a "just leave it behind us" mentality regarding Nazi war crimes. Increasingly, it undermined denazification and implemented an amnesty law—with the Western Allies' approval—exempting from further punishment some one hundred fifty thousand former lower-level *SS* and other Nazi officials. Many of the arbitrarily pardoned had been involved, in varying virulent degrees, in violent Nazi crimes.

Similarly, with considerable success, Adenauer, the government, and the West German public pressured the United States and Britain to free the war criminals convicted and imprisoned by the Allies. Cold War politics intervened heavily in favor of war criminals. The Korean War, beginning in 1950, had intensified Western fears of Communism and prompted Britain and the United States to discuss the future rearmament of West Germany and its admission into the North Atlantic Treaty Organization (NATO). Adenauer maintained to the Western Allies that to achieve German support for such a significant action they had to fulfill two conditions: the halting of the defamation, in his view, of the German soldier, and a satisfactory settlement of sentences for war crimes.

While intractably demanding the Allies' sympathetic consideration and outright disregard of clear crimes against humanity, the only concession that Adenauer extended to victims of the Final Solution was his government's conclusion of a treaty in March 1953 with Israel, where, by then, several hundred thousand Jewish survivors had managed to settle. In the agreement Bonn promised to pay 3.5 billion marks to the Jewish state as "compensation" for the Holocaust. In Adenauer's view, postwar Germany would prosper if it paid not only the few reparations owed to the Western Allies, but also some to Israel. But barely 11 percent of West Germans approved of the agreement. Still, the United States pressed Adenauer to complete the accord by indicating that doing so would assist the Federal Republic in joining NATO.

Clearly, Best and other German war criminals confined in Denmark benefited from the rapidly changing political climate in Western and Central Europe. The Danish government released its prisoners—murderers and accomplices all—though most had served only half their sentences. Immediately on his arrival in Germany at the end of August 1951, Best began a fanatical quest to rehabilitate himself, hoping to exploit the widespread German campaign to redeem war criminals in general.

But his success required first that he avoid further prosecution in Munich for his role in the killing (on June 30, 1934) of Nazi storm trooper (*SA*) leaders. During the proceeding, Achenbach intervened via a letter, dated September 6, 1951, to Thomas Dehler, the federal minister of justice. The lawyer argued that choosing to prosecute Best, whom the Danes had just released, would severely damage German-Danish relations as well as German efforts to encourage the United States and Britain to grant far-reaching pardons to war criminals.

Eventually, and expectedly, the prosecution suspended its investigation, citing a lack of evidence incriminating Best and declaring Hitler's decree amnestying the June 30 killers applicable to the case (as if the Führer's directives still held the vaguest vestige of legal credibility). The outcome left Best ecstatic, feeling secure that he'd nothing more to fear in his Nazi past from German judicial authorities.

During the fall of 1951, Best began working for Achenbach's legal office in Essen. Soon, he directed the office's crusade to persuade Bonn to press the Western Allies for a "general amnesty" of war criminals convicted by Allied courts. His campaign, in alliance with Achenbach, followed a first wave of amnesty demands begun in the late 1940s, which two prominent German churchmen, both of whom the Nazis had imprisoned in Dachau for several years, had headed.

Protestant clergyman Martin Niemöller and Catholic bishop Johannes Neuhäusler had lobbied U.S. military authorities heavily not only for commuting death penalties given to Nazi war criminals by American tribunals but also for releasing the convicts. The pressure from the churchmen and the German public forced the United States to grant clemency to most of the criminals on death row. Niemöller and Neuhäusler even attempted to save four of the worst perpetrators of the Holocaust, including Ohlendorf and Blobel, whom the Americans finally executed in June 1951.

By the time Best returned to Germany a few months later in 1951, of the 1,558 war criminals the U.S. military courts and commissions had convicted and imprisoned in Germany, nearly half had already been discharged. During the first months of 1952, the United States released over one hundred more. The British conducted a clemency policy along similar lines.

Best developed an argument favoring the wholesale pardon of all such criminals—whether freed or still in prison. He'd worked originally on his view while imprisoned in Denmark. In pro-amnesty propaganda he sought to distinguish between "political crimes" ordered by the state, whose perpetrators, he insisted, deserved a full pardon, and those common, privately motivated crimes committed for personal advantage (of which, unsurprisingly, he was innocent).[63]

For this campaign he and Achenbach mobilized every means at their disposal: recruiting the rabidly pro-Nazi FDP branch in North Rhine-Westphalia, other political and legal connections, and corporate funds. Numerous former *SS* and *Gestapo* officers contacted Best. In July 1952 he wrote to one of them, observing that many of their comrades "had landed in the local area" and had "more or less established a foothold." Moreover, he continued, "comrades communicate with me from all parts of Germany. One could create a pretty extensive group, but I am presently against any organizational amalgamation."[64]

In January 1953 the general amnesty campaign collapsed quickly. The West German government outlawed a neo-Nazi party that had gained seats in Lower Saxony's state parliament. At the same time, British military police arrested a group of former Nazi functionaries, led by Werner Naumann, who'd joined the North Rhine-Westphalia FDP and had ties to both Achenbach and Best. The group demanded that the FDP put forth an extreme nationalist political program that would provide Germany with "compensation for the wrong done to National Socialism, produced by the despotism of the victors and denazification. We say free us from the judgments of the Allies, who have discriminated against our people, and especially their soldiers."[65]

The radicalism, which raised fears in the United States and Britain of a resurgence of Nazism, quickly frayed relations between the federal Ministry of Justice in Bonn and the Achenbach-Best amnesty movement. Although many Germans had criticized what they viewed as a violation of German sovereignty by the British occupation power in arresting former Nazis, the Ministry of Justice ordered its officials to keep their distance from Best. The minister, Dehler, realized that Best and Achenbach represented part of an old Nazi coterie and had helped open the doors for such elements to FDP branches in the Rhineland and Ruhr regions. The ministry had collected considerable evidence revealing the extent of the former Nazis' infiltration of that portion of the party.

The Naumann and neo-Nazi scandals torpedoed not only Best's relationship with Achenbach, whose law office he no longer worked for, but also ruined his chances for further professional rehabilitation. The government rejected his request for reinstatement in the foreign ministry as well as his application for a pension. And, further, he was denied a license to practice law.

Despite thousands of former Nazis whom West German federal and state governments had hired, Bonn, as ascendant government, feared Best. In his re-emergence in politics, the federal government saw a danger to itself at home and abroad. Following the suicide of Himmler, the assassination of Heydrich, and the hanging of Kaltenbrunner, Best—Heydrich's former deputy—was the highest-ranking living member in West Germany of the former *Gestapo* and *RSHA*.

But if the government saw him as *persona non grata* for a return to the civil service, his friends in the business world viewed him differently. Like many other Germans, including the Adenauer government, they, too, cared little about remembering—let alone rectifying—the past. German business provided jobs, some quite lucrative, for numerous former National Socialists, including Best. What had happened only a decade earlier to the victims of the Holocaust seemed very far away.

14

Eichmann, Jerusalem, and Eichmann's Henchmen

Incredibly, at war's end in 1945 both Allied military intelligence and the Jewish Agency in Palestine—which had represented since 1929 the economic and other interests of Jews living in Palestine to the local British mandate government—barely had a name for him. Neither group had his photograph. They knew him only as the innocent-sounding "head of the Gestapo department responsible for Jews," not as the zealously efficient but consciously anonymous bureaucrat of mass racial murder.

Adolf Eichmann ranked among the most powerful of Nazi Germany's vast number of "desk murderers," persons who, like Werner Best, had helped implement the Final Solution not as its executioners but as its facilitators. Such individuals included, at nearly every level, German railroad officials as well as administrators, clerks, and functionaries in the *SS*, police, and numerous government and Nazi Party officials.

Even before the war, Eichmann had served as a specialist on "Jewish affairs" in the *SD*. One of a number of young, self-confident activists in the Security Service, Eichmann pressed the agency to take an ever greater role in the Reich's official policy of persecuting the German Jews and forcing their emigration from Germany. By late 1937, this policy encountered something of a crisis, with unrest in the Arab countries helping to curtail Jewish immigration to Palestine and with many countries tightening their immigration policies.

In response, the *SD* sent Eichmann on a fact-finding mission to Egypt and Palestine that produced few results. During 1938 and 1939, amid the German annexation of Austria and takeover of Czechoslovakia, Himmler placed Eichmann in charge of offices in Vienna, Prague, and Berlin that forced Jews to emigrate through a combination of terror and chicanery, but not before bleeding them dry financially.

With the onset of war and Poland's defeat and division between Germany and the Soviet Union, Eichmann initiated the first German deportation of Jews, as part of Himmler's broader plan to resettle in German-occupied Poland ethnic Germans from lands under (or about to fall under) Soviet rule. Like Hitler, the *Reichsführer SS*, and other top Nazi officials, Eichmann viewed the war principally as a struggle against Jews and alleged that they formed a powerful global enemy that had to be combated relentlessly.

Immediately, he organized the transport of 4,700 Jews from the former Czechoslovakia, Polish Silesia, and Austria to a town called Nisko, located on the border between German and Russian Poland. Many of the deported died in miserable conditions of starvation and neglect.

But on October 20, 1939, the *RSHA* suspended the Nisko transports, mainly because they clashed with other parts of Himmler's large-scale resettlement scheme. Nevertheless, the barbarous Nisko experiment provided a model for the much larger deportations then planned by the *SS* of Jews from the whole area of the Reich to Lublin, in the German-occupied Polish territory called the Government General.

In December 1939 Heydrich transferred Eichmann to the main *RSHA* headquarters in Berlin and placed him in an office designated IVD4, with responsibility for "emigration and evacuation." Heydrich called Eichmann his "special officer" for "the evacuation of the Eastern provinces" and made him responsible for all the deportations planned for occupied Poland.[1] During the following months Eichmann participated in *SS* efforts to expel vast numbers of Poles and Jews from areas of western Poland incorporated into the Reich to make room there for the resettlement of ethnic Germans.

Initially Eichmann and the *RSHA* sought to evacuate the Poles and Jews to the Government General. But overcrowding there helped produce by the summer of 1940 Nazi plans to send the Jews falling under Nazi rule elsewhere, more specifically to Madagascar, a primitive island off the eastern coast of Africa. But the Nazis' so-called Madagascar Plan failed the reality test quickly. In addition, massive overcrowding increased in the former Poland, where the Germans had begun forcing many of the three million Jews into ghettos and continued their attempt to resettle ethnic Germans in the western districts.

By early 1941, such problems led Hitler and Himmler to commission Heydrich to prepare a plan for the "solution" to the so-called Jewish question in Europe. To assist Heydrich in this regard, the latter moved Eichmann's Department IVD4 formally under the *Gestapo*, and in March the department received a new designation, IVB4, for "Jewish Affairs and Evacuation."[2] The German invasion of the Soviet Union in June paved the way for the eventual decision by the Nazi leadership to implement the Final Solution—first, to murder all Soviet Jews, and then, to extend the killing to all Jews elsewhere in Europe. In December the *SS* rewarded Eichmann with a promotion to the rank of lieutenant colonel.

Between 1942 and 1944, he played a key role in the Final Solution. In January 1942 he assisted Heydrich in planning the Wannsee Conference that recruited the cooperation of numerous German government agencies in what, a few months earlier, Hitler and Himmler had begun ordering—the extermination of the Jews. Thereafter, the enthusiastic lieutenant colonel organized the deportation of several million Jews from all over Europe—many in some two thousand huge trainloads—to their death at Auschwitz and other large killing centers in the East.

He did so by sitting in his office in Berlin at Kurfürstenstraße 116 and signing documents or making telephone calls. Also he had a "team" of fanatical subordinates, most of them Austrians, whom he sent to supervise deportations nearly everywhere in Nazi-occupied Europe. They included Dieter Wisliceny, Alois Brunner, and Franz Novak; the latter two are discussed later in this chapter.

Eichmann and his men had no illusions about the deported's fate. Eichmann traveled constantly among Berlin, Vienna, and Prague and visited his men in the field as well as the killing sites. On many occasions he visited Auschwitz, he watched naked Jews herded into a gas van at Chelmno, and he observed a mass shooting at Minsk. The orders from Auschwitz purchasing Zyklon-B gas for use in its gas chambers passed through Department IVB4. At least once, he helped supply Jewish prisoners to Nazi doctors who murdered them for use in studying human skeletons and, specifically, the "skulls of Jewish-Bolshevik commissars."[3]

Always he demanded the deaths of as many Jews as possible. He helped to establish the ghetto at Theresienstadt near Prague and to develop Nazi propaganda advertising it as an "old people's home" in order to lull German Jews and the world into complacency about the deportations. Repeatedly, he intervened to limit the type and number of Jews exempted from the transports. In German-occupied Greece, between mid-March and mid-May 1943, some forty-five thousand Jews were deported to and murdered in Auschwitz.

Also he pressed hard for extending the deportations to Jews in the Italian-occupied zone of Greece. In France during mid-1943, he pushed to speed up the deportations of local Jews to Auschwitz, in large part because of German military setbacks in the war; he wished to conclude the deportations before the war's end and pressure the French to collaborate.

But only in Budapest, after March 1944, when German troops occupied Hungary and installed a new pro-German government there, did Eichmann appear in public to supervise roundups of Hungarian Jews and their deportation. Since at least 1942, Hitler had held the idea of gaining hold of and killing the Jews of Hungary. Once Eichmann arrived there, he headed a special *SS* commando comprising his trusted lieutenants in Department IVB4, and participated directly, with the help of many Hungarians, in the collecting of local Jews for transport to Auschwitz-Birkenau. By the fall of 1944, with nearly two-thirds of Hungary's 725,000 Jews already shipped to the camp and murdered, and with the war grinding toward its end and a looming German defeat, Eichmann showed—in the words of his most recent biographer, David Cesarani—"unmistakable signs of fanaticism in his efforts to deport the remnant" of that country's Jews.[4] He even quarreled with Himmler, who had suspended some deportations and who hoped to use the Jews to bargain with the Western Allies for the *Reichsführer*'s own safety.

While still in the Hungarian capital, Eichmann boasted to an *SS* subordinate that the number of Jews killed in the war was nearly six million. He intended to remain in Hungary as long as needed to send as many local Jews as possible to their death. Living lavishly and drinking and smoking heavily, he only finally left Budapest on Christmas Eve 1944, just hours before the Red Army encircled the city and closed the last escape route.

During the first months of 1945 he returned to a Berlin of mountainous, bombed-out rubble and busily arranged for the destruction of incriminating files of Department IVB4. Germany's surrender found him in Prague. When he heard that his *RSHA* chief, Ernst Kaltenbrunner, had left for the Austrian mountains near Altaussee, he traveled there to make a final report. By then, neither Kaltenbrunner nor most other *SS* associates wanted much to do with him. He was "damaged goods" in light of his role in the Holocaust, something even he knew would eventually make him a top war criminal.

In early May he complained bitterly to *SS* intelligence officer Wilhelm Hoettl about Kaltenbrunner who, along with the latter's cohorts, did not want "this apocalyptic memento of their own sins" anywhere near them.[5] Nevertheless, at his superior's orders, Eichmann assembled hastily in the mountains a band of Nazi partisans, mostly *SS* and police who had fled to the region and who intended to make a last-ditch armed stand against the Allied enemy.

When such heroic pretensions failed to materialize, he followed the example of most other *SS* men. He disappeared, as he said later, "to the extent that I didn't tell everybody who I was."[6] He made his way down from the mountains to visit his wife Vera in Altaussee but didn't stay long.

ALIASES OF EVIL

Eventually, Eichmann returned to Germany. Once there, he managed to hide in plain sight in several U.S. internment camps by using false papers and aliases, one of them "Second Lieutenant Otto Eckmann."[7] U.S. interrogators failed to uncover his identity, though apparently some fellow prisoners knew it. He remained cautious, not writing to his wife and instead leading her and other relatives to believe that he'd died. But later, Austrian authorities denied Vera a death certificate when they learned that the only "eyewitness" to her husband's alleged demise was her brother-in-law.

By October 1945, the world had begun to identify and focus on Adolf Eichmann. The UNWCC had identified him but possessed erroneous information about his personal appearance and background. When the IMT opened, prosecutors and others mentioned his name regularly. In January 1946 one of his former *Gestapo* staff, Dieter Wisliceny, had served as a witness for the prosecution and testified that his boss had once shown him a written directive, signed by Himmler but based on an "order from the Fuehrer," for the "final solution of the Jewish question." That meant, Wisliceny explained, "the biological annihilation of the Jews."[8]

Wisliceny, who had once studied theology, knew well what *final solution* meant. He had joined the Nazi Party in 1931 and the *SS* and *SD* in 1934. He was the driving force behind the deportation of Slovakian Jews in 1942 and of Greek Jews in 1943 and 1944 and was one of Eichmann's reliable cohorts in assuring that the Hungarian deportations would be a murderous success. His corrupt, opportunistic, bribe-hungry character led him to accept payments to save Jews, but the *SS* major almost never delivered on his side of the arrangements. After his testimony at Nuremberg, the Americans handed him over for trial to Czechoslovakia, which condemned Dieter and hanged him in February 1948.

But during his IMT testimony, Wisliceny recalled a chilling conversation with Eichmann in February 1945 about what would happen to the two when the war ended. "I laugh," he quoted Eichmann as telling him, "when I jump into the grave because of the feeling that I have killed 5,000,000 Jews. That gives me great satisfaction."[9]

Despite the gradual illumination of the shadowy Eichmann to Allied investigators, near the end of 1945 U.S. intelligence—still failing to uncover him in internment camps and based on the testimony of two former *SS* men—concluded that Eichmann had somehow escaped the Allied dragnet and was on the run. Thereafter, U.S. interest in him faded, especially once the Cold War (a covert struggle with the Soviet Union for military secrets and political influence in Europe) emerged, leaving the United States less inclined to divert its intelligence or other resources to find even one of the central figures among Hitler's mass murderers. Later on, U.S. intelligence agencies captured and employed a number of Eichmann's former *Gestapo* aides in the conflict with the Russians.

By early 1946, Eichmann decided that he'd better remove himself from Allied custody. Living in U.S. camps had become increasingly dangerous because delegations of Jewish survivors, wishing to identify their earlier tormentors, kept visiting. In February he escaped from the last camp, at Ober-Dachstetten in Franconia, with the help of fellow officer-prisoners. Because of the honor code among the former *SS* officers, they agreed to assist him.

Supplied with a new false identity, forged papers, and civilian clothing, he fled north and settled near Hamburg. There, using the alias of "Otto Henninger,"[10] he worked for three years as a lumberjack for the brother of one of his previous fellow prisoners. When his employer went bankrupt, he leased a small plot of land and, echoing the early career of his superior Himmler, raised chickens for nearly a year.

All this time Eichmann passed unnoticed by the authorities. Shrewdly, he'd chosen to hide in northern Germany, in the British zone, where relatively few military intelligence officers and field police searched for known Nazi criminals. The British had much less enthusiasm than the Americans for war crimes trials and by 1949 had renounced any intention to prosecute war criminals in West Germany.

Nevertheless, Allied interest in Eichmann hadn't faded entirely. In April 1946, Rudolf Höß provided an affidavit for the IMT on behalf of Kaltenbrunner that implicated Eichmann in the workings of Auschwitz-Birkenau. During the next couple of years the Allies accumulated substantial information about Eichmann, though to the public he remained largely unknown.

Apparently, by the spring of 1950, he had noted a newspaper story about his escape several years earlier from Ober-Dachstetten and had heard of a raid by authorities on his wife's home in Altaussee. In late 1946, both the CIC and local Austrian gendarmerie—acting on a tip from the indefatigable Wiesenthal, whose landlady knew of Eichmann—visited the wife. She claimed, however, that she hadn't seen her husband since before the war's end and was now divorced from him. She had adopted, as a result, her maiden name, Vera Liebl. Nor did she have photographs. Her stonewalling proved highly effective; thereafter, both the Americans and Austrians appeared to forget about her as well as Eichmann.

During the summer of 1950, Eichmann left Germany finally and went abroad, hoping that one day his wife and three young sons could join him. Cut off from his family for several years, he was tired of hiding so near to potential captors. He left his chicken farm in northern Germany and, like thousands of other Nazi fugitives, escaped along a well-established "rat line" that led south through Italy to South America. One found in South America large ethnic German communities, often sympathetic to Nazism.

He'd planned his getaway much earlier. Most prominent in his decision to flee Germany, he had received in 1948 official papers to enter Argentina. The documents, including a landing permit, bore the name of yet another alias, "Ricardo Klement,"[11] and remained valid for only two years. Eichmann—now "Klement"—had to arrive in Argentina in 1950, before the permit expired.

He'd acquired the papers bearing the new alias in northern Italy. They'd come to him largely through the covert postwar operation established in Europe by a former *SS* officer and the Perónist government in Buenos Aires. A year earlier, likely the same "rat line" had aided the escape of Mengele through Rome to Argentina. Eichmann/Klement would recall later: "In the press, on the radio and in books my name was being constantly mentioned. I heard of the existence of some organizations which had helped others leave Germany."[12]

Eichmann/Klement traveled in the spring of 1950 through southern Germany and into Italy. Along the way he found lodging and other assistance in Catholic monasteries and convents. One, a brotherhood in Bavaria, had helped Jewish converts to Catholicism to emigrate from Nazi Germany, which prompted Eichmann's then-*Gestapo* office to watch it closely. But now, after the war, according to Cesarani, the community turned with apparent ease and lack of conscience "to assisting the men who had once persecuted them."[13] Within a few weeks Eichmann arrived in Genoa. There, with the help of a Franciscan priest, acting on behalf of Hudal, the pro-Nazi bishop in Rome, Eichmann acquired a Red Cross passport, on which the local Argentine consulate stamped a visa.

He left Genoa by ship on June 17 and landed in Buenos Aires a month later. Immediately, the network of *SS* and Perónist government officials that had facilitated his escape from Europe found him—as it had numerous other former Nazis—both lodging and employment. Within a few months he moved beyond—and at a safe distance from—the Argentine capital to a small mountain village to the north, where he worked undisturbed for nearly three years delivering survey reports for a hydroelectric plant. No one, he noted with satisfaction, troubled him with awkward questions or checks on his background.

By December 1950, he felt secure enough to contact his wife. He wrote her via his parents, advising her in code that he was alive and well. The communication not only signaled her to prepare to join him but also showed his accurate perception that the world's interest in him had dwindled. Primarily because of growing Cold War politics, the Western Allies, as well as German and Austrian authorities, had called off the search for Eichmann. The United States found itself embroiled in the Korean War and more fearful than ever of the potential spread of Communism. The Americans sought to win West Germany for a partner—eventually a partially rearmed one—against the Soviet Union by amnestying convicted Nazi war criminals and by expending scant effort to find other suspected criminals who'd escaped.

Eichmann's whereabouts, therefore, held the attention of only a few private individuals, uppermost Wiesenthal and another Holocaust survivor and Nazi pursuer, Tuvia Friedman. During the war, Friedman, a Polish Jew and survivor of forced-labor camps and the liquidation of the ghetto in his hometown, Radom, had joined anti-Nazi partisans. When liberated by the Red Army, he entered the Polish militia for a time and in 1945 left for Austria, where he began tracking war criminals.

When Wiesenthal urged American friends to help search for Eichmann, he received, in various forms, the weary reply: "We've got other problems."[14] But slowly, working from his documentation center in the northern Austrian city of Linz and collaborating with Friedman, Wiesenthal learned bits of information about Eichmann, some of which he gleaned from the testimony at the IMT and the war crimes trials in Czechoslovakia of Wisliceny and other former *SS* officers.

Still, neither he nor anyone else looking for Eichmann possessed a photograph of the fugitive. Eventually, Wiesenthal secured the coveted picture from one of Eichmann's postwar mistresses. Much earlier, he'd concluded that Eichmann remained alive, particularly when Vera attempted unsuccessfully to have Adolf registered as dead. In Wiesenthal's view she sought by her action to protect—and to deceive the world about—her husband, the mass murderer.

Meanwhile, no one in Austria kept the wife or any of her husband's other family members under surveillance. Only by accident in 1952 did Wiesenthal learn that she and the children had left the country. Incredibly, she'd received a visa to enter Argentina from its embassy in Vienna (albeit under her maiden name) without raising any apparent suspicions.

In early July the family arrived in Buenos Aires and joined "Ricardo Klement." Later, Eichmann and his wife would inform their still young sons of the true identity of "Klement." According to Cesarani: "The waning interest in Nazi-era criminals allowed Eichmann and his family several years of relative peace and quiet in Argentina."[15]

In March 1953, Wiesenthal received a crucial piece of information, which came from a fellow stamp collector, an elderly Austrian baron, in Linz. The baron had worked during the Nazi era in German military counterintelligence; his "Catholic-monarchist views," he told Wiesenthal, had made him "skeptical of the Nazis." He showed Wiesenthal a letter from a former army comrade then living in Buenos Aires. What the Nazi hunter saw made him gasp. The last paragraph read: "I saw that miserable swine Eichmann, the one who was in charge of the Jews, he's living near Buenos Aires and works for a water plant."[16]

Armed with what he'd learned about Eichmann, an excited Wiesenthal contacted both the Israeli government and the World Jewish Congress (WJC) requesting their help in locating and capturing the war criminal. Each, however, refused his plea. Wiesenthal could barely hide his bitter disappointment. "American Jews," he told himself, "probably had other worries." As for the Israelis, they "no longer had any interest in Eichmann; they had to fight for their lives against the Arabs." He realized that "I was quite alone."[17]

Still he persisted, despite the fact that he ran short of money and failed to persuade the WJC to support his work financially. Lacking the resources to retain his Linz office, in 1954 he shipped his files on Nazi criminals to Jerusalem's Yad Vashem, the new Holocaust museum, archive, and memorial.

Meanwhile, life for Eichmann/Klement and his family remained uneventful. Although he moved from one low-paying job to another, which he resented deeply, and had to return to Buenos Aires, his wife bore him another son. He associated—and often drank heavily—with former *SS* men, including, briefly, the Auschwitz physician-murderer Josef Mengele.

Hoping to earn badly needed money for himself, he collaborated with another *SS* officer in producing a planned book that would allegedly justify the Final Solution. Although no such publication ever resulted, Eichmann made clear in related interviews that he remained a wholly unreconstructed, unapologetic Nazi. About the extermination of the Jews, he declared: "No, I have no regrets at all and I am not eating humble pie at all. . . . [M]y innermost being refuses to say that we did something wrong."[18]

CAPTURE

Finally in 1957, for the few persons in Europe still looking for Eichmann, a break came in the case. West German prosecutor Fritz Bauer—a Jew determined to bring as many Nazi war criminals to trial as possible—received from Argentina a tip on Eichmann's whereabouts, including even his address in a Buenos Aires suburb. The information came from a German Jewish émigré whose daughter had dated one of Eichmann's sons.

In an unusual move, Bauer decided not to inform his own judiciary. He feared that among the numerous ex-Nazis employed in it, some might alert Eichmann. Instead, he took the matter to the Israeli government. Only because of Bauer's dogged persistence with Mossad (the Israeli secret service), which apparently had little interest in Eichmann and no unit to track Nazi criminals, did it begin an investigation.

Almost simultaneously, in April 1959, Wiesenthal discovered in a Linz newspaper a death notice for Eichmann's stepmother that listed her daughter-in-law, Vera Eichmann, as one of the mourning relatives. Wiesenthal asked himself, why had Vera Liebl, supposedly divorced from her supposedly dead husband, now readopted his name? In February 1960, when Eichmann's father died, another obituary appeared in the newspaper; it, too, cited Vera Eichmann, identifying her as a "daughter-in-law."

Hoping to uncover more proof, Wiesenthal sent an assistant to visit Vera Eichmann's real mother, who believed apparently that telling a half-truth would best continue helping conceal her daughter's hiding place. Her daughter, she told the visitor, had married in South America a man called "Klems" or "Klemt."[19] Immediately, Wiesenthal dispatched the information to the Israeli government.

By then, Israeli investigators in Buenos Aires had already identified Eichmann positively as "Ricardo Klement" and begun moving to capture him. Unwittingly, their prey aided the mission. At the beginning of 1960, Eichmann and his sons had completed building a new residence for him in a rural, desolate marshland outside Buenos Aires at the address of 14 Garibaldi Street. The historian Cesarani suggests that Eichmann moved into the isolated area to give the former Nazi "a sense of security" and "a clear field of vision for 360 degrees." But instead, the location provided the Israelis "the perfect place for an abduction."[20]

Leading the several-member party of Israeli secret agents sent to Argentina to seize Eichmann was Zvi Aharoni, a German Jew who had left Germany in 1938 and settled in Palestine. Initially, he arrived in Buenos Aires on March 1, 1960, and within eleven days he located and began monitoring Eichmann's house. On April 3, he managed to have Eichmann photographed while the latter worked in his garden.

Aharoni returned to Israel with the evidence he had gathered and, receiving the final go-ahead for "Operation Eichmann," he traveled back to Argentina, along with other Mossad agents, and made final preparations. Even the head of the secret service, Isser Harel, arrived in Buenos Aires in early May to take overall responsibility for the venture. The Israelis worked in the utmost secrecy, knowing that in the city former Nazis and Nazi sympathizers pervaded the large local German community of eighty thousand as well as the Perónist movement that still had major influence in Argentine politics.

On the evening of May 11, the agents took up positions around Eichmann's house. When a bus carrying him home from work dropped him off, one of the Israelis, Peter Malkin, pounced on him. Two other agents helped Malkin push the struggling and screaming Eichmann onto the floor of a waiting automobile. They bound him, threw a blanket over him, and sped off to a pre-established safe house in Buenos Aires. There they placed the captive in a specially built cell and began interrogating him.

Under intense questioning, they got him to admit: "My name is Adolf Eichmann."[21] Three days later, after further questioning, Eichmann signed a statement saying he was prepared to stand trial in Israel. On May 19, using carefully forged travel documents and drugging Eichmann so he could walk, with aid, but not speak, the Israeli agents managed to move him and themselves through airport security and aboard an Israeli El Al jetliner. The plane arrived in Israel on May 22, around 7:35 in the morning.

The next day, the Israeli government announced that its agents had tracked down Eichmann in the Argentine capital and secretly abducted him to Israel, where several hundred thousand Holocaust survivors lived. The government made public its intention to try its infamous captive for crimes against the Jewish people and against humanity in general.

TRIAL AND EXECUTION

Eichmann's abduction triggered a minor international crisis. Both Argentina and the United Nations' Security Council condemned Israel's violation of Argentine sovereignty. Some critics of the abduction suggested that the crime of violating Argentina's borders equaled Eichmann's alleged wrongdoing—a claim that outraged Israelis.

Both in Argentina and elsewhere, the affair produced an upsurge in anti-Semitism, some of it expressed in violent attacks on Jews. Fearing worse outbreaks of such hatred, several Jewish leaders in the United States and Europe pleaded with the Israeli government to abandon its intention of prosecuting Eichmann. But Israel, determined to try him, eventually reached a compromise with Argentina, whereby the two countries issued a joint statement condemning the actions by "citizens of Israel" that "violated the fundamental rights" of Argentina.

Publicly, David Ben Gurion, Israel's president, who had approved the abduction, defended the decision to try Eichmann "so that the younger generation growing up and being educated in Israel, which has only a pale idea of the unthinkable cruelties committed, can learn what really happened." Privately, Ben Gurion expressed an even more ambitious purpose for the trial. "The Jewish state," he told an American Jewish leader, "is heir of the six million murdered, the *only* heir."

Those Jews, he claimed, would have come to Israel if they hadn't been slaughtered. "You ask what we shall gain from the Eichmann trial. We shall gain nothing, but we shall be fulfilling our historic duty towards six million of our people who were murdered." About the president's view, Cesarani observed: "The trial would be a symbolic assertion of Israel's right to represent Jews past and present, a display of Jewish sovereignty that had been impossible before 1948, when Jews could only seek redress as individuals in the courts of whichever country they inhabited."[22]

To his captors and his pretrial interrogator, and later at his trial in Jerusalem, Eichmann joined the overwhelming majority of other former Nazis responsible for the Final Solution who, when questioned about their actions, maintained they'd done nothing wrong. The lengthy pretrial interrogation, begun on May 29 and done by Avner Less, a highly experienced Tel Aviv police officer, produced 275 hours of tape and a transcript of 3,564 pages; in addition, Eichmann wrote a 127-page "memoir" that he completed in mid-June 1960.

Eventually, Eichmann commented on some four hundred pages of Nazi documents, many written and signed by him. Later, Less, whose own father had been sent to Theresienstadt and then Auschwitz, commented on the interrogation:

> When Eichmann sat facing me for the first time, he was a bundle of nerves. The left half of his face twitched. He hid his trembling hands under the table. I could feel his fear, and it would have been easy to make short work of him. . . .
>
> As I watched Eichmann sitting there in this condition, I suddenly had the feeling I was holding a bird in my hand, a creature who felt completely at my mercy. But that impression soon passed. His statements and the documents we examined together revealed the cold sophistication and cunning with which he had planned and carried out the extermination of the Jews. Occasionally, this filled me with such loathing that I couldn't bear to be near him and would cast about for excuses to postpone the next hearing to another day, just to avoid having to follow his horrible descriptions or listen to his brazen lies.[23]

When the trial opened on April 11, 1961, in Beit Ha'am, Jerusalem's new cultural center, over seven hundred people filled the room. About the trial and worldwide publicity it attracted, Lipstadt has commented: "This was not the first Nazi war crimes trial. Yet there were more reporters in Jerusalem than had gone to Nuremberg. . . . At Nuremberg victors had sat in judgment. Now the victims' representative [Israel] would sit in judgment."[24]

During the trial, Eichmann's appearance in the courtroom, in which he sat in a bulletproof-glass booth, shocked observers of the proceedings, some of them Holocaust survivors. They saw no powerful, diabolical, and arrogant *Gestapo* leader. Instead, as Moshe Pearlman, a journalist and immigrant from Britain, commented later:

> The biggest surprise was the very ordinariness of the man, the mildness of his appearance, "Mr. Average," in his middle fifties, with receding hair on a balding head, the sides grey and apparently freshly barbered, thick horn-rimmed glasses on a stark nose, the mouth small and thin-lipped, and the pallid skin of his clean-shaven face creased with lines of worry or age, or both. . . . But the crimes attributed to Eichmann were of such unprecedented callousness and magnitude that one expected, as the door opened to the glass dock, to see some monster lumber in. . . .

> It was also a far cry from the swaggering Gestapo officer in shiny Nazi uniform whom some of the witnesses, who would later be giving evidence, had seen before and during the war. This man did not seem a member of that vaunted *Herrenvolk* who had suppressed a continent and murdered millions of its people because they were considered vermin. Two members of this race of "vermin" now sat behind him as guards. . . . A more striking contrast would be difficult to imagine. It somehow made Eichmann look just a little more nondescript, and the tattered Nazi racial doctrines even more ludicrous.[25]

Repeating what he had said in the interrogation, Eichmann resorted to lying, evasion, and outright denial when the prosecution confronted him with incriminating evidence. Shown Nazi documents—some bearing his own signature—that contradicted his portrayal of himself as wholly innocent, he denied their authenticity or lied about them. For example, he testified that during the summer of 1941, Heydrich had told him Hitler "ordered the physical extermination of the Jews." Heydrich had then directed him to visit the *SS* leader Globocnik in the Government General, to "take a look at how far he has got with his plans [for the killings]."

Soon thereafter, Eichmann said, he had visited several extermination facilities. While some historians have used his statements as evidence that Hitler had decided on the Final Solution during the summer and/or fall of 1941, Longerich concludes that Eichmann traveled to the extermination sites in the spring of 1942 and misstated purposely the dates to conceal his role in the decision to implement the Final Solution:

> There is in fact much to suggest that Eichmann was sent to the extermination sites, the destinations of the deportations that he had organized, in order to assess the murder capacity of the camps and then to establish the pace and extent of the deportation. It is also conceivable that the result of his inspection trips was itself the precondition for the decision to begin the deportations on a European scale. At any rate, after the war one would have been able to draw the conclusion from his travels that he played a far more active part in the "Final Solution" than he, always presenting himself as a subordinate receiver of orders, was prepared to admit.[26]

Eichmann's "memoirs," which he began writing while in Argentina and which *Life* magazine serialized at the end of 1960, brimmed with the same arrogant self-justification and unrepentance the author had always shown. *Life's* editorial staff strained to justify publication, claiming even that Eichmann had something to tell the world about the Soviet Union, since he "had a great degree of company" among "Communists and other totalitarians."[27]

For the first time the trial showcased for the world the horrific crimes of the Holocaust—something that the many Nuremberg and other earlier war crimes trials, so embroiled in postwar policy and Cold War politics, had failed to accomplish. The court found Eichmann guilty on all charges and sentenced him to death by hanging.

Some Jews and others, both in Israel and abroad, protested the death sentence and state-sanctioned killing. Eichmann, via his defense counsel, asked for clemency, but Ben Gurion rejected the plea. Since no other crime in Israel carried the death sentence and since nothing like Eichmann's trial and conviction had happened there before, workers hurriedly built a gallows in a third-floor room of the heavily guarded prison housing the condemned.

During the evening of May 31, 1962, officials informed him that the execution would happen within a couple of hours, at midnight. Even at this extremis, Eichmann refused to repent of his monstrous crimes and continued to try to parse their magnitude to a more palatable size. Earlier, when a clergyman visited and reminded him of Hans Frank's "confession" of guilt, the prisoner noted derisively, "[H]e repented, but he was guilty. He was a general, he gave the commands and orders. He needed to repent, but I am not guilty." During his trial, when cross-examined by the prosecutor, Eichmann had claimed: "Regrets do not do any good, regretting things is pointless, regrets are for little children."[28]

He had requested a bottle of wine, which he drank with his last meal. When the guards arrived to escort him, they found the "desk murderer" tipsy, though nowhere as drunk as he'd been during the apex of his career, in Hungary, when he had personally supervised the brutal deportations of hundreds of thousands of Jews. Then, he had often reeked of brandy. The clergyman again appealed to the prisoner to repent, but Eichmann dismissed him with these parting words: "Guten abend. You look very sad. Why are you sad? I am not sad."

Around 11:45, prison guards led him, handcuffed and shackled, to the newly created execution room. His gait was unsteady, due more to the shackles and wine than fear. En route, his nose began to leak mucous, and a guard had to wipe it. When they arrived, the wooden gallows weren't yet finished and they had to wait. Finally, the hangmen placed the noose around his neck. He refused the offer of a hood.

Much to the disappointment of the clergyman, Eichmann's last words were entirely in line with his unrepentant life. "Long live Germany," said the condemned killer, "long live Argentina, long live Austria. These are the three countries with which I have been most connected [he conveniently forgot to mention Hungary] and which I will never forget. I greet my wife, my family and my friends. I am ready. We'll meet again soon. So is the fate of all men. I die believing in God."[29]

With these trite words, reflecting not grandeur and dignity, but a willful, obstinate unawareness, Adolf Eichmann was hanged. Immediately following the execution, silence pervaded, its perfection marred only by the slowly decreasing creak of the rope and the dripping sound of his bodily fluids trickling down his legs and splattering the floor.

Ironically, Eichmann's request that his body be cremated added a grotesque posthumous footnote. Because Jewish law forbids cremation, the Israelis had to quickly build a crematorium in order to incinerate the corpse. Early the following morning, as dawn broke over the waves, his ashes were tossed into the international waters of the Mediterranean Sea.

Assisting in Eichmann's capture represented for Wiesenthal what he and others termed his most "brilliant success." The arrest and prosecution, he believed,

> reminded the world of the tragedy of the Jews at the time when it seemed to be being repressed and forgotten. After the Eichmann trial, no one could doubt any longer the extent of the tragedy. . . . Since then the world has been familiar with the concept of the "murderer at his desk": we now know that fanatical, near-pathological sadism is not necessary for millions of people to be murdered; that all that is needed is dutiful obedience to some "leader"; that mass murderers need not be—indeed should not be—asocial types; that large-scale murder in fact presupposes a socially integrated murderer.[30]

Similarly, German-Jewish émigré Hannah Arendt, who covered the trial for *The New Yorker* and later wrote a controversial book on the proceedings, depicted Eichmann as a colorless, obedient bureaucrat, an example of the "banality of evil."[31] She played down the role of anti-Semitism in Eichmann's participation in the Holocaust and instead claimed that he had acted from the tendency of ordinary people to obey orders and conform to popular opinion with little thought to the results of their action or inaction.

During the trial a shameless Vera Eichmann, in Munich, told a reporter for the London *Daily Express*: "I'm convinced my Adolf is not guilty. It is ridiculous to charge him with these killings. . . . We never discussed his work. . . . In the home politics were never discussed." Yet, about the arch "desk murderer," Cesarani concludes:

> There is no evidence in his youth of violence or brutal Jew-hatred and he could not have joined the SD in 1935 out of an intention to wage war on the Jews. . . . He had to overcome revulsion [to mass killing] and chose to be a *génocidaire*. And he could do this because the Jews were "the enemy" and the Reich was now at war on all fronts. The language and thinking of warfare merged with racial eugenics to neutralize any reservations.[32]

Indeed, ideology and fanaticism had played a role in Eichmann's involvement in the horror he had helped to perpetrate.

Not surprising, the Jerusalem trial caught the attention of Holocaust deniers as much as it did the world's rational populace. A French denier, Paul Rassinier, seized on Eichmann's denunciation of documentary evidence against him to condemn not only Eichmann's conviction and execution but also the earlier Nuremberg war crimes trials. Continuing such trials, Rassinier claimed in 1962, represented part of a Jewish and Communist conspiracy to divide and demoralize Europe.

Also Eichmann's effort to discredit evidence that incriminated him inspired the American Harry Elmer Barnes, a so-called revisionist historian, to move from his previous assertion that the Allies were the real culprits in World War II to denying outright that the Holocaust had happened. Barnes, writing in 1967, borrowed a page from Eichmann's attack on the court's documentation. He declared that the charges against Eichmann and Nazi Germany were based on "fundamental but *unproved assumptions* that what Hitler and the National Socialists did in the years after Britain and the United States entered the war revealed that they were . . . vile, debased, brutal and bloodthirsty gangsters."[33]

Eichmann's defense at his trial also caught the attention of another denier, Arthur Butz, an American engineering professor. Eichmann had attempted to prove that during the war, the German public had found his behavior acceptable. No one, he testified, had "reproached" him for anything in the performance of his duties. Not even a German Protestant pastor, Heinrich Gruber, he continued, who had tried repeatedly amid the war to persuade Eichmann to improve the treatment of the Jews, "claims to have done so." Eichmann admitted that Gruber had sought to lessen Jewish suffering but had "not actually object[ed] to the very performance of my duties as such." The defendant argued that because Gruber had not specifically said "Stop the extermination," the pastor approved of it.

Butz, a decade later, used—in Lipstadt's words—"the same tangled kind of thinking [as Eichmann] to try to make a situation [involving the Holocaust] appear to be other than it was." Butz published a book in 1977 denying the Holocaust had happened. To allegedly support his claim, he cited a 1948 report of the International Committee of the Red Cross (ICRC) that surveyed the committee's wartime attempts to assist Jews and others interned in Nazi camps. The report had discussed the German "extermination" programs and referred to some Jews imprisoned in the Theresienstadt Ghetto near Prague as "transfer[ed] to Auschwitz." According to Lipstadt, "Given the report's repeated references to extermination, there was little doubt as to what that statement meant." However, Butz, "because the ICRC report did not explicitly mention extermination in relation to 'transfer to Auschwitz,'" alleged "those words meant nothing sinister."[34]

Eichmann's gruesome shadow in history reemerged in March 2000, again in association with Holocaust denial. That month, Israel released a 1,300-page manuscript he had written nearly forty years before, while in prison and on trial. Eichmann had written it seeking to diminish his role in the Holocaust. Israel released a typescript copy at the request of lawyers for Lipstadt involved in the highly publicized libel trial in London brought by David Irving against her for calling him a Holocaust denier. As Lipstadt hoped, the manuscript provided statements from Eichmann's own hand that "demonstrate[d] that Irving denied the very things that those who had engaged in the killings freely admitted."[35] Eichmann alluded to the enormity of the crime against the Jews, but distorted and downplayed his involvement in it. Had he not understood fully what he had been involved in? "In the newly released memoir," Lipstadt concluded later, "Eichmann expressed himself as an inveterate Nazi and anti-Semite. . . . [T]he memoir reveals a man who considered his Nazi leaders to be his 'idols' and who was fully committed to their goals."[36] Her side in the trial presented massive documentation of Irving's culpability that delivered her an overwhelming victory in the case.

EICHMANN'S MEN

Alois Brunner

Some had called him Eichmann's "best tool."[37] Born in the Austrian Burgenland in 1913, he had joined the Nazi Party in 1931 and the *SA* a year later. After living for a time in Germany, in March 1938 he entered the *SS* and became a staff member in Vienna of the Central Agency for Jewish Emigration.

His rabid anti-Semitism appealed to Eichmann, who hired Alois Brunner as his personal secretary. Brunner's efficiency won him a promotion in 1939 to director of the agency. He impressed his superiors with his eagerness to use threats and violence against the Jews to force them to leave Austria—and to leave behind whatever wealth they owned.

When the war started, Brunner assisted his boss, Eichmann, in organizing the brutal transport of several thousand Jews to Nisko, during which hundreds of deportees died. While still serving as director of the agency in Vienna, beginning in late 1941, Alois no longer implemented the policy of coercing emigration. Instead, both he and the agency participated in the Final Solution—in the forced deportation of some forty-seven thousand Austrian Jews to ghettos and death camps. Similar to Eichmann and numerous other key officials involved in exterminating the Jews, Brunner knew the fate of the deported. By late 1942, he held the *SS* rank of captain and headed the Central Agency for Jewish Emigration in Berlin.

In February 1943, Eichmann sent his favorite troubleshooter to Salonika, the second-largest city in Greece that also enjoyed the biggest prewar Jewish community in that country, to supervise the transport of some forty-four thousand Jews from Greece to Auschwitz. Shortly after arriving there, Brunner wrote to a *Gestapo* colleague in Vienna expressing satisfaction—even delight—with his work preparing for the deportations.

He and several other "Eichmann men"—in the words of Austrian historian Hans Safrian—formed a "special commando" that descended on the ancient Salonika Jewish community with the utmost cruelty and use of terror. Many community members had ancestors that included Jews expelled centuries earlier from Spain and Portugal.

In a letter Brunner wrote at the end of February to a "comrade" in Vienna, he mocked the Jews and revealed his hatred for them:

> The weather is beautiful. And our work continues along first class. On 25.2 the yellow star here began to twinkle. So many countrymen said, oh dear, mine also wore a star. The Greek population is so pleased over the marking and ghettoization [of the Jews] that I told myself it was a crime that no previous such measures had been taken up. Inflation and the black market could never have reached such proportions if any eye had been kept on the Jews. At the moment there is hardly a business where a Jewish sign hangs outside. And when we first move them off [to Auschwitz] we will unleash jubilation among the Greeks.[38]

Brunner participated in the massive plunder of the Jews in Salonika. Following their ghettoization in March, using spies and torture he and other Eichmann henchmen, including Wisliceny, forced the defenseless people to confess where they had hidden jewelry and money. Eventually, the looters filled cellars in one of Salonika's major boulevards with piles of riches. Also Brunner and his staff, along with the *Wehrmacht* and with assistance from local Greek officials, seized some twelve tons of gold from Salonika's Jews.

Brunner and Wisliceny, with the help of the threatened and terrified Jewish Council in Salonika, headed by the chief rabbi, Zvi Koretz, organized the deportations to Auschwitz. The trains to Auschwitz began leaving on March 15 and ran for several months; all told, Brunner would deport to their deaths 43,850 Jews. Although 11,200 weren't gassed immediately, most of those perished during the life of the camp. Dr. Karl Clauberg selected some of Salonika's Jewish women as subjects in his agonizing, inhuman sterilization experiments. Of the 50,000 Jews in prewar Salonika, only 1,950 had survived by 1945.

The *Wehrmacht* in Greece used most of the murdered Jews' gold to pay for its occupation of the country—the very same army that would later hide its crimes behind the chimera of its "honor" and its "meticulous" respect for the rules of warfare. The German army sold the gold to Greek traders and speculators, who paid the *Wehrmacht* with huge sums of paper drachmas (the Greek currency). As the tide of war turned against Germany in 1942, the *Wehrmacht* spent enormous sums of Greek currency to fortify the Greek coast and nearby Crete, which held strategic importance for the Germans, who used them as bases for launching attacks in the eastern Mediterranean on the British navy.

On July 2, 1943, Eichmann dispatched Brunner to France to head a command unit and take control, outside Paris, of the Drancy transit camp, a converted apartment complex and major assembly point from which, during the war, approximately seventy thousand Jews were deported from the country. During the following year he sent approximately twenty-four thousand Jews to the East. Many of those who remained died from disease and starvation, including French poet and painter Max Jacobs, who breathed his last on March 5, 1944. On September 10, the *SS*, under Brunner's command, entered Nice, in the former Italian-occupied zone of southern France, to round up further Jews.

On April 6, 1944, Klaus Barbie, the "Butcher of Lyon," and the *Gestapo* raided an orphanage in Izieu, a village forty miles east of Lyon, just as its residents were sitting down to enjoy a cup of hot chocolate. Barbie and his men tossed their crying, screaming victims into the backs of waiting trucks. They sent forty-four children, from age four to age seventeen, to Drancy, from where Brunner would dispatch them onward to Auschwitz. All would die.

But Brunner didn't care. At Drancy he beat elderly women and ordered prisoners to prepare postcards for sending home to relatives and friends saying that all was well with them. The cards were mailed to their addressees, but only after the writers had been sent off and gassed. Also Brunner went out of his way to deport women, especially pregnant ones or those with infants.

As late as July 31, 1944, he organized roundups of Jewish children hiding in France and sent the last convoy of Jews from Paris to Auschwitz. Altogether, since mid-1942 some seventy-six thousand Jews had been deported from France, and another four thousand had died in camps or been murdered inside the country. A quarter of the Jews living in France had become victims of the Holocaust.

During the fall of 1944, Eichmann sent Brunner to Slovakia. From September—shortly after the Germans crushed an anti-Nazi insurrection in that country and occupied the former German satellite—until March 1945, when Soviet troops nearly overran Slovakia, Brunner deported some fourteen thousand local Jews, most to their death at Theresienstadt and Auschwitz. Until the war's final days, he continued to sabotage the efforts of foreign Jewish leaders to rescue Slovakian Jews and, at the country's main concentration camp, Sered, personally carried on the selections for deportations, the last of which happened on April 13, 1945. Brunner appeared nearly everywhere at once, roaring out orders and beating prisoners with his own hands.

A former prisoner at Sered, a Czech Jew, Liesel Goldner, recalled after the war "that in the camp many people were shot—we heard the shots, but some prisoners were forced to watch the shootings." Goldner remembered also how Brunner had persuaded numerous Jews to surrender to him voluntarily their money, jewelry, and other valuables. He promised that if they did so, he would permit such families to live together in the camp and travel together in a "communal transport" train on which other families would be separated in groups in the train's rear cars that would eventually be disconnected and sent to different, less attractive destinations.

"During the trip," Goldner said, as she and her husband traveled together at the front of the train, "we watched where the rear cars with the separated families would be disconnected. But they were not disconnected. The 'communal transport' was an extortion device of Brunner, because around midnight we all arrived at Theresienstadt."[39] It's estimated that altogether during the war, nearly 150,000 European Jews were deported under Brunner's direct supervision.

The postwar chaos and confusion served Brunner well. Like so many other former members of the *SS*, he concealed himself in a *Wehrmacht* uniform and, under an assumed identity, claimed to be just an ordinary soldier. Like Mengele, he lacked the *SS* blood-type tattoo, which made his gambit easier.

A former *SS* colleague claimed that he saw Brunner, dressed in "the uniform of an ordinary infantryman" and with a newly grown "long black mustache" at the end of June 1945 in a POW transport in Linz.[40] Around the same time, an incident occurred that increased the likely success of his deceptive efforts: the Soviets had arrested an *Anton* Brunner (also an *SS* captain) in Vienna and, assuming him to be Alois, executed his near namesake. For a long time after, Eichmann's right-hand man was presumed dead.

The U.S. Army had interned Brunner, but with his new identity, the army employed him as a driver at a military base. Brunner didn't remain in captivity long. It's unclear whether he escaped or whether his captors failed to learn his real identity and released him.

In any case, by the late summer, he'd surfaced in Vienna under a false name. Soon, he fled the city with his wife. For nearly two years, sheltered by a friend and local hotel owner, they lived in a small Austrian town between Linz and Passau. In 1947 he settled in western Germany; he registered in Essen-Heisingen using the name "Alois Schmaldienst,"[41] an alias that he'd borrowed from a cousin in Austria. But in early 1950 a government permit office in Vienna, supervised by U.S. occupation authorities, recognized as bogus an Austrian passport bearing Schmaldienst's name. Inquiries with the real Alois Schmaldienst revealed that the photograph on the phony document belonged to his cousin—Alois Brunner.

Thereafter, assuming a new alias, "Dr. Georg Fischer,"[42] Brunner made plans to escape to the Middle East. Nearly everywhere he found both people and governments (either wittingly or not) willing to assist him. Most incredibly, since the late 1940s he had collaborated with the U.S.-subsidized and controlled West German foreign intelligence service, headed by Reinhard Gehlen, one of Hitler's former general staff officers and military intelligence analysts.

The so-called Gehlen Organization, which received millions of dollars in funding from the United States and evolved later into the West German Secret Service, recruited numerous former *Gestapo* and *SS* officers—like Brunner—as spies and collaborators against the Soviet Union. (In his memoirs, published in 1971, Gehlen claimed, unconvincingly, that Germany's invasion of Russia was, in fact, an anti-Bolshevik act of liberation.)

In 1954, Brunner/Fischer fled to Syria at just about the time a French military court tried and condemned him in absentia to two death sentences for his role in the Final Solution in France. Living in Damascus, he received immediate protection from the Syrian government. Along with another former Nazi involved in the Final Solution, the foreign ministry official Franz Rademacher, he worked as an adviser to the country's Ministry of Interior on torture and repression techniques. Both Germans had contacts, directly or indirectly, with other intelligence agencies, notably in the Soviet Union, Egypt, and Algeria.

Brunner would continue living in Syria, eventually becoming the world's highest-ranking Nazi war criminal still alive. He was able to do so despite massive evidence accumulated in the West of his wartime criminality and despite requests for his extradition. But the Western Allies, West Germany, and Israel placed, at best, only half-hearted diplomatic pressure on Syria to surrender him.

Nevertheless, he lived this life not without cost. In 1960, presumably Mossad sent Brunner a letter bomb, which reportedly took his left eye, and in 1980 another letter bomb blew off three fingers of his left hand. But in general, the Syrians provided him with strong political and physical protection. In 1968 Israel and Austria requested his extradition; it would take Germany sixteen more years to request the same in 1984.

During the summer of 1982, Brunner's security and freedom began to erode, when Nazi hunter Beate Klarsfeld, whose husband's father was one of Brunner's victims and gassed in Auschwitz, traveled to Syria posing as a Nazi sympathizer and managed to phone Brunner before the Syrians deported Klarsfeld. In March 1983, the *Times* (London) located Brunner's residence

(7 Rue Haddad) in Damascus, though Syrian authorities still denied that he lived in the country. The Anti-Defamation League urged both the Austrian and West German governments to press Syria to extradite him.

In December 1984 the Federal Republic requested Brunner's extradition, but Syria refused. The Damascus government claimed that no one named Alois Brunner/Georg Fischer lived in Syria. However, during the summer of 1985, the West German magazine *Bunte* published an interview with the longtime fugitive from justice. The article not only identified his street address in Damascus but also quoted him as saying that he "had no bad conscience" about his role in the extermination of European Jewry, or as he put it, "getting rid of that garbage."

In 1987 in a phone interview, he reiterated his views to a *Chicago Sun-Times* reporter, "The Jews deserved to die. I have no regrets. If I had the chance, I would do it again." In August 1987 "a bitter and temperamental" Brunner claimed to an interviewer that his last sentence had referred to his "deportation work," not to exterminating Jews—but the parsing is pointless, since they were, essentially, one and the same, and the former *SS* captain was fully aware of that reality.[43]

Soon, the United States, including senators like Edward Kennedy of Massachusetts, supported the Bonn government's request for Brunner's extradition, but officials at the U.S. embassy in Damascus never delivered Washington's demarche. Apparently, the embassy and U.S. Department of State feared that the "Brunner affair" could jeopardize more urgent American concerns in the Middle East—terrorism, hostages, and missiles—than genocide.

In August 1987, Interpol issued an international arrest warrant for Brunner, but to no avail. During January 1988, West German foreign minister Hans-Dietrich Genscher, while visiting Damascus, asked Syrian president Hafez Al-Assad about Brunner. Assad denied any knowledge of the former Nazi's whereabouts. Hardly had the West German official returned home when the Syrian government publicly condemned the raising of the issue as "inappropriate" and "in bad taste."

Continued efforts into the 1990s failed to move the Syrians to give up Brunner. In 1991 the European Parliament condemned Syria for offering refuge to the war criminal. In 1995 German prosecutors offered a $330,000 reward for information leading to his capture. The U.S. embassy concluded:

> Damascus is too embarrassed to admit his presence and has a perverse sense of pride which would prohibit turning the former Nazi over to any [W]estern authority, since this would be perceived locally as giving in to Israeli pressures. Brunner is old and frail and the Syrians are confident that nature will eliminate the issue in the not too distant future.[44]

Despite unconfirmed reports that Brunner had fled to Brazil or had died in 1996, hope continued in Europe, the United States, and Israel that he remained alive and that someone could still bring him to justice. The last credible sighting of Brunner was in 1992 when he left his house in Damascus and was taken away in an ambulance. In March 2001—when Brunner would have been eighty-eight years old—another French court tried him *in absentia* for war crimes and crimes against humanity, including the deportation of 250 French children who were gassed within twenty minutes of arriving at Birkenau, and sentenced him to life imprisonment.

The long Brunner saga had reflected—and continued to do so—the world's indifference toward the victims of the Holocaust. Recently, a group of historians studying the affair concluded that Brunner's "apparent ability, not only to remain in Syria for decades, but even to apply his Gestapo experience there, is, in effect, a Syrian endorsement of Nazi cruelty and anti-Semitism even in the late twentieth century."[45]

In July 2007, the Austrian Ministry of Justice offered a belated reward of fifty thousand euros for information leading to the capture of Brunner, ninety-five years old by then if still alive. Although it had more hope of catching Genghis Kahn, the ministry cited "indications" that he was "possibly still alive" and that "one should seize this potentially last opportunity" to bring him to justice.[46]

No chance existed that Syria would cooperate in the renewed search for Brunner, termed by the Simon Wiesenthal Center in Los Angeles the most wanted of remaining Nazi war criminals. As Wiesenthal stated in his memoirs, "Among Third Reich criminals still alive, Alois Brunner is undoubtedly the worst. In my eyes, he was the worst ever. While Adolf Eichmann drew up the general staff plan for the extermination of the Jews, Alois Brunner implemented it."[47]

Franz Novak

The young man's dependability and fanatical devotion to authority and Nazi ideology had caught his boss's attention and earned him the infamous title, "Stationmaster of Death." A long-faced former Hitler Youth member with chiseled features, a high forehead, widow's peak, strong nose, and full, almost feminine lips began working for Eichmann in Vienna in 1938 at the Central Agency for Jewish Emigration.

Soon, Eichmann transferred Franz Novak to the agency's office in Prague. From then on, the highly valued and ambitious subordinate, who reached eventually the *SS* rank of captain, provided the core of Eichmann's team that would help implement the Final Solution.

Like most other "Eichmann men," Novak, a native of Wolfsberg, Austria, and son of a locomotive driver, was in his twenties and already a longtime Austrian Nazi. In July 1934 he had participated in the abortive Nazi coup to seize power in Vienna. He escaped capture and arrest by Austrian authorities (though they stripped him of his citizenship) by fleeing to Germany, where, during 1938, he joined the *SS* and *SD*.

Novak's subsequent career followed in step, almost in sync, with Eichmann's. In March 1941, Eichmann appointed him as transportation specialist in the *Gestapo's* newly created Department IVB4. For the most part, Novak scheduled the deportation—or in Nazi vocabulary "special"—trains. He worked as follows: once the department received orders for an *Aktion* (roundup of Jews for deportation) and the number of victims to be involved, Novak consulted with the *SS* Economic-Administrative Main Office (*WVHA*) in Berlin, which decided on the destination of the deported to the east. The *WVHA*, established in 1942, developed swiftly into a huge economic enterprise that generated income for the *SS* by supplying labor to German industry and by managing most of the concentration camps, including Auschwitz-Birkenau and Maidanek. The *WVHA* sent Jews to camps and ghettos needing their labor or where the killing machinery had the capacity to murder them.

Once Novak learned the destination of the deportees, he contacted the *Reichsbahn* (German state railway) to negotiate for the trains required to haul the specific number of Jews. Nearly always, he competed successfully for the trains against the demands of the German army, which needed rolling stock to ship troops and supplies to the military fronts. He then drew up a timetable for the "special trains" in cooperation with officials at the Reich Ministry of Transport.

According to Cesarani: "Given the competing demands on the finite and diminishing transport resources of the Third Reich, this was the hardest part of the process and needed all Novak's mastery of detail and persuasive powers."[48] On average, Novak's office scheduled two full trains nearly every day that carried Jews eastward.

During 1944 he joined Eichmann and other veterans of Department IVB4 in Hungary to participate personally in the rounding up and deporting of 434,351 Hungarian Jews to Auschwitz; another 21,000 from southern Hungary were transported to Vienna to build fortifications. Many other Hungarian Jews were shot by the Arrow Cross (Hungarian Nazis) and their bodies tossed into the Danube River.

Even the heroic efforts in Budapest of Raoul Wallenberg of the Swedish legation or Carl Lutz of the Swiss legation, who together saved some one hundred thousand Jews, could only mitigate the deportations, not end them. In the Hungarian capital, Novak conferred with both local and German railway and police officials to fix the train routes and schedules.

After the war, Novak and several other "Eichmann men" fled to Austria, to near Hitler's birthplace, Braunau am Inn. He worked as a farmhand, and with the help of a friend in nearby Wolfsberg, he obtained falsified documents that allowed him to live under an assumed name. Not long thereafter, he moved with his family to a Vienna suburb and worked as a printing shop employee.

In 1957, he applied for and received Austrian citizenship from the local government in Wolfsberg. He commented later:

> There wasn't much asked about the reason for removal of the citizenship. Indeed, half of Wolfsberg had participated in the [Austrian Nazis'] putsch in 1934. . . . [E]veryone had known precisely that I had participated actively in the putsch. . . . It was obvious that one wanted to draw a line through the past, and thus I received Austrian citizenship once again.[49]

He also received back his real name. All this passed almost wholly unnoticed by the Western Allies and Austrian authorities. But Eichmann's capture and trial four years later led quickly to a series of arrests and trials of Novak and other former confederates in Department IVB4. By the time of Eichmann's trial, Austrian officials had remanded Novak to a Vienna court for investigation.

In May 1961, he provided a deposition for the Israeli court trying his former Nazi boss. He testified, as had so many other former perpetrators of the Holocaust, that he had no knowledge of what had happened to the Jews until after the war. Although he admitted to working in the *Gestapo*'s Department IVB4 for Eichmann and remembered "transports of Jews taking place from Theresienstadt to Auschwitz," he claimed that he had been only "an assistant Specialist Officer" taking orders from superiors "to draw up the timetables for the specific train journeys" and "prepare the requisite documents for the Reichsbahn (Reich Railways) about the means of transport." His assignment accompanying Eichmann to Budapest in 1944 "was to receive the timetables for special trains for evacuating Jews from Hungary." But Novak lied unabashedly about what he had known of the trains: "I did not know that the persons in the these transports were to be liquidated in Auschwitz. The transports were ordered so as to employ Jews for labour or to evacuate them."[50]

He needn't have worried. At the time, Austria was settling into a long period of fervent belief in its national myth that it was actually not Nazism's first accomplice, but rather its first victim. The vast majority of Austrians remained uninterested either in punishing Nazi war criminals or in the fate of Jewish survivors of the Holocaust.

During the Nazi era Austria's far-reaching, deeply rooted anti-Semitism had played a prominent role in its people's broad support of Hitler. Before the war the country had actively courted its annexation by Germany, and when that occurred in 1938 enormous crowds of Austrians welcomed the event in displays of near ecstasy, including Hitler's triumphal entry into Vienna. Between 1938 and 1943 the Nazi Party enrolled proportionately far more members in Austria than in the Germany of pre-1938 borders.

Austrians like Novak—as well as Eichmann, Brunner, Stangl, Kaltenbrunner, and numerous others mentioned in this book—made up some 40 percent of persons involved in the huge Nazi wartime killing operations, both in the euthanasia program and in the wholesale extermination of the Jews. Of the roughly 130,000 Jews in Austria at the war's beginning, 65,459 (or roughly 50 percent) perished in the Final Solution.

After the war, despite the establishment of a parliamentary democracy in the country, the so-called Second Republic, extensive anti-Semitism persisted. Of the approximately 4,500 Jewish concentration camp survivors who returned to Austria beginning in the summer of 1945, almost all of them received scant sympathy. This utter lack of empathy, a deficiency of remorse, resulted, in part, because some six hundred thousand former Austrian members of the Nazi Party, *SS*, and *SA* lived in the country and, with their immediate families, comprised one-quarter of the population.

Most Austrians blamed the Germans they had once welcomed so enthusiastically for their postwar suffering and for the Holocaust. The postwar Austrian government confronted the problem of longtime anti-Semitism within its borders either by denying it existed or by promising to curtail it. The latter approach was never pursued with any degree of commitment or thoroughness.

Austrians rarely, if ever, reexamined their own strong prejudices or pernicious collaboration with the Germans. Instead, according to historian Michael Thad Allen, most Austrians believed in the so-called victim myth,

> a myth not entirely of their own making. The Allies had identified Austria as "the first free country to fall a victim to Hitlerite aggression" in the Moscow Declaration of October 30, 1943. Statesmen seized on this definition of their country. Other passages demanded accountability for participation in the Nazi regime but received far less attention.[51]

Both during and after the Allied occupation of Austria, which ended in 1955 with the reestablishment of Austrian sovereignty, the nation's federal and state governments had an extremely weak record for denazification and for trying notorious Nazi war criminals. Allen observed that the Second Republic made some effort after 1945 "to confront its Nazi past" by establishing the so-called People's Courts.

The courts initiated nearly 137,000 cases (some 108,000 of which began before March 1948) against former Nazis until the tribunals' abolition in 1955 by a series of amnesties that freed the convicted. Other forms of denazification removed 7.5 percent of the workforce, seized the assets of Nazis, and levied fines on their incomes. But, Allen concludes, "Many former Nazis recovered quickly and found their way back to positions of influence and wealth."[52]

After 1955, Holocaust survivors in Austria had little success in persuading their government to prosecute the murderers still in their midst. The government initiated only forty-six trials, one a little-known Auschwitz proceeding in Vienna that ended in March 1972 with the release of both its defendants, Fritz Ertl and Walter Dejaco. The two had served as members of a team of *SS* architects that designed and built the gas chambers at Birkenau.

Also, only slowly did Vienna agree to pay reparations to Jews and other victims of persecution in the war, and it compensated persons who were nonresidents with barely a fraction of their property's value. Even before the victims were compensated, the government had restored in 1952 the property of former Austrian Nazis.

Novak benefited immensely from the Austrian public's aversion to dealing with its country's past. Four trials were required before a court successfully convicted him. In 1964, a Vienna court sentenced him to eight years in prison. Upon his appeal of the verdict, the Supreme Court overturned the lower court's decision. A new trial in 1966 ended in the jury acquitting him on all counts when it accepted his defense of being duty bound to obey superiors' orders. Nevertheless, he was tried again in 1969 and received nine years in prison, but his lawyer managed to get the decision declared invalid, and Novak served no time.

Three years later, a fourth trial found him guilty, but the jury, although denying explicitly his defense of having to obey binding orders, didn't convict him on the charge of "accessory to murder." Instead, it charged him with committing "public violence under aggravating circumstances," because he had transported Jews knowing full well that no provisions for water, food, or sanitation were being allotted them.[53] As a result of convicting him of the lesser charge instead of the more serious one, the final sentence of the "Stationmaster of Death" was a mere seven years. But shortly thereafter, the Austrian government issued him a pardon.

Thus, despite his long-belated prosecution, Novak escaped nearly unpunished for his key role in arranging to transport more than a million Jews to their deaths. Wiesenthal estimated that Novak, for each victim he had sent to Auschwitz to die, had served in prison only three minutes and twenty-one seconds.

Interestingly, however, after Novak's pardon, Wiesenthal likely saved Novak's life. When an elderly Jew from England, a Holocaust survivor who had once been loaded on to Novak's trains headed to Auschwitz, threatened to shoot Novak, Wiesenthal convinced the armed man not to do so. The Nazi hunter told him: "Revenge killings cannot and must not be a way of administering justice. We differ from the Nazis precisely in that we accept the judgments of courts of law, even if we consider them monstrous or unjust. If you are convinced that Novak is a murderer then you shouldn't become Novak's murderer."[54]

Throughout the trials Novak insisted on his innocence. He'd only been "a small subordinate wheel" in Eichmann's department, he told investigators and interrogators. Nor had he hated Jews, he claimed, or known that they were being exterminated at camps such as Auschwitz. Only forced labor—he'd supposedly thought—had awaited the deported victims. "Auschwitz," he insisted, "was for me only a rail station."[55]

Nevertheless, he justified the Jewish persecution with a grotesque defense based on his and Germany's alleged victimization. He claimed that Germans had suffered commensurately during the war "persistent air-raid warnings, and we were always rescuing those buried alive and hauling away the dead."[56]

But other evidence from prosecution witnesses (some of whom German or Austrian authorities had tried and punished already for their involvement in Nazi crimes) contradicted Novak. They underscored how heavily he lied to protect himself. Richard Hartenberger, a former collaborator of Eichmann and Novak who brought the Jews' mail to the Berlin office to be censored, testified that "already in 1941 or 1942" information about the massacre of Jews had trickled through "from people who came to our office from the camps" and from "reading for ourselves the documents at our office." He continued: "Also while nothing official had been communicated, it was known to everyone in Referat [Department] IVB4 that the Jews were being gassed, and not only the SS members knew, but also, for example, the female typists."[57]

At Novak's trial in 1969 a former department secretary corroborated Hartenberger's claim. Erika Scholz recalled starting work in all innocence until "[l]ater I understood that the Final Solution of the Jewish Question meant the destruction and extermination of the Jews. Everyone else in Referat IVB4 must have known what I knew. I didn't speak about it with the other members of Referat IVB4."[58] Novak, indeed, had known. But against the urgency of his ambition, he simply hadn't cared.

15

Hunting the Comfortable

It wouldn't have happened after Eichmann's capture and trial and the resulting awakening of much of the world to the Holocaust and many of its perpetrators living in freedom and unpunished. But twelve years earlier, in 1949, no one seemed even the slightest bit interested, neither the police in Austria nor the Allied authorities occupying the country. Theresa Stangl prepared to leave for Syria to meet her husband—a former Nazi death camp commandant and refugee from Austrian justice. On May 6, Frau Stangl visited her local police station in Wels, completed a required certificate requesting permission for her and her three daughters to leave the country, and applied for a passport.

"There was no secret whatever about our leaving," she thought later. "Everybody knew we were going to join Paul in Damascus."

Even atop the packing crates, along with his address she painted her husband's name in large bold letters: FRANZ PAUL STANGL. She gave the police the same information, explaining to them openly why she wanted to leave the country: "To join my husband who escaped." When she applied for a Syrian visa through the Swiss consulate, she felt relieved that "there was no problem about it at all."[1]

Four years after the war's end, hardly anyone knew of or suspected Franz Stangl's significance as one of Hitler's principal exterminators of Jews. In 1950, when Simon Wiesenthal, working from his headquarters in Austria, checked out Stangl's family in Wels, neighbors informed him that Frau Stangl, along with her children, had left the country months earlier "for an unknown destination."[2]

THE HAPPY STANGL COUPLE

Unlike several other former Nazi mass murderers hiding in Syria, Stangl didn't remain there long. Not even the slightest risk existed that Syria would extradite him or any other war criminal; the Syrians viewed them as soul mates and experts in the Arab League's bitter war against Israel. Nevertheless, by then, details about the Treblinka extermination camp had emerged in Europe and made Stangl one of the most wanted of former Nazis. He no longer believed himself safe.

Nor did he and his wife discuss the past. When she arrived in Damascus nearly a year after he'd gone there, she found him "the happy sweet man he had been years before all the horror." Apparently in denial about the real "horror"—her husband's role in the wartime murder of nearly a million Jews—she decided "not to talk to him again about Treblinka," but instead "let him regain his peace of mind." She rationalized the choice, telling herself that "the awful things that had been done were done, and my thoughts now had to be for the children, for our life together, for the future."

Except for occasional fears about Stangl's security, the family lived comfortably. Initially, he worked in a textile mill at the job the pro-Nazi Bishop Hudal in Rome had secured for him; he'd saved enough money to pay for his family's trip to Syria. In December 1949 a knitting company hired him as a mechanical engineer at a good salary. He and the family moved into a large dwelling in the Syrian capital. Frau Stangl later boasted about the residence: "We were the first German family there to have our own home, and *all* the Germans visited us."[3] She enjoyed the luxury of traveling in the Middle East, of visiting museums and archaeological excavations of ancient ruins.

But anxiety soon arose about her husband's situation. The Damascus police president, who lived in the front of Stangl's house with "his harem," showed a more-than-casual interest in Stangl's middle daughter, then twelve and already "very blonde and very pretty." The Stangls panicked. Not only did they wish to remove their daughter from the situation, but they also worried that whatever they did would anger the police chief. Would he arrest Stangl?

Immediately, Stangl decided to leave Syria for South America, a place much farther from Europe and where, he knew, numerous other former Nazis had fled. Large German communities existed there as well. The family worked through the Brazilian consulate in Beirut and received visas to enter Brazil. Much to their surprise, the police chief did nothing to prevent their departure.

Traveling by ship via Italy, the family arrived on the Brazilian coast, at Santos, in 1951. Hardly had the ship docked when a thief stole much of their money after Frau Stangl had "stupidly," as she acknowledged, trusted a stranger to exchange it for Brazilian currency. But soon the Stangls felt at home in the new country. Within a week he found a job in a textile firm in São Paulo, Sutema, working first as a weaver and then as a machine engineer. Much of the next two years he spent traveling for the company.

Many years later, he recalled in an interview with Gitta Sereny an unusual encounter while traveling on business, one which indicated that even for perpetrators involved in the ordinary moment-by-moment demands of living, their past crimes were often—just below the surface—very much present:

> When I was on a trip once, years later in Brazil, my train stopped next to a slaughterhouse. The cattle in the pens, hearing the noise of the train, trotted up to the fence and stared at the train. They were very close to my window, one crowding the other, looking at me through that fence. I thought then, "Look at this; this reminds me of Poland; that's just how the people looked, trustingly, just before they went into the tins [gas chambers].". . . I couldn't eat tinned meat after that. Those big eyes . . . which looked at me . . . not knowing that in no time at all they'd all be dead.[4]

Eventually, he changed jobs twice, fell ill in 1955, and started a small workshop in his house that produced bandages for hospitals. To supplement his income, Frau Stangl worked for Mercedes-Benz. By the summer of 1959, his health had improved, and he went to work for Volkswagen, a job his wife had helped facilitate. In short order the company paid him a hefty salary that, coupled with his wife's income, permitted him and the family to move into a large new two-storey house they built in one of São Paulo's upper-class districts.

Stangl lived there even under his own name. In 1954 both he and his wife had registered themselves and the family at the Austrian consulate in São Paulo. Several years later, when two of his daughters married and needed copies of their father's certificates of Austrian birth and citizenship, the consulate provided the documents. Frau Stangl wrote home to Austria regularly to relatives and friends; everyone there had the family's address. Life for the Stangls couldn't have been much better. "This was a very good time for us," Theresa thought.

While in São Paulo, the Stangls "rarely, rarely spoke" of his wartime background. If she even mentioned the subject, Stangl cut her off: "Are you starting on that again?"

She'd stop immediately. "After all," she thought, "I too didn't *want* to think about it any more."

She would claim remorse, yet she would defend what her husband and other Nazis had done. About the death camps her husband had commanded, she told herself that the men—prisoners—in the camps "had been killed . . . like soldiers at the front":

> They [the Nazis] killed them—I said to myself—because of the war. Oh, deep down I knew it wasn't so. But that's how I rationalized it for myself. I never never allowed myself to think that women and children had been killed. I never asked him about that and he never told me. . . . If my thinking as I know now was illogical, then it was because that was how I wanted, how I needed, how I had to think in order to maintain our life as a family and, if you like—for I know this also now—my sanity.[5]

She seemed as well to excuse her husband's enormous criminality by viewing him as "an incredibly good and kind father. He played with the children by the hour. He made them dolls, helped them dress them up. He worked with them; he taught them innumerable things. They adored him—all three of them. He was sacred to them."[6]

Neither she nor Stangl saw any incongruity between his love for his own children and his participation in the cold-blooded murder of some several hundred thousand Jewish children at Hartheim, Sobibor, and Treblinka. To the postwar happy couple in São Paulo, Jews hadn't really been—and still were not—human. Plus, Stangl reassured himself that in killing Jews, whom he had viewed merely as "cargo" at Sobibor and Treblinka, he'd followed the orders of superiors and done his national duty in wartime.

MENGELE: FROM FREEDOM TO AN ACCIDENTAL DEATH

During April 1948, following an American trial at Nuremberg of *SS* and other German physicians, which had decreed death sentences for seven of the twenty-three defendants (including a couple of his Auschwitz colleagues), Mengele prepared to leave Germany. After visiting his hometown Günzburg briefly, he had crossed in April 1949 from Germany into Austria and continued on to northern Italy, where he acquired an International Red Cross travel document—with a whole new fake identity—in order to enter Argentina.

Apparently, he received the papers through a postwar clandestine operation established in Europe by a onetime *SS* officer, an Argentine of German parentage, living in Spain. The officer, who established bases in Italy and Switzerland, through which fugitive *SS* men could flee Europe, had the support in Argentina of Juan Perón's government. The Perónists hoped to recruit Nazi technicians to develop their country's air force and other military units. It's unclear whether this was part of *ODESSA* that allegedly assisted *SS* men fleeing Germany and Austria. Much more likely the operation that aided Mengele comprised a so-called rat line that served the same function and received support from groups such as "Edelweiss," an organization of former Nazi officers operating in the Tyrol.

Once in Italy, he managed to reach Rome, in all likelihood helped by Catholic Church sources whose anti-Communist and anti-Jewish sympathies made them willing to assist former Nazis. In the Italian capital the German bishop, Hudal, numbering among the most notorious of such churchmen, made no secret after the war that he harbored and enabled Nazi war criminals to escape Europe by providing them with money, false credentials, and passenger ship tickets.

Mengele arrived in Argentina in June 1949 under the alias "Helmut Gregor."[7] His phony papers passed him off as an ethnic German from the Alto Adige in northern Italy. Living in Buenos Aires, he worked as a physician and acted as a representative of his family's farm machinery company, which provided him with money and a comfortable living. A family friend in Günzburg, Hans Sedlmeier, managed the business in Germany and would serve for years as a contact for Mengele with his relatives. While in the Argentine capital, Mengele met and socialized with numerous other former Nazi escapees, including, for a time, Eichmann, who had fled in 1950 to Argentina.

Apparently, during the early 1950s, Mengele visited Perón, the country's autocratic president, and advertised himself to the Argentine leader as a "specialist in genetics." Mengele entertained Perón with stories about his work with cattle, "where all the cows gave birth to twins." The president knew him only as "Doctor Gregor," but termed him a "stiff-backed Bavarian, highly cultured, proud of his land."[8]

By 1956, reflecting the world's failure to pursue him, Mengele began using his real name. The German embassy in Buenos Aires issued him a passport stamped with it. The ambassador, Werner Junkers, disclaimed later any responsibility for the passport and insisted, "I didn't know who Mengele was."[9] But Junkers had belonged formerly to the Nazi Party, had served as a senior aide to Hitler's foreign minister, Ribbentrop, and had worked in the murderous, pro-Nazi Croatian regime during 1944–1945.

Using the new document, Mengele traveled to Switzerland, where he met his son Rolf. On his return to Buenos Aires, he purchased part ownership in a pharmaceutical company, the profits of which soon made him a rich man and prominent member of the large local German expatriate community. But in the spring of 1960, Mengele left for Paraguay.

By then, several factors had shaken his sense of security. Perón's regime had fallen, and Mengele could no longer count on the sympathy—and protection—of Argentina's government. In West Germany, as Mengele's family there learned from sympathetic police officials, the authorities, at last bowing to the pressure of world opinion, had begun compiling evidence of his crimes. Now they worked toward extraditing him.

As a result, he sought and received Paraguayan citizenship, a legal status in the country that protected him from deportation. He owed much of his newly found security to Hans Rudl, a neo-Nazi former *Luftwaffe* ace pilot and personal friend of Paraguay's dictator, Alfred Stroessner, who helped Mengele obtain the cherished citizenship. Also by then, a sister-in-law, the widow of Mengele's younger brother, joined him there. They married. (His first wife, Irene, had divorced him in 1954. According to his biographers, Gerald Posner and John Ware, Mengele had agreed to the divorce, having "signed and notarized a power of attorney in Buenos Aires so that a local attorney in Günzburg could represent him and process the divorce by proxy."[10])

Following the Israeli capture of Eichmann in May 1960, interest in finding Mengele intensified. The Israelis planned to abduct Mengele as well, but he managed to elude his pursuers and disappear. In the words of an Argentine writer: "From now on he would spend every remaining moment of his life looking over his shoulder."[11] After Eichmann's trial in Jerusalem, the Israelis twice attempted to capture the former Nazi doctor; however, international complications in the aftermath of Eichmann's abduction halted the effort.

Meanwhile, Mengele moved again—this time to Brazil. By then, West German authorities, always a step behind their quarry, had issued a warrant for his arrest and demanded his extradition from Argentina. Two years later, the Federal Republic made a similar request to Paraguay. In the interim, Israeli intelligence continued to track Mengele in Paraguay, but in 1963 it concluded that he'd left for Brazil.

For many years thereafter, Mengele's trail went cold. Neither German nor Israeli authorities learned that Mengele's son, Rolf, had flown in 1977 from Germany to Brazil to visit his father. The thirty-three-year-old Rolf questioned his father at length about Auschwitz, but the latter lied, remaining wholly unrepentant. Later, after returning to Germany, the son recounted their exchange:

> He told me he did not "invent" Auschwitz and that he was not personally responsible for the incidents there. Auschwitz already existed. He wanted to help but that was very limited. He couldn't help everyone. For instance, on the platforms, he asked me what was he to do when the half-dead and infected people arrived? It was beyond one's imagination to describe the circumstances there. He said his job was to clarify only "able to work" and "unable to work." He tried to grade the people as "able to work" as often as possible. He thinks he saved the lives of several thousand people in that way. He didn't order the extermination and he was not responsible.
>
> He said the twins owe their lives to him. He said he never harmed anybody personally, and he got very excited at this point. He asked me if I—his son—believe the lies in the newspapers.[12]

Rolf's visit lasted two weeks. In the end, he realized, it was impossible to discuss the concepts of evil or guilt because his father had no such feelings:

> I tried. These allegations, these facts left me speechless; I tried to tell him that his presence in Auschwitz alone was unacceptable to me. I was hoping he'd say, "I tried to get a transfer to the front. I did this, I did that." But it didn't come to this preliminary agreement. Unfortunately, I realized that he would never express any remorse or feeling of guilt in my presence.[13]

Nor in the presence of anyone else.

Meanwhile, Nazi hunters—especially the Austrian-based Jewish Holocaust survivor, Wiesenthal—continued to look for Mengele. During June 1979, following the Bonn government's elimination of its statute of limitations on Nazi war crimes, it insisted that Paraguay revoke Mengele's citizenship.

The West Germans hoped the protofascist, right-wing dictatorship in Asuncion would deport Mengele. Although its president, Stroessner, claimed to know nothing of Mengele's whereabouts, the government—in a move grudgingly calculated to appease Western public opinion—revoked the former Nazi's citizenship. But Stroessner, a rabid anti-Semite, saw in the affair a crypto-Jewish-Communist plot. The entire issue, he complained in a long tirade to the U.S. ambassador in Asuncion, represented "an international scandal . . . raised by [a] communist conspiracy out to blacken the reputation of Paraguay."[14]

Unknown at the time to nearly everyone except Mengele's family in Günzburg, the former "Angel of Death" had drowned in Brazil in February 1979. In the interim, in both the West German and American press, he remained a much-discussed subject. During January 1985 the U.S. government released information to the public at the request of the Simon Wiesenthal Center in Los Angeles, the foundation named for the famous Nazi pursuer.

The information revealed that the U.S. Army had arrested and detained Mengele shortly after the war's end—only to release him. The explosive news unleashed a torrent of criticism against the United States. In February the U.S. attorney general ordered a special investigations unit (established in 1979 in the Department of Justice to identify suspected former war criminals living in the United States) to investigate Mengele's postwar activities and, if possible, his present whereabouts.

But hardly had that initiative begun when, on June 6, 1985, in the Brazilian village of Embu near São Paulo, local police, with West German support, discovered Mengele's remains in a grave marked for a man named "Wolfgang Gerhard."[15] German authorities had located the grave after searching Hans Sedlmeier's home in Günzburg. Letters found there suggested that Mengele had died of a stroke six years earlier, while swimming in the ocean near São Paulo.

Amid the stunning discovery, forensic experts in West Germany, the United States, Israel, and Brazil examined not only the bones unearthed in the grave but also the letters ostensibly written by Mengele. All were his. Thanks largely to a world with little concern—or remorse—for what had happened, one of the most notorious villains of the Nazi Reich had gotten away. Unrepentant for his crimes and unpunished.

THE TIGHTENING NOOSE AROUND STANGL

When Israeli secret service agents seized Eichmann in Argentina in 1960, Stangl became rightfully nervous. He followed avidly the subsequent, highly publicized Eichmann trial. Almost daily, he sat in his favorite armchair reading everything that both the Brazilian and local German papers wrote about the proceeding. But to his wife and daughters, who noticed his conspicuous fixation, he "never commented" on the events in Jerusalem. Frau Stangl realized that, like everything else associated with his wartime activities, this also "was taboo."[16]

Doubtless because of the trial's international notoriety, during 1961 the Austrian government placed Stangl's name for the first time on its official list of "wanted criminals" under the heading of "Subject Treblinka." Apparently for thirteen years, Vienna had judged it irrelevant or unnecessary to place the former commandant on the list, even after he'd escaped in 1948 from the prison in Linz, where the authorities—presumably—were holding him for trial for his complicity in the euthanasia murders at Hartheim. Only an arrest warrant for Stangl from the Linz provincial court existed.

From October 1964 to August 1965, Stangl's name figured prominently in the first Treblinka trial in West Germany of ten *SS* men who'd served at the death camp. The Brazilian and foreign press mentioned him frequently. The trial's main defendant, Kurt Franz, was originally a cook for the *SS* and at the chancellery of the Führer, but by the time he became Stangl's deputy camp commandant at Treblinka, his reputation had grown considerably. By then, he was regarded among prisoners as the "doll" for his good looks but was equally known for his dominating presence and extreme cruelty—he beat, shot, and killed inmates at every opportunity. He and three others received sentences of life in prison for their involvement in the immense crimes at the camp, including the collective murder of at least three hundred thousand people. Five others were sentenced to prison terms of from three to twelve years, and one defendant was acquitted.

Throughout the trial in Düsseldorf and even after, however, official circles in both Austria and Germany never acted on the fact that Stangl was living openly and under his own name in Brazil. Apparently, and appallingly, the Austrian consulate in São Paulo never checked the "wanted list" in Vienna. Nor did anyone at Volkswagen, where he worked, ask any questions, though—according to Sereny—"both his co-workers and the management at least knew his name and presumably read the papers" where that name was often mentioned in connection with euthanasia and extermination.

More damning still, no one at Volkswagen ever questioned the oddness of the precise expression Stangl would use during his "wild" outbursts at incompetent co-workers, whom he described as "idiots" and "morons." Stangl "would open [his] mouth too wide and let them have it." He'd yell, "My God, euthanasia passed *you* by, didn't it."[17] But such tragic failures of action were not surprising. Numerous former Nazis—likely thousands—resided undisturbed in Brazil and other South American countries.

During the mid-1950s, Stangl had applied to Vienna to receive his pension, but apparently without success. Regarding the former death camp commandant, during over two decades following the war's end, the Austrians made no effort—except for imprisoning him briefly in 1948—to capture and place him on trial. Most Austrians, for reasons discussed near the end of the previous chapter, had little interest in revisiting the Nazi era in any fashion.

If anyone had so desired to apprehend Stangl, such a goal would have been vastly more straightforward than seeking to arrest an Eichmann or Mengele, both of whom made consistent efforts to distort their backgrounds and dissemble their identities. But Stangl was never really hiding. In his own words, expressed long after the war:

> But you know, in Brazil I never hid. I lived and worked there from the beginning under my own name. I registered at the Austrian consulate—first, because my papers read that way, as Paul Franz Stangl. Later, when I had to get a copy of my birth certificate through them, from Austria, I changed it and it was entered correctly as Franz Paul Stangl. Anybody could have found me.[18]

The question was never whether or not Stangl was a fugitive, in the sense of someone constantly on the run with justice in hot pursuit, but the sorry fact that no one (besides a couple of people) was really looking.

Still, Stangl endured a sense of fatalism about the inevitability of someone apprehending him. "You see, it's unavoidable," he said repeatedly to himself and his wife. Later, he admitted, "I had always expected it."

He realized initially in February 1964 that he was being hunted. His former son-in-law, Herbert Havel, whom his middle daughter had divorced, showed him an Austrian newspaper report that said Wiesenthal had begun searching for him. Then Havel remarked, in a less-than-veiled threat, that he "had sent his Jewish uncle to see Wiesenthal." Shortly thereafter, Havel saw a photograph in a Vienna paper that left him with little doubt—as he informed Stangl—that the latter "was the man Wiesenthal was seeking." Allegedly, Havel threatened—in Stangl's words—to "destroy us all" unless the daughter returned to him.[19]

Wiesenthal recalled in his memoirs that he had been gathering information on Stangl's Nazi career since 1950, when by a few months he missed finding Theresa in Altaussee. Years later at a press conference in Vienna, he mentioned Stangl to journalists as an example of the link in Nazi Germany between the euthanasia institutions and the mass extermination in the death camps. The euthanasia staff, he explained, "who had learned to live with the stench of cremated corpses at those institutions were, almost without exception, promoted to leading posts in the extermination camps."[20]

For many years, the Nazi hunter knew only that Stangl had left Damascus for an "unknown destination." Finally, on February 21, 1964, he had a major breakthrough in the case. By then, Stangl's name had been appearing increasingly in the European press, in part as a result of the decision of a West German court in Düsseldorf to open in a few months the Treblinka trial of ten of Stangl's former *SS* men at the camp, including Kurt Franz. Wiesenthal provided the press with information about Stangl's criminality.

That day Wiesenthal received a visit at his office from a woman who identified herself as Frau Stangl's cousin. Speaking about Stangl, the woman claimed tearfully, "I had no idea my cousin Theresa was married to such a terrible man." Wiesenthal, not wishing to show too much excitement, asked her, "And where is Theresa now?"

"Why, in Brazil, of course," the woman replied.[21] Then, suddenly realizing that she'd said too much, she hardly spoke again and left hurriedly. She remained anonymous. Wiesenthal had a rule never to ask or demand the name or address of anyone who volunteered information to him.

Only a few days later, another fortuitous opportunity befell Wiesenthal. What he termed "an evil-looking, unkempt type" called at his office. Whether or not Havel had sent the man is unclear; later Wiesenthal both claimed and denied such a connection with Havel. The man identified himself as a former member of the *Gestapo*, but someone, he assured his host, who hadn't done "anything bad."

Never once looking Wiesenthal in the eye, he continued, "Anyway, what could I have done? I'm one of the little ones who get the stick for everything." He'd come to talk about Franz Stangl, he said.

"The fat cats, the Stangls and Eichmanns, they got all the backing they needed. They were smuggled out, they got money and papers. But who'll help me? Look at my shirt, my suit. No work, no money. Can't even afford a drop of wine."

Wiesenthal, as he listened to the vile visitor's stream of complaints, had to restrain himself. He had no sympathy for the man. Instead, he thought to himself, the Nazis had made him, Wiesenthal, a Jew, "one of the little ones who'd got the stick." And the man couldn't "even afford a drop of wine"? His breath reeked with the smell of schnapps.

Finally, the man got to the point. "Look here," he said. "I know where Stangl is. I could help you find him. Stangl never helped me." But, he added, "it will cost you something."

First, he asked for "twenty-five thousand dollars" for information on Stangl's whereabouts. Wiesenthal, by this time, was outraged by the former *Gestapo* man's presence and by his heavy-handed attempt at bribery, but he still sought to pry the information from the man, though he refused the offer.

The man tried to bargain. "All right, I'll make you a special price. How many Jews did Stangl do in?"

"We'll never know exactly how many people lost their lives during the time that he was commandant of Treblinka. It could have been 700,000."

The man thought for a moment, then replied, "I want one cent for every dead person. Seven hundred thousand cents . . . that's seven thousand dollars . . . a steal of a price."

Wiesenthal boiled with anger. He clutched his desk firmly with both hands, knuckles whitening, so as not to hit the man. Only slowly did he regain control of himself: "The commandant of Treblinka, the murderer of 700,000 Jews, was more important than this filthy man, who was now standing before me expectantly, no doubt considering whom to turn to if I declined his offer."

He told the man, "You don't get a penny from me today, but if Stangl is arrested on the strength of your information, you shall have the money." Would the Nazi pursuer, the man asked, "not try to find out who he [the visitor] was"? For Wiesenthal, "Franz Stangl was worth such a promise." Finally, after a few more minutes of negotiating, the visitor produced his information: "Stangl is working as a mechanic at the Volkswagen plant in São Paulo in Brazil."[22] Within a few weeks a Brazilian contact of Wiesenthal ran a "credit check" on Stangl. It provided the wanted Nazi's address and lifestyle but did so without alerting anyone.

KLAUS BARBIE: A U.S. COLD WAR SPY

The U.S. Army employed him after the war and even assisted his escape from Europe. Thanks to a serious failure in judgment of U.S. military intelligence, the need for an alleged Cold War espionage agent took precedence over the obligation of punishing a former leading Nazi official for war crimes.

Klaus Barbie's wartime victims in France—whether dead by the war's end or still alive—had known him in the Vichy city of Lyon as the *Gestapo*'s "butcher" of French Jews and other "unwanted" persons. A native of Bad Godesberg in western Germany and member of the Hitler Youth from 1933 to 1935, Barbie had joined the *SS* and *SD* in 1935; by 1940, he'd reached the *SS* rank of first lieutenant.

From 1942 to 1944, Barbie served in Lyon as *Gestapo* chief. Until his final days there in 1944, he continued to deport French and refugee Jews to their death and repress the French resistance, including the betrayal, capture, torture, and murder of Jean Moulin, a key figure in the Resistance. By the spring of 1944, with German setbacks blatantly noticeable on nearly every military front, French authorities showed increasing reluctance to cooperate in German arrests, seizures, and deportations of French Jews. This position forced the Nazi police in France, including the *Gestapo*, to rely on their own resources. To hunt down Jews, the police staged raids on arbitrary targets without much regard for the actual identities or nationalities of the victims.

Barbie carried out the policy to the letter. Under his direction, in the early morning hours of April 6, 1944, Security Police in the Lyon district had forced their way into a children's home in Izieu-Ain, a village forty miles east of Lyon, and seized fifty-one persons, including five women and over forty children, some as young as three or four years old. All the children perished, and only one adult survived. In this instance, the police were unable to engage in their customary plundering of victims. Barbie's men had failed—according to his report on the raid filed with *Gestapo* superiors in Paris—to secure cash or other valuables.

Barely a week later, and only four months before the Germans would lose France to the Western Allies' D-day invasion, a German police directive—likely from or through Alois Brunner, head of Eichmann's "resettlement" commando in Paris—ordered the seizure of all remaining Jews of French nationality except for those in mixed marriages. The resulting final phase of deportations of French Jews—including a number in Lyon under Barbie's supervision—netted six thousand victims. Three deportation transports left for Auschwitz—even after the Allied invasion of France had started.

Postwar, Barbie fell into the U.S. Army's custody. But in the spring of 1947, the army's Counterintelligence Corps (CIC) hired him as a spy. By the late 1940s, the initial stages of the Cold War had produced among the Western Allies a growing mistrust and uncertainty regarding Soviet intentions in Europe. The Russians had overrun and seized control of most of Eastern Europe, and during 1948–1949 they established a blockade around West Berlin, divided among the British, Americans, and French. Barbie assisted the CIC in operating an extensive network of informants reporting on Soviet activities in the U.S. and Soviet zones of Germany, as well as on former *SS* officers, French intelligence, and the French occupation zone.

Not only did the CIC protect Barbie from arrest by the French for his war crimes, but it also shielded him from the French government's first call in June 1949 for his extradition from Germany. In fact, Barbie remained a CIC employee throughout 1950 and lived in a Bavarian safe house. There, the army concealed him deliberately from the Office of the High Commissioner in the U.S. zone, as well as from the U.S. Department of State. Finally, at the end of 1950, the CIC arranged to have Barbie removed from Europe. He traveled under false papers and the alias "Klaus Altmann" and, a year later, arrived in Bolivia.[23]

Thereafter, the U.S. government had to deal with the embarrassing legacy of the U.S. Army's employment of Barbie and its assistance in helping him escape Europe. Already in June 1950, the State Department's top officials had urged handing Barbie over to France regardless of his ties to the U.S. Army. "Franco-American relations," Secretary of State Dean Acheson warned, "[would] be affected more adversely by refusal to extradite than [would] be [the] case if he is extradited."[24]

Unwilling still to experience public humiliation on the matter and to press for the arrest of Barbie, Washington did nothing until 1972. What little it did do, it didn't do voluntarily. In January, Nazi hunter Beate Klarsfeld made public the U.S. connection to Barbie. Arriving in Bolivia, she claimed that Klaus Altmann was, in fact, Barbie and that the United States had refused in 1950 to hand over Barbie to France.

Within weeks both France and the United States requested that the Bolivian government allow Barbie to be extradited to France. But the appeal failed. The nationalist dictatorship in La Paz defined the issue as a "Bolivian matter" and argued as well that no legal proof existed that Altmann was Barbie. Only its court system, the Bolivians claimed, could decide Altmann's identity and, if necessary, extradite him.

France twice tried him *in absentia*, in 1952 and 1954. When, believing that earlier the United States had furnished Barbie a new identity as Altmann, France asked Washington for documentary support, the Pentagon refused to provide the necessary records. According to a State Department official exasperated with the military, the latter "refused to disclose the material available or to offer any justification for withholding it." For the next eleven years Barbie remained free, even though, as a Bolivian official observed, "everyone knew that Altmann was Barbie."[25]

The situation changed suddenly in 1983. A new democratic government in La Paz arrested Barbie for failing to pay a tax debt. Immediately, Bolivian officials transferred him into French custody, bypassing the right-wing Bolivian courts that for the past decade had protected him. On February 8, Barbie arrived in Paris, an object of intense interest in the French press and public. The French government had encouraged the Bolivians to extradite him by providing Bolivia with economic incentives. The United States placed heavy diplomatic pressure on the new La Paz government not to allow Barbie to escape justice again.

Another interested observer, the West German government, nearly botched the chance to remove Barbie from Bolivia. With Barbie under arrest, and before Bolivia handed him over to France, Bonn refused a Bolivian offer to extradite him to Germany for prosecution. The Germans claimed—speciously—that there existed no aircraft that could move Barbie nonstop from La Paz to German soil. Landing in a third country to refuel, said Bonn, would trigger legal problems. The Americans, with their own scandalous record in the Barbie affair, remained unconvinced and visibly fearful that the German attitude would result in Barbie's ultimate release and subsequent disappearance.

Most likely, Germany's national election, scheduled for March 1983, influenced the West German response. The forthcoming election left Helmut Kohl's conservative government, which had gained power in Bonn only a few months earlier, with little enthusiasm to deal with a notorious former Nazi war criminal. The early 1980s in the Federal Republic had witnessed an upsurge of nationalist and neo-Nazi revivalism.

When Western journalists speculated on Barbie's connections with U.S. intelligence, Washington had to determine how honestly it would respond. The issue provided the Soviet Union with choice propaganda material. During the Cold War, Moscow had argued that the West, especially NATO (the Western military alliance), had employed former German war criminals. Soviet newspapers now charged that the United States had raised the concealment of such criminals to a "matter of state policy."[26]

In August 1983 the U.S. Department of Justice published a report of its investigation of the Barbie affair. The 240-page document found that between 1945 and 1950, U.S. Army CIC officers had employed Barbie, protected him from extradition to France, where he was wanted for war crimes, and organized his escape to South America. The report emphasized that often there is a need for information that necessitates dealing with criminals, former enemies, and other undesirable persons. U.S. intelligence units, lacking a network of agents targeted against its former ally, the Soviet Union, turned to European anti-Communist resources to fill information gaps. These included former German and East European intelligence operatives and East European émigré political groups. Among them were Nazis (including *Gestapo* and *SS* members) and members of East European fascist organizations, whom the CIC considered valuable informants. The State Department sent copies of the report to numerous governments along with an apology to Paris—one much too long in the making to the French and to many Jews, French or otherwise, whose families and friends had numbered among Barbie's victims.

In 1987 the "Butcher of Lyon" was indicted for raiding in February 1943 the headquarters of the *Union Générale des Israélites de France*, arresting eighty-five Jews there and sending them to Auschwitz; for deporting the more than forty children and their adult companions from the orphanage in Izieu; and for ordering on August 11, 1944, the last transport from Lyon to Auschwitz.

During the trial, Barbie's grandstanding legal team, conducted by Jacques Verges, prepared a grotesque postmodernist defense. It equated Barbie's Nazi crimes with France's behavior toward the native peoples in its former colonies in Vietnam and Algeria and with Western imperialism and racism in general. Discussing the comparison, Lipstadt called it later "[s]hades of Holocaust denial" in "attempting to diminish the significance of the Holocaust." Using such "slight-of-hand attempts at moral equivalence constitute[d] a basic tactic of those who hover on the periphery of Holocaust denial."[27]

But such efforts to indict and try "the West," rather than Barbie, failed utterly. The court sentenced Klaus Barbie to life in prison. The long-delayed justice, however, produced a trial much less sensitive to the crimes of the "Butcher of Lyon" than if it had been conducted in the late 1940s or 1950s. None of Barbie's surviving victims had the opportunity to confront him directly; in addition, French prosecutors mentioned little or nothing of Barbie's relationship with French collaborators. Barbie died in September 1991, with slight notice in France or elsewhere. His capture and trial had done almost nothing to assist the French in dealing with their relationship to Nazism. Yet for much of this, a highly insensitive and opportunistic postwar U.S. government remained largely responsible.

STANGL'S ARREST

The Nazi hunter, whose role in Eichmann's capture had made him a celebrity to many in the world, strove for nearly three years to make certain his next move would succeed in catching, in his words, another "of the worst murderers of Jews." Having just learned Stangl's address in São Paulo, Wiesenthal had to plan carefully the former killer's arrest and extradition to Austria—both with the Austrian and Brazilian governments.

By early 1964, Austria wanted Stangl not merely as a result of the Hartheim trials and for escaping from custody in 1948, but also for his command of Sobibor and Treblinka. Wiesenthal faced a dilemma:

> If I'd gone to the Austrian Ministry of Justice, a dozen people there and in the Ministry of Foreign Affairs would have known about it. And then in Brazil, at least double that number in the Austrian Embassy, the Brazilian ministries, and the Brazilian police would have had advance notice of Stangl's arrest. Now you don't have to believe in ODESSA to be absolutely certain that Stangl would have been warned and even people who didn't know him personally would have helped him to disappear. And then there would be—and, as I told you, there were!—others who wanted to make him disappear for me and just bring me his ears. But I wanted him alive![28]

First, Wiesenthal had to lay the groundwork in Brazil. He alerted several friends in Rio de Janeiro that he sought the help of someone in their country both influential and sympathetic "to our cause," though he didn't mention Stangl. Working through his Rio friends, in December 1966 he met in Zurich an important Brazilian politician then traveling in Europe. The acquaintance gave Wiesenthal "assurance that he would be of assistance in this case" and that he'd help "find a way to shorten the procedure of the extradition request coming from Austria to Brazil." About the plans Wiesenthal recalled later: "We agreed that a success would only be possible if one could cut down the number of the people let into the secret. So we reduced with the help of that politician the number of those persons down to six."[29]

After a month had passed, Wiesenthal visited the Austrian minister of justice, a trustworthy Tyrolean. Working with a handful of the minister's loyal aides, they gathered a mass of evidence on Stangl: a thousand-page dossier and the warrants for his arrest. Wiesenthal was waiting for further documentation from Düsseldorf, where earlier a court had tried ten of Stangl's Treblinka subordinates, including Kurt Franz. In the meantime, he sent a personal courier and assistant to Rio de Janeiro with his documentation center's own file on Stangl.

The courier, a young Brazilian woman, met Wiesenthal's high-level Brazilian connection and handed him the file personally. Before the courier left Brazil in mid-February 1967 to return to Vienna, the political contact had a police friend shadow Stangl unofficially. But the contact sent, through the courier, a word of warning to Wiesenthal that Stangl's arrest had to occur by March 1 or "anything could happen."[30]

Wiesenthal moved fast. He arranged with the Austrian minister of justice the preparation for Brazil of the documentary case against Stangl, including the arrest warrant and extradition request, and its translation into Portuguese. On February 23, 1967, the Ministry of Justice delivered the file to the Austrian foreign ministry, which had a trusted official of the Brazilian embassy verify and notarize the translation. To keep the dossier as secret as possible, Wiesenthal and the few Austrian officials involved with it agreed to send it to the Austrian embassy in Rio de Janeiro, via express airmail in a special envelope. The outside of the packet alerted embassy officials that only the ambassador should open it.

On February 27, the embassy delivered the parcel to the Brazilian foreign ministry. The Brazilian government and police, as well as the governor of São Paulo, acted quickly. The next night, police in São Paulo surrounded Stangl's house in one of the city's upper-class areas and waited. Stangl, on his way home from work, had stopped at a bar with youngest daughter Isolde for a beer.

Meanwhile, at the house, from the front window Frau Stangl saw "a lot of cars around. Our street was full of them." Only later did she remember that she'd noticed the activity but had "thought nothing of it" at the time. When she heard "a commotion outside," she rushed again to the window:

> Police cars were drawn across the street, blocking it off on each side; our car was surrounded by crowds of police. Paul was pulled out of the car—handcuffed—Isi fell to the ground shouting for us; that's what I had heard, and rushed to the window; but the police car with Paul in it, followed by a string of others, was off before I could even get out of the door. Isi was almost incoherent with shock. She said Paul's face went yellow when it happened.[31]

On the night of March 1, the governor of São Paulo announced officially Stangl's arrest. Finally—nearly a quarter of a century after his multitude of crimes—one of Nazi Germany's worst mass murderers in the Holocaust had been captured. However, for his apprehension the world could hardly thank the governments of Austria or West Germany.

Stangl blamed his arrest on Havel, his former son-in-law, even though the evidence did not support that suspicion. When Stangl's wife and daughters sought unsuccessfully to visit him in a local prison, police told Frau Stangl that she "should be glad they had taken him—if they hadn't, the Israelis would have picked him up."[32]

Stangl, too, appeared terrified when taken into custody. He believed that Jewish commandos, acting as Brazilian police, had kidnapped him. He felt visibly relieved when the police placed him in a jail cell. A source told Wiesenthal that Stangl "remembered what had happened to Eichmann and considered himself lucky."[33]

Immediately, West Germany and Poland, in addition to Austria, asked for Stangl's extradition. But Brazil had never before extradited a Nazi criminal, despite the fact that a number of them had fled there after the war. The greatest pressure on the Rio government to surrender Stangl came from the United States. Robert F. Kennedy, the senator from New York and former U.S. attorney general, while visited by Wiesenthal and at the latter's urging, telephoned the Brazilian ambassador to the United States. Kennedy made clear that he'd view any refusal of extradition with disfavor. "What's at stake," he told the ambassador, "is justice for enormous crimes. Brazil now has an opportunity to gain millions of friends."[34]

Meanwhile, Theresa and her daughters visited Stangl, whom police had transferred to a military prison in Brasilia for maximum security against the possibility of a rescue or escape attempt. The prisoner, who had once overseen the killing of nearly one million Jews, complained to his wife about his "dreadful" fate. He even cried.

She asked him about Treblinka because, as she noted later, "by this time, you know, we had read so much" that he hadn't told her. He denied everything: "I don't know what pictures you saw, perhaps you saw pictures of other camps." Theresa did nothing to press him about what she'd read. Nor about telling her—finally—the truth. Instead, she made his denial her own.

She felt victimized by Stangl's arrest, thinking only of the "traumatic experience" for her daughters seeing him behind bars and of how "he was so wonderful with them."[35] She grieved that the girls had lost their father. But no one in Stangl's family thought even remotely of the roughly one million persons (including hundreds of thousands of children) who'd lost their lives during the former commandant's tenure at Treblinka.

16

Four Faces Long after the War

What Didn't Happen

Since the 1960s and 1970s, the Holocaust has become easily the best documented of all genocides. Still, despite the plethora of publications on the subject and the establishment of so many Jewish and Holocaust-focused museums, despite the film documentaries and scholarly research, despite the Holocaust's continuing legacy of controversy, denial, and remembrance, thousands of victims have slipped through the cracks of history, forgotten except for a name, if that, while thousands of perpetrators have likewise slipped through those cracks into the oblivion of ordinary lives.

This chapter is about what did not happen to four of the principal Nazi perpetrators, discussed initially in chapter 1. Each, in one way or another, escaped the punishment he deserved for his criminality, continuing to the end to insist on his innocence in what is one of the single worst mass crimes in human history.

STANGL: FINALLY THE ACCUSED

During the trial that began on May 13, 1970, for his crimes at Treblinka, Stangl's behavior and attitude at Sobibor also became part of the official record. Each of the few Sobibor survivors, appearing as prosecution witnesses before the court, commented on how he had often attended the unloading of transports of Jews "dressed in white riding clothes."

What was his excuse for preferring riding clothes to his uniform? His skin was sensitive to the sand flies that plagued Sobibor in the summer. He placated himself later by asserting, "Not everyone [i.e., the Jewish prisoners] was as sensitive to them as I." And why did he parade in this jaunty outfit on the platform as Jews were herded to their death? "It was hot."[1]

As the trial unfolded, the issue so tiresomely familiar in so many other cases involving German prosecution of Nazi criminals arose—that of whether to rule the defendant a perpetrator or an accomplice. Of all the survivors of Treblinka and Sobibor who testified during the proceeding, "very nearly the only one that linked the defendant directly to a personal act of violence" and "weighed heavily at Stangl's trial," was Stanislaw Szmajzner, a young Polish Jew who had escaped from Sobibor in October 1943 and who lived after the war in Brazil. He described to the court what he'd seen in May 1942 on his arrival at the camp by train:

> When the door of our car was pushed open, all we could think of was to get out into the air. . . . We looked around desperately, but the hurry, the noise, the fear and confusion were indescribable; it was impossible to find anyone. About twenty metres away, across the "square," I saw a line of SS officers and they were shooting. I especially noticed Stangl, because he wore a white jacket—it stuck out. He was shooting too. I can't say whether he killed anyone, or in fact whether anyone was killed by these shots or not, but they were certainly shooting.[2]

Unknown to the newly arrived teenager, Szmajzner, the *SS* sent his parents—along with most others on the transport—directly from the train to the gas chamber. His family was murdered and their corpses plundered in under an hour. The youth survived Sobibor by working as a goldsmith, a valuable trade in a hell where gold was so prevalent, even if some were wedding rings from dead couples and some were crowns or fillings from the teeth of the murdered.

Stangl himself had brought him "small quantities of gold to melt down" and to fashion into jewelry. Szmajzner recalled:

> All of them [*SS* officers] brought gold—later it was gold fillings with the flesh and blood still on them, the way they had been torn out of people's mouths. . . . Stangl was always cheerful and treated me with kindness. . . . I certainly thought that the gold he brought was for his personal use. He had not needed to send other people or to hide. . . . I never saw Stangl hurt anyone. What was special about him was his arrogance. And his obvious pleasure in his work and his situation.[3]

When Szmajzner had asked Stangl repeatedly about his father, the commandant always replied, "He is fine; don't worry about him: just do your work."

On the stand the former commandant denied—lied about—nearly everything that Szmajzner and other prosecution witnesses testified about him.

Above all, in the words of Gitta Sereny, who attended the trial and later wrote about it and the mass murderer:

> Stangl, insisting that he had never shot into a crowd of people, appeared to be more indignant about this accusation than about anything else, and to find irrelevant the fact that, whether he shot into the group or not, these very same people died anyway, less than two hours later, through actions ultimately under his control. . . . It is, I think, because of this universal acceptance of a false concept of responsibility that Stangl himself (until just before he died), his family and—in a wider but equally, if not even more, important sense—countless other people in Germany and outside it, have felt for years that what is decisive in law, and therefore in the whole conduct of human affairs, is what a man *does* rather than what he *is*.[4]

On December 22 the court sentenced Stangl to life imprisonment for his co-responsibility in murdering some nine hundred thousand people at Treblinka. The evidence failed to show that Stangl himself had committed specific acts of murder, but it did prove that by virtue of his attitude, presence, the orders he gave, and his role as camp commandant, he had enforced, approved, and/or participated actively in murdering prisoners.

Simon Wiesenthal, who'd played a part in Stangl's capture, viewed the latter's conviction by the Germans at least as important as Eichmann's by the Israelis: "The Stangl case provided West Germany with their most significant criminal case of the century. If I had done nothing else in my life but get this evil man, I would not have lived in vain." The German prosecutor in the case made clear: "Stangl is the highest ranking official of a death camp we have been able to try."[5]

Following the trial, Sereny visited Theresa Stangl in her home in Brazil. The wife of the mass killer defended both him and herself as innocent of any wrongdoing. Her husband, she claimed, "never gave the impression of being a Nazi, never even showed the slightest sympathy for them. . . . And he never said anything against Jews. I never heard him say a word like that."

Above all, she continued feeling victimized by Stangl's arrest and imprisonment: "I didn't see Paul for three years. He wrote me once a week. All we did—all we could do—was hope. I still didn't believe he had been Kommandant; he denied it to me to the end."

But her husband wasn't the only one in denial. When asked whether she might've influenced her husband to leave his odious deadly job by insisting that she'd leave him if he did not, Frau Stangl at first admitted that she could have done so, most likely successfully. But her acknowledgment of her own culpability so upset her that, after a sleepless night, she wrote Sereny a letter—in which she "beg[ged] to correct" her earlier answer and refused to accept that she could've exerted any influence over Stangl and his career choices—and rushed her revisionist reply to the historian's hotel. As Sereny realized with her usual astute insight, "[T]he truth can be a terrible thing, sometimes too terrible to live with."[6]

But Frau Stangl's sister, who lived in Vienna, when asked about the Stangls, responded, "Do I think she could have stopped him? I think she was ambitious too. . . . Resi always wanted to get to the top. Well, I suppose in a way she did get there."[7]

Frau Stangl also recalled how, since her husband's arrest, his former deputy commandant at Sobibor, the coarse Gustav Wagner, Stangl's close friend and longtime sidekick who had also escaped to Brazil, had pressed her to marry him. Wagner was not easily forgotten by the survivors of Sobibor.

Stanislaw Szmajzner viewed with terror the huge, powerfully built man with a severely deformed shoulder. When he learned that Wagner lived in Brazil, he cried:

> It is the worst, the most terrible shock you could have given me. That man. Here in Brazil. To think that I am now breathing the same air as he—it makes me feel terribly, terribly ill. . . . I would not know how to find words to describe to you what a terrible—a truly terrible man that is. Stangl—he is good by comparison, very good. But Wagner—he should be dead.[8]

It was little wonder that Frau Stangl rejected his advances. She viewed him as "vulgar." Certainly, she didn't refuse his hand because of his criminal career at Sobibor, where, as chief of the selections, he ordered the deaths of hundreds of thousands of Jews as well as supervised the death camp's routines and daily life. No less a person than Himmler decorated and promoted him in September 1943 for his efficient slaughter of Jews.

He had wholly enjoyed killing. A Sobibor survivor, Moshe Bahir, testified at a postwar trial that Wagner's "lust to kill knew no bounds. . . . He would snatch babies from their mothers' arms and tear them to pieces in his hands. I saw him beat two men to death with a rifle, because they did not carry out his instructions properly, since they did not understand German." On another occasion, Bahir had witnessed Wagner beating a youth "all over his body"; when Wagner "grew weary of the blows," he "took out his revolver and killed [the boy] on the spot." For Bahir, such "terrible scenes" gave him "nightmares to this day."[9]

But even though the Nuremberg trials had condemned Wagner to death *in absentia*, he and Stangl, with the help of the Catholic Church, escaped via Rome and Syria to Brazil, which granted Wagner permanent residency on April 12, 1950. From September 6, 1965 to December 20, 1966 the West German court tried eleven of the *SS* men who'd served at Sobibor for crimes against humanity. One committed suicide, one received a life sentence, five were given prison terms of between three and eight years, and four were acquitted.

Yet Wagner escaped even this paltry show of supposed justice. Using the alias Günther Mendel, Wagner lived happily and freely in a Bavarian-style house outside São Paulo. His situation remained unaffected for three decades until April 20, 1978, when newspaper reporters from Rio de Janeiro recognized him among guests at a party of former Nazis to celebrate what would've been Hitler's eighty-ninth birthday. Wagner was arrested on May 30, 1978, but the Brazilian government rejected requests from Israel, Austria (where he held citizenship), Poland, and West Germany that he be extradited.

Still a dedicated Nazi, he showed no regret for his crimes. In a secretly taped conversation for a BBC documentary, aired on June 18, 1979, about the exterminations at Sobibor, Wagner commented: "I had no feelings. . . . It just became another job. In the evening we never discussed our work, but just drank and played cards."[10]

In October 1980, Wagner's lawyer announced that his client had committed suicide. But did he follow the sterling examples of former superiors like Hitler, Goebbels, Göring, and other vanquished Nazi leaders? Even this seeming closure is uncertain. Reportedly Wagner was discovered with a knife sticking out of his chest—not the most common or efficient method of killing oneself. But perhaps his was not the hand that held the knife.

After Stangl's trial, Sereny interviewed at length the mass murderer himself, then sixty-three years old, in a Düsseldorf prison. He awaited the result of his appeal against the life sentence. During their final meeting on June 27, 1971, in response to questions about his culpability in the extermination of the Jews, he uttered four sentences, each spaced by long moments of silence, and the whole statement an apparent deconstruction of his defenses of denial and equivocation. "My conscience is clear about what I did, myself. . . . I have never intentionally hurt anyone myself. . . . But I was there. So yes, in reality I share the guilt."

Then, looking dejectedly around the little prison room, the tall, graying figure added, "I have no more hope." Then again, neither did his dead victims. He died the next day. After barely four years spent behind bars.

Sereny believed that she'd extracted from Stangl a genuine admission: "I think he died, because he had finally, however briefly, faced himself and told the truth."[11]

But had he really? As pioneering and valuable as her conversations with Stangl had been, his "deathbed confession" mentioned only the word "guilt." He expressed no regret for his horrible crimes or remorse over his victims. And certainly no sense of feeling for what they had suffered. In the end, the cold-blooded murderer of nearly one million people had pity solely for himself.

BEST ELUDES PUNISHMENT

He wanted others to forget. And since the war's end, he'd done his utmost to make it happen—in part, he hoped, to help pave the way for his own political and professional rehabilitation. No longer involved in amnesty politics in a former fellow Nazi's West German law office, Werner Best turned for work to the business world. In early 1954 German industrialist Hugo Stinnes Jr. hired Best as a legal adviser and member of his company's board of directors. Deeply involved in the Free Democratic Party's (FDP) rightist and pro-Nazi faction in the Rhineland, Stinnes had known Best since the Nazi years. During 1956 Best moved to the Ruhr city of Mülheim, the company's headquarters.

Despite his new job and apparent security from possible future legal problems connected to his Nazi past, Best had failed to achieve something he coveted desperately—to rehabilitate himself with and win acceptance from the political elite of the new West German state. Consequently, like many other former Nazis, he spent substantial time seeking to justify his past and even to exonerate himself of it.

Primarily for that purpose, he wrote several lengthy manuscripts that he planned eventually to publish. In 1953 he completed an essay on the *Gestapo*. He intended it for use in helping reintegrate into public service former Nazi functionaries, including himself, particularly those who had served in the *Gestapo* and other police organizations. Numerous such persons, many his onetime Nazi subordinates, had bombarded him with requests for his assistance.

In May 1951, regarding the issue and responding to widespread pressure from the German public, the Bonn government had implemented a new law. Article 131 stipulated that some 150,000 persons who'd belonged to the civil service and armed forces at the end of World War II and who'd lost their positions as a result, primarily through denazification proceedings, were entitled to pensions and possible reemployment in their former posts.

The law had thrown open the door to a mass influx of onetime Nazis whom denazification boards hadn't incriminated into both the West German federal and state bureaucracies. But Article 131, lenient and forgiving as it was, excluded—permanently—from such reemployment all former *Gestapo* and *Waffen-SS* members, as well as persons classified by denazification trials as "major offenders" (categories I and II).

Best, in his writings on the *Gestapo*, sought to revise the IMT's classification of Hitler's political police as a "criminal organization." He did so by both denying and lying about its enormous police and judicial powers as well as its role in the Holocaust. His writings, he believed, would provide a rationale for amending Article 131 to make former *Gestapo* officials (such as Werner) eligible for reappointment to public service.

The *Gestapo*, he insisted, had differed little from agencies such as the U.S. Federal Bureau of Investigation or the French *Sureté*. The Nazi political police, he alleged, had functioned as a "normal technical authority" that aimed at securing the Nazi state against its enemies, who operated "consciously or unconsciously" as "instruments" of Soviet Communism and the Western powers.

He described the *Gestapo*'s collaboration in deporting Jews as a "task alien to the police." Mentioning nothing of Eichmann's *Gestapo* Department IVB4, he maintained that the political police hadn't initiated the deportations, but instead, during such operations, only received orders from and cooperated with other Reich authorities. The police, he argued, had as little involvement in administrating concentration camps as in murdering Jews in death camps.

Nor, he claimed, did the *Gestapo* associate much with the *Einsatzgruppen*. Judiciously silent about his role in organizing *Einsatzgruppen* in Poland, he justified the activity of such units there and in Russia "as defensive measures against the illegal attacks by civilian terrorists and provocateurs on the [German] occupation." The units, he argued, had engaged in the mass shootings of Jews, both in retaliation for similar "illegal actions" and in "the necessity to obey orders."[12] Incredulously, he compared the units to the American pilots who had dropped atomic bombs on the Japanese cities of Hiroshima and Nagasaki.

Most of Best's lies and omissions, which he never published but nevertheless shared with former Nazi cohorts and others, went unchallenged. At the time few *Gestapo* records—beyond those used at the Nuremberg trials—had been uncovered to help cement the Allies' classification of the agency as a "criminal organization." But with memory of the Nuremberg trials fading almost completely from the consciousness of the West German public, and with few survivors residing in Germany capable of reminding the more forgetful Germans, numerous local police and other political pressure groups adopted many of Best's claims. During the summer of 1953, the groups forced an amendment to Article 131. It permitted appointment and reappointment of most former *Gestapo* and *Waffen-SS* officials to public, and especially police, service.

Not surprising, during the mid- and late 1950s a flood of such persons moved into well-paid and secure positions. About this highly questionable development, a German scholar comments:

> In 1945 there had been individuals in Germany who looked forward to the permanent dissolution of the corrupted elite structures and a basic democratization of state and society. To many—particularly those who had been persecuted by the Nazis—it must have been very depressing a few years later to observe the return en masse of the civil servants. For hardly ten years after it was all over, the same people who, as it were, made Hitler's state were back at work, if not tidily pensioned.[13]

Things were looking up for Best, too. He hoped to use the newly revised law to benefit himself, for he was nothing if not ignoble. He applied to receive state financial benefits for the period of his Danish imprisonment as well as an appointment to the West German foreign ministry. But the ministry—already the subject of a parliamentary investigation into its reemployment of numerous former Nazi diplomats and fearing a storm of opposition from Denmark if it hired Best—searched for an incontrovertible reason to reject his application. Eventually, it refused the request because Best hadn't undergone denazification proceedings.

Immediately, he initiated a lawsuit against the government. No longer steeped in self-pity and depression, his resurgent arrogance got the better of him. Believing himself safe from prosecution, he pursued the lawsuit. Apparently in response, a denazification board in Berlin opened proceedings against him, an action that not only surprised Best and stopped his lawsuit from going forward, but that also threatened—significantly—his financial well-being. The Berlin board's judge had a reputation for levying extremely heavy fines on defendants who didn't live in Berlin; Best owned only a tiny parcel of land in the city.

In September 1958 the board classified Best as a "major offender" and directed him to pay a fine of seventy thousand marks (roughly sixteen thousand dollars).[14] But Best would not admit defeat. He used his influence with the powerful FDP in his home state of North Rhine-Westphalia to prevent its finance ministry from providing information to the Berlin board regarding Best's actual assets. Once again, what had seemed to be his certain undoing (not residing in Berlin) turned out to be his salvation. The board saw itself forced to refigure the fine downward to almost nothing, based on the small property Best owned in Berlin.

Best was one lucky former Nazi. But his good fortune was all too common among perpetrators. In February 1962, the board closed the proceeding and collected 104 marks (twenty-five dollars) from him.

By this time, however, one of West Germany's first major trials of Nazi war criminals had received widespread German and Western media attention. In 1958 a court in Ulm convicted several former *Einsatzgruppen* members of the mass murder of Lithuanian Jews.

The press reports must have stunned an "insider" like Best. The same West German society that only a few years earlier had responded with a tidal wave of indignation at the execution of several *Einsatzgruppen* commanders convicted by the Americans at Nuremberg now expressed astonishment at and disapproval of the mass murders by officials of the *Einsatzgruppen*.

Several more events helped scandalize the Nazi past in West German public opinion. These included: the painting of swastikas on the Cologne synagogue in December 1959; the East German Communist regime's publication of the so-called *Brown Books*, which, though denounced in Bonn as anti-West German propaganda, identified thousands of former Nazis holding political, economic, and military positions in the Federal Republic; and the fact that the Ludwigsburg "central office" (*ZS*), established in 1958 to investigate Nazi crimes, initiated during its first year four hundred inquiries involving further murderous actions of the *Einsatzgruppen* and the mass killing at death camps in German-occupied Poland.

In September 1964, the so-called Treblinka trial ended with one acquittal and convictions for nine of ten defendants charged with participating in the murder of more than three hundred thousand people. The sentences, including life imprisonment for Kurt Franz (Stangl's deputy commander at the camp) and three other former camp officials, remained unchanged.

A year later, the lengthy Auschwitz trial resulted in convictions for seventeen former *SS* officials at the camp, in acquittals for three others, and in the dropping of charges against two others. Simultaneously, investigations began of former *RSHA*, *Gestapo*, and other police and *SS* officials suspected of involvement in deporting Jews and murdering foreign workers. During the inquiries, numerous defendants called on Best to testify or to provide affidavits on their behalf, witnessing to their supposed innocence.

But something else appeared that worried Best and his former police colleagues equally as much as the growing number of investigations: during the mid-1960s the United States began returning to West Germany masses of captured Nazi records taken initially to Washington after the war for identification, cataloging, and microfilming. The unexpected return and sudden availability of such materials threatened to expand the information of West German prosecutors and courts and to strengthen the cases against former Nazis and collaborators.

Best acted quickly. To research and report to him on the contents of Nazi records at the U.S. National Archives in Washington, D.C., he hired a young American historian. During 1968 she provided him with a document that, as arrogant and grandiose as ever, he hoped would discredit and bring about the fall from power of West Germany's new Christian Democratic Union (CDU) chancellor, Kurt Kiesinger, a former official in the Nazi foreign ministry but, unlike Werner, wasn't banned from government. Best—whose numerous efforts to minimize and to exonerate himself fully of his Nazi past had failed—resented Kiesinger's rise in the CDU and Bonn government. If Best couldn't work in the foreign ministry, then Kiesinger wouldn't be permitted his plum position.

But the document that Best, so eager to wreak havoc for the sake of his "aggrieved" ego, procured didn't undermine the chancellor. Instead, it achieved the opposite of Best's desired outcome. It was a November 1944 report to the *RSHA* accusing Kiesinger of stopping planned anti-Jewish propaganda measures in the foreign ministry. The report denounced him as "representative of political tendencies . . . opposed to the foreign policy of the Führer."[15] Kiesinger could hardly have wished for a better endorsement.

Similarly, Best sought unsuccessfully to garner funding from West German business and other groups to establish an extensive "document service" that would provide information to former Nazi officials and would help defend them against war crimes charges. In a letter to potential donors Best denounced Robert Wolfe, head of the U.S. National Archives' captured German records branch, as "Jewish" and for permitting filming of Nazi documents housed in the West German foreign ministry archive.

According to Best, a widespread global conspiracy existed, not to seek justice for abominable crimes, but to persecute poor former Nazis and, in the process, to bring injury to Germany. His allegations resembled earlier Nazi claims as well as postwar assertions by Holocaust deniers and other anti-Semites:

> Next to determined American circles, especially Israel and world Zionism as well as the Eastern bloc, particularly the DDR [the East German Communist regime] (probably even more than Moscow), are interested in non-stop trials of war criminals and preventing a general amnesty. In judging the danger, it is inconsequential whether the chief motives are hate, diplomatic strategy, or the search for reasons to demand reparations [from the Federal Republic].[16]

His arrest on March 11, 1969, and imprisonment in Berlin didn't surprise him. Four years earlier, the Berlin public prosecutor had opened an investigation of him in connection with a whole complex of other inquiries into the activities of former *RSHA* officials and of the *Einsatzgruppen* in Poland. Although no one had interrogated Best personally, he had received intimations from several sources that the Berlin investigation encompassed him.

The prosecutor's 750-page report on the investigation's results contained evidence from a wide range of *Einsatzgruppen* and other Nazi records culled from archives in Germany, Poland, the United States, and Israel, as well as testimony from two hundred witnesses and thirty-eight of the accused. The report identified Best as the chief defendant (i.e., perpetrator) responsible for the murders during late 1939 and 1940 of some ten thousand Poles and Polish Jews. In his role as an *RSHA* office head during the war's first months, he was accused of having organized, equipped, and instructed the *Einsatzgruppen* and *Einsatzkommandos* that carried out mass murders in Poland.

But prosecutors didn't interrogate Best until after arresting him, four years since the opening of the investigation. Why had they waited so long? For one thing, the authorities viewed him as a formidable adversary—the most well informed (legally and historically)—of the Holocaust's surviving so-called desk killers.

Also they knew of his extensive connections to politicians and judicial and other well-positioned officials—many of them former Nazis—who, if they learned he was under investigation, might seek to stop it. But most importantly, with Best being the highest-ranking former member of the *RSHA* still alive, the prosecution wished to avoid, at all costs, any move that might result in the failure of the wide-ranging investigation and impending trial.

Shortly after the arrest, the police searched his home in Mülheim. They found a substantial correspondence between him and other former *RSHA* and police officials that discussed in detail the chain of command and responsibility in the huge former security agency. Further witnesses verified the information. As a result, Best's defense, from its start, remained relatively weak.

The prosecution (with the documentation available to it) held absolute proof that Best, as Heydrich's deputy between September and December 1939, had functioned as the organization's virtual chief of the *RSHA*. The prosecution also possessed solid evidence that Best, from his office in Berlin, had led the selection and organization of the *Einsatzgruppen* in Poland and had determined the units' routes of advance and locales of deployment. The *Aktion* organized by Best had operated under the cover name "Tannenberg."

Despite the overwhelming case against him, despite his repeated denials that he had anything to do with "Tannenberg," and despite his assertion that responsibility for it lay with *Gestapo* chief Heinrich Müller, who had vanished at war's end, never to be brought to justice, uncertainty existed over the issue of whether the West German judicial system would convict Best as a "perpetrator." In most previous trials of those involved in the *Einsatzgruppen* killings in Poland and later in the Soviet Union, the courts had judged the accused merely as "accomplices" or guilty of enacting such orders rather than engendering them. The outcome was mild prison sentences or no punishment at all.

What would the judiciary, therefore, do with Best? He had not personally murdered anyone, nor had he issued—at least as much as current evidence indicated—a direct order to kill. The prosecution, to bolster further its already powerful case against him, gathered evidence stretching far back into his career that demonstrated his longtime dedication to Hitler, Himmler, Heydrich, and the Nazi police.

But in the spring of 1971, a series of wholly unexpected events intervened. First, a new magistrate assigned to the case lifted the order for Best's arrest temporarily, citing as justification the testimony of Best and his defense counsel and a recent amendment to the German penal code. The prosecution, for its part, had little doubt that the intrusion on Best's behalf was politically motivated, done by a judge sympathetic to the accused.

Best and his lawyer claimed that once the world war and violence had begun, *Aktion* "Tannenberg" had contributed nothing "original" or different to the wartime deaths in Poland. Although the prosecution could show that Best knew of the *Einsatzgruppen* killings at least by November 1939, the judge ruled such evidence exhibited only "aiding and abetting [of the crimes] without particular base motives."[17]

Consequently, Best's case fell under a 1968 amendment to the penal code, which apparently did not accord with the wishes of German lawmakers at the time the amendment became law but had been overlooked by them. The amended law ruled that after May 1960 "an accessory to a crime [aiding and abetting such] merely acting under orders could only be punished if it was demonstrated that his contribution to the crime sprang from base motives [racial hatred] or that he was aware of the cruel or malicious nature of the crime at the time of its commission."[18]

Thus, it was no longer possible to bring to trial "desk murderers" like Best who had acted—in the opinion of the courts—as an accessory to a Nazi-inspired killing rather than its perpetrator. The situation was farcical, if not tragic: it meant that one of the highest-ranking office chiefs of the *RSHA* was therefore an "accomplice" to the *Einsatzgruppen* commanders "subordinate to him."[19] If the court confirmed such a view, it would destroy much of the foundation for the legal proceedings against the numerous remaining former *RSHA* officials.

Immediately, on that basis, the prosecution appealed the court's decision to lift the order for Best's arrest. Four weeks later, the court reinstated the order, and Best returned again to the Berlin prison to await trial. But now, with his conviction as a "perpetrator" nearly a certainty (despite his denials, disclaimers, and distortions), suddenly he and his lawyer changed their defense strategy. The lawyer requested that the court release Best for reasons of ill health and declare him incapable of imprisonment.

The sixty-seven-year-old Best had worked exceedingly hard until his arrest, but once in prison he complained of alleged weakening health. Symptoms included long periods of nervousness, anxiety, and deteriorating memory. They were hardly life threatening or incapacitating, but that didn't stop the new magistrate from continuing his earlier display of considerable consideration. Lacking medical confirmation of the dubious claims, the court went ahead anyway and freed Best from prison—again. Immediately, a war of physicians ensued to decide whether Best could endure further imprisonment and a trial.

On October 27, 1971, the court returned him to prison. Best's efforts to escape his impending trial by claiming an inability to participate in his defense and to handle prison were nothing new. Much too frequently, West German courts permitted numerous Nazi criminals to employ that ruse successfully to avoid trial, including several discussed earlier in this study.

Moreover, numerous of Best's former criminal colleagues in the *RSHA* and Nazi Security Police had evaded postwar punishment by alleging ill health. The only thing new was that this time, Best didn't cry. Since his earlier postwar troubles with his wife, their relationship had stabilized; his children appeared to support him as well.

In February 1972 the prosecution brought an indictment against Best accusing him of perpetrating, "commonly with Hitler, Göring, Himmler, Heydrich and [Heinrich] Müller," the murders of at least 8,723 persons in Poland during the first weeks of the world war. At 1,032 pages long, the indictment was the single most extensive document of its kind in West German judicial history. It contained massive evidence demonstrating that Best, in both "his nature and position," had been "one of the most significant National Socialists" and the "model" of the so-called desk murderer.[20]

The trial, however, never happened. New testimony by medical personnel again placed in question the defendant's ability to endure a lengthy judicial proceeding. Experts described him as suffering from depression and anxiety and as unable to follow along in a trial for more than two hours per week.

Consequently, the court decided on August 2, 1972, to halt the proceeding and to release Best from prison. Continued efforts by the prosecution to reopen the case (transferred to a court in Duisburg) nearly succeeded at the end of the 1970s. But medical experts testified again that Best, then nearly eighty years old, was too ill to stand trial.

Yet his work schedule made such testimony a farce. He wrote numerous manuscripts in which he sought to justify his Nazi career. In 1988 a Danish editor published a book of Best's recollections, which included his false claim that he'd rescued the Danish Jews—a distortion of history that he did his utmost to transform into a legendary fact. Best's book barely mentioned the Jewish persecution in Nazi Germany and France, the *Einsatzgruppen*, and the death camps. Why would it? Such information was counterproductive to his spin on the past.

In September 1987, he made a serious mistake that nearly led to a new court proceeding against him. Following his appearance on the witness stand in the trial of a former Nazi police official accused of deporting French Jews during World War II, he ended his testimony, a press report noted, "with a suggestive click of the heels and a bow in the direction of the judge's bench." But what was most striking to prosecutors wasn't his heel clicking but rather the obvious reality that in his two-hour interrogation, he made "an astonishingly fresh impression—mentally as well as physically."[21]

Immediately, the prosecution in Duisburg requested an assessment of his health from yet another medical expert, who, much to Best's chagrin, judged him completely capable of standing trial. On July 5, 1989, the Duisburg court indicted Best and moved toward opening a trial against him for the murder of 8,723 Poles and Polish Jews.

But—apparently unknown to the court—he had died from natural causes on June 23. In the end, the brutal anti-Semite and "desk killer" remained—like nearly every other perpetrator of damning inhuman deeds—unpunished for his role in the Holocaust and wholly without regret for what he'd done. For over four decades he had breathed, taken strolls, tasted good food and better wine, indulged his desires and ego, and witnessed great human events that his victims had never lived to see.

BACH-ZELEWSKI: NOTHING TO HIDE?

He had worked closely with Himmler in the Final Solution. During the fall of 1945, a few months after the *Reichsführer*'s suicide, the U.S. Army captured him. The Americans had no idea what a major war criminal they held.

Unfortunately, even long after evidence had surfaced of his bloody wartime activities, neither the Americans, nor the other Allies, nor the Germans would place him on trial for his principal bureaucratic function—commanding mobile police units that killed Jews (often collaborating with *Einsatzgruppe* B) in Byelorussia. Historian Richard Breitman shows how only in 1983 did British intelligence finally provide its own government and the United States with knowledge of its wartime decoding of secret radio messages of the German police, which showed the deadly activities of Erich von dem Bach-Zelewski, some of his *SS* comrades, and police units on the Eastern Front. The decoded messages were declassified in the 1990s.

After the war, when the Allies interviewed him, Bach-Zelewski—lacking any remorse or even a sense of wrong for what he'd done—professed total ignorance of the Holocaust. "I didn't realize," he said in an ingratiating, but pompous, tone, "until after the war that all of the Jews were dead." Who was responsible? "The whole crowd have blood on their hands," he claimed to a U.S. prison psychologist, naming Hitler, Himmler, and other leading Nazi officials. "But I have none."[22]

The work of Bach-Zelewski and most of the other German killers in the East had ended in late 1943 and 1944, as the Red Army expelled German forces from western Russia and substantial portions of Eastern Europe. Like many other Nazi perpetrators of the Holocaust who killed on the Eastern front, Bach-Zelewski despised Jews, Communists, anti-German partisans, and "looters." His attitude made his murderous actions seem to him as normal as breathing.

During the war's final months he recuperated from food poisoning in a hospital. Once he'd recovered and avoided arrest by the Allies, he made his way to his family on the German-Swiss border. In August 1945 he surrendered to the Americans, claiming that he had "a clear conscience and nothing to hide." Later, while a witness for the Allied prosecution at the IMT, he told an American interviewer that he had "participated in the Russian campaign" since 1941 but had "ordered that there be no persecution of the Jews, no ghettos."[23] He maintained that he'd even saved ten thousand Russian Jews from death.

Had he ever seen Jews executed? "Yes, I saw executions, however not only of Jews, but others."

While testifying on January 7, 1946, before the tribunal, Bach-Zelewski avoided assiduously any discussion of the Final Solution. He mentioned nothing of how *SS* and police units in Byelorussia under his command rounded up and murdered tens of thousands of Jews. Nor did he admit that his superior, Himmler, had ordered him—along with other *SS* and police leaders in the East heading killing units, including the *Einsatzgruppen*—to associate Jews automatically with "Bolsheviks," Soviet "partisans," and "looting." This widely cast association had helped target all Soviet Jews for death.

Instead, he claimed to the court that he had commanded only one police regiment and occasionally an *SS* cavalry brigade that conducted only operations against Soviet "partisans." Not only did he agree with an interrogator that "it was not quite clear what was to be understood by the term 'partisan,'" which "was never during the entire [war] clearly defined," but also he maintained that Jews formed an "exception" in participating in partisan activities.[24] He left the court with the wholly misleading impression, therefore, that his so-called antipartisan units had nothing or little to do with Jews.

Anyway, he claimed erroneously, he had felt sympathy for the partisans, alleging that the *Wehrmacht* and his superiors in the *SS* had provided no "detailed instructions as to the methods to be used in antipartisan operations." This had resulted "in a wild state of anarchy" in such activities.[25] But in fact such "anarchy" characterized primarily the many German massacres of Soviet Jews, whom the Nazis identified purposely as "partisans." Also, during the war the only concern he had expressed—to Himmler in Minsk in mid-August 1941—was for the psychological repercussions on his police of their mass killing of Jews and other Soviet groups.

He blamed the crimes in the East on the *Einsatzgruppen*, which he insisted erroneously that he had no control over, whose "principal task" was "the annihilation of the Jews, gypsies, and political commissars."[26] The Soviet deputy prosecutor, Colonel Y. V. Pokrovsky, asked him whether he had contact with Arthur Nebe, the commander of *Einsatzgruppe* B, which operated in Byelorussia. Did he not "receive Nebe's reports" of his unit's activities? "Not directly," came the evasive reply, "but I managed to see them."

What, Pokrovsky followed up, had Bach-Zelewski known "of the activities of Einsatzgruppe B?" Not much, only hearsay, he responded: "Einsatzgruppe B was located in Smolensk, and operated in precisely the same way as all the other Einsatzgruppen. One heard everywhere in conversation that the Jews were being rounded up and sent to ghettos."[27] The witness was neither asked, nor did he reveal on his own, whether his *SS* and police units had also rounded up Jews. He knew that a truthful answer to this, as well as to the previous questions, would likely send him to the gallows.

Thus, like the vast majority of other Holocaust participants, Bach-Zelewski lied to and shamelessly deceived the postwar world. He benefited also from his captors' mistakes and naïveté. They remained persuaded by his claims both then and long after the war—victims of their refusal to share among themselves valuable information about him and other perpetrators, of their lack of knowledge about and concern for Jews as the principal objects of Nazi hatred and genocide, and of Bach-Zelewski's eager willingness to testify against and blame former superiors for war crimes for which he, too, was responsible.

Following his testimony, those on trial denounced him openly. Göring stormed and raged so that his place in the dock could hardly contain him. "Why, that dirty, bloody, treacherous swine!! That filthy skunk! Goddam, *Donnerwetter*, the dirty blankety-blank sonofabitch!!! He was the bloodiest murderer in the whole goddam setup! The dirty, filthy *Schweinehund*, selling his soul to save his stinking neck!!"[28]

Also while at Nuremberg, Bach-Zelewski told Leo Alexander, an American psychiatrist and professor, that Polish and Soviet Jews in World War II were completely unprepared to resist the German annihilation of them. "The mass of the Jewish people," he said,

> were taken completely by surprise. They did not know at all what to do; they had no directives or slogans as to how they should act. That is the greatest lie of anti-Semitism because it gives the lie to the slogan that the Jews are conspiring to dominate the world and that they are so highly organized. In reality they had no organization of their own at all, not even an information service. . . . The Jews in the old Poland, who were never communistic in their sympathies, were, throughout the area of the Bug eastward, more afraid of Bolshevism than of the Nazis. This was insanity. They could have been saved. . . . After the first anti-Jewish actions of the Germans, they thought now the wave was over and so they walked back to their undoing.[29]

Eventually Bach-Zelewski, as part of his postwar effort to exculpate himself of his crimes, donated his war diary to the West German Federal Archives (*Bundesarchiv*) at Koblenz. There was, however, as Breitman discovered, "a slight problem": it was revealed later that the entries covering 1941–1942 "were not the originals" but "were heavily doctored" or rewritten to protect the author.[30]

Except for spending a few years in West Germany under house arrest as ordered by a denazification court, Bach-Zelewski enjoyed complete freedom and lived a safe, comfortable life. Married, he resided in Roth, near Nuremberg. Many of his neighbors and former Nazis protected him. He escaped extradition to the Soviet Union for his crimes, and neither the Allies nor postwar West Germany would prosecute him for his role in the Jewish massacres.

Although in April 1952 he denounced himself for his wartime actions, no prosecutor investigated him. Apparently he believed himself—correctly, as it turned out—safe from legal action. But in 1961, he was arrested and tried for his participation in the killing in 1934 of *SA* leaders—including the commander, Ernst Röhm—and sentenced to four and a half years in prison.

In May 1961, while in prison in Nuremberg, he provided testimony in Eichmann's trial. He sought in a deposition to distance himself as much as possible from the former *Gestapo* leader. He "did not knowingly make the acquaintance of Eichmann in person," he asserted, admitting only that it "is possible that he [Eichmann] knows me and saw me once in Budapest, but he did not speak to me."[31]

A bit later in the deposition, he testified that Hitler had sent him in October 1944 to Budapest to help establish "a military government" there.[32] But he mentioned nothing of how, at the time, Eichmann and the new fascist and fanatically anti-Semitic Hungarian government—that Bach-Zelewski helped place in power—rounded up and deported the last of the country's Jews, some eighty-five thousand in Budapest, to Auschwitz.

In fact, he continued denying—as he had done at the IMT fifteen years before—nearly any knowledge during the world war of the killing of Jews or of the *SS* bureaucracy that had organized and carried out the genocide. "Until the end of the war," he insisted, "I was not familiar with the organization of the Head Office for Reich Security."

About the *Einsatzgruppen* operating in the Soviet Union on orders of the *RSHA*, he claimed to know little or nothing. Because of his "position" as a Higher *SS* and Police Leader in Central Russia, beholden directly to Himmler, from June 1941 to the fall of 1943, he had only "received information"—and nothing more—about the "illegal activity on the part of these Operations Units." He "understood" the work of the units "to be the liquidation of underground movements and the extermination of Jews." But, he insisted, "I was not informed as to the complete extent of this activity. Only after the end of the War did I become aware of that."[33] He added, continuing to lie: "I myself never had anything to do with the treatment of the Jews."[34]

Moreover, when he described the visit to him in Minsk in mid-August 1941 by Himmler and the latter's aide, Karl Wolff, his version differed sharply from the facts of the meeting uncovered many years later by historians. He claimed that during the visit, while the three men watched, "twenty or thirty people" were shot, including "two or three Jews." "Himmler," he added, "was very pale during the executions."[35] But research has indicated that a firing squad killed at least a hundred prisoners, many of them Jews and women, accused of partisan activity, and that Bach-Zelewski complained to Himmler about the psychological impact on his killers of this and the many other similar shootings they were carrying out.

He ended the deposition by trying to make himself look even more innocent of participation in the mass murder of Jews: "I myself was constantly remonstrating with Himmler about unjustified executions, and I was instrumental in the demotion of Higher SS and Police Leaders."[36] What did he mean by "unjustified executions?" For whom? Not for the victims.

The following year, another West German court sentenced him to life in prison for his role in the 1933 death of six German Communists. The convictions suggested that the courts and West German public viewed only the murder of ethnic Germans—not tens of thousands of Jews—an unpardonable crime. Nevertheless, West German authorities interrogated him in April 1966, during which he testified that barely three weeks into the German invasion of Russia, in early July 1941, Himmler had told the commander of *Einsatzgruppe* B operating in Byelorussia, Nebe, that "every Jew in principle [must] be regarded as a partisan," and therefore killed.[37]

Twenty years before at the IMT, seeking to protect himself from Allied prosecution for his admitted antipartisan activity, he had claimed that no one in the Nazi leadership had defined "partisans"—meaning, above all, Jews. In 1971 Bavarian authorities discovered him furloughed from prison—by a sympathetic judge, allegedly because of the prisoner's ill-health—and resting in a private clinic in Nuremberg. Imprisoned again, he died a year later—but of natural causes.

WALTHER RAUFF: NO REMORSE IN CHILE

At his surrender in April 1945, the U.S. Army's CIC had called him a "menace" and recommended his "life-long internment" in an Allied prison.[38] But it did not happen. In December 1946, together with several other prisoners, former *SS* Colonel Walther Rauff escaped from American internment at

Rimini, Italy. He claimed later that a Catholic priest in Naples had aided his flight and helped him make his way to Rome.

Apparently while in northern Italy during 1944 and early 1945, heading Nazi operations to kill local partisans, Rauff had established valuable contacts for the future. Throughout 1947 and much of the following year, he eluded efforts to recapture him by hiding out in the convents of the Holy See, apparently under the protection of Bishop Hudal. The pro-Nazi churchman hid him in Milan and in convents of the Holy See, including in Rome.

From there, Rauff, the co-innovator of the murderous gassing van, organized the escape for some of his fellow Nazi comrades and war criminals from Europe through the so-called Roman route. Rauff, the Vatican, the church relief agency Caritas, and even (unknowingly) the Red Cross assisted these former Nazis, a few of them "good Catholics" from Eastern Europe, and provided them with false identity papers, visas, and transportation from Italy to South America. Some Jewish and other groups searching for Nazi criminals thought Rauff had founded and led *ODESSA*, the postwar clandestine organization that assisted the escape of numerous former *SS* men, though the evidence is much more circumstantial than irrefutable.

To finance his own escape, Rauff possessed substantial amounts of forged Nazi banknotes that another former *SS* official had exchanged for real foreign currency. In November 1948, he and his family left for Damascus, where the Syrian government hired out-of-work German military and/or police specialists to assist the country in making war on Israel. Apparently appointed a Syrian government commissioner of security, he reorganized local intelligence agencies and modeled the Syrian secret police along the lines of the former *Gestapo*.

In late 1949 a military coup in Damascus led to his arrest, reportedly on charges of "terrorism" in which he attempted to extract information from people (presumably Jews) suspected of being connected with a "Jewish bombing incident." Other reports from the U.S. Central Intelligence Agency (CIA) said Rauff had been arrested because members of the Syrian military leadership disliked him and resented his influential position, and that he was suspected of involvement with the "Syrian Communist movement."[39] He fled Syria, staying briefly in Beirut, Lebanon, and returned in late 1949 to Italy.

But once he landed on Italian soil, the Allies did nothing to apprehend him. Some evidence indicates that he may have worked briefly for Israeli intelligence, which sought to use him with other former Nazis to infiltrate Arab countries. From there, he and his family resettled in Ecuador, where the CIA learned that he worked as a salesman for the Parke-Davis and Bayer corporations. During the interwar years, while in the German navy, he had spent time in South America.

In October 1958 he received permanent residency in Chile, and by 1960 he felt secure enough to travel to West Germany on a Chilean passport, though under an assumed name. While in Munich, he visited with other former *SS* officers. Apparently, German authorities suspected nothing and did little to hinder or capture him, even though most likely they knew he resided in Chile, and substantial documentation and information about his bloody and ruthless activities in the Holocaust had surfaced initially at the Nuremberg trials.

During 1961 Rauff's name emerged in the Eichmann trial in Israel. Only then did West Germany, pressed by Wiesenthal and others, begin seeking to extradite Rauff for war crimes. The Nazi hunter had first learned about Rauff in the early 1950s while reading a bundle of captured *SS* records. In one document, a letter of June 5, 1942, a subordinate of Rauff, in inspecting the deadly gassing vans used by *Einsatzgruppen* A and D in Russia, had reported to his boss a number of technical changes that made it possible to squeeze more victims into the vans. In one load, most vans could carry from forty to sixty people.

The next sentence in the letter Wiesenthal had to read three times to believe: "Since October 1941, 97,000 [persons] were processed in the three trucks in use without any faults appearing in the vehicles."[40] The word *processed* meant *killed*. The dogged Nazi pursuer held, moreover, Rauff's entire correspondence with Berlin's Gaubschat Company, which had manufactured special airtight chambers for the vans.

When Wiesenthal informed the West German authorities of Rauff's address in Chile, an official investigation began that would lead in 1963 to a formal request for the former Nazi's extradition. However, the publicity about Rauff ended his relatively comfortable life only briefly. A Chilean law prohibited any prosecution of murder charges after fifteen years; Rauff's crimes stretched back at least eighteen.

In April 1963 the Chilean Supreme Court rejected the application for his extradition. During 1971, Wiesenthal asked the Santiago government to consider deporting Rauff, who hadn't yet obtained Chilean citizenship, but before the government could act on the request, military strongman Augusto Pinochet seized control of the regime.

Meanwhile, in June 1972, Rauff gave a deposition voluntarily in Santiago at the local West German embassy, for a criminal investigation in Hamburg of former *SS* officer Bruno Streckenbach. The Soviets had captured Streckenbach at the war's end, sentenced him to twenty-five years in prison, and then released him in 1955, whereupon he had settled in Bavaria. In June 1941 Streckenbach, while an *SS* lieutenant colonel and head of the personnel department in the *RSHA*, had joined Heydrich in giving orders to commanders of the *Einsatzgruppen* to destroy the Jews in the Soviet Union. As the German armies on June 22 began their massive invasion of the Soviet Union, the killing units had followed, ready to strike their victims.

Hardly surprising, regarding Streckenbach's role in the matter, Rauff's testimony shed little light. Who, after all, wanted to incriminate himself? About his own involvement in the Final Solution, Rauff admitted that he had known during the war about the *Einsatzgruppen* and "[o]f the measures against the Jews in Russia." Already during the Polish campaign in September 1939, he said, he "had heard of liquidation measures against the Jews."

But he mentioned nothing of his work in the *RSHA* in helping equip and supply the *Einsatzgruppen* in Russia with munitions. Also, in discussing the gas vans he did his best to lie about the central role he played in supervising the development, testing, and then use of them on their victims:

> Regarding the annihilation of Jews in Russia, I know that gas vans were used for this purpose. I cannot say, however, from when on and to what extent this happened. I used to think that the thing with the gas vans started at the time when I was at the navy [from early 1940 to the start of 1941]. Today I have doubts about this and consider it possible that this matter only got going after I had returned from the navy. At any rate I now [know] that at some time after my return I saw two of these gas vans standing in the yard, which [Friedrich] Pradel [Rauff's subordinate in Section IID of the *RSHA*] showed to me. Somehow I then also learned that the gas vans were used for the execution of sentences and for the killing of Jews.
>
> I consider it impossible that Pradel should have carried out the development of the gas vans on his own initiative. He must have received an order for this either from me or from another superior standing above me.[41]

The Pinochet coup in Chile provided Rauff with both a friend and a cause that he could serve. Apparently, he aided Pinochet's regime by assisting in the torture and possibly even killing of numerous Chileans who opposed the dictator's iron-fisted rule. The French paper *Le Monde* reported that Rauff served as chief of the Chilean intelligence service. But as late as March 1976, the CIA remained unclear on exactly what, if any, connections existed between Rauff and the Chilean government. Meanwhile, a West German judge visited Rauff in Chile to gather his testimony for an investigation of Friedrich Pradel, the former *SS* official with whom Rauff had collaborated in developing the infamous gas van.

In April 1983, during a personal interview, Wiesenthal urged U.S. president Ronald Reagan to become involved in the Rauff affair. Later Wiesenthal recalled that the president "did inform the State Department, which asked us to make our entire file on Rauff available to them." Also, Wiesenthal met with West German chancellor Helmut Kohl; the latter mentioned "that he would talk to his Ministry of Justice to see if a new extradition application might not be made."[42] Soon after, the United States joined West Germany in pressuring Chile to extradite the former Nazi for trial. But still nothing happened.

Finally, Santiago indicated its willingness to consider handing over Rauff. It feared damage to its image in the world and appeared concerned about rumors that the United States might implement an economic boycott of Chile if Pinochet continued to harbor the builder of the Nazi gas van that had "processed" several hundred thousand Jews. Such concerns were not without justification. In January 1984, Beate Klarsfeld, a French Nazi hunter, arrived in Santiago and launched a loud, conspicuous campaign for Rauff's extradition; a few weeks later, Klarsfeld received Israel's official support. On February 19 the European Parliament issued a resolution calling on Chile to hand over Rauff.

But on May 14, 1984, two days before a courier was scheduled to leave West Germany for Chile with a new arrest warrant and request for Rauff's extradition, news arrived that Rauff had died at his home of heart failure and, accompanied by neo-Nazi demonstrations, had been buried in Santiago. He'd escaped punishment for his crimes for nearly forty years because a post–World War II world—most notably, quoting an essay on the subject by several scholars, "American negligence in the immediate postwar period; active assistance from certain officials of the Catholic church; and longstanding protection by several different Chilean governments"[43]—cared little or nothing for what he and others had done in the Holocaust. And neither had Rauff.

17

The Post-Holocaust World

Even a distinguished historian seemed surprised at Maurice Papon's French trial and conviction in 1997. Papon, a post–World War II government minister and Paris police chief under Charles de Gaulle, was found guilty of aiding the Germans during the war in rounding up Jews in Bordeaux for deportation. The court proceedings, Tony Judt wrote in 2006,

> revealed no new evidence—except perhaps about the man [Papon] himself, who displayed an astonishing absence of pity or remorse. And of course the trial came fifty years too late: too late to punish the octogenarian Papon for his crimes; too late to avenge his victims; and too late to save the honour of his country.[1]

But was the "absence of pity or remorse" of such a perpetrator really "new evidence"? Or "astonishing"? Hardly. Because for well over a half century, since the war's end, in similar trials and investigations—that also often came much "too late"—or in other circumstances where perpetrators escaped justice entirely, nearly every perpetrator had "displayed" the same or even greater lack of "pity or remorse." Indeed, while they admitted that the Holocaust had happened, most had denied their role in it and considered themselves victims of the Allies, other postwar authorities, and/or "international Jewry." If this sad fact apparently eluded Judt, a prolific British scholar who died in 2010, it has surely escaped much of the rest of the world.

Indeed, one suspects that a majority of people today believe or assume that Holocaust perpetrators could not possibly have failed to learn from their crimes, to regret them, and that, in turn, their hatred for their victims had been lessened or banished. But no such regret or similar sentiment passed the postwar lips of the perpetrators. Instead, their postwar lives and claims helped stoke an ever-greater prejudice in the post-Holocaust world.

Since World War II ended nearly seven decades ago, Holocaust deniers and other anti-Semites who come close to denial have spun their web of deceit and fabrication. From 1945 to 1950, first-generation deniers watched closely the war crimes trials and testimony of Nazi perpetrators; they denounced each proceeding as unjust and began publicizing their allegations. Their anti-Semitic and other claims portraying Germany as the major victim in the war and the Jews as responsible for what had happened to them reflected almost exactly what most perpetrators, with their denials of involvement in the Holocaust, had asserted both in courtrooms and elsewhere.

Indeed, a close ideological affinity existed between perpetrator and denier. With their attacks on the truth, with both using many of the same falsehoods, they engaged—and deniers to whatever degree continue to do so—in a relentless anti-Jewish propaganda crusade. This book has brought to light the perpetrators' shadowy side of this campaign, in which, more often than not, they defended Nazi anti-Semitism and the Holocaust it produced.

Göring probably had the greatest influence on denial mythology when he claimed at his well-publicized trial before the IMT that he and Hitler had not known about the Holocaust during the war and that the Germans had no "policy that aimed at the extermination of the Jews." Perpetrators like Karl Wolff and Erich von Manstein asserted that the number of Jews killed in the Holocaust was exaggerated. Other perpetrators—Göring, Irma Grese, Kaltenbrunner, and Rosenberg come most to mind—disavowed the evidence used to prosecute them, much of it documents from their own hand. Ohlendorf, during his Nuremberg trial in 1947 with other *Einsatzgruppen* members, blamed the Jews, including women and children, for the wartime genocide that befell them.

Many perpetrators maintained that they and Germany had been victims of someone else. The alleged victimizers included a powerful "world Jewry" that collaborated often with another conspirator against Germany and its people—the Allies. Best termed the Nuremberg and other war crimes trials a "farce" and unjustified. As late as 1968, he declared that a conspiracy of the United States, "Israel and world Zionism," and East Germany sought to continue persecuting former Nazis. Ohlendorf compared his mobile firing squads in the Soviet Union to what he termed the "press-button killers" who had dropped atom bombs on Japan. Nor was this the extent of the perpetrators' litany of excuses for their criminal behavior in the Holocaust. Many of them insisted they had merely obeyed orders from their superiors.

Since the late 1940s, all of these and other anti-Semitic and anti-Allied claims have filled the publications of deniers and quasi-deniers. The history of this hate-filled movement is chronicled by, among others, Lipstadt, British historian Richard Evans, and American writers Michael Shermer and Alex Grobman. The only major difference between the perpetrators and deniers is that the former didn't deny the Holocaust happened.

As this final chapter is written, anti-Semitic and denial websites—featuring the old vile and hateful articles by Julius Streicher, one of the Nazis' most vulgar Jew haters, now born anew in a medium, the Internet, he could never have imagined—proliferate exponentially. Deniers continue to try to minimize the casualties caused by Nazism, to mitigate its lethal intent, or to deny the genocide outright.

In 2006 the Iranian government sponsored a Holocaust denial conference held in Teheran—"an event," according to American writers David Dalin and John Rothmann, "unprecedented in the annals of modern anti-Semitism. . . . Never before had an assemblage of Holocaust deniers been given the respectability of state sponsorship." In 2008, Dalin and Rothmann published a study of Haj Amin al-Husayni, a radical Palestinian Arab cleric and nationalist who allied with Hitler, lived during the war in Germany, collaborated with Himmler, and knew about and approved of the Holocaust. The authors conclude that al-Husayni's venomous hatred of Jews—including his demand on German radio in 1943 that Muslims "Kill the Jews. . . . This pleases God, history and religion"—has

> inspired generations of radical Islamic terrorists, from Yasser Arafat and Osama bin Laden to Ahmed Omar Saeed Sheikh, the Muslim terrorist who masterminded the brutal kidnapping and barbaric murder of Daniel Pearl [an American Jew and journalist] in Pakistan. As the founding father of radical Islamic anti-Semitism in the twentieth century, al-Husseini remains the inextricable and enduring link between the old anti-Semitism of pre-Holocaust Europe and the Jew hatred and Holocaust denial that now permeates the Muslim world.[2]

The Nazis also beamed Arab-language broadcasts to the Middle East during the world war and Holocaust. The many propaganda transmissions revealed Nazi Germany's determined efforts to recruit allies, supporters, and collaborators among the Arabs and Muslims. In analyzing the broadcasts, historian Jeffrey Herf has demonstrated how, despite military defeat,

> Nazism left traces behind, especially traces of hatred of the Jews that drew on the distinctly European traditions of radical anti-Semitism. The evidence of the immediate postwar years in the Middle East . . . lends plausibility to the thesis of continuity and lineages between Nazism's Arabic-language propaganda, on the one hand, and radical Islam in the subsequent decades, on the other. . . .

> The diffusion of Nazi ideology and in particular of radical anti-Semitism struck a nerve [among Arabs] because it expressed ideas that connected to the indigenous traditions being selectively received and accentuated by Arab and Islamist ideologues.[3]

The postwar Muslim Brotherhood and other leaders in the Arab world displayed attitudes toward Israel and the West that were in keeping with the conspiracy theories wartime Radio Berlin had broadcast daily to Arabs. Such broadcasts claimed repeatedly that the United States, Britain, and the Jews "are all conspiring against Arab interests."[4] Postwar Arab conspiracy views have extended beyond the Islamist fringe and included even moderate Muslim leaders.

A similar continuum of radical anti-Semitism characterized the postwar statements and actions of most Nazi perpetrators of the Holocaust. They, too, "left traces behind" of "hatred of the Jews." Both their participation in the Holocaust and in their postwar disavowals that they had done so left Islamic militants and other Jew haters with an example of violence committed against Jews unprecedented in the long history of anti-Semitism. Nor did some perpetrators fail to exploit the close tie of Nazism to the Arab world. Brunner, Rauff, Stangl, Wagner, and other war criminals escaped permanently or for a lesser time to Syria, which welcomed the Nazis as allies against Israel.

In 2002, Islamic radicals in Pakistan, as anti-Semitic as any *SS* fanatic, beheaded the American Jewish journalist Daniel Pearl and filmed the horrifying spectacle for a rapt audience for no other reason than that he was Jewish. In a Pew Global Attitudes project, released in August 2005, 60 percent of Turks, 88 percent of Moroccans, 99 percent of Lebanese Muslims, and 100 percent of Jordanians held negative views of Jews and Israel.

In much of the Muslim world, anti-Zionist propaganda echoes the anti-Semitic hate of Hitler, Himmler, Göring, Goebbels, and Streicher—all of whom knew Haj Amin al-Husayni intimately along with other Arab radicals. Arab nations like Syria and Iran still deny the Holocaust happened and speak of eliminating Jews and eradicating Israel. Age-old anti-Semitic rumors reappear in slightly different or updated garb and circulate across the globe: the Jews are an international power elite bent on world domination and destruction—even death—of Muslims and others; the Jews orchestrated the 9/11 World Trade Center and Pentagon attacks for their own nefarious purposes; and the Jews control media resources and therefore influence public opinion disproportionately.

Anti-Zionist propaganda also compares the Israelis' treatment of Palestinians to the Nazis' treatment of Jews. The Saudi Ministry of Education uses textbooks, supposedly sanitized of anti-Semitism, that employ harsh rhetoric. They teach the infamous forgery, *The Protocols of the Elders of Zion*, as historical fact, assert that "Jews and Christians are the enemies of the [Muslim] believers," and promise that in the end, Muslims will vanquish the Jews, to whom the textbooks refer as "apes."[5] The leading imam of Saudi Arabia, Abdul Rahman Al-Sudais, has called Jews "the scum of the human race whom Allah cursed."[6]

Nor is the Western world immune to a persistent, and at times violent, anti-Jewish sentiment. During the past decade, Europe has seen a resurgence of the hatred. Holocaust denial raised its ugly head in a major international trial held in a London court from January through March 2000. In April the judge, Justice Gray, rejected overwhelmingly the libel suit of British writer David Irving against Lipstadt and the publisher of her book *Denying the Holocaust* for calling Irving "one of the most dangerous spokespersons for Holocaust denial." About the judge's verdict, the *Guardian* commented: "Much more than the fate of David Irving was decided yesterday. The High Court also drove a stake through the heart of 'revisionism'—the right-wing credo which says the Jews have mounted a con-trick on the rest of humanity by inventing a tragedy. Gray has nailed that lie."[7]

In a shocking event for Jews and other concerned observers, in January 2009 Pope Benedict XVI rehabilitated a Catholic bishop who denied the Holocaust had happened. The British-born bishop, Richard Williamson, had made a number of statements denying the full extent of the Holocaust. In comments to a Swedish television station, he said, "I believe there were no gas chambers," and that only up to three hundred thousand Jews had perished in Nazi camps instead of nearly six million.

Jewish leaders in both Europe and America denounced Williamson; a French Jewish group called him "a despicable liar whose only goal is to revive the centuries-old hate against Jews." But the Vatican defended Benedict's lifting of Rome's 1988 excommunication of Williamson from the Church by insisting that the bishop's "personal opinions" were "totally extraneous" to the rescinding of the excommunication.[8] Meanwhile, the Holy See continued to support the wartime pope, Pius XII, who had turned a blind eye to the Holocaust (discussed in chapter 10), for sainthood.

Recently, Britain's chief rabbi, Sir Jonathan Sacks, warned of an ever-rising anti-Semitism across the globe, including in the United Kingdom. In June 2009, he told the *Times* (London) that Britain found itself "in the grip of a 'virulent' new strain of anti-Semitism," a "new mutation" of anti-Jewish sentiment different from the hatred promoted by Hitler but "dangerous" because "it was international." A worrying alliance had developed, Sacks said, "between radical Islamists and anti-globalisation protesters." The previous January, he continued, "the number of anti-Semitic incidents reached the highest level [in Britain] since records began. Jews have been physically attacked, schools targeted and cemeteries desecrated."[9]

The rise in the number of attacks happened at the same time as Israel's assault on Hamas in Gaza. Repeatedly Britain has seen a surge of anti-Semitic attacks when turmoil has broken out in the Middle East. Additionally, in Germany, despite the government's vigilance, it is still necessary to surround synagogues and Jewish community centers with heavy security, making German Jews feel increasingly unsafe. In September 2007, a Muslim of Afghan origin attacked Frankfurt am Main rabbi Zalman Gurevitch on a street and stabbed him repeatedly while calling him a "Jewish pig."[10] Anti-Semitism remains an open problem as well in post-Soviet Russia.

In the United States the potent anti-Jewish sentiment that in 1915 permitted and encouraged the kidnapping from prison and lynching of Leo Frank (an American Jew falsely charged and wrongfully convicted of raping and murdering a thirteen-year-old female employee) by a mob of distinguished citizens, including a former governor, a senator's son, lawyers, and a prosecutor, still endures in the twenty-first century. (Frank's sensationalized trial helped revive the Ku Klux Klan as well as lead to the founding of the Anti-Defamation League.)

Jew hatred not only endures but percolates in American popular culture. For example, in January 2002, two radio "shock jocks" in New York, Opie (born Gregg Hughes) and Anthony (surname Cumia), interviewed seventy-five-year-old actor Robert Clary, a French Jew and Holocaust survivor, about the memoirs of his remarkable life, *From the Holocaust to Hogan's Heroes*. During the "interview" Opie and Anthony not only insinuated that Clary was gay (the Nazis also despised homosexuals and eliminated many of them), but as he recounted his concentration camp experiences at Buchenwald, where he was shipped along with twelve members of his immediate family, all of whom perished in the gas chambers, Opie and Anthony proceeded to play sound effects in the background: a ping-pong game and a canned laugh track. Clary hung up, only to be coaxed by a persuasive producer to get back on the phone, at which point the radio hosts ridiculed him for returning to the airwaves after such abuse and suggested that his only motive—being a Jew and all—was to sell his book and make money. When they played a recording of one of Hitler's speeches, Clary hung up for good, at which point uncontrollable laughter filled the studio.

Did Opie and Anthony lose their lucrative jobs and celebrity? No. Although a few people expressed dismay and disgust, in particular Richard Johnson of the *New York Post*, the radio station did nothing, the majority of people didn't care, and those listeners who did thought the segment a "classic" and that "playing Hitler speeches while interviewing a Holocaust survivor was really funny."[11] Opie and Anthony were fired only when in August 2002, they sponsored a contest that led to the arrest of two people for having sex at St. Patrick's Cathedral.

But such behavior isn't the sole preserve of America's more sophomoric citizens. Leading up to the Iraq War, U.S. politicians on both sides of the aisle of Congress uttered remarks that resembled closely the accusations of the pro-Nazi, anti-Semitic Charles Lindbergh, who claimed early in World War II that a Jewish minority was driving America into the war against its interests. In 2004 Democratic senator Ernest Hollings of South Carolina announced that the war with Iraq was being pursued "to secure Israel" and to "take the Jewish vote from the Democrats."[12] Republican pundit Pat Buchanan stated that "a cabal" was determined "to snare our country in a series of wars that are not in America's interests."[13]

According to an Anti-Defamation League survey in 2005, 14 percent of U.S. residents held anti-Semitic views; that number increased significantly when considered by race, with 36 percent of African Americans holding strongly anti-Jewish views. In April 2006 the U.S. Commission on Civil Rights released its finding that anti-Semitic incidents are a serious problem across American college campuses.

On July 28, 2006, at the Seattle Jewish Federation, Naveed Afzal Haq shot six women, killing one; the police classified the shooting a hate crime based on Naveed's statements. In September of that year, Yale University founded the Yale Initiative for Interdisciplinary Study of Anti-Semitism, the first North American university-based center seeking, according to its director, Charles Small, "to understand the current manifestation of this disease."[14] A few months later, a young Holocaust denier assaulted Auschwitz survivor and Nobel Peace laureate Elie Wiesel in a San Francisco hotel.

Is anti-Semitism a disease? Or a plague? Or both?

To continue seeking answers, in July 2008, the U.S. Holocaust Memorial Museum in Washington, D.C., sponsored a workshop for its patrons and visitors entitled "Studying Antisemitism in the 21st Century." Two of the workshops examined "the new anti-Semitism" in the United States, which columnist Victor Davis Hanson had defined in September 2006 "as a strange mixture of violent hatred by radical Islamists and the more or less indifference to it by Westerners." Hanson, like Rabbi Sacks in Britain, warned:

> The dangers of this post anti-Semitism is [*sic*] not just that Jews are shot in Europe [at synagogues in Istanbul] and the United States [at a Jewish center in Seattle], or that a drunken celebrity [Mel Gibson] or demagogue [Louis Farrakhan, leader of the "Nation of Islam"] mouths off. Instead, ever so insidiously, radical Islam's hatred of Jews is becoming normalized.[15]

In 2009, the Southern Poverty Law Center, a nonprofit civil rights organization headquartered in the South, counted 932 active hate groups in the United States. The vast majority of the groups preach a bigoted and dangerous mix of white supremacist, neo-Nazi, and anti-Semitic ideas. In June, an eighty-eight-year-old white supremacist and Holocaust denier in Washington, D.C., James von Brunn, shot and killed a security guard inside the U.S. Holocaust Memorial Museum.

Two years later, the recent effort to analyze and understand anti-Semitism in its various forms and guises received a serious blow. In June 2011, Yale University eliminated its five-year-old center for the "interdisciplinary study of anti-Semitism." A university official defended the move, saying the center had failed "to serve the research and teaching interests" of the school's faculty. One of the numerous critics of the university's decision, the *New York Post*, concluded that the school "almost certainly" ended the center "because [the center] refused to ignore the most virulent, genocidal and common form of Jew-hatred today: Muslim anti-Semitism."[16] A representative of the Palestine Liberation Organization in America had complained to Yale's president about the attention the center paid to anti-Semitism among Palestinians and Muslims.

To be sure, many sources, past and present, exist that fuel the persistence of widespread racial, anti-Semitic, and other prejudice in the world. But one can only wonder whether, had the Allies and others after World War II pursued and punished the perpetrators of the Holocaust more aggressively, and in doing so made a powerful effort to discredit racism (and with it, anti-Semitism), contemporary attitudes nearly everywhere toward Jews—and other minorities—might have moved more significantly in the direction of toleration. Would Holocaust denial have become such a potent—and dangerous—myth? And would a major campaign to round up and prosecute the Nazi and other perpetrators have lessened the world's general indifference to and lack of regret for other later genocides, like that in Cambodia and those more recently in Rwanda, the former Yugoslavia, and Darfur in Sudan?

Today, occasionally a Holocaust perpetrator is still uncovered, brought to trial, and imprisoned. The most notorious case has involved John Demjanjuk, a retired ninety-one-year-old U.S. autoworker of Ukrainian descent. He had entered the United States illegally after the war and settled in Cleveland, Ohio. When the United States discovered the situation, Washington deported Demjanjuk to Israel, where a court convicted him on charges that he had killed Jews while serving as a guard at Treblinka and acting as someone known to camp prisoners as "Ivan the Terrible." In 1993, however, evidence persuaded the court that while Demjanjuk had been a camp guard somewhere, he was not at Treblinka. The court reversed the conviction and freed him. In 1999 the United States reopened the case against him after learning that he had worked for the *SS* in Sobibor. A decade later the United States deported him to Germany.

In May 2011, a Munich court convicted Demjanjuk of being an accessory to the murder of 28,060 people at Sobibor in 1943, when the court said evidence showed he had served as an auxiliary guard at the camp. He had trained for the job at an *SS* facility. The court sentenced him to five years in prison. Like so many other Holocaust perpetrators, Demjanjuk insisted on his innocence, claiming he was a victim of the Nazis—first, he said, wounded as a Soviet soldier fighting German forces, and then captured and held as a prisoner of war. Efriam Zuroff, the chief Nazi hunter at the Simon Wiesenthal Center in Jerusalem, called the conviction "a very important victory for justice" and hoped it would open the door for other similar cases in Germany.[17]

Some observers question whether it's worth the time and effort to prosecute such war criminals, now usually in their eighties, in their final, frail years. But in 2003 Richard Kurland, a lawyer for the Canadian Jewish Congress, answered this query. He reminded the world, "Dead people are dead forever. But if we can incarcerate a murderer for even a short period at the end of life, it does go a long way to bring a measure of justice for the victims. These were acts of evil, pure and simple."[18]

About such evil, what provided the greatest impetus for it? Based on the findings of the present book, it is difficult to argue with historian Sean McMeekin's recent analysis of anti-Semitism. He has linked anti-Semitism to a "toxic self-pitying disease" that had infected Germans both during and after World War I.[19] Hitler and the Nazis capitalized on such hatred and, during World War II, threatened with it to destroy Western civilization. After the German defeat in 1945, nearly every Nazi perpetrator of the Holocaust, despite his or her culpability in horrific crimes, refused to accept responsibility for them and instead wallowed in claims that the Jews and Allies had victimized each perpetrator and Germany. Given the post–Holocaust era's connections between perpetrators and Holocaust deniers—which the foregoing pages have identified—it is hardly surprising that the anti-Semitism of denial, whether among Arabs or Westerners, is based on a similar pitying of oneself and of blaming Jews, Israel, and/or Anglo-Americans for every evil one confronts.

Unfortunately, if history reveals anything to mankind, it is that humans are often very poor students. Especially, we appear to learn little from our hatreds—whether fanaticism or indifference—toward others and what they do to those whom we hate. That held true for the majority of Nazi perpetrators of the Holocaust, who survived without Hitler into the postwar era, a few briefly and most for many years, with dangerous consequences for anti-Semitism and many Jews but also for other groups singled out for hatred for their different racial make-up, religion, culture, or lifestyle.

Neither the perpetrators nor the world experienced an extensive, badly needed reckoning for what, between 1939 and 1945, nearly physically wiped out an entire people in Europe. Tragically, the post-Holocaust world had little sympathy for the victims and thus little will to punish the perpetrators and persuade them to tell the truth about their role in what happened. Mankind is much less human for it.

Notes

Note: As a general rule, only quotations in the text receive a citation in the notes. Other sources used in the text are listed in the bibliography.

PREFACE

1. Raul Hilberg, *The Destruction of the European Jews*, rev. and def. ed., 3 vols. (New York and London: Holmes & Meier, 1985), 3:1090.

2. Rebecca Wittmann, *Beyond Justice: The Auschwitz Trial* (Cambridge and London: Harvard University Press, 2005), 5.

3. To borrow from a noted quote: "When war is declared, truth is the first casualty," from Arthur Ponsonby, *Falsehood in War-Time* (London: George Allen & Unwin, 1928) and other versions attributed to various persons.

4. Deborah E. Lipstadt, *Denying the Holocaust: The Growing Assault on Truth and Memory* (New York: Free Press, 1993), 22. The book remains the single most important study of its subject.

5. Ibid., 52.

6. Deborah E. Lipstadt, *The Eichmann Trial* (New York: Nextbook, Schocken, 2011), xx.

7. "Romanians Are Told of Nation's Role in Mass Killing of Jews," *New York Times*, July 2, 1991, http://www.nytimes.com/1991/07/02/world/romanians-are-told-of-nation-s-role-in-mass-killing-of-jews.html.

8. Gerhard L. Weinberg, *Germany, Hitler & World War II: Essays in Modern German and World History* (Cambridge and New York: Cambridge University Press, 1995), 220, from an essay published originally in U.S. Holocaust Memorial Council, ed., *Fifty Years Ago: Revolt amid the Darkness. Days of Remembrance, April 18–25, 1993*, ed. U.S. Holocaust Memorial Council (Washington, D.C.: U.S. Government Printing Office, 1993), 1–15.

9. Adolf Hitler, *Hitler's Second Book: The Unpublished Sequel to* Mein Kampf, ed. Gerhard L. Weinberg, trans. Krista Smith (New York: Enigma Books, 2003; originally published in German in 1961), xxiii.

10. John Bartlett, *The Shorter Bartlett's Familiar Quotations: A Collection of Passages, Phrases, and Proverbs Traced to Their Sources in Ancient and Modern Literature*, 17th printing (New York: Pocket Books, 1964), 62.

11. Brian K. Feltman, "Legitimizing Justice: The American Press and the International Military Tribunal, 1945–1946," *The Historian* 66, no. 2 (Summer 2004): 318.

CHAPTER 1: WORLD WAR II AND ALLIED PROMISES

1. The best study of the war is Gerhard L. Weinberg, *A World at Arms: A Global History of World War II* (Cambridge and New York: Cambridge University Press, 1994).

2. Arieh J. Kochavi, *Prelude to Nuremberg: Allied War Crimes Policy and the Question of Punishment* (Chapel Hill and London: University of North Carolina Press, 1998), 142.

3. Gerhard L. Weinberg, *Germany, Hitler & World War II: Essays in Modern German and World History* (Cambridge and New York: Cambridge University Press, 1995), 219, from an essay published originally in *Fifty Years Ago: Revolt amid the Darkness. Days of Remembrance, April 18–25, 1993*, ed. U.S. Holocaust Memorial Council (Washington, D.C.: U.S. Government Printing Office, 1993), 1–15.

4. Alexander Victor Prusin, "'Fascist Criminals to the Gallows!' The Holocaust and Soviet War Crimes Trials, December 1945–February 1946," *Holocaust and Genocide Studies* 17, no. 1 (Spring 2003): 4.

5. "German Use of Motor Cars for Mass Suffocations Noted," *New York Times*, July 16, 1943, p. 7.

6. Prusin, 6.

7. Ibid.

8. See the entry for January 17, 1944, in Alexander Cadogan, *The Diaries of Sir Alexander Cadogan 1938–1945*, ed. David Dilks (New York: Putnam, 1972), 597.

9. Robert S. Wistrich, *Hitler and the Holocaust* (New York: Modern Library, 2001), 190.

10. Joseph W. Bendersky, *The "Jewish Threat": Anti-Semitic Politics of the U.S. Army* (New York: Basic Books, 2000), 315.

11. "W.M. (45) 43rd Conclusions. Conclusions of a Meeting of the War Cabinet Held at 10, Downing Street, S.W. 1, on Thursday, 12th April 1945, at 3:30 p.m.," Public Record Office, London/Cabinet 65/50, frames 23–24.

12. Raul Hilberg, *The Destruction of the European Jews*, rev. and definitive ed., 3 vols. (New York and London: Holmes & Meier, 1985), 3:1063–65.

13. Weinberg, *World at Arms*, 483.

14. Kochavi, 133.

15. "Indictment," in *The Trial of Josef Kramer and Forty-Four Others (The Belsen Trial)*, ed. Raymond Phillips (London: William Hodge, 1949), 4–5.

16. A copy of the law is in "The Einsatzgruppen Case," *Trials of War Criminals before the Nuernberg Military Tribunals under Control Council Law No. 10*, 15 vols. (Washington, D.C.: Government Printing Office, 1952; repr., Buffalo, N.Y.: William S. Hein, 1997), 4:xviii–xxi. Citations are to the Hein edition.

17. Kochavi, 169.

18. Donald Bloxham, *Genocide on Trial: War Crimes Trials and the Formation of Holocaust History and Memory* (Oxford: Oxford University Press, 2001), 2.

19. Ibid., 5.

CHAPTER 2: FOUR FACES OF GENOCIDE: WHAT HAPPENED IN THE WAR

1. Yitzhak Arad, *Belzec, Sobibor, Treblinka: The Operation Reinhard Death Camps* (Bloomington and Indianapolis: Indiana University Press, 1987), 80.

2. Henry Friedlander, *The Origins of Genocide: From Euthanasia to the Final Solution* (Chapel Hill and London: University of North Carolina Press, 1995), 205.

3. Gitta Sereny, *Into That Darkness: From Mercy Killing to Mass Murder* (New York: McGraw-Hill, 1974), 58.

4. Friedlander, 93.

5. Sereny, 126–27.

6. Ibid., 157.

7. Arad, 184.

8. Sereny, 200.

9. Quoted in Arad, 186.

10. Ibid., 97.

11. Ibid., 162.

12. Ibid., 167–68.

13. Ulrich Herbert, "The German Military Command in Paris and the Deportation of the French Jews," in *National Socialist Extermination Policies: Contemporary German Perspectives and Controversies*, ed. Ulrich Herbert (New York: Berghahn Books, 2000), 146.

14. Ibid., 138.

15. Ibid., 142.

16. Ulrich Herbert, *Best. Biographische Studien über Radikalismus Weltanschauung und Vernunft, 1903–1989* (Bonn: Verlag J. H. W. Dietz, 1996), 283.

17. Herbert, "German Military Command," 143.

18. Military Commander in France (Administrative Section) to Chiefs of German Security Police and Security Service Paris (Concerning: Deportation of Jews and Communists), January 6, 1942, signed by Best, Doc. 967-F, *Trial of the Major War Criminals before the International Military Tribunal (Nuremberg, 14 November 1945–1 October 1946)*, 42 vols. (Nuremberg, n.p., 1949), 37:387–88.

19. Herbert, "German Military Command," 151–52.

20. Herbert, *Best*, 231.

21. Ibid., 239.

22. Gerhard L. Weinberg, *A World at Arms: A Global History of World War II* (Cambridge and New York: Cambridge University Press, 1994), 192.

23. Richard Breitman, *The Architect of Genocide: Himmler and the Final Solution* (New York: Knopf, 1991), 192.

24. Ibid., 196.

25. Peter Longerich, *Holocaust: Nazi Persecution and Murder of the Jews* (New York: Oxford University Press, 2010), 531n13.

26. Ibid., 221.

27. Christopher R. Browning, with contributions by Jürgen Matthäus, *The Origins of the Final Solution: The Evolution of Nazi Jewish Policy, September 1939–March 1942* (Lincoln and Jerusalem: University of Nebraska Press and Yad Vashem, 2004), 288–89.

28. Raul Hilberg, *The Destruction of the European Jews*, rev. and definitive ed., 3 vols. (New York and London: Holmes & Meier, 1985), 1:328.

29. Affidavit of Walter Blume, 29 June 1947, "The Einsatzgruppen Case," *Trials of War Criminals before the Nuernberg Military Tribunals under Control Council Law No. 10*, 15 vols. (Buffalo, N.Y.: William S. Hein, 1997, first pub. 1952), 4:140.

30. Browning, *Origins*, 355.

31. "Interrogation Protocol [Walther Rauff Deposition]," March 1, 1972, Nizkor Project, Shofar FTP Archive File, http://www.nizkor.org/ftp.cgi/people/r/ftp.py?people/r//rauff.walter/Rauff-deposition-translation.

32. Browning, *Origins*, 356.

33. Ibid.

34. Becker to Rauff, May 16, 1942, Doc. 501-PS, International Military Trials, Office of U.S. Chief of Counsel for Prosecution of Axis Criminality, *Nazi Conspiracy and Aggression*, 8 vols. 12 pts. (Washington, D.C.: U.S. Government Printing Office, 1946), 3:418.

35. Ibid.

36. Jeffrey Herf, *Nazi Propaganda for the Arab World* (New Haven and London: Yale University Press, 2009), 126.

37. Ibid., chapters 6–7.

38. Richard Breitman, with Norman J. W. Goda and Paul Brown, "The Gestapo," in *U.S. Intelligence and the Nazis*, ed. Richard Breitman, Norman J. W. Goda, Timothy Naftali, and Robert Wolfe (Washington, D.C.: National Archives Trust Fund, 2004), 153.

CHAPTER 3: LEAVING AUSCHWITZ

1. Hans Frankenthal, in collaboration with Andreas Plake, Babette Quinkert, and Florian Schmaltz, *The Unwelcome One: Returning Home from Auschwitz*, trans. John A. Broadwin (Evanston, Ill.: Northwestern University Press, 2002), 63.

2. Ibid., 64–73.

3. Leversen to Jewish Committee for Relief Abroad (London), May 6, 1945, Jews in Germany, General (Relief Workers' Reports), Doc. Ref. No. HA6A-1/9, Wiener Library, London, Gale Digital Collections (Post-War Europe: Refugees, Exile and Resettlement, 1945–1950, http://www.tlemea.com/postwareurope/index.htm).

4. Trieger deposition, in *Trial of Josef Kramer and Forty-Four Others (The Belsen Trial)* (hereafter *TJK*), ed. Raymond Phillips (London: William Hodge, 1949), 690.

5. Lebowitz deposition, Ibid., 673.

6. Bialek deposition, Ibid., 657.

7. Robert J. Lifton, *The Nazi Doctors: Medical Killing and the Psychology of Genocide* (New York: Basic Books, 1986), 343.

8. Helena Kubica, "The Crimes of Josef Mengele," in *Anatomy of the Auschwitz Death Camp*, ed. Yisrael Gutman and Michael Berenbaum, published in association with the U.S.

Holocaust Memorial Museum (Bloomington and Indianapolis: Indiana University Press, 1994), 319.

9. Ibid., 320.

10. Olga Lengyel, *Five Chimneys: The Story of Auschwitz* (New York: Howard Fertig, 1983; first published 1947), 40.

11. Ruth [Huppert] Elias, *Triumph of Hope: From Theresienstadt and Auschwitz to Israel*, trans. Margot Bettauer Dembo, published in association with the U.S. Holocaust Memorial Museum (New York: Wiley, 1999), 147–51.

12. Grese statement, *TJK*, 711.

13. Grese testimony, 16 October 1945, *TJK*, 251.

14. Grese statement, 711.

15. Donald L. Niewyk, ed., *Fresh Wounds: Early Narratives of Holocaust Survival* (Chapel Hill and London: University of North Carolina Press, 1998), 67.

16. Ibid., 68.

17. Kopper statement, *TJK*, 705–6.

18. "Defendants Lose Impassivity" and "Belsen Woman Guard Weeps, Denies Guilt," *New York Times* (hereafter *NYT*), September 20 and October 17, 1945, respectively.

19. Grese statement, 711.

20. Ibid., 712.

21. "Belsen Woman Guard Weeps."

22. Opening Speech for the Defendants Grese, Lothe, Lohbauer and Klippel, October 16, 1945, *TJK*, 244.

23. Deborah E. Lipstadt, *Denying the Holocaust: The Growing Assault on Truth and Memory* (New York: Free Press, 1993), 50.

24. "Wife Says Kramer Knew He Did Wrong," *NYT*, October 11, 1945, 4.

25. Closing Speech for the Prosecution, November 13, 1945, *TJK*, 599.

26. Gerald L. Posner and John Ware, *Mengele: The Complete Story*, with a new introduction by Michael Berenbaum (New York: Cooper Square Press, 2000, first published in 1985), 68–69.

27. Ibid., 65.

28. Ibid., 66.

29. Telford Taylor, *The Anatomy of the Nuremberg Trials: A Personal Memoir* (Boston: Little, Brown, 1992), 301.

30. Hermann Langbein, *People in Auschwitz*, trans. Harry Zohn, published in association with the U.S. Holocaust Memorial Museum (Chapel Hill and London: University of North Carolina Press, 2004), 332.

31. Rebecca Wittmann, *Beyond Justice: The Auschwitz Trial* (Cambridge, Mass. and London: Harvard University Press, 2005), 137.

32. Langbein, *People*, 178.

33. Ibid., 388.

34. The episode is recounted in Wittmann, 88.

35. Langbein, *People*, 507.

36. Ibid., 508.

37. Ibid., 507.

38. Wittmann, 3.

39. Langbein, *People*, 514.

40. Ibid., 509.

CHAPTER 4: A LIBERATION OF CONTRASTS

1. This account of the family's rescue is in U.S. Holocaust Memorial Council, ed., *Fifty Years Ago: Revolt amid the Darkness. Days of Remembrance, April 18–25, 1993* (Washington, D.C.: U.S. Government Printing Office, 1993), 251–53.

2. Ulrich Herbert, *Best. Biographische Studien über Radikalismus Weltanschauung und Vernunft, 1903–1989* (Bonn: Verlag J. H. W. Dietz, 1996), 370.

3. Peter Longerich, *Holocaust: Nazi Persecution and Murder of the Jews* (New York: Oxford University Press, 2010), 399.

4. "Sweden Offers Aid to Denmark's Jews," *New York Times*, October 3, 1943, 3.

5. Herbert, *Best*, 321.

6. Ibid., 362.

7. Longerich, 398.

8. Ibid.

9. Herbert, *Best*, 359.

10. Longerich, 399.

11. Herbert, *Best*, 369.

12. Ibid., 364.

13. Longerich, 400.

14. Kevin Mahoney, ed., *1945: The Year of Liberation* (Washington, D.C.: U.S. Holocaust Memorial Museum, 1995), 125.

15. Ibid.

16. Sington testimony, September 19, 1945, *Trial of Josef Kramer and Forty-Four Others (The Belsen Trial)*, ed. Raymond Phillips (hereafter *TJK*; London: William Hodge, 1949), 47.

17. Leversen to Jewish Committee for Relief Abroad (London), May 6, 1945, Jews in Germany, General (Relief Workers' Reports), Doc. Ref. No. HA6A-1/9, Wiener Library, London, Gale Digital Collections (Post-War Europe: Refugees, Exile and Resettlement, 1945–1950, http://www.tlemea.com/postwareurope/index.htm.

18. Sington testimony, 47–48.

19. Ibid., 49.

20. Ibid.

21. Kramer testimony, October 8, 1945, *TJK*, 157. For the exchanges recounted in the next several paragraphs, between Kramer and his counsel and the prosecution, see pp. 173–82.

22. Deborah E. Lipstadt, *Denying the Holocaust: The Growing Assault on Truth and Memory* (New York: Free Press, 1993), 50.

23. Indictment, *TJK*, 4–5.

24. Donald Bloxham, *Genocide on Trial: War Crimes Trials and the Formation of Holocaust History and Memory* (Oxford: Oxford University Press, 2001), 100–101.

25. See the discussion of the trial's press coverage in ibid., 97–100.

26. Herbert, *Best*, 400.

27. "Midday Situation Report, November 19, 1943," in *Hitler and His Generals: Military Conferences 1942–1943. The First Complete Stenographic Record of the Military Situation Conferences, Stalingrad to Berlin*, ed. Helmut Heiber and David M. Glantz (New York: Enigma, 2003), 300.

28. Herbert, *Best*, 388.
29. Ibid., 410.
30. Ibid., 410–12.

CHAPTER 5: SOVIET "LIBERATORS"

1. Maria Epstein, "Memoirs 1940–1980," 34, RG-02 (Survivor Testimonies), 132, U.S. Holocaust Memorial Museum Archives, Washington, D.C., 34.
2. Ibid., 35.
3. Ibid., 18.
4. Ibid.
5. Vasily Grossman, *A Writer at War: Vasily Grossman with the Red Army, 1941–1945*, ed. and trans. Antony Beevor and Luba Vinogradova (New York: Pantheon, 2005), 208. Apparently the reference is to the *SS* experimenting with a new poison.
6. Ibid., 249–50.
7. Ibid., 251.
8. Ibid., 281.
9. Nikita S. Khrushchev, *Khrushchev Remembers*, with introduction, commentary, and notes by Edward Crankshaw, trans. and ed. Strobe Talbott (Boston: Little, Brown, 1970), 263.
10. Arno Lustiger, *Stalin and the Jews: The Red Book: The Tragedy of the Jewish Anti-Fascist Committee and the Soviet Jews*, trans. Mary Beth Friedrich and Todd Bludeau (New York: Enigma, 2003), 161.
11. Ibid., 168–69.
12. Zvi Gitelman, *Bitter Legacy: Confronting the Holocaust in the Soviet Union* (Bloomington: Indiana University Press, 1997).
13. Richard Overy, *Russia's War* (New York: Penguin, 1997), 309.
14. This quote and others used subsequently are from the report, which is reprinted in Kevin Mahoney, ed., *1945: The Year of Liberation* (Washington, D.C.: U.S. Holocaust Memorial Museum, 1995), 41–48.
15. Alexander Victor Prusin, "'Fascist Criminals to the Gallows!': The Holocaust and Soviet War Crimes Trials, December 1945–February 1946," *Holocaust and Genocide Studies* 17, no. 1 (Spring 2003): 7–9.
16. Raul Hilberg, *The Destruction of the European Jews*, rev. and definitive ed., 3 vols. (New York and London: Holmes & Meier, 1985), 1:296–97, 361n75.
17. Peter Longerich, *Holocaust: Nazi Persecution and Murder of the Jews* (New York: Oxford University Press, 2010), 296–97.
18. "Interrogation of Friedrich Jeckeln," December 14, 1945, Nizkor Project, Shofar FTP Archive File: people//j/jeckeln.friedrich/jeckeln-interrogation.1245.
19. Prusin, 11.
20. Timothy R. Vogt, *Denazification in Soviet-Occupied Germany: Brandenburg, 1945–1948* (Cambridge, Mass. and London: Harvard University Press, 2000), 42–43.
21. Ibid., 64.
22. Ibid., 88.
23. Alexander von Plato, "Zur Geschichte des sowjetischen Speziallagersystems in Deutschland. Einführung," in *Sowjetische Speziallager in Deutschland 1945 bis 1950*,

ed. Sergei Mironenko, Lutz Niethammer, and Alexander von Plato, in collaboration with Volkhard Knigge and Günter Morsch, 2 vols. (Berlin: Akademie Verlag, 1998), 1:24, 35.

24. Adalbert Rückerl, ed., *The Investigation of Nazi Crimes, 1945–1978: A Documentation*, trans. Derek Rutter (Hamden, Conn.: Archon Books, 1980), 72.

25. Rebecca Wittmann, *Beyond Justice: The Auschwitz Trial* (Cambridge, Mass. and London: Harvard University Press, 2005), 15.

26. Hilberg, 3:942.

27. Ibid., 3:943.

28. "A Jewish Woman-Doctor in the Clauberg-Block," 1943–45, Eyewitness Accounts, The 'Final Solution' (September 1939–1945), Doc. Ref. No. 054-EA-1006, Wiener Library, London Reference: P.III.h.No. 1061 (Auschwitz), Gale Digital Collections (Testaments to the Holocaust), http://www.tlemea.com/testaments/index.htm.

29. "Testimony in the Criminal Proceedings against the Late Prof. Carl Clauberg," 1941–43, Eyewitness Accounts, The 'Final Solution' (September 1939–1945), Doc. Ref. No. 054-EA-0979, Wiener Library, London Reference: P.III.h.No.870 (Auschwitz), Gale Digital Collections (Testaments to the Holocaust), http://www.tlemea.com/testaments/index.htm.

30. Robert J. Lifton, *The Nazi Doctors: Medical Killing and the Psychology of Genocide* (New York: Basic Books, 1986), 277.

31. Ibid.

CHAPTER 6: IN THE CUSTODY OF LENIENCY

1. Gitta Sereny, *Into That Darkness: From Mercy Killing to Mass Murder* (New York: McGraw-Hill, 1974), 249.

2. Ibid.

3. Ibid., 261.

4. Ibid., 262.

5. Frau Stangl's encounter with the drunken *SS* man, Ludwig, and with her husband is in ibid., 135–37.

6. Ibid., 264.

7. Leonard Mosley, *The Reich Marshal: A Biography of Hermann Goering* (Garden City, N.Y.: Doubleday, 1974), 322–23.

8. Leon Goldensohn, *The Nuremberg Interviews: Conducted by Leon Goldensohn*, ed. and introduced by Robert Gellately (New York: Knopf, 2004), 116–17.

9. Ibid., 113.

10. J. Noakes and G. Pridham, eds., *Nazism, 1919–1945: A Documentary Reader*, 3 vols. (Exeter, UK: University of Exeter Press, 1982–1988), 3:1104.

11. Edward B. Westermann, *Hitler's Police Battalions: Enforcing Racial War in the East* (Lawrence: University Press of Kansas, 2005), 145.

12. Peter Longerich, *Holocaust: Nazi Persecution and Murder of the Jews* (New York: Oxford University Press, 2010), 203.

13. Richard Breitman, *The Architect of Genocide: Himmler and the Final Solution* (New York: Knopf, 1991), 190–91.

14. Goldensohn, 277.

15. Ibid., 278.

16. Caron Cadle, "Kurt Daluege—Der Prototyp des loyalen Nationalsozialisten," in *Die Braune Elite 2: 21 weitere biographische Skizzen*, ed. Ronald Smelser, Enrico Syring, and Rainer Zitelmann (Darmstadt: Wissenschaftliche Buchgesellschaft, 1999), 78–79.
17. Sereny, 264.
18. Ibid., 265.
19. Quoted in Alan Levy, *Nazi Hunter: The Wiesenthal File* (New York: Carroll & Graf, 2002, first published 1993), 359.
20. Sereny, 267.
21. Ibid., 271–72.
22. Ibid., 273.
23. Jochen von Lang, *Top Nazi SS General Karl Wolff: The Man between Hitler and Himmler* (New York: Enigma Books, 2005), viii.
24. See "'. . . a "Delousing Van" . . . ': Euphemism for Murder," April 11, 1942, Holocaust History Project, http://www.holocaust-history.org/19420411-turner-wolff.
25. The exchange of correspondence is in von Lang, 189–90.
26. Ibid., 318.
27. Deborah E. Lipstadt, *Denying the Holocaust: The Growing Assault on Truth and Memory* (New York: Free Press, 1993), 49.
28. Donald Bloxham, *Genocide on Trial: War Crimes Trials and the Formation of Holocaust History and Memory* (Oxford: Oxford University Press, 2001), 195.
29. Von Lang, 321, 328.
30. Ibid., 337.
31. Breitman, *Architect*, 8.
32. Ibid.
33. Ibid., 9.
34. Ibid., 7.
35. Hannah Arendt, *Eichmann in Jerusalem: A Report on the Banality of Evil* (New York: Viking, 1963), 94.
36. See Breitman's book of that title.
37. Sereny, 273.
38. Robert S. Wistrich, *Who's Who in Nazi Germany* (New York: Macmillan, 1982), 330.
39. Sereny, 275.
40. Michael Phayer, *The Catholic Church and the Holocaust, 1930–1965* (Bloomington: Indiana University Press, 2000), 168.
41. Ibid.
42. Sereny, 289–91.
43. Ibid., 290.

CHAPTER 7: NUREMBERG, NUMBER TWO, AND THE SUBSTITUTE

1. Ulrich Herbert, *Best. Biographische Studien über Radikalismus Weltanschauung und Vernunft, 1903–1989* (Bonn: Verlag J. H. W. Dietz, 1996), 414.
2. Ibid.

3. "Testimony of Werner Best, July 31, 1946," in *Trial of the Major War Criminals before the International Military Tribunal (Nuremberg, 14 November 1945–1 October 1946),* 42 vols. (hereafter *TMWC*; Nuremberg, n.p., 1949), 20:133.

4. Ibid., 20:135–36.

5. Ibid., 20:138.

6. Ibid., 20:153.

7. Ibid., 22:177.

8. Herbert, *Best*, 417–18.

9. Robert S. Wistrich, *Who's Who in Nazi Germany* (New York: Macmillan, 1982), 226.

10. "Testimony of Otto Ohlendorf, January 3, 1946," *TMWC*, 4:316–18.

11. Ibid., 4:318–19.

12. Ibid., 4:319–20.

13. Ibid., 4:322.

14. Ibid., 4:337.

15. Ibid., 4:353–54.

16. Ibid., 4:333.

17. Joseph Goebbels, *The Goebbels Diaries, 1942–43*, ed. and trans. Louis P. Lochner (Garden City, N.Y.: Doubleday, 1948), 266, the entry for March 2, 1943.

18. G. M. Gilbert, *Nuremberg Diary* (New York: Da Capo Press, 1995, first published 1947), 4.

19. Deborah E. Lipstadt, *Denying the Holocaust: The Growing Assault on Truth and Memory* (New York: Free Press, 1993), 45.

20. Gilbert, *Nuremberg Diary*, 101.

21. Leonard Mosley, *The Reich Marshal: A Biography of Hermann Goering* (Garden City, N.Y.: Doubleday, 1974), 342–43.

22. "Testimony of Hermann Göring, March 18, 1946," *TMWC*, 9:441.

23. "Testimony of Hermann Göring, March 21, 1946," *TMWC*, 9:619.

24. Mosley, 343.

25. Ibid.

26. "Testimony of Hermann Göring, March 19–20, 1946," *TMWC*, 9:507–9.

27. "Testimony of Hermann Göring, March 20, 1946," *TMWC*, 9:515.

28. Ibid., 9:519–20.

29. Ibid., 9:538.

30. Mosley, 344.

31. Brian K. Feltman, "Legitimizing Justice: The American Press and the International Military Tribunal, 1945–1946," *The Historian* 66, no. 2 (Summer 2004): 310.

32. Gilbert, *Nuremberg Diary*, 206.

33. "Testimony of Hermann Göring, March 21, 1946," *TMWC*, 9:617–19.

34. Ibid., 9:646.

35. Ibid.

36. Gilbert, *Nuremberg Diary*, 208.

37. See James Donovan's introduction of the film, November 29, 1945, *TMWC*, 2:431–32.

38. Gilbert, *Nuremberg Diary*, 49.

39. Peter R. Black, *Ernst Kaltenbrunner: Ideological Soldier of the Third Reich* (Princeton, N.J.: Princeton University Press, 1984), 258.

40. Gilbert, *Nuremberg Diary*, 5.

41. Leon Goldensohn, *The Nuremberg Interviews: Conducted by Leon Goldensohn*, ed. and introduced by Robert Gellately (New York: Knopf, 2004), 140.

42. Leni Yahil, *The Holocaust: The Fate of European Jewry*, trans. Ina Friedman and Haya Galai (New York and Oxford: Oxford University Press, 1990), 650.

43. Telford Taylor, *The Anatomy of the Nuremberg Trials: A Personal Memoir* (Boston: Little, Brown, 1992), 360.

44. Gilbert, *Nuremberg Diary*, 255.

45. "Testimony of Ernst Kaltenbrunner, April 11, 1946," *TMWC*, 11:241, 269.

46. Ibid., 11:274–76.

47. Black, 150.

48. The affidavit is in "Testimony of Ernst Kaltenbrunner, April 12, 1946," *TMWC*, 11:318–19, 324–25.

49. Joshua M. Greene, *Justice at Dachau: The Trials of an American Prosecutor* (New York: Broadway Books, 2003), 141–42.

50. See the affidavit in "Testimony of Ernst Kaltenbrunner, April 12, 1946," *TMWC*, 11:331.

51. Ibid., 11:332, 335.

52. Affidavit of Alois Höllriegel, November 7, 1945, Doc. 2753-PS, International Military Trials, Office of U.S. Chief of Counsel for Prosecution of Axis Criminality, *Nazi Conspiracy and Aggression* (hereafter *NCA*), 8 vols. 12 pts. (Washington, D.C.: U.S. Government Printing Office, 1946), 5:393.

53. "Testimony of Ernst Kaltenbrunner, April 12, 1946," *TMWC*, 11:338–39.

54. "Testimony of Rudolf Höß, April 15, 1946," *TMWC*, 11:415, 416.

55. "Testimony of Dieter Wisliceny, January 3, 1946," *TMWC*, 4:359.

56. Black, 149, 150.

57. Ibid., 150–51.

58. Ibid., 151, 173–74.

59. Ibid., 152.

60. Ibid., 157–58.

61. Kaltenbrunner (Chief of Security Police and Security Service) to Mayor of Vienna (Blaschke), 30 June 1944, Doc. 3803-PS, *NCA*, 6:738.

62. Raul Hilberg, *The Destruction of the European Jews*, rev. and definitive ed., 3 vols. (New York and London: Holmes & Meier, 1985), 2:847.

63. Gilbert, *Nuremberg Diary*, 255, 261.

64. Black, 271.

65. Herbert, *Best*, 419, 420.

66. Ibid., 421.

CHAPTER 8: NUREMBERG: "KING FRANK"

1. Gerhard L. Weinberg, *A World at Arms: A Global History of World War II* (Cambridge and New York: Cambridge University Press, 1994), 898–99.

2. Hans Frank, *Im Angesicht des Galgens*, 2nd ed. (Neuhaus bei Schliersee: Eigenverlag Brigitte Frank, 1955), 40, 331.

3. Ian Kershaw, *Hitler 1889–1936: Hubris*, paperback ed. (New York and London: Norton, 2000), 8.

4. Martyn Housden, *Hans Frank: Lebensraum and the Holocaust* (London: Palgrave, 2003), 4.

5. Ibid., 85.

6. Ibid., 1.

7. Peter Longerich, *Holocaust: Nazi Persecution and Murder of the Jews* (New York: Oxford University Press, 2010), 157.

8. Christopher R. Browning, with contributions by Jürgen Matthäus, *The Origins of the Final Solution: The Evolution of Nazi Jewish Policy, September 1939–March 1942* (Lincoln and Jerusalem: University of Nebraska Press and Yad Vashem, 2004), 45.

9. Longerich, 172.

10. Ibid., 175.

11. Ibid., 176.

12. Browning, *Origins*, 360.

13. Ibid., 360–61.

14. Longerich, 293.

15. Frank Diary, 1941 Oct.–Dec. Cabinet Session, Tuesday 16 December 1941 in the Government Building at Krakow, Speech of the Governor General Closing the Session, Doc. 2233-D, International Military Trials, Office of U.S. Chief of Counsel for Prosecution of Axis Criminality, *Nazi Conspiracy and Aggression* (hereafter *NCA*), 8 vols. 12 pts. (Washington, D.C.: U.S. Government Printing Office, 1946), 4:891–92.

16. Longerich, 308, 309.

17. Browning, *Origins*, 409.

18. Longerich, 309.

19. Ibid., 338–39.

20. Frank Diary, Conference Volume, Cabinet session in Cracow on 24 August 1942, Subject: A new plan for seizure and for food [Ernaehrung] of the General Gouvernement, Doc. 2233-E-PS, *NCA*, 4:900.

21. Frank Diary, Official Meetings, 1943, Warsaw, 25 January 1943, Present: Dr. Hans Frank and others, Doc. 2233-AA-PS, *NCA*, 4:916–17.

22. Joseph Goebbels, *The Goebbels Diaries, 1942–43*, ed. and trans. Louis P. Lochner (Garden City, N.Y.: Doubleday, 1948), 283–84, the entry for March 9, 1943.

23. Housden, 146.

24. Ibid., 184.

25. Frank Diary, 1944. Loose Leaf Volume covering period from 1 January 1944 to 28 February 1944—speech delivered by Hans Frank in Berlin 25 January 1944 before the Representatives of the German Press, Doc. 2233-F-PS, *NCA*, 4:902.

26. Housden, 152.

27. Ibid., 217–18.

28. Leon Goldensohn, *The Nuremberg Interviews: Conducted by Leon Goldensohn*, ed. and introduced by Robert Gellately (New York: Knopf, 2004), 19.

29. Robert E. Conot, *Justice at Nuremberg: The First Comprehensive Dramatic Account of the Trial of the Nazi Leaders* (New York: Harper & Row, 1983), 79.

30. G. M. Gilbert, *Nuremberg Diary* (New York: Da Capo Press, 1995, first published 1947), 5.

31. See Donovan's presentation of the film on December 13, 1946 in *Trial of the Major War Criminals before the International Military Tribunal (Nuremberg, 14 November 1945–1 October 1946)* (hereafter *TMWC*), 42 vols. (Nuremberg, n.p., 1949), 3:536.

32. Walsh's presentation is in ibid., 3:537–39.

33. Ibid., 3:551, 569.

34. Ibid., 3:569.

35. Gilbert, *Nuremberg Diary*, 69.

36. See Baldwin's presentation, January 10, 1946, *TMWC*, 5:78.

37. Ibid., 5:79.

38. Ibid., 5:89, 90.

39. Housden, 227.

40. "Testimony of Hans Frank, April 18, 1946," *TMWC*, 12:13.

41. Telford Taylor, *The Anatomy of the Nuremberg Trials: A Personal Memoir* (Boston: Little, Brown, 1992), 370.

42. The exchange is in "Testimony of Hans Frank, April 18, 1946," *TMWC*, 12:33–35.

43. Gilbert, *Nuremberg Diary*, 265.

44. Frank, *Im Angesicht des Galgens*, 409, 331.

45. Ibid., 411.

46. Niklas Frank, *In the Shadow of the Reich*, trans. Arthur S. Wensinger with Carole Clew-Hoey (New York: Knopf, 1991), 1, 21.

CHAPTER 9: NUREMBERG: "FRED" THE "ENDOWED SEER" AND VERDICTS AND SENTENCES

1. Alfred Rosenberg, *Memoirs of Alfred Rosenberg*, with commentaries by Serge Lang and Ernst von Schenck, trans. Eric Posselt (Chicago: Ziff-Davis, 1949), 299.

2. Eugene Davidson, *The Trial of the Germans: An Account of the Twenty-Two Defendants before the International Military Tribunal at Nuremberg* (New York: Collier, 1966), 126.

3. Rosenberg, 30.

4. Ibid., 10.

5. Ibid., 171.

6. Christopher R. Browning, with contributions by Jürgen Matthäus, *The Origins of the Final Solution: The Evolution of Nazi Jewish Policy, September 1939–March 1942* (Lincoln and Jerusalem: University of Nebraska Press and Yad Vashem, 2004), 236.

7. Ibid., 284.

8. "Testimony of Alfred Rosenberg, April 17, 1946," *Trial of the Major War Criminals before the International Military Tribunal (Nuremberg, 14 November 1945–1 October 1946)* (hereafter *TMWC*), 42 vols. (Nuremberg, n.p., 1949), 11:549–51.

9. Peter Longerich, *Holocaust: Nazi Persecution and Murder of the Jews* (New York: Oxford University Press, 2010), 212.

10. Ibid., 293.

11. Browning, *Origins*, 403.

12. Ibid.

13. Max Domarus, ed., *Hitler: Speeches and Proclamations, 1932–1945*, trans. Chris Wilcox and Mary Fran Gilbert, 4 vols. (Wauconda, Ill.: Bolchazy-Carducci, 1992–2004), 3:1449.

14. Top secret memorandum, "About Discussions [of Rosenberg] with the Fuehrer on 14 December 1941," Doc. 1517-PS, International Military Trials, Office of U.S. Chief of Counsel for Prosecution of Axis Criminality, *Nazi Conspiracy and Aggression*, 8 vols. 12 pts. (Washington, D.C.: U.S. Government Printing Office, 1946), 4:55–56.

15. Longerich, 297–98.

16. Rosenberg, 294.

17. Ibid., 297.

18. G. M. Gilbert, *Nuremberg Diary* (New York: Da Capo Press, 1995, first published 1947), 5.

19. Leon Goldensohn, *The Nuremberg Interviews: Conducted by Leon Goldensohn*, ed. and introduced by Robert Gellately (New York: Knopf, 2004), 197–99.

20. "Testimony of Alfred Rosenberg, April 15–16, 1946," *TMWC*, 11:454, 458, 485, 486.

21. Ernst Piper, *Alfred Rosenberg, Hitlers Chefideologe* (Munich: Karl Blessing Verlag, 2005), 624–25.

22. Ibid., 624.

23. "Testimony of Alfred Rosenberg, April 16, 1946," *TMWC*, 11:514–15.

24. Ibid., 11:468.

25. This lengthy exchange is in ibid., 11:552–55.

26. The exchange is in ibid., 11:556–62.

27. Deborah E. Lipstadt, *Denying the Holocaust: The Growing Assault on Truth and Memory* (New York: Free Press, 1993), 42.

28. Rosenberg, 112.

29. Ibid., 112, 113.

30. Ibid., ix.

31 The final words of Göring, Kaltenbrunner, Rosenberg, and Frank are in *TMWC*, 22:366–68, 378–85.

32. See the judgments against the four, October 1, 1946, in *TMWC*, 22:524–27, 536–38, 539–41, 541–44.

33. Gilbert, *Nuremberg Diary*, 431–32.

34. See "Judgment, September 30, 1946," *TMWC*, 22:411–523; and the section "Persecution of the Jews," 491–96.

35. Tony Judt, *Postwar: A History of Europe since 1945* (New York: Penguin, 2006), 805.

36. Donald Bloxham, *Genocide on Trial: War Crimes Trials and the Formation of Holocaust History and Memory* (Oxford: Oxford University Press, 2001), chapter 2.

37. Ibid., 65–66.

38. Much of the foregoing, describing Göring's suicide, is based on the account in Leonard Mosley, *The Reich Marshal: A Biography of Hermann Goering* (Garden City, N.Y.: Doubleday, 1974), 352–57, which used an official report issued by the Allied Control Council (that administered postwar occupied Germany) that reconstructed the former *Reichsmarschall*'s final hours.

39. Telford Taylor, *The Anatomy of the Nuremberg Trials: A Personal Memoir* (Boston: Little, Brown, 1992), 621–24.

40. Ann Tusa and John Tusa, *The Nuremberg Trial* (New York and Lanham, Md.: Cooper Square Press, 2003, first published 1983), 487.

41. The executions are described in Taylor, 610–11.

CHAPTER 10: POLAND: OCCASIONAL TRIALS AMID A CONTINUING HOLOCAUST

1. Anna Cichopek, "The Cracow Pogrom of August 1945," in *Contested Memories: Poles and Jews during the Holocaust and Its Aftermath*, ed. Joshua D. Zimmerman (New Brunswick, N.J. and London: Rutgers University Press, 2003), 233–34.

2. Jan T. Gross, *Fear: Anti-Semitism in Poland after Auschwitz* (New York: Random House, 2006), xiv.

3. Victor Klemperer, *The Lesser Evil: The Diaries of Victor Klemperer, 1945–59*, trans. Martin Chalmers (London: Phoenix, 2004), 387, entry for May 5, 1952.

4. Gladwin Hill, "Flight of Few Jews Left Is in View as Polish Anti-Semitism Strikes," *New York Times* (hereafter *NYT*), October 27, 1945, 6.

5. Raul Hilberg, *The Destruction of the European Jews*, rev. and definitive ed., 3 vols. (New York and London: Holmes & Meier, 1985), 2:399–400.

6. "Trial of Gauleiter Artur Greiser," June 21–July 7, 1946, Case no. 74, ed. United Nations War Crimes Commission, *Law Reports of Trials of War Criminals* (hereafter *LRTWC*), 14 vols. (London: His Majesty's Stationery Office, 1949), 13:105.

7. Ibid., 13:90.

8. Ibid., 13:94–95.

9. Ibid., 13:104–6.

10. Peter Longerich, *Holocaust: Nazi Persecution and Murder of the Jews* (New York: Oxford University Press, 2010), 291.

11. Ernst Klee, Willi Dressen, and Volker Riess, eds., *"The Good Old Days": The Holocaust as Seen by Its Perpetrators and Bystanders*, trans. Deborah Burnstone, foreword by Hugh Trevor-Roper (New York: Konecky and Konecky, 1991), 218–19, 222–23.

12. "Trial of Gauleiter Artur Greiser," 13:102.

13. "15,000 Poles Watch Greiser Execution," *NYT*, July 22, 1946, 1.

14. "Pope Asked Poles to Spare Greiser," *NYT*, July 23, 1946, 12.

15. Gross, *Fear*, 35.

16. Ibid., 87.

17. Ibid., 90.

18. Quoted in ibid., 91.

19. Yitzhak ("Antek") Zuckerman, *A Surplus of Memory: Chronicle of the Warsaw Ghetto Uprising*, ed. and trans. Barbara Harshav (Berkeley and Los Angeles: University of California Press, 1993), 662.

20. Quoted in Gross, *Fear*, 145.

21. "Trial of Hauptsturmführer Amon Leopold Goeth, September 2–5, 1946," Case no. 37, *LRTWC*, 7:4.

22. Ibid., 7:3.

23. Ibid.

24. Ibid., 7:1.

25. Ibid., 7:4.

26. "Trial of Obersturmbannführer Rudolf Franz Ferdinand Hoess, March 11–29, 1947," Case no. 38, *LRTWC,* 7:12.

27. Aleksander Lasik, "Rudolf Höss—Manager of Crime," in *Anatomy of the Auschwitz Death Camp*, ed. Yisrael Gutman and Michael Berenbaum, published in association with the U.S. Holocaust Memorial Museum (Bloomington and Indianapolis: Indiana University Press, 1994), 296.

28. "Testimony of Rudolf Höß, April 15, 1946," *Trial of the Major War Criminals before the International Military Tribunal (Nuremberg, 14 November 1945–1 October 1946),* 42 vols. (Nuremberg, n.p., 1949), 11:415, 416.

29. Ibid., 11:417.

30. Ibid., 11:416–17.

31. Gilbert, *Nuremberg Diary*, 250–51.

32. Ibid., 267–69.

33. Ibid., 260, 269.

34. "Trial of Obersturmbannführer Rudolf Franz Ferdinand Hoess," 7:17.

35. Rudolf Höß, *Death Dealer: The Memoirs of the SS Kommandant at Auschwitz*, ed. Steven Paskuly, trans. Andrew Pollinger, new foreword by Primo Levi (New York: Da Capo Press, 1996), 27.

36. Ibid., 7.

37. Ibid., 197.

38. Ibid., 164.

39. Ibid., 6.

40. Aleksander Lasik, "Postwar Prosecution of the Auschwitz SS," in *Anatomy of the Auschwitz Death Camp*, ed. Yisrael Gutman and Michael Berenbaum, published in association with the U.S. Holocaust Memorial Museum (Bloomington and Indianapolis: Indiana University Press, 1994), 589.

CHAPTER 11: MEMORY IN WEST GERMANY: LONG AND SHORT

1. Victor Klemperer, *I Will Bear Witness: A Diary of the Nazi Years*, trans. Martin Chalmers, 2 vols. (New York: Random House, 1999), 2:473, entry for May 4, 1945.

2. Ibid., 2:478, entry for May 11, 1945.

3. Ibid., 2:493, entry for May 25, 1945.

4. Ibid., 2:28, entry for March 16, 1942.

5. Ibid., 2:41, entry for April 19, 1942.

6. Ibid., 2:155, 156, entries for October 17 and 23, 1942.

7. Alan Levy, *Nazi Hunter: The Wiesenthal File* (New York: Carroll & Graf, 2002, first published 1993), 71.

8. Ibid., 72.

9. Ibid., 74, 75.

10. Katharina von Kellenbach, "Vanishing Acts: Perpetrators in Postwar Germany," *Holocaust and Genocide Studies* 17, no. 2 (Fall 2003): 305.

11. Ibid., 305, 306.

12. Ibid., 307.

13. Ibid., 307–8.

14. Ibid., 308.
15. Ibid., 320.
16. Ibid., 308–11.
17. Michael Thad Allen, "Realms of Oblivion: The Vienna Auschwitz Trial," *Central European History* 40, no. 3 (September 2007): 403.
18. Von Kellenbach, 311, 312.
19. Ibid., 314, 319, 320.

CHAPTER 12: PSEUDO-PURGES AND POLITICS

1. Hans Frankenthal, in collaboration with Andreas Plake, Babette Quinkert, and Florian Schmaltz, *The Unwelcome One: Returning Home from Auschwitz*, trans. John A. Broadwin (Evanston, Ill.: Northwestern University Press, 2002), 82–84.
2. Much of this section is based on Raul Hilberg, *The Destruction of the European Jews*, rev. and definitive ed., 3 vols. (New York and London: Holmes & Meier, 1985), 3:1081–86.
3. Eric A. Johnson, *Nazi Terror: The Gestapo, Jews, and Ordinary Germans* (New York: Basic Books, 2000), 75–77, 463–67.
4. Ibid., 478.
5. Ibid., 482.
6. Tom Bower, *Blind Eye to Murder: Britain, America and the Purging of Nazi Germany—A Pledge Betrayed* (London: Granada, 1983), 2.
7. Harold James, *The Deutsche Bank and the Nazi Economic War against the Jews: The Expropriation of Jewish-Owned Property* (Cambridge and New York: Cambridge University Press, 2001), 64.
8. Ibid., 213.
9. Ibid., 98.
10. Ibid., 90.
11. Ibid., 132, 216.
12. Ibid., 154.
13. Bower, 5.
14. James, 216–17.
15. Bower, 1–2, 13–14.
16. Ibid., 14–15.
17. Ibid., 403.
18. James, 89–90, 102–4, 217.
19. Bower, 403.
20. "German Bank Linked to Death Camp," February 5, 1999, BBC News, http://news.bbc.co.uk/2/hi/europe/272860.stm.
21. Manfred Pohl, "Abs und Auschwitz," *Die Zeit*, November 2, 1999.
22. "Deutsche Bank Denies Hiding Nazi Deals," February 6, 1999, CNN.com, http://www.cnn.com/WORLD/europe/9902/06/deutsche.bank.
23. Jonathan Petropoulos, *The Faustian Bargain: The Art World in Nazi Germany* (London and New York: Allen Lane/Penguin, 2000), 5.
24. Ibid., 286 n49.
25. Ibid., 33–36.

26. Ibid., 43.
27. Ibid., 49, 51.
28. Ibid., 49–50.

CHAPTER 13: OTHER TRIALS AND AMNESTY

1. Ulrich Herbert, *Best. Biographische Studien über Radikalismus Weltanschauung und Vernunft, 1903–1989* (Bonn: Verlag J. H. W. Dietz, 1996), 421.
2. Ibid., 626 n40.
3. Ibid., 421.
4. Extracts from the Testimony of Defendant Ohlendorf, October 8–9 and 14–15, 1947, "The Einsatzgruppen Case," *Trials of War Criminals before the Nuernberg Military Tribunals under Control Council Law No. 10* (hereafter *TWC*), 15 vols. (Buffalo, N.Y.: William S. Hein, 1997, first published 1952), 4:291.
5. Ibid., 4:244–45.
6. Peter Longerich, *Holocaust: Nazi Persecution and Murder of the Jews* (New York: Oxford University Press, 2010), 188–89.
7. Ibid., 227.
8. Opening Statement for the Defendant Ohlendorf, October 6, 1947, "The Einsatzgruppen Case," *TWC*, 4:59 (defense counsel's italics).
9. Extracts from the Testimony of Defendant Ohlendorf, 4:356.
10. Ibid., 4:356–57.
11. Ibid., 4:355.
12. Ibid., 4:388, 390.
13. Nikolaus Wachsmann, *Hitler's Prisons: Legal Terror in Nazi Germany* (New Haven, Conn. and London: Yale University Press, 2004), 203–4 (Wachsmann's italics).
14. Raul Hilberg, *The Destruction of the European Jews*, rev. and definitive ed., 3 vols. (New York and London: Holmes & Meier, 1985), 2:403.
15. Schlegelberger to seven Nazi party and government agencies on "The Final Solution of the Jewish Problem," April 5, 1942, Doc. 4055-PS, "The Justice Case," *TWC*, 3:649.
16. Annegret Ehmann, "From Colonial Racism to Nazi Population Policy: The Role of the So-called Mischlinge," in *The Holocaust and History: The Known, the Unknown, the Disputed, and the Reexamined*, ed. Michael Berenbaum and Abraham J. Peck (Bloomington: Indiana University Press, 1998), 128.
17. Wachsmann, 214.
18. Opening Statement for Defendant Schlegelberger, "The Justice Case," *TWC*, 3:127.
19. Final Statements of the Defendants: Schlegelberger, "The Justice Case," *TWC*, 3:941.
20. Opinion and Judgment: Franz Schlegelberger, "The Justice Case," *TWC*, 3:1086.
21. Opinion and Judgment, "The Justice Case," *TWC*, 3:985.
22. Wachsmann, 344.
23. Herbert, *Best*, 423.
24. Ibid., 423, 425.
25. Ibid., 434.
26. Martin Gilbert, *The Holocaust: A History of the Jews of Europe during the Second World War* (New York: Holt, Rinehart and Winston, 1985), 615.

27. "Trial of Hanns Albin Rauter," May 4, 1948, Case no. 88, ed. United Nations War Crimes Commission, *Law Reports of Trials of War Criminals* (hereafter *LRTWC*), 14 vols. (London: His Majesty's Stationery Office, 1949), 14:93.

28. Ibid., 14:106–7.

29. Hilberg, 2:571.

30. Anne Frank, *The Diary of a Young Girl: The Definitive Edition*, ed. Otto H. Frank and Mirjam Pressler, trans. Susan Massotty (New York: Doubleday, 1995), 303, 304.

31. "Trial of Hanns Albin Rauter," 14:93.

32. Ibid., 14:94.

33. Ibid., 14:94–95.

34. Ibid., 14:106.

35. "France's Nuremberg," *NYT*, April 24, 1946, 7.

36. Johnpeter Horst Grill, *The Nazi Movement in Baden, 1920–1945* (Chapel Hill: University of North Carolina Press, 1983), 519.

37. Longerich, 172.

38. Ibid.

39. Grill, 518.

40. Wolfram Wette, *The Wehrmacht: History, Myth, Reality*, trans. Deborah Lucas Schneider (Cambridge, Mass.: Harvard University Press, 2006), 74.

41. Ibid., 75.

42. Ibid., 75–76.

43. Glenna Whitley, "In the Wolf's Mouth: SMU's Bryan Mark Rigg Uncovers the Story of Hitler's Jewish Soldiers," February 26, 2004, *Dallas Observer*, http://www.dallasobserver.com/2004-02-06/news/in-the-wolf-s-mouth/print.

44. "Testimony of Erich von Manstein, August 9, 1946," *Trial of the Major War Criminals before the International Military Tribunal (Nuremberg, 14 November 1945–1 October 1946)* (hereafter *TMWC*), 42 vols. (Nuremberg, n.p., 1949), 20:599.

45. "Testimony of Erich von Manstein, August 10, 1946," *TMWC*, 20:616–19.

46. Ibid., 633.

47. Telford Taylor, *The Anatomy of the Nuremberg Trials: A Personal Memoir* (Boston: Little, Brown, 1992), 519.

48. "Testimony of Erich von Manstein, August 10, 1946," *TMWC*, 20:639–42.

49. Taylor, 520.

50. Tom Bower, *Blind Eye to Murder: Britain, America and the Purging of Nazi Germany—A Pledge Betrayed* (London: Granada, 1983), 275.

51. Ibid., 288.

52. Donald Bloxham, *Genocide on Trial: War Crimes Trials and the Formation of Holocaust History and Memory* (Oxford: Oxford University Press, 2001), 166.

53. Bower, 293.

54. Ibid., 294.

55. Deborah E. Lipstadt, *Denying the Holocaust: The Growing Assault on Truth and Memory* (New York: Free Press, 1993), 52.

56. Bower, 295.

57. Ibid., 299.

58. Erich von Manstein, *Lost Victories*, ed. and trans. Anthony G. Powell, foreword by B. H. Liddell Hart (Chicago: Henry Regnery, 1958), 176.

59. Gerhard L. Weinberg, *Germany, Hitler & World War II: Essays in Modern German and World History* (Cambridge and New York: Cambridge University Press, 1995), 307.
60. Herbert, *Best*, 445.
61. Ibid., 446.
62. Ibid., 447.
63. Ibid., 458.
64. Ibid., 464–65.
65. Ibid., 465.

CHAPTER 14: EICHMANN, JERUSALEM, AND EICHMANN'S HENCHMEN

1. David Cesarani, *Becoming Eichmann: Rethinking the Life, Crimes, and Trial of a "Desk Murderer"* (New York: Da Capo Press, 2004), 81.
2. Ibid., 92.
3. Ibid., 154.
4. Ibid., 13.
5. Uki Goñi, *The Real Odessa: How Perón Brought the Nazi War Criminals to Argentina* (London and New York: Granta Books, 2002), 296.
6. Cesarani, 199.
7. Ibid., 202.
8. "Testimony of Dieter Wisliceny, January 3, 1946," *Trial of the Major War Criminals before the International Military Tribunal (Nuremberg, 14 November 1945–1 October 1946)*, 42 vols. (Nuremberg, n.p., 1949), 4:358–59.
9. Richard Overy, *Interrogations: The Nazi Elite in Allied Hands, 1945* (New York: Viking, 2001), 192.
10. Cesarani, 204.
11. Goñi, 299.
12. Ibid., 298.
13. Cesarani, 209.
14. Simon Wiesenthal, *Justice Not Vengeance*, trans. Ewald Osers (New York: Grove Weidenfeld, 1989), 74.
15. Cesarani, 215.
16. Wiesenthal, 76.
17. Ibid., 77.
18. Cesarani, 219.
19. Wiesenthal, 77.
20. Cesarani, 221.
21. Ibid., 231.
22. Ibid., 239–40.
23. Adolf Eichmann, *Eichmann Interrogated: Transcripts from the Archives of the Israeli Police*, ed. Jochen von Lang in collaboration with Claus Sibyll, trans. Ralph Manheim, introduction by Avner W. Less, new foreword by Michael Berenbaum (New York: Da Capo Press, 1999, first published 1983), xx.
24. Deborah E. Lipstadt, *The Eichmann Trial* (New York: Nextbook, Schocken, 2011), xi, xii.

25. Moshe Pearlman, *The Capture and Trial of Adolf Eichmann* (New York: Simon & Schuster, 1963), 88–89.

26. Peter Longerich, *Holocaust: Nazi Persecution and Murder of the Jews* (New York: Oxford University Press, 2010), 262–63.

27. Cesarani, 326.

28. Ibid., 237, 321.

29. Ibid., 321.

30. Wiesenthal, 78.

31. Hannah Arendt, *Eichmann in Jerusalem: A Report on the Banality of Evil* (New York: Viking, 1963).

32. Cesarani, 16, 329.

33. Deborah E. Lipstadt, *Denying the Holocaust: The Growing Assault on Truth and Memory* (New York: Free Press, 1993), 76.

34. Ibid., 133–34.

35. Lipstadt, *Eichmann Trial*, xviii.

36. Ibid., xix.

37. Mary Felstiner, "Alois Brunner: Eichmann's Best Tool," in *Simon Wiesenthal Center Annual* (White Plains, N.Y.: Kraus Publications, 1986), 3: 1–41.

38. Hans Safrian, *Die Eichmann-Männer* (Vienna/Zurich: Europaverlag, 1993), 15–16.

39. "Deportation of a Czechoslovakian Jewess to Theresienstadt," 1938–44, Eyewitness Accounts, The "Final Solution" (September 1939–1945), Doc. Ref. No. 059-EA-1330, Wiener Library, London Reference: P.III.h.No. 479 (Theresienstadt), Gale Digital Collections (Testaments to the Holocaust), http://www.tlemea.com/testaments/index.htm.

40. Safrian, 324.

41. Ibid.

42. Ibid.

43. Richard Breitman, with Norman J. W. Goda and Paul Brown, "The Gestapo," in *U.S. Intelligence and the Nazis*, ed. Richard Breitman, Norman J. W. Goda, Timothy Naftali, and Robert Wolfe (Washington, D.C.: National Archives Trust Fund, 2004), 161–62.

44. Ibid., 163.

45. Ibid., 164.

46. "Search Renewed for Nazi Fugitives," July 14, 2007, *The Tribune* (Ames, Iowa).

47. Wiesenthal, 233.

48. Cesarani, 122.

49. Safrian, 322–23.

50. "Franz Novak, 31 May 1961 [Examination of Witness]," Nizkor Project, Shofar FTP Archive File: people/e/eichmann.adolf/transcripts/Testimony-Abroad/Franz_Novak -01 and 02.

51. Michael Thad Allen, "Realms of Oblivion: The Vienna Auschwitz Trial," *Central European History* 40, no. 3 (September 2007): 404–5.

52. Ibid., 402.

53. Wikipedia in German, s.v. "Franz Novak," http://de.wikipedia.org/wiki/Franz_Novak.

54. Wiesenthal, 18.

55. Wikipedia, "Franz Novak."

56. Safrian, 331–32.

57. Ibid., 332.

58. Ibid.

CHAPTER 15: HUNTING THE COMFORTABLE

1. Gitta Sereny, *Into That Darkness: From Mercy Killing to Mass Murder* (New York: McGraw-Hill, 1974), 339.

2. Simon Wiesenthal, *Justice Not Vengeance*, trans. Ewald Osers (New York: Grove Weidenfeld, 1989), 82–83.

3. Sereny, 340–41.

4. Ibid., 342–44, 201.

5. Ibid., 347–48.

6. Ibid., 348.

7. Gerald L. Posner and John Ware, *Mengele: The Complete Story*, with a new introduction by Michael Berenbaum (New York: Cooper Square Press, 2000, first published in 1985), 90–91.

8. Uki Goñi, *The Real Odessa: How Perón Brought the Nazi War Criminals to Argentina* (London and New York: Granta Books, 2002), 279–80.

9. Posner and Ware, 113.

10. Ibid., 108.

11. Goñi, 291.

12. Posner and Ware, 30.

13. Ibid., 280.

14. Norman J. W. Goda, "Manhunts: The Official Search for Notorious Nazis," in *U.S. Intelligence and the Nazis*, ed. Richard Breitman, Norman J.W. Goda, Timothy Naftali, and Robert Wolfe (Washington, D.C.: National Archives Trust Fund, 2004), 431.

15. Posner and Ware, 291.

16. Sereny, 352.

17. Ibid., 363.

18. Ibid., 349.

19. Ibid., 351–52.

20. Wiesenthal, 84.

21. Alan Levy, *Nazi Hunter: The Wiesenthal File* (New York: Carroll & Graf, 2002, first published 1993), 369.

22. The encounter is in Wiesenthal, 84–85.

23. Goda, 426–27.

24. Ibid., 427.

25. Ibid., 428.

26. Ibid., 429.

27. Deborah E. Lipstadt, *Denying the Holocaust: The Growing Assault on Truth and Memory* (New York: Free Press, 1993), 11.

28. Levy, 373–74.

29. Ibid., 374.

30. Ibid., 375.

31. Sereny, 355.

32. Ibid., 356.

33. Levy, 376.

34. Wiesenthal, 86–87.

35. Sereny, 356.

CHAPTER 16: FOUR FACES LONG AFTER THE WAR: WHAT DIDN'T HAPPEN

1. Gitta Sereny, *Into That Darkness: From Mercy Killing to Mass Murder* (New York: McGraw-Hill, 1974), 117–18.
2. Ibid., 122.
3. Ibid., 130–31.
4. Ibid., 124.
5. Alan Levy, *Nazi Hunter: The Wiesenthal File* (New York: Carroll & Graf, 2002, first published 1993), 378.
6. Sereny, 47, 358, 360–62.
7. Ibid., 358–59.
8. Ibid., 130.
9. Quoted in Yitzhak Arad, *Belzec, Sobibor, Treblinka: The Operation Reinhard Death Camps* (Bloomington and Indianapolis: Indiana University Press, 1987), 191.
10. Robert S. Wistrich, *Who's Who in Nazi Germany* (New York: Macmillan, 1982), 330–31.
11. Sereny, 364–65.
12. Ulrich Herbert, *Best. Biographische Studien über Radikalismus Weltanschauung und Vernunft, 1903–1989* (Bonn: Verlag J. H. W. Dietz, 1996), 485–86.
13. Norbert Frei, *Adenauer's Germany and the Nazi Past: The Politics of Amnesty and Integration*, trans. Joel Golb (New York: Columbia University Press, 2002), 64.
14. Herbert, *Best*, 490.
15. Ibid., 503.
16. Ibid., 505–6.
17. Ibid., 513–15.
18. Adalbert Rückerl, ed., *The Investigation of Nazi Crimes, 1945–1978: A Documentation*, trans. Derek Rutter (Hamden, Conn.: Archon Books, 1980), 64.
19. Herbert, *Best*, 515.
20. Ibid., 517.
21. Ibid., 520–21.
22. Leon Goldensohn, *The Nuremberg Interviews: Conducted by Leon Goldensohn*, ed. and introduced by Robert Gellately (New York: Knopf, 2004), 272.
23. Ibid., 268–69.
24. "Testimony of Erich von dem Bach-Zelewski, January 7, 1946," *Trial of the Major War Criminals before the International Military Tribunal (Nuremberg, 14 November 1945–1 October 1946)*, 42 vols. (Nuremberg: n.p., 1949), 4:487, 490.
25. Ibid., 4:478.
26. Ibid., 4:476.
27. Ibid., 4:480.
28. G. M. Gilbert, *Nuremberg Diary* (New York: Da Capo Press, 1995, first published 1947), 114.
29. Raul Hilberg, *The Destruction of the European Jews*, rev. and definitive ed., 3 vols. (New York and London: Holmes & Meier, 1985), 3:1030–31.
30. Richard Breitman, *Official Secrets: What the Nazis Planned, What the British and Americans Knew* (New York: Hill & Wang, 1998), 223.

31. "Testimony of Erich von dem Bach-Zelewski, May 29, 1961," The Nizkor Project, Shofar FTP Archive File: people/e/eichmann.adolf/transcripts/Testimony-Abroad// Erich_Von_Dem_Bach_Zelewski-01-02.

32. Ibid.

33. Ibid.

34. Ibid.

35. Ibid.

36. Ibid.

37. Peter Longerich, *Holocaust: Nazi Persecution and Murder of the Jews* (New York: Oxford University Press, 2010), 198.

38. Richard Breitman, with Norman J. W. Goda and Paul Brown, "The Gestapo," in *U.S Intelligence and the Nazis*, ed. Richard Breitman, Norman J. W. Goda, Timothy Naftali, and Robert Wolfe (Washington, D.C.: National Archives Trust Fund, 2004), 153.

39. Ibid., 155.

40. Simon Wiesenthal, *Justice Not Vengeance*, trans. Ewald Osers (New York: Grove Weidenfeld, 1989), 60.

41. "Interrogation Protocol: Walther Rauff, June 28, 1972," The Nizkor Project, Shofar FTP Archive File: people/r//rauff.walter/Rauff-deposition-translation.

42. Wiesenthal, 63–64.

43. Breitman, with Goda and Brown, 159.

CHAPTER 17: THE POST-HOLOCAUST WORLD

1. Tony Judt, *Postwar: A History of Europe since 1945* (New York: Penguin, 2006), 819.

2. David G. Dalin and John F. Rothmann, *Icon of Evil: Hitler's Mufti and the Rise of Radical Islam* (New York: Random House, 2008), 108, 126, 127.

3. Jeffrey Herf, *Nazi Propaganda for the Arab World* (New Haven and London: Yale University Press, 2009), 266.

4. Ibid., chapters 7 and 8.

5. Hudson Institute, Center for Religious Freedom, *2008 Update: Saudi Arabia's Curriculum of Intolerance* (Washington, D.C.: Center for Religious Freedom, 2008), 5.

6. Wikipedia, s.v. "Abdul Rahman Al-Sudais," http://en.wikipedia.org/wiki/Abdul_Rahman_Al_Sudais.

7. Quoted from the inside cover promotion of *The Irving Judgment: Mr. David Irving v. Penguin Books and Professor Deborah Lipstadt* (London and New York: Penguin Books, 2000).

8. "Pope Rehabilitates Holocaust Denier," January 24, 2009, *New York Times*, http://www.nytimes.com/reuters/2009/01/24/world/international-us-pope-jews.html?.

9. "Virulent New Strain of Anti-Semitism Rife in UK, Says Chief Rabbi," *Times* (London), June 20, 2009, http://www.timesonline.co.uk/tol/comment/faith/article6539415.ece.

10. "Germany Jails Attacker of Rabbi," BBC News, May 20, 2008, http://news.bbc.co.uk./2/hi/europe/7410180.stm.

11. "Peril, Profit in Ranting for Ratings," August 23, 2002, *New York Daily News*, http://articles.nydailynews.com/2002-08-23/news/18204469_1_opie-and-anthony-anthony-cumia-animal-cruelty.

12. Edward Alexander, "The Democratic Party's Anti-Semitism Problem," *Seattle Times*, August 9, 2004, http://seattletimes.nwsource.com/html/opinion/2001999939_alexander09.html.

13. "Pat Buchanan's Iraq Conspiracy," April 17, 2003, *Time*, http://www.time.com/time/columnist/jaroff/article/0,9565,444259,00.html.

14. John Christoffersen, "Yale Creates Center to Study Anti-Semitism," boston.com, September 19, 2006, http://www.boston.com/new/education/higher/articles/2006/09/19/yale_creates _center_to_study_anti_semitism.

15. Victor Davis Hanson, "The New Anti-Semitism," *Jewish World Review*, September 27, 2006, http://www.JewishWorldReview.com.

16. Abby Wisse Schachter, "Yale's Latest Gift to Anti-Semitism," *New York Post*, June 21, 2011, http://www.nypost.com/p/news/opinion/opedcolumnists/yale_latest_gift_to_anti_semitism_MVRL7G363U30EcMrxe15UM.

17. "Demjanjuk Convicted in Nazi Camp Deaths," *USA Today*, May 13, 2011, p. 7A.

18. Quoted in "Michael Seifert, SS Guard at Camp in Italy, Dies at 86," *New York Times*, November 8, 2010, http://www.nytimes.com/2010/11/09/world/europe/09seifert.html.

19. Sean McMeekin, *The Berlin-Baghdad Express: The Ottoman Empire and Germany's Bid for World Power* (Cambridge: Belknap Press of Harvard University Press, 2010), 366.

Bibliography

Note: To the extent possible, I have limited the sources in the bibliography to those available in English.

ARCHIVAL SOURCES

United Kingdom. Public Record Office. CAB 65/50.

United States Holocaust Memorial Museum Archives, Washington, D.C. RG-02 (Survivor Testimonies). 132 (Memoirs 1940–1980 by Maria Epstein).

Wiener Library, London. Folder: Jews in Germany, General (Relief Workers' Reports), Doc. Ref. No. HA6A-1/9. Gale Digital Collections: Post-War Europe: Refugees, Exile and Resettlement, 1945–1950. http://www.tlemea.com/postwareurope/index.htm.

———. Foreign Office, United Kingdom. Department: Northern. Subject: Situation in Denmark. TNA No. FO/32760-0003, FO 371/36791-0007. Gale Digital Collections: Conditions and Politics in Occupied Western Europe, 1940–1945. http://www.tlemea.com/conditionsandpolitics/index.htm.

———. Section: Eyewitness Accounts. Detail: From the "seizure of power" to the outbreak of war (1933–39): Economic elimination (Dr. Leon Stein). Reference: P.II.b. No. 1145. Gale Digital Collections: Testaments to the Holocaust. http://www.tlemea.com/testaments/index.htm.

———. Section: Eyewitness Accounts. Detail: The "Final Solution" (September 1939–1945): Concentration Camps: Alphabetical Order. Reference: P.III.h (Auschwitz) no. 1061; P.III.h (Auschwitz) no. 870. Gale Digital Collections: Testaments to the Holocaust. http://www.tlemea.com/testaments/index.htm.

———. Section: Eyewitness Accounts. Detail: The "Final Solution" (September 1939–1945): Concentration Camps: Alphabetical Order. Reference: P.III.h No. 1039 (SS Troop- Maintenance Camp Riga). Gale Digital Collections: Testaments to the Holocaust. http://www.tlemea.com/testaments/index.htm.

———. Section: Eyewitness Accounts. Detail: The "Final Solution" (September 1939–1945): Concentration Camps: Alphabetical Order. Reference: P.III.i. No. 628 (Belgium). Gale Digital Collections: Testaments to the Holocaust. http://www.tlemea.com/testaments/index.htm.

———. Section: Eyewitness Accounts. Detail: The "Final Solution" (September 1939–1945): Concentration Camps: Alphabetical Order. Reference: P.III.h No. 479 (Theresienstadt). Gale Digital Collections: Testaments to the Holocaust. http://www.tlemea.com/testaments/index.htm.

PRINTED ORIGINAL SOURCES

". . . a 'Delousing Van'. . . : Euphemism for Murder." April 11, 1942. Holocaust History Project. http://www.holocaust-history.org/19420411-turner-wolff.

Arad, Yitzhak, Yisrael Gutman, and Abraham Margaliot, eds. *Documents on the Holocaust: Selected Sources on the Destruction of the Jews of Germany and Austria, Poland, and the Soviet Union.* 5th ed. Jerusalem: Yad Vashem, 1993.

Arad, Yitzhak, Shmuel Krakowski, and Shmuel Spector, eds. *The Einsatzgruppen Reports: Selections from the Dispatches of the Nazi Death Squads' Campaign against the Jews in Occupied Territories of the Soviet Union, July 1941–January 1943.* New York: Holocaust Library, 1989.

Domarus, Max, ed. *Hitler: Speeches and Proclamations, 1932–1945.* Translated by Chris Wilcox and Mary Fran Gilbert. 4 vols. Wauconda, Ill.: Bolchazy-Carducci, 1992–2004.

Eberle, Henrik, and Matthias Uhl, eds. *The Hitler Book: The Secret Dossier Prepared for Stalin from the Interrogations of Hitler's Personal Aides.* Translated by Giles MacDonogh. New York: Public Affairs, 2005.

Eichmann, Adolf. *Eichmann Interrogated: Transcripts from the Archives of the Israeli Police.* Edited by Jochen von Lang in collaboration with Claus Sibyll. Translated by Ralph Manheim. Introduction by Avner W. Less. New foreword by Michael Berenbaum. New York: Da Capo, 1999.

"The Einsatzgruppen Case." *Trials of War Criminals before the Nuernberg Military Tribunals under Control Council Law No. 10.* 15 vols. Buffalo, N.Y.: William S. Hein, 1997, first published 1952. Vol. 4.

"Erich Von Dem Bach Zelewski, 29 May 1961 [Examination of Witness]." Nizkor Project. Shofar FTP Archive File: people/e/eichmann.adolf/transcripts/Testimony-Abroad/Erich_Von_Dem_Bach_Zelewski-01 and 02.

"Franz Novak, 31 May 1961 [Examination of Witness]." Nizkor Project. Shofar FTP Archive File: people/e/eichmann.adolf/transcripts/Testimony-Abroad/Franz_Novak-01 and 02.

Goldensohn, Leon. *The Nuremberg Interviews: Conducted by Leon Goldensohn.* Edited and introduced by Robert Gellately. New York: Knopf, 2004.

Hackett, David A., ed. *The Buchenwald Report.* Translated by David A. Hackett. Boulder, Colo.: Westview, 1995.

Heiber, Helmut, and David M. Glantz, eds. *Hitler and His Generals: Military Conferences 1942–1945, The First Complete Stenographic Record of the Military Situation Conferences, Stalingrad to Berlin.* New York: Enigma, 2003.

Hitler, Adolf. *Hitler's Second Book: The Unpublished Sequel to* Mein Kampf. Edited by Gerhard L. Weinberg. Translated by Krista Smith. New York: Enigma Books, 2003; originally published in German in 1961.

International Military Trials. Office of United States Chief of Counsel for Prosecution of Axis Criminality. *Nazi Conspiracy and Aggression.* 8 vols. 12 pts. Washington, D.C.: U.S. Government Printing Office, 1946.

"Interrogation of Friedrich Jeckeln." December 14, 1945. Nizkor Project. Shofar FTP Archive File. http://www.nizkor.org/ftp.cgi/people/ftp.py?people//j/jeckeln.friedrich/jeckln-interrogation.1245.

"Interrogation Protocol [Walter Rauff Deposition]." March 1, 1972. Nizkor Project. Shofar FTP Archive File. http://www.nizkor.org/ftp.cgi/people/r/ftp.py?people/r//rauff . walter/Rauff-deposition-translation.

The Irving Judgment: Mr. David Irving v. Penguin Books and Professor Deborah Lipstadt. London and New York: Penguin, 2000.

"The Justice Case." *Trials of War Criminals before the Nuremberg Military Tribunals under Control Council Law No. 10.* 14 vols. Buffalo, N.Y.: William S. Hein, 1997, first published 1952. Vol. 3.

Klee, Ernst, Willi Dressen, and Volker Riess, eds. *"The Good Old Days": The Holocaust as Seen by Its Perpetrators and Bystanders.* Translated by Deborah Burnstone. Foreword by Hugh Trevor-Roper. New York: Konecky and Konecky, 1991.

Kogon, Eugen, Hermann Langbein, and Adalbert Rückerl, eds. *Nazi Mass Murder: A Documentary History of the Use of Poison Gas.* Translated by Mary Scott and Caroline Lloyd-Morris. New Haven and London: Yale University Press, 1993.

Langbein, Hermann. *Der Auschwitz-Prozeß. Eine Dokumentation.* 2 vols. Vienna/Frankfurt/Zurich: Europa Verlag, 1965.

Mahoney, Kevin, ed. *1945: The Year of Liberation.* Washington, D.C.: U.S. Holocaust Memorial Museum, 1995.

Marrus, Michael R., ed. *The Nuremberg War Crimes Trial 1945–46: A Documentary History.* Boston and New York: Bedford, 1997.

Niewyk, Donald L., ed. *Fresh Wounds: Early Narratives of Holocaust Survival.* Chapel Hill and London: University of North Carolina Press, 1998.

Noakes, J., and G. Pridham, eds. *Nazism, 1919–1945: A Documentary Reader.* 3 vols. Exeter, U.K.: University of Exeter Press, 1982–1988). Vol. 3.

Overy, Richard. *Interrogations: The Nazi Elite in Allied Hands, 1945.* New York: Viking, 2001.

Phillips, Raymond, ed. *Trial of Josef Kramer and Forty-Four Others (The Belsen Trial).* London: William Hodge, 1949.

Rückerl, Adalbert, ed. *The Investigation of Nazi Crimes, 1945–1978: A Documentation.* Translated by Derek Rutter. Hamden, Conn.: Archon Books, 1980.

Smajzner, Stanislaw. "Extracts from the Tragedy of a Jewish Teenager." Holocaust Education and Archive Research. http://www.holocaustresearchproject.org/ar/sobibor/smajzner.html.

"Trial of Gauleiter Artur Greiser." Case no. 74. Edited by the United Nations War Crimes Commission. *Law Reports of Trials of War Criminals.* 14 vols. London: His Majesty's Stationery Office, 1949. Vol. 13.

"Trial of Hanns Albin Rauter." Case no. 88. Edited by the United Nations War Crimes Commission. *Law Reports of Trials of War Criminals*. 14 vols. London: His Majesty's Stationery Office, 1949. Vol. 14.

"Trial of Hauptsturmführer Amon Leopold Goeth." Case no. 37. Edited by the United Nations War Crimes Commission. *Law Reports of Trials of War Criminals*. 14 vols. London: His Majesty's Stationery Office, 1948. Vol. 7.

"Trial of Obersturmbannführer Rudolf Franz Ferdinand Hoess." Case no. 38. Edited by the United Nations War Crimes Commission. *Law Reports of Trials of War Criminals*. 14 vols. London: His Majesty's Stationery Office, 1948. Vol. 7.

"Trial of Robert Wagner and Six Others." Case no. 13. Edited by the United Nations War Crimes Commission. *Law Reports of Trials of War Criminals*. 14 vols. London: His Majesty's Stationery Office, 1948. Vol. 3.

Trial of the Major War Criminals before the International Military Tribunal (Nuremberg, 14 November 1945–1 October 1946). 42 vols. Nuremberg, 1947–1949.

United States Holocaust Memorial Museum, ed. *Fifty Years Ago: Revolt amid the Darkness. Days of Remembrance, April 18–25, 1993*. Washington, D.C.: U.S. Government Printing Office, 1993.

DIARIES, LETTERS, AND MEMOIRS

Bechler, Margaret. *Warten auf Antwort. Ein deutsches Schicksal*. Expanded ed. Berlin: Ullstein, 1998.

Bradley, Omar N. *A Soldier's Story*. New York: Modern Library, 1999, first published 1951.

Cadogan, Alexander. *The Diaries of Sir Alexander Cadogan 1938–1945*. Edited by David Dilks. New York: Putnam's, 1972.

Clay, Lucius D. *Decision in Germany*. Garden City, N.Y.: Doubleday, 1950.

Dodd, Christopher J., with Larry Bloom. *Letters from Nuremberg: My Father's Narrative of a Quest for Justice*. New York: Crown, 2007.

Elias, Ruth [Huppert]. *Triumph of Hope: From Theresienstadt and Auschwitz to Israel*. Translated by Margot Bettauer Dembo. Published in association with the U.S. Holocaust Memorial Museum. New York: Wiley, 1999.

Frank, Anne. *The Diary of a Young Girl: The Definitive Edition*. Edited by Otto H. Frank and Mirjam Pressler. Translated by Susan Massotty. New York: Doubleday, 1995.

Frank, Hans. *Im Angesicht des Galgens*. 2nd ed. Neuhaus bei Schliersee: Eigenverlag Brigitte Frank, 1955.

Frank, Niklas. *In the Shadow of the Reich*. Translated by Arthur S. Wensinger with Carole Clew-Hoey. New York: Knopf, 1991.

Frankenthal, Hans, in collaboration with Andreas Plake, Babette Quinkert, and Florian Schmaltz. *The Unwelcome One: Returning Home from Auschwitz*. Translated by John A. Broadwin. Evanston, Ill.: Northwestern University Press, 2002.

Gehlen, Reinhard. *The Service: The Memoirs of General Reinhard Gehlen*. Translated by David Irving. Introduction by George Bailey. New York: World Publishing, 1972.

Gilbert, G. M. *Nuremberg Diary*. New York: Da Capo, 1995, first published 1947.

Goebbels, Joseph. *The Goebbels Diaries, 1942–43*. Edited and translated by Louis P. Lochner. Garden City, N.Y.: Doubleday, 1948.

Grossman, Vasily. *A Writer at War: Vasily Grossman with the Red Army, 1941–1945*. Edited and translated by Antony Beevor and Luba Vinogradova. New York: Pantheon, 2005.

Harris, Whitney. *Tyranny on Trial: The Evidence at Nuremberg*. Dallas, Tex.: Southern Methodist University Press, 1954.

Höß, Rudolf. *Death Dealer: The Memoirs of the SS Kommandant at Auschwitz*. Edited by Steven Paskuly. Translated by Andrew Pollinger. New Foreword by Primo Levi. New York: Da Capo, 1996.

Kesselring, Albert. *The Memoirs of Field-Marshal Kesselring*. Foreword by James Holland. Introduction by Kenneth Macksey. Barnsley, U.K.: Greenhill Books, 2007.

Khrushchev, Nikita S. *Khrushchev Remembers*. Introduction, commentary, and notes by Edward Crankshaw. Edited and translated by Strobe Talbott. Boston: Little, Brown, 1970.

Klemperer, Victor. *I Will Bear Witness: A Diary of the Nazi Years*. Translated by Martin Chalmers. 2 vols. New York: Random House, 1999. Vol. 2.

———. *The Lesser Evil: The Diaries of Victor Klemperer, 1945–59*. Translated by Martin Chalmers. London: Phoenix, 2004.

Lengyel, Olga. *Five Chimneys: The Story of Auschwitz*. New York: Howard Fertig, 1983, first published 1947.

Levi, Primo. *The Drowned and the Saved*. New York: Vintage, 1989, first published in English 1988.

———. *Moments of Reprieve: A Memoir of Auschwitz*. Translated by Ruth Feldman. New York: Penguin, 1987, first published in English 1986.

———. *The Periodic Tables*. New York: Schocken, 1995, first published in English 1984.

———. *The Search for Roots: A Personal Anthology*. Translated and with an introduction by Peter Forbes. Afterword by Italo Calvino. Chicago, Ill.: Ivan R. Dee, 2002.

———. *Survival in Auschwitz: The Nazi Assault on Humanity* (original title: *If This Is a Man*). Translated by Stuart Wolf. New York: Simon & Schuster, 1996, first published in English 1987.

Manstein, Erich von. *Lost Victories*. Edited and translated by Anthony G. Powell. Foreword by B. H. Liddell Hart. Chicago: Henry Regnery, 1958.

Nyiszli, Miklos. *I Was Mengele's Assistant*. Oswiecim, Poland: Oswiecim, 2001.

Perl, Gisella. *I Was a Doctor in Auschwitz*. Manchester, N.H.: Ayer, 1948.

Prüfer, Curt. *Rewriting History: The Original and Revised World War II Diaries of Curt Prüfer, Nazi Diplomat*. Edited by Donald M. McKale. Translated by Judith M. Melton. Kent, Ohio: Kent State University Press, 1988.

Rosenberg, Alfred. *Memoirs of Alfred Rosenberg*. With commentaries by Serge Lang and Ernst von Schenck. Translated by Eric Posselt. Chicago: Ziff-Davis, 1949.

Schecter, Jerrold L., and Vyacheslav V. Luchkov, eds. *Khrushchev Remembers: The Glasnost Tapes*. Foreword by Strobe Talbott. Translated by J. L. Schecter and V. V. Luchkov. Boston: Little, Brown, 1990.

Taylor, Telford. *The Anatomy of the Nuremberg Trials: A Personal Memoir*. Boston: Little, Brown, 1992.

Wiesel, Elie. *Night*. Translated by Stella Rodway. Foreword by François Mauriac. Twenty-fifth anniversary edition. New preface by Robert McAfee Brown. New York and London: Bantam, 1982.

Wiesenthal, Simon. *Justice Not Vengeance*. Translated by Ewald Osers. New York: Grove Weidenfeld, 1989.

Zuckerman, Yitzhak ("Antek"). *A Surplus of Memory: Chronicle of the Warsaw Ghetto Uprising*. Edited and translated by Barbara Harshav. Berkeley and Los Angeles: University of California Press, 1993.

MEDIA ARTICLES

Alexander, Edward. "The Democratic Party's Anti-Semitism Problem." *Seattle Times*, August 9, 2004. http://seattletimes.nwsource.com/html/opinion/2001999939_alexander09.html.

Chandler, Robert. "Vasily Grossman." *Prospect Magazine* 126 (Sept. 2006). http://www.prospect-magazine.co.uk/printarticle.php?id=7739.

Christoffersen, John. "Yale Creates Center to Study Anti-Semitism." *boston.com News*, September 19, 2006. http://www.boston.com/new/education/higher/articles/2006/09/19/yale_creates_center_to_study_anti_semitism.

"Demjanjuk Convicted in Nazi Camp Deaths." *USA Today*, May 13, 2011, p. 7A.

"Deutsche Bank Denies Hiding Nazi Deals." CNN, February 6, 1999. http://www.cnn.com/WORLD/europe/9902/06/deutsche.bank.

"German Bank Linked to Death Camp." BBC News, February 5, 1999. http://news.bbc.co.uk/2/hi/europe/272860.stm.

"Germany Jails Attacker of Rabbi." BBC News, May 20, 2008. http://news.bbc.co.uk/2/hi/europe/7410180.stm.

Hanson, Victor Davis. "The New Anti-Semitism." *Jewish World Review*, September 27, 2006. http://www.JewishWorldReview.com.

Kershner, Isabel. "Women's Role in Holocaust May Exceed Old Notions." *New York Times*, July 18, 2010, p. 8.

"Michael Seifert, SS Guard at Camp in Italy, Dies at 86." *New York Times*, November 8, 2010. http://www.nytimes.com/2010/11/09/world/europe/09seifert.html.

New York Times. "Belsen and Dachau," December 15, 1945, p. 16.

———. "Belsen Girl Guard Blames All of SS," October 6, 1945, p. 7.

———. "Belsen Woman Guard Weeps, Denies Guilt," October 17, 1945, p. 6.

———. "Defendants Lose Impassivity," September 20, 1945, p. 5.

———. "15,000 Poles Watch Greiser Execution," July 22, 1946, p. 1.

———. "Flight of Few Jews Left Is in View as Polish Anti-Semitism Strikes," October 27, 1945, p. 5.

———. "France's Nuremberg," April 24, 1946, p. 7.

———. "German Use of Motor Cars for Mass Suffocations Noted," July 16, 1943, p. 7.

———. "Kramer and 10 Others Hanged for Belsen-Oswiecim Atrocities," December 15, 1945, p. 1.

———. "Pope Asked Poles to Spare Greiser," July 23, 1946, p. 7.

———. "SS Killed 4,000,000 at Oswiecim, Prosecutor Says at Kramer Trial," September 18, 1945, pp. 1, 9.

———. "Sweden Offers Aid to Denmark's Jews," October 3, 1943, p. 3.

———. "Wife Says Kramer Knew He Did Wrong," October 11, 1945, p. 4.

"Pat Buchanan's Iraq Conspiracy." *Time*, April 17, 2003. http://www.time.com/time/columnist/jaroff/article/0,9565,444259,00.html.

"Peril, Profit in Ranting for Ratings." *New York Daily News*, August 23, 2002. http://articles.nydailynews.com/2002-08-23/news/18204469_1_opie-and-anthony-anthony-cumia-animal-cruelty.

Pohl, Manfred. "Abs und Auschwitz." *Die Zeit*, November 2, 1999.

"Pope Rehabilitates Holocaust Denier." *New York Times*. January 24, 2009. http://www.nytimes.com/reuters/2009/01/24/world/international-us-pope-jews.html.

"Romanians Are Told of Nation's Role in Mass Killing of Jews." *New York Times*, July 2, 1991. http://www.nytimes.com/1991/07/02/world/romanians-are-told-of-nation-s-role-in-mass-killing-of-jews.html.

Schachter, Abby Wisse. "Yale's Latest Gift to Anti-Semitism." *New York Post*. June 21, 2011. http://www.nypost.com/p/news/opinion/opedcolumnists/yale_latest_gift_to_anti_semitis m_MVRL7G363U30EcMrxe15UM.

"Search Renewed for Nazi fugitives." *Tribune* (Ames, Iowa), July 14, 2007.

"Suspect Charged in Holocaust Museum Attack." MSNBC, June 6, 2009. http://www.msnbc.msn.com/id/31237522.

"Virulent New Strain of Anti-Semitism Rife in UK, Says Chief Rabbi." *Times* (London), June 20, 2009. http://www.timesonline.co.uk/tol/comment/faith/article6539415.ece.

Whitley, Glenna. "In the Wolf's Mouth: SMU's Bryan Mark Rigg Uncovers the Story of Hitler's Jewish Soldiers." *Dallas Observer*, February 26, 2004. http://www.dallasobserver.com/2004-02-06/news/in-the-wolf-s-mouth/print.

GENERAL HISTORIES, DICTIONARIES, AND ENCYCLOPEDIAS

Benz, Wolfgang. *The Holocaust: A German Historian Examines the Genocide*. Foreword by Arthur Hertzberg. Translated by Jane Sydenham-Kwiet. New York: Columbia University Press, 1999.

Bergen, Doris L. *War & Genocide: A Concise History of the Holocaust*. Lanham, Md.: Rowman & Littlefield, 2003.

Boatner, Mark M., III. *The Biographical Dictionary of World War II*. Novato, Calif.: Presidio Press, 1996.

Enzyklopädie des Holocaust. Die Verfolgung und Ermordung der europäischen Juden. Edited by Eberhard Jäckel, Peter Longerich, and Julius H. Schoeps. 2nd ed. 4 vols. Munich and Zurich: Piper, 1998.

Friedlander, Saul. *The Years of Extermination: Nazi Germany and the Jews, 1939–1945*. New York: Harper Perennial, 2008.

Friedman, Saul S. *A History of the Holocaust*. London and Portland, Ore.: Vallentine Mitchell, 2004.

Gilbert, Martin. *The Holocaust: A History of the Jews of Europe during the Second World War*. New York: Holt, Rinehart and Winston, 1985.

Hilberg, Raul. *The Destruction of the European Jews*. Rev. and definitive ed. 3 vols. New York and London: Holmes & Meier, 1985.

Laqueur, Walter, ed., and Judith Tydor Baumel, assoc. ed. *The Holocaust Encyclopedia*. New Haven and London: Yale University Press, 2001.

Longerich, Peter. *Holocaust: Nazi Persecution and Murder of the Jews*. New York: Oxford University Press, 2010.

McKale, Donald M. *Hitler's Shadow War: The Holocaust and World War II*. First paperback ed. Lanham, Md.: Taylor Trade, 2006.

Niewyk, Donald, and Francis Nicosia, eds. *The Columbia Guide to the Holocaust*. New York: Columbia University Press, 2000.

Wistrich, Robert S. *Hitler and the Holocaust*. New York: Modern Library, 2001.

———. *Who's Who in Nazi Germany*. New York: Macmillan, 1982.

Yahil, Leni. *The Holocaust: The Fate of European Jewry*. Translated by Ina Friedman and Haya Galai. New York and Oxford: Oxford University Press, 1990.

SECONDARY SOURCES

"Abdul Rahman Al-Sudais." Wikipedia. http://en.wikipedia.org/wiki/Abdul_Rahman_Al_Sudais.

Aharoni, Zvi, and Wilhelm Dietl. *Operation Eichmann: The Truth about the Pursuit, Capture, and Trial*. Translated by Helmut Bogler. New York: Wiley, 1997.

Allen, Michael Thad. "Realms of Oblivion: The Vienna Auschwitz Trial." *Central European History* 40, no. 3 (September 2007): 397–428.

Aly, Götz. *Hitler's Beneficiaries: Plunder, Racial War, and the Nazi Welfare State*. Translated by Jefferson Chase. New York: Holt, 2006.

Arad, Yitzhak. *Belzec, Sobibor, Treblinka: The Operation Reinhard Death Camps*. Bloomington and Indianapolis: Indiana University Press, 1987.

Arendt, Hannah. *Eichmann in Jerusalem: A Report on the Banality of Evil*. New York: Viking, 1963.

Astor, Gerald. *The Last Nazi: The Life and Times of Josef Mengele*. New York: Dutton, 1985.

Bartlett, John. *The Shorter Bartlett's Familiar Quotations: A Collection of Passages, Phrases, and Proverbs Traced to Their Sources in Ancient and Modern Literature*. 17th printing. New York: Pocket Books, 1964.

Bartov, Omer. *Erased: Vanishing Traces of Jewish Galicia in Present-Day Ukraine*. Princeton, N.J.: Princeton University Press, 2007.

Bendersky, Joseph W. *The "Jewish Threat": Anti-Semitic Politics of the U.S. Army*. New York: Basic, 2000.

Benz, Wolfgang, ed. *Dimension des Völkermords. Die Zahl der jüdischen Opfer des Nationalsozialismus*. Munich: Deutsche Taschenbuch Verlag, 1996.

Bessel, Richard. *Nazism and War*. New York: Modern Library, 2004.

Black, Peter R. *Ernst Kaltenbrunner: Ideological Soldier of the Third Reich*. Princeton, N.J.: Princeton University Press, 1984.

Bloxham, Donald. *Genocide on Trial: War Crimes Trials and the Formation of Holocaust History and Memory*. Oxford: Oxford University Press, 2001.

Borwicz, Michal M. "Polish-Jewish Relations, 1944–1947." In *The Jews in Poland*, edited by Chimen Abramsky, Maciej Jachimczyk, and Antony Polonsky. Oxford and New York: Basil Blackwell, 1986.

Bower, Tom. *Blind Eye to Murder: Britain, America and the Purging of Nazi Germany—A Pledge Betrayed*. London: Granada, 1983.

Breitman, Richard. *The Architect of Genocide: Himmler and the Final Solution*. New York: Knopf, 1991.

———. *Official Secrets: What the Nazis Planned, What the British and Americans Knew.* New York: Hill & Wang, 1998.

Breitman, Richard, with Norman J. W. Goda and Paul Brown. "The Gestapo." In *U.S. Intelligence and the Nazis*, edited by Richard Breitman, Norman J. W. Goda, Timothy Naftali, and Robert Wolfe. Washington, D.C.: National Archives Trust Fund, 2004, 137–72.

Browder, George C. *Foundations of the Nazi Police State: The Formation of Sipo and SD.* Lexington: University Press of Kentucky, 1990.

Brown, Daniel Patrick. *The Beautiful Beast: The Life and Times of SS-Aufseherin Irma Grese.* Ventura, Calif.: Gordon West Historical Publications, 2004.

Browning, Christopher R. *Ordinary Men: Reserve Police Battalion 101 and the Final Solution in Poland.* New York: Harper Perennial, 1998.

———. *The Path to Genocide: Essays on Launching the Final Solution.* Cambridge: Cambridge University Press, 1992.

Browning, Christopher R., with contributions by Jürgen Matthäus. *The Origins of the Final Solution: The Evolution of Nazi Jewish Policy, September 1939–March 1942.* Lincoln and Jerusalem: University of Nebraska Press and Yad Vashem, 2004.

Bukey, Evan Burr. *Hitler's Austria: Popular Sentiment in the Nazi Era, 1938–1945.* Chapel Hill: University of North Carolina Press, 2000.

Cadle, Caron. "Kurt Daluege—Der Prototyp des loyalen Nationalsozialisten." In *Die Braune Elite 2: 21 weitere biographische Skizzen*, edited by Ronald Smelser, Enrico Syring, and Rainer Zitelmann. Darmstadt: Wissenschaftliche Buchgesellschaft, 1999, 66–79.

Cesarani, David. *Becoming Eichmann: Rethinking the Life, Crimes, and Trial of a "Desk Murderer."* New York: Da Capo, 2004.

Cichopek, Anna. "The Cracow Pogrom of August 1945." In *Contested Memories: Poles and Jews during the Holocaust and Its Aftermath*, edited by Joshua D. Zimmerman. New Brunswick, N.J. and London: Rutgers University Press, 2003, 221–38.

Conot, Robert E. *Justice at Nuremberg: The First Comprehensive Dramatic Account of the Trial of the Nazi Leaders.* New York: Harper & Row, 1983.

Cornwell, John. *Hitler's Pope: The Secret History of Pius XII.* New York: Penguin, 2008.

Courtois, Stéphanie, Nicolas Werth, Jean-Louis Panné, Andrzej Paczkowski, Karel Bartosek, and Jean-Louis Margolin. *The Black Book of Communism: Crimes, Terror, Repression.* Translated by Jonathan Murphy and Mark Kramer. Cambridge, Mass. and London: Harvard University Press, 1999.

Czech, Danuta. "The Auschwitz Prisoner Administration." In *Anatomy of the Auschwitz Death Camp*, edited by Yisrael Gutman and Michael Berenbaum. Published in association with the U.S. Holocaust Memorial Museum. Bloomington and Indianapolis: Indiana University Press, 1994, 363–79.

Dalin, David G., and John F. Rothmann. *Icon of Evil: Hitler's Mufti and the Rise of Radical Islam.* New York: Random House, 2008.

Dallin, Alexander. *German Rule in Russia, 1941–1945.* New York: Macmillan, 1957.

Davidson, Eugene. *The Trial of the Germans: An Account of the Twenty-Two Defendants before the International Military Tribunal at Nuremberg.* New York: Collier, 1966.

De Mildt, Dick Welmoed. *Die westdeutschen Strafverfahren wegen nationalsozialistischer Tötungsverbrechen, 1945–1997.* Amsterdam: Holland University Press, 1998.

———. *In the Name of the People: Perpetrators of Genocide in the Reflection of Their Postwar Prosecutions in West Germany: The Euthanasia and Aktion Reinhard Trial Cases.* The Hague: Martinus Nijhoff, 1996.

Dennis, Mike. *The Rise and Fall of the German Democratic Republic, 1945–1990*. Harlow, England: Longman, 2000.

Deschner, Günther. *Reinhard Heydrich: A Biography*. Translated by Sandra Bance, Brenda Woods, and David Ball. New York: Stein & Day, 1981.

Dwork, Debórah, and Robert Jan van Pelt. *Auschwitz: 1270 to the Present*. New York and London: Norton, 1996.

Ehmann, Annegret. "From Colonial Racism to Nazi Population Policy: The Role of the So-called Mischlinge." In *The Holocaust and History: The Known, the Unknown, the Disputed, and the Reexamined*, edited by Michael Berenbaum and Abraham J. Peck. Bloomington: Indiana University Press, 1998, 115–34.

"Elie Wiesel." Wikipedia. http://en.wikipedia.org/wiki/Elie_Wiesel.

Evans, Richard J. *Lying about Hitler: History, Holocaust, and the David Irving Trial*. New York: Basic, 2001.

Felstiner, Mary. "Alois Brunner: Eichmann's Best Tool," in *Simon Wiesenthal Center Annual*. White Plains, N.Y.: Kraus Publications, 1986. Vol. 3, 1–41.

Feltman, Brian K. "Legitimizing Justice: The American Press and the International Military Tribunal, 1945–1946." *The Historian* 66, no. 2 (Summer 2004): 300–319.

Frei, Norbert. *Adenauer's Germany and the Nazi Past. The Politics of Amnesty and Integration*. Translated by Joel Golb. New York: Columbia University Press, 2002.

Friedlander, Henry. *The Origins of Genocide: From Euthanasia to the Final Solution*. Chapel Hill and London: University of North Carolina Press, 1995.

Gall, Lothar. *Hermann Josef Abs. Eine Biographie*. Munich: C. H. Beck Verlag, 2004.

Gellately, Robert. *Backing Hitler: Consent and Coercion in Nazi Germany*. Oxford and New York: Oxford University Press, 2001.

Gitelman, Zvi. *Bitter Legacy: Confronting the Holocaust in the Soviet Union*. Bloomington, Ind.: Indiana University Press, 1997.

Goda, Norman J. W. "Manhunts: The Official Search for Notorious Nazis." In *U.S. Intelligence and the Nazis*, edited by Richard Breitman, Norman J. W. Goda, Timothy Naftali, and Robert Wolfe. Washington, D.C.: National Archives Trust Fund, 2004, 419–42.

Goñi, Uki. *The Real Odessa: How Perón Brought the Nazi War Criminals to Argentina*. London and New York: Granta Books, 2002.

Greene, Joshua M. *Justice at Dachau: The Trials of an American Prosecutor*. New York: Broadway Books, 2003.

Grill, Johnpeter Horst. *The Nazi Movement in Baden, 1920–1945*. Chapel Hill: University of North Carolina Press, 1983.

Gross, Jan T. *Fear: Anti-Semitism in Poland after Auschwitz*. New York: Random House, 2006.

———. *Neighbors: The Destruction of the Jewish Community in Jedwabne, Poland*. Princeton: Princeton University Press, 2001.

Grossman, Vasily. *Life and Fate*. Translated and with an introduction by Robert Chandler. New York: New York Review Books, 2006.

"Hanns Albin Rauter." Wikipedia in German. http://de.wikipedia.org/windex.php?title=Hanns_Albin_Rauter.

Hayes, Peter. "The Deutsche Bank and the Holocaust." In *Lessons and Legacies III: Memory, Memorialization, and Denial*, edited by Peter Hayes. Evanston, Ill.: Northwestern University Press, 1999, 75–90.

———. *Industry and Ideology: IG Farben in the Nazi Era*. New ed. Cambridge and New York: Cambridge University Press, 2001, first published in 1987.

Henkys, Reinhard. *Die nationalsozialistischen Gewaltverbrechen. Geschichte und Gericht*. Stuttgart and Berlin: Kreuz-Verlag, 1964.

Herbert, Ulrich. *Best. Biographische Studien über Radikalismus Weltanschauung und Vernunft, 1903–1989*. Bonn: Verlag J. H. W. Dietz, 1996.

———. "The German Military Command in Paris and the Deportation of the French Jews." In *National Socialist Extermination Policies: Contemporary German Perspectives and Controversies*, edited by Ulrich Herbert. New York: Berghahn Books, 2000, 128–62.

Herf, Jeffrey. *Divided Memory: The Nazi Past in the Two Germanys*. Cambridge, Mass. and London: Harvard University Press, 1997.

———. *Nazi Propaganda for the Arab World*. New Haven and London: Yale University Press, 2009.

Höhne, Heinz. *The Order of the Death's Head: The Story of Hitler's SS*. Translated by Richard Barry. New York: Penguin, 2000, first published in English 1969.

Housden, Martyn. *Hans Frank: Lebensraum and the Holocaust*. London: Palgrave, 2003.

Hudson Institute, Center for Religious Freedom. *2008 Update: Saudi Arabia's Curriculum of Intolerance*. Washington, D.C.: Center for Religious Freedom, 2008.

Isaacson, Walter. *Einstein: His Life and Universe*. New York: Simon & Schuster, 2008.

James, Harold. *The Deutsche Bank and the Nazi Economic War against the Jews: The Expropriation of Jewish-Owned Property*. Cambridge and New York: Cambridge University Press, 2001.

Johnson, Eric A. *Nazi Terror: The Gestapo, Jews, and Ordinary Germans*. New York: Basic Books, 2000.

Judt, Tony. *Postwar: A History of Europe since 1945*. New York: Penguin, 2006.

Kellenbach, Katharina von. "Vanishing Acts: Perpetrators in Postwar Germany." *Holocaust and Genocide Studies* 17, no. 2 (Fall 2003): 305–29.

Kellogg, Michael. *The Russian Roots of Nazism: White Émigrés and the Making of National Socialism, 1917–1945*. Cambridge: Cambridge University Press, 2005.

Kershaw, Ian. "Arthur Greiser—Ein Motor der 'Endlösung.'" In *Die Braune Elite 2: 21 weitere biographische Skizzen*, edited by Ronald Smelser, Enrico Syring, and Rainer Zitelmann. Darmstadt: Wissenschaftliche Buchgesellschaft, 1999, 116–27.

———. *Hitler 1889–1936: Hubris*. Paperback ed. New York and London: Norton, 2000.

Klee, Ernst. *Was sie taten—was sie wurden. Ärzte, Juristen und andere Beteiligte am Kranken oder Judenmord*. Frankfurt am Main: Fischer Taschenbuch Verlag, 1994, first published 1986.

Koch, H. W. *In the Name of the Volk: Political Justice in Hitler's Germany*. London: I. B. Tauris, 1989.

Kochavi, Arieh J. *Prelude to Nuremberg: Allied War Crimes Policy and the Question of Punishment*. Chapel Hill and London: University of North Carolina Press, 1998.

Koehl, Robert Lewis. *The Black Corps: The Structure and Power Struggles of the Nazi SS*. Madison: University of Wisconsin Press, 1983.

Kogon, Eugen. *The Theory and Practice of Hell: The German Concentration Camps and the System behind Them*. Introduction by Nikolaus Wachsmann. Translated by Heinz Norden. New York: Farrar, Straus & Giroux, 2006, first published in English 1950.

Königseder, Angelina, and Juliane Wetzel. *Waiting for Hope: Jewish Displaced Persons in Post-World War II Germany*. Evanston, Ill.: Northwestern University Press, 2001.

Kubica, Helena. "The Crimes of Josef Mengele." In *Anatomy of the Auschwitz Death Camp*, edited by Yisrael Gutman and Michael Berenbaum. Published in association with the U.S. Holocaust Memorial Museum. Bloomington and Indianapolis: Indiana University Press, 1994, 317–37.

Kurtz, Michael J. *America and the Return of Nazi Contraband: The Recovery of Europe's Cultural Treasures*. New York: Cambridge University Press, 2006.

Lagnado, Lucette Matalon, and Sheila Cohn Dekl. *Children of the Flames: Dr. Josef Mengele and the Untold Story of the Twins of Auschwitz*. New York: Penguin, 1992.

Lang, Jochen von. *Top Nazi SS General Karl Wolff: The Man between Hitler and Himmler*. New York: Enigma, 2005.

Langbein, Hermann. *People in Auschwitz*. Translated by Harry Zohn. Published in association with the U.S. Holocaust Memorial Museum. Chapel Hill and London: University of North Carolina Press, 2004.

Lasik, Aleksander. "Postwar Prosecution of the Auschwitz SS." In *Anatomy of the Auschwitz Death Camp*, edited by Yisrael Gutman and Michael Berenbaum. Published in association with the U.S. Holocaust Memorial Museum. Bloomington and Indianapolis: Indiana University Press, 1994, 588–600.

———. "Rudolf Höss—Manager of Crime." In *Anatomy of the Auschwitz Death Camp*, edited by Yisrael Gutman and Michael Berenbaum. Published in association with the U.S. Holocaust Memorial Museum. Bloomington and Indianapolis: Indiana University Press, 1994, 288–300.

Lavsky, Hagit. *New Beginnings: Holocaust Survivors in Bergen-Belsen and the British Zone in Germany, 1945–1950*. Detroit, Mich.: Wayne State University Press, 2002.

Less, Avner W., ed. *Schuldig. Das Urteil gegen Adolf Eichmann*. Foreword by Jochen von Lang. Frankfurt am Main: Athenäum, 1987.

Levy, Alan. *Nazi Hunter: The Wiesenthal File*. New York: Carroll & Graf, 2002, first published 1993.

Liddell Hart, B. H. *History of the Second World War*. New York: Putnam, 1970.

Lifton, Robert J. *The Nazi Doctors: Medical Killing and the Psychology of Genocide*. New York: Basic Books, 1986.

Lipstadt, Deborah E. *Denying the Holocaust: The Growing Assault on Truth and Memory*. New York: Free Press, 1993.

_____. *The Eichmann Trial*. New York: Nextbook, Schocken, 2011.

Lustiger, Arno. *Stalin and the Jews: The Red Book: The Tragedy of the Jewish Anti-Fascist Committee and the Soviet Jews*. Translated by Mary Beth Friedrich and Todd Bludeau. New York: Enigma, 2003.

Malkin, Peter, and Harry Stein. *Eichmann in My Hands*. New York: Warner Books, 1990.

Mallmann, Klaus-Michael, and Martin Cüppers. *Nazi Palestine: The Plans for the Extermination of the Jews in Palestine*. Translated by Krista Smith. New York: Enigma, 2010.

Manvell, Roger. *Hermann Göring*. New York: NAL Mentor, 1974.

Manvell, Roger, and Heinrich Fraenkel. *Himmler*. First American ed. New York: Putnam, 1965.

Marks, Steven G. *How Russia Shaped the Modern World: From Art to Anti-Semitism, Ballet to Bolshevism*. Princeton, N.J.: Princeton University Press, 2003.

McKale, Donald M. *Hitler: The Survival Myth.* Updated ed. New York: Cooper Square Press, 2001.

McMeekin, Sean. *The Berlin-Baghdad Express: The Ottoman Empire and Germany's Bid for World Power.* Cambridge: Belknap Press of Harvard University, 2010.

Mosley, Leonard. *The Reich Marshal: A Biography of Hermann Goering.* Garden City, N.Y.: Doubleday, 1974.

Müller, Ingo. *Hitler's Justice: The Courts of the Third Reich.* Translated by Deborah Lucas Schneider. Cambridge, Mass.: Harvard University Press, 1991.

Naftali, Timothy. "The CIA and Eichmann's Associates." In *U.S. Intelligence and the Nazis*, edited by Richard Breitman, Norman J. W. Goda, Timothy Naftali, and Robert Wolfe. Washington, D.C.: National Archives Trust Fund, 2004, 337–74.

———. "Reinhard Gehlen and the United States." In *U.S. Intelligence and the Nazis*, edited by Richard Breitman, Norman J. W. Goda, Timothy Naftali, and Robert Wolfe. Washington, D.C.: National Archives Trust Fund, 2004, 375–418.

Nicholas, Lynn. *The Rape of Europa: The Fate of Europe's Treasures in the Third Reich and the Second World War.* New York: Knopf, 1994.

Overy, Richard. *Russia's War.* New York: Penguin, 1997.

Padfield, Peter. *Himmler: Reichsführer-SS.* Rev. ed. London: Cassell, 2001.

"Page Six (from the *New York Post*) by Richard Johnson 1/12/02." Robert Clary. http://www.robertclary.com/pagesix.html.

Pearlman, Moshe. *The Capture and Trial of Adolf Eichmann.* New York: Simon & Schuster, 1963.

Pendas, Devin O. *The Frankfurt Auschwitz Trial, 1963–1965: Genocide, History, and the Limits of the Law.* New York: Cambridge University Press, 2006.

Petropoulos, Jonathan. *The Faustian Bargain: The Art World in Nazi Germany.* London and New York: Allen Lane/Penguin, 2000.

Phayer, Michael. *The Catholic Church and the Holocaust, 1930–1965.* Bloomington: Indiana University Press, 2000.

Piper, Ernst. *Alfred Rosenberg. Hitlers Chefideologe.* Munich: Karl Blessing Verlag, 2005.

Plato, Alexander von. "Zur Geschichte des sowjetischen Speziallagersystems in Deutschland. Einführung." In *Sowjetische Speziallager in Deutschland 1945 bis 1950*, edited by Sergei Mironenko, Lutz Niethammer, and Alexander von Plato, in collaboration with Volkhard Knigge and Günter Morsch. 2 vols. Berlin: Akademie Verlag, 1998, 1:19–75.

Ponsonby, Arthur. *Falsehood in War-Time.* London: George Allen and Unwin, 1928.

Posner, Gerald L., and John Ware. *Mengele: The Complete Story.* With a new introduction by Michael Berenbaum. New York: Cooper Square Press, 2000.

Prusin, Alexander Victor. "'Fascist Criminals to the Gallows!' The Holocaust and Soviet War Crimes Trials, December 1945–February 1946." *Holocaust and Genocide Studies* 17, no. 1 (Spring 2003): 1–30.

Reitlinger, Gerald. *The SS: Alibi of a Nation, 1922–1945.* New York: Da Capo, 1989.

Rhodes, Richard. *Masters of Death: The SS-Einsatzgruppen and the Invention of the Holocaust.* New York: Vintage, 2003.

Rigg, Bryan Mark. *Hitler's Jewish Soldiers: The Untold Story of Nazi Racial Laws and Men of Jewish Descent in the German Military.* New ed. Lawrence: University Press of Kansas, 2004.

Rosenbaum, Joe, and David Kohn. *Defy the Darkness: A Tale of Courage in the Shadow of Mengele*. Westport, Conn.: Praeger, 2000.

Safrian, Hans. *Die Eichmann-Männer*. Vienna and Zurich: Europaverlag, 1993.

Sereny, Gitta. *Into That Darkness: From Mercy Killing to Mass Murder*. New York: McGraw-Hill, 1974.

Shermer, Michael, and Alex Grobman. *Denying History: Who Says the Holocaust Never Happened and Why Do They Say It?* Berkeley: University of California Press, 2000.

Smelser, Ronald, and Edward J. Davies II. *The Myth of the Eastern Front: The National-Socialist War in American Popular Culture*. New York: Cambridge University Press, 2008.

Southern Poverty Law Center. "Hate Map." http://www.splcenter.org/get-informed/hate-map.

Steinacher, Gerald. *Nazis on the Run: How Hitler's Henchmen Fled Justice*. New York: Oxford University Press, 2011.

Steinlauf, Michael C. "Poland." In *The World Reacts to the Holocaust*, edited by David S. Wyman. Baltimore and London: Johns Hopkins University Press, 1996, 81–155.

Stern, Kenneth S. "Why Campus Anti-Israel Activity Flunks Bigotry 101." New York: American Jewish Committee, 2002.

Sydnor, Charles W., Jr. "Executive Instinct: Reinhard Heydrich and the Planning for the Final Solution." In *The Holocaust and History: The Known, the Unknown, the Disputed, and the Reexamined*, edited by Michael Berenbaum and Abraham J. Peck. Bloomington: Indiana University Press, 1998, 159–86.

Tusa, Ann, and John Tusa. *The Nuremberg Trial*. New York and Lanham, Md.: Cooper Square Press, 2003, first published 1983.

Vogt, Timothy R. *Denazification in Soviet-Occupied Germany: Brandenburg, 1945–1948*. Cambridge, Mass. and London: Harvard University Press, 2000.

Wachsmann, Nikolaus. *Hitler's Prisons: Legal Terror in Nazi Germany*. New Haven, Conn. and London: Yale University Press, 2004.

Walters, Guy. *Hunting Evil: The Nazi War Criminals Who Escaped and the Quest to Bring Them to Justice*. New York: Broadway Books, 2009.

Ward, Mark Lee, Sr. "Deadly Discourse: Negotiating Bureaucratic Consensus for the Final Solution through Organizational and Technical Communication." PhD diss., Clemson University, 2010.

Wegner, Bernd. *The Waffen-SS: Organization, Ideology and Function*. Translated by Ronald Webster. Oxford and Cambridge, Mass.: Basil Blackwell, 1990.

Weinberg, Gerhard L. *Germany, Hitler & World War II: Essays in Modern German and World History*. Cambridge and New York: Cambridge University Press, 1995.

———. *A World at Arms: A Global History of World War II*. Cambridge and New York: Cambridge University Press, 1994.

Werner, Sebastian. "Werner Best—Der völkische Ideologe." In *Die Braune Elite 2: 21 weitere biographische Skizzen*, edited by Ronald Smelser, Enrico Syring, and Rainer Zitelmann. Darmstadt: Wissenschaftliche Buchgesellschaft, 1999, 13–25.

Westermann, Edward B. *Hitler's Police Battalions: Enforcing Racial War in the East*. Lawrence: University Press of Kansas, 2005.

———. "'Ordinary Men' or 'Ideological Soldiers'? Police Battalion 310 in Russia, 1942." *German Studies Review* 21 (February 1998): 41–68.

Wette, Wolfram. *The Wehrmacht: History, Myth, Reality*. Translated by Deborah Lucas Schneider. Cambridge, Mass.: Harvard University Press, 2006.

Wiener, Anita. *Expanding Historical Consciousness: The Development of the Holocaust Educational Foundation*. Skokie, Ill.: Holocaust Educational Foundation, 2002.

Wistrich, Robert S. *Hitler and the Holocaust*. New York: Modern Library, 2001.

Wittmann, Rebecca. *Beyond Justice: The Auschwitz Trial*. Cambridge, Mass. and London: Harvard University Press, 2005.

Wykes, Alan. *Himmler*. New York: Ballantine, 1972.

Index

About the Author

Donald M. McKale was born in 1943 in Clay Center, Kansas. He retired in 2008 as the Class of 1941 Memorial Professor and Professor Emeritus of History at Clemson University. He is the author or editor of seven books, among them *Hitler's Shadow War: The Holocaust and World War II* and *Hitler: The Survival Myth*. He is also the author of some forty articles, chapters, and other publications. He lives with his wife, Janna, in Clemson, South Carolina.